Orders to Kill

Orders to Kill

*The Truth Behind
the Murder of
Martin Luther King*

William F. Pepper

Carroll & Graf Publishers, Inc.
New York

Carroll & Graf Publishers, Inc.
260 Fifth Avenue
New York, NY 10001

Library of Congress Cataloging-in-Publication Data as available.

ISBN: 0-7867-0253-2

Manufactured in the United States of America.

95   96   97   5   4   3   2   1

This book and my underlying investigation are
dedicated to:

The Reverend Dr. Martin Luther King, Jr.
James Earl Ray
and
The People of America,
Victims All.

Contents

The Principal Players   vii
Introduction   xxiii
Glossary   xxix

Part I: Background to the Assassination

1. Vietnam: Spring 1966–Summer 1967   3
2. Death of the New Politics: 8
   Summer 1967–Spring 1968
3. Memphis: The Sanitation Workers' Strike,   12
   February 1968–March 1968
4. Enter Dr. King: March–April 3, 1968   17

Part II: The Assassination

5. The Assassination: April 4, 1968   27
6. Aftermath: April 5–18, 1968   34

 7. Hunt, Extradition, and Plea: 38
    May 1968–March 10, 1969

Part III: The Initial Investigation

 8. Reentry: Late 1977–October 15, 1978   51
 9. The Visit: October 17, 1978   66
10. James Earl Ray's Story: October 17, 1978   70
11. Pieces of the Puzzle: 1978–1979   83
12. Brother Jerry on the Stand: November 30, 1978   106
13. The HSCA Report: January 1979   111
14. Following the Footprints of Conspiracy: 131
    January–September 1979
15. Disruption, Relocation and Continuation: 145
    1978–1988
16. More Leads, More Loose Ends: 158
    Spring–Summer 1989
17. James Earl Ray's Legal Representation   166
    Reexamined

Part IV: The Television Trial of James Earl Ray

18. Preparations for the Television Trial of   179
    James Earl Ray: November 1989–September 17, 1992
19. Pretrial Investigations: September–October 1992   192
20. Corroboration and New Evidence: November 1992   207
21. Making A Case: December 1992   233
22. The Trial Approaches: January 1993   249
23. The Eve of the Trial: January 24, 1993   272
24. The Trial: January 25–February 5, 1993   281
25. The Verdict: February–July 1993   303

Part V: The Continuing Investigation

26. Loyd Jowers's Involvement: August–December, 1993   311
27. Breakthroughs: January–April 15, 1994   331
28. Setbacks and Surprises: April 16–October 30, 1994   348
29. Raul: October 31, 1994–July 5, 1995   372
30. Orders to Kill   411
31. Chronology   462
32. Conclusion   493

Appendix   497
Notes   503
Acknowledgments   507
Index   511

THE PRINCIPAL PLAYERS

The Memphis Police Department (MPD) in 1968

Frank C. Holloman	former FBI agent and Director of Memphis Police and Fire Departments
J. C. MacDonald	Chief of police
William O. Crumby	Assistant Chief
Sam Evans	Inspector—head of all Special Services including the emergency tactical units (TACT)
Don Smith	Inspector in charge of Dr. King's personal security in Memphis in the 1960s
N. E. Zachary	Inspector—homicide

Eli H. Arkin   operational head of the intelligence
                               bureau

J. C. Davis   detective in the intelligence bureau

Emmett Douglass   driver of TACT 10 cruiser on
                               afternoon of April 4, 1968

Joe B. Hodges   patrolman/dog officer

Barry Neal Linville   homicide detective

Marrell McCollough   undercover intelligence officer
                               assigned to infiltrate the Invaders

Ed Redditt   black detective seconded to
                               intelligence bureau

Willie B. Richmond   black intelligence bureau officer

Jim Smith   officer assigned to Special Services
                               and detailed to intelligence; later
                               attorney general's investigator

Tommy Smith   homicide detective

Jerry Williams   black detective

The Memphis Fire Department in 1968

Carthel Weeden   captain in charge of station 2

Lt. George Loenneke   second in command station 2

William King   fireman station 2

Floyd Newsom   black fireman station 2

Norvell Wallace   black fireman station 2

The Judges

Preston Battle, Jr.   Shelby County Criminal Court trial
                               judge in 1968

Joe Brown, Jr.   Shelby County Criminal Court trial
                        judge in 1994–95

The Prosecutors

Phil Canale   Shelby County District Attorney
                        General in 1968–69

John Pierotti   Shelby County District Attorney
                        General in 1993–95

James Earl Ray's Lawyers

Arthur Hanes Sr. &   James Earl Ray's first lawyers
Arthur (now Judge)
Hanes Jr.

Percy Foreman   James Earl Ray's second lawyer

Hugh Stanton Sr.   court appointed defense co-counsel
                        with Percy Foreman in 1968–69

James Lesar   James Earl Ray's lawyer in the early
                        1970s

Jack Kershaw   James Earl Ray's lawyer in the mid
                        1970s

Mark Lane   James Earl Ray's lawyer from 1977 to
                        the early 1980s

William F. Pepper   (Author) chief counsel 1988 to
                        present

Wayne Chastain   Memphis attorney—defense associate
                        counsel 1993 to present; Memphis
                        Press Scimitar reporter in 1968

The U.S. Government

Executive Branch in 1967–68

Lyndon Baines Johnson   President

Robert S. McNamara   Secretary of Defense

The FBI in 1967–68

J. Edgar Hoover   The director

Clyde Tolson   associate director; close friend and
                              heir of J. Edgar Hoover

Cartha DeLoach   assistant Director

William C. Sullivan   assistant director in charge of
                              Domestic Intelligence Division and
                              expansion of COINTELPRO
                              (Counter-Intelligence Program)
                              operations

Patrick D. Putnam   special agent seconded to U.S. army
                              Assistant Chief of Staff for
                              Intelligence

Robert G. Jensen   special agent in charge (SAC)
                              Memphis field office

William Lawrence   special agent in charge of
                              intelligence for the Memphis field
                              office

Joe Hester   Memphis field office special agent in
                              charge of coordinating the
                              Memphis area investigation

Al Sentinella   FBI special agent in the Atlanta field
                              office who controlled SCLC
                              informant James Harrison in 1967–68

Arthur Murtagh   FBI agent assigned to the Atlanta
                              field office in 1967–68

The CIA in 1967–68

Richard M. Helms　　　　　Director

U.S. Army in 1967–68

OFFICE OF CHIEF OF STAFF

Gen. Harold Johnson　　　　Chief of Staff

ARMY INTELLIGENCE

Brigadier General William H. Blakefield	Commanding officer United States Army Intelligence Command
Major General William P. Yarborough	Assistant Chief of Staff for Intelligence ("ACSI")
Gardner (pseudonym)	key aide of 902nd Military Intelligence Group
Col. F. E. van Tassell	Commanding Officer, ACSI office security and Counter-Intelligence Analysis Board ("CIAB")
Gardner's aide (pseudonym)	Gardner's aide—his number two
Herbert (pseudonym)	staff officer ACSI's office, Pentagon
Col. Robert McBride	Commanding officer 111th Military Intelligence Group, Ft. McPherson, Georgia

20TH SPECIAL FORCES GROUP (20TH SFG) IN 1967–68,
HEADQUARTERS, BIRMINGHAM, ALABAMA

Col. Henry H. Cobb, Jr.	Commanding Officer
Major Bert E. Wride	second in command

Capt. Billy Eidson (dec.)	Alabama contingent
Second Lt. Robert Worley (dec.)	Mississippi contingent
Staff Sgt. Murphy (pseudonym)	Alabama contingent
Staff Sgt. Warren (pseudonym)	Alabama contingent
Buck Sgt. J. D. Hill (dec.)	Mississippi contingent

PSYCHOLOGICAL OPERATIONS (PSY OPS'')

Reynolds (pseudonym)	photographic surveillance officer
Norton (pseudonym)	photographic surveillance officer

The House Select Committee on Assassinations (HSCA)

Louis Stokes	Chairman of the HSCA
Richard Sprague	former Pennsylvania prosecutor and first HSCA chief counsel in 1976
Robert Blakey	chief counsel of the HSCA 1977–79
Walter Fauntroy	Chairman sub-committee on the Assassination of Martin Luther King, Jr. in 1976–79

Southern Christian Leadership Conference (SCLC) Officials in 1967–68 Who Were Witnesses To Significant Events Or On The Scene

Rev. Dr. Martin Luther King, Jr.	president

Rev. Dr. Ralph D. Abernathy	vice president/treasurer
Rev. Andrew Young	executive vice president
Rev. Hosea Williams	chief field organizer
Rev. James Orange	field organizer
Rev. James Lawson	Memphis representative who invited Dr. King to Memphis

The Invaders in 1967–68

Charles Cabbage

Dr. Coby Smith

"Big" John Smith

Charles "Izzy" Harrington

Calvin Taylor

Other Significant Figures

Lavada (Whitlock) Addison	owner of a restaurant frequented by Frank C. Liberto in 1978
Willie Akins	friend of Loyd Jowers
Amaro ("Armando") ———	cousin of Raul ———
Walter Bailey	owner/manager of the Lorraine Motel in 1968
Clifton Baird	Louisville, Kentucky police officer in 1965
Arthur Baldwin	Memphis topless club owner in the 1970s

Myron Billet

occasional driver for Chicago mob leader Sam Giancana in the 1960s

Kay Black

reporter for the Memphis *Press Scimitar* in 1968

Ray Blanton

Governor of Tennessee in 1976 when Ray escaped from prison

Earl Caldwell

New York Times reporter at the Lorraine Motel on April 4, 1968

Carson (pseudonym)

associate/friend of Sgt. J. D. Hill of 20th SFG

Sid Carthew

British merchant seaman who visited the Neptune tavern in Montreal in 1967

Cheryl (pseudonym)

acquaintance/associate of Amaro ———— and his cousin Raul ———— from 1962–1979

Joe "Zip" Chimento

Marcello New Orleans associate and coordinator of Marcello weapons trading and gunrunning in 1967–68

Chuck (pseudonym)

six year old boy in 1968, alledgedly sitting in parked car on Mulberry Street at the time of the shooting

Morris Davis

FBI/DEA informant in 1968 and HSCA informant/researcher in 1977–78

Daniel Ellsberg

former defense department specialist who released the *Pentagon Papers*

Hickman Ewing, Jr.

former U.S. attorney and chief prosecuting counsel for the television trial of James Earl Ray

April Ferguson

associate of Mark Lane in 1978 and defense co-counsel for the television trial of James Earl Ray

Marvin E. Frankel

former U.S. federal District Court

	judge and judge for the television trial of James Earl Ray
Eric S. Galt	employee in 1967–68 at Union Carbide Corporation's Toronto operation with U.S. government Top Secret security clearance; the identity used by James Earl Ray in 1967–68
Lewis Garrison	Memphis attorney for Loyd Jowers
Memphis Godfather	Carlos Marcello's principal associate in Memphis
James Harrison	SCLC controller in 1967–68 and paid FBI informant
Ray Alvis Hendrix	eyewitness who left Jim's Grill ten to fifteen minutes before the shooting on April 4, 1968
Kenneth Herman	Memphis private investigator
O. D. Hester "Slim"	friend of Ezell Smith
Frank Holt	trucker's helper employed by M. E. Carter in 1968
Charles Hurley	Memphis resident who picked up his wife in front of the rooming house on the afternoon of April 4, 1968
Solomon Jones	Dr. King's driver in Memphis in 1968
Loyd Jowers	owner of Jim's Grill on South Main Street in Memphis in 1968
Jim Kellum	Memphis private investigator for the defense
(William) Tim Kirk	inmate at Shelby County Jail 1978, and at Riverbend Maximum Security Prison in 1992–present
Reverend Samuel "Billy" Kyles	Memphis minister

James Latch   Vice president of Memphis LL&L Produce Company and partner of Liberto in 1968

Frank Camille Liberto   President of LL&L Produce Company in Memphis in 1968

Phillip Manuel   investigator for the Permanent Sub-Committee on Investigations of the United States Senate in 1968

Carlos Marcello   New Orleans, mafia leader in 1967–68

John W. ("Bill") McAfee   Memphis photographer covering Dr. King on assignment from network television on April 4, 1968

James McCraw   Yellow Cab driver in 1968, driving on the evening of April 4

John McFerren   Somerville, Tennessee businessman and civil rights leader in 1968

Sheriff Bill Morris   Shelby County Sheriff in 1967–68

Red Nix   Marcello organization contract killer

Oliver Patterson   FBI and HSCA informant in 1977–78

Paul ____   Yellow Cab driver in 1968, driving on the evening of April 4

Raul ——   shadowy figure whom James Earl Ray met in the Neptune Bar in Montreal in July 1967

James Earl Ray   the alleged assassin of Dr. Martin Luther King, Jr. who has as of March 10, 1995 been in prison for 26 years

Jerry Ray   youngest brother of James Earl Ray

John Ray   younger brother of James Earl Ray

William Zenie Reed   eyewitness who left Jim's Grill ten to fifteen minutes before the shooting on April 4, 1968

Randy Rosenson	man whose name was on a business card found by James Earl Ray in the Mustang in 1967
Jack Saltman	Thames Television producer of the Trial of James Earl Ray in 1993
William Sartor	*Time* magazine stringer and investigative reporter, died mysteriously in 1971
Bobbi Smith	waitress at Jim's Grill in 1967–68
Ezell Smith	employee at a Liberto family business in Memphis in 1968
Betty Spates	mistress of Loyd Jowers in 1967–68 and waitress at Jim's Grill
Dr. Benjamin Spock	pediatrician, author, political activist and potential vice president candidate on a proposed King-Spock ticket in 1968
Gene Stanley	former U.S. Attorney and Knoxville lawyer for Randy Rosenson in the 1970s
Charles Quitman Stephens	422½ South Main Street rooming house tenant in room 6-B and State's chief witness against James Earl Ray in 1968
Maynard Stiles	deputy director of the Memphis Public Works department in 1968
Alexander Taylor	senior Florida intelligence officer in 1968
Steve Tompkins	Memphis *Commercial Appeal* reporter in 1993
Ross Vallone	Houston associate of Carlos Marcello in 1967–68
Louie Ward	Yellow Cab driver in 1968, driving on the evening of April 4

Nathan Whitlock   son of Lavada (Whitlock) Addison
                             who met Frank C. Liberto in 1978
                             in his mother's restaurant

John Willard   alias used by James Earl Ray for
                             renting a room at 422½ South
                             Main Street on April 4, 1968

Glenn Wright   prosecution co-counsel in the
                             television trial of James Earl Ray

Walter Alfred "Jack"   U.S. army Vietnam Special
Youngblood   Operations Group operative, pilot,
                             intelligence agent and mercenary

Introduction

LIKE MOST PEOPLE, I accepted the official story about how Dr. Martin Luther King, Jr., was murdered. I believe this was the result of my naiveté or perhaps the desire to put the loss of a friend behind me. In any case, when Dr. Benjamin Spock, the pediatrician and antiwar activist, and I traveled to Memphis for the memorial march on April 8, 1968, four days after the assassination, so far as I was concerned it was in the hands of the police.

In the following years, I heard about inconsistencies in the state's case and rumors of a conspiracy in which James Earl Ray was framed for Dr. King's murder. Then in 1977–1978, at the Rev. Ralph Abernathy's request I prepared for and then conducted a five-hour interview of James Earl Ray. Since that time, the mystery of Dr. King's assassination has dominated much of my life. In no small measure I suppose this is because of the responsibility I feel for having initially prompted him to oppose the Vietnam War—for that stand was a major factor contributing to his death.

The intervening years have only strengthened my belief that Dr. King's assassination constituted the greatest loss suffered by the republic this century. To understand his death it is essential to realize that though he is popularly depicted and perceived as a civil rights leader, he was much more. A nonviolent revolutionary, he personified the most powerful force for long overdue social, political, and economic reconstruction of the nation.

Those in charge of the United States intelligence, military, and law enforcement machinery understood King's true significance. They perceived his active opposition to the war and his organizing of the poor as grave disruptions to the stability of a society already rife with unrest, and took the position that he was under communist control.

The last year of his life was one of the most turbulent in the history of the nation. Much of the civil unrest took the form of nationwide urban riots and was clearly the result of racial tensions, frustrations and anger at oppressive living conditions and the endemic hopelessness of inner-city life. However, one cannot consider these explosions without taking into account the pervasive presence of the war, its legitimization of violence, and its overall impact on the neighborhoods of the nation.

By July 1967, the number of riots and other serious disruptions against public order had reached ninety-three in nineteen states. In August there were an additional thirty-three riots which occurred in thirty-two cities in twenty-two states.

Dr. King was at the center of it all. His unswerving opposition to the war and his commitment to bring hundreds of thousands of poor people to a Washington D.C. encampment in the spring of 1968 to focus Congress's attention on the plight of the nation's poor, turned the government's anxiety into utter panic. I believe that there was no way Dr. King was going to be allowed to lead this army of alienated poor to Washington to take up residence in the shadow of the Washington memorial.

When army intelligence officers interviewed rioters in Detroit after the July 25, 1967 riot—which left nineteen dead, eight hundred injured, and $150 million of property damage—they were amazed to learn that the leader most respected by those violent teenagers was not Stokely Carmichael nor H. Rap Brown but Dr. Martin Luther King, Jr.

Six weeks after the Detroit riot the National Conference for New Politics (NCNP) scheduled a national convention over the Labor Day weekend in Chicago. The gathering of 5,000 delegates from all around the country and from every walk of life was expected to support a third-party presidential ticket of Dr. King and Dr. Spock. We now know how much shock this prospect caused at the highest levels of government.

So caught up were we in the fight for social change that we didn't appreciate the strength and determination of the opposition. It has become clear to me that by 1967 a siege mentality had descended on the nation's establishment forces, including its federal law enforcement, intelligence and military branches. At the best of times, official Washington and its appendages throughout the country are highly insular and protective. In 1967–1968, with the barbarians, as they would have regarded them, gathering just outside the gates of power, any move in defense of the system and its special economic interests would have been viewed as a patriotic duty. All significant organizations committed to ending the war or fostering social or economic change were infiltrated, subjected to surveillance, and/or subverted.

This book has been in development since 1978 and reflects a long-term effort to uncover the truth about the assassination. It does not cover the full scope of the investigation since many leads were examined and discarded and much information, however interesting, ultimately turned out to be superfluous to the central story. In 1988, I agreed to represent James Earl Ray, and by 1990 I had become convinced that the only way to end his wrongful imprisonment would be to solve the case. The investigation on which the book is based has been focused on that goal. However, for a period of nearly seven years prior to publication, I've tried in every way possible to put evidence of James's innocence before a court. Frustrated at every turn, I now turn to the court of last resort—the American people.

This story has taken twenty-seven years to unfold. This is

largely the result of the creation and perpetration of a cover-up by government authorities at local, state, and national levels.

I've become convinced that, had they not met obstruction from within their own ranks, some of the honest, competent Memphis homicide detectives I've come to know over the years could have ferreted out enough evidence to warrant indicting several Memphians on charges ranging from accessory before and after the fact, to conspiracy to murder, to murder in the first degree. Among those indicted would have been some of their fellow officers. Even without official obfuscation, however, it's unlikely that these detectives could have traced the conspiracy further afield to its various well-insulated sources.

As will become increasingly clear, it was inevitable that such a local police investigation wouldn't be allowed and that each and every politically sponsored official investigation since 1968 would disinform the public and cover up the truth.

Years of investigation led to an unscripted television trial in 1993 that resulted in a not-guilty verdict. My subsequent investigation has unearthed powerful new evidence. The stories of several key witnesses, silent for twenty-seven years, are revealed for the first time. Although we will never know each and every detail behind this most heinous crime, we now have enough hard facts to overwhelmingly support James Earl Ray's innocence. The body of new evidence, if formally considered, would compel any independent grand jury—which, as of the time of this writing, we have been seeking for a year and a half—to issue indictments against perpetrators who are still alive. Even as this book goes to press we are pursuing all possible avenues through the courts to obtain justice and free James, as well as to bring to account those guilty parties whom we have identified.

Ultimately, there are many victims in this case: Dr. King; James Earl Ray; their families, and the citizens of the United States. All have been victimized by the abject failure of their democratic institutions. The assassination of Martin Luther King and its coverup extends far and wide into all levels of government and public service. Through the extensive control of information and the failure of the system of checks and balances, government has inevitably come to serve the needs of powerful special interests. As a result, the essence of democracy—government of, by, and for the people—has been terminally eroded.

Thus, what begins as a detective story ends as a tragedy of unimagined proportions: Dr. Martin Luther King, Jr., is dead; James Earl Ray remains in prison; many of the guilty remain free, some even revered and honored; and our faith in the United States of America is shaken to the core.

William F. Pepper
London, England

Glossary

ACLU American Civil Liberties Union

ACSI Assistant Chief of Staff for Intelligence

agency Central Intelligence Agency

Alpha 184 Team Operation Detachment Alpha 184 Team. Special Forces Field Training Team in specialized civilian disguise selected from 20th SFG

AFSCME Association of Federal, State, County and Municipal Employees Union

agent provocateur covert operative used to infiltrate a targeted group and influence its activity

AUTOVON first generation fax machine—state of the art in 1967

ASA Army Security Agency

asset government independent contract agent whose actions may be officially denied

behind the fence operation covert, officially deniable operations

body mass assassin's human target area—the chest area

BOP Black Organizing Project (companion organization of the Invaders)

bureau   Federal Bureau of Investigation
center mass   another term for "body mass" (see above)
CIA   Central Intelligence Agency
CIAB   Counterintelligence Analysis Board
CINCSTRIKE   Commander–in–Chief U.S. Strike Command
C.O.   Commanding Officer
COINTELPRO—FBI counterintelligence program aimed at
   targeted dissenting/protest groups.
COME   Community on the Move for Equality (coalition of labor
   and civil rights groups in Memphis formed at the time of
   the sanitation workers strike spearheaded by an interracial
   committee organized by local clergy)
COMINFIL   FBI designation for a communist infiltration
   investigation of a targeted group
committee   House of Representatives Select Committee on
   Assassinations
CONUS   Continental United States
D.A.   District Attorney
DEA   Drug Enforcement Agency
DEFCON   Acronym for national security emergency with
   seriousness expressed in ascending order, e.g. DEFCON 2,
   3, 4
DIA   Defense Intelligence Agency
ELINT   electronic intelligence surveillance
FBI   Federal Bureau of Investigation
HSCA   House of Representatives Select Committee on
   Assassinations
HUMINT   Human Intelligence Source (informer)
IEOC   Intelligence Emergency Operation Center—army
   intelligence communications and deployment centre which
   was established in an area where civil unjest was anticipated
Invaders   small militant black organizing group in Memphis,
   oriented toward self-help
IRR   Investigative Records Repository—army intelligence records
   repository at Fort Holabird where intelligence files on
   civilians were kept
LAWS   light anti–tank weapon rockets
LL&L   Liberto, Liberto & Latch (produce company owned by
   Frank C. Liberto)
MIGs   Military Intelligence Groups (counterintelligence)
MPD   Memphis Police Department

NAACP National Association for the Advancement of Colored People

NAS Millington Naval Air Station

NCNP National Conference for New Politics

NLF National Liberation Front

NSA National Security Agency

ONI Office of Naval Intelligence

Operation CHAOS CIA program for the collection of information on citizens and groups through the interception and reading of mail, and the placement of informants and covert operators in dissenting organizations

Operation MINARET NSA watch–list program collecting information on individuals and organizations involved in civil disturbances, antiwar movements and military deserters

OS Office of Security—department in CIA from which a variety of super secret covert operations was mounted, often involving members of organized crime

Project MERRIMAC CIA SOG project which focused on infiltration of and spying on ten major peace and civil rights groups

Project RESISTANCE 1967 OS project designed to infiltrate meetings of antiwar protestors, recruit informants and report on black student activities in cooperation with local police

Psy Ops Psychological Operations

recon. reconnaissance

SAC FBI Special Agent in Charge—ranking officer in any field office

SCLC Southern Christian Leadership Conference

SFG Special Forces Group a.k.a. the Green Berets

SNCC Student Non Violent Coordinating Committee

SOG Special Operations Group—small covert often interservice operations groups formed for a particular purpose

TACT (TAC) emergency tactical units deployed in Memphis at the time of the sanitation workers strike which consisted of twelve men in three or four vehicles

TBI Tennessee Bureau of Investigation

USAINTC U.S. Army Intelligence Command (the overall army intelligence organization)

USIB United States Intelligence Board

THE SCENE OF THE ASSASSINATION

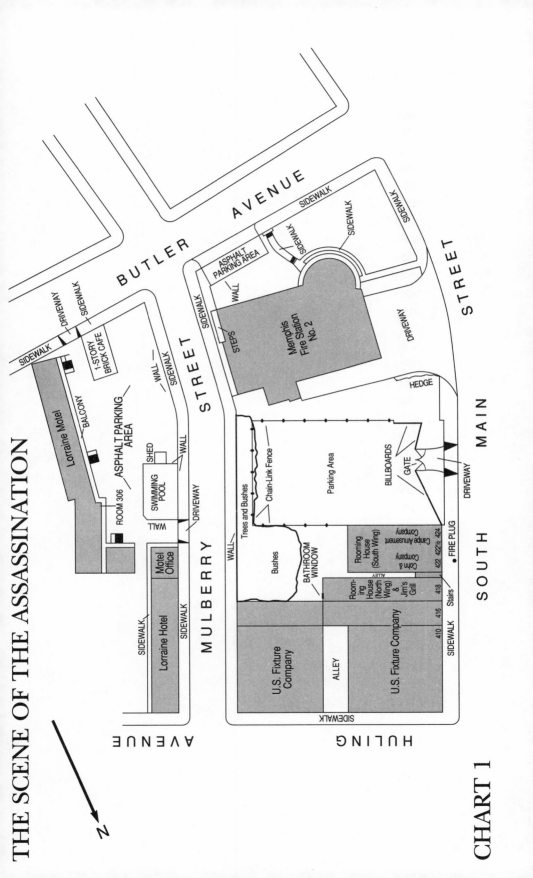

CHART 1

PART I

Background to the Assassination

1

Vietnam: Spring 1966– Summer 1967

THIS STORY BEGINS IN VIETNAM, where I had gone as a freelance journalist in the spring of 1966.

Soon the picture became clear. Wherever I went in South Vietnam, from the southern delta to the northern boundary (I corps), U.S. carpet bombing systematically devastated the ancient, village-based rural culture, slaughtering helpless peasants. Time and again, in hospitals and refugee camps, children, barely human in appearance, their flesh having been carved into grotesque forms by napalm, described the "fire bombs" that rained from the sky onto their hamlets.

After a time in the field, I suffered a minor injury in a crash landing near Pleiku caused by ground fire. I returned to Saigon, where I went to a party held by some casual friends. I was tired and upset. For several days in the Central Highlands I had been confronted with one atrocity after another. Because I was far from a battle-hardened correspondent, I wasn't taking it very well. Soon I was approached by a young Vietnamese woman who solicited information from me. Aided by a few drinks, I expressed my disgust with the U.S. involvement in the war. The woman appeared sympathetic. After that evening, I never saw her again.

The next day I was summoned by Navy Commander Madison, the press accrediting officer, who my colleagues advised was an intelligence operative. He commented on my absence from the daily Saigon press briefings (at which the military line was disseminated) and stated that he had received reports of unacceptable remarks made by me. He advised me that my accreditation was going to be revoked.

I returned home and began to prepare articles for publication and testimony to be given before Sen. Edward M. Kennedy's Subcommittee to Investigate Problems Connected with Refugees and Escapees. My article "The Children of Vietnam" was published by *Ramparts* in January 1967, during which time Dr. Martin Luther King, Jr., was becoming increasingly concerned over the Johnson administration's plans to reduce its domestic antipoverty spending in order to channel more funds to the war effort.

Dr. King hadn't yet categorically broken with the White House over the issue, but soon after the *Ramparts* article appeared he received calls from Yale chaplain William Sloane Coffin, *Nation* editor Carey McWilliams, Socialist Party leader Norman Thomas, and others, urging him to take a more forceful antiwar stand and, indeed, to even consider running as a third-party presidential candidate in 1968. I would later learn that wiretaps of the conversations in which the candidacy was discussed were relayed to FBI director J. Edgar Hoover and, through him, to Lyndon Johnson.

On Saturday, January 14, King flew to Jamaica, where he had planned to work on a book about one of his most ardently held beliefs—the idea of a guaranteed income for each adult citizen. He was accompanied by his friend and associate Bernard Lee. While having breakfast he began to read the January *Ramparts*. According to Lee, and also recorded by David Garrow in his historical account, *Bearing the Cross*,[1] Dr. King was galvanized by my account of atrocities against civilians and the accompanying photographs. Although he had spoken out against the war before, he decided then and there to do everything in his power to stop it.

Dr. King's new commitment to oppose the war became his priority. He told black trade unionist Cleveland Robinson and longtime advisor Stanley Levison that he was prepared to break with the Johnson administration regardless of the financial consequences and even the personal peril.[2] He saw, as never before, the necessity of tying together the peace and civil rights movements, and soon became involved in the antiwar effort. He spoke at a forum sponsored by the *Nation* in Los Angeles on February 25, 1967, joined Benjamin Spock (a proposed running mate in his possible third-party candidacy) in his first antiwar march, through downtown Chicago on March 23, and began to prepare for a major address on the war to be presented at the April 15 Spring Mobilization demonstration in New York.

From the beginning of the year, he began to devote more time to the development of a new coalition. He had come to believe it was time to unite the various progressive, single-issue organizations to form a mighty force, whose power would come from increased numbers and pooled funds. The groups all opposed the war and all wanted equal rights for blacks and other minorities, but their primary concern was eliminating poverty in the wealthiest nation on earth. These common issues formed the basis of the "new politics," and the National Conference for New Politics (NCNP) was established to catalyze a nationwide effort. I was asked to be its executive director.

Though our emphasis was on grassroots political organizing, our disgust with the "old politics," particularly as practiced by the Johnson administration, compelled the NCNP to consider developing an independent presidential candidacy. To decide on this and adopt a platform, a national convention—to be attended by delegates from every organization for social change across the land—was scheduled for the 1967 Labor Day weekend at the Palmer House in Chicago.

In New York on Tuesday, April 4, exactly twelve months before his death, Dr. King addressed an audience of more than three thousand at Riverside Church and made his formal declaration of opposition to the war. He expressed his concern that his homeland, the Great Republic of old, would never again be seen to reflect for the world "the image of revolution, freedom and democracy, but rather come to mirror the image of violence and militarism." He called for conscientious objection, antiwar demonstrations, political activity, and a revolution of values whereby American society would radically shift from materialism to humanism.

Response to the speech was prompt and overwhelmingly condemnatory. Old friends (such as Phil Randolph and Bayard Rustin) either refused to comment publicly or disassociated themselves from King's position. The domestic economic and civil rights progress of Lyndon Johnson was strongly supported by liberals and civil rights leaders who were loathe to alienate the president by opposing his war effort. I noted Dr. King's increasing pessimism that resulted from continued sniping from civil rights leaders like Roy Wilkins of the National Association for the Advancement of Colored People (NAACP) and Whitney Young of the National Urban League. (We didn't know at the time that Wilkins was meeting and working with the FBI's assistant director, Cartha DeLoach,[3] throughout this period.) Even some of King's closest longstanding personal advisors were opposed to the speech. For example, it was ironic that Stanley Levison, long labeled by the FBI as the strongest "communist" influence on Dr. King, attempted in every way possible to restrain King's efforts to oppose the war formally.

The reaction from newspaper editorials was virtually always negative. The *Washington Post*, the *New York Times*, and *Life* magazine joined the chorus of criticism.

During the run up to the April 15 antiwar demonstration, Dr. King and I discussed not only the effect of the U.S. war effort in Vietnam but also political strategy in general and particular details of the demonstration. Five days before the demonstration, the NAACP board of directors passed a resolution attacking King's effort to link the peace and civil rights movements. Martin said to me in a moment of frustration, "They're all going to turn against me now, but still we must press on. You and the others must not only be steadfast, but constantly so."

He and others asked me to put forward the idea of a King-Spock ticket at the demonstration. He didn't want to appear to be explicitly seeking such a nomination, for the media would certainly paint him as engaging in a self-serving quest, to the detriment of his professed calling and cause. If, on the other hand, he was pressed or drafted into the race, he could answer the call and run—not to win, but to heighten national debate and awareness.

On April 15, as Dr. King concluded his speech by calling on the government to "stop the bombing," the crowd had grown to about 250,000 cheering and chanting partisans. When I put forward the notion of a King-Spock ticket, the assembled mass exploded as one in support. For many of us the end of that demonstration marked the first step in the establishment of a "new politics" in the United States.

On April 23, 1967, as Martin and I rode together to Massachusetts to announce, with Ben Spock, the beginning of a grassroots organizing project called Vietnam Summer, a man whose name meant nothing to us at the time but whose life was to become inextricably intertwined with ours, was being helped into a bread box in the kitchen of the Missouri State Penitentiary in Jefferson City. The box was loaded onto a delivery truck that would take James Earl Ray through the gates to freedom.

2

Death of the New Politics: Summer 1967– Spring 1968

THE NCNP CONVENTION ON LABOR DAY WEEKEND 1967 began with great enthusiasm and expectation. Many of us believed that nothing less than the nation's rebirth was on the agenda. Dr. King's rousing keynote address, calling for unity and action, brought forth an overwhelming response from the 5,000 delegates. It was the most political speech he would ever give.

There was, however, an ominous presence. A small aggressive group had pressed each arriving black delegate into a self-styled Black Caucus. Dr. King's safety was in danger from this group, which had threatened to take him hostage, so he had to depart quickly under guard as soon as he finished speaking.

Torn by dissension, the convention descended into a fiasco; any chance of achieving a unified political movement was destroyed.

More than a decade would pass before we would become aware of the extent of the government's role in the disaster. And not until later than that would we realize that a coalition of private and public forces had orchestrated it.

For example, we would learn that a CIA operation, named Operation CHAOS, had been put in place to enable the subversion of dissent and undermine such gatherings of dissenting citizens. Operation CHAOS involved the collection of information on private citizens and groups through the interception and reading of mail, and the placement of informants and covert operators in dissenting organizations. At the NCNP convention, the tactic used was to divide the black and white delegates using the so-called Black Caucus, which we thought at the time was a natural outgrowth of the legitimate Black Power movement.

Black Caucus delegates voted *en bloc* and used outrageous techniques—provoking strident emotionalism; playing on white guilt, divisiveness, and intimidation; calling for the use of arms; and introducing blatantly anti-Semitic resolutions. Years later we learned that they were organized by the government and backed by federal funds, filtered through Chicago Mayor Richard Daley's antipoverty organization, and that the members included individuals from one of Chicago's most feared street gangs—the Blackstone Rangers.

The convention became hopelessly embroiled in animosity and walkouts by some leading liberal sponsors of the New Politics movement itself. Some, like Martin Peretz (the Harvard instructor, who was one of the moving forces) felt personally betrayed, understandably so considering the amount of time and resources they had expended on the convention. We didn't admit it at the time, but the NCNP died as a political force that weekend. Its focus permanently changed from national political activity to fragmented local political organizing efforts.

The inevitable weakening of these disparate efforts made them easy marks for infiltration by groups of *agents provocateurs*. (One such organization, the Invaders, would emerge in Memphis. This group of twenty or so black men and women developed a series of programs designed to address local needs by providing services where none had previously existed. The Invaders were significant because of their proximity to Dr. King in the weeks leading up to his assassination. They were infiltrated by intelligence operatives and subjected to surveillance out of all proportion to any threat they might have posed to the Memphis power structure.)

DR. KING AND I KEPT IN TOUCH AFTER THE CONVENTION. Though he was immensely disappointed by the Chicago catastrophe, he nevertheless increased his antiwar efforts. He also threw himself into the development of the Poor People's Campaign, scheduled to assemble in Washington in the late spring of 1968. The first phase of this campaign would bring to Washington up to several hundred thousand blacks, Hispanics, American Indians, poor whites, and compatriot students and intellectuals from all over the country. A tent city would be set up and civil disobedience tactics would be taught and used, if necessary, to get the attention of the White House, Congress, and various government agencies.

This combination of opposition to the war and a call for redistribution of the nation's wealth served to increase King's unpopularity with the government. It also antagonized segments of the black and white middle class as well as the black church. No doubt it confirmed the belief held by certain public and private forces that King was a serious threat to the very order and system of U.S. government. No one could predict what would happen when he led a massive wave of alienated citizens to take up residence in the nation's capital.

Those close to Dr. King noticed how the pace of his radicalization increased in the last year of his life. His analysis of the problems of American society had become much broader. His growing belief in the necessity of dissent against powerful special interests was, in fact, much like Jefferson's assertion that ultimate power should always flow from the people, otherwise tyranny results.

This perspective was driven home to me in the course of our last meeting. The last time I saw him alive was in Dean John Bennett's study at Union Theological Seminary in New York

City. It was March 1968, and Andrew Young, executive director of the Southern Christian Leadership Conference (SCLC) and Ben Spock were also present. Spock was seeking Martin's active support for draft resistance, since Martin believed that the war was tantamount to genocide by conscription. At this time Martin was becoming fully involved in a strike of sanitation workers in Memphis. He spoke about the necessity of empowering such urban blacks through nonviolent action.

3

Memphis: The Sanitation Workers' Strike: February 1968– March 1968

BEGINNING IN FEBRUARY 1968, Dr. King had received regular reports from his friend, Memphis clergyman James Lawson, pastor of Centenary Methodist Church, about the sanitation workers' dispute in that city. Ninety percent of the thirteen hundred sanitation workers in Memphis were black. They had no organization, union or otherwise, to defend their interests and no effective means to air grievances or to seek redress. However, to most of the citizens of Memphis, black and white, a strike against the city was nothing less than rebellion.

In a bitter and frustrating setback for the black community, Henry Loeb, who had been the mayor from 1960 to 1963, defeated incumbent William Ingram, who was regarded as friendly to black Memphians, in the mayoral election. Considering the new mayor's history and reputation, there was no reason for black workers to hope that their working conditions or salaries might improve.

The grievances were many. Salaries were at rock bottom, with no chance of increase. Men were often sent home arbitrarily, losing pay. Much of the equipment was antiquated and poorly maintained. In early 1968 two workers, thirty-five-year-old Echole Cole and twenty-nine-year-old Robert Walker, were literally swallowed up by a malfunctioning "garbage packer" truck. These trucks were over ten years old and in the process of being phased out. There was no workmen's compensation and neither man had life insurance. The city gave each of the families a month's pay and $500 toward funeral expenses. Mayor Loeb said that this was a moral but not a legal necessity. After the deaths of Cole and Walker, talk of a strike was widespread.

Maynard Stiles, who was second-in-command at the Memphis Public Works Department, told me, years after the event, that T. O. Jones, the head of the local union, called him the night before the strike with what Stiles regarded as a very reasonable list of demands. Stiles said that Jones wanted him to go along to the union meeting scheduled for that night and announce the city's agreement with the terms. An elated Stiles called Loeb to advise him that a settlement was at hand on very reasonable terms. Loeb ordered him not to dignify any such meeting with his presence and insisted that no terms be accepted under any circumstances. The union meeting went ahead that evening without Stiles. The next day the strike was on.

The national office of the Association of Federal, State, County and Municipal Employees (AFSCME) sent in professional staff to handle the negotiations, which the mayor insisted on conducting in public, giving neither side any opportunity to change position. With no solution in sight, an interdenominational group of clergy intervened but made no progress.

The deadlock led to a protest march on February 23, which got out of control in the face of heavy police provocation. Ultimately, the police used Mace on men, women, and children—marchers and bystanders alike. Afterward, a strike strategy committee was formed with the Rev. James Lawson as its chairman. Rev. Lawson had been one of the founders of the

SCLC and had worked with the organization for a decade. Dr. King regarded him highly.

Meanwhile, Dr. King was closing a leadership conference in Miami. While knowing that most of his audience disagreed with the Poor People's Campaign, he insisted that the nation had to be awakened to the issues of poverty and hunger. The shantytown he planned to erect in Washington would ensure that the plight of the American poor would be foremost in the consciousness of the people of the nation, even the world.

"We are Christian ministers and . . . we are God's sanitation workers, working to clear up the snow of despair and poverty and hatred. . . ." he told them.

In Memphis, a city injunction against the strike intensified the black community's support for the sanitation workers, and consumer boycotts and daily marches through the downtown area were organized. The director of the Memphis police and fire departments, Frank Holloman, who had agreed that he would allow the marches if they were peaceful, withdrew many of the visible, uniformed police. Holloman had been a special agent of the FBI for twenty-five years. For seven of those years (1952–1959), he had been in charge of director J. Edgar Hoover's Washington office. In Memphis he had no support from the black leaders. Internally he relied heavily on his chief, J. C. MacDonald (who in 1968 was close to retirement), a group of seven assistant chiefs, Inspector Sam Evans who was in charge of all Special Services, and Lieutenant Eli H. Arkin of the police department's intelligence bureau.

THE GROWING INVOLVEMENT OF YOUNG BLACKS, particularly high school students who were being organized by the Invaders and their parallel organization, the Black Organizing Project (BOP), brought an increased volatility to the strike. During a boycott of local merchants, these young people harassed blacks who made purchases in downtown stores. The militants made themselves heard throughout the dispute, and various Invaders were arrested for disorderly conduct, for trying to persuade students to leave school, and for blocking traffic. In retrospect, the Invaders' actions seem mild in comparison with those of other black power groups in other parts of the country.

Community on the Move for Equality (COME), a coalition of labor and civil rights groups spearheaded by an Internal Committee of local clergy, which was now running the strike, sought national as well as local publicity, scheduling nationally prominent leaders to speak in Memphis in support of the workers. The local NAACP chapter asked Roy Wilkins to come; the local union sought to bring in longtime civil rights leader Bayard Rustin; and the Rev. Lawson raised the possibility of bringing Dr. King to Memphis. Wilkins and Rustin finally agreed to come on March 14.

Lawson, who had been keeping Dr. King abreast of developments, approached him in late February when the civil rights leader was close to physical exhaustion. It was around this time that his doctor had ordered complete rest.

AT FIRST KING HAD BEEN RELUCTANT to become directly involved. He had delivered speeches in Memphis but had never headed any civil rights activity there aside from leading the so-called "march against fear," which was organized in response to the Mississippi shooting of James Meredith, the first black to enroll at the University of Mississippi. But even though some SCLC executive staff wanted to stay away from the strike, Dr. King came to see it as being directly relevant to the national campaign.

What group could be more illustrative of the exploitation he sought to dramatize than these lowliest nonunion workers who daily took the garbage away from the city's homes? King's involvement was potentially a high-profile activity (though with some risks) that would lead naturally into the Washington Poor People's Campaign. Because Memphis contained a small, militant, black organizing group (the Invaders) as well as the more conservative, southern black congregations, it was, in his view, a microcosm of the nation, with all of the attendant problems and obstacles to the development of a successful coalition. How could he turn his back on the real, current struggle of the Memphis sanitation workers?

In early March the Rev. Lawson made the announcement that the city had been waiting for. The SCLC had transferred a March 18 staff meeting scheduled for Clarksdale, Mississippi, to Memphis, and on that evening Dr. King would address a gathering of strike supporters.

4

Enter Dr. King: March–April 3, 1968

ALTHOUGH DR. KING had experienced problems and setbacks, particularly concerning his position against the war, no one approached his stature on the national scene as a spokesman for the black and poor of America. His involvement would inevitably focus national attention on the strike, its issues, and its nonviolent tactics.

On March 18, the Mason Temple overflowed. Crowds sat on the floor, on the stairs, in the aisles and doorways; scores of others stood in the street. Dr. King entered through a side door, and a human wedge of burly volunteers swept him along to the podium. The sound of applause and stamping feet increased to a deafening roar. Reverend Ralph Abernathy, vice president of SCLC, told me it was one of the most moving welcomes he had ever seen.

When King advocated a general work stoppage in Memphis, the Temple nearly burst into pandemonium. He sat down to tumultuous applause and then received a note, initialed by Andy Young and Ralph Abernathy, suggesting that he return to lead a march on the day of the work stoppage.

Dr. King returned to the microphone and said that perhaps the Poor People's Campaign could begin in Memphis. If the people wanted him to, he would lead such a march to city hall. The response was predictable. The date was set for March 22, four days later. Organizers began to spread the word that Dr. King would return to Memphis to lead a march on Friday from Clayborn Temple to city hall. Ten thousand marchers were expected.

White apprehension rose. Hate literature was circulated throughout the city. Then, incredibly, on the day before the march, the city, whose average annual snowfall was only 5.6 inches, was buried by a blizzard that dumped 16.2 inches of snow, the second-largest snowfall ever recorded in Memphis. The city was virtually shut down and the march had to be postponed until Thursday, March 28. Early on the morning of the march, King left New York City for Memphis.

Organizers began to intercept students on the way to school or even at the school gates, urging them to join the march. A confrontation between police and students at Hamilton High School resulted in a student being injured. Word spread that the police had killed a girl at the school, and the young people's anger grew. It was not an auspicious start for Dr. King's nonviolent march.

The Memphis police department (MPD) was completely mobilized that morning, with over 300 officers supplemented by fifty sheriff's deputies committed to the general march area. Emergency mobile TACT units run by Inspector Sam Evans were also standing by. Each unit consisted of twelve sheriff's deputies and MPD officers, with three cars and four men to each car. This was the first use of a TACT squad in Memphis. Since there weren't enough shotguns to go around, a number of officers carried their personal weapons.

The police were anxious. Riot training had been virtually nonexistent in Memphis, except for a special, elite group. Their own constantly circling helicopter only added to the uneasiness.

Dr. King was late and the crowd became increasingly restless. Some leaders, such as the Rev. Samuel "Billy" Kyles, wanted to start the march without King, but Reverend Lawson insisted on waiting. For a long time Lawson had tried to involve Kyles in the strike support planning sessions but finally agreed with the others that it was a waste of time—for Kyles rarely, if ever, showed up; though he frequently attended the public meetings.

Dr. King and Ralph Abernathy finally arrived at the march site just before 11:00 a.m., having been driven directly from the airport. They led the march, linking arms with local ministers, but signs of unrest were everywhere. Trouble began in short order as the line of march proceeded up Beale to Main. The sounds of glass breaking, isolated at first, got louder and more frequent. Youths ran alongside the line of march, ignoring the marshals' instructions. Chaos descended, and Dr. King was persuaded to leave the area. A car was flagged down and he was taken to the Rivermont Hotel at the direction of the police, being escorted by motorcycle officer Lt. Marion Nichols. He was given lodging even though he had no reservation at that hotel (rooms having been reserved at the Peabody Hotel).

After Dr. King had been spirited away, Lawson moved through the line of march with a bullhorn, urging everyone to return to the church where they had begun. As thousands began to turn around, the sounds of breaking glass continued. Youths darted from one store to another, shattering windows. Some began looting, but eyewitnesses maintain that they were followed by older, more experienced hands who quickly and efficiently took advantage of the window-breaking, entered the stores, and came away with goods. The police moved in behind the disorganized crowd and fired Mace and tear gas.

Around 11:30 a.m. Frank Holloman and Mayor Loeb called Gov. Buford Ellington and requested the Tennessee National Guard. By noon, a contingent of the State Highway Patrol was on the way to Memphis and the first National Guard units were assembling.

The police and the sheriff's officers randomly clubbed a number of onlookers and customers of stores, pool halls, restaurants, and lounges, which, under the orders of Inspector

Sam Evans, were forcibly closed. A sixteen-year-old boy, Larry Payne, was shot and killed by the police who claimed he was a looter, and when cornered, had pulled a knife. An eyewitness said that Payne had his hands up when shot. A knife was allegedly found at the scene, but no fingerprints were on it. That evening, a curfew was put in place and Guardsmen descended on the city from all over western Tennessee, accompanied by eight armored personnel carriers.

By Friday morning, 282 persons had been arrested and held without bond; sixty-four persons were treated in hospital emergency rooms by midnight Thursday, with another ten coming in over the weekend. Dr. King was savagely attacked by the media and the Washington establishment. Congressmen tripped over each other in their haste to condemn him and to demand that on the basis of the Memphis experience the Poor People's Campaign in Washington be called off.

Dr. King's SCLC aides, who had had no hand in planning the march, believed that local incompetence had set them up for this disaster. Rev. Lawson believed that the young militants, who hadn't been involved in planning the march either, would have to be brought in with the SCLC. Dr. King met with three leaders of the Invaders (Charles Cabbage, Calvin Taylor, and Charles "Izzy" Harrington) the morning after the march, and it was agreed that the Invaders would be fully involved in the planning and development of strategy for the next one. Though depressed over the violence, Dr. King was buoyed by the meeting. At an afternoon press conference he expressed confidence in the new working relationship. He also confirmed that he would take time out from his schedule to prepare for the Washington campaign, and once again return to Memphis to lead a large nonviolent march. This time the SCLC would assist in the planning. Meanwhile, the boycott and local marches would continue. Nonviolence was still seen as the only viable strategy.

The following Saturday, March 30, SCLC staff and some board members met in Atlanta to discuss whether to continue in Memphis. Some in the SCLC staff (including newcomer Jesse

Jackson) counseled him to cut his losses and turn his attention to the Poor People's Campaign.

Ralph Abernathy told me that King privately had made the decision to march again in Memphis, but understandably he wanted the SCLC's support. Finally Dr. King obtained the support he wanted. The decision to return became official on Saturday afternoon, March 30, 1968.

On March 31, in an act that I long regarded as unrelated to the events of this story, Lyndon Johnson announced before a nationwide radio and television audience that he wouldn't seek reelection. Fifteen days earlier Robert Kennedy had announced his intention to challenge Johnson for the presidency. I would learn years later that FBI director J. Edgar Hoover had informed Johnson around that time that Kennedy had been attempting to reach Dr. King to advise him of his decision. Kennedy was seeking King's support and participation in what promised to be a difficult and bitter campaign.

SCLC organizers—including James Bevel, James Orange and Jesse Jackson—went ahead to Memphis to take over the arrangements for the march, the date of which was firmly set for April 5. Six thousand union members from all over the country were to come to Memphis. One after another, labor and civil rights groups announced their support.

On Monday, April 1, Mayor Loeb announced the end of the curfew, and units of the National Guard slowly began to leave, ready to be called up quickly if needed for the next march. The funeral for Larry Payne, the sixteen-year-old casualty of the first march, was held at the Clayborn Temple the next day, followed by a speech by Ralph Abernathy that evening to an overflow crowd. He checked in at the Peabody that evening, but the next day would transfer to the Lorraine when Dr. King arrived.

On Wednesday morning, city attorney Frank Gianotti appeared in U.S. district court before Judge Bailey Brown and requested a temporary restraining order against certain named out-of-state residents (King, Abernathy, Hosea Williams, James Bevel, James Orange, and Bernard Lee) to prevent them "from organizing in or engaging in a nuisance parade or march in the city of Memphis." Judge Brown issued the restraining order but set it down for a hearing the next morning.

Dr. King's flight arrived in Memphis at 10:33 a.m., having been delayed by a bomb threat. His party was picked up and taken straight to the Lorraine Motel. After checking in, they went to the Rev. Lawson's church to meet with clergy and union leaders and with one set of lawyers. Then they adjourned to the Lorraine Motel to eat in the restaurant and meet with the BOP group around 4:00 p.m. At that meeting Dr. King agreed to assist in the funding of a black cooperative and a "liberation" school.

The Lorraine, today the National Civil Rights Museum, is a two-story building at 406 Mulberry Street, located in a rundown warehouse and rooming house area of the city, five blocks south of Beale Street and a block east of South Main (see Chart 1, the front's piece). It had been black-owned and operated from its beginning. Walter and Lorraine "Lurlee" Bailey took it over in 1955 when it was a fourteen-room structure. By 1965 it had nearly fifty new units and a swimming pool. It was a family-run motel, with Bailey and his wife doing most of the work and cooking.

Checking in with the SCLC advance staff on April 2 were James Laue of the Justice Department's Community Relations Service (room 308) and photographer Joseph Louw, who had been traveling with Dr. King while working on a documentary about the Poor People's Campaign (room 309).

Dr. King was scheduled to address a mass meeting at the Mason Temple, and, in spite of a storm, several thousand people were expected. Ralph Abernathy told me that King was tired and wanted to stay at the motel and meet and talk to a few people. As he had done the night before, he asked Ralph Abernathy to stand in for him and address the group.

Abernathy remembered entering the side door of the temple, drawing applause as he was recognized. The applause subsided when the crowd failed to see Dr. King behind him. He didn't even attempt to speak but instead went around the side of the hall to a telephone in the vestibule from which he called Dr. King and told him, "Your people are here tonight and you ought to come and talk to them. This isn't my crowd. It's your crowd. I can look at them and tell you that they didn't come tonight to hear Abernathy. They came tonight in this storm to hear King.''

King came.

Tornado warnings had been issued. The storms swept out of Arkansas and across Tennessee and Kentucky, leveling houses, barns, utility lines, and trees. It left twelve people dead and more than 100 injured. The wail of civil defense sirens sounded across the city, adding to the eerie and expectant atmosphere inside the Mason Temple. Dr. King arrived around 9:00 p.m. to rapturous applause.

Dr. King's speech, his last, was one of his most famous, and certainly, his most prophetic, ending:

> . . . *Like anybody, I would like to live a long life.*
> *Longevity has its place.*
> *But I'm not concerned about that now.*
> *I just want to do God's will.*
> *And he's allowed me to go up to the mountain and I've looked over and I've seen the Promised Land.*
> *I may not get there with you.*
> *But I want you to know tonight*
> *THAT WE AS A PEOPLE WILL GET TO THE PROMISED LAND.*
> *So I'm happy tonight.*
> *I'm not worried about anything, I'm not fearing any man.*
> *MINE EYES HAVE SEEN THE GLORY OF THE COMING OF THE LORD!*

PART II

The Assassination

5

The Assassination:
April 4, 1968

THURSDAY, APRIL 4, was the fifty-third day of the strike. While Dr. King slept, Judge Bailey Brown began to hear arguments on whether the temporary restraining order should be made permanent, thus making it illegal for the march which had been rescheduled for April 8 to go ahead. The legal team representing Dr. King and his colleagues requested a dismissal or a modification of the existing order and proposed a series of restrictions on the march, acceptable to Dr. King. Around 4:00 p.m. that afternoon, Judge Brown announced that he was going to let the march proceed, subject to those restrictions.

In the late morning Dr. King met with some of the Invaders and then met with Abernathy over lunch in their room, 306. Abernathy recalled that after the meal, Dr. King and his younger brother, Alfred Daniel "A. D." King, who had arrived unexpectedly, joked with their mother on the telephone to Atlanta, probably from A. D.'s room, 201. Shortly afterward the executive staff meeting began in room 306. Hosea Williams has told me that at that meeting Dr. King took him to task for attempting to put some of the Invaders on the SCLC staff (Hosea was always a keen strategist, and he saw the usefulness of co-opting some of the Invader leadership to their side). Dr. King said that he couldn't appreciate anyone who hadn't learned to accept nonviolence, at least as a tactic in the struggle if not in one's way of life. He said he didn't want the SCLC to employ anyone who didn't totally accept nonviolence.

The meeting was in full swing when Andy Young returned from court to give his report. He was later than expected and had also neglected to call in and give a report on how the proceedings in court were going, as King had asked him to do. He was jokingly taken to task. Hosea remembers Dr. King tussling with him in the room, saying, "I'll show you who the leader is."

JUST ABOUT THE TIME that the staff meeting was heating up in the motel, less than three hundred feet away a man calling himself John Willard was registering for a sleeping room in the rear of the South Main Street rooming house whose back faced the Lorraine. Also during this time, one of the SCLC's senior field organizers, the Rev. James Orange, went off to do some shopping, driven by Invader Marrell McCollough. On the way back to the motel they picked up James Bevel at Clayborn Temple.

About two hours later, J. Edgar Hoover was about to have the first of his predinner martinis at his usual table at Harvey's Restaurant in Washington. The fact that he attended Harvey's for dinner as usual on that day would be cited by defenders of the FBI as indicating a lack of knowledge of the events that were to take place in the next half hour.

Reverend Kyles stated that he arrived at the motel around 3:00 p.m. and went from room to room for a period of time, visiting with various people. Dr. King and about fourteen other aides were to go to his house for a buffet dinner organized by his wife, Gwen. In *At the River I Stand*,[4] Joan Beifuss records in detail Kyles's comments on his activity during the last hour of Dr. King's life, which have now become accepted as fact. In light of what I learned later, I believe it useful to quote verbatim from her transcription of Kyles's story:

Ralph was dressed when I got in [to room 306] and Martin was still dressing. . . . Ralph said, "All right now, Billy. I don't want you fooling me tonight. Are we going to have soul food? Now if we go over there and get some filet mignon or T–bone, you're going to flunk. . . ." Martin says, "Yeah, we don't want it to be like that preacher's house we went to in Atlanta, that great big house. We . . . had some ham—a ham bone—and there wasn't no meat on it. We had Kool Aid and it wasn't even sweet. . . ." I said, "You just get ready. You're late." I had told them 5:00 and I told my wife 6:00. I said, "Hurry up. Let's go."

He was in a real good mood. . . . It may have been from what they accomplished in the staff meeting. . . . When Martin's relaxed he's relaxed. . . . He'd put his shirt on. He couldn't find his tie. And he thought that the staff was playing games with him, but we did find it in the drawer. When he put the shirt on, it was too tight. And I said, "Oh, Doctor, you're getting fat!" He said, "Yeah, I'm doing that.". . .

Ralph was still doing something. He's very slow. And we went back out together, Dr. King and myself, and stood side by side. . . . Solomon Jones [King's local driver] said something about it was getting cool and to get your coat. . . . I was greeting some of the people I had not seen. . . . Martin was leaning over the railing. . . .

I called to Ralph to come on. They were getting ready to load up. I said, "I'll come down. Wait a minute. Somebody can ride with me." As I turned and got maybe five steps away this noise sounded. Like a firecracker.

Some minutes after the shot, photographer Joseph Louw snapped the picture flashed around the world that showed a group of SCLC staff, including Andy Young, standing on the balcony pointing in the direction of the back of the rooming house. In the photograph a person is kneeling at the feet of the others, apparently checking Dr. King for life signs. At the time no one seemed to know who this person was.

The first call for help to the police department's dispatcher was recorded at 6:03 p.m. Calls went out from police dispatch and fire station 2 diagonally opposite the Lorraine, where patrolman Willie B. Richmond had sounded the alert.

Lt. Judson E. Ghormley of the Shelby County Sheriff's Department commanded TACT unit 10 (TACT 10) that afternoon. They were in place with three cars at fire station 2 on South Main and Butler. The TACT units each consisted of twelve officers from the MPD and the Shelby County sheriff's department. All, except officer Emmett Douglass, who was sitting in the unit's station wagon monitoring the radio, were inside the fire station drinking coffee, playing ping-pong, making phone calls, or talking. When the shot rang out and Richmond called out, "Dr. King has been shot!" all of the men ran out the north exit of the station and around to the rear of the building. Ghormley said he stopped at the concrete wall at the rear of the fire station, turned around, ran back to the front of the station, and headed north up South Main toward the rooming house, arriving in front of the recessed doorway of Canipe Amusement Company at 424 South Main within two minutes of the shot. There he found a bundle that contained a gun inside a cardboard box and several other items, including nine 30.06 unfired rifle bullets. One of the two customers in Canipe Amusement Company and Canipe himself described hearing a thump as the bundle was dropped and said that they noticed a young man pass by and a white Mustang parked just south of the shop pull away.

Sheriff's deputy Vernon Dollahite apparently arrived shortly after Ghormley from the opposite direction, having continued from the motel around the block up to South Main. He entered Jim's Grill located directly beneath the rooming house where John Willard had rented a room. (See Chart 1, page xxxiii). Dollahite ordered Loyd Jowers, the owner and manager of the grill, to lock the door and let no one in or out.

According to those present, Dr. King was lifted onto a stretcher and carried down the stairs to a waiting ambulance.

Ralph Abernathy rode with him to St. Joseph's Hospital. Bernard Lee, Andy Young, and Chauncey Eskridge, King's personal lawyer, followed behind in a car driven by Solomon Jones, a driver for the R. S. Lewis Funeral Home who had been provided to Dr. King as his chauffeur when he was in Memphis.

At that time Mayor Henry Loeb was on his way, driving south on Interstate 55 for a speaking engagement at the University of Mississippi. He spotted Sheriff Bill Morris's car. Morris told him what had happened. After the news was confirmed by MPD director Holloman, Loeb's car turned around and headed back to Memphis.

Around 6:30 p.m. a police dispatcher, William Tucker, received a call from a patrol car that supposedly was chasing a white Mustang across the northern part of the city.

Upon hearing about the shooting, Lorraine Bailey had screamed, run to her room, and collapsed on her bed. She suffered a cerebral hemorrhage and was rushed to St. Joseph's Hospital. She never regained consciousness and died the following Tuesday, just as the funeral for Dr. King began in Atlanta.

Rev. A. D. King had been in the shower when the shooting occurred. He was dressing when the ambulance left, and he remained at the motel, waiting for word from the hospital and keeping in touch with his parents in Atlanta.

At St. Joseph's, King was worked on feverishly by a team of five or six doctors in the emergency room while police sealed off the hospital. Early on it became apparent to the medical team that the high-velocity bullet had entered the right lower facial area around the chin, penetrated downward, and severed the spinal cord in both the lower neck, upper chest, and back regions.

Andy Young and Chauncey Eskridge waited in a small anteroom. Ralph Abernathy and Bernard Lee stood against the wall of the small emergency room, waiting while the doctors worked. Finally, neurosurgeon Frederick Gioia approached Abernathy and told him that there was no hope. The only life function remaining was King's heartbeat. Finally, that too ceased. Dr. Martin Luther King, Jr., was pronounced dead at

7:05 p.m. The hospital chaplain, Faith Coleman Bergard, reached the emergency room shortly afterward, and while Dr. King's aides prayed in the anteroom, he bent over the body, prayed, and closed the dead man's eyes.

Having heard about the shooting, Coretta King was on her way to board a plane for Memphis when the news of his death reached her. She returned home to be with their four children.

Around this time I was pulling into the driveway of my parents' home in Yonkers, New York. A bulletin announcing Dr. King's shooting came over the radio. Stunned, I sat immobile for several minutes.

For one bright moment back there in the late 1960s we actually believed that we could change our country. We had identified the enemy. We saw it up close and we had its measure—and we were very hopeful that we would prevail. The enemy was hollow where we had substance; shallow to our depth; callous, cruel, and unfeeling in the face of unashamed caring and love. All our dreams were instantly gone, destroyed by an assassin's bullet. To me they were as dead as the man who in my lifetime had been their prophet and whose remains were by now lying lifeless on a Memphis hospital operating table.

Shortly afterward I called Ben Spock. We arranged to travel together to Memphis for the memorial march the following Monday and then go to Atlanta for the funeral.

FEAR AND UNCERTAINTY PREVAILED in Memphis that evening. Telephone communications broke down in the central city. Though a curfew had been imposed and the meeting at Mason Temple, at which Dr. King was to speak, had been called off, masses of blacks, some unknowing, some in defiance, converged on the temple. By 8:15 p.m. window-breaking and rock-throwing incidents were increasing. By 9:00 sniper fire was reported in northern Memphis, and by 10:00 a building supplies company, just north of downtown, was the scene of a major fire. Rioting and looting became rampant, with liquor stores the main target. The first contingent of a four-thousand-strong National Guard force moved into the streets, joining the police, sheriff's deputies, state highway patrol, and fifty Arkansas highway patrolmen.

Eventually, Ralph Abernathy, Andy Young, Hosea Williams, and the other SCLC staff members regrouped at the motel and met into the early hours of Friday, April 5. All pledged loyalty to Ralph Abernathy as Dr. King's appointed successor.

By Friday morning the autopsy by Shelby County's medical examiner, Dr. Jerry Francisco, had been completed at John Gaston Hospital. Dr. King's body was then taken to R. S. Lewis and Sons Funeral Home, where people came to pay their respects.

Coretta King was on her way from Atlanta to escort the body home, and the SCLC staff gathered at the funeral home to take the body to the airport when she arrived. She and her children never left the private jet Sen. Robert Kennedy had chartered for her. Attorney General Ramsey Clark visited her on board and publicly announced, "All of our evidence at this time indicates that it was a single person who committed this criminal act."

6

Aftermath:
April 5–18, 1968

ON THE MORNING OF FRIDAY, April 5, President Johnson met with twenty-one civil rights leaders called to Washington from across the country. He then went to the National Cathedral and attended a memorial service for Dr. King in the midst of the ongoing insurrection and civil disorder in the capital.

Compared with the spontaneous violence of the night before, Friday in Memphis was relatively calm, as though the city had spent its anger in one short burst. The situation across the country was very different. By evening at least forty cities were in trouble; states of emergency were declared in Washington D.C., Chicago, Detroit, Pittsburgh, Baltimore, Wilmington, Delaware, and Newark.

Within twenty-four hours of the killing, the 30.06 Remington 760 Gamemaster rifle found in the bundle near the scene was traced, by its serial number, to the Aeromarine Supply Company in Birmingham, Alabama. The manager, Donald Wood, told investigators that a person named Harvey Lowmeyer had first bought a .243 Winchester on March 29 and then, strangely enough, exchanged it for the Remington the next day. On the rifle was a Redfield 2 × 7 telescopic sight which had been mounted at Lowmeyer's request.

A pair of binoculars also found in the bundle in front of Canipe's shop was traced by Memphis police to the York Arms Company, located a few blocks north of the rooming house on Main Street.

The rifle was packed in a Browning rifle box, along with a Remington Peters cartridge box containing nine 30.06 cartridges—four military type and five Remington Peters soft points. The rifle box had been wrapped in a bedspread, along with a zippered plastic overnight bag containing toiletries, a pair of pliers, a tack hammer, a portable radio, two cans of beer, and a section of the April 4 Memphis *Commercial Appeal.* In the rifle was an unejected cartridge case.

The Memphis City Council passed a resolution expressing condolences to Dr. King's family and issued a reward of $50,000 for information leading to the capture and conviction of the assassin. Since the *Commercial Appeal* and the *Press Scimitar* had also each pledged $25,000, the reward offer came to $100,000.

The march scheduled for Monday, April 8, was to go ahead as a memorial to Dr. King, with a rally in front of city hall, subject to the restrictions previously agreed upon and handed down by Judge Bailey Brown. On that cloudy Monday, Dr. Spock and I joined some forty thousand people, mostly local blacks, and slowly marched between the ranks of the five thousand National Guardsmen who lined the route from Hernando Street to City Hall.

Eventually Dr. Spock and I mounted the specially erected platform and joined the family, Ralph Abernathy, and others who would address the large outpouring of mourners. We went to Atlanta the next day for the funeral. There were about 100,000 mourners, including Vice Pres. Hubert Humphrey, walking slowly behind a mule-drawn caisson to the campus of Morehouse College for a service and then on to the burial in South View Cemetery. Prominent individuals who had increasingly turned their backs on Dr. King when during his last year he most needed them turned up at his funeral. The hypocrisy sickened me.

That evening, Robert Kennedy invited a number of us to a gathering in his hotel suite. I did not go—I regarded the senator's politically motivated actions as distasteful. I had long ago come to expect that from the Kennedys as a result of my previous experience as Robert Kennedy's Westchester County, New York, citizens chairman during his senatorial campaign in 1964. (We would learn years later that a less mature Attorney General Kennedy had given in to Hoover's pressure to permit the wiretapping of Dr. King.)

Negotiations aimed at settling the Memphis sanitation workers' strike would soon resume under intense presidential pressure for a settlement. An agreement was reached on April 16: the union was recognized and a pay raise was agreed to, as were the procedures for a dues checkoff through the Public Workers Federal Credit Union. The strike had lasted sixty-five days.

ON APRIL 10, Mrs. John Riley, in apartment 492 of the Capitol Homes Housing Project in Atlanta, telephoned the local FBI field office to report a Mustang that had been left in a small parking space near her building. She described it as white with a 1968 Alabama plate in the back and two Mexican tourist stickers on the windshield. She had heard that the police were looking for a man driving a white Mustang in connection with the killing of Dr. King. The Mustang, she reported, had been parked in that space since April 5.

A quick check showed that the car was registered in the name of Eric S. Galt, 2608 South Highland Avenue, Birmingham. The ashtray was overflowing with cigarette butts and ashes.

On April 12, the Miami FBI office issued and then immediately withdrew a statewide police bulletin calling for the location—though not the apprehension—of one Eric Starvo Galt.

A handwriting comparison indicated that Galt was also the man calling himself Harvey Lowmeyer who bought the rifle at the Aeromarine store in Birmingham. An analysis of fibers found in the trunk of the Mustang matched those on the pillow and sheets in room 5B of the rooming house rented by John Willard on April 4.

From interviews with acquaintances of Galt, the FBI learned that he had attended the International School of Bartending on Sunset Boulevard in Los Angeles. Tomas Reyes Lau, its director, provided a photograph of the man. Money orders cashed in the Los Angeles area, found to have been bought at the Bank of America by Eric S. Galt, were made out to the Locksmithing Institute of Bloomfield, New Jersey. The records of that institute showed that Galt had been receiving lessons by mail beginning in Montreal on July 17, 1967, with the latest lesson having been sent to 113 14th Street, Atlanta.

Local FBI agents descended on those premises on April 16. Learning that Galt still had ground-floor room number 2, they established physical surveillance for twenty-four hours. Author Gerold Frank maintained that when no one appeared, two agents acting under instruction from Cartha DeLoach, the FBI's assistant director in Washington, disguised themselves as hippies and rented a room adjoining No. 2 from James Garner, the landlord.[5] The connecting door was padlocked from the other side, so, according to Frank, DeLoach gave instructions to take the door off the hinges to get in (DeLoach has denied this). Thus, they obtained—possibly illegally because no warrant had been issued—a variety of items from the room, including a map of Atlanta with a clear left thumb print. Someone—apparently J. Edgar Hoover himself—suggested that the available fingerprints be compared against the prints of white men, under fifty, wanted by the police—the fugitive file. There were reportedly fifty-three thousand sets of prints in this category.

On April 17, the Birmingham FBI office sought a federal fugitive warrant for Eric Starvo Galt pursuant to an indictment charging a conspiracy to violate Dr. King's civil rights.

Beginning on the morning of April 18, the FBI specialists undertook the task of fingerprint comparison; by the next morning, the seven hundredth card matched. It belonged to a fugitive from a Missouri penitentiary. His name was James Earl Ray. It was clear: Galt and Ray were the same man.

7

Hunt, Extradition, and Plea: May 1968– March 10, 1969

WITH THE DEATH OF DR. KING, the media quite naturally turned their attention to the FBI-led search for the killer. The manhunt officially started on April 17 with the Birmingham indictment. From that time, the FBI ("the bureau") purported to mount an all-out campaign to search for Dr. King's murderer.

During this time, the bureau selectively leaked information to the media. One such leak was noted very early on by Martin Waldron of the *New York Times*. In his article entitled "The Search" published on April 20, 1968, he stated:

"Earlier there had been information leaks from the FBI that the fingerprints found on the rifle dropped on the Memphis street had been tested and had been found to be those of Ray."

On May 1, the *San Francisco Chronicle,* quoting certain "unimpeachable sources" of the *Los Angeles Times,* said that the FBI had found or obtained a map of Atlanta with "the area of Dr. Martin Luther King's residence and church circled and ... linked to accused assassin James Earl Ray." The article went on to state that "the map tends to support a theory by some investigators that Ray stalked Dr. King for some time before fatally shooting him on April 4." (On May 22, the Scripps-Howard newspaper chain carried the same story across the nation.) So, shortly after being identified, a leak, clearly from the bureau, portrayed Ray in the national media as a killer who consciously stalked his prey and left behind tangible evidence of his stalking.

Praise for the bureau manhunt also appeared in print. It was widespread and appears to have first been declared by nationally syndicated columnist and Hoover friend Drew Pearson in a column written with Jack Anderson that appeared on May 6, 1968:

> We have checked into the operations of the FBI in this respect and are convinced that it is conducting perhaps the most painstaking, exhaustive manhunt ever before undertaken in the United States.
>
> Its G-men have checked every bar ever patronized by James Earl Ray, every flop-house he ever stopped at, every cantina in Mexico he ever visited. It has collected an amazing array of evidence, all linking Ray with the murder.

In early May, as a matter of routine, the FBI asked the Royal Canadian Mounted Police (RCMP) to examine its files to assess whether anyone resembling the fugitive James Earl Ray might have applied for a passport recently. (A similar exercise under way in the United States had been unproductive.)

A task force of constables compared Ray's photograph with nearly a quarter of a million photographs submitted with passport applications from April 23, 1967 (the day of Ray's escape from prison).

On May 20, a young constable saw a photograph that looked like Ray. It was attached to the application of one Ramon George Sneyd, a thirty-five-year-old native of Toronto. The passport had been issued on April 24, 1968, and sent on that date to Sneyd care of the Kennedy Travel Bureau in Toronto.

Mr. Sneyd turned out to be a Toronto policeman who was clearly not the man in the photograph accompanying the passport application. Sneyd said that around the first of May he had a call from someone who claimed to be with the passport division inquiring whether he had lost his passport. When he said he had never had a passport the caller apologized, saying that it must have been a mistake, and then hung up.

The RCMP forwarded the passport application to the FBI laboratory in Washington for a handwriting comparison with the Galt signature. They matched.

Backtracking Ray's movements, the RCMP discovered he had apparently arrived in Toronto on April 8 and explored using not one but two new identities: Sneyd and Paul Edward Bridgeman, a thirty-five-year-old man who had some resemblance to Ray. Bridgeman had also received a telephone call asking if he had lost his passport. (He had had one eight years earlier.)

The RCMP also discovered that there was a Toronto citizen named Eric St. Vincent Galt who was the only Eric Galt listed in the Canadian telephone directories in 1968. He worked for Union Carbide, the U.S. defense manufacturer.

The RCMP quickly learned from the Kennedy Travel Bureau that Ray, as Sneyd, had left for London on a BOAC flight on May 6. Scotland Yard was contacted and every port of entry into the United Kingdom was alerted. The official reason was that Ramon George Sneyd, traveling on a Canadian passport, had violated the Alien Immigration Act. If apprehended he was to be held for questioning.

On the same day he flew to London, Ray flew to Portugal, where he obtained a new passport from the Canadian embassy that corrected a misspelling in the last name from "Sneya" to "Sneyd." He flew back to London on the 17th of May.

MEANWHILE, the U.S. media continued their coverage of the case. In a May 20 *Time* article, "acquaintances" reportedly re-

ferred to Ray as ". . . an obsessive racial bigot, an abrasive patron, who belted screwdrivers, dozed on the bar stool and
bickered with anyone around."

Time carried the FBI line on the death slug, stating that "the
unjacketed slug had been too badly marked for a definite comparison to be made."

A May 20 *Newsweek* article cited the FBI's comments on an
ad placed by Ray and another ad that he answered by sending
a Polaroid photograph in which he looked fatter than usual.
Newsweek reported that "bureau insiders said he was taking amphetamines off and on and his weight might well have fluctu-
ated sharply as a result." The article noted that the bureau
had released another photograph of Ray taken with a prostitute
in Mexico, but she was "clipped out." The article continued:

> Still, the fact of her presence—plus Galt/Ray's pathetic try
> for mail-order romance—yielded telling insights, and thus
> helped fill out his emerging portrait as an ingrown, emotion-
> ally stunted loner. The more investigators find out about their
> man, in fact, the less they see him as the conspiratorial type.
> "You take five guys who don't know each other and put them
> in a room," said one. "Four of them would start talking small
> talk to each other. Ray would sit by himself." He picked up
> the suspect's mug shot. "This is our man," he said. "He
> killed King."

Hence, in this one leak to *Newsweek* the bureau conveyed to
the American public, some two weeks before Ray's capture, that
the man being sought for the killing of Dr. King was a vice-
ridden loner and was certainly guilty.

Jeremiah O'Leary, a frequent mouthpiece for the bureau,
in an article in the *Washington Star* quoted unnamed convicts
interviewed by unnamed investigators (who could only have
been FBI agents tracking Ray) as saying that "Ray was a racist
and a habitual user of amphetamines while in prison." O'Leary
also maintained that "some of his fellow prisoners described
him as an anti-negro loner who spent much of his time in jail
reading sex books and girlie magazines."

Other wire service syndicated pieces were equally damning.

For example, one story under the leader "Ray Talked Of Bounty On King: Friend"[6] put out by UPI quoted a convict named Raymond Curtis, allegedly a friend of Ray, as saying that Ray told him that if there was a bounty on Dr. King, he would collect it if he got out. Curtis also alleged that Ray used dope, bragged about picking up lots of women, and was a loner.

It is difficult to imagine more damaging depictions of an accused person who hadn't yet even been apprehended, much less given a chance to tell his story.

ON SATURDAY, June 8, Ray, wearing a beige raincoat and shell-rimmed glasses, presented his Canadian passport at the desk at Heathrow Airport at approximately 11:15 a.m. He had been scheduled to fly on a British European Airways flight to Brussels at 11:50. Immigration officer Kenneth Human noticed a second passport when Ray pulled the first from his jacket and asked to see that one as well. It was identical except that it had been issued in Ottawa on April 4, and the last name was "Sneya." Ray explained the misspelling and stated that he had had no time to get it corrected before leaving Canada, requiring him to take care of it in Lisbon.

Ray was approached by Detective Sgt. Philip Birch of Scotland Yard, who asked to see the passports. He took Ray (as Sneyd) to a nearby room and telephoned Scotland Yard. Detective Chief Superintendent Thomas Butler and Chief Inspector Kenneth Thompson were notified and headed toward Heathrow. Ray was searched by Sergeant Birch, and the officer extracted a .38 revolver from his back right pocket, the handle of which was wrapped in black electrical tape. The six-chamber gun was loaded with five rounds.

Ray explained that he was going to Rhodesia and thought the gun might be needed because of the unrest there. Birch informed him that he was committing an offense for which he could be arrested. Shortly after 1:00 p.m., Butler and Thompson arrived, when Ray was placed under arrest for possession of a gun without a permit and was taken to Cannon Row police station, fingerprinted, and placed in a cell. Later Butler and Thompson told him that they had reason to believe he was not in fact a Canadian citizen but an American wanted in the United States for various offenses including murder with a firearm.

Solicitor Michael Eugene was appointed to represent Ray. Extradition was routinely opposed. Ray wrote to U.S. attorneys F. Lee Bailey of Massachusetts and Arthur J. Hanes of Birmingham, indicating that he was interested in seeking legal services in the event of his return to Memphis to stand trial on a murder charge. Bailey, who had been friendly with Dr. King, wasn't willing to act, but Arthur Hanes and his son Arthur, Jr., were interested and went to England in an effort to visit their new client. During their first trip, in June 1968, they were denied access, but soon afterward they were allowed to see him.

The extradition requests from the states of Tennessee and Missouri were based largely on the affidavit of one Charles Quitman Stephens, a resident of the South Main Street rooming house, who had emerged as the state's chief witness. He had provided a tentative eyewitness identification of Ray as a person he allegedly saw in the hallway of the rooming house around the time of the killing.

Extradition was granted. Ray appealed. Subsequently, on the advice of his new lawyer, Arthur Hanes, Sr., he dropped the appeal. While the extradition proceedings were in process, an entire cell block in the Shelby County Jail in Memphis was prepared for Ray in consultation with the federal government. When Ray was formally extradited to the United States on July 19, 1968, he was placed in the specially arranged facilities.

The Drew Pearson and Jack Anderson column on July 22, 1968, stated that Ray was a lone gunman. It began:

"It now looks as if the FBI has exploded the generally prevalent theory that the murder of the Rev. Dr. Martin Luther King involved a conspiracy."

The column went on to confirm that the FBI had "found a robbery where Ray probably got his money." It continued, "The FBI has been checking very carefully, and one of the robbers answers the description of James Earl Ray. He had the same long hair, the same height and the same physical makeup."[7]

Thus surfaced—for the first time—the Alton, Illinois, bank robbery story. This claim enabled the bureau in 1968 to explain how James covered his living expenses during his period as a fugitive. If he had obtained funds from this source, it could be contended that he had no help from anyone else. (Years later we would learn that not only had Ray nothing to do with this robbery but that there were other prime suspects.)

From that date, the Hanes father-and-son team, aided by local private investigator Renfro Hays, began to prepare for trial. Then a surprising thing happened. On November 10, just two days before the trial and after a visit from Texas attorney Percy Foreman, Ray dismissed Hanes and retained Foreman. On November 12, Foreman obtained an extension based on his coming into the case so late.

On December 18, concerned by Foreman's irregular attendance, the court appointed public defenders Hugh Stanton, Sr., and Hugh Stanton, Jr., to assist Foreman and ordered them to be ready to try the case if Foreman wasn't available because of his poor health. On January 17, the next court date set after the appointment of the Stantons, Foreman was indeed absent because of illness. The judge said that if Foreman was unable to handle the case, the Stantons would have to try it. The date was confirmed for March 3.

The Stantons assigned two investigators, George King and George Getz, to interview witnesses and work on the case. Foreman was sick for part of January, and the Stantons were obviously concerned about whether he would be able to carry on. They advised the court that they weren't going to be ready to go to trial on March 3. The trial was put off for another month.

Ultimately, the case never came to trial because James Earl Ray entered a plea of guilty on Monday, March 10, 1969.

THE MATTER WAS HEARD BEFORE JUDGE PRESTON BATTLE. When Judge Battle asked Ray if he understood that the charge of murder in the first degree was being levied against him in this case "because you killed Dr. Martin Luther King under such circumstances that it would make you legally guilty of murder in the first degree under the law as explained to you by your lawyers," Ray responded, "Yes, legally yes." After Ray affirmed that the plea of guilty was made freely and voluntarily with full understanding of its meaning and consequences, twelve names were called from the jury pool.

After the seating of the jury, Phil M. Canale. Jr., the district attorney general of Shelby County, introduced himself, his executive assistant, Robert Dwyer, and his assistant attorney general, James Beasley. His presentation to the court recommended punishment of a term of ninety-nine years. Canale indicated that even though the defendant had consented to the plea, accepted the stipulations, and verified the free and voluntary nature of his undertaking in the *voir dire*, the state was still obligated to provide fundamental proof to the judge and jury.

He concluded by saying that the investigation had been conducted by local police, national police organizations, and international law enforcement agents, and that his office had examined over three hundred items of physical evidence. His chief investigator had traveled thousands of miles throughout the United States and to foreign countries, and there was no evidence of any conspiracy involved in this killing, no proof that Dr. Martin Luther King, Jr., was killed by anyone other than or in addition to James Earl Ray. Canale pledged that if any evidence was ever presented that showed there was a conspiracy, he would take "prompt and vigorous action in searching out and asking that an indictment be returned, if there were other people, or if it should ever develop that other people were involved."

Percy Foreman then addressed the jury and said it had taken him a month to convince himself that there was no conspiracy. He maintained that he talked with his client for more than fifty hours and estimated that most of that time was spent in cross-examination, "checking each hour and minute and each expenditure of money down to seventy-five cents."

After his presentation, Foreman then asked each juror whether he was willing to subscribe to the verdict of ninety-nine years. Each juror answered, "Yes, sir." At the end of the polling the jury was officially sworn and witnesses called. Testimony was then taken from Reverend Kyles, Dr. King's personal lawyer Chauncey Eskridge, Coroner Dr. Jerry Francisco, homicide chief N. E. Zachary, and FBI special agent in charge Robert G. Jensen.

After a recess, Assistant Attorney General Beasley set forth the agreed-upon stipulation of facts that the state would prove, in addition to the testimony previously heard. Beasley summarized the state's interpretation of the actual killing and the details of the flight of James Earl Ray, his trip overseas, his apprehension, and his return.

Judge Battle asked the jury to raise their hands if they accepted the compromise and settlement on a guilty plea and a punishment of ninety-nine years. The jury was unanimous, and the verdict was signed. Ray was sentenced to ninety-nine years in the state penitentiary.

On the face of it, it was difficult to imagine how Ray could have so clearly admitted guilt if in fact he didn't commit the crime. (Only many years later would I learn about the extraordinary circumstances surrounding the guilty plea.) At one point in the proceedings he appeared to object to what was being said and done. After both sides accepted the jury, he interrupted the proceedings by saying:

"Your Honor, I would like to say something. I don't want to change anything that I have said, but I just want to enter one other thing. The only thing that I have to say is that I can't agree with Mr. Clark."

"Mr. who?" asked the court.

"Mr. J. Edgar Hoover, I agree with all these stipulations, and I am not trying to change anything."

"You don't agree with whose theories?"

"Mr. Canale's, Mr. Clark's, and Mr. J. Edgar Hoover's about the conspiracy. I don't want to add something on that I haven't agreed to in the past."

Then Mr. Foreman said, "I think that what he said is that he doesn't agree that Ramsey Clark is right, or that J. Edgar Hoover is right. I didn't argue that as evidence in this case, I simply stated that underriding the statement of [Attorney] General Canale that they had made the same statement. You are not required to agree with it at all."

Though the general public was made well aware of the guilty plea, Ray's equivocation at the hearing went largely unnoticed.

It was all over by lunchtime. Within three days of arriving at the penitentiary, Ray had written to the court requesting that his plea of guilty be set aside and that he be given a trial.

Three days after Ray's letter to the court, on March 16, the *Washington Post* led off a front-page national news section with the heading "Ray Alone Still Talks of a Plot."

After quoting Memphis prosecutors who had "access to the massive investigative files of the FBI" and who see "Ray as a man who had a general hatred of Negroes and at best an unspecific and unstructured desire to harm King," the article went on to assert that Ray remained the only person associated with the case who believed that there was a conspiracy.

The fact that many others—including Dr. King's widow, Ralph Abernathy, and other associates—believed in the existence of a conspiracy was ignored.

PART III

The Initial Investigation

8

Reentry: Late 1977–
October 15, 1978

DURING THE NEXT NINE YEARS I had virtually nothing to do with
the civil rights or antiwar movements, having walked away after
Dr. King's funeral. I had no hope that the nation could be
reconstructed without Martin King's singular leadership. There
quite simply was no one else. Ralph Abernathy and I had had
only sporadic contact during those nine years. I had completed
degree studies in education and law and written two books,
and he had taken on and then been forced to give up, with
some bitterness, the leadership of the SCLC.

IN LATE 1977, during a telephone conversation, Ralph told
me he wasn't satisfied by the official explanation of Dr.
King's murder and wanted to have a face-to-face meeting
with the alleged assassin of his old friend. He said he would
welcome an opportunity to hear Ray's story and assess it di-

rectly for himself. Would I arrange such a meeting and accompany him?

His interest in the case was clearly motivated by the activity of the House Select Committee on Assassinations (HSCA). HSCA investigations into the murders of President Kennedy and Dr. King were in progress at the time.

The HSCA had been formed in 1976 in response to a growing public disbelief in the conclusions of the report of the Warren Commission on the assassination of President Kennedy. Public confidence in government had been shaken early on by the allegations of New Orleans district attorney Jim Garrison, the Watergate scandal, and the 1973 Senate Judiciary Sub-Committee Report (detailing the widespread surveillance of American civilians by army intelligence). This was followed by the Rockefeller Commission Report issued in June 1975 (detailing CIA domestic activities against American civilians) and the findings of the 1975 House Judiciary Committee (detailing the FBI's counterintelligence program [COINTELPRO]). Confidence in the government sank even farther, if possible, as a result of the 1976 Church Committee Report (which contained one hundred pages devoted to FBI and other government agency harassment and surveillance of Dr. King), and the 1976 House Intelligence Committee report (covering the domestic activities of the CIA).

Walter Fauntroy, a former colleague of Abernathy and King, was chairman of the HSCA subcommittee investigating King's assassination. Although I was skeptical of such committees, having experienced congressional investigations of the antiwar movement a decade earlier, there was a general air of expectation that perhaps, at last, some of the hitherto unanswered questions would be addressed. It occurs to me now that Abernathy may well have been looking for a way to make his presence felt in this process.

To properly assist Ralph, I knew I had to do a considerable amount of preparation. I agreed to help him as long as no meeting took place until I believed that we were ready. I wasn't going to become involved in any way that would embarrass King's memory or allow Ralph to be used by a clever lawyer of Ray's. I believed we were likely to have only one opportunity to put some serious questions to Ray and I wanted us to make the most of it. It was clear that Ralph would be interviewed by the press at the end of our session, and any position he took would have to be based on solid information. If this were not the case, his renewed interest in the case could well prove to be an embarrassment to himself and a disservice to Ray's latest effort to obtain a trial. Ray had been trying to get a trial for nearly ten years. If the man was innocent, I certainly didn't want to hurt his chances for release. Ralph agreed to these ground rules, as did Mark Lane, Ray's lawyer at the time.

I read everything I could find about the killing, but there wasn't a great deal available. One of the earliest and most prominent works was Gerold Frank's *An American Death*,[8] which became, in effect, the official account of the case. Years later, I came across an internal FBI document dated March 11, 1969, the day after Ray's guilty plea hearing. This memo to Hoover's number two and closest confidant, Clyde Tolson, came from Assistant Director Cartha DeLoach. Specifically, he wrote:

Now that Ray has been convicted and is serving a 99-year sentence, I would like to suggest that the Director allow us to choose a friendly, capable author, or the *Reader's Digest,* and proceed with a book based on this case.

A carefully written factual book would do much to preserve the true history of this case. While it will not dispel or put down future rumors, it would certainly help to have a book of this nature on college and high school library shelves so that the future would be protected.

[Underneath this is handwritten the words "Whom do you suggest?"]

I would also like to suggest that consideration be given to advising a friendly newspaper contact, on a strictly confidential basis, that Coretta King and Reverend Abernathy are deliberately plotting to keep King's assassination in the news by pulling the ruse of maintaining that King's murder was definitely a conspiracy and not committed by one man. This, of course, is obviously a rank trick in order to keep the money coming in to Mrs. King, Abernathy, and the Southern Christian Leadership Conference. We can do this without any attribution to the FBI and without anyone knowing that the information came from a wire tap.

Respectfully,
C. D. DeLoach[9]

On the very next day, DeLoach transmitted an addendum in which he stated the following:

If the Director approves, we have in mind considering cooperating in the preparation of a book with either the Reader's Digest or author Gerold Frank. . . . Frank is a well known author whose most recent book is "The Boston Strangler." Frank is already working on a book on the Ray case and has asked the Bureau's cooperation in the preparation of the book on a number of occasions. We have nothing derogatory on him in our files, and our relationship with him has been excellent.[10]

At the bottom of this addendum is handwritten the word "O.K." and the initial "H."

Also at the bottom of DeLoach's letter to Tolson is a handwritten reference to George E. McMillan, which apparently refers to the bureau passing certain documentation to author George E. McMillan. McMillan, who had well-known intelligence connections, published a book on the case, *The Making of an Assassin,* which was allegedly a psychological profile of Ray and very much supported the bureau's lone assassin theory.[11]

Gerold Frank brought to light a few issues of interest. He revealed the presence of Memphis police detectives in the fire station across the street monitoring activity at the Lorraine, and the withdrawal on the afternoon of April 4 of one of them, Ed Redditt, ostensibly for his own safety after there had apparently been a threat on his life. He also mentioned the absence of an all points bulletin (a general alert describing the suspect) and a citizens band broadcast that drew police attention away from the downtown area where the shooting took place. He attributed the broadcast to a teenage hoaxer. Frank also disclosed a rumor that an eleven-year-old boy had seen the shooting and run into the fire station.

William Bradford Huie's book, *He Slew the Dreamer,* published in 1968, was compromised from the outset because the author had entered into contracts with two of Ray's lawyers, agreeing to pay them in exchange for information and leads that the defendant would provide in response to written questions carried to him by the lawyers.[12] Initially, Huie clearly accepted the existence of a conspiracy, even stating that the state's main witness, Charlie Stephens, was too drunk to be transported by cab driver James McCraw around the time of the shooting. Huie abruptly switched positions, however, to contend that Ray was a lone assassin.

During the early years after the killing, these books and the mass media gave prominent voice to significant aspects of the state's case. The prosecution's scenario was put out to the world as the final word.

The State's Case

The accused assassin was described as a racist whose motives for the crime were a hatred of blacks—Dr. King in particular— and a desire to achieve the recognition that responsibility for such a crime provided. The state rejected out of hand the existence of a shadowy figure named Raoul who Ray claimed set him up and directed his movements from the moment of their first meeting in August 1967 until the afternoon of the killing. (James never learned how the man spelled his name and spelled it differently at various times, eventually adopting the spelling "Raoul," although the more prevalent spelling of that Latin name is "Raul" which I have elected to use throughout.) The state claimed that Ray had allegedly stalked Dr. King for some time, beginning the weekend of March 17, 1968, when Dr. King arrived in Los Angeles.

Around March 22, Ray was in Selma, Alabama, near where Dr. King was scheduled to organize for his Poor People's Campaign. He was placed in Atlanta during the last week in March, leaving on March 30 to purchase the rifle. The state alleged that on March 31 he returned to Atlanta, where he left clothes at a local laundry on April 1. The Atlanta map discovered with Ray's belongings left behind in the Atlanta rooming house allegedly had markings around the locations of Dr. King's house, church, and office. Carrying the murder weapon with him, Ray arrived in Memphis on April 3, the same day on which Dr. King began his final visit to that city.

On April 4, Ray drove to the downtown area and rented a room under the alias John Willard in the seedy rooming house at 422 ½ South Main Street. While being shown around by landlady Bessie Brewer, he would reject one "housekeeping room" in the south wing of the house for a smaller "sleeping room" in the rear of the north wing. This room had a view of the Lorraine Motel, where, allegedly, Dr. King always stayed when he was in Memphis. The old rooming house had separate entrances for each wing. The room chosen by Ray, 5-B, which adjoined that of two long-term residents—Charles Quitman Stephens and Grace Walden—was at the end of a hall and near a rear-facing bathroom overlooking the motel balcony where Dr. King was standing when he was killed. (See chart 2, page 57.)

At one point during that fateful afternoon, Ray bought a pair of binoculars at the York Arms Store on South Main, allegedly driving there, and on his return parked his car in front of Canipe Amusement Company, just south of Jim's Grill. (See chart 3, page 58.) He then returned to his room, where he allegedly moved furniture around, placing a chair near the window so that he could better surveil the motel. Later on he allegedly entered the bathroom at the end of the hall and locked the door. He knocked a screen from the window down to the backyard area behind the rooming house. This overgrown yard ended at an eight-foot wall that rose up from Mulberry Street directly opposite the balcony. Standing in the bathtub (where scuff marks were left) and waiting for the right moment, he rested the rifle on the windowsill. At 6:01 p.m. he fired a single shot, the recoil from which dented the windowsill, and in his haste he neglected to eject the spent cartridge. The shot traveled just over two hundred feet, striking Dr. King in the lower right side of his face, the bullet

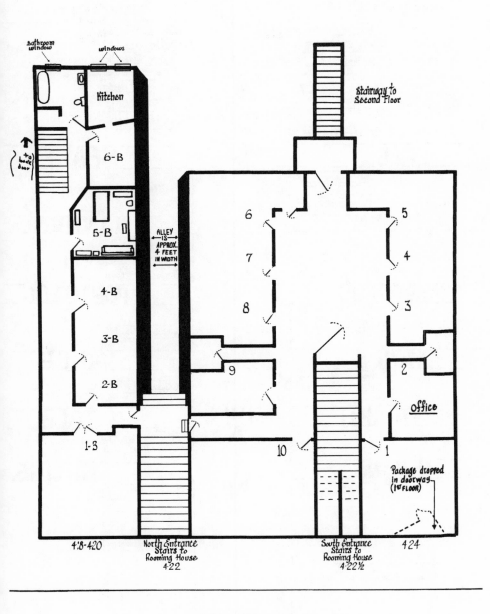

Bathroom
window

windows

kitchen

0

6-B

to
back
door

5-B

ALLEY
IS
APPROX.
4 FEET
IN WIDTH

4-B

3-B

2-B

1-B

4:8-420

North Entrance
Stairs to
Rooming House
4:22

Stairway to
Second Floor

6   5

7   4

8   3

9   2

Office

10   1

South Entrance
Stairs to
Rooming House
4:22½

Package dropped
in doorway
(1ˢᵗ FLOOR)

424

— SOUTH MAIN STREET —

CHART 2

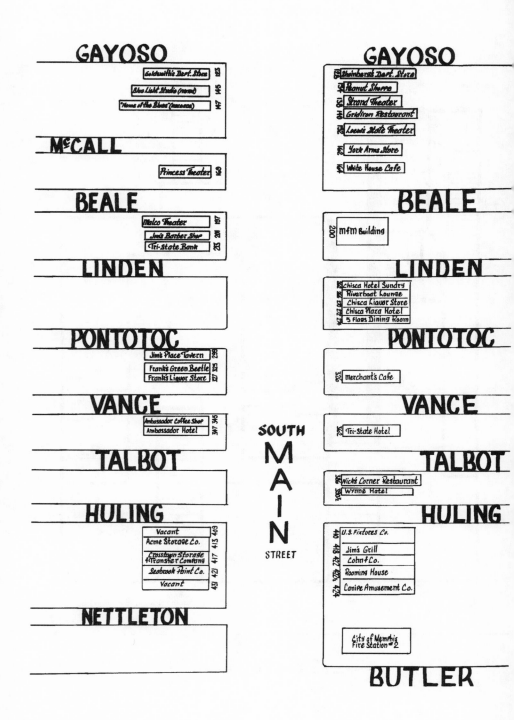

CHART 3

traveling downward and breaking his jaw, damaging his upper spine, and coming to rest just under the skin below the left shoulder blade.

Immediately after the shooting, Ray allegedly ran to his room, gathered his few belongings into a bundle, and ran down the front stairs, being viewed, as he ran, by Charles Stephens. (Another tenant, Willie Anschutz, also saw a man, whom he couldn't identify, run from room 5-B down the hall carrying some sort of package.) The state would say that, once on the street, Ray saw a police car parked facing the street near the sidewalk in the driveway of the fire station which caused him to panic and drop the bedspread-wrapped bundle in the recessed doorway of Canipe Amusement Company. He then jumped into his white Mustang just south of Canipe's and drove to Atlanta, where he abandoned the Mustang.

Ray then made his way to Canada and eventually to England as Ramon George Sneyd, in whose name he was able to obtain a passport. The state contended that in his determination to get as far away as possible, and in line with his racist inclinations, he explored the possibility of going to Rhodesia. When he was unable to arrange this during a trip to Portugal, he returned to England, where he robbed a bank. He was finally apprehended at Heathrow Airport while on his way to Brussels, where he had intended to explore other African emigration possibilities.

As to the funds he needed to live on during his fugitive period beginning April 23, 1967, the state contended that he committed various robberies, first in Canada and later in the United States. No evidence whatsoever existed of Ray receiving assistance from anybody, except perhaps members of his own family.

The picture of James Earl Ray that emerged then—as put out by the authorities from the time he was first identified on April 19, 1968, until he entered a plea of guilty on March 10, 1969, and ever after—was that of a dangerous career criminal who was also a bitter racist and a loner.

The Dissent

The only substantial dissenting voice in print in the early years after the assassination was that of investigative writer Harold Weisberg, who relied heavily on the findings of journalist Matt Herron (who was on the scene), news reports, articles, and telephone interviews.

Weisberg's book, *Frame Up*,[13] published in 1971, raised a number of new issues. They included the following:

- Eyewitness evidence of chauffeur Solomon Jones seeing someone in the brush immediately after the shot.
- A last-minute change of Dr. King's hotel from the Rivermont to the Lorraine and a change of his originally assigned room at the Lorraine.
- The presence of another white Mustang, parked in front of Jim's Grill, within one hundred feet of the Mustang parked in front of Canipe Amusement Company.
- The inability of the FBI laboratory to conclusively match the death slug to the alleged murder weapon.
- The absence of any fingerprints of Ray in the rooming house.
- The transfer of black firemen from the fire station near the scene the evening before the killing.
- The CB "hoax" broadcast that took place moments after the shooting, which Weisberg found indicative of the existence of a conspiracy.

He also briefly discussed a Louisiana state trooper named Raul Esquivel, whose Baton Rouge barracks contained a telephone whose number Ray had allegedly called. Weisberg obtained the number from *Los Angeles Times* reporter Jeff Cohen, who said he was given it by Charles Stein, whom Ray met in California and who rode with him from Los Angeles to New Orleans in December 1967. Stein allegedly had seen Ray dial the number and wrote it down.

Weisberg drew attention to the potential conflict of interest arising out of the literary contracts signed by Ray, his successive lawyers, and author William Bradford Huie. He also discussed at length the hostility of Hoover and the FBI toward Dr. King and the harassment he suffered at their hands. He developed early on a case for a conspiracy, with Ray as a pawn manipulated by a man named Raul.

Mark Lane's book, *Code Name Zorro,* published in 1977, provided other new information pointing to leads and discrepancies in the state's case.[14] Lane referred to the fact that a "screen" of bushes behind the rooming house had been cut down some time after the shooting. He disputed the official reason given by the MPD that the order to remove detective Redditt from his post shortly before the shooting was a result of a threat on Redditt's life. Redditt also told him that the Invaders were infiltrated by a black undercover cop who was an *agent provocateur* for violence and illegal activity. Redditt met him years later when the agent, who was undercover, pleaded for his cover not to be blown, saying that he was currently working for the CIA.

Lane's account further disputed the official story by contending that Dr. King had never previously stayed at the Lorraine. He quoted Memphis reporter Kay Black, who had covered some of Dr. King's earlier visits. She said that she remembered him staying at the Claridge Hotel, and before his last visit she didn't even know where the Lorraine Motel was located. Lane also questioned what had happened to the rooming house's register, which had long since disappeared.

Clearly only the secondary press attempted to raise the issues of the case and generate discussion about Ray's guilt or innocence.

Quietly and behind the scenes, as other commitments allowed, I began to investigate. When I became aware that on September 10, 1976, the MPD burned all the files of its intelligence bureau, despite an effort by the American Civil Liberties Union (ACLU) to prevent their destruction, I realized that a reconstruction of the events leading up to the assassination was going to be that much more difficult.

I TURNED WITH NEW INTEREST TO THE ACTIVITY OF THE HSCA. The first year of its work had been turbulent. Its first chief counsel, former Pennsylvania prosecutor Richard Sprague, a tough, honest professional, had been summarily replaced by Cornell University law professor G. Robert Blakey in early 1977.

Following Sprague's removal in the wake of concerted personal attacks against him by the press, it was evident that the scope of the subcommittee inquiry on Dr. King's death had become restricted solely to James Earl Ray and his brothers, John and Jerry.

In an interview with Sprague shortly after his dismissal, he told me he had taken the job because he was promised a free hand by the Ninety-fifth Congress, yet hardly had the committee been organized when House Speaker Tip O'Neill demanded, in order to justify additional funds, that it "prove" to the Congress there was a conspiracy. Sprague maintained that after he left, the committee's approach changed drastically. Whereas he had been committed to an open-ended, formal investigation for as long as it took and regardless of where it led, the new chief counsel clearly favored an approach that Sprague termed "evaluative" (as opposed to "investigative"), which focused on closing rather than opening doors. Articles, books, and stories were evaluated individually, without cross-referencing, so they couldn't be used as sources for new information. Sprague was cynically resigned to the fact that the public didn't care. He believed that Congress and the executive branch were at best never interested in a real investigation and at worst committed to covering up the truth. Chief deputy counsel Robert Lehner eventually resigned, disagreeing with Blakey's decision to limit the investigation to the Ray brothers.

During the HSCA investigation, the media again turned their focus on Ray. *Time* set the tone in its January 26, 1976 issue with an article variously referring to him as a "narcotics addict" and a "narcotics peddler," based on George McMillan's book.[15] Missouri Corrections Department chief George M. Camp tried to contact McMillan for details about the allegation in his book that Ray financed the killing of Dr. King by selling drugs as an inmate. Camp stated publicly that McMillan's charges were "totally unsubstantiated" and that he wanted McMillan to "either put up or shut up."[16] Aside from the *St. Louis Post-*

Dispatch's coverage, Camp's refutation was ignored around the country.

A UPI wire service release on January 25, 1978—at the beginning of the last year of the investigation—also variously referred to Ray as having gone "insane" (1963–1964), sending an "obscene letter" to the post office (1967–1968), constantly reading "girlie magazines," harassing "two women with late night telephone calls" (1967–1968), being involved with "drug traffic" and even having "cheated fellow prisoners in crooked card games."

ROBERT BLAKEY WAS A PURPORTED EXPERT ON ORGANIZED CRIME who had taught at both Notre Dame and Cornell law schools. At Cornell he was the director of its Institute of Organized Crime, and previously he served as a special attorney with the Organized Crime and Racketeering Section of the U.S. Department of Justice under Robert Kennedy.

As my investigation proceeded during these early days, I reviewed a copy of a most unusual affidavit executed by Blakey on February 4, 1976.[17] It was prepared and submitted to the court in a civil action brought by Cleveland-Las Vegas crime syndicate leader Morris Dalitz against *Penthouse* magazine as a result of an article that alleged the involvement of organized crime in the development of Rancho La Costa California resort.[18] The allegation of criminal involvement was tied to Dalitz's involvement with the project.

Blakey, as an expert witness, contended that Moe Dalitz had no connection with organized crime.[19] This was extraordinary because it was by then a well-established fact that Dalitz was a long-time major syndicate operator. Subsequently, on September 10, 1979, the *Wall Street Journal* noted that Dalitz had long been identified by federal authorities as an ongoing senior advisor to organized crime.

Because the murder of Dr. King could well have involved elements of organized crime, I was concerned that the counsel steering the investigation would take such a position only a short time before he took over control of the HSCA. (Blakey's expert opinion was ultimately not accepted and *Penthouse*'s defense of the piece was successful.)

I was also very uneasy with the new chief counsel's apparently cozy relationship with the CIA and the FBI, which moved him to give the intelligence agencies influence over his staff's requests for files, documents, and records. Other factors were unsettling as well: the early removal of twenty-eight staffers, the insistence on secrecy (even the requirement that all staff sign nondisclosure agreements, with harsh penalties for violation), the instruction to staff members that they were to have no contact with critics without Blakey's personal authorization, and the absence of accountability of committee consultants to anyone beyond the immediate committee leadership. I was thus led to conclude early on that the reconstituted committee leadership had no intention of conducting an independent investigation.

My misgivings about the HSCA were reinforced when in the summer of 1978 I learned about a clandestine assignment given to previous FBI informer and HSCA undercover agent Oliver Patterson to establish a relationship with Ray's brother Jerry, and to provide as much information as possible from these contacts. He was instructed to obtain hair samples from Jerry and to go through his personal things from time to time, looking for anything that might be of interest, including correspondence.

In August 1978 Patterson was instructed to publicly discredit Mark Lane, who was James Earl Ray's lawyer at the time.

In a sworn statement dated August 14, 1978, Patterson stated that his HSCA handlers instructed him to give a private interview to *New York Times* reporter Anthony J. Marro on Monday, August 7, 1978, in which he was told to accuse Mark Lane of being gay, state that Lane had told him that he knew there was no person named Raul, and further allege that his [Patterson's] own undercover work had confirmed James Earl Ray's guilt.

When Lane (tipped off by Susan Wadsworth, a friend of Patterson's) uncovered the plot and confronted Patterson, Patterson agreed to cooperate with him. Consequently, when Marro arrived at noon at the designated St. Louis hotel he found himself walking into a room filled with news cameras and reporters. He ran from the room with Lane behind him asking whether he wanted the truth. Lane then addressed a press conference, and with Patterson and Wadsworth present revealed the history of the HSCA's illicit use of Oliver Patterson. Affidavits setting out details about this matter were executed by Wadsworth, and another friend of Patterson, Tina Denaro.

Chief counsel Blakey subsequently issued a statement in which he said that a complete investigation of Patterson's allegations would be made but that on the basis of a preliminary investigation, "the Committee categorically denies each and every allegation of wrongdoing. It states with assurance that no federal, state, or local law, or any rule of the House or of the Committee has been violated by the investigator or by any other member of the Committee staff."

Patterson never repudiated his allegations against the committee.

9

The Visit:
October 17, 1978

By MID-OCTOBER 1978 I was ready to meet Ray at the Brushy Mountain prison in Tennessee. Mark Lane agreed to arrange for as long a session as we wished, which we could record in any way we chose. Our group was to include Ralph Abernathy, psychiatrist Howard Berens of Boston, who specialized in interpreting body language, and two photographers.

I had learned as much as possible about our subject's life. James Earl Ray was born on March 10, 1928, in Alton, Illinois. He and his family, which included his two brothers, Jerry and John, moved some six years later to Ewing, Missouri, where his father gave the family the name of "Rayns" to avoid an association with some of James's uncle's petty criminal activities. Thus Ray's first alias was provided to him by his own father when he was six.

Ray finished elementary school (eighth grade) and promptly dropped out. He moved back to Alton, and at age sixteen he worked at the International Shoe Tannery in East Hartford, Illinois. He enlisted in the army in January 1946. Eventually, he was stationed in West Germany.

In December 1948, he received a general discharge, which cited his "inaptness and lack of adaptability to military service." He returned to Alton and soon began drifting from job to job.

In September 1949, he left Chicago for California, and in October he was arrested for a minor burglary, a charge he has always denied. He was sentenced to ninety days in prison. After returning to Illinois in 1950, he worked in supermarkets and factories and attempted to earn his high school diploma by going to night school. In May 1952, he robbed a cab driver of eleven dollars. He was sent to the state penitentiary at Joliet and later transferred to the state prison farm in Pontiac, where he remained until he was released on March 12, 1954.

Though he stayed out of trouble for a while, at a bar he met Walter Rife, who persuaded him to help sell U.S. postal money orders Rife had stolen. They were caught, and on July 1, 1955, Ray was sentenced to forty-five months at the federal penitentiary at Leavenworth, Kansas. It is interesting to note that Rife, who apparently turned informer, received a lesser sentence even though he had actually stolen the money orders. In a subsequent interview (March 12, 1979) Ray would reflect philosophically on the issue of informing, saying that he didn't want to end up like Joe Valachi, the mob informant. He felt that if someone else wanted to inform that was their business, but he would neither inform nor assist in the prosecution of anyone. Over the years, I have become impressed with the strength of this commitment. For Ray, this is more than a way to stay alive in prison. He believes it is wrong and will not relent. In this respect Ray is an old-fashioned con, respected wherever he has done time.

He was paroled from Leavenworth in early 1959, only to be tried and convicted for a grocery store robbery in St. Louis in December 1959. In March of 1960 he began serving a twenty-year sentence at the Missouri State Penitentiary.

He was always on the lookout for ways to escape. After two unsuccessful attempts he succeeded on April 23, 1967, when he began the odyssey that was to end over a year later with his extradition from the United Kingdom. After being convicted and eventually incarcerated at Brushy Mountain, Ray again tried to escape. His second attempt there was successful. On June 10, 1977 he went over the wall but was caught and returned in just over two days. At that time it had become clear that the HSCA (the future of which had been in doubt) was going to continue. I was uneasy when I learned that a large number of FBI agents appeared extraordinarily quickly on the scene.

On October 16, the day before our meeting was to take place, the members of our small group gathered at a hotel on the outskirts of Knoxville. Late that evening we were joined by Mark Lane and one of his assistants, Barbara Rabbito. For several hours that evening Ralph and I went over questions I had drafted, preparing for the next day's interview.

The next morning, we were joined by Ray's wife, Anna. She had been an NBC courtroom artist sketching scenes at the trial following Ray's escape attempt in 1976, apparently was smitten with him, and began to visit him regularly. They eventually were married by Martin's old friend, Jim Lawson, who shared Mark Lane's belief that Ray was not the killer. (In March 1993, James and Anna divorced acrimoniously.)

Around 10:00 that morning we set out for Petros, the remote home of Brushy Mountain State Penitentiary. Mark Lane, Ralph Abernathy, Dr. Howard Berens and I visited with James in a small interview room outside the maximum security area. From what I had read about him I was prepared to meet a racist, hardened criminal whose tendency for violence lay not far below the surface. I was very surprised. He seemed serious and shy, almost diffident, and shook hands weakly. He was trim but exceedingly pale, for he had been doing much of his time in solitary "for his own safety" as a result of an escape attempt. By that time he had been in prison for eight years and seven months. He sat down at the head of a small table, and after Dr. Berens and I arranged the tape recorders, Abernathy began the session with a prayer.

Ralph's prayer did little to ease the tension that had been

building from the moment we passed through the prison gate. As a result of my research I leaned toward the belief that Ray had not killed Dr. King; I hoped that he would be able to convince us of his innocence. I suppose that this hope stemmed, at least in part, from an unwillingness to accept that such a singular life and work as Dr. King's could be snuffed out so unceremoniously by a "lone nut" who was by all appearances a nonentity. I knew, however, that if Ray's answers didn't measure up and we came to believe he was guilty, then Ralph would have to declare as much in his statement to the media. To do or say anything else would be like spitting on Martin's grave.

10

James Earl Ray's Story: October 17, 1978

THE STORY WE GOT FROM JAMES EARL RAY THAT DAY, confirmed by him over the years, is significantly different from the one that would be embodied in the conclusions of the HSCA.

When Ray escaped from Missouri State Penitentiary in Jefferson in 1967, he had escaped by concealing himself in a bread box, being taken out with the delivery to the prison farm. When he left he had approximately $1,250 in cash, a small transistor radio, and a social security number in the name of John L. Rayns that his brother John had given him.

He eventually made his way to Chicago, where he found a job working at the Indian Trail restaurant in Winnetka. Under the Rayns name he obtained some identification papers, bought an old car, and acquired a temporary driver's license. During this period he was in contact with his brother Jerry.

Concerned about staying too long in the area, Ray left the job after approximately six weeks and decided to go to Canada to get a false passport and then leave the country. He got a pistol from an ex-con he knew, sold his car, bought another, and drove to Montreal. Upon arriving in Canada, Ray began using the name Eric S. Galt (he wasn't clear as to how he came to choose the name).

In Montreal, he robbed a brothel of $1,700. Soon after, he called a travel agency to find out what documents were necessary to get a Canadian passport. He was told he had to have someone vouch for him who had known him for two years, which he later found not to be true. He intended to travel to a country in Africa or South America from which he could not be extradited. He also started hanging out around the docks and local bars, seeking passage out of Canada on a freighter, or perhaps hoping to find some drunken sailor from whom he might steal merchant marine documents.

One of these waterside taverns was the Neptune Bar at 121 West Commissioner's Street. Here in August 1967 he met the shadowy character Raul, who Ray insists was to coordinate and direct his activity from that day through April 4, 1968. The meeting at the Neptune was the first of eight or ten. Eventually, Ray told Raul that he needed identification and passage out of the country. Raul replied that he might be able to help if Ray would help with some smuggling schemes at the U.S. border. Ray had no way of contacting Raul at this time. They simply made arrangements to get together, usually at the Neptune. (Over the years, Ray's description of Raul has varied slightly, but he has basically described him as being of Latin extraction, weighing between 145 and 150 pounds, about 5'9" tall, and having dark hair with a reddish tint.)

Eventually discarding the idea of finding a guarantor, Ray resumed meeting with Raul and tentatively agreed to help smuggle some unspecified contraband across the border from Windsor to Detroit. Raul promised him travel papers and money for this service. Ray said he expected to receive only a small payment for the operation, but he never negotiated or even asked about his fee. This was typical of Ray's behavior throughout. He didn't believe he was in a position to ask questions—he was being paid to follow instructions.

Ray was told by Raul that if he decided to become further involved he would have to move to Alabama, where Raul would buy him a car, pay his living expenses, and give him a fee. In return, Ray would be expected to help Raul in another smuggling operation, this time across the Mexican border.

Shortly afterward he met Raul at Windsor, and in two separate trips smuggled two sets of packages across the border to Detroit. He thought the first trip was a dry run to test him. On the second trip he was stopped at customs, but the inspector was interrupted by his superior and sent elsewhere. The second official discontinued the search and simply had him pay the $4.50 duty for a television set he had declared.

When he got to Detroit, Raul nervously asked why he had been delayed. Ray showed him the receipt from the customs officer. Raul gave him about $1,500 and a New Orleans telephone number where a message could be left. He told Ray that if he would continue to cooperate, he would eventually obtain not only travel documents but more money as well.

Raul told Ray to get rid of his old car and go to Mobile, Alabama, where they would meet at a place to be decided. Ray said that he convinced Raul to go to Birmingham instead because it was a larger city and Ray thought he'd be more anonymous there. Raul said that he would send a general delivery letter to Birmingham with instructions on where and when to meet.

Some time after his arrival in Birmingham, Ray picked up a general delivery letter from Raul that instructed him to go to the Starlight Lounge the same evening. There Raul reminded Ray that he was going to need a reliable car. Ray saw an advertisement in the paper for a used Mustang, and Raul gave him $2,000 in cash to buy it.

After this, Raul asked him to buy some photography equipment. He also gave Ray a new number in Baton Rouge, Louisiana, which he could call for instructions as a backup to the New

Orleans number. Raul gave him $1,000 for the photography equipment and his living expenses, and at Raul's request Ray gave him a set of keys to the Mustang. He ordered the photography equipment by mail from a Chicago firm but didn't understand why Raul wanted it.

Ray had previously received his driver's license and a set of Alabama tags under the name of Eric S. Galt. He kept the old Rayns license in a rented safe deposit box at a local bank, along with some of the cash Raul had given him and a pistol he had bought through a classified ad two or three weeks after he arrived in Birmingham.

Some time in late September or early October, Ray received a general delivery letter from Raul asking him to call New Orleans, which he did. This would be the first of several such calls he would make. Raul himself never got on the phone, but Ray instead always talked with a man who knew where Raul was and who relayed instructions. Ray never met the man he spoke to on the phone and didn't think he could now identify his voice, but he had the impression that the contact kept tabs on persons other than Raul. Ray was told to drive to Baton Rouge and make another phone call to receive instructions for a rendezvous in Mexico.

When Ray got to Baton Rouge, Raul was gone, having left instructions for Ray to go directly to a motel in Nuevo Laredo, Mexico, just across the border. Ray checked in there on October 7. Raul joined him and they went back across the border to the United States carrying some kind of contraband inside the spare tire. Ray surmised that it was drugs or jewelry. Raul gave him $2,000 and assured him that he would get the travel documents next time, along with enough money for Ray to go into business in another country. Raul gave him a second New Orleans number to replace the first and told him that his next operation would involve transporting guns and accessories. Raul said he would contact him again, when the time came, through general delivery.

After traveling in Mexico for some time, Ray headed for the California border. Before crossing over, however, he went through the car to see if there was anything that might make

customs agents suspicious. Down the left side of the front passenger seat he found a cigarette packet with a business card
slipped into it. On the front of the card was printed a name
that had been inked out, the name of a city (a two-word name
that appeared to be New Orleans), and "L.E.A.A." Written on
the back was the name Randy Rosen. There were some additional letters after Rosen that James couldn't identify (he later
came to believe that the name was Rosenson) and an address,
1180 Northwest River Drive, Miami.

Ray wasn't certain how the card got in the car but believed
that somehow it was connected to Raul—perhaps the cigarette
packet had slipped out of Raul's pocket. Ray only threw it away
in Los Angeles after copying the information. Subsequently
Ray's brother Jerry and others spent a fair amount of time and
energy trying to find Rosenson.

Ray arrived in Los Angeles on or about November 19, believing he was through with Raul. He had given up hope that
Raul would get him the travel documents, and he was determined to try to get merchant seaman's papers on his own. He
lived for a while in an apartment on North Serrano Street. He
began looking for papers and a job, and he even placed a
classified in the *Los Angeles Times* advertising himself as available
for "culinary help." He didn't have a social security card, and
because seaman's papers required fingerprints he was worried
that his efforts could result in his exposure as a fugitive. He
enrolled in a bartending course, took dancing lessons, and had
psychological, hypnotic counseling for a period of time, spending about $800 on these activities.

He also contacted a number of organizations he thought
might help him to emigrate. He sent out photographs that
weren't good likenesses (his face appeared fatter than it was),
which later would be used by the media to accuse him of being
on amphetamines. He also had plastic surgery on his nose to
alter his appearance.

By early December he was short of cash. He called the New
Orleans number and the contact suggested he go to New Or-
leans. Marie Martin, a barmaid at the Sultan Club in the St.
Francis Hotel, hooked him up with her cousin, Charles Stein,

who wanted a ride to New Orleans and back. Before leaving Los Angeles, Ray dropped Marie Martin and Charles and Rita Stein off at the local George Wallace independent presidential campaign headquarters so they could register to vote. Soon after, Ray and Stein set off. Ray described Stein as a sort of "hippie" type.

In New Orleans, Ray checked into the Provincial Motel in the Latin Quarter at Stein's suggestion. He met Raul at Le Bunny Lounge. Raul told him that they would be running guns into Mexico and that Ray could end up in Cuba. There he could book himself passage to anywhere in the world. Raul gave him $500 and said that he would contact him in Los Angeles in a few months.

After returning to Los Angeles with Charlie Stein around the middle of January Ray moved into the St. Francis Hotel. On March 17, following instructions from Raul, he left for New Orleans, arriving a day late. He found that Raul had gone to Birmingham, leaving word that he would meet him at the Starlight Lounge the next day. Somehow Ray got lost on the way to Birmingham and wound up in Selma. Since it was dark by that time, he spent the night there.

Ray arrived in Birmingham on the following day, March 23, once again running somewhat behind schedule, and went straight to the Starlight, where he met Raul. Raul seemed to be in a hurry to go to Atlanta, though he didn't say why. They set out immediately.

On arriving in Atlanta they drove to the Peachtree and 14th Street area, where Ray rented a room from the very drunk landlord, James Garner. After a meal at a local diner Raul left, saying he'd be back in the morning.

The next morning, Ray took the room for a week. He was able to get his room free because he convinced Garner that he had paid him in advance the night before. Later, on the telephone, Raul told Ray not to get too far away in case he needed him quickly; he might be required to drive to Miami in a few days. Raul wanted to be able to come and go freely from his confederate's room without being seen by the landlord or anyone else. Ray was unable to duplicate a door key for him (though he had taken a locksmithing course), so he agreed to leave the side door open. This didn't work too well, however, because the landlord's sister kept locking it.

Raul apparently left town, telling Ray he'd be back in a couple of days. Some six days later he returned, saying he was now ready to put the gunrunning operation into full gear. He instructed Ray to get a large-bore deer rifle fitted with a scope, plus ammunition, and to ask about the price of cheap foreign rifles. Raul originally wanted the gun to be bought in Atlanta, but Ray suggested that he could buy a rifle in Alabama more easily, since he had an Alabama ID. Raul agreed.

With that part of the operation set, Ray packed up some of his belongings; he left other things behind at the rooming house: his pistol, some clothes, a television set, and a typewriter. He fully expected to return. Raul and Ray drove together to Birmingham, where Ray rented a room in the Travelodge motel. There Raul briefed him further on the gun purchase and gave him money. They went to a tavern, probably the Starlight Lounge, where Raul told him to go to Aeromarine Supply to buy the rifle.

At Aeromarine Supply, Ray told the clerk he was going hunting with his brother-in-law, looked at a number of rifles, and finally selected one and asked to have a scope mounted on it. He asked the salesman to "throw in" some ammunition. Ray purchased the gun under the alias Harvey Lowmeyer, the name of a former criminal associate in Quincy, Illinois. At the last minute he believed it would be safer to buy the gun under another alias. If the clerk requested identification, he would go elsewhere to purchase the rifle under his verifiable alias, Eric S. Galt.

He took the rifle back to the motel and showed it to Raul. To Ray's surprise Raul said it wouldn't do. Ray had picked up some brochures in the store, so Raul marked the rifle he wanted and told Ray to try to make an exchange. Ray called Aeromarine Supply, said that his brother-in-law didn't like the rifle, and asked if he might exchange it for another; the store said the rifle could be exchanged but he would have to wait until the next day.

The next morning, March 30, Ray picked up the new rifle (which we know was a Remington 760 Gamemaster). The salesman threw in some ammunition free of charge. Raul approved. (At the time of our interview, Ray appeared to be genuinely ignorant about the brand, type, and make of the gun bought on the 29th, as well as the one obtained in exchange on the 30th—even now, long after the details have been publicly revealed, Ray seems not to recall these details). Before leaving the motel Raul instructed him to check into the New Rebel Motel on Lamar Avenue in Memphis on April 3 and to bring the gun with him.

Ray set out from Birmingham and proceeded as instructed toward Memphis at a leisurely pace, spending the night at a motel in Decatur. On the 31st he stayed at another motel in the Tuscumbia-Florence area. On April 1, he spent the night in a motel in Corinth, Mississippi (which he subsequently identified as the Southern Motel). He spent the night of April 2 in the DeSoto Motel in Mississippi, just south of Memphis. (Harold Weisberg told me some years later that in 1974, while working for attorneys Bud Fensterwald and James Lesar in preparation for an evidentiary hearing for Ray, he spoke to the manager and some cleaning staff, who confirmed that Ray was at the DeSoto Motel as he claimed. The manager claimed that the records had been turned over to FBI agents when they visited shortly after the assassination.)

On April 3, Ray drove across the Mississippi-Tennessee state line and checked into the New Rebel Motel in Memphis. Late in the evening, Raul appeared at the doorway wearing a raincoat, and Ray let him in. Ray didn't know where he came from or how he got there. Raul told him they were going to rent a room near the river. There they would work the first stage of the gunrunning deal.

At the time, Ray figured that Raul wanted the room in a rundown part of Memphis because they'd be less conspicuous. As usual, he didn't ask Raul any questions. Raul wanted Ray to rent the room using the Galt alias, but Ray was uncomfortable with this and suggested using an alias he had used previously— John Willard.

Raul then wrote out the address of a tavern named Jim's Grill and instructed Ray to meet him there at 3:00 the next afternoon.

Earlier in the day, Ray had brought the rifle in its box into the room wrapped in a sheet or bedspread. Just before Raul left, Ray gave him the gun, and Raul left with it under his coat. He had no idea why Raul wanted to take the gun. James Earl Ray has remained adamant that after turning the gun over to Raul at the New Rebel Motel on the evening of April 3 he never saw it again.

After checking out of the New Rebel Motel on April 4, Ray stalled for some time, did some shopping, changed a slowly leaking tire, and then drove downtown. He left the car in a parking lot and proceeded on foot to look for Jim's Grill. He first went into a tavern on Main Street called Jim's Club and noticed a fellow in the tavern who looked at him "kind of funny," then eventually located Jim's Grill down the street, at 418 South Main Street. Not seeing Raul inside, he retrieved the car and parked it at the curb just outside the grill around 3:30 p.m. By then Raul had arrived. Ray remembers Raul asking him where the car was. Ray pointed to it.

Ray rented a room in the rooming house above the grill for a week, using the name John Willard. There Raul told him to get a pair of infrared binoculars; the people who were buying the guns wanted them too, he said. When Ray asked for them at the York Arms Store on South Main Street, he was told they could only be bought at an army surplus store, so instead he bought a pair of regular binoculars.

When he returned, he noticed that the man whom he had first seen at Jim's Club was inside the grill. He apparently didn't notice Ray, who didn't go inside but went up to the room where Raul was waiting.

Ray tried to tell Raul about the man downstairs, but Raul ignored him and told him he was going to meet a very important gunrunner and that they were going to the outskirts of town to try out the rifle. Raul told him to bring his stuff upstairs, so Ray got his bag out of the Mustang. He also brought a bedspread up in case he had to spend the night there, because he didn't want to sleep on the one in the room. Raul gave him $200 in cash and told him to go to the movies and come back in two or three hours. Ray was instructed to leave the Mustang where it was because Raul said he would probably use it.

Ray went downstairs for the last time around 5:20 p.m. He had talked to Raul for about forty-five minutes. Back in the street, he looked in at Jim's Grill and didn't see the man he suspected had been following him. He remembered that the Mustang had a flat spare tire and decided to have it fixed so that Raul wouldn't have any trouble if he used the car later.

Ray said he was uneasy about the man, who he thought had followed him, and concluded that he was either a federal narcotics agent or the "international gunrunner" Raul had mentioned. He drove to a gas station to have the tire repaired, arriving there sometime between 5:50 and 6:00 p.m. Since there were a lot of customers, he simply waited, because he was in no hurry. Finally an attendant came over and told him that he didn't have the time to change his tire. Ray remembered that an ambulance raced by with its siren blaring.

Driving back, he was confronted by a policeman who had blocked off the street about a block away from the rooming house. The policeman motioned to him to turn around. The policeman's presence told him that something was wrong, and his inclination, as always in such circumstances, was to get out, so he drove south toward Mississippi, intending at first to get to a telephone and call the New Orleans number. It wasn't until he had almost reached Grenada, Mississippi, that he heard on the radio that Martin Luther King had been killed.

When he heard that the police were looking for a white man in a white Mustang, he realized he might have been involved with a man or men who had conspired to kill King. He took back roads rather than the interstate highway because he was afraid he might be the object of a search. On his way he stopped and threw away the photography equipment and then drove straight to Atlanta, where he abandoned the car.

Ray made his way by bus out of the United States into Canada, reaching Toronto on April 6. He went to a local newspaper to check birth announcements of people who would have been slightly younger than him since he thought he looked younger than he was. He picked out some names, including Ramon George Sneyd and Paul E. Bridgeman. He called each to find out whether either had applied for a passport, pretending that it was an official inquiry. Sneyd hadn't applied for a passport, but Bridgeman had, so Ray decided not to use Bridgeman's name for the passport, only for local use.

On April 8 he registered as Paul Bridgeman at a rooming house on Ossington Street. He would leave the house every morning at 8:30, returning each evening around 5:30. (He subsequently stated that he took another room in a second rooming house on Dundas Street, where he would spend most of the day, pretending that he had a night job. He registered there under the Sneyd name).

Ray flew to England on May 8 and from there he made a quick trip to Portugal to try to get to one of the Portuguese overseas territories—Angola or Mozambique. Unsuccessful, he returned to England, planning to go eventually to Belgium to explore the possibilities of taking another route. As we know, he was apprehended at Heathrow Airport on June 8, 1968, and extradited to the United States on July 19, 1968.

We asked Ray why he had pleaded guilty. He insisted that he had been greatly pressured and coerced. I would later learn the details of the extent of the pressure on him and the history of his extraordinary legal representation. (This is discussed in chapter 17.) We finished our session with Ray around 4:00 p.m., some five hours after we began.

Dr. Berens and I agreed that during the interview Ray displayed a vagueness and apprehensive equivocation relating to any connection with persons or places in Louisiana. There was also a curious general change in tone and manner when we began to probe about why he went for psychological, hypnotic counseling. Only during this experience did he use his real name (for fear of it coming out during hypnosis). He has dismissed that experience as a kind of extracurricular preoccupation that he undertook while awaiting instructions from Raul.

The possibility of Ray being subjected to mind control occurred to me.

As for Raul, the extensive details that Ray provided convinced us that such a person did indeed exist, despite the authorities' consistent public statements to the contrary. Though Ray did not mention it during our interview, I subsequently learned that in early 1978 he said that his brother Jerry had anonymously been sent a photograph of an individual whom Ray positively identified as Raul. This identification was reported by the local media at the time. On the back of the photograph was written the name Carlos Hernandez Rumbaut. James said that he sent the photograph to his brother John in St. Louis and asked him to check it against picture archives at the main library. In particular he asked him to compare it with photographs of alleged drug dealers. John made a copy of the photo and sent the original back in a package with other materials. Ray said when he opened the package the photo was missing. A few days later federal marshals arrested John Ray on a parole violation; when he was released he found that his house had been rifled and numerous things taken, including the photograph. (Years later I would learn that Rumbaut was an asset of the Drug Enforcement Administration [DEA] and that he had also been implicated in drug dealing. I obtained his photograph—it was clear that Rumbaut was not the man whom James had identified in 1978 as Raul. With hindsight, it appeared possible that by putting his name on the back of the the real Raul's picture, someone could have been trying to set James up to wrongly identify Rumbaut as Raul.)

ABERNATHY AND I LATER AGREED with Dr. Berens's assessment that Ray was basically telling the truth. However, I believe that James Earl Ray has never revealed all that he knows. He has been the target of at least one murder attempt in prison and has probably decided that to say more is dangerous. We didn't know what, if any, role he had played but we thought he was an unlikely candidate for the assassin.

Ralph Abernathy felt that Ray didn't show any signs of the

compulsive hatred of blacks common in the South. Ralph, like the rest of us, was, I believe, genuinely surprised at this. We had all heard and read the mass media's reports about Ray's alleged racism which was, after all, put forward as his primary motivation for the murder.

As we left the prison, a phalanx of television and print journalists was waiting. Ralph's statement left no doubt as to his conclusions following the interrogation: "James Earl Ray's answers to my questions convinced me more than ever that it was a conspiracy that took the life of Dr. Martin Luther King, Jr., and that James Earl Ray should get a new trial."

The session left me intrigued and troubled. The James Earl Ray I had read and heard about was not the man I saw in that tiny room. The man I saw was not a nut, nor was he a flaming racist. In fact, there was a gentleness about him that I didn't think could have been feigned. Could an innocent man have spent nearly nine years in prison with the truth never having been revealed? I decided to continue my investigation.

11

Pieces of the Puzzle: 1978-1979

BEGINNING IN 1978, as time and my legal practice allowed, I gradually became immersed in the case. In early 1978, as a result of a Freedom of Information Act lawsuit brought by Morton Halperin of the Center for National Security Studies in Washington, I discovered the interest that the CIA's little-known Office of Security (OS) had in Dr. King during the 1960s. Some of the agency's most covert operations were mounted from the OS. Through an elaborate network of assets (independent contract agents whose acts may be officially denied), it coordinated a wide range of operations, including assassination efforts, the most infamous being the collaboration with organized crime through Sam Giancana and John Roselli in attempts to assassinate Fidel Castro in the early 1960s.

I learned that some of the key personnel of the OS were former FBI agents, and that J. Edgar Hoover and the FBI had a good working relationship with the OS. Incredibly, OS consultant Lee Pennington prepared Hoover's personal income tax returns. Also, the OS had run a little-known program called Project RESISTANCE, which, along with Operation CHAOS (mounted in 1967 at President Johnson's request), was responsible for domestic surveillance and intelligence-gathering against thousands of Americans who opposed the Vietnam War.[20] During this period, CIA agents were also infiltrating protest and antiwar groups, and provided training programs, services, and equipment to local police departments in exchange for surveillance and break-ins on the agency's behalf. Throughout the 1960s and early 1970s the OS coordinated this activity, often in conjunction with the FBI and army intelligence, which had similar operations.[21]

Documents reflected the Agency's fear that Dr. King was influenced by a "Peking line" of communist thinking, and it was considering how derogatory information could be used to discredit him. Dr. King had been under Operation CHAOS, Project RESISTANCE, and other agency surveillance programs for a number of years. The agency had also recruited assets in the 1960s to infiltrate, spy on, and subvert civil rights groups.

One such infiltrator was informant A, mentioned often in memos issued by OS director Howard Osborn and OS Security Research Staff (SRS) chief Paul Gaynor. Informant A was subsequently identified as Jay Richard Kennedy, who referred to Dr. King as a "Maoist." In a memo dated October 5, 1967 (released to the public on March 13, 1978), Kennedy also referred to the New Politics (NCNP) convention. In a gross misinterpretation of the events, he reported that the Black Caucus and the Communist Party "virtually wrecked the Convention" but failed to get support for a King-Spock presidential ticket. The government's reliance on such an out-of-touch informant is frightening.

In a memorandum for the SRS chief dated November 29, 1975, the following disclaimer was put on the record: "A thorough review of cited Office of Security files disclosed no evidence that the Office of Security has ever conducted any investigation, including wiretaps, surveillance, mail cover, or field investigation regarding listed subjects (one of whom was

Dr. King). No inquiry was made outside the Office of Security and no DOD records were reviewed or checked." (DOD [Domestic Operations Division] coordinates the agency's operations inside the United States.)

In fact, the OS intercepted King's mail and probably entered his hotel rooms illegally to obtain photocopies of credit card receipts, business cards, and telephone messages, which were included in the documents released. Even though Operation CHAOS was supposedly begun in 1967, many of the Freedom of Information Act documents on Dr. King were dated in the spring and summer of 1965, and purloined receipts and telephone messages dated from the spring of 1966.

Finally, from the memos that the OS sent the FBI, it's obvious that at least during the last year of Dr. King's life they worked jointly against him. An OS memo dated March 15, 1968, issued within three weeks of Dr. King's assassination, closed with the statement: ". . . FBI liaison has been most cooperative and effective in providing the office with timely information about the various domestic militants and protest groups."[22]

Throughout the 1960s and in particular for the two years following the appointment of Richard Helms as CIA director in June 30, 1966, the congressional and the executive branches of government, supported on national security grounds by the Supreme Court whenever necessary (following the 1959, 5-4 decision in the case of *Barr v. Matteo*), generally abdicated their responsibility to check the agency and effectively gave the green light for its conduct of covert special operations (SOG activity) inside the United States.

As a result of the agency's interest in and surveillance of Dr. King in the mid 1960s, I was interested in learning as much as possible about its domestic activity during that critical period leading up to the assassination. Much of the history was well known and fairly widely published, since there had been in previous years the occasional exposure of covert domestic activity.

The agency was established by the National Security Act, passed on September 18, 1947. In proposing the creation of the CIA, President Harry Truman emphasized the nation's unawareness leading up to the raid on Pearl Harbor, which he thought illustrated the need for a central intelligence entity capable of providing prompt and effective warning about any such enemy attack. Administration witnesses continually stressed the position that the CIA was to be strictly limited to overseas operations. To meet certain congressional apprehension the bill was amended to provide that "the agency shall have no police, subpoena, law-enforcement powers or **internal security functions**" (emphasis added).

Nevertheless, in the 1960s the agency became increasingly involved in domestic affairs. The list of distinguished persons and entities which came to be used in covert activities reads like a roster of the American establishment. More than one analyst has noted that the coalition of lawyers, businessmen, and financiers, which constituted the "establishment" during those years, consolidated silent control over the course of U.S. public policy.[23]

Though the nation was publicly assured, and it was commonly believed, that CIA activities were confined to international operations, by 1964 its domestic activity had become so extensive that a special section—the Domestic Operations Division—was secretly created to handle it. Its office at 1750 Pennsylvania Avenue was one block from the White House. The division's purpose, as reflected by its very name, belied the official line that the agency was not engaged in any domestic activity.

As this growth developed, former President Truman, who sponsored the original establishment of the agency, declared in 1963, "I never had any thought . . . when I set up the CIA that it would be injected into peacetime cloak-and-dagger operations. Some of the complications and embarrassment that I think we have experienced are in part attributable to the fact that this quiet intelligence arm of the President has been so removed from its intended role. . . . I . . . would like to see the CIA be restored to its original assignment as the intelligence arm of the President, and whatever else it can properly perform in that special field—and that its operational duties be terminated or properly used elsewhere. We have grown up as a nation respected for our free society. There is something about the way the CIA has been functioning that is casting a shadow over our historic position and I feel that we need to correct it."[24]

As happened with President Eisenhower's final warning about the danger to American democracy of the burgeoning "military industrial" complex, Harry Truman's words went unheeded.

On June 30, 1966, Richard McGarrah Helms, a career intelligence professional, was appointed director of the CIA by Lyndon Johnson. As director he succeeded Vice Admiral William P. "Red" Raborn who had previously been vice president for project management at the defense industry contractor Aerojet-General Corporation of California.

By 1967 the CIA had offices and installations all over America. It even publicly listed them in New York City, Chicago, Los Angeles, Detroit, Philadelphia, San Francisco, Miami, Pittsburgh, Houston, St. Louis, New Orleans, Denver, and Minneapolis. Many others existed under front companies and names. Gradually, a number of domestic activities and operations began to surface, and American taxpayers became aware of the range of activities that they had been unwittingly financing.

In February 1967 (the month following my piece on Vietnam), *Ramparts* published an article by Mike Wood (who later became NCNP's on-site convention coordinator in Chicago), which revealed the extensive relationship between the CIA and the American academic community through a plethora of contracts and grant arrangements with American colleges, universities, and research institutes. Wood's article focused on the infiltration of the National Student Association, but that liaison was only the tip of the iceberg which extended to faculty members and departments in dozens of institutions. Peripheral to these revelations was the occasional reference to even more deeply covert army involvement in such activity.

After Wood's disclosures it gradually emerged that during this period the agency was involved in virtually every segment of U.S. domestic life—business; labor; local, state and national law enforcement and government; universities; charities; the print and press media; lawyers, teachers, artists, women's organizations, and cultural groups. The publicly known list alone was staggeringly extensive.[25] Grants were given, projects were funded, covers were provided, studies were commissioned, projects were mounted, training programs were run, and books were published. The arrangements were wide and varied. In its 1976 report the Senate Select Committee on Intelligence Activities said that by 1967 the agency had sponsored, subsidized, or produced over 1,000 books, with 200 being turned out in 1967 alone. Analysts have noted the practice whereby one CIA operative or asset would write a book and others review it for selected newspapers and magazines.[26]

By 1967 the CIA was spending 1.5 billion dollars a year without any effective fiscal control over individual expenditures on operations. Covert domestic activities and operations were paid for by "unvouchered funds" (expenditures without purchase orders or receipts). As a result of the 1949 Central Intelligence Act, Director Helms had the authority to spend money "without regard to the provisions of law and regulations relating to the expenditure of government funds." Helms's signature on any check, no matter how large, drawn on any CIA bank account was deemed to be sufficient. Interagency cooperation, particularly with the army and/or the state department, was frequently necessary and this was accomplished through the establishment of Special Operations Groups (SOG) created for particular projects or missions. SOG operations conducted inside Vietnam and across into Cambodia and Laos against "Charlie"—the Viet Cong—were frequent during the escalation of the war, and well-known. SOG activity inside the United States against "Willie" (blacks and dissidents) was not publicized or known.

ON OCTOBER 17, 1978, just before we had left Knoxville to interview Ray, Mark Lane had given me a copy of an affidavit issued by Daniel Ellsberg, the man who leaked the Pentagon Papers and thus revealed to the American public some harsh truths about the war in Vietnam. The affidavit detailed a conversation

Ellsberg had had four months earlier with Brady Tyson, then an aide to UN ambassador Andrew Young.

On June 16, 1978, while at the United Nations to talk with members and staff of the UN-Special Assembly on Disarmament, Ellsberg became quite friendly with Tyson. As they left Tyson's office one day, the subject of King's assassination came up.

In the affidavit Ellsberg stated, "I asked Tyson whether he thought there had been a conspiracy and who he thought might have done it. He said very flatly to me, **'We know there was a conspiracy and we know who did it.'** . . . I asked him who it was, if he would feel free to say, and he said again in a way that was very surprising to me in its lack of equivocation or reservation, 'It was a group of off-duty and retired FBI officers working under the personal direction of J. Edgar Hoover.' He said further that this was a group working secretly and known to almost no one else in the FBI. This group Tyson said included 'a sharpshooter,' who had actually done the shooting."

Ellsberg was startled. He pressed Tyson to tell him his source. Reluctantly, Tyson said, "That has turned up in Walter Fauntroy's [HSCA] investigation and he's told us." "Us," Ellsberg emphasized, included Ambassador Young, another aide, Stoney Cooks, and Tyson himself.

The affidavit continued: "I got the impression from things he subsequently said that Ambassador Young and his associates had actually gone over a good deal of the evidence directly and had not simply been told this in general terms." He quoted Tyson as saying, "We are eighty percent sure that **we know who they are.** We're eighty percent sure that we know the names of all the people who were involved, and . . . it's all circumstantial but very detailed."

Tyson said he didn't know what was going to be done because, "we don't have courtroom proof of this, of the names."

Ellsberg was struck by Tyson's lack of caution. "Tyson himself did not at any time caution me either to be silent about this or even so much as show discretion by what I did with it . . . I even inferred to some degree that he might want me to pass it along, using discretion, to people who in my judgment ought to know it. His [Tyson's] actual position impressed me; his closeness to Young, to King, his concern for the subject, and the fact that he was an official of the U.S. government, the first friendly one I had seen in some seven years. A story that would have been a run-of-the-mill assertion in the mouths of the myriad of conspiracy theorists ... had enormous weight coming from him."

Tyson left Ellsberg with the impression that they all hoped it would come out in the hearings. Tyson also said that when the HSCA was being formed Fauntroy informed Carl Albert, then Speaker of the House of Representatives, that he wanted to be on a committee to investigate Dr. King's death or even, if possible, to head the committee. Albert said to him, "Walter, you don't want that job." To which Fauntroy replied, "But I do want it; why not?" Albert whispered, "Walter, they will kill you ... , the FBI."

When the facts revealed to Ellsberg failed to come out in the 1978 summer hearings and the committee began to move in a different direction, Ellsberg decided to make his information known to James Earl Ray's lawyer; hence the affidavit.

After the Ray interview I spoke with Ellsberg, who confirmed the statement. Jim Lawson, who had a long-established relationship with Andy Young, Stoney Cooks, and Brady Tyson, agreed to seek confirmation from them. When he telephoned Stoney Cooks about the allegations, Cooks said, "Andy and I had hoped that the House Select Committee would release these matters and open them up."

"As I listened to him," Lawson told me, "I realized that he was confirming Ellsberg's affidavit. He clearly indicated that there were names not released, information related to the death that the public did not know and that was not consistent with the theory that James Earl Ray was the lone assassin." Lawson had no doubt that this information had privately been relayed to Andy Young and his staff aides by Walter Fauntroy.

When Jim Lawson subsequently asked Tyson about Ellsberg's statements, Tyson replied that he didn't remember all he had told Ellsberg but that he believed that he was an honest and significant witness. He even suggested that Ellsberg was "unimpeachable."

As we reviewed this series of events, Lawson also recalled that many many months earlier Dr. Joseph Lowery, Abernathy's successor as president of the SCLC, had described to him a discussion with Fauntroy that appeared to confirm the Ellsberg account. At a subsequent meeting in Los Angeles, Lowery repeated the story with both Lawson and Mark Lane present. Later that fall, in a telephone conversation primarily concerned with my upcoming address at SCLC's national convention, Lowery also confirmed to me that Lawson was telling the truth. He said that he still hoped that the HSCA would eventually uncover all the facts.

I became convinced that there was enough basic substantiation for the Ellsberg affidavit to warrant submitting it to the HSCA. In retrospect, I suppose we couldn't have expected the committee to confirm Ellsberg's allegations, but we were curious as to how they would explain them away. So on the morning of October 27, Abernathy, Reverend Lawson, activist/comedian Dick Gregory, and I, joined Mark Lane for a private session in Walter Fauntroy's office to present the new information to the committee leadership and senior staff. As we arrived, we saw to our surprise, an assemblage of reporters and photographers standing just outside the doorway of his office suite.

We were never sure how the media had found out about the meeting. It wouldn't serve the committee's purpose to publicize it in any way. It was also contrary to counsel Robert Blakey's style. He always preferred simply to disclose carefully prepared information. Although he never acknowledged it, we intuited that Mark Lane had tipped off the media. I felt this was unfortunate. The untimely public disclosure of information could close some doors that had partially opened for us.

We were ushered into Fauntroy's inner office. Chairman Stokes, Blakey, and two staff members were waiting for us. In his introductory statement Lane tore into the committee, its staff, and its leadership. He accused them of not following up leads and ignoring significant facts, and then he attacked Blakey personally and professionally. Blakey angrily objected and left the meeting, not returning until he was certain that Lane had finished.

As the Ellsberg revelations were set out for the committee, I noticed Fauntroy squirming in his chair. He denied ever having expressed any of the opinions attributed to him by any of the people mentioned. Fauntroy said he couldn't understand how Tyson and Cooks, nor surely Andy Young, could ever attribute the statements in question to him. He said that it was his job to investigate every fact and allegation brought before the committee, and that he was determined to do this to the best of his ability. He said that because of his admiration for Dr. King, and all the years they had served together in the struggle for civil rights, he could never participate in anything but a full and complete investigation.

Lawson was to note later, however, that Fauntroy equivocated considerably in the way he dismissed Ellsberg's contentions. He would glance sideways at Abernathy, only to look quickly away. He never once looked directly at Jim Lawson.

Throughout the rest of the meeting, the staff and chairman insisted that there was nothing worth considering in the Ellsberg allegations. They tried to put our group on the defensive by asserting that our promise of new information was a ruse to call the press. However, there was no effort to discredit Ellsberg's version of Tyson's remarks, nor was there any attempt to refute Jim Lawson's corroboration. Instead we simply met a stone wall.

After the meeting, an argument erupted between Blakey and Lane. I stepped between them as Blakey was telling Lane that if he kept it up there was no question that he'd be taken care of once and for all. I was shocked.

We left Fauntroy's offices and were met by a barrage of photographers and television journalists. Lane and Abernathy made brief statements. Abernathy, in his offhand manner, informed them that, yes, we had had a very productive meeting with the staff and leadership of the committee; we hoped that they would go on and complete their work; and we had given them certain information implicating the FBI in the killing of

Dr. King. I was amazed that none of the press picked this up: there was virtually no response.

The next morning, I left a copy of the Ellsberg affidavit at former Attorney General Ramsey Clark's law office. Ramsey agreed to have a word with Brady Tyson. After he spoke to Tyson, it was evident that something had changed. He told me that Tyson hadn't repudiated Ellsberg's comments but indicated that he didn't recall saying the specific things alleged. I would learn more about this Fauntroy-Tyson story later.

FROM NEW YORK I went to Memphis to study the scene of the crime and talk with some of the people who were close to the tragic events.

There was no doubt that Dr. King was standing on the second-story balcony in front of room 306 when he was shot. Mark Lane was skeptical about the MPD and the FBI official conclusion that the shot had been fired from the bathroom window on the second floor of the rooming house. Author/investigator Harold Weisberg also disputed this finding, saying that the shot most likely came from the area of the parking lot that bordered the fire station on one side and the rear yard of the rooming house on the other (see Chart 1, page xxxiii).

At the time of the shooting, a row of brush trees, a larger tree, and apparently other bushes provided a type of screen between the rooming house, the parking lot and the motel on the other side of the street. This backyard area sloped upward about five or six feet from an eight-foot retaining wall on Mulberry Street, and was actually higher than the balcony on which Dr. King was standing at the time he was shot, though this fact appeared to have been largely overlooked.

I thought that an analysis of the trajectory of the shot might help, but at that time I couldn't carry this out. There was also the problem of Dr. King's posture at the time he was hit. Just prior to the shot he was observed to be leaning slightly on the rail, but there was disagreement as to whether he had actually straightened up before being hit.

*   *   *

THE STATE'S CHIEF WITNESS in 1968 was Charlie Stephens. He and his common-law wife, Grace Walden, were both in their room (6-B, which adjoined the bathroom) at the time of the shooting. Stephens had provided the affidavit used for extradition, which had tentatively identified Ray's profile as being that of a man he saw going down the front stairs after the shooting. When I talked with Walden, she said Charlie didn't see anyone or anything. However, she said that when she was lying in bed around the time of the shot she herself saw a small man with "salt and pepper" hair wearing an open army jacket and a plaid sports shirt hurrying down the rear stairway leading to the back door. The description didn't fit Ray in any way. Her story would vary significantly from time to time over the years (on one occasion she described the man as being black) except regarding one fact—that Charlie Stephens didn't see anything.

Wayne Chastain agreed. As a reporter for the Memphis *Press Scimitar,* Chastain had been one of the first people on the scene on April 4. He told me that minutes after the shooting he saw an excited Solomon Jones, who said the shot came from the bushes "over there," pointing across Mulberry Street to the thick brush behind the rooming house. "Catch me later at the hospital," Solomon said.

Chastain then went around the front of the building and had a brief word with Judson "Bud" Ghormley, the deputy sheriff who was in charge of TACT 10, the emergency unit on break at the fire station when the shooting happened, and who apparently found the bundle in front of Canipe's. He then entered the rooming house from the front and climbed to the second floor and went to the rear to try to get a view of the brush area below.

When he stuck his head in the door of room 6-B, he saw Walden lying on a sofa off to the right and asked her if he could look out of her rear window. She asked what the commotion was all about, and he told her that Dr. King had been shot. She said, "Oh, that was what I heard, I thought it was a firecracker." She took him into the kitchen area of the run-down suite, where the rear windows overlooked the Lorraine and the brush below. As he entered this part of the room he saw Charlie Stephens sitting at the kitchen table fiddling with a radio. He said Charlie may have mumbled a word or two but basically he and Charlie—who appeared to be in a stupor— didn't speak.

When he looked out the window Chastain could see the Lorraine balcony, but the combination of brush and trees below was so thick that he didn't have a clear view of the motel parking area or driveway. As he turned to leave he noticed that Charlie had passed out with his head on the table.

After leaving the rooming house that evening Chastain went to St. Joseph's Hospital, where they had taken Dr. King. There, along with a battery of media people, he listened to Solomon Jones describe what he had seen. Jones maintained that he was standing by the car, having just told Dr. King that he would need a coat that evening, when the shot came. Jones ducked down and turned to look in the direction of the sound, and he saw a man in the bushes with a white sheet or hood over or around his face. Jones said at that time that this man rose up from the bushes, appeared to throw something to the side, walked to the wall, jumped down, and began to mingle with the crowd. He was wearing a jacket and plaid shirt and came within about twenty-five feet of Jones, who was shocked and frightened. As the man began to walk away, Jones got into his car and tried to follow him but was frustrated by the growing crowd of people and cars. In a short time the ambulance arrived.

Chastain returned to the rooming house the next morning between 7:30 and 8:00 to see Bessie Brewer, the manager. She said that the FBI told her not to talk to anyone. Chastain was approached by an old "codger" he knew only as Major, who was drunk even at that hour, but he asked Chastain to come back to his room. He told Chastain that he saw who had done it. He said, "It was a nigger," but that he would never testify against him. His room was in the southern section of the rooming house where the Brewers also lived and where the office was located. Stephens and Walden lived on the other side; a four-foot alleyway separated the two sections. Chastain didn't take Major very seriously because his window looked out into the alley (although it also allowed one to look directly into room 5-B on the other side—the room rented by Ray).

Around 11:00 a.m. Chastain's editor sent him back to the rooming house to interview Charlie Stephens. Charlie had sobered up, and as they were talking the Major came up to them and told Charlie that he had told Chastain it was a nigger who did it. "Yeah, it was a nigger," Charlie agreed. Chastain gave no credence to either man. Bessie Brewer said that they were both drunk and didn't see anything.

Some time later, Loyd Jowers, the owner of Jim's Grill, told Chastain that he had refused to serve Stephens in the grill after 4:00 on the day of the killing because he was too drunk. He did, however, sell him two quarts of beer to take upstairs to his room.

The day after the shooting, Grace Walden told Chastain the same story she told me ten years later about the small man with the salt-and-pepper hair whom she saw, from her bed, going down the back stairs. It was not clear to Chastain, however, that she could have seen anything from where her bed was located.

Chastain was astounded when in the following months Stephens emerged as the state's main witness against James Earl Ray. In light of Stephens's condition, which must have been apparent to any police investigation, he couldn't have testified to anything. Assistant District Attorney James Beasley's representation at the guilty plea hearing of what Charlie Stephens would have testified, had there been a trial, made no sense to Chastain. Beasley had told this to the court:

> In the meantime, back upstairs at 422 ½ South Main, Charles Quitman Stephens, who occupied these two rooms adjacent to a bathroom here [indicating], Mr. Stephens, who earlier in the afternoon had observed Mrs. Brewer as she talked to the Defendant . . . heard movements over in the apartment 5-B rented to the Defendant. . . . At approximately 6:00 p.m., Mr. Stephens heard the shot coming apparently through this wall from the bathroom [indicating]. He then got up, went through this room out into the corridor in time to see the left profile of the Defendant as he turned down this passageway. . . .

I would learn that Charlie Stephens was placed under close control by the MPD right after the murder; apparently he hoped to receive the reward being offered by the Memphis *Commercial Appeal* newspaper and the city of Memphis. After Ray was brought back to the United States, Stephens was held in protective custody by the MPD, and Grace Walden was placed in a mental hospital. Bessie Brewer was removed as manager of the rooming house and left the scene. The rooming house itself was put under lock and key.

Chastain also referred me to an interview of Stephens conducted by CBS correspondent Bill Stout shortly after the killing, which, curiously enough, didn't air until 1976. Stout showed Stephens a picture of James Earl Ray that the authorities were circulating:

BILL STOUT: Mr. Stephens, what do you think of that picture? Does that look like the man?

CHARLES STEPHENS: Well—[clears throat]—Excuse me—from the glimpse that I—that I got of his profile, it doesn't.

STOUT: It doesn't?

STEPHENS: Certainly— No, sir, it certainly doesn't. For one thing, he's too heavy. His face is too full. He has too much hair, and his nose is too wide—from the glimpse that, as I said, that I got of his profile. But that definitely, I would say, is not the—the guy.

Neither Charlie Stephens nor Solomon Jones were available to me in 1978, both having dropped out of sight.

CHASTAIN RAISED THE QUESTION of Dr. King's last-minute room change at the Lorraine. He recounted a Saturday night conversation with the owner of the Lorraine, Walter Bailey. Bailey said that on April 2, the day before Dr. King was to arrive, his wife had been visited by an SCLC "advance man," who insisted that the ground-level, courtyard room wouldn't do, and that Dr. King had to have a second-floor balcony room overlooking the swimming pool (even though it was empty). Bailey said that his wife described the visitor as being about six feet tall, built

like a football player, and "Indian" in appearance, with high
cheekbones.

ANOTHER *Press Scimitar* reporter, Kay Black, told me in two interviews that early on the morning of April 5 she received a call
from former mayor William Ingram, who told her that some
trees or brush behind the rooming house from which Dr. King
was supposed to have been shot were being cut down. He suggested that she go over and take a look. When she got to the
rooming house later in the day she found that the brush had
indeed been cut. An official at the Public Works Department
told her it was a routine cleanup.

Reverend James Orange, who had been in the parking area
of the Lorraine at the time of the shooting, told me that the
memory of the brush area stuck in his mind because immediately after Dr. King was shot he saw smoke rise from "a row of
bushes right by the fire station." (I thought he must have been
mistaken about the exact loction of the smoke, since the angle
of the shot appeared to be wrong and the bushes extended all
the way to the northern end of the rooming house rear yard.)
"It could not have been more than five or ten seconds after
the shot," he said. Just prior to the shot he and Jim Bevel arrived
back at the Lorraine, driven by Invader Marrell McCollough. Exiting McCollough's car, they began to "tussle" just below the balcony where Dr. King was standing when he was shot. The next
morning Rev. Orange noticed that the bushes were gone.

Increasingly, I viewed the early morning alteration of this
area as sinister. It was inexplicable to me that the MPD, the
FBI, and the HSCA investigations didn't follow up on this lead
begging for attention. James Orange told me that no one connected with any enforcement or investigative body had asked
him about what he saw. When he tried to alert the police officers on the scene they told him to stay out of the way.

IN EARLY NOVEMBER 1978, shortly after our HSCA meeting in
Walter Fauntroy's office, Dan Ellsberg told me that he had
recently met Fauntroy at an ACLU affair. He said Fauntroy still
denied mentioning the FBI to Tyson, Cooks, and Young, but

when pressed, he expressed his opinion that the FBI "not only set the tone for Dr. King's assassination through their harassment but, in fact, played a role in carrying out the conspiracy," and that "it would not have been beyond J. Edgar Hoover to have personally approved, if not ultimately directed, the operation."

On Friday, November 17, 1978, Walter Fauntroy, Brady Tyson, Andy Young, and Stoney Cooks, all testifying before the HSCA, denied any knowledge of FBI involvement and refuted Daniel Ellsberg's statement. Their testimony was in response to a front-page article in the *Knoxville New Sentinel* on November 11, in which Mark Lane and Anna Ray released the contents of the Ellsberg affidavit, alleging that the Ellsberg-Lowery statements proved "without a doubt" that FBI director Hoover ordered the assassination. I felt that Lane had gone too far in his interpretation of the information.

Fauntroy categorically denied having received any evidence of FBI involvement, and Young denied receiving such information from Fauntroy. However, Young did at one point admit that, "there were strange connections that we were all concerned about, and it was one of the things we wanted this Committee to look into." He also acknowledged having a concern about official involvement in a conspiracy. Since no member followed up on those remarks, they were simply left hanging, and Young's testimony was summarized as being a denial of Ellsberg's allegations.

Brady Tyson testified that he and Ellsberg had at first spoken generally about assassinations and then, when the conversation turned to the King killing, he told Dan Ellsberg about his "pet theory"—that a clandestine group within the FBI, though not an official or authorized operation, might have carried out the plot.

Following suit, Stoney Cooks also denied knowledge of any FBI involvement. In response to a question from Congressman Harold Ford about Tyson's reputation at the UN, Cooks stated that his colleague was kind of a "missionary," and in seeking to provide Dan Ellsberg with the warmest possible welcome he probably "was a bit overzealous in his conversations."

I believed that Brady Tyson had probably been loose-tongued but truthful in his remarks to Dan Ellsberg. Fauntroy had probably shared his information in-house with Young and his aides, without any expectation that an outsider would hear the story and repeat it. When it came out after Ellsberg became convinced that the HSCA wasn't going to act, the wheels were set in motion to deny it ever happened. Under pressure, Young and his aides denied hearing the story of Hoover's possible involvement and Fauntroy himself (since he was a senior member of the committee and had to maintain the appearance of loyalty) had no choice, unless he was willing to resign.

Dan Ellsberg's revelation constituted not only the first real indication of FBI involvement in Dr. King's murder but, even more ominous, it was an initial indication that the HSCA was not prepared to allow such evidence to become public or even to acknowledge what appeared to be its own information.

MORE DETERMINED THAN EVER TO EXAMINE THE OFFICIAL STORY, I went back to Memphis and turned my attention to Jim's Grill. In 1968, Loyd Jowers told Chastain about a mysterious stranger who was in the grill on the afternoon of April 4 and again the following morning, ordering eggs and sausage both times. Jowers described him as well-dressed and definitely out of place. Following police orders, when the man appeared on the 5th Jowers called the police, who arrived and took the man in, only, apparently, to release him soon afterward.

Wayne Chastain maintained that many of the black people who had been in the grill at the time of the shooting had never been identified. He had tried unsuccessfully to locate and interview each of the black waitresses on duty that afternoon, one of whom, Betty, he had heard had particular significance. Jowers seemed unable to assist him in finding Betty and one other waitress but arranged for him to interview a third waitress—Rosie Lee Dabney—who had waited on the stranger on the afternoon of April 4.

Chastain had become aware, as a result of the activities of writer William Sartor, a stringer for *Time* magazine, and investigator Renfro Hays, that both Jowers and Rosie Lee Dabney had identified the "eggs and sausage" man from photographs that Sartor had shown them. The photographs depicted a government intelligence asset with ties to army intelligence and the CIA; his name was Walter Alfred "Jack" Youngblood. Chastain told me, however, that some five years later, when he and reporter Jeff Cohen showed the same photographs to Jowers in a diner one night, Jowers changed his mind. He said that he didn't think that was the man after all. When reminded about his earlier identification he simply said he thought it wasn't the man.

Chastain said that MPD assistant chief Henry Lux denied taking Youngblood in, but Frank Holloman acknowledged that a man was detained, as did FBI special agent in charge (SAC) Robert Jensen. Jensen insisted that the man was a gun collector and that his presence had nothing to do with the killing.

Chastain believed that this "eggs and sausage" man was Jack Youngblood, and was the same mysterious person who he heard had visited attorney Russell X. Thompson and local ministers James M. Latimer and John Baltensprager a week or so after the killing. Reverend Latimer identified Youngblood as his mysterious visitor from a photograph Chastain showed him, and attorney Walter Buford (a college classmate and friend of Youngblood) said that Youngblood had called him while in town during that time. I resolved to pursue the story myself.

I located and interviewed Loyd Jowers, a thin, almost anemic man in his late sixties. Puffing on a cigarette, Jowers confirmed Chastain's account of the arrest. I showed him photographs of Jack Youngblood and he said, "Yup, that's him all right."

Attorney Russell Thompson told me that around 10:00 p.m. on April 10, 1968, he received a call from a man with a Western accent. The caller said that he had just flown into Memphis from his home in Chicago, had heard of Thompson from some friends, and needed to talk to him immediately but that it was important to speak with him alone. They agreed to meet early the next morning.

He described his visitor as being about six feet tall, about thirty-five years old, with light hair and wearing a sombrero. He also had a tattoo of the letters "T" over "S" on his arm, which Thompson recalled he could make disappear. He didn't give his name (although he later used the alias Tony Benavites) and maintained that a Denver roommate of his, a professional gun (as was he) whom he called Pete, shot Dr. King. He said that only a fool would attempt to carry out the killing from a second-floor bathroom window at the end of a corridor, because the trees could so easily have deflected a bullet. He said that Pete fired from the bushes, broke the rifle down, putting the barrel down his back, jumped from the wall, and disappeared in the confusion. Thompson was struck by the precise description of the brush and the trees behind the rooming house. This led him to believe that the man knew the area well and could even have been there when it happened.

In an offhand way he asked Thompson to represent his friend should he be charged. Benavites said that he himself had been picked up "last Friday" (the day the stranger in Jim's Grill was arrested) and was turned loose after being taken up to the rooming house.

Thompson heard from this man only once more in a brief phone call in which he said it didn't appear that legal assistance would be required after all. Thompson gave a full report to MPD inspector N. E. Zachary and William Lawrence of the FBI.

Less than four hours after the mysterious stranger left Thompson's office on April 11, the Rev. James Latimer, pastor of the Cumberland Presbyterian Church at the time, received a telephone call just as he was heading off to lunch with his friend Rev. John Baltensprager. The caller said he needed some "spiritual guidance" or else he was going to "commit suicide."

The two ministers went to a steak house called Jim's Place and met a rather smartly dressed man wearing tinted sunglasses, a blue sports coat, dark trousers, and boots. He was described as having dark wavy hair, long sideburns, and a dark complexion. He was about six feet tall and had an athletic build. At Latimer's suggestion they went to Robilio's Cafeteria in South Memphis, where there was more privacy. The man identified himself as J. Christ Bonnevecche and said that on the afternoon that Dr. King was killed he was employed as a runner for the Mafia.

Latimer asked Bonnevecche whether he had killed Martin Luther King. The man said, "No, but I know who did." He seemed to be implying that there was an organized crime connection with the killing, but it didn't really make much sense to the ministers. He said that he was a drug addict and rolled up his sleeves to show the ministers a scar on the inside of his elbow. As he did so, they noticed an intertwined tattoo, "T" over "J," similar to the "T" over "S" that attorney Thompson had noticed. Bonnevecche reportedly also said that his friend "Nick" killed Dr. King. He said that Nick was very much like himself in personality and interests. He told them that Nick had entered and left town on a motorcycle and that when he exited he had the murder weapon strapped onto his back, having previously discarded the rifle stock.

Reverend Latimer indicated, however, that a good deal of the discussion focused on the Kennedy assassination, which he said Bonnevecche maintained was a Mafia hit. His mysterious visitor also said that Robert Kennedy was next, and that he would definitely be assassinated if he won the California primary.

This, of course, is exactly what happened. Reverend Latimer also reported this conversation to Inspector Zachary, who promised, as he had with Thompson, to "check it out."

I wouldn't be able to speak with Reverend Latimer for a number of years, but Russell Thompson talked with him about this incident. Thompson said he had no doubt that the man who visited him was the same person who spoke with the ministers. Thompson said he never received a satisfactory explanation or a report back from Inspector Zachary or the FBI, and when I showed him Jack Youngblood's picture he seemed uncertain but thought that he could have been the man. Though his visitor was about the right age, Thompson had described him as being light-haired. All the photographs I had of Youngblood were of a dark-haired man. If Youngblood had been his visitor, he must have been in disguise.

Youngblood did appear to match the description of a man who appeared at the St. Francis Hotel in Los Angeles shortly after the assassination. This man was with a James Earl Ray

look-alike who appeared to have a great deal of money to throw
around and who openly spoke of a second killing that was soon
to take place. (Remember that during his stay in Los Angeles
in late 1967 to early 1968 Ray had lived for some time at the
St. Francis Hotel and was known there.)

Months later I would meet Jack Youngblood on two occasions. He said that he knew some people who had direct information about the killing. They were now living outside of the
country and for a sum of money he might be able to get them
to tell their story.

When pressed as to why these overseas contacts would be
willing to sit down and reveal what they knew about this case,
considering that there is no statute of limitations for murder,
he said the main reason was because they were disenchanted
after having provided long and effective service to their government. They now felt that they were being sold down the river,
forgotten. He claimed that he had an oil-company plane at
his disposal.

Because of his intelligence connections and activity it was
possible that he knew people who were involved. At the end
of the day I came to believe it was unlikely that he had any
direct involvement in the case. It seemed that either he was
acting on behalf of the government spreading false information
("disinformation") in order to confuse and divert the investigation away from the truth, or he was holding out the promise
of information in an effort to hustle money. Though I arranged
some funds for him, he never produced the mysterious expatriate government operatives.

OF ALL THE INDICATIONS of government involvement I encountered during my first investigatory period, none was more bizarre than the actions of William Bradford Huie. In 1978 Jerry
Ray had told me that in 1976, as the HSCA was being formed,
James Earl Ray's Nashville attorney Jack Kershaw was invited to
attend a meeting in Nashville with author William Bradford
Huie and two other persons.

Huie asked him to take an offer to his client: a payment of

$220,000, a pardon from the governor of Tennessee, a waiver of the outstanding detainer (escape warrant) on him from the Missouri Department of Corrections, and a new identity, in exchange for his unequivocal admission of guilt in the murder of Dr. King. Kershaw delivered the offer to his client, who rejected it out of hand.

A short time later, when Mark Lane had replaced Kershaw, Huie repeated the offer to Jerry Ray in the course of two telephone conversations which Jerry tape recorded. Ray's response was the same.

Not long afterward I obtained copies of the transcript of the tape. In the October 29, 1977, 12:15 a.m. conversation, the following exchange took place:

Jerry Ray ". . . So when this deal came up with James and Kershaw said you'd pay so much money if he'd, you know, plead guilty and confess.

William Bradford Huie: "Yeah, that's right. But let me tell you one thing clearly. I'm not talking about just a statement. I'm talking about something that James has never done in his life before. I'm talking about a story that says how and why. And he explains . . ."

Nine and a half hours later, a second conversation took place:

Huie: "You're talking about $200,000 here, Jerry. The only thing that will be of any value for both a book and film and put this right in your mind —*Why and How I killed Dr. King.* I, by James Earl Ray. With the help of William Bradford Huie."

12

Brother Jerry on the Stand: November 30, 1978

JERRY RAY TESTIFIED before the HSCA in open session on Thursday, November 30, 1978. Mark Lane was not permitted to represent Jerry because he already represented James and there might be a conflict of interest. Jerry had asked me to consider appearing with him. There were two problems. First of all, I was obviously concerned that my appearance on his behalf—special appearance though it was—not be construed as a commitment at that stage to the unequivocal innocence of his brother. Second, my family feared that this overt action would be unwise. Nevertheless I decided to represent Jerry for the specific purpose of protecting his rights.

I overrode family opposition by inviting New York lawyer, feminist, and civil rights activist Florynce Kennedy to be co-counsel. As one of the nation's most prominent black women lawyers, with considerable experience in opposing abuse of process, Flo added considerable strength to the witness table.

I believed that the question of James's and his brothers' alleged involvement in a 1967 bank robbery in Alton, Illinois (James's birthplace), was likely to be a key element of the committee's interrogation. In attempting to disprove the existence of Raul and thus the existence of a conspiracy, the committee would most likely claim that the money James received during his time on the run had been obtained from the $27,000 robbery of the Alton bank.

It was evident that after July 13, 1967, and during his stay in Canada, James Earl Ray had acquired money. The Alton bank robbery occurred on the day before some of his purchases began, and had thus been seized upon as the explanation for the source of his funds. James, however, said he initially obtained funds in Canada by robbing a Montreal brothel, and that Raul subsequently gave him money. The HSCA speculated that rather than James escaping from prison, spending two and a half months in the States, traveling to a strange city in Canada in a destitute condition, and committing an armed robbery, it would be more reasonable to assume that he escaped from prison, made contact with his brother John in St. Louis, got a job while they planned a crime, then, after committing the robbery in a familiar area, fled to Canada.

On November 17, 1978, the *New York Times* published a front-page article by Wendel Rawls, Jr., stating that the results of a *Times* investigation agreed with the conclusions of a separate investigation by the HSCA that the Ray brothers, including Jerry, were guilty of robbing the Alton bank.

On Wednesday, the 29th, the day before Jerry's appearance before the HSCA, I placed a call to East Alton police lieutenant Walter Conrad. I advised him that in an effort to put to rest the continuing allegations that my client had been a participant in that robbery, I had counseled him to return once again to East Alton and offer to be charged and stand trial (Jerry had previously surrendered himself on August 18, 1978, offered to waive the statute of limitations, take a lie detector test, and, if charged, stand trial for the robbery). I then told Lieutenant Conrad about the *New York Times* article.

Lt. Conrad said that he had told Jerry Ray during his August visit that neither he nor his brothers were suspects, nor had they ever been suspects in that crime. He told me explicitly that neither he nor any member of the Alton police department, nor, to the best of his knowledge, any employee or official of the Bank of Alton, had ever been questioned by the *New York Times* or any investigator of the HSCA. He said that he couldn't imagine what the basis was for the *Times*'s claims or the committee's allegations.

Accordingly, he advised me that there would be no need for Jerry Ray or any of his brothers to return to Alton.

I later acquired an FBI "airtel" of July 19, 1968, sent to the SAC of Memphis from director Hoover, which gave a report of an analysis of all fingerprint impressions relating to unsolved bank robberies at that time. The report concluded that a comparison of the prints of James Earl Ray didn't match with **any** prints on the Alton bank robbery file.

A further FBI teletype of August 1, 1968, to the director from the Springfield SAC, recited details of an interview conducted in Madison County Jail in Edwardsville, Illinois, with a suspect in the Alton robbery. The report of this interview states that the individual being questioned "meets physical description . . . in above bank robbery; has history of using automatic pistol similar to that used by op. sub. Number 1 and was employed part time for cab company which had stand directly across street from Bank . . . and invested heavily in cabs shortly after Bank robbery."

In my view, there was no question that on August 1, 1968, the FBI was on the trail of the suspects for the Alton robbery, and that those suspects didn't include the Ray brothers. Yet in August 1978 the HSCA, through Counsel Blakey, contacted Philip Heymann, assistant attorney general of the Criminal Division of the Justice Department, seeking the prosecution of John Ray for allegedly giving false testimony to the HSCA regarding the Alton bank robbery.

Before formally referring this matter to the Department of Justice, Mr. Blakey met with U.S. Attorney Earl Silberg and a representative of the Criminal Division on May 24, 1978. Blakey admitted that the primary reason he wanted John Ray charged with perjury was to convince James Earl Ray to testify before the committee concerning his knowledge of the assassination of Martin Luther King. Blakey tried to persuade the Justice Department that John Ray had, in fact, committed perjury in denying his participation with his brothers in the robbery.

In a letter reply to the HSCA (obtained through a Freedom of Information Act application years later), Assistant Attorney General Heymann and Alfred L. Brantman, chief of the General Crimes Section of the Criminal Division, forcefully declined to consider any prosecution, declaring that "there is no existing or anticipated or other evidence to link John Ray or James Earl Ray to that robbery."

He also stated that "returning an indictment against John Ray in order to pressure his brother James Earl Ray into cooperating could and should be viewed as an abuse of process. It is one thing to use the criminal laws to pressure an individual into cooperating with the government. It is another thing to use the criminal laws against someone to pressure another individual into cooperating with the Government. This is particularly true when the individuals involved are close family relatives such as brothers."

During Jerry Ray's appearance on November 30, HSCA Counsel Mark Speiser did indeed focus one aspect of his questioning on the Alton bank robbery. I informed Speiser that Jerry was not and had never been a suspect in that case and that this had been confirmed to me by the Alton authorities as late as the previous day. I also put on the record Jerry's willingness to waive the statute of limitations and stand trial for that crime if any authority was willing to try him.

Jerry explicitly denied any participation in the robbery, pointing out that at the time of the Alton robbery he was working at the Sportsman's Club in Northbrook, Illinois. His employment records would confirm that in the three years he worked there he never missed a day and that he frequently worked seven nights a week, making it impossible for him to have been in Alton at the time of the crime. Jerry's factual responses fell on deaf ears.

Throughout the hearing Flo and I frequently locked horns

with the committee counsel. They continually attempted to tie Jerry and John to James during the time James was a fugitive. Any facts to the contrary would be ignored.

Though Flo and I believed as counsel that we had taken some of the bite out of the HSCA's persistent attack on the facts, we expected the HSCA report to confirm the committee's predetermined conclusions.

We were right.

13

The HSCA Report: January 1979

BY THE END of the final set of public hearings, I felt convinced that the HSCA had already formed its conclusions and was probably well advanced in writing its final report. In fact, a first draft was finished by December 13, 1978, about two weeks after the hearings.

Disinformation was produced at a high cost to the taxpayers (the total cost of the King and Kennedy investigations was $5.5 million). Clearly, the committee could have done a proper job. Counsel Blakey reported that in conducting both investigations staff completed 562 trips to 1,463 destinations—including Mexico, Canada, Portugal, and Cuba—during a total of 4,758 days. Three hundred and thirty-five witnesses were heard in public or private sessions, and some 4,924 interviews were conducted.

The last official act of the committee, in December 1978, was to approve its findings and recommendations. The final report was published in January 1979. It is essential to distinguish between the report itself—which was widely disseminated, even published commercially—and the material contained in the accompanying thirteen volumes, which had a very limited print run and distribution. One frequently finds information buried in the volumes that conflicts with conclusions in the report itself.

Among the most valuable historical information was the account of the FBI's wide-ranging legal and illegal communist infiltration investigation (COMINFIL) and counterintelligence programs and activities (COINTELPRO) conducted before and after the assassination. These were designed to tie Dr. King and the SCLC to the influence of the Communist Party and to discredit Dr. King.

As early as 1957, at the time of the founding of the SCLC, FBI supervisor J. K. Kelly stated in a memo that the group was "a likely target for communist infiltration."[27] As the SCLC mounted an increasingly high-profile challenge to segregation and the denial of voting rights to blacks across the South, the bureau began actively infiltrating meetings and conferences.[28]

On October 23, 1962, Hoover sent a memo authorizing the Atlanta and New York field offices to conduct a general COMINFIL investigation of the SCLC. The memo also inquired about whether the SCLC had any branches in New Orleans and asked the New Orleans office to explore COMINFIL possibilities in that city.[29]

As for the COINTELPRO activities specifically aimed at Dr. King which began in late October, 1962, the HSCA report noted that a 1976 Justice Department report explicitly stated that the bureau's campaign embodied a number of felonies. The HSCA report only summarized these activities, with the full scope of the illegal activity only being revealed by the documents contained in Volume six.

In December 1963, less than a month after the assassination of President John F. Kennedy, bureau officials attended a Washington conference to analyze the avenues of approach aimed at "neutralizing King as an effective Negro leader."[30] The conference focused on how to "produce the best results without embarrassment to the Bureau."[31] Those present discussed the possibility of using Dr. King's housekeeper, Mrs. King, or selective plants in the SCLC. From then on, agents in the field were challenged to come up with proposals for humiliating, discrediting, or even merely inconveniencing Dr. King and the SCLC.

Officials at the meeting agreed with domestic intelligence chief William C. Sullivan's suggestion that microphones be placed surreptitiously in Dr. King's hotel rooms as he traveled. These would complement the wiretaps already in place at his home and office in Atlanta. The bureau hoped to pick up information about extramarital sexual activity, which could then be used to tarnish his reputation or even blackmail him.

The bureau carried out this surveillance at numerous hotels nationwide from late 1963 through the end of 1965. Documents reveal that the wiretaps on the SCLC's Atlanta offices ran from October 24, 1963, to June 21, 1966;[32] Dr. King's home was tapped from November 8, 1963, to April 30, 1965, when he moved.[33]

In 1966 FBI director Hoover, becoming fearful of a congressional inquiry into electronic surveillance, ordered this monitoring of Dr. King discontinued—but in such a way that it could be reinstalled at short notice.[34]

When in 1967 the SCLC and Dr. King turned their attention to Vietnam and the Poor People's Campaign in Washington, the bureau asked Attorney General Clark to approve renewed telephone surveillance. He refused.[35] I was skeptical that electronic surveillance on King ceased, but thought it unlikely that evidence of such rogue activity would ever surface.

The bureau also engaged in surreptitious activities and burglaries directed against Dr. King and the SCLC. The HSCA estimated that twenty such events took place between 1959 and 1964.[36] These illegal operations began at least three years prior to any security file being officially opened.

The bureau would maintain that Dr. King was not officially a COINTELPRO target until late 1967 or early 1968. In fact, a massive campaign was underway from 1964 with the purpose of destroying him and even, at one point, apparently trying to induce him to commit suicide. In its campaign the bureau left few areas untouched.

Bureau Contacts with Political Leaders

The FBI, often with direct personal contact of an agent or SAC in the relevant area, met with a number of political leaders to advise them about information it had obtained on Dr. King's allegedly indiscreet personal life and the communist influence on him. Those approached included, among others, the following:

- U.K. prime minister Harold Wilson (whom Dr. King was to visit on his return trip from Oslo, after receiving the Nobel Peace Prize)
- New York governor Nelson Rockefeller
- Former Florida governor LeRoy Collins, then director of the U.S. Justice Department's Community Relations Service
- Massachusetts governor John A. Volpe (Dr. King was to be honored in Massachusetts in 1965)
- Speaker of the House of Representatives John McCormack (briefed on August 14, 1965)
- Director of the CIA; Secretary of State Dean Rusk; chairman of the Joint Chiefs of Staff; Maj. Gen. Carl C. Turner, Provost Marshal, U.S. Army; and Gen. Leonard E. Chapman, Commandant, U.S. Marine Corps (all of these leaders received a bureau-prepared monograph on March 19, 1968, entitled "Martin Luther King Jr., A Current Analysis"; it contained carefully selected discrediting material on Dr. King that the bureau had compiled by that time, about two weeks before his death[37]

Bureau Manipulation of the Media

By late 1964 the bureau began to put out the word to news-people that Dr. King's personal life was unsavory. A whisper campaign was aimed at the media in general, and trusted reporters were offered an opportunity to read the transcripts of the surveillance or to listen to the allegedly damaging tape recordings. The HSCA confirmed a number of approaches Hoover made to the media through Crime Records Division head Cartha DeLoach.

U.S. News & World Report was one of the bureau's favorite media outlets. Like some select others, it was provided with the full text of an extraordinary three-hour meeting between Hoover and a group of women reporters, at which Hoover declared, "I consider King to be the most notorious liar in the country." A summary report of this comment also found its way to the first page of the *New York Times,* on November 19, 1964.[38]

In November 1966 the bureau also successfully used the media to cause Dr. King to cancel a meeting with Teamsters leader Jimmy Hoffa. (At this time Hoffa was in the final stages of appealing his conviction and sentence on a charge of jury tampering, stemming from his earlier trial in Nashville. His appeal was finally denied in January 1967, and he entered prison on March 7.) Any alliance between Dr. King and the powerful labor leader would have greatly concerned the bureau and the federal government because Hoffa had an enormous work force and a virtually unlimited treasury. His support of King would have greatly enhanced the SCLC's effectiveness. Consequently, the Crime Records Division prepared an article for public release and also recommended that "a Bureau official be designated now to alert friendly news media of the meeting once the meeting date is learned so that arrangements can be made for appropriate press coverage of the planned meeting to expose and disrupt it."[39] Hoover's "OK" appeared below that recommendation.

Upon learning of the imminent date of the meeting, the Crime Records Division notified a national columnist for the New York *Daily News* as well as selected news photographers and wire service reporters, to ensure maximum publicity. The *Daily News* broke the story, causing Dr. King to decide not to meet Hoffa. The bureau then tipped off a number of reporters that King was traveling to Washington. As he came off the plane, he was besieged by reporters asking about the proposed meeting. The Crime Records Division reported that it had been successful in thwarting the SCLC receiving any funds from the

Teamsters. Hoover scribbled "Excellent" at the bottom of the memo.[40]

In March 1967, Hoover approved a recommendation by the Domestic Intelligence Division to furnish "friendly" reporters with questions designed to exploit King's growing opposition to the war in Vietnam. Reporters were also furnished with off-the-record embarrassing questions they might put to Dr. King at press conferences.[41]

Following the UN rally on April 15, 1967, newspapers began to speculate on the possibility of a third-party King-Spock presidential ticket. We had no doubt that this ticket would be a matter of serious concern to the sitting president, who would be concerned about the split liberal vote resulting in Nixon being elected. Such a ticket would also be a matter of concern to the FBI and the intelligence community because of the resulting debate about the war and their roles in support of it. (This was subsequently confirmed by Freedom of Information Act materials and other researchers.)[42] However, we never anticipated the degree of fear that Dr. King's activities and plans in 1967–1968 instilled in the intelligence, defense, and federal law enforcement apparatus.

The bureau's concern was heightened when it learned that we had scheduled a convention in Chicago for September. Its field office recommended that flyers, leaflets, cards, and bumper stickers be used in conjunction with the voices of a number of political columnists or reporters, to discredit the ticket.[43] The Chicago memo stressed that "this person . . . [the journalist chosen] . . . should be respected for his balance and fair mindedness. An article by an established conservative would not adequately serve our purposes." (We would later learn of the existence of a heavily deleted CIA memo dated October 5, 1967, which noted that the communists had been blocked in their efforts to obtain a King-Spock peace and freedom ticket. The deletions were justified on the grounds of protecting "intelligence activities, sources or methods."[44])

In October 1967, the FBI's Domestic Intelligence Division recommended that an editorial be placed in a "Negro magazine" to reveal King as "a traitor to his country and his race" and thus reduce his chances of gaining much income from a series of SCLC fund-raising shows scheduled around that time by Harry Belafonte. This recommendation was also approved by Hoover and marked "Handled 10/28/67."[45]

In early March 1968 the bureau began to disseminate information to the press aimed specifically at hurting the SCLC's fund-raising for the Poor People's Campaign. One such story the bureau circulated was "that King does not need contributions from the 70,000 people he solicited. Since the churches have offered support, no more money is needed and any contributed would only be used by King for other purposes."[46]

On March 28, 1968, the day the Memphis demonstration broke up in violence (which I have come to believe was caused by *agents provocateur*), a Domestic Intelligence Division memo detailed the outbreak of violence and had attached to it an unattributable memo that it was suggested could be made available by the Crime Records Division to "cooperative media sources." It also carried Hoover's "OK" and the notation "handled on 3/28/68." This effort resulted in the widely published articles depicting Dr. King as a coward for fleeing the scene of the violence.

For example, five days before King's death, the Memphis *Commercial Appeal* (March 30, 1968) asserted in an editorial that "Dr. King is suffering from one of those awesome credibility gaps. Furthermore, he wrecked his reputation as a leader as he took off at high speed when violence occurred."

The next day (March 31) the paper stated in an article headed "Chicken à la King" that "Dr. Martin Luther King Jr. fled from the rioting and looting in the downtown area Thursday. . . ." His efforts to climb aboard a meat truck were rebuffed but the motorist next in line picked him up."

On March 30 and 31 the *Globe-Democrat,* in an editorial supplied virtually verbatim by the FBI and headed "The Real Martin Luther King" stated that "King sprinted down a side street to an awaiting automobile and sped away." Dr. King was termed a deceiver who would no longer be able to "hoodwink intelligent Americans." It labeled him "one of the most menacing men in America." On the opposite page was a cartoon caricature of Dr. King shooting a gun, with the caption, "I'm not firing it—I'm only pulling the trigger." In fact, King was reluctant to leave the scene of the violence on March 28. He virtually had to be forced to leave.

Then, as Dr. King prepared to go to Memphis for what would be his last visit, the Domestic Intelligence Division, in a memorandum issued on March 29, 1968, recommended that the following article be furnished to a "cooperative news source":

> Martin Luther King, during the sanitation workers' strike in Memphis, Tennessee, has urged Negroes to boycott downtown white merchants to achieve Negro demands. On 3/29/68 King led a march for the sanitation workers. Like Judas leading lambs to slaughter King led the marchers to violence, and when the violence broke out, King disappeared.
>
> The fine Hotel Lorraine in Memphis is owned and patronized exclusively by Negroes but King didn't go there for his hasty exit. Instead King decided the plush Holiday Inn Motel, white owned, operated and almost exclusively patronized, was the place to "cool it." There will be no boycott of white merchants for King, only for his followers.

Thus, five days before the assassination the bureau was looking to place an internally prepared article whose message was that Dr. King should stay at a black-owned hotel instead of a white establishment. In particular, "the fine Hotel Lorraine" was singled out.

In volume four of the HSCA report,[47] the committee stated that the "FBI did as a part of its propaganda campaign against Dr. King prepare a press release on March 29, taking him to task for staying at the Holiday Inn. In turn, this criticism was echoed in newspapers around the country, although the investigation was unable to determine concretely if the news stories were the direct result of the FBI release. . . ."

In its Saturday morning (March 30) edition the *Commercial Appeal* made a point of stating that Dr. King was "staying in a $29 a day room at the Holiday Inn Rivermont, also known as the Rivermont Hotel." This of course was the hotel to which he was rushed and registered by the police after the march broke up.

The HSCA accepted Ralph Abernathy's recollection that Dr. King's normal practice was to stay at the Lorraine, though reporter Kay Black's memory differed. The contention that Dr. King normally stayed at the Lorraine made no sense in light of the active campaign of criticism aimed at him for staying at white-owned hotels. Such criticism would have been hollow if in fact the Lorraine was his usual motel in Memphis. The committee didn't discuss or even refer to the changing of Dr. King's room at the Lorraine.

THE HSCA REPORTED that the bureau's media efforts to discredit Dr. King even continued after he was killed. In March 1969, when it was learned that Congress was considering declaring Dr. King's birthday a national holiday, the Crime Records Division recommended briefing the members of the House Committee on Internal Security, who had the power to keep the bill from being reported out of committee. A plan was developed, but Hoover was concerned that any efforts to discredit King posthumously be handled "very cautiously."[48]

Though not covered specifically by the HSCA report, one of the most blatant ways the bureau tried to tarnish Dr. King's image after his death was by spreading the story to the media that he might well have been shot on the orders of a husband of a former lover. Jack Anderson, one of the columnists who was fed the FBI information, revealed in 1975 how he had been contacted by Hoover in 1968, when he was, in his words, "on good terms with the old FBI curmodgeon [sic]":

> The FBI vendetta against Dr. Martin Luther King Jr. didn't end with his murder. FBI Director J. Edgar Hoover, who had tried to blacken King's name while he was alive, also tried to tarnish it after his death.
>
> Not long after King was gunned down on the balcony of his Memphis motel on April 4, 1968, Hoover sent word to me that the motive behind the murder was cuckoldry, that the assassin apparently had been hired by a jealous husband . . .

who had become enraged by the discovery that his wife had borne King's child. The intermediary identified the Los Angeles couple and showed me supporting data, including an FBI report describing a passionate interlude between the wife and Dr. King in a New York City hotel. . . .

I flew to Los Angeles and did my damnedest to confirm the FBI leads. . . . I could find absolutely no evidence that contradicted the couple's own explanation that Dr. King was an honored friend of the family, a frequent guest in their home and nothing more.

I also discovered with deepening apprehension that there were no FBI agents on this trail that was supposed to be so hot. I returned to Washington satisfied that the FBI story was erroneous and half convinced that it was a deliberate hoax.[49]

In 1968 Anderson was indeed on good terms with Hoover, receiving and publishing bureau information such as that appearing in his columns on May 6, 1968 (lauding the bureau's search for Ray and pronouncing his guilt), and March 25, 1969 (denying the existence of either a conspiracy or the handler named Raul).

Bureau Influence with Religious Leaders

In his testimony before the HSCA in open hearing, bureau assistant director C. D. Brennan confirmed that the FBI also strove to discredit Dr. King in the eyes of prominent religious leaders. A number of confidential bureau memos substantiated this assertion.

The bureau was particularly incensed over the possibility of Dr. King meeting with the pope in late September 1964. In an effort to prevent this audience, Assistant Director John Malone provided an extensive briefing to one of the bureau's most reliable friends—Francis Cardinal Spellman of the New York diocese. His Eminence was long known to be one of the Roman Catholic Church's most virulent anticommunists and a long-term supporter of U.S. intervention in Vietnam. He reportedly "immediately advised" the Vatican secretary of state that no audience be given to Dr. King in light of "very serious, but highly confidential information which had come to his attention but which he could not discuss in detail over the telephone."[50] For whatever reason, the effort failed, and Dr. King did meet with the pope on September 18, 1964.

The bureau had more luck in its contact with the Baptist World Alliance, which had scheduled Dr. King to speak at its congress in Miami Beach, Florida, in June 1965. After the alliance was presented with certain "facts" about Dr. King, his speech was canceled.

The FBI mounted similar campaigns in late 1964 and early 1965 designed to damage Dr. King's relations with the National Council of Churches and Archbishop Cody of the archdiocese of Chicago.

Campaign to Prevent the Award of Honorary Degrees to Dr. King

Every time the bureau learned that a university was planning to award Dr. King an honorary degree, it strove to dissuade senior officials from making the award. Usually these efforts failed. One notable success apparently involved Marquette University in 1964. Hoover had himself received an honorary award from Marquette in 1950 and considered the prospect of King getting the same award a personal insult. The bureau pulled out all stops, and the award was canceled.

Attempts to Neutralize Dr. King's Leadership and Replace Him

In 1964 the bureau undertook a plan to promote an alternative figure as a black leader. A moderate, acceptable replacement was to emerge after the discrediting and destruction of Dr. King was complete. A memo dated December 1, 1964, proposed that Cartha DeLoach organize a meeting of a number of the more amenable civil rights leaders. These leaders would be positively informed about the bureau's civil rights activity as well as about the negative aspects of Dr. King. In effect, the so-called potential replacements would treat King like a pariah.

The "Suicide Project"

One of the bureau's most venal actions against King took place in October 1964 after it was announced that he was going to receive the Nobel Peace Prize. U.S. ambassadors in London, Stockholm, Oslo, and Copenhagen were briefed about his personal life and communist associations, in case any of them contemplated receiving him. In addition, the FBI made a tape that allegedly contained ribald remarks made by Dr. King, and sounds of people apparently engaging in sexual activity. An agent flew the tape to Tampa, Florida, and mailed it anonymously to the SCLC from that city, along with a letter threatening to expose the alleged sexual indiscretions.

The letter, mailed in late November, was designed to drive King to despair:

> King look into your heart. You know you are a complete fraud and a greater liability to all of us Negroes. . . . You are no clergyman and you know it. I repeat you are a colossal fraud and an evil, vicious one at that. . . . You, even at an early age have turned out to be not a leader but a dissolute, abnormal moral imbecile. We will now have to depend on our older leaders like Wilkins[,] a man of character[,] and thank God we have others like him. But you are done. Your "honorary" degrees, your Nobel Prize (what a grim farce) and other awards will not save you. King, I repeat you are done. . . .

The HSCA concluded that the final paragraph "clearly implied that suicide would be a suitable course of action for Dr. King":[51]

> King, there is only one thing left for you to do. You know what it is. . . . There is but one way out for you. You had better take it before your filthy, abnormal fraudulent self is bared to the nation.[52]

As a result of this action by the bureau, Dr. King and his colleagues became aware for the first time of the extensive surveillance of them. From then on, they had no doubt about the lengths to which Hoover would go to silence King.

SCLC Infiltration

Former agent Arthur Murtagh testified before the HSCA that he himself had many informants whom he used to gather information about the SCLC. They were part of the "black probe" operation. He noted that the field office's primary informant was a member of the SCLC's executive staff controlled by agent Al Sentinella, who sat directly across from him in the Atlanta field office. In addition to the monthly bureau payment, this informant further supplemented his income by embezzling organization funds. Sentinella warned him about this but took no other action. The informant informed on the SCLC and Dr. King, sometimes daily, right up to the day of the assassination. Among other information, details of Dr. King's itinerary and travel plans were provided.

The official abuses, though orchestrated by Hoover, were supported and carried out by bureau and field office personnel in every section of the country. Murtagh said that in Atlanta 90 percent of their time was spent on investigating and attempting to denigrate Dr. King. This focus reflected a hatred that seemed to permeate the bureau from top to bottom.

Murtagh's HSCA testimony revealed that on April 4, 1968, as he left the Atlanta field office around 6:30 p.m. with Special Agent Jim Rose, his fellow agent virtually "jumped for joy," exclaiming, "We [or "They"—Murtagh's recollection here is hazy] finally got the son of a bitch!"

(In his testimony before the HSCA, Rose couldn't recall any words that he uttered at the time. When asked whether it was possible that he made the statement alleged by Murtagh, he said, "It is possible.")[53]

As horrendous as this campaign was in the HSCA's view, the committee didn't view it as indicative of the bureau's involvement in the assassination itself, but as appearing to create an atmosphere in which the assassination could take place. Summarizing the HSCA conclusions, Counsel Blakey declared that, "as it turned out, the House Select Committee found no evidence of complicity of the CIA, FBI **or any government agency** in either assassination." (emphasis added.)

Just as chilling as the HSCA's efforts to deflect attention from
government involvement in King's death were its efforts to sidestep questions about a conspiracy by putting forward a highly
questionable theory of its own. The HSCA firmly rejected the
FBI's conclusion that Ray was a racist and that his racism was
the motive for the assassination. It would be difficult to construct a more convoluted scenario than the one the HSCA advanced: Two alleged conspirators, St. Louis racists named John
Sutherland and John Kauffmann—both dead by the time the
HSCA was formed, and whose supposed involvement was raised
for the first time in the final report—were alleged to have
offered a bounty on Dr. King, which Ray somehow heard about,
taking it upon himself to earn it. It was acknowledged, however,
that Ray had never met the two men. No explanation was provided as to why he never collected nor tried to collect his payment, nor even how he imagined he would be paid.

The HSCA suggested possible ways James Earl Ray could have
learned about the alleged offer. They tried, for example, to
show that he could have heard about it from another prisoner
or even a medical officer with whom he had had contact during
his Missouri incarceration. Finally the committee admitted that
its investigation failed to confirm any such connection. In fact,
both the prisoner, John Paul Spica, and the doctor, Hugh
Maxey, denied ever having heard of the alleged Sutherland-
Kauffmann offer.

The committee then attempted to establish that John Ray,
at his Grapevine Tavern in St. Louis, passed information to
James about the contract. Since John Ray had in late 1967
and early 1968 allegedly been a supporter of the presidential
campaign of Alabama governor George Wallace and his American Independence Party, and both Sutherland and Kauffmann
also supported the party, the HSCA believed there was a link.
The Grapevine, according to the committee, was a source of
Wallace literature. The committee also claimed that brothers
John and Jerry were quite active in Wallace campaign activity.
John Ray denied under oath knowing either Sutherland or
Kauffmann and further denied ever hearing or participating in
conversations at the Grapevine about the offer.

Though the committee admitted that its extensive investigation of the St. Louis conspiracy proved frustrating and that it could produce no direct evidence that Ray had ever even heard of the money offer to kill Dr. King, or even that such an offer existed, it alleged that through his participation in the Alton bank robbery Ray was physically present in the St. Louis area around July 1967.

The HSCA concluded that Ray was a lone gunman, acting with full knowledge of what he was doing, probably stalking Dr. King for a period immediately preceding the assassination. Raul, as described by Ray, didn't exist, so Ray couldn't have been a fall guy manipulated by others. However, if there was a Raul he was likely either or both of Ray's brothers, with whom he had ongoing contact and assistance. The HSCA stated that strong circumstantial evidence existed about the consultative role of one of the brothers in the purchase of the weapon itself. (The only scintilla of evidence provided was Aeromarine store manager Donald Wood's comment that when he bought the rifle Ray said he was going hunting with his brother. In fact Ray has said that his cover story for the purchase was that he was going hunting with his brother-in-law.)

To shore up the committee's conclusions about the involvement of the Ray brothers, Counsel Blakey continued to press for a prosecution of John Ray for perjury for denying that he participated in the Alton bank robbery. As noted earlier, the U.S. attorney general's office summarily refused, citing a lack of evidence.

The HSCA then sealed, for fifty years, all the investigative files and information it elected not to publish. This included all field investigative reports, interviews, documents, and data. Counsel Blakey also invited the CIA, the FBI, and the MPD intelligence division to place their files on the case under congressional cover so that they would be protected from any Freedom of Information Act requests. This they did.

With all of its speciousness and shortcomings, the HSCA report raised a number of questions and identified a number of witnesses who had varying types of involvement and stories to tell. In most cases the committee prepared brief explanations and summaries to implement its door-closing objective.

The committee accepted the MPD's official explanation for the removal of Detective Redditt from his surveillance post at the fire station. Under cross-examination, however, Redditt admitted that his role was not to provide security for Dr. King, as he had previously maintained, but rather to surveil him and provide intelligence reports. The report noted that upon being removed from his post Redditt was personally brought by MPD intelligence officer Lt. E. H. Arkin to a meeting in police headquarters where he was informed by Director Holloman of a threat on his life. However, the report also revealed, without explanation, the presence at that meeting of one Phillip Manuel, an investigator for the U.S. Senate Permanent Subcommittee on Investigations, chaired by Arkansas senator John McClellan. Supposedly, Manuel had told Redditt's superiors about the threat on Redditt's life.

The HSCA discussed the removal of the two black firemen, which early investigators had found curious, but passed it off as being motivated by the MPD's concern with the security of their surveillance posts and having nothing to do with the existence of a conspiracy.

The report also dealt with rumors surrounding the removal of a personal security detail assigned to Dr. King and accepted Inspector Don Smith's explanation that since the SCLC party wasn't willing to cooperate with the detail it was disbanded late in the afternoon of April 3.

As to Solomon Jones's insistence that he saw someone in the bushes right after the shooting, the HSCA concluded that it was unlikely that what Solomon saw was a person but that if it were a man it was likely to have been a quick-responding MPD policeman, already on the scene.[54] (This appears incredible considering Solomon had described the man as wearing a jacket and plaid shirt.)

The HSCA further noted the MPD's failure after the shooting to issue an all points bulletin (general alert describing the suspect) as well as a "Signal Y" alert (instructing cars to block off city exit routes). Pages were devoted to discrediting Grace

Walden and hence her denial that a man she saw exiting the bathroom around the time of the shooting was James Earl Ray. In so doing the committee gave credibility to Charlie Stephens's account of seeing someone running down the hallway after the shot. The committee maintained that it didn't rely on him for an identification. The HSCA attacked Wayne Chastain's report of his interview with Walden and his observations of a drunken Stephens as "improbable, if not an outright fabrication"[55] (despite including in the volumes MPD detective lieutenant Tommy Smith's affidvait stating that Stephen was indeed drunk).

The report also raised the names of three individuals with intriguing possible connections to the case. One was Herman Thompson, a former East Baton Rouge, deputy sheriff. Ray had told the committee that Thompson was the owner of the Baton Rouge telephone number given to him by Raul. (Ray had discovered this by comparing the number he had with the phone numbers in the Baton Rouge telephone directory, beginning with the last digit. Eventually he matched the number he had with that listed for a Herman Thompson.) The second individual was Randy Rosenson, whose name was on the business card Ray said he had found in the Mustang before crossing the border from Mexico into California. The third person was Raul Esquivel, the Louisiana state trooper whose Baton Rouge state police barracks had allegedly been called by Ray in December 1967 on his trip with Charlie Stein from Los Angeles to New Orleans.

The HSCA reported that all three people denied knowing Ray and concluded that none of them had any connection with a conspiracy to kill Dr. King. They noted that Esquivel's work records made it impossible for him to have been Ray's Raul.

The information contained in the ancillary volumes published by the HSCA was much more valuable than the report itself. Though carefully edited, the ancillary volumes included sworn statements and documents that provided a useful place for me to start to analyze issues. For example, the HSCA staff interview of Aeromarine Supply Store manager Donald Wood on March 10, 1977, revealed Wood's account of the conversation he had with Ray when the latter requested the change of rifle. He said that he remembered the man said "that he had, and I'm pretty sure these were his exact words, he had been talking to someone and that's not the gun he wanted." Wood then recalled that the man said what he really wanted was a Remington Model 760 Gamemaster pump-action rifle. He said he had the impression that the caller was probably reading it from something, since very few people ever referred to the gun as a "Gamemaster." (This was compatible with Ray's recollection of Raul pointing out the rifle from a brochure Ray gave him).

The HSCA ballistics panel reported that they test-fired the evidence rifle and examined the markings on the test-fired bullets. They found that the markings on **most** of the test fired bullets varied from one to another. They concluded that no meaningful comparison could be made between the test-fired bullets and the death slug.

The FBI laboratory had conducted neutron activation analysis tests on the evidence bullets and the death slug (such tests analyze the composition of lead in a bullet). The HSCA panel stated that the bureau's April 29, 1968 report stated that the elemental composition of the bullets varied and therefore no meaningful comparison with the death slug could be made. The panel didn't conduct its own neutron activation analysis.

The panel noted that somehow the rifle and the scope were misaligned, resulting in the weapon not firing straight. It also noted that the death slug was originally delivered to the FBI in one piece but was received by the panel in three fragments produced as a result (so the panel believed) of the bureau's laboratory testing procedures.

The fingerprints report showed that Ray's prints were found on the following items in the discarded bundle: the rifle, the scope, the binoculars, a beer can and the *Commercial Appeal* newspaper. There were none of Ray's prints in the bathroom, the room he rented, nor elsewhere in the rooming house. The report also conceded that there were many unidentified fingerprints in the relevant areas of the rooming house and on Ray's Mustang.

A Memphis City Engineers analysis of the bullet's trajectory couldn't conclude whether it came from the bathroom window of the rooming house or the elevated brush area behind the rooming house. This uncertainty was due not only to confusion over Dr. King's posture but also to the fact that the medical examiner, Dr. Francisco, hadn't traced the path of the bullet in Dr. King's body. When asked about this departure from normal procedure, Francisco took the curious position that he was loathe to cause further mutilation for no good reason.

The HSCA discussed the possibility that the shot had been fired from the brush and also the contention that the brush had been cut down the next morning. It concluded that the bullet had been fired from the bathroom, discounting (as noted earlier) Solomon Jones's statement. Also, after supposedly reviewing the work records of the Memphis Sanitation Department and the Department of Parks it concluded that no cutting had taken place. The committee didn't interview Kay Black or James Orange.

Occasionally, some testimony before the committee appeared to contradict Ray's story. For example, Estelle Peters, an employee of the Piedmont Laundry in Atlanta, contended that her records indicated that Ray left laundry with her on April 1. If this was the case, it could be alleged that Ray was in Atlanta with the alleged murder weapon at the same time as Dr. King, and could have been stalking him. Ray maintained that he had put in the laundry earlier and that he was nowhere near Atlanta on April 1, having been well along on his trip to Memphis and spending that evening at a motel in Corinth, Mississippi.

Often, more questions were raised than answered.

The MPD agent whom Redditt had told Mark Lane had infiltrated the Invaders was revealed to be Marrell McCollough. Under oath, McCollough admitted that he furnished regular reports on the Invaders' activity to Lieutenant Arkin, his MPD intelligence bureau control officer. One of the first people to reach Dr. King after the shooting, McCollough had been in the parking area of the Lorraine, having just dropped off SCLC staffers Orange and Bevel. He immediately raced up the stairs after the shot. During his HSCA testimony, McCollough acknowledged that he was the mysterious figure kneeling over the fallen Dr. King on the balcony, apparently checking him for life signs. He also admitted to subsequently being involved as an *agent provocateur* in a number of illegal activities for which various Invaders were convicted and sentenced. He explicitly denied being connected, at the time of the assassination, to any federal agency. When I tried to locate McCollough later, I learned he had disappeared from Memphis; it was rumored that he had gone to work for the CIA.

The HSCA raised the issue of the withdrawal of some MPD TACT units from the area of the Lorraine. This had been confirmed in an affidavit provided to the HSCA by MPD chief William O. Crumby, who attributed the withdrawal to a request made by a person in Dr. King's group. This withdrawal contributed to the reduced police presence in the immediate area of the assassination.

Several conspiracy scenarios, some implicating the Mafia, were covered and dismissed in the HSCA report. I was interested in some of the scenarios, if only for the leads provided and resolved to follow them up.

THE HSCA'S REPORT had only strengthened my growing conviction that Dr. King's murder had not been solved.

14

Following the Footprints of Conspiracy: January–September 1979

IN THE EARLY MONTHS OF 1979 I commuted to Memphis to follow up on some issues only summarily covered by the HSCA.

First was a meeting with John McFerren, the owner of a gas station/grocery store in Somerville, Tennessee. I had been trying to meet with him for over four months, ever since Jim Lawson had told me about his story. Lawson said that McFerren had been a courageous and reliable black civil rights leader in Fayette County, whose activities had put his life under constant threat and caused his insurance to be canceled and his store to be periodically blacklisted by white suppliers. On the afternoon of February 8, 1979, I traveled with two associates of Mark Lane—April Ferguson, a lawyer, and Barbara Rabbito, a stenographer—to the small town of Somerville, about forty miles outside of Memphis.

When we reached McFerren's store around 6:15 p.m., I was immediately struck by the impression of a place under siege.

The huge plate glass window in front of his store was cracked from top to bottom and taped together, the result, McFerren said, of a drive-by shooting, one of many he had experienced since 1968. Not long ago, he told us, he shot and wounded a man contracted by the Mafia to kill him. He said that he was tipped off three weeks before the attempt and was waiting for the hit man—a black who was not from the area. Unshaven and dressed in working clothes with an old baseball cap, McFerren stood about 5'8". Solidly built and very alert, he peered cautiously over his glasses at us.

Although he knew we were coming and led us to a back room furnished with only a crude table and a couple of chairs, he seemed increasingly uneasy. He had closed the store and shut off the lights, but there was still a steady stream of traffic in and around the gas station. As it grew dark, his nervousness increased. Though his old friend Jim Lawson had arranged the meeting, it was obvious that McFerren didn't completely trust the three white strangers in front of him. We would accomplish little on that visit, and we left with the understanding that Lawson would be back in touch to arrange for a more secure meeting. Three more weeks of sporadic contact followed. He refused to talk on any local phones, being convinced that they were tapped.

Finally, I got McFerren's story after another face-to-face meeting was arranged. McFerren maintained that on the afternoon of April 4, 1968, while he was shopping at the Liberto, Liberto and Latch (LL&L) Produce Company in Memphis, he saw the company's president, Frank Liberto, talking on the telephone, having been handed the phone by one of the bosses who had answered it. As McFerren went to the back of the store, where there was an office on the other side of the wall, he heard Liberto's conversation through the open door. He insisted that he heard Liberto say, "I told you not to call me here. Shoot the son of a bitch when he comes on the balcony." Liberto told the caller that he should collect his money from Liberto's brother in New Orleans after he had finished. The sum of $5,000 was mentioned.

McFerren had heard rumors that Frank Liberto had some

underworld connections; this was none of McFerren's business, he thought, and so he just put the conversation out of his mind. He was jolted, however, when just an hour later, after he arrived back in Somerville, he heard of Martin Luther King's assassination.

After agonizing for two days, McFerren called Baxton Bryant, the executive director of the Tennessee Council on Human Rights, at his home in Nashville. Bryant, a Methodist minister, had been involved behind the scenes trying to mediate the garbage strike. McFerren asked Bryant to come to Somerville.

When Bryant got to Somerville and heard McFerren's story, Bryant insisted that he tell it to the FBI. McFerren was reluctant until Bryant promised him that either his name would be kept secret or he and his family would receive protection.

That night Bryant drove to Memphis, where he telephoned Frank Holloman at home and insisted on seeing him immediately. Around midnight they met in Holloman's office at police headquarters; soon after, homicide chief N. E. Zachary and FBI agent O. B. Johnson arrived. The three listened to Bryant's story and asked to see McFerren at once.

Bryant, knowing that McFerren wouldn't talk on the telephone, drove back the forty miles to Somerville and managed to convince his friend to get out of bed and go to Memphis. On Monday, April 8, at 3:00 a.m., Zachary and Johnson began interrogating McFerren in Bryant's room at the Peabody. Also present was David Caywood, an ACLU attorney.

They finished around 5:00 a.m. Zachary and Johnson taped McFerren's account and had him sketch the office in which he had seen Liberto and another one of the bosses, down to its furnishings, the position of the men, and where he himself had stood in the corridor, listening. They promised to check it out thoroughly.

Three days later, Bryant was told that the FBI believed that if McFerren overheard the telephone call at all, it wasn't related to the assassination. McFerren told me that as a result of the way he was treated he was most uncomfortable. He felt he was looked on as a criminal himself.

The HSCA had uncovered another independent reference

to the possible involvement of a Frank Liberto (the story told by Morris Davis, summarized below), noted Liberto's well-known racial bias, and even ascertained that his brother, Salvatore, who lived in Louisiana, was indirectly connected to organized crime leader Carlos Marcello (a fact that was unknown to McFerren). Nevertheless the HSCA elected to dismiss McFerren's story, just as the MPD and the FBI had. Shortly after the assassination, *Time* magazine stringer William Sartor had investigated McFerren's story. He concluded that organized crime was responsible for the killing, having connected to his own satisfaction Memphis produce dealer Frank C. Liberto with Carlos Marcello, the New Orleans Mafia leader. The HSCA concluded, after what it termed an extensive investigation, that no evidence existed to tie either Liberto or Marcello to the assassination.

I had previously obtained an affidavit dated February 21, 1977, sworn by Morris Davis of Birmingham, Alabama. I would have dismissed Davis's account out of hand had I not heard about McFerren's allegations. His independent reference to the involvement of a Frank Liberto was troubling. Davis maintained that in early 1968 he became aware of a plot to kill Dr. King which involved a local Birmingham doctor/gunrunner named Gus Prosch, a Mafia-connected man named Frank Liberto from Memphis and also, incredibly, King's close friend Ralph Abernathy and Birmingham SCLC leader Fred Shuttlesworth. Davis said he observed Abernathy and Shuttlesworth meeting with Prosch and Liberto on two occasions in the parking lot of the Gulas Lounge in Birmingham, and that late on the afternoon of April 3 Prosch actually showed him the gun that he said was to be used in the killing.

DURING ONE OF MY trips to Memphis in early 1979 I learned about Arthur Baldwin, a Memphis topless club owner who had become a very useful asset of the federal government. Previously in trouble with the law, he had received leniency in exchange for being the government's chief witness against high-ranking officials in Governor Ray Blanton's administration, exposing a "pay for pardon" operation and other corrupt practices. Baldwin came to my attention in connection with the assassination, or rather its cover-up. On February 16, 1979, Mark Lane's associates Ferguson and Rabbito executed affidavits resulting from a visit conducted a few days before with William "Tim" Kirk, an inmate of the Shelby County Jail. According to the affidavits, Kirk had called their office several times to request that Mark Lane visit him at the jail. He said he had some information that might be of value. Since Lane was unavailable, Ferguson and Rabbito went out to see him the next day. He declined to let them tape the conversation or use his name, but he permitted them to take notes. Kirk stated that he had been in and out of the Shelby County Jail since 1972 on robbery and extortion charges. Between October 15, 1977, and February 1978, while in jail, he befriended Arthur Baldwin, another prisoner. He kept in occasional contact with Baldwin after Baldwin was released.

In June or July of 1978 Baldwin mentioned a murder contract for $5,000. The target was James Earl Ray. Kirk, who was in jail at the time, believed that he wasn't necessarily being asked to do the job himself but that the $5,000 was for putting out the contract and making the appropriate connections for Baldwin so that it could be carried out.

Kirk remembered being puzzled as to why Baldwin who had a comfortable home on Balboa Circle, occasionally took rooms at the Executive Plaza Inn near the airport for business meetings. Baldwin's wife had told Kirk to call her husband at that hotel; it was at that number that he had the conversation about the contract on Ray. Kirk did some checking. From talking to other inmates who had worked for Art Baldwin, Kirk concluded that Baldwin, who he believed had soon after been officially removed from the Tennessee area and placed with a new identity in a new location, was a member of the federal government's Witness Protection Program as a result of his participation in an operation being mounted against certain state officials. He further concluded that the offer against Ray put out by Baldwin could have originated only with the government, because someone in Baldwin's position, being a significant government informant, would be completely under their control. He said that he had heard from contacts at Brushy Mountain prison that James Earl Ray was "good people." He therefore decided to get the word to Ray's attorney at the time, Mark Lane.

It was evident to both Ferguson and Rabbito that Kirk was in a state of considerable anxiety. He didn't stand to benefit; in fact, it was a statement against his own interest. He didn't ask for anything in exchange for the information, only emphasizing that his name should not be used.

I MET WITH ARTHUR HANES, SR., Ray's first lawyer, in February 1979 in his Birmingham law offices. He was cordial and cooperative. He said that he first viewed the balcony at the Lorraine from the bathroom in early September 1968. He said that even then it would have been extremely difficult to sight and shoot accurately through the remaining tree branches and tall bushes. Hanes noted that in September the foliage would have been fuller than it was in April, but nevertheless the tree branches themselves would have been an obstacle to challenge even the most competent marksman, which he said Ray certainly was not.

Arthur Hanes said, "We were ready. We thought we had a terrific chance to win the case and we were very disappointed when we were released. We felt like the state's case was largely circumstantial. In fact, I have not heard one new piece of evidence since we left the case. I believe I can fairly say we developed every piece of evidence that is available to this good day. As we neared trial time, of course, don't forget the burden was not on us to prove or disprove anything. We were trying to use the holes in the state's case to create the doubt it merited. . . . There was really no good testimony available to the state that the shot came from anywhere except those bushes. . . . And then you have the natural inconsistencies of the state's case. The ballistics, the state couldn't match this gun that Jimmy purportedly bought with a slug that was found in King's body. . . . Then there was the package in Guy Canipe's doorway. Mr.

Canipe would say the package was thrown down there some two to five minutes **before** the shot was fired."

This extraordinary statement, if true, meant that Ray was well and truly set up. Hanes told me that Canipe would have been a highly important witness for the defense.

Hanes went on to tell me that when he had worked for the FBI, he had taken training in ballistics evidence. He said that he had examined the slug removed from Dr. King and that "there was certainly enough rifling left on the bullet to link it with a particular gun if the gun could have been found."

Under oath, in his attempt to set aside the guilty plea in Ray's 1974 habeas corpus proceeding, Hanes testified that there was no question "that was a perfect evidence slug. If it had matched the rifle that was found in Canipe's amusement shop, the FBI testimony—and of course we have seen dozens of times—the FBI testimony would have been in my judgment, that the gun, to the exclusion of all others, fired this shot. What the testimony was going to boil down to was that this was a 30.06 rifle, and this was a 30.06 slug, and we were prepared to prove how many other 30.06's there were in the United States at the time, and in Memphis at the time, and in effect, completely investigate the firearms business."

Ray, of course, didn't go to trial on November 12, 1968, but instead two days earlier dismissed Arthur Hanes and retained Percy Foreman. To this day, Ray maintains that that was a mistake.

IN THE SUMMER OF 1979, Anna Ray insisted that I visit Knoxville lawyer Gene Stanley, a former assistant U.S. attorney for eastern Tennessee, who she learned had been attorney for Randy Rosenson, the man whose name was written on the government (L.E.A.A.) business card Ray had found. The L.E.A.A. stood for the Law Enforcement Administration, which at the time was sponsoring a number of pilot projects in selected cities. Anna had been tipped off by the manager of the Andrew Johnson Hotel in Knoxville. The manager had been approached by the HSCA, which was looking for Rosenson, who had previously stayed there while recovering from a car accident. The manager also told her that Stanley had previously represented Rosenson. Ray had always believed that there must be some connection between Raul and Rosenson, and in his search over the years for Raul, he tried unsuccessfully on several occasions to locate Rosenson, even having his brother Jerry and a Tennessee lawyer go to New Orleans to pursue leads.

In July 1979, Anna, Mark Lane, and I met with Stanley in his Knoxville offices. Stanley appeared nervous, although he had voluntarily agreed to see us. He had represented Rosenson when the latter was involved in a car accident in 1977, and later on a drug charge. He next heard from Rosenson in October 1977, when he was arrested and detained in Richmond, Virginia, on an Ohio warrant connected to a drug charge filed in the congressional district of the HSCA chairman, Louis Stokes.

At that time, Stanley said, HSCA attorney Robert Lehner and staff investigators flew to Richmond to interview Rosenson. Stanley represented him during the interrogation and during a further two days of questioning by HSCA investigators in Atlanta. Stanley told us that Rosenson was connected to organized crime and had formed his associations in Miami and New Orleans as a result of drug use. He was employed in smuggling drugs and, while ostensibly in the import-export business, brought in a variety of wild animals to sell. He owned a pet shop and was involved in other types of contraband smuggling. When Rosenson was questioned about specific organized crime figures, he indicated that he knew them well.

The HSCA continued its interrogation in Atlanta on October 26. According to Stanley, this time Lehner wasn't present and Chief Investigator Edward Evans and two other staff investigators conducted the extensive interrogation. Stanley maintained that the main line of questioning focused on Raul. He said he came away from the sessions with no doubt that the HSCA knew that there was a Raul, knew his identity, and believed that his operation was identical to the one Ray described.

In informal conversations, the investigators told Stanley they had traced the man whom Ray referred to as Raul to Monterey,

Mexico, claiming that he used the alias of "Raul de (or da) Gasso". They said that he smuggled contraband, particularly heroin, along a Mexico-Montreal-New Orleans triangle. Rosenson was able, said Stanley, to corroborate names, dates, and places of his contacts with this person, even to the point of identifying him from a portfolio of photographs the investigators showed him, although he didn't know him by the name they used.

Stanley said he was mystified and greatly disappointed when the HSCA reported that, although it had found evidence that Randy Rosenson was in many of the same cities as James Earl Ray, it found no evidence that his former client had contact with Raul. He was disturbed that the committee even explicitly quoted Rosenson as saying that he knew nothing about "a Raul."

I was excited about the confirmation of Raul's existence, but Anna Ray was upset. She said that Stanley had previously told her that the HSCA investigators had told him they believed Raul had been killed in a car accident in Mexico in or around 1972.

DURING THIS TIME I acquired what might have been a hot tip or a piece of disinformation: a photocopy of a photograph of a building. I tried unsuccessfully to locate the source of this photocopy. In the top margin there was a handwritten note indicating that the building, which was within blocks of the scene of the crime, was owned by a relative of an organized crime figure and was where the rifle purchased by Ray was stored until April 4, 1968.

IN THE DEFENSE FILE I came across the statements of two witnesses who seemed to provide Ray with an alibi and was astounded that no mention had ever been made of them. These statements were made by Ray Alvis Hendrix, a member of the Corps of Engineers working on a barge on the river; and William Zenie Reed, a photographic supplies salesman. The two men had been drinking together in Jim's Grill on the

afternoon of April 4. Hendrix and Reed were staying at the
nearby Clark's Hotel on Second Avenue. They left the bar
sometime between 5:30 and 5:45. Hendrix realized that he left
his jacket in the bar and went back in to retrieve it. Meanwhile,
Reed, waiting outside, examined a Mustang parked in front of
Jim's Grill. Since he was considering buying a car and was interested in the model, he gave it a fairly close look. When Hendrix
emerged, the two men walked north on South Main, reaching
Vance Avenue a couple of blocks away. They were about to
cross the street when a white Mustang, also going north on
South Main, caught up with them and made a right turn on
to Vance. If they hadn't stopped, they could have been struck,
though the car wasn't moving very fast. Reed observed that it
was being driven by a young dark-haired man. Just a short time
later, after they had reached their hotel, they heard sirens.
Reed stated that while he couldn't be certain, the car turning
on to Vance seemed to be the same car that he had been
inspecting. Hendrix recalled that Reed had commented to
that effect.

The statements of Reed and Hendrix appear to corroborate
Ray's story that he parked his Mustang in front of the grill and
that he drove it away prior to the shooting to see about having
a tire repaired.

IN THE AUTUMN OF 1979, I was able to meet with the Louisville,
Kentucky, police officer, Clifton Baird, whose story I had come
across in the HSCA report. His allegations were so credible that
their dismissal by the HSCA was on its face incomprehensible.
Everyone who had worked with Baird or had known him agreed
that he was an honest, diligent cop who played strictly by the
rules. The HSCA agreed.

On September 18, 1965, Louisville police officer Arlie Blair
accepted Baird's offer to drive him home at the end of the
3–11 p.m. shift. As they had done on previous occasions, the
two rode to Blair's house, parked for a while in the driveway
around midnight, and talked. Arlie Blair was unaware that, on
some of these occasions, Baird had taped their conversations

with a recorder that he placed in a rear speaker with the microphone under his seat. Baird had come to distrust Arlie. Fearful of any kind of setup, for some time he had regarded his growing collection of tapes as a kind of insurance.

Blair said he belonged to an organization that wanted Martin Luther King dead and was willing to pay $500,000 to accomplish this. He wanted to know whether Baird would participate in such a conspiracy. Baird told him he wanted no part of it and advised his fellow patrolman to stay away from such activity. At the time he was approached, Baird was himself under intense investigation by the FBI and police officials in his home town of Owensboro, Kentucky, in connection with the operation of a "dynamite ring" in western Kentucky. Consequently, he believed that the FBI and certain fellow police officials might have been preparing to compel him to take part in the King assassination plot by holding the investigation over him. He was also concerned that they might be trying to set him up. The investigation of Baird was completed long before the HSCA was formed, having concluded that he had no involvement whatsoever in the "bombing conspiracy." Sources close to the committee were quoted in a *Scripps-Howard* syndicated article published on March 28, 1977, as saying that Baird's claims of attempted blackmail "would explain why a veteran but low ranking policeman would have been approached by the alleged King conspirators."

At afternoon roll call the day after he recorded Blair's offer, he saw Blair talking to a group of men, some of whom he recognized as Louisville police officers and others as FBI agents who, over a period of some sixteen years or more, had developed a close relationship with members of the force. He identified the FBI agents he knew as special agents William Duncan (the FBI liaison with the Louisville Police Department) and Robert Peters. The HSCA has also reported that the Louisville special agent in charge, Bernard Brown, was present. Baird told me that was possible because he didn't know Brown; there were other "men in suits" he didn't recognize. As he watched, one of the agents was introduced to Blair, and the entire group went into a room and closed the door. Listening in from outside the room, Baird heard the offer discussed in heated tones. He also heard himself referred to as a "nigger lover."

Determined to get more information, Baird drove Arlie home the next evening, September 20, 1965. Once again, he tape recorded Blair's account and the reference to the $500,000. The tape that was made on September 18 has somehow disappeared, so the recording of September 20 is the only account in existence. Baird told me that he kept a copy and provided the original to the HSCA.

He testified before the HSCA in executive session on November 30, 1977. Special agent Duncan admitted that the discussion took place but maintained that it was a joke inspired by Louisville police sergeant William Baker, deceased at the time of the hearings, and that agents Peters and Brown would confirm his account. Contrary to Duncan's prediction, Peters and Brown denied any knowledge of the offer, as did Blair, who, however, admitted that the voice on the Baird tape recording was his own. Blair attributed his failing memory to physical and mental deterioration due to alcoholism.

The committee completed a thorough background check of Clifton Baird, concluding that he was highly credible. A technical evaluation of the tape verified that it was of a type used in 1965. Nevertheless, the HSCA refused to connect in any way the subject of Baird's testimony—the offer made on September 18, 1965—with the assassination of Dr. King in 1968. The committee dismissed it as a joke or, in any event, unrelated to later events.

In a three-hour interview with me at the Louisville airport on September 5, 1979, Baird said he has never doubted that those agents were coordinating an offer to kill Dr. King, who was a frequent visitor to Louisville (King's brother A. D. lived there). He said they clearly used Arlie Blair in an attempt to involve him in what he called a "serious business." Baird didn't believe they wanted him to be the gunman—as he said, "they have access to professionals for that"—but possibly they wanted him to be a "patsy . . . like James Earl Ray probably was."

As for Sergeant Baker's alleged joke, Baird said that it was incredible. Baker was assigned to Juvenile at that time and would have had little or no contact with those involved. He said he believed that Baker was named because "dead men make sorry witnesses." He also wondered why, if it was just a joke, ranking officers of the Louisville police department and the local FBI office would be involved; and why Peters and Brown would deny it ever happened?

During our interview, Baird recounted numerous incidents from the summer of 1965 through spring of 1968 when at odd times and places—the hospital, the police parking lot, and elsewhere—he would be confronted by four FBI agents he knew who would block his path just staring impassively at him, as though trying to "spook" him. He also found indications that his mail was being opened. He believed that he was being watched and warned to keep quiet. Then, after Dr. King was killed, the harassment stopped; the pressure was off.

Baird also told me that there was an unprecedented wholesale transfer of all the Louisville FBI agents to other field offices just before the assassination. He remembers the move coming as a real surprise because the staff had remained unchanged for such a long time. He believed that when the assassination plans had been formulated Hoover found it desirable to move the agents who had been involved in the previous attempt out of Louisville. (It was bureau policy that no agent be transferred without Hoover's personal approval.)

Clifton Baird's account of his experience left me with little doubt that there was a serious effort made in September 1965 to organize an assassination attempt on Dr. King in Louisville. Although it wasn't clear who the sponsors were, federal agents were involved and they sought the assistance of their friends on the Louisville police force.

The timing of this effort made sense. In 1965 Dr. King's prestige was considerable. Despite the efforts of the bureau and its allies within the previous year, and to the manifest outrage of bureau chief J. Edgar Hoover, King had received the Nobel Prize and had successfully fought off every subversive effort to discredit him.

As I left the Louisville airport that day, I couldn't help but wonder when the decision to eliminate King was initially made and how many other scenarios had preceded the one carried out in Memphis on April 4, 1968. It occurred to me later that Clifton Baird's story may have been the basis for the information received and provided by Daniel Ellsberg, since Brady Tyson had referred to "a group of off duty FBI agents" assigned the task of organizing the assassination of Dr. King.

As this initial stage of my research drew to a close, sadly it was becoming ever more clear to me that the HSCA's failure to look closely at a number of leads guaranteed that the major questions surrounding Dr. King's murder had not been considered much less answered.

15

Disruption, Relocation and Continuation: 1978–1988

In 1975–1977 CONSULTING PROJECTS I undertook in a large New England city resulted in a massive reorganization of a school system rife with corruption and the closing of the largest residential juvenile justice facility in the area. Many of those who lost their jobs as a result were connected to, or had a relative who was connected to, the organization of Raymond Patriarca, the undisputed Mafia leader in New England. Consequently, I became a marked man. I received threatening phone calls and strange men dressed in business suits paraded up and down outside my rural home. All my consulting contracts were either canceled or not renewed. Fabricated charges appeared from nowhere, and investigations of me and the various consulting services being run down were mounted. When it came down to hard facts, however, there were none. The allegations eventually disappeared into thin air.

Since I was increasingly engaged in the practice of international law, which frequently took me to Europe, my family and I moved to England in June of 1981. Except for telephone discussions and the gathering and consideration of documents, my work on the King case stalled for a time. Not until 1988 did I again begin to focus on the case more fully.

In the spring of 1988 I was finally able to follow up a story summarized and dismissed by the HSCA in its final report as not being credible. Using the services of a reporter with law enforcement contacts (T. J.), I was able to trace Sam Giancana's driver Myron "Paul Bucilli" Billet to a small apartment in Columbus, Ohio. Accompanied by my assistant, Jean Obray, I was greeted by an old man in his pajamas who suffered from emphysema so badly that he was hooked up to an oxygen tank.

Entering a gloomy sitting room/bedroom and following Myron as he shuffled along into the kitchen, we noticed a teddy bear propped up on a pillow on his bed.

He said that he had been a "gofer" for the Chicago mob in the fifties and sixties. Sam Giancana, the Chicago boss, had taken a liking to him and given him the name Paul Bucilli. (Elsewhere, in personal notes and letters written eleven years earlier which he provided to me, he said the name was given to him by Ben "Bugsy" Siegel, whom he met in Los Angeles.) He would drive Sam to different places and accompany him on various trips, being available if needed as another pair of hands.

In January 1968 Billet was working at the Whitemarsh country club outside of Chicago when Sam asked him to take off a few days and drive him to Apalachin, New York, for a meeting. (This town had been the site of a major meeting of organized crime leaders in 1957. It was accidentally discovered by a New York state policeman, conclusively establishing that there was a national organized crime syndicate despite J. Edgar Hoover's previous vociferous denials of its existence.) Billet described in some detail the restaurant in town where they had driven after arriving, and the layout and location of their motel. According to Billet, those present were himself, Sam Giancana, Carlo Gambino, John Roselli, and three federal agents who he believed were from the FBI and CIA. The agents were known to the mob leaders since they had worked with them on previous gunrunning and other Cuban operations. The meeting was convened to review the working relationship between the criminal families and government agencies represented there. At one point one of the "feds" announced there was a contract on offer for the murder of Martin Luther King with a price of one million dollars. Giancana immediately responded, "No way." He made it clear that so far as he was concerned his bunch wasn't going to become involved with that assignment. The agents said it was no big issue, that other arrangements would be made. After that brief exchange, the meeting continued with other business, and the subject wasn't broached again.

It isn't clear from Billet's account whether the federal agents were simply communicating the availability of the contract or principally involved in ensuring that the job was done. Myron remembered the names of two of the agents—Lee Leland and Martin Bishop. In his earlier writings Billet also put a name to the third agent (Hunt), whom he had seen before. (It occured to me that he could have been referring to CIA agent E. Howard Hunt.)

When I showed Myron some photographs, including those of Giancana, Gambino, and Roselli, without naming them, he recognized and named each of the mobsters. When he looked at Giancana's photograph he smiled affectionately. "Yeah, that's Sam."

My subsequent documentary research revealed that during much of late 1967 and early 1968 Sam Giancana was in Mexico. The meeting Billet referred to could have taken place only during one of his trips back to the United States, of which there were a number. Billet was in prison at the time he told his story to the HSCA, charged with concealing a body he had accidentally discovered. He remembered that the HSCA chairman himself, Louis Stokes, was with the group that interviewed him. The committee ultimately dismissed his allegations, but when he was released from prison and took up residence in Columbus some strange things began to happen.

First, a man would appear regularly in the small shop on the ground floor of his building to ask about him. This man's demeanor was such that Billet was sure he wanted him to know he was being watched.

Second, at one time Billet had a heart attack. Sometime later a hospital administrator said that an official of the U.S. government had appeared at the hospital with instructions to remain outside Billet's door until he was out of danger. Billet took this to mean that someone was concerned about preventing any death-bed revelations.

Though suffering from some memory lapses which interfered with a detailed recollection of the twenty-year-old events, I believed Myron Billet to be sincere and his description of the working relationship between the mob and the federal government to be accurate.

After leaving Billet, we went to visit Ray at Brushy Mountain Penitentiary. During the nearly ten years that had passed since I had last seen him, he had written a book, *Tennessee Waltz,* telling his side of the story. His account pulled together many of his previous recollections of his activity after his escape from prison on April 23, 1967.

Ray had recently been denied an evidentiary hearing by the Memphis federal district court magistrate, but he was convinced he would have a chance with the Sixth Circuit Court of Appeals. He was desperately looking for someone to represent him on the appeal. Mark Lane had long ago ceased to represent him. I offered to approach Russell Thompson, the Memphis attorney who had been involved in some peripheral legal and investigatory work when Art Hanes was Ray's defense lawyer. Thompson said he would consider getting involved if I would assist and if April Ferguson, now a federal public defender, would help. I began to review a copy of Ray's petition to the court.

While in Memphis, I met for the first time with Art Hanes's local investigator, Renfro Hays. Since he was also an investigator for Memphis attorney Walter Buford, who knew Jack Youngblood, he had come to learn about the government operative and mercenary. He maintained that Youngblood had been in Memphis a few days before the killing. Hays considered him to be very dangerous. He recalled that Youngblood owned a pickup truck and that the day before the killing he stood on it to cut down a tree branch at the rear of the rooming house that was obscuring a clear view from the bathroom window to the balcony of the Lorraine. It was not at all clear to me how Renfro knew this and I was skeptical, having become aware of earlier stories of his which mixed fact and fiction.

Hays also went on about Raul Esquivel, the Louisiana state policeman stationed in Baton Rouge, who he thought was the salt-and-pepper-haired man Grace Walden allegedly saw in the rooming house. He believed that Esquivel, who he told me had once been a bodyguard for Louisiana governor Huey Long, was the shooter. Although it is of questionable reliability, Grace Walden identified a photograph of Raul Esquivel as the salt-and-pepper-haired man in front of Hays, Wayne Chastain, and her attorney at the time, Charles Murphy.

I was intrigued. Hays seemed to be both sincere and fearful. He also mentioned the Baton Rouge telephone number he said had been given to Ray by Raul, which was the number of the state police barracks in Baton Rouge where Esquivel was assigned. As discussed earlier, this number had been referred to as early as 1969 by Jeff Cohen and Harold Weisberg. Later I obtained a credit report on Esquivel that showed a fairly large deposit in 1968. I found no verification that he had ever been a bodyguard for Huey Long.

Hays also contended that a twelve-year-old black boy had seen the shooter and run up Mulberry to Butler and into the fire station, where he told his story to one of the firemen, who later informed the police. The police came and took the boy away; he wasn't heard from again. Hays said that the fireman was having an affair with a local married woman and that he had told her his story. (I later tried to confirm Hay's story by speaking to the woman he mentioned. Now remarried to a local lawyer, she denied even having known a fireman, much less having had an affair with one. I dropped that line of inquiry. Although I later spoke to most of the firemen on duty at the time, none of them recalled the incident.)

Hays also mentioned Harvey "Ace" Locke, a sometimes shoe repairman and safecracker of no fixed address who would often stop by the South Main Street rooming houses looking for a room where he could "squat" for the night. A day or so before the killing he had been told about 5-B being vacant, and on April 4, not knowing it had just been rented, he opened the door in the late afternoon to see three or four persons already there, none of them resembling James Earl Ray. He quickly closed the door and went away. Though I searched hard for Locke, I was unable to find him, and eventually came to believe that he had died. As we parted company, Hays said to me, "You're a nice young man. Why do you want to get involved with these people—they're really dangerous. You'll get yourself killed."

I interviewed Floyd Newsom, one of the black firemen removed from the fire station diagonally across from the Lorraine the evening before the killing. He told me he received a phone call the night of April 3 ordering him to report not to his home fire station 2 but to a firehouse in the northern, all-white section of the city, making him an extra man while leaving his home station a man short. He said he never got a proper explanation, even when he later left the department and it was revealed to him that this transfer was at the request of the police. It made no more sense than the similar transfer from fire station 2 of black fireman Norvell Wallace, who also left the station a man short and made an extra man where he was sent.

BACK IN ENGLAND I learned that Russell Thompson had decided against handling Ray's appeal. My primary interest continued to be learning the truth about the murder, but there were some important constitutional issues that cried out to be raised. I reluctantly agreed to take the appeal on myself. (This appeal is discussed in a later chapter.)

ON MY NEXT VISIT TO MEMPHIS, Renfro Hays introduced me to Ken Herman, another local investigator, whose services I engaged. Herman and some of his contacts introduced me to a

Circulation Summary
Northern Woods Library
Mon, Apr 29, 2013 12:57 PM

Books are free - Please don't steal them
------------------------Patron------------------------
    Name: SHAW, LARRY
    ID: 00065614
------------------------Checkouts------------------------
Orders to kill   May 20, 2013
Webster's New World diction May 20, 2013
------------------Available Holds------------------
None

Thank-you, Please come again

number of current and retired MPD officers. Until the end of October 1988, when I formally filed Ray's appeal with the Sixth Circuit Court of Appeals, I was introduced as an overseas writer doing some historical research on the assassination.

It was in this context that I interviewed retired inspector Sam Evans. My interest in Evans centered on the pull back of the MPD TACT units on the afternoon of April 4. In particular I was interested in TACT 10 which was originally based at the Lorraine Motel and pulled back to fire station 2 on South Main Street. At our first session he acknowledged that these emergency units were under his direct command, but was reluctant to admit he had given any orders that they be pull back. He tried to change the subject at one point, recounting how he had slaughtered a big brown bear that had escaped from the zoo; with nothing less than boastful glee he described how he killed the animal with a machine gun. Returning to the TACT issue, I reminded him of Chief Crumby's affidavit provided to the HSCA in 1978, which confirmed that the units were pulled back. He finally remembered that they had probably been pulled back, but only as a result of the request of someone in Dr. King's group. He said he couldn't remember who had made the request. He said he was personally familiar with local colleagues of Dr. King, and that he used to chair the regular morning meetings with Reverend Lawson and the others during the strike. He said that he had a number of close contacts in that group who were leaders in the black community and who regularly provided him with information. It was clear that he was talking about valuable local informants. In this context he spoke of Solomon Jones and Walter Bailey, the owner of the Lorraine. In a subsequent session, Evans boasted that he knew Rev. Billy Kyles very well and that they spoke frequently, leading me to believe that Kyles was one of his sources of information in the black community. According to writer Philip Melanson, in 1985 Evans had admitted to him that the request to move the TACT units came from Kyles, although Kyles had emphatically denied making any such request.[3]

Chief Crumby later confirmed that the request to pull back the TACT units had come the "day before" from someone in

Dr. King's group, and that the units were under the direct command of Sam Evans.

Considering that Reverend Kyles had no role in Dr. King's organization, it is unlikely that he would have been authorized to make such a request. It is also unlikely that the MPD would have acceded to any such suggestion because the TACT units were primarily antiriot forces and the city was expecting the worst.

Some MPD officers who had worked with Marrell McCollough, the undercover officer attached to the Invaders, told me they had found him very much an outsider. He was originally from Mississippi and joined the police force after serving with the military in Vietnam. It was rumored that he went to work for the CIA some time in the early 1970s and was last heard of being in Central or South America.

To FIND OUT MORE about the so-called hoax broadcast, Ken Herman took me to interview the people who were principal MPD dispatchers during the time of the assassination. The most informative was Billy Tucker, who said that he had handled the entire broadcast. In our noon meeting on October 29, 1988, he set out his recollections quite clearly.

It was officer Rufus Bradshaw, Tucker said, who relayed the details of a chase in the northeast side of the city involving a blue Pontiac in pursuit of a white Mustang. At first Bradshaw said he was in pursuit himself, but later it became clear that he was relaying information from a CB operator—William Austein—who was parked alongside him. Austein was supposedly taking the details of the chase directly from the driver of the blue Pontiac, narrating over his CB. Soon it became obvious to Tucker that there was neither a chase nor a blue Pontiac but that the broadcast was designed to divert police attention toward the northeast area of Memphis. Tucker also confirmed that no all points bulletin, (general alert describing the suspect) or Signal Y alert (instructing cars to block off city exit routes) were issued.

Many of the other MPD interviews led nowhere. Officers

whom one would have thought to be in a position to know details of what had happened were often graciously unhelpful.

IN A RUN-DOWN ROOMING HOUSE on Peabody we found former taxi driver James McCraw, the driver who shortly before the killing had refused to transport the heavily intoxicated State's chief witness Charlie Stephens. In his mid-to-late sixties McCraw spoke through a voice box that he held to his throat. He said that he was driving a taxi on the afternoon of April 4 and was dispatched to the rooming house to pick up Charlie Stephens in room 6-B on the second floor. He said that he arrived shortly before 6:00 p.m. and double-parked in front of the rooming house opposite the northernmost door. As he left his cab to go inside he noticed a delivery van parked outside and two white Mustangs parked within one hundred feet of each other, one in front of Jim's Grill and the other just south of Canipe Amusement Company.

He entered Stephens's room and saw "old Charlie" passed out on his bed. He left, saying that he wasn't going to "haul him." He remembered seeing that the hall bathroom door was open and that the bathroom was apparently empty, both as he approached and as he left Stephens's room. He said he got into his cab and went to pick up another fare. He hadn't gone very far when an announcement came over his radio from the dispatcher about the shooting of Dr. King with an instruction for all drivers to stay away from the downtown area. McCraw insisted that he couldn't have been gone from the rooming house more than a few minutes when he heard the announcement.

This was an exciting discovery. If true, as the degree of detail indicated was likely, then the MPD, FBI, and HSCA's conclusion about the shot coming from the bathroom made no sense at all. McCraw had been telling this story for a number of years and said he had told each and every investigator who asked him about the empty bathroom. His confirmation of Charlie Stephens's drunken state within minutes of the shooting was further evidence which both supported Ray's contentions and contradicted the official scenario.

VERNON DOLLAHITE, stuffed into his desk chair in full deputy sheriff's uniform with gun belt and holster, said he found the bundle in front of Canipe's after the shooting. He said he was with TACT 10 on break at the fire station and when he heard about the shooting ran out the northeast door and jumped over the fence and onto the sidewalk on Mulberry Street. He raced to the motel parking lot, dropped his gun, picked it up, and continued north on Mulberry to Huling, where he proceeded west to South Main, leaving a fellow officer to stay in the vicinity of Huling and Mulberry. He stopped briefly at Jim's Grill and told everyone to remain there until he returned. He then continued south past Canipe's, returning to find the bundle. He was joined shortly by Lt. "Bud" Ghormley, the TACT 10 unit leader. Ghormley took charge of the bundle and Dollahite retreated to the other side of the street.

Dollahite said his entire run took him less than two minutes, and he was certain he didn't see the bundle before he entered Jim's Grill when he was coming up South Main. He also didn't see anyone or any car leaving the scene.

Herman and I looked at each other. Dollahite had to have missed the bundle and must have been mistaken about the time it took him to complete his run. From what he said it would have been impossible for an assassin fleeing the rooming house to drop the bundle after shooting Dr. King, then get into the Mustang parked in front of Canipe's and drive off without being seen by him. Something was wrong. Either Dollahite was off in his timing or he had spent more time than he realized in Jim's Grill. I had read the statement given by Ghormley (who was dead by 1988); he maintained that he found the bundle after first heading in the same direction as Dollahite, deciding against jumping the wall, and went back out to South Main, going north to Canipe's. Ghormley too estimated it took him around two minutes to arrive at the scene of the discarded evidence. He also didn't see anyone or any car leaving. The two stories conflicted, but on balance it appeared to me more likely that Ghormley reached Canipe's and the bundle first.

I had also read the statements of Guy Canipe and two customers—Bernell Finley and Julius Graham. Individually and together they told a story of hearing a thud when the bundle was dropped and seeing a white male walking briskly by in a southerly direction. Very soon after, they said a white Mustang pulled away from the curb heading north. Julius Graham remembered hearing what he thought was a shot before all this happened.

I remembered Art Hanes telling me Canipe would testify that the bundle was dropped minutes **before** the shot, but I was unable to speak with Canipe, who has since died. I was, however, able to locate an account of an interview with him by George Bryan, which appeared in the April 11, 1968, *Commercial Appeal.* Bryan wrote that Canipe said he saw a man drop a bundle in the doorway of his store and then continue walking. Canipe left his two customers, who were in the rear, and walked to the door, looked out, and saw the back of the man walking away. Within a minute his customers, apparently hearing some noise outside which could have been the shot, ran to the front of the store as the man was driving away in a white Mustang that was parked about twenty feet south of the store.

If the state's contentions were to be believed, then the timing of this escape was incredibly fine. Apparently it had to have taken place within a minute of the actual shot.

The MPD investigation concluded that there was only one Mustang, as by implication did that of the HSCA. I was about to gain firsthand further evidence that this conclusion was wrong.

Ray has pretty consistently maintained that he didn't move the Mustang he parked in front of Jim's Grill until he finally left the area before 6:00 p.m. He said that he walked to the York Arms, a few blocks north of the grill, when he was sent by Raul to buy binoculars. The Mustang was also there, according to McCraw, when he entered the rooming house shortly before 6:00.

I located and interviewed Peggy and Charles Hurley. Back in

1968 Peggy Hurley worked for the Seabrook Wallpaper Company, directly across the street from the rooming house. Each day her husband, Charles, would arrive to pick her up when she finished work around 5:00. He would park virtually in front of Canipe's until she came out. On that Thursday afternoon, a fellow worker told Peggy that her husband had arrived around 4:45, earlier than usual. When she looked out the window she saw that the car that had just pulled up wasn't their white Falcon but a white Mustang—and the young, dark-haired man sitting in it certainly was not Charles.

Mr. Hurley told me that he remembered arriving that afternoon and having to park just behind a white Mustang. He also noticed a young man wearing a dark blue windbreaker sitting inside it and that it had Arkansas plates. Ray's car, of course, had Alabama plates with white letters on a red background and Ray was dressed in a dark suit, white shirt and dark tie on that afternoon. This Mustang, Charles Hurley said, had red letters on a white background. He recalled noting this because someone at work also had a Mustang with Arkansas plates. When Peggy Hurley came out a few minutes later, and they left, the young man was still sitting in the Mustang.

At the suggestion of both Kay Black and Wayne Chastain, I met former Memphis *Press Scimitar* photographer/reporter Jim Reid. He told me that about three days before the assassination he'd seen a tree branch that could have obstructed a clear shot from the rooming house bathroom window being cut and had taken a photograph of it. He said he even mentioned it to a friend who was with the CIA and who exclaimed, "How the hell did you know about that?" I asked him to look for the photograph.

Shortly after the killing, Reid interviewed Willie Green, who was working at an Esso station in the area of Linden and Third. In a front-page article that included Green's photograph, Jim had described how the man reacted excitedly when he was shown a photo of Ray and asked if he remembered seeing him around 6:00 p.m. that evening. Green positively identified Ray as a man who had come into the gas station at that time. The gas station no longer existed by 1988.

IT HAD BEEN TEN YEARS since I had last seen Loyd Jowers, the owner of Jim's Grill in 1968. I visited him at his latest business, a slot-and-pinball machine arcade on Union Street. He talked to me while keeping an eye on business and also with a long barreled pistol not too far from his hand and ready for use, as he said was occasionally necessary.

Jowers went over some familiar ground. He remembered the Mustang in front of the grill when he came to work around 4:00 that afternoon. He also remembered selling beer to Charlie and insisting that he take it to his room because he was so drunk. At the time of the shooting Jowers said he was in the front of the grill and when he heard the shot he thought that a pot had fallen in his kitchen. He said he went back there and peered in but saw nothing unusual, so he came back out to the front. A short time later a sheriff's deputy came through the door and ordered everyone to stay inside.

Jowers acknowledged that waitresses were on duty on the afternoon of April 4. I had long wanted to interview them, particularly Betty, having learned about her from Wayne Chastain back in 1978. Jowers said that she had had a number of husbands and used various names. He told me generally where he thought she lived, and Ken Herman and I set out to find her. I quickly became convinced that Loyd had deliberately led us astray.

16

More Leads, More Loose Ends: Spring–Summer 1989

IN THE SPRING OF 1989 I changed the focus of my investigation, heading for Atlanta to visit with Ralph Abernathy and Hosea Williams, neither of whom I'd seen in several years. Hosea was pleased to hear that I was representing James Earl Ray on an appeal and looking again into some unanswered questions surrounding the case. He had never been satisfied with the result of the official investigations.

We also discussed a particularly sensitive matter. I had learned from David Garrow's research that the FBI's paid informant on the SCLC's executive staff was its comptroller, James Harrison, who had joined the organization in October 1964, working directly under Ralph Abernathy's supervision.[4] Harrison reported to agent Al Sentinella in the Atlanta field office from autumn of 1965, and was still doing so on the day of Dr. King's killing. It was a bitter shock to Hosea when the story broke about Harrison, because they had been college fraternity brothers and were roommates in 1967–1968. He was also embarrassed and worried that others might believe that he was in league with Harrison and the government against Dr. King. He was chagrined that Harrison had managed to con him into tape recording some SCLC staff meetings, ostensibly so that Hosea could protect his job, which Harrison convinced him was in danger. In fact, Hosea had no idea about Harrison's informant activities; he didn't know, for example, that when Harrison traveled with them to Memphis on April 3, 1968, he had dutifully checked in with Memphis FBI SAC Jensen and then spent the rest of the day with the SCLC group before returning to Atlanta.

Reviewing the events of April 4, Hosea confirmed what I already knew—that Martin spent most of the afternoon in an executive staff meeting at the Lorraine. The meeting lasted until about ten to fifteen minutes before the shot. It was briefly interrupted between 4:00 and 4:30 when Andy Young returned from court to tell them about the judge's ruling in favor of the march. He also remembered a brief "tussle" between Martin and Andy, before they resumed. Billy Kyles, who wasn't at the meeting, knocked on the door sometime shortly before 6:00 P.M. and reminded them that they were already forty-five minutes late for supper at his home. Martin then told everybody to go to their rooms and quickly get ready to go. Hosea left, made one quick stop, and then went to his room on the ground level under Dr. King's room. He remembers being right next to Solomon Jones's limousine and hearing Solomon, who was standing by the driver's side of the car with one foot inside and one foot outside, telling Dr. King to wear his coat since it was a cool evening.

Hosea said that as he was putting the key in the lock of the door to his room he heard Dr. King say, "You're right, Jonesey, I'll get my coat." Then he heard the shot and saw Martin's leg dangling from the balcony.

I then raised Kyles's claim that he had been in Martin's room for the better part of an hour before the shooting. Hosea said that was impossible because the executive staff meeting broke up only minutes before the shot. Kyles wasn't a member of SCLC staff and wouldn't have been present at such a meeting.

The next day, following the Wednesday Holy Week service at West Hunter Street Baptist Church where Ralph Abernathy had been pastor for as long as I'd known him, Ralph and I discussed the last trip he and Martin made to Memphis.

Ralph's description of King's last hour was virtually identical to Hosea's. He and Martin began to get ready for dinner sometime around 5:30–5:45, after the staff meeting broke up. Martin was ready first and went outside. Ralph remembers hearing Solomon Jones tell Martin, just before the shot, that he might want his coat because it was cool that evening.

Regarding Billy Kyles's testimony Ralph said angrily, "If Billy Kyles said that, then Billy Kyles is a liar." Ralph said Kyles had at no time been in the room with them. Ralph had just slapped some cologne on his face when he heard the shot and ran outside to cradle his friend in his arms. Kyles was on the balcony. Ralph told him to go inside and phone for an ambulance. He recalled that in the rush of events Andy Young knelt beside him and said, "Ralph, it's all over, it's all over." He told Andy, "It's not all over, Andy, don't you say that." Moments later he entered the room to find Kyles lying on the bed sobbing. Ralph told him this was no time for hysterics and to call an ambulance. Kyles said, "Ralph, the lines are all busy."

A few years later I gained access to the surveillance report of Memphis patrolman Willie Richmond, who was assigned to watch King's party at the Lorraine. His report confirmed what Ralph and Hosea had told me.

Why had Kyles lied? Was he simply trying to boost his stock as a civil rights leader by establishing himself as important enough to have been close to King just before his death? I had previously obtained a copy of the register of the Lorraine for the week through April 5, 1968, and found it curious that though he lived locally, Kyles had taken room 312 on April 3 and 4.

Ralph died in 1992. That meeting was the last time I saw him.

IN EARLY SUMMER 1989 I became involved in assisting the production of a BBC documentary on the assassination, *Inside Story:*

Who Killed Martin Luther King? At Ray's suggestion, English television producer John Edginton of Otmoor Productions had
approached me earlier that year. He was horrified by the HSCA
revelations of the COINTELPRO activity against Dr. King. I
believed that such activity, including electronic surveillance,
continued right up to his death but that we would probably
never uncover any hard evidence of it. I shared with Edginton
the results of my work to date and suggested that he might
want to interview Myron Billet and John McFerren.

I took Edginton and his team to see Billet. He found his
story credible and set out to see if he could corroborate the
details. He traveled to Apalachin, New York, and found the
motel and the restaurant where Billet said they had dinner the
night before the meeting. Both were just as Myron described
them. Edginton was impressed, as was I. Billet was a dying old
man who had embraced religion and become concerned with
the afterlife—he had no reason to lie.

Billet died of a heart attack soon after the BBC program
aired. His closest friend, Rev. Maurice McCracken of Cincinnati, insisted that he had died a happy man. At last he was able
to get someone to listen to his story.

At John McFerren's general store/gas station one afternoon,
Edginton's production unit waited for three hours while I tried
unsuccessfully to persuade McFerren to talk. His fear was still
strong enough to prevent him from coming forward again.

After the documentary aired, McFerren told me that even
though he didn't participate, an official of one of the major
petroleum companies who supplied products to him called him
aside one day and said that he had better be careful because
"Old Pepper is stirring things up."

IN JUNE 1989, I received a report from T.J., my Southern re-
porter contact, on Raul Esquivel, Sr. and Raul Esquivel, Jr. T.J.'s
New Orleans source told him that in 1968 Esquivel Sr. was a
Louisiana state trooper based at the Troop B Barracks in Baton
Rouge who was allegedly associated with Jules "Ricco" Kimbel
and Sal Liberto. Kimbel's name has frequently appeared on

the periphery of both the John Kennedy and the King cases. His possible involvement had been discussed and dismissed by the HSCA, which became convinced that Kimbel wasn't in Canada at the same time as Ray. The HSCA also noted his lack of cooperation with the committee. Sal Liberto was a relative of the Memphis produce company owner Frank Liberto whom McFerren had mentioned in his statement. Esquivel was of Spanish descent—originally from Belize—5'9", 175 lbs, and in 1968 he was forty-two years old. He also had served in both the army and the navy during World War II.

Though he appeared to have some potentially relevant connections in New Orleans, there was no hard evidence of his involvement. Indeed when I eventually spoke with Charlie Stein in the autumn of 1994, he categorically denied seeing the telephone number James dialed in the course of their trip to New Orleans in December 1967.

The Edginton team also made contact with Kimbel. Former New Orleans district attorney Jim Garrison told Edginton that everything Kimbel had told him about the Kennedy assassination turned out to be true. The BBC team visited Kimbel in the Three Rivers federal penitentiary in Texas.

He told an extraordinary story. He had worked for the government as an FBI/CIA asset and for organized crime. His FBI handler was an agent named Clement Hood Sr. in New Orleans. He said that the mob and the agency worked together like one organization. The mob would handle contract work for the Agency, which could then plausibly deny any connection or knowledge of events should they become public. He was always paid in cash for his work, which he implied was strong-arm activity, including murder. He told the BBC team that Dr. King was hated by powerful wealthy individuals in the South, specifically Louisiana right-wing leader Leander Perez and Texas oilman H. L. Hunt. In this, he said, they were on common ground with the CIA and the FBI.

Though he would later say he was mistaken, he originally stated that in the summer of 1967, on the instructions of Clement Hood, Sr., he flew James to Canada where he helped get James false identification. A former CIA agent told the BBC that the Agency did have an identities specialist based in Toronto who could have operated throughout Canada during this period. His name was Raul Maori.

In subsequent interviews with the BBC team in December 1989, however, Kimbel told of a considerably greater involvement in the King case. He maintained that he flew two shooters from Montreal to Memphis and flew them back after the killing. He alluded to "dry runs" in the South Main Street area and an operational base just over the line in Mississippi, and even admitted to picking up sniper rifles for the assassins. James Earl Ray was not the killer, he maintained, but only a decoy. He said that Frank Liberto played a minor role in the assassination and that his brother Sal was more prominently involved. It would obviously take considerable effort to investigate Kimbel's story.

The BBC documentary also included an interview with New York *Daily News* columnist Earl Caldwell, who as a young reporter covering Dr. King for the *New York Times* in 1968 had been in room 215 of the Lorraine Motel on April 4. He said that immediately after the shot he came out of his room and saw the figure of a white man crouching in the bushes behind the grill and the rooming house. No one from the FBI, MPD, or HSCA had ever tried to talk to Caldwell, and his observations contradicted the official position of the state that the shot came from the bathroom window. The Edginton production also provided expert testimony further rebutting that possibility, including the discrediting of the theory that a dent in the bathroom windowsill could have been made by a rifle barrel (the HSCA had also discounted the windowsill evidence).

In his BBC interview, Inspector Sam Evans—in direct contradiction of his admission to me and apparent admission to writer Philip Melanson—denied that TACT units had been withdrawn or pulled back. He said they could have been removed only if he gave the order, which he never did. I marveled.

My investigation in Memphis continued sporadically. In the summer of 1989 Herman and I eventually found Betty (whose last name we learned was Spates), the former waitress in Jim's

Grill whom I had especially wanted to see. Betty was an attrac-
tive black woman in her late thirties, with fearful eyes and a
soft voice. Coming out of her house to meet with us, she appeared nervous. She admitted being at work in the grill on the
day of the assassination but didn't want to talk about it. When
I told her I was Ray's lawyer she declared, "There is no doubt
that man [Ray] did not kill Dr. King. I know that for a fact."
She refused to discuss how she knew. She told me that every
time she changed her job, she was visited by a man who "just
came by to let me know that he knew where I was." Once she
said she was offered money and a new identity if she would
agree to leave the area. She refused because all her family and
her children were in Memphis. She could not be persuaded to
talk more, so we left, saying we would keep in touch.

Had Loyd Jowers been unhelpful in our effort to find Betty
in order to protect her? That seemed out of character for Jowers who appeared coldhearted. When we discussed the case he
always appeared to be on edge. The word was that he had
become a very heavy drinker over the last ten years. By his own
admission he had not seen Betty for a long time, and he pre-
tended to have no interest in or knowledge about her. Why,
then, would he be protective?

My concern about Jowers deepened when I discovered that
he had told the Edginton team that no waitresses were on duty
on the afternoon of April 4—that he was all alone in the grill.
He had previously acknowledged to me, as he had to Chastain
on various occasions, that, in fact, there were waitresses working
that afternoon. However, at other times he had insisted to
Chastain that he was alone. There was also his change of position back and forth over the years as to whether or not Jack
Youngblood was the "eggs and sausage man." The man was
not senile. He had all of his faculties. I became more convinced
than ever that this wasn't a memory problem, and he hadn't
been drinking when he admitted to me, a short while before
the BBC interview, that waitresses had been working on the
day of the assassination. What was going on?

In a conversation with one of Edginton's researchers, James
McCraw had offhandedly referred to a gun being in Jim's Grill

around the time of the murder. I visited with McCraw and he told me that late in the morning the day after the shooting Jowers showed him a rifle that was in a box on a shelf under the counter in the grill. Jowers told him that he had found it "out back" after the killing. He said he was going to turn it over to the police and later Jowers confirmed to McCraw that he had done so.

I found this new disclosure startling. Was this second gun in fact the murder weapon? If Jowers had been telling him the truth, it was clear that the shot came from the brush area behind the rooming house and not from inside. But the police were all over the area within minutes of the shooting. Why had they not found the gun or mentioned it? Why had Jowers never raised it in any of our numerous conversations, and why was there no indication of it in the HSCA report? What had happened to it? Had Jowers in fact turned it over?

Could this be why Betty Spates was frightened? Had she also seen the gun, or did she know something about it?

17

James Earl Ray's Legal Representation Reexamined

To MOST EFFECTIVELY PREPARE JAMES'S APPEAL I had to understand the entire history of his representation, including the circumstances surrounding the guilty plea. I began at the beginning.

Arthur Hanes, Sr., had told me that he believed James sought him out because he had tried a similar case, the defense of Alabama residents charged with the killing of a Detroit woman, Mrs. Viola Liuzzo. Mrs. Liuzzo had been gunned down from a side window of an overtaking car, on a dark road outside of Selma during the time of the historic Selma-to-Montgomery march. She was driving black marchers (as was I) out of Montgomery on that night. Hanes said that it was not unusual for him to be approached in such matters, for as mayor of Birmingham he had proved to be a conservative on racial issues. (Recall, however, that James's other choice was F. Lee Bailey, a Boston lawyer strongly identified with liberal politics.)

Hanes and his son Art, Jr., were contacted by author William

Bradford Huie of Huntsville, Alabama, who wanted exclusive rights to write James's story. Huie had told Hanes that he could present the accused in a favorable light and that the sale of his writing would be the means of raising money for the defense.

In early July 1968, Hanes made a trip to London, taking with him documents furnished by Huie. One was a very broad power of attorney, bestowing on Hanes the authority to act for James. In another document, James transferred to Hanes any monies that he would receive as a result of a subsequent agreement with Huie. These two documents were signed July 5, 1968.

On July 8, 1968, Hanes and Huie executed an agreement giving Huie exclusive rights to produce literary material dealing with the case.

After several days James decided to sign the agreement because he thought there was no other chance to raise money for his defense. Huie agreed to pay Hanes and James each 30 percent of the gross receipts from the literary works. James's money was to go directly to Hanes for his defense. In September 1968, at James's request, the July 8 agreement was amended whereby Hanes would receive a flat fee of $20,000 plus expenses. James asked for the change because he came to understand that Hanes was employed to handle the case only at the trial level, and he wanted to have available financial reserves for an appeal if necessary.

The English magistrate's decision to grant extradition was based largely on the affidavit of the state's "eyewitness" Charles Q. Stephens. Having finally decided against an appeal on Hanes's advice, James was extradited and flown to the United States on July 19, arriving at the Shelby County Jail early that morning.

The conditions of James's eight-month (July 19, 1968–March 10, 1969) confinement in the specially prepared jail cell were extraordinary. Guards were present at all times. Closed-circuit television cameras monitored every move, including the exercise of his natural bodily functions. Since multiple microphones allowed for total audio surveillance, in order to communicate privately James and Hanes had to get down on their hands and knees and whisper in each other's ears. The cell area was brightly lit twenty-four hours a day; to sleep, James had to cover his eyes with a cloth. There was no natural light, no fresh air. The guards kept a log that recorded all visitors. In addition to the constant surveillance, all of James's mail was screened, including correspondence with his attorneys, with copies provided to the prosecutor's office. Trash from the cell, including James's notes prepared for discussions with his attorney, was also periodically screened and turned over to the prosecutor.

The impact of these conditions eroded James's physical and mental health to the point that by late February 1969 his capacity to resist pressure (from his second attorney, Percy Foreman) to enter a plea, had become greatly diminished.

Art Hanes and his son told me that they were ready to go to trial by November 12, 1968. They felt that they had prepared their case well and believed that the state wouldn't be able to prove James guilty beyond a reasonable doubt. The senior Hanes stressed that James never authorized him to plea bargain with the attorney general. **He always insisted on a trial.** Hanes recalled that at an early stage the state did offer a life sentence in exchange for a plea. James refused.

During the pretrial period, Huie asked James questions through Arthur Hanes. Hanes would deliver Huie's inquiries to his client. When James responded in writing, Hanes would take the answers back to Huie. After some time Huie invited Jerry Ray to visit him at his home in Huntsville, paying his way. At that meeting he asked Jerry to talk with his brother to convince him not to take the stand in his own defense. Jerry was convinced that Huie didn't want James to testify because any testimony he gave would be in the public domain and therefore decrease the value of Huie's book.

Jerry, furious, told James that Hanes was in collusion with Huie and advised his brother to get another lawyer. He suggested Percy Foreman (the so-called Texas Tiger) because of his reputation as an aggressive criminal defense lawyer. James said he didn't want Foreman, but the local Memphis lawyer they contacted, Richard J. Ryan, indicated that the case was too big for him. Jerry then contacted Percy Foreman on his own. Foreman agreed to take the case but wanted a letter from James requesting a visit before he would go down and see him. James refused, saying he would go to trial with Arthur Hanes.

Jerry again called Foreman who asked him to bring copies of the contracts James had signed with Hanes and Huie and meet with him. On November 10, two days before the trial was to begin, Jerry and John Ray met Percy Foreman at the Memphis airport. Foreman read the contracts and said, "I can break these, let's get a cab and go and see your brother."

James had always wondered how Foreman actually got in to see him that first time. Art Hanes answered the question for me. He said that Sheriff Bill Morris had told him that when Foreman appeared at the jail that first time, the jailer called him and then put the visit on hold while Morris consulted with Judge Battle. To Morris's surprise, Battle was receptive to the visit and told Morris to let the Texas lawyer go in and talk to James. Thus it appears that for whatever reason, the trial judge actually facilitated the removal of the Haneses from the case on the eve of the trial.

In the course of that meeting Foreman told James that if he continued with Hanes, he would probably be "barbecued." Foreman promised not to get involved in any type of book contract until the trial was over. He quoted a fee of $150,000 including appeals.

James had become convinced that Hanes was working for Huie and Huie was releasing information to the FBI because the bureau was somehow able to follow leads he provided to Huie, turning up promptly after he had provided him with the confidential information. Foreman capitalized on this, putting enormous pressure on James to retain him, passionately criticising the relationship between Hanes and Huie as a conflict of interest that was probably going to cost James his life.

On the evening of November 10, Hanes was handed a letter summarily dismissing him. He offered Foreman his time and the benefit of his experience in preparing the case but Foreman didn't seem interested. Because Judge Battle perceived Foreman to be unwell and was concerned about his frequent absences from the court, he appointed public defender Hugh Stanton Sr. as associate defense counsel on December 18, 1968.

Eventually Stanton's status was elevated to that of co-counsel. Foreman obtained an extension of the trial date and then moved to establish his own contractual relationship with Huie, which was concluded on January 5, 1969. He also suggested that Jerry meet with writer George MacMillan, who, along with his wife, has long been associated with U.S. intelligence.

To this day, James regrets having retained Foreman. If nothing else, Foreman's poor health was an obvious impediment to competent representation. During this time Foreman was on three types of medication daily as a result of a car accident. He had fairly recently testified under oath that it was impossible for him to sleep properly or to sit and concentrate for any period of time. Consequently, he stated, he was not able to take any major cases by himself. He was also in trouble with the federal government on tax and other charges.

After a couple of weeks Foreman contacted Hanes in Birmingham, asking for a meeting. Hanes, Sr., told me that they spent two or three hours with him, then took him to dinner, surprised by his nonchalance and lack of specific thoughts in preparing for the trial.

In a drastic change of position, on February 13, 1969, Foreman brought a letter summarizing his advice to his client to plead guilty, with a list of reasons. A surprised James signed the letter, not in agreement but only in acknowledgment of having received the advice, making it clear to his agitated lawyer that he had no intention of entering a plea. From then on Foreman began pressing James to enter a plea of guilty.

James was completely opposed to the idea. In fact on February 17, in a letter to his brother Jerry, James wrote:

Dear Jerry:

I thought I would answer your letter. I guess you read that they postponed the trial until April 7. I look forward to going to trial sometime in April, probably the last part.

Undeterred by James's recalcitrance, Foreman brought him fifty-six stipulations of fact prepared by the prosecutor and aggressively pressed him to agree to all of them and plead guilty.

He hammered away at James relentlessly, telling him, "They're gonna fry your ass if you don't" (despite the fact that no one had been executed in Tennessee in many years, that the overriding political sentiment in the state was against the death penalty, and that the King family had expressed their opposition to using it in the case). Foreman also assured him that his aging father would be sent back to Idaho, where he had been a minor parole violator, forty-odd years earlier, if James did not plead guilty. He stated that the press had convicted him anyway and that no Memphis jury would acquit him. Finally, and according to James most importantly, he told him that if he went to trial he couldn't guarantee to put forward his best effort as defense counsel.

James ultimately came to believe that Foreman would throw the case if he didn't agree. He was certain that the judge wouldn't let him substitute another attorney so late in the proceedings, but he reasoned that if he made a deal he could get rid of Foreman, get another lawyer, and open up the case all over again. He finally agreed to enter the plea in exchange for Foreman paying a sum of money to his brother Jerry so that they could hire a new attorney and open up the case. This they indeed did, hiring local attorney Richard Ryan shortly after the hearing.

On Friday, March 7, Foreman arrived at the jail at 7:45 a.m. to make sure that James was in the proper frame of mind and that everything was ready for a smooth entry of the plea. Foreman agreed in writing to provide Jerry with a loan of $500 "contingent upon the plea of guilty and sentence going through on March 10, 1969, without any unseemly conduct on your [James's] part in court."

The transcript of the March 10, 1969, court hearing supports James's assertion that all he meant to do was plea bargain on the charge without admitting guilt. He admits that there was overwhelming evidence that he was in the area and somehow involved, however unknowingly. Thus being tied to the events and having bought a gun found at the scene, he believed that he might indeed be "legally" guilty. At one point, in response to a question of guilt, he explicitly said, "Yes, legally, yes." He made a point of interrupting the proceedings at one stage to refute the popular notion that there was no conspiracy.

James was sentenced on March 10, 1969, to ninety-nine years, the most severe sentence aside from death that he could receive. Three days later he began a struggle for a trial, shortly thereafter hiring attorney Ryan.

On March 31, 1969, Judge Battle was considering James's motion to vacate his plea and obtain a trial, when he died of a heart attack at his desk. In fact, he was found with his head on James's motion papers. The law at the time in Tennessee stated that if a judge died while considering such a motion, the motion was automatically granted. In the only other case where a judge died while considering such a motion, the petitioner was given a new trial. Technically speaking James's motion for a trial also encompassed setting aside his guilty plea, but the principal aim of the statute—to grant the relief sought when the judge most familiar with the issues is removed from the scene—surely applies in such a case. However, James's motion was denied in 1969, as was each and every subsequent petition for relief. By 1988 James had accumulated a history of refusals by the courts to hear new evidence.

I was amazed at the predicament James had found himself in. Foreman had backed him into a corner, where he felt the only way out was to enter a plea to get rid of him and be paid for doing so to have funds to hire another lawyer, who would then have to undo the plea. Despite the conflict of interest, Hanes had conducted a serious investigation and was confident that he would obtain an acquittal, whereas it appeared that Foreman had never intended to go to trial. As to the sufficiency of the defense investigation of the case, Foreman would later contend under oath that he had some six or eight student investigators working on the case, but he was unable to remember their names and he admitted that he didn't keep any written notes or pay records. He said he paid them in cash.[5] He maintained that he himself continued interviewing witnesses "just up until the day Ray told me he thought it was best to enter a plea of guilty in consideration of a waiver of the death penalty and that was in the first few days of February. . . ."[6]

This contention must be viewed in the light of the letter which James wrote to his brother much later—February 17, 1969—in which he said he was looking forward to going to trial in April.

Foreman also maintained that James told him he had intentionally placed fingerprints all over the gun. "He told me he didn't wipe them off, that he wrapped the gun up to keep the fingerprints from being wiped off.[7] He told me why. He wanted the boys back at Jefferson City to know that he had done it."

These statements were unlike any other version of the events and issues. In all the sessions I spent with James Earl Ray, he never agreed with the position put forth by Percy Foreman, and it is inconceivable to anyone else I know who has been close to the case, including the Haneses, that he could have made these remarks.

Foreman maintained that at their first meeting James told him that Arthur Hanes wanted him to plead guilty but that he did not want to. This is the only time I ever heard it alleged that James thought Hanes wanted him to plead guilty. This unsubstantiated allegation is vehemently denied by the Haneses and calls forth the greatest anger from James, who has consistently maintained that the man he came to call Percy "Four-flusher" harassed and tormented him until he agreed to enter the plea.

Twelve years after the guilty plea, James discovered further behind-the-scenes maneuverings. He learned of the existence of certain handwritten notes made during the course of the guilty plea negotiations by the district attorney general, Phil Canale, who finally provided them to the HSCA in 1978. James was not able to obtain a copy of the notes until around 1981. They revealed that Judge Battle had appointed public defender Hugh Stanton, Sr., as associate counsel with Foreman on December 18, 1968, and within hours of being appointed Stanton was in Canale's office offering to plead his new client, whom he had never seen. The negotiations continued for more than two months without James's knowledge. Prosecutor Canale's notes also made it clear that Judge Battle himself played an active role in these discussions; Foreman subsequently confirmed that he had regular direct *ex parte* discussions with the judge. At one point, the notes indicate that Judge Battle actually passed messages from Foreman to Canale. For a trial judge, this activity was clearly improper and demonstrates the lengths to which all sides—with the exception of the actual defendant—were willing to go to avoid a trial.

The Canale notes also revealed that Stanton had a conflict of interest stemming from his previous representation of the state's primary witness against James—Charles Q. Stephens— and that the district attorney general raised this issue in passing with Stanton, who dismissed it out of hand.

James's latest petition for relief and his eventual appeal were founded largely on the revelations contained in the notes and on the fact that the notes were withheld from him. There were material constitutional arguments in support of James's appeal.

Hugh Stanton's conflict of interest was a classic. He had been appointed to represent James (and in light of the concern about Foreman's health had been raised to the status of co-counsel) by Judge Battle, the same judge who at an earlier hearing in July 1968, when the state sought a protective custody order against Stephens, had appointed him to represent Stephens.

Thus we had a defense co-counsel who had, in the same case, within the previous six months represented the primary prosecution witness against the defendant. In addition, Charlie Stephens had applied for the publicly offered reward for providing identification of James and thus also had a financial interest in the conviction of the person he identified. Obviously, vigorous cross-examination of Stephens would be required at trial for an effective defense. This meant the case couldn't go to trial because if it did Stanton would be precluded from examining Stephens because he had no waiver from him. Thus James would have been unable to confront the main witness against him.

This scenario appeared to be a blatant violation of James's Sixth Amendment rights to independent counsel and the right to confront an accuser. The Supreme Court has thrown out and condemned convictions where lesser conflicts of counsel have existed.

Thus, I felt I had good cause to hope the appeal I filed on James's behalf would succeed, yet the attorney general's answer brief ignored the major issues of law that were raised. My first reaction was that the state's brief was neither carefully nor thoughtfully prepared, and I was therefore inclined to believe that the state knew something I didn't.

I prepared and filed a brief and then a reply brief with the Sixth Circuit Court of Appeals and waited for oral argument to be scheduled. I was looking forward to the opportunity of advancing the principal issues to the three-judge appellate panel in Cincinnati. It seemed that the state had no effective rebuttal, and it was my intention to drive this point home to the court.

There was no chance. The court ruled that the appeal be denied and that oral argument was unnecessary. I applied for a hearing and reconsideration *en banc*—before the full court. This was denied.

Subsequently, on June 19, 1989, I filed a petition for a review by the U.S. Supreme Court (*certiorari*). This was a last resort. If the Supreme Court denied James's appeal, it would be fundamentally changing the law by denying the timeless right of the accused to confront his accuser. This would make a mockery of the U.S. justice system and give prosecutors and trial judges everywhere unprecedented power to deprive a person of his liberty. In any other case this would be unthinkable.

In addition to the petition filed, the producers of the BBC television documentary *Inside Story: Who Killed Martin Luther King?* which was aired in September 1989 and which raised many of the unanswered questions about the case, sent a video copy of the program to each member of the Supreme Court. All fell on deaf ears. *Certiorari* was denied on October 30, 1989. The trial that James Earl Ray had so long been denied seemed to be as far away as ever.

PART IV

The Television Trial of James Earl Ray

18

Preparations for the Television Trial of James Earl Ray: November 1989– September 17, 1992

I WAS DISAPPOINTED, saddened and angry. The court's refusal to consider the serious issue of defense counsel's conflict of interest was demoralizing, not only in respect of James's case but also in its denial of what I had always regarded as a fundamental right of a criminal defendant. More than ever I became convinced that inevitably such politically sensitive cases were subject to different standards of law and procedure and that James would not be set free unless his actual innocence was proven.

If the Supreme Court would not grant James a trial, I would find another way to get his case heard. During 1989 I began to flesh out the bones of the idea of a television trial. It would have to be unscripted, featuring real evidence, witnesses, judge, and counsel before an independent jury. It would also have to be conducted strictly according to Tennessee law and criminal procedure. James liked the proposal from the outset. He knew that the revelations of one or another documentary had never generated enough public support from which he could benefit. He believed that if he could tell his story to an independent jury he had a good chance of winning, even though material evidence contained in federal government files pertaining to the case continued to be sealed and unavailable to the defense.

I spent two years getting nowhere. Finally, Thames Television in London expressed interest in producing the program. However, since Thames was to lose its franchise the following year and thus not be able to broadcast the program, it would have to arrange a sale to another broadcaster. In addition, a U.S. joint venture partner was needed to share the costs.

In early 1992 I signed a contract with Thames. It was agreed that both counsel and the judge would be paid reasonable professional fees. I insisted that the Ray family also be paid a fee. Thames promised that the investigation on both sides would be amply and equally funded. This commitment included funds not only for the extensive field investigation required but also the costs connected with the travel and accommodation of the defense team and witnesses. Eventually, however, the defense expense allocation was substantially less than what was required, so I had to personally subsidize the defense costs.

In Memphis I introduced Thames producer Jack Saltman to my local investigator, Ken Herman, who would provide him and his team with a wide range of introductions and assistance during this period of the project.

Saltman finally settled on former U.S. attorney Hickman Ewing, Jr., as the prosecutor. Hickman had been the U.S. attorney for the Western District of Tennessee for about ten years. Before that he had been the assistant U.S. Attorney with primary trial responsibility and was an experienced prosecutor. To maximise credibility I had hoped that Hickman might involve, as second chair or in some other capacity, Robert "Buzzy" Dwyer or Jim Beasley, who had been the front-line prosecutors in 1968. However, Hickman selected as second chair Glenn Wright, a black former Shelby County assistant attorney general who was then in private practice. My second chair was April Ferguson, a U.S. federal public defender at the time.

For the judge, Hickman accepted my proposal of Marvin E. Frankel, a federal district court judge now practicing law in New York City. Judge Frankel had also previously taught evidence at Columbia Law School and was well regarded in New York legal circles. I understand that from the outset he was excited about the idea.

The jury was selected from a pool of citizens initially secured by a consultant search group. They came from Illinois, Nebraska, Iowa, and Texas and completed questionnaires and submitted to videotaped interviews. Hickman and I eventually agreed on twelve jurors and two alternates.

In Memphis, we found support and encouragement for the project. By now the city had a black administration. In addition to a black mayor and a black director of police and fire, the criminal court clerk's office, where all of the physical evidence in the King case was held, was administered by a black, elected clerk—Minerva Johnican—who offered to do everything she could to assist.

However, John Pierotti, the Shelby County district attorney general, was white. Though he had ultimately succeeded his mentor Phil Canale, who was the attorney general in 1968, Pierotti told us early on that he had no interest in covering up any aspect of the King case and offered whatever support he could give. Saltman was ecstatic. I was much more guarded, expecting doors to close at any moment.

We gained access to the attorney general's investigatory file because James had previously obtained a court order to that effect. I hoped to undertake extensive ballistics and neutron activation tests on the rifle, the evidence bullets, and the death slug and to arrange for DNA testing on certain other items.

The American cable producers Home Box Office (HBO) and Thames requested access to and the right to use, if not conduct tests upon, the physical evidence in the clerk's office. The application to the criminal court went before Judge John P. Colton, Jr., who at the outset was enormously positive and receptive.

He had a reputation for fairness and openness. Local counsel told us we were fortunate to be in his particular court.

The motion was delayed to give the state attorney general an opportunity to reply. The office responded by stating that it had no objection to the production having access to the evidence inside the clerk's office but that it was opposed to any removal of evidence from that office and also to any testing of the rifle, the evidence bullets, or any other items. It became clear that this was the best agreement we were going to get from the attorney general's office; practically speaking, every indication was that the attorney general's opposition would be upheld by the Tennessee courts. A consent order was drawn up and agreed to by the attorney general and ourselves, allowing limited access to the evidence within the clerk's office.

With agreement by all parties, and no opposition in sight, I traveled from England to Memphis, arriving around 4:00 p.m. on Friday, June 5, 1992. I was met by Ken Herman, whose first words, ''Maybe they'll listen to you now,'' stopped me in my tracks. Barely an hour earlier, Judge Colton had, on his own motion, ordered that the evidence not be made available at all, for any purpose. This inexplicable action confirmed that twenty-five years later, nothing had really changed.

Among the reasons for Colton's ruling was his purported concern that James could be prejudiced in the event that a real trial was granted one day, and that James had an appeal pending before the state supreme court. The fact that James had earlier submitted an affidavit stating that he supported the proposed access to the evidence and waiving any future right to complain, was dismissed by the judge who went so far as to question James's mental state, unbelievably expressing concern about whether he was able to give informed consent. It was ironic: we were attempting to gain access to evidence to provide a television trial precisely because James had been unable to get an official trial for twenty-four years, yet this judge, whose predecessors and court had denied every post-conviction relief petition during that period, denied even the most minimal access to evidence, purportedly to protect James in the event he one day got an official trial.

The judge also seemed to ignore the fact that other media representatives had been routinely given permission to view and photograph the evidence, which after all was all that our consent order allowed.

The court's action stunned everyone. Had something or someone caused Colton to do a dramatic and uncharacteristic about-face? Even some of his friendliest colleagues couldn't explain his action.

Early the next morning we drove furiously to the Riverbend maximum security prison in Nashville where James had been transferred. James decided to withdraw his pending appeal, thus eliminating one alleged objection set out by the judge. I was impressed by his calm, indeed philosophical, reaction. He immediately saw the political nature of the judge's decision. For him it was one more example of the double standard that had long hindered his case.

At the subsequent hearing, with all parties in agreement, the judge listened politely, complimented counsel on their presentations, and reserved his decision. Ten days later he denied the motion and made his order permanent.

HBO pursued an appeal. Given the scheduling of cases, I knew that this would get us nowhere, and the lawyers' bills would further drain the budget.

Shortly afterward we discovered that after issuing an order in our case, Judge Colton had allowed a television station to film the evidence. We promptly requested equal right of access. He couldn't deny our request, and we were finally able to examine and photograph the physical evidence within the confines of the clerk's evidence room.

Early on I insisted that we take James's testimony in the prison before the beginning of the production. I wanted to have him undergo direct and cross-examination, under oath, before the judge, just in case, for whatever reason, the state authorities decided not to allow him to participate. We also wanted to safeguard against anything happening to him before his actual testimony.

Meanwhile, Ken Herman was sent to find out whether Charlie Stephens was still alive. There was a rumor that he had been seen in a Memphis tavern within the last year. We and others had believed that Stephens had been dead for a number of years. Herman was unable to find Stephens. Then, at the dirt-floor house where Stephens's brother and closest living relatives still lived, he learned that two FBI agents had come down there with Charlie in the late 1970s and had stayed for about two weeks in the area. Eventually, a job had been arranged for Charlie in Fort Smith, Arkansas, and he moved there. The family told us that they had received word from Little Rock in the summer of 1979 that Charlie had died of a heart attack, but they never saw the body, which had been cremated. Ken went to Little Rock and concluded that Stephens had in fact died there in August 1979.

In New York in early August I visited and interviewed Earl Caldwell, who was currently writing for the New York *Daily News*. His description of events surrounding the killing cast much doubt on the official version. Caldwell, who had previously been interviewed for the BBC documentary, was a *New York Times* reporter in 1968 assigned to cover Dr. King's April visit to Memphis. He told me that the *Times* national editor, Claude Sitton, said he had heard Dr. King had lost control of his group, and that he wanted Caldwell to "nail" him. Caldwell was dumbfounded. He decided he would simply do his job. He certainly was not about to play a part in any effort to "nail" Martin Luther King.

Caldwell stayed in room 215 on the ground level of the Lorraine, near the southern end, or Butler Street side of the motel (see Chart 1, page xxxiii). At about 6:00 p.m. on April 4 he was standing in the doorway of his room in his shorts when he heard what he thought at first was a bomb explosion. He was looking at the brush area at the rear of the rooming house on the other side of Mulberry Street and saw a figure in the bushes, a white male wearing what appeared to be coveralls. The man was crouched or semicrouched in the midst of the high bushes and was staring at the balcony. Caldwell was astonished when told (and shown pictures) later on that there was no brush; that the area was actually wide open and that a sniper would have had no place to hide.

He didn't see a gun in the hands of the man, and he was quickly distracted by Solomon Jones, who began driving the car back and forth frantically in the driveway of the motel. When Caldwell looked back to the brush area, the man had disappeared. He soon learned that Dr. King had been shot. (Though Caldwell was unaware of it, soon after the shooting Solomon Jones told the assembled national media that he had seen a man come out of the bushes at the time of the shooting, make his way over the wall, actually enter the Lorraine property, and then slip away. Desperate to follow, he tried to find a way out of the Lorraine Motel parking area, becoming hysterical when he couldn't find a clear path to drive out, because he believed that the shooter was getting away—hence the furious maneuvering back and forth of the car, seen but not understood by Earl Caldwell.)

Caldwell said that at various times he had written about what he had seen, although not in the *Times* because it had a policy of not allowing reporters to inject their views into a news story. He was never interviewed by the FBI or any other police authority and was not called to testify by the HSCA, so his observations were effectively buried.

IN AUGUST 1992 I began reviewing and copying the attorney general's files, a process that would go on for months. With each visit to Memphis the list of names of people to be interviewed grew.

The four-drawer metal cabinet containing the files had about eight thousand pages of documents, reports, and materials developed from the MPD and FBI investigations of the case. I initially focused on material that would be relevant to James's testimony. Much of the documentation in the form of copies of James's receipts, canceled checks, and correspondence simply corroborated his version of events.

The primary document was the 1968 MPD investigation report and its many supplements, which contained statements from the police and firemen on duty in the area of the murder scene that day; it also had statements of other people who were in and around the South Main Street area at the time. Its conclusion: that the shot was fired from the bathroom and that the killer ran down the north, front stairs of the rooming house carrying a bundle of belongings that included the murder weapon, exited through the front door, and headed south toward his car, which was parked in front of Canipe's. It postulated that he saw a police car, which was part of TACT unit 10, whose members were then on break at the fire station, parked up to the sidewalk in the driveway of the fire station, panicked, and dropped the bundle in Canipe's doorway and then got into the Mustang and drove off. All this must have been accomplished in under two minutes of the shooting, because that was how long it took Lt. Bud Ghormley to reach the bundle, with Deputy Vernon Dollahite arriving from the opposite direction soon after. (There was no mention of the other Mustang that James McCraw and others saw in front of Jim's Grill, which was where James said he had parked and left his car until he drove away shortly before 6:00. The report concluded that James had driven his car to the York Arms Store when he went to purchase the binoculars and then returned and parked in front of Canipe's.)

MY ASSISTANT, JEAN, flew in from London to help with my sessions with James, which began on Saturday, August 22. Our preparation lasted ten or more hours a day. We intensively went over his story and the various statements he had made over the years. The inevitable memory lapses concerning various details had to be confronted and explained. We began in the beginning, with his childhood.

I wanted James to emerge as the type of person I knew him to be rather than the violent racist the media had portrayed. While growing up, he had little contact with blacks, but he remembered shooting dice with blacks at the bus stop on his way home from the shoe factory when he was working there. He evinced no hostility toward blacks whatsoever and his employers at the Indian Trails restaurant in Illinois had said he got along very well with his fellow workers, most of whom were minorities. They were sorry to see him go.

James was basically shy, with average intelligence and an understated sense of humor. He bought a gun only when he needed it for a job; he didn't routinely carry a weapon. His source, inevitably, was one or another "fence." He had no experience with a rifle outside of his army training. In the army he qualified as a marksman, which was the lowest rating possible and a requirement of basic training.

He had never fired at another person and in fact only ever loaded his six-shot pistols with five bullets, leaving the firing chamber empty, which would require pulling the trigger twice to fire the gun. (For example, as mentioned earlier, when he was arrested at Heathrow Airport he had only five bullets in his six-chamber revolver.) He followed this practice to avoid accidentally discharging the gun, which was a real possibility as far as he was concerned. Early in his criminal activity, when approaching the scene of a planned burglary, the owner of the premises yelled at him and he fled frantically, tripping and discharging the weapon, shooting himself in the foot.

There was no doubt that he was an incompetent, petty criminal—a bungler. On more than one occasion he either failed to get to the scene of a planned crime, got there too late, or was arrested soon after fleeing. Once, while robbing a store, he took off his shoes to move about quietly. He saw police outside and panicked, running away in his stocking feet and carrying on for miles before putting on a pair of women's shoes that he found along the way. He did this, he said, because he didn't want to look conspicuous as he approached a town. He was picked up soon after. He was easily led and had a proclivity for meeting in bars his various companions in crime who would propose illegal operations. This tendency was particularly important in light of his assertion in the King case that he was a patsy following the instructions of a handler named Raul whom he also met in a bar—the Neptune in Montreal.

I asked James about the Atlanta map found in his apartment in Birmingham. Although he said he did mark the map, he denied making any marks associated with Dr. King's residence, church, and SCLC office. He said that he invariably bought a map when he traveled to a new area and would routinely mark it to get his bearings.

Regarding his movements on the afternoon of the killing, he basically confirmed his earlier story. He said he had walked to the York Arms Store to buy the binoculars, ending up covering the ground twice since he didn't go far enough the first time, and returned to ask Raul for further instructions.

The sessions with James continued until Saturday, August 29, when we met with the judge, the prosecutor and representatives of Thames and HBO, to hammer out a set of policies and procedures covering all aspects of the trial and preparation.

One problem that confronted me resulted from my status as the attorney for the defendant, now representing him in a trial for television. This was probably an unprecedented position for a U.S. attorney.

My position that the defendant's interests were primary required me frequently to be uncooperative with the production team. Requests that would in my view materially compromise the defense case or detract from the rights that the defendant would have in a real trial were unacceptable unless the benefit of the proceeding itself was commensurate with the concession. The greatest area of contention focused on the element of surprise, a primary asset of the defense in any criminal proceeding but anathema to a tightly timed film production schedule. The production team wanted us to disclose to the producer and the prosecution the names of every defense witness and a summary of their testimony so that the number of side bar disputes would be minimized. This would have unacceptably contravened the defendant's interests, so a compromise schedule of disclosure was agreed upon and producer Saltman gave us a pledge of confidentiality with respect to all defense evidence and leads incurred in our investigation.

On the sensitive issue of remuneration for witnesses it was agreed that they would be paid a nominal amount, forty dollars, with compensation for expenses and any loss of earnings, which would necessarily vary from person to person.

Eventually a manual of procedures was developed for the trial. It was agreed that to the maximum extent possible the

Tennessee Rules of Criminal Procedure (TRCP) would be followed. The most significant deviations from these rules were ultimately the following:

- Since a number of witnesses had died or were otherwise unavailable, it was agreed that their prior statements could be put on the record if they were taken under oath, made to a law enforcement official, or otherwise deemed reliable and relevant by the judge. Any prior inconsistent statements could also be provided at the same time as a substitute for cross-examination.

- The judge ruled that with the exception of our security witnesses we had to give the prosecution full disclosure of our case. The judge reasoned that although the defense had not formally requested discovery of the state's case, it had been allowed access to the district attorney general's 1968 file. This of course didn't take into account the embargo of a wide range of other evidence and documentation, such as that produced by the HSCA, which is sealed until 2029.

- A *sine qua non* condition of the trial was the understanding that the defendant would take the stand, testify, and submit to cross-examination. Since James had wanted this opportunity for twenty-four years, he readily agreed and in fact testified for thirteen hours.

- We agreed that each side would give notice (according to an agreed-upon schedule) to the other side regarding the various categories of defense witnesses: regular, surprise and security. We were concerned primarily with security witnesses John McFerren, Tim Kirk, and Betty Spates, who feared for their personal safety. We were certain that they wouldn't testify unless their identities were protected at least prior to their testimony.

- The producers believed that James's guilty plea had to be dealt with in some way. Eventually it was agreed that I would deliver a twenty-minute speech to the jury, explaining the reasons and conditions surrounding the plea, and Hickman would then be given five minutes to rebut.

- We would insist that the defense investigation be entirely independent from the prosecution and the producers, and would share information with the production team (which was agreed to be in confidence) only to the extent that it was absolutely essential to do so. Thus we operated on a strictly need-to-know basis whenever possible.

James's examination was scheduled to begin at 9:00 a.m. the following Tuesday, September 1. That morning we crowded into a relatively small prison conference room, made even smaller by the presence of the camera equipment. My direct examination lasted all of that day. When at one point during a break the judge made an adverse comment about prison food, suggesting going out to eat, James shyly said, "Take me with you," and then, amid laughter, added, "I'll even pay."

Hickman cross-examined James for most of the following day, after which I conducted redirect, then Hickman began his re-cross-examination.

One morning while we were preparing for James's testimony, I arranged to interview inmate Tim Kirk.

I asked Kirk if he would agree to testify or give a statement about the offer of a contract to kill James that was communicated to him by Arthur Baldwin back in 1978. Kirk wanted to help James but was very reluctant because of the high profile he would get and the impact such assertions might have on his potential parole and, indeed, his safety inside the prison. Finally, on a subsequent visit, he refused to testify publicly but agreed to provide a current statement or affidavit if I could arrange for his name to be withheld.

With the examination of James completed on September 2, I resumed my review of the attorney general's file in Memphis. There were a number of photographs of the scene, most of which appeared to have been taken the day after the crime. The brush area was shown to be clear, and piles of cut twigs and branches were scattered around. Some photographs taken from the Lorraine balcony showed the rooming house and the open bathroom window. In most photographs a large tree branch prominently hung over the retaining wall at the edge of the brush area. (See photographs #12 and 13.)

Photographs of footprints near the top of the alleyway were

of immediate interest. Also in the file was a statement listing three officers on the scene shortly after the shooting as patrolmen Torrence N. Landers, Carroll Dunn, and J. B. Hodges. They had apparently climbed up onto the wall from Mulberry Street, made their way through the bushes to the edge of the building, and near the top of the alleyway between the two wings of the rooming house stumbled on the large (13½"–14") footprints in the wet soil heading toward the door to the building. This door at the end of the alleyway opened on to a landing that led to the basement and off to the right into Jim's Grill. Landers's statement said that they proceeded down the alley but only perfunctorily checked the basement underneath the rooming house and the grill because they did not have a flashlight. I thought it was extraordinary that the basement wasn't inspected.

Though the footprints had been photographed and a plaster cast made of them, this evidence was ignored.

Before returning home to London, Jean and I went to see witness James McCraw, the former cab driver, only to be told that he had been rushed to the hospital. There McCraw expressed his concern that he might not make it to late January, when the trial was scheduled to be held, because of his failing health. His evidence was vitally important: the state of intoxication of the state's chief witness, the fact that the bathroom was empty minutes before the shooting, and the existence of a second rifle which had never been disclosed before.

We decided to take a declaration under oath from him as soon as he was released from the hospital. Though by taking his statement we would have to provide it to the prosecution in advance of his testimony, at least then his information would be preserved.

HBO issued its final commitment to the project on September 17, and Thames confirmed that we could proceed. A filming date for the trial was fixed for January 25, 1993, with international airing scheduled for the twenty-fifth anniversary of Dr. King's death, April 4, 1993. We had three-and-a-half months to investigate and prepare for trial. Considering the enormity of the task, it was no time at all.

19

Pretrial Investigations: September–October 1992

AT THE OUTSET we had no illusions about our task. It would not be enough to show reasonable doubt of James's guilt because the media had already convicted him. We would have to prove his innocence beyond a reasonable doubt. The strategy would be twofold. We would seek to introduce evidence that directly contravened each significant aspect of the state's case and then, to the extent possible, attempt to show how the killing actually occurred. We intended to go well beyond the actual murder to demonstrate the existence and extent of a cover-up. There was no shortage of material and leads, but how much could be turned into hard evidence to put before a jury?

Hickman and his prosecution team had an opportunity to conduct a fresh investigation of the case. It was thus conceivable that he could come up with a theory different from that advanced by the state in 1969. Eventually, we came to believe that he would prosecute the case along the lines set out in the MPD/FBI reports, relying largely on circumstantial evidence.

There were several outstanding leads from my previous investigatory work to follow up. Top of the list was Betty Spates. I had previously instructed Ken Herman to keep in touch with her from time to time, hoping that she would develop enough trust to reveal whatever it was that she knew. A number of other people had to be located, including: Randy Rosenson; Solomon Jones, who had been missing from Memphis for years; William Reed and Ray Hendrix (Jim's Grill customers who left the grill shortly before 6:00 p.m.); and service station attendant Willie Green—all of whom were potential alibi witnesses as to James's whereabouts at the time of the killing; and of course, rooming house manager Bessie Brewer.

I wanted to interview each person we could identify as being in Jim's Grill that afternoon, as well as each person who was in the rooming house, each fireman on duty at fire station 2, each member of TACT 10 on rest break in the fire station at the time, and the employees of the Tayloe Paper and Seabrook Wallpaper companies across the street from the rooming house.

It was obviously important to interview any police officers who were at the scene or involved in the investigation in any way, as well as members of Dr. King's entourage and the staff at the Lorraine, and a number of other persons who were in the area.

Then there were the individual members of the Invaders, the local black civil rights leadership, and ordinary community people who had never previously been properly interviewed. Further afield, the stories of people like Morris Davis and Jules "Ricco" Kimbel needed to be further checked out, and James's movements in Montreal and Toronto would have to be looked at.

It was obviously essential to obtain information about the role of organized crime. The conversation John McFerren accidentally overheard in Frank C. Liberto's office provided a rare insight into its potential involvement, but I knew it wasn't going to be easy to break into that closed community.

Ultimately, of course, there was the question of where the conspiracy went and who provided the money. This would inevitably require that the investigation extend to organized crime's structure beyond Memphis and in particular Carlos Marcello's organization in New Orleans. I knew that we would have to "follow the money," because mob involvement would have been for money.

SINCE JAMES HAD TRAVELED extensively in the year following his escape from Jefferson City, I had to organize an investigation that not only blanketed Memphis and rural Tennessee but extended to California in the west, Toronto and Montreal in the north, Texas in the southwest, and virtually every area of the South, though with a focus on New Orleans, Atlanta, Birmingham, and Miami. I would also need to obtain information from former prisoners and staff at Missouri State Penitentiary as well as selective others at Brushy Mountain.

I had to assemble a team of investigators. Assignments would be given to each of them on a need-to-know basis, with most of them not knowing one another and no one else privy to the overall scope of the work. Most of them would be licensed private investigators in their particular areas. My team rapidly grew to twenty-two.

Separating the relatively few valuable pieces of material in the attorney general's files from the overwhelming amount of irrelevant and false information and accusations was time-consuming. We made notes of leads that appeared to have possible significance. Frequently, these seemed not to have been followed up.

Certain documents in the attorney general's files related to what Betty Spates might know about the murder. One was a report of a claim by Memphis bailbondsman Alexander Wright, who had come to know Betty Spates in 1969 when he was arranging bail for her brother, Eddie Lee Eldridge. The report was dated February 3, 1969, and issued by Detective J. C. Davis of the MPD intelligence division. Davis wrote that:

Information from a reliable source has been received by the above and this information is that Mr. WRIGHT at State Surety Bonding Company was quoted as saying, "I know two women who were working in the building where the shot came from that killed King. They told me that RAY was across Main Street and not in the building when the shot was fired. The man who killed King is the owner of the flop house, and not RAY." Mr. Wright also stated that policemen were in the building when the shot was fired that killed King and that they had been coming there prior to the day that King was killed.

After these two women were questioned by the police and FBI they were fired by their boss, the man who killed Dr. King. They are willing to take the witness stand in court.

A handwritten note under the typed report initialed by the attorney general's chief investigator John Carlisle stated:

We have a tape in our offices that was taken from a tape that O'Neil [Wright's boss, who recorded Betty's comments] brought to this office on January 30.

The second document relating to Betty Spates was Mr. Carlisle's report of an interview he conducted with James Alexander Wright on February 10, 1969. Mr. Wright confirmed that Betty told him Ray was not guilty because she knew about his movements that afternoon and that her "boss man" [Loyd Jowers] was out in the back and was the only one who could have killed Dr. King.

The third document purports to be an interview with Betty Spates on February 12, 1969, in which she appears to deny ever making the statement alleged by Wright. It is curious that this statement is unsigned, although a space was left for the signature of "Mrs. Betty Spates."

Wright's description of Spates's account of James's movements on the afternoon of April 4 didn't agree with what I knew about the case, but I remembered that when I spoke with her some four years earlier she was adamant about James's innocence, though she refused to provide details. It appeared to me that, however clumsy her effort, she had tried back in 1969 to provide James with an alibi because she knew he was innocent. As I suspected, she had indeed seen the gun and now I better understood her fear. I wondered what else she knew.

Wright confirmed his story to me, adding that Betty had told him that a number of MPD plainclothes and uniformed policemen came to the grill, apparently to inspect the place, during the week leading up to the killing. After the killing she spoke to him again and said that she knew Ray couldn't have done it because he was upstairs drunk and that they had found the gun within fifteen feet of the killing out in the back by the corner of the building. (It occurred to me that this was the area where the footprints leading into the alley were found.)

CHARLES CABBAGE, one of the founding leaders of the Invaders and the BOP back in the 1960s, agreed to contact each available former member of the Invaders and try to arrange a session with me.

Former firemen Floyd Newsom and Norvell Wallace agreed to testify about their unexpected transfer from fire station 2 on April 4. Though it was likely that the prosecution would attempt to dismiss it as a coincidence, I believed it was one of a number of inexplicable official actions indicative of a conspiracy.

Olivia Hayes, who worked at the Lorraine as a receptionist during 1968, reluctantly told me that Dr. King was supposed to be in room 202 on the ground level but somehow was switched to the balcony room, 306. She didn't admit to knowing why. Here was further confirmation of the room change. When I pressed her, perhaps too insistently, she clammed up.

THE TAYLOE PAPER COMPANY was located across the street from Jim's Grill in 1968. A number of its employees used to stop in the grill after work for a beer and a game of shuffleboard or pinball. Two of those persons, Kenneth Foster and David Wood, gave statements at the time confirming that they observed a white Mustang parked in front of Jim's Grill, but they were not available in 1992.

Steve Cupples, who had worked at Tayloe Paper back in 1968 and had been in Jim's Grill on the evening of April 4, agreed to be interviewed. He remembered leaving work on April 4 sometime between 5:00 and 5:20, parking his car across the street from Jim's Grill.

"Sure, I remember a Mustang in front of the bar," he said. "I got dust on my new blue suit squeezing between its rear and the front bumper of the car parked tightly behind it." He said he was certain that the Mustang was there at 5:15 or 5:20 and that its back bumper was "virtually even" with the north entrance door of the rooming house. (See chart 4 for the lineup of cars in the rooming house area on South Main at 5:30 on April 4.)

Cupples recalled that the FBI visited him on four occasions, twice at home and twice at work. They asked him the same questions every time, showed him photographs of the same person, whom he didn't recognize, and he believes they asked him not to speak with anyone about what he saw. When asked about other persons who "hung out" in the area, he commented that there was a black street artist who used to "hang out" in the grill. This artist was almost a "fixture" but Cupples didn't remember the familiar figure being there that day. He agreed to help us in any way he could.

Jimmy Walker, deputy coroner for the city of Atlanta in 1992, had also worked at Tayloe. He vaguely recalled that on the afternoon of April 4 he had to park just behind the fire hydrant, in front of Canipe's, and he periodically opened the door of the grill to check his car. He noticed the white Mustang in front of the grill because it was in the area where he usually tried to park. He agreed to come to Memphis and undergo hypnosis in an effort to sharpen his memory. When he did so in early 1993, he confirmed his story.

Another Tayloe employee, Franklin Ray, also remembered the Mustang being parked in front of the grill. So then, there were four available Tayloe employees and statements by two others who said they saw a white Mustang parked in front of the grill, at the same time that the state and other independent

Diagram depicting the lineup of cars in the rooming house area of South Main Street at 5:30 P.M. on April 4.

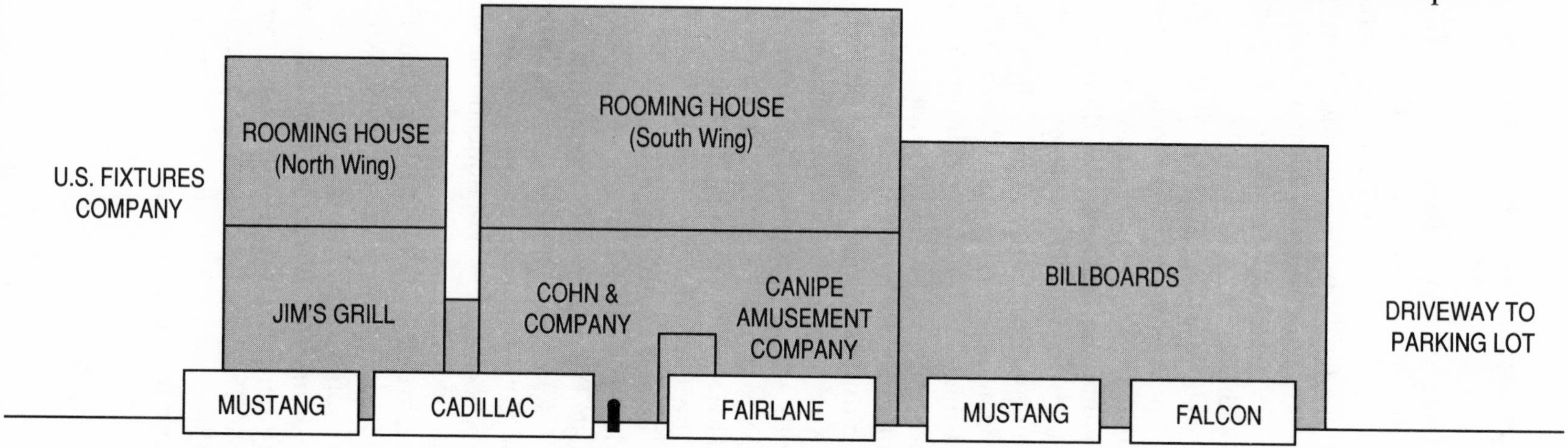

DRIVEWAY TO PARKING LOT

BILLBOARDS

ROOMING HOUSE (South Wing)

CANIPE AMUSEMENT COMPANY

COHN & COMPANY

ROOMING HOUSE (North Wing)

JIM'S GRILL

U.S. FIXTURES COMPANY

FALCON

MUSTANG

FAIRLANE

CADILLAC

MUSTANG

CHART 4

witnesses (McCraw and the Hurleys) confirmed that a similar white Mustang was parked in front of Canipe's. The facts pointed to the presence of two identical white Mustangs, parked within seventy-five to one hundred feet of each other, around the time of the shooting. Here was another "coincidence" for the prosecution to address.

Yet another coincidence was the hoax CB radio broadcast on the evening of the assassination. On Saturday morning, October 24, 1992 I met Carroll Satchfield who had legally changed his name to Carroll Carroll. On April 4, while in his electronics and communications shop on Union Avenue near Cooper, he had turned on channel seventeen of his CB radio and heard "We are now at the corner of Summer and East Parkway." It was, he thought, a police chase, and as he listened he noticed that although the broadcast was reporting the cars going ever farther away from him, the signal remained constant throughout the thirty-five-minute broadcast, as though coming from a fixed location. "Phoney," he thought—a practical joke.

Eventually he learned that he was listening to the voice of a hoaxer whose account was being picked up by William Austein, who had flagged down MPD car number 160, driven by officer Rufus Bradshaw. Austein proceeded to relay the account of the "chase" to officer Bradshaw, who in turn passed it on verbatim to MPD dispatcher Willie Tucker.

I knew that if we could develop the details surrounding this event—which diverted all police attention immediately after the shooting to the northern end of the city, away from the scene of the crime and the logical escape route to the south combined with the MPD's failure to follow their standard emergency procedures (no all points bulletin or Signal Y). I might be able to convince the jury it was one more indication of a conspiracy.

THE NEXT DAY, October 25, I had my first opportunity to examine the physical evidence in clerk Minerva Johnican's criminal court clerk's office. Certain key items of evidence were not as described.

The bullets found in the bundle, which were described in

the clerk's inventory as having been test-fired, were clearly never fired. The casings of the unfired bullets were sliced, and thus it was obvious to me that neutron activation or other trace element analysis tests had been performed on them, which was consistent with the HSCA forensic report that the FBI conducted such an examination back in 1968. In that test a sample of lead would have been taken from each bullet to compare with lead from the death slug to determine whether the bullets and the death slug came from the same batch. If they did, this would mean that the bullets in the evidence bundle (which contained other personal items belonging to Ray) likely had been bought at the same time and place as the actual death slug itself.

Yet there was no report of the results to be found anywhere. Neither was there any mention of the test, nor any report in the attorney general's files. What happened to the report? Other forensic test reports were turned over to the attorney general. Why not this one?

A number of maps had been found among James's belongings recovered in Atlanta, either in the Mustang or in his room at the Garner rooming house. He had obviously acquired them as he entered a new state or city. As James told us was his practice, he had made markings on virtually every one of them, including the Atlanta map. However, the markings on the Atlanta map seemed to have little bearing on Dr. King's home or church, focusing primarily on the 14th Street area near the rooming house.

Cigarette butts and ashes collected by the FBI from the Mustang after it was found in the Capitol Homes parking lot in Atlanta were missing. James didn't smoke, so the presence of cigarette butts pointed to someone else having been in the car at some time. Eyewitness reports in the attorney general's file taken at the time the abandoned white Mustang was found in Atlanta described the ashtray as overflowing, yet the evidence from the Mustang contained only one butt and a minuscule amount of ash.

I asked Johnican to raise the question of the tampered-with and missing evidence with the attorney general. The deliberate or negligent destruction of the evidence had most likely occurred before Johnican took office, and I hoped that she might raise the issue of her predecessor's custodial reponsibility. I also hoped she would consider undertaking some forensic tests on her own account and authority, but such was not to be.

I interviewed fireman William B. King. He remembered being in the back of fire station 2 looking out of the window in the door when the shot was fired. Dr. King was standing straight up, he said, though he had been bent over a few seconds earlier. He said that fireman Charles Stone was lying on top of the lockers looking out the window at the moment of the shooting. William King believed that only he and Stone actually saw the shooting. He recalled MPD detective Redditt leaving earlier. After the shot, William King called his wife and went outside to the rear of the firehouse and looked over toward the brush area behind the rooming house which was about one hundred feet north of where he was standing. He said that he noticed freshly cut white wood.

As mentioned earlier, the terrain of the rooming house backyard sloped slightly downward toward the wall. The eastern area, closest to the wall, was engulfed with a mixture of untamed mulberry bushes and small trees. Most of the small trees were between ten and fifteen feet tall, but at least one extended to a height of about twenty-five feet, and there was one sycamore tree which was much taller. The thicket of mulberry bushes extended for some distance from the wall back into the yard, eventually giving way to high grass and weeds.

He added that, at the time, the FBI and the attorney general's office told him not to discuss what he had seen with anyone. He was never questioned by the HSCA, and no defense counsel or investigator had talked to him in the intervening years.

William King said that a few days later he walked down Mulberry Street to the Lorraine driveway and confirmed that the freshly cut wood was still there. How would the prosecution explain this? I believed William King may have been talking about a sizable branch, which I recalled seeing depicted in various photographs over the years and more recently in an

8" × 10" glossy in the attorney general's file. (See photograph #13.)

Whether cut before or after the shooting, in its original upright position the branch could have come between the bathroom window of the rooming house and the balcony on which Dr. King was standing when he was shot. (Even from the official photographs we examined, there is serious question as to whether a clear shot existed.) William King would take the stand.

Retired fire lieutenant George Loenneke also told me how he had seen Dr. King at the moment he was shot. He said that Richmond had been away from the window at the time and that he, Loenneke, had raised the alarm.

Loenneke then surprised me. He said that some days after the shooting, he talked with a sales girl who worked on the ground floor in Seabrook's offices directly opposite the rooming house. She told him that around 5:30 on the afternoon of the shooting she saw a man pull up in a white Mustang and park it just south of Canipe's. She observed the man leave the car soon after and go upstairs, entering the rooming house through the northernmost door adjacent to Jim's Grill. She was certain that the man was not James Earl Ray. Loenneke didn't know the girl's name. Could she be found? If so there might be further evidence not only of the second Mustang but of another person (apparently the same person seen by the Hurleys) driving and parking it just south of Canipe's.

Fireman Charles Stone was in the rear of fire station 2 at the time of the shooting. He was on top of the lockers, looking out through the small windows located between the lockers and the ceiling. Only he and William King actually saw Dr. King hit by the bullet, he said. George Loenneke was "messing about with his locker" and probably didn't see anything.

On October 29, Ken Herman and I went to Central Church, where Rev. James Latimer was pastor. I had wanted to meet with him for some time, having heard years earlier about his strange visitor a week after the killing who supposedly needed "spiritual guidance" in the matter of the King killing or he would "commit suicide." Latimer confirmed the account Russell Thompson had given me of the incident and said that he had told his story to Inspector N. E. Zachary of the MPD, and to the FBI. They promised to "check it out." He heard nothing. In August he was visited by two men who showed him credentials and emphasized that they were from the Tennessee Bureau of Investigation (TBI), not the FBI. They showed him photographs that closely resembled the man who visited him, but that was the last Latimer heard about it. I showed him a mug shot of Jack Youngblood and he said that this did not appear to be the man. Subsequently I visited him with Wayne Chastain and showed him a proper photograph of Youngblood and he hesitated but still could not positively identify him. Wayne reminded him that he had previously identified Youngblood closer to the time. Latimer shrugged and said, "It's been twenty-five years."

No one familiar with TBI procedures could explain the TBI involvement. They wouldn't usually become involved in a Shelby County/Memphis investigation, being used as a rule in smaller towns without the facilities available in Shelby County.

I INTERVIEWED RETIRED NEW YORK CITY POLICEMAN LEON COHEN, who was a private investigator in Memphis in 1968. In the course of his work he had befriended the owner of the Lorraine, Walter Bailey. On April 5, he saw Bailey at the Lorraine and found him deeply distressed. His wife had suffered a stroke immediately after the shooting of Dr. King and was near death in St. Joseph's Hospital.

Bailey told Cohen that he had arranged for Dr. King to be placed in room 202 on the ground floor when a call from Atlanta came through with a request that he be moved to room 306. Bailey protested, maintaining that the ground-floor room facing an inner courtyard was more secure, but the caller insisted on the change.

Cohen's conversation with Walter Bailey substantiated Olivia Hayes's recollection that Dr. King was to have been housed on the ground floor and then was moved. However, it differed from Wayne Chastain's account of a conversation with Bailey in 1970 or 1971 when Bailey told him that his wife had been visited by a dark-skinned advance man with an Indian appearance who insisted on the change.

Why the different stories? Since Walter Bailey has been dead for a number of years, it is only possible to speculate. If an advance man actually organized the switch, Mrs. Bailey would have realized what role she had unwittingly played at the time of the shooting. It would have been natural at the time for her husband to try to protect her by mentioning a call. Another explanation, of course, is that later on Bailey may have shifted the blame from himself at a time when he couldn't be contradicted. This occurred to me sometime later, when William Ross, who used to drive Walter Bailey, told me that at one point Bailey told him that he regarded his wife's death as a sort of sacrifice, explaining that he had come to associate her death with Dr. King's own passing. He said Dr. King had to die because he was taking on forces, including government, he couldn't overcome. If he hadn't been killed in Memphis at the Lorraine on April 4, 1968, it would have been somewhere else and some other time. But it was a pity, Bailey said, that his wife became so closely involved.

When I later interviewed the Baileys' daughter, Carolyn Champion, and her husband, they were adamant that Mrs. Bailey had been declared in excellent health by their family doctor around the time of the stroke. They were convinced that for some reason she had taken a measure of personal responsibility for the assassination. They didn't know why.

WE WERE UNABLE TO FIND WILLIE GREEN, the black service station attendant who might have seen James around 6:00 on April 4 when, as James claimed, he had gone to a gas station to get a spare tire repaired. This was supported by an FBI report on the examination of the Mustang that confirmed the spare tire was indeed flat. Memphis investigator Cliff Dates eventually convinced us that Green was dead.

Around this time I became immersed in the mysteries surrounding the work and death of William Sartor. As mentioned

earlier, Sartor became deeply involved with the case after following up on John McFerren's story. Until his death he increasingly believed organized crime was involved in the murder—in
particular the Carlos Marcello organization in New Orleans. He
spent considerable time in New Orleans meeting with Marcello
contacts, including the man's nephew, Little Joe.

In 1971, suddenly and unexpectedly, Bill Sartor died, ostensibly
from an overdose, though he wasn't a drug user. Dale Dougherty,
who had been a boyhood friend of Sartor, and Bill Sartor's
mother had long considered the death suspicious. The night
before he died, he told Dougherty that someone had agreed
to talk to him in Memphis, and he was looking forward to the
meeting. In recent days he had been acting fearfully, often
sitting in his mother's home watching the road with a shotgun
at the ready. But that last evening when he stopped off where
she worked, he was in good spirits. He told her that he was
going to stop at the Hickory Stick bar for a couple of drinks
and then go to bed. He asked her to wake him early. She
couldn't rouse him the next morning. He was rushed to the
hospital but never regained consciousness.

She had never been able to obtain a postmortem report. The
death certificate stated the cause was undetermined. Try as she
might, no one would cooperate. Even her family physician,
after making a few phone calls, told her to leave it alone.

There it rested until I spoke with Dougherty, who had become the trustee of Bill Sartor's notes and manuscript, a copy
of which had been provided to the HSCA. I began to explore
what appeared to be the more relevant of Sartor's leads. He
noted that produce man Frank Liberto flew to Detroit the night
that James Earl Ray was extradited from London. He learned
this following a telephone conversation between Sartor's girlfriend (and future wife) who placed the call, and Liberto's
partner, James Latch, who told her that since Ray was being
brought back that night Frank would be nowhere around. I
found this interesting because it showed apprehension on Liberto's part and also revealed that he had some family or contacts in Detroit, a city near the Canadian border. I also agreed
to help Dougherty and Mrs. Sartor get some answers about

Sartor's death. Dougherty, in turn, agreed to come to Memphis and attempt to interview one Pat Lyons, a former friend of Sartor's wife, who had assisted them in their work on the case.

Pat Lyons was one of the last persons to speak with Bill Sartor, who had called him from Waco the evening before his death about his visit to Memphis. When Dougherty went to Memphis in November, Lyons flat-out refused to speak with him. Later one of our local investigators surveilled the house in which Lyons lived with his mother, which appeared to be permanently sealed, with all the windows closed and the blinds drawn.

This man was frightened. Sartor had written that at one point in 1969–1970 a local hood held a knife to Lyons's throat and told him that he was under instructions to kill him. The order, according to Sartor, resulted from Lyons's help in his King investigation. Lyons told Sartor the order came from an associate of Frank C. Liberto, and he was only able to get out of the immediate danger by pleading with his assailant to put him on the phone with Liberto's associate or even Frank Liberto himself and then convincing him that he was not helping Sartor but just trying to find out what he knew so that he could relay the information.

By 1992 Liberto had been dead for fourteen years. Yet Lyons was still terrified.

Meanwhile Dougherty worked at full speed in his effort to get an autopsy report on Sartor. He enlisted the assistance of the Waco district attorney, Ken Abels, and one of his investigators, J. C. Rappe.

20

Corroboration and New Evidence: November 1992

I INTERVIEWED PHOTOGRAPHER JOHN "BILL" McAFEE, who in 1968 was covering Dr. King's involvement with the garbage strike on network assignments. McAfee set up his camera at the Lorraine just before noon on April 4, noticing as he arrived MPD chief J. C. MacDonald "lurking" around the Butler Street driveway entrance of the Lorraine, walkie-talkie in hand. He recognized MacDonald, having photographed him many times, and he was surprised to see him since the chief rarely left his office.

McAfee left the Lorraine at around 5:00 to drive the reporter he was working with to the airport. Waiting for him at home there was a message from ABC assigning him to cover the immediate aftermath of the assassination. He bolted out the door and drove back to the South Main Street area, stopping briefly to pick up a sound man and some equipment at his brother's audio shop on Second Street, one block from Mulberry Street.

As he entered the shop he heard the local AM station actually being overridden by a powerful CB broadcast. He realized that in order for this to occur the CB broadcast must have been transmitting from a base in the immediate area. What he heard was the hoax broadcast, and this was the first time there had been any indication that it might have originated from the immediate vicinity of the shooting.

I subsequently called Carroll Carroll, who confirmed that for a CB transmission to override an AM signal it had to originate close to the receiving set. Thus the possibility that the broadcast was a prank carried off by a CB hoaxer in a distant part of the city, as had been concluded by the MPD, made no sense.

McAfee was willing to testify.

IN LATE OCTOBER AND EARLY NOVEMBER, with the help of Sarah Teale of Teale Productions, I visited CBS, NBC, and ABC studios in New York to view all the available library film taken at that time. I was most interested in Earl Wells's NBC interview with gas station attendant Willie Green, as well as in locating photographs of the bush area behind the rooming house before it was cut.

Ernest Withers, a black Memphis photographer, also agreed to provide contact sheets of photographs of the scene at the time. In addition, he agreed to attempt to identify and locate a black woman who was a senior at LeMoyne College in the spring of 1968 who was referred to in Hugh Stanton's investigation notes as allegedly seeing a man (possibly, I thought, the same person described by Solomon Jones) leaving the scene right after the shooting. The young woman apparently screamed at the police to go after the man.

Neither Teale nor Withers was able to produce any clear photographs of the bushes taken on the day of the shooting, nor was Withers able to locate the LeMoyne student. I also tried to find Mary Hunt who was in the Joseph Louw photograph of the people on the balcony pointing in the direction of the back of the rooming house. She appeared to be focusing her gaze on some point further to her left (south) than the others. I eventually discovered that she had died of cancer.

One of our priorities was to gain a conclusive understanding of what happened to the backyard area of the rooming house.

By 1992 the area was vastly different from the way it was in 1968. Then, the common backyard area of the connected wings of the rooming house led to a four-foot-wide alley running to a door that led down to the basement and, from the inside landing to the right, into Jim's Grill.

The backyard sloped slightly downward toward a high wall (about 7'6"–8') rising from the Mulberry Street sidewalk. As mentioned previously, the area closest to the wall was engulfed with a thicket of untamed mulberry bushes, small trees of up to twenty-five feet in height, untended grass and weeds, and a tall sycamore tree. The thick bushes extended for some distance from the wall back into the yard.

We needed to interview as many people as we could who remembered the yard at the time. Wayne Chastain had gone up to the second floor of the rooming house on April 4 shortly after the shooting to get a view of the bushes and the backyard. He said he looked through the Stephens's kitchen window and saw a very thick growth of bushes and brush.

Press Scimitar reporter Kay Black repeated what she had told me in 1978 about the telephone call she received on April 5 from former mayor William Ingram, in which he said that there was a work crew behind the rooming house cutting down all the bushes and high brush and grass in the area. Ingram appeared to be suspicious of the purpose behind this activity.

Later that morning, Black went over to the area and saw that the cutting and clearing had been completed. The bushes were gone, the brush was removed and debris was neatly raked and stacked in piles. No satisfactory reason was ever given to her, although there was some mention of a concern that tourists not be offended. Black agreed to testify. (SCLC field organizer James Orange had noticed the bushes at the time of the shooting and that they were gone the next morning. I made a mental note to contact him.)

Cab driver James McCraw, who was familiar with the area and went out there occasionally through the rear door of the grill, said it was completely overgrown and never cared for or tended at all. While not knowing the exact time, McCraw did recall that the area was cut and cleaned by the city shortly after the shooting.

Former MPD captain (lieutenant in 1968) Tommy Smith who had refused for a very long time to be interviewed, finally agreed. In our 1992 meeting he vividly remembered the state of overgrowth in the rooming house backyard. He described a "thicket" of mulberry bushes, which impeded him considerably as he attempted to gain access on the evening of the shooting.

As to the presence of a person in the bushes, Earl Caldwell agreed to testify at the trial. I believed that the defense had found in him the strongest available witness that the shot had come from the brush area behind the rooming house. We were still looking for Solomon Jones, who had been away from Memphis for a number of years. It was rumored that he was in Atlanta, and since he had previously worked for funeral homes we began to check out the funeral homes there.

HAVING LEARNED ABOUT THE FOOTPRINTS near the top of the alleyway between the two buildings and that three patrolmen had been in that area shortly after the shooting, I had been trying to locate the only one who was still alive—dog officer J. B. Hodges. He had long ago moved from Memphis out into the country. Since he had been in that area immediately after the shooting, I believed that if we could find him he would be able to give us a good description.

In addition, I wanted to locate Maynard Stiles, who had been deputy director of the Memphis City Public Works Department in 1968. Since he was in charge of day-to-day operations it was likely that he would have been responsible for giving the orders for any cutting and cleanup activity.

IT HAD OFTEN BEEN RUMORED that a tree branch was cut some time shortly before April 4. Jim Reid, the former Memphis *Press Scimitar* reporter/photographer who had told me fourteen years earlier that he had taken a picture of the cutting, was still unable to come up with the photograph.

After many attempts, on November 30 I caught up with Captain Ed Atkinson, who in 1968 had been a staff assistant to Memphis fire and police director Frank Holloman. I thought that he might have seen or had access to some significant documentation. He didn't, but he remembered being present in the aftermath of the killing at a discussion in police headquarters with two other officers. One of the officers said that he was present with two FBI agents at the bathroom window at the rear of the rooming house after the killing; one of the agents said that a tree branch would have to be cut, because no one would ever believe that a shooter could make the shot from that point with the tree in the way. The branch was cut down the next day. Atkinson didn't remember who the officers were.

Weeks later, Atkinson underwent hypnosis to enhance his memory. For some time he described two featureless faces, though he said one of the voices sounded familiar. Slowly he began to recognize the owner of the familiar voice and he identified him as Earl Clark (an MPD captain). Then he discerned that the other officer who was recounting the conversation he had witnessed was a sergeant. He wasn't able to identify him, though he described him as wearing thick-rimmed glasses, and having a moustache.

EVEN THOUGH JAMES NEVER DENIED BUYING THE GUN found in the bundle in front of Canipe's, we obviously needed to learn as much as possible about that purchase.

When Ken Herman interviewed Aeromarine Supply store manager Donald Wood in his Birmingham store, Mr. Wood more or less repeated his statements to the HSCA, saying that the buyer, whom he photo-identified as James Earl Ray, knew nothing about guns. He added that the buyer said he was going deer hunting in Wisconsin with his brother-in-law. Then, curiously enough, he volunteered that he had always believed that one of his customers, a Dr. Gus Prosch, was somehow involved in the killing. He said that Prosch had bought a lot of guns from him, was involved with gun dealings, and had also been involved in racial problems. When, months later, I interviewed Wood he confirmed his earlier statement to my investigator. Prosch's name had surfaced on the periphery of the case before, in the affidavit of Morris Davis. We knew that for some reason his fingerprints had been compared by the FBI with some of the unidentified prints in this case with no success. Prosch had rebuffed Herman's earlier attempt to interview him. Subsequently, I extensively interviewed Prosch, alone and in Morris Davis's presence. He categorically denied any involvement.

I also instructed Herman to try to confirm James's movements between March and April 1, 1968, since I believed that the prosecution was going to contend that he had stalked Dr. King in Atlanta during that time. The motels James said he had stayed in on his trip from Birmingham to Memphis either no longer existed or had long ago discarded their records. We met similar frustration in Atlanta where potential witnesses were either dead or missing.

Jim Kellum, a local investigator, had at my request developed a file on topless-club owner Art Baldwin, who had been named by inmate Tim Kirk as the person who put out the contract on James in June or July 1978. Kellum's documents independently confirmed Baldwin's connections with organized crime through mob leader Frank Colacurcio in Seattle and Carlos Marcello in New Orleans, as well as his role as an informant and witness for the federal government against Tennessee governor Ray Blanton and members of his staff.

Kellum, however, had no success in arranging access to produce man Frank Liberto's mistress, or in pinpointing information about his organized crime associates referred to by writer William Sartor.

Then suddenly, on November 17, 1992, Kellum asked to be released of any further work, saying some of his contacts weren't taking kindly to the thrust of my investigation. I understood. I discreetly approached private investigator Gene Barksdale, who had been close to the Liberto clan, for information on Frank Liberto's activities. I pressed him to talk to Liberto's mistress and for information on Liberto's organized crime associates, one of whom, Sam Cacamici, I learned had died. Barksdale told me that some of his old friends in the Liberto family started behaving strangely when he approached them on these issues. He also got no cooperation from the mistress in his initial efforts.

The investigation of the Liberto connections to the killing

was complicated by the fact that in 1968 there were no fewer than three Frank Libertos in Memphis alone, each with extended family connections in New Orleans. The first Frank Liberto (Frank Camille Liberto), the primary target of the investigation, was the produce dealer overheard by John McFerren who died in 1978. The second Frank Liberto had also been dead for over ten years. In 1968 he owned Frank's liquor store and the Green Beetle Tavern on South Main Street, just up the block from Jim's Grill. The third and probably wealthiest Frank Liberto was over 80 in 1992. Barksdale told me that despite his age he was still active in his automobile business. So in 1968 we had no fewer than three Frank Libertos with some, as yet unclear, family relationship. There was also another member of the Liberto family, apparently related to Frank C. Liberto, who owned and ran a business a short distance from the Lorraine.

John McFerren told me about Ezell Smith, who worked for this business and around the time of the assassination saw a rifle being put together there. McFerren said Ezell learned later that this was the gun used to kill Martin Luther King.

As noted earlier, in 1978 I had somehow acquired a photograph of a building with a note along the top margin indicating that a building within blocks of the scene of the crime owned by a relative of an organized crime figure, was where the rifle bought by Ray was stored until April 4, 1968.

Ken Herman photographed the building where Ezell had worked. It was the same building as in the photograph sent to me. I saw this as the first crack in the silence that kept closed the involvement of local organized crime in the killing. We looked for Ezell, without success. The frustration of not being able to capitalize on such a tip was overwhelming.

WE NEXT SOUGHT OUT Emmett Douglass, the policeman whose car the MPD report states spooked James as he allegedly fled. The MPD report concluded that he entered the sidewalk looking south on South Main Street and saw Douglass's "emergency cruiser" parked near the sidewalk at the north front side of the fire station. At that point he supposedly panicked, throwing the bundle down in Canipe's recessed doorway before driving away in the Mustang parked nearby.

The HSCA report hedged. It stated that James probably saw the Douglass cruiser that was parked "adjacent" to the station and pulled up to the sidewalk (a physical impossibility since the front of the station was set back about sixty feet from the sidewalk) or possibly saw policemen exiting from the fire station.

A TACT 10 cruiser driven by Emmett Douglass was indeed parked at the north side of the fire station but not near the sidewalk. Douglass was sitting in the station wagon monitoring the radio during the break that afternoon, while the other members of his unit were in the fire station.

On a chilly late November evening, Captain Douglass went with me to the fire station and showed me exactly where he was parked late in the afternoon of April 4, 1968. He insisted that he was not parked up to the sidewalk but was directly in front of the northwest side door of the station about sixty feet back from the sidewalk of South Main Street. (See Chart 5, p. 215.) In 1968, a set of billboards with frames that extended from the ground to a considerable height were located on the north side of the parking lot, right next to the rooming house building. These structures would have blocked the view of anyone looking toward his position from that spot.

It was rumored that there had also been a hedge that ran between the edge of the fire station driveway and the parking lot next door extending out to the sidewalk, which would have impeded the view of anyone looking from the sidewalk near Canipe's to the spot where the MPD alleged that Douglass's car was parked. If the rumors were true that the hedge had been cut down soon after the shooting, it could have been done to bolster the MPD claim that James was frightened upon seeing the police wagon parked near the sidewalk.

Douglass told me that he never told the MPD or the FBI that he was parked up near the sidewalk; it would have made no sense for him to park up where he would have obstructed both pedestrian and incoming vehicular traffic. By parking farther back alongside the building and opposite the door, he

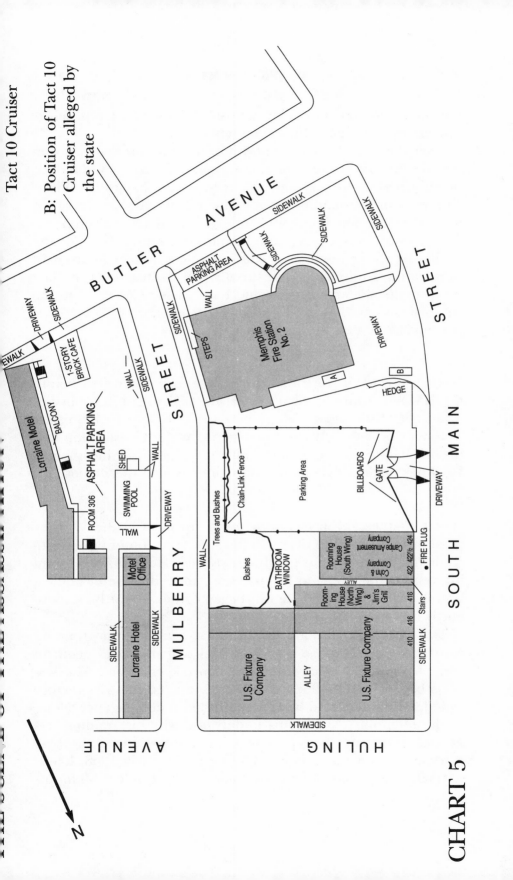

Tact 10 Cruiser

B: Position of Tact 10 Cruiser alleged by the state

CHART 5

was out of the way yet readily accessible to his TACT unit fellow officers in the event of an emergency.

After the shot, Douglass got out of the car and began to run toward the rear of the station, but, remembering his radio duty, he returned to the car and called in to headquarters. Others had exited the station through the northeast side door and went over the low fence and wall. Douglass remembered two officers, one with a gun drawn, running from the front of the station, crossing his line of vision about sixty feet in front of him within a minute of the shooting. If he had been parked up near the sidewalk, they would have passed very close to the front of his car. They were nowhere near him.

Douglass agreed to testify.

FORMER FBI AGENT ARTHUR MURTAGH, who had testified before the HSCA as to the bureau's extensive COINTELPRO activities against Dr. King, agreed to take the stand. His profound disillusionment over the bureau's disregard for the Constitution and his first-hand knowledge of the bureau's illegal activities against Dr. King made Murtagh an invaluable asset to the defense.

WHEN I HAD BEGUN MY EXAMINATION OF THE FILES in the attorney general's office in the Criminal Justice Center Building, Investigator Jim Smith was assigned to assist me. He had a long-term interest in the case, and his assistance proved to be of immeasurable value. Gradually, Smith began to talk about his experiences in 1968.

As a young policeman, he attended a clandestine training course run in Memphis. It covered such activities as riot control and physical and electronic surveillance techniques. The sessions began in late 1967 and were conducted in strict secrecy by federal trainers paid by one or another federal agency. None of the Memphis participants understood why the training was necessary, because Memphis had never experienced the type of riots seen in other cities. The events of early 1968, like a self-fulfilling prophecy, caused some of those select Memphis policemen to rethink their reactions at the time. Perhaps Holloman knew something that they didn't. Some of this training was conducted in secret facilities, the location of which was not even known by the participants, who were picked up at police headquarters and driven in a van (from which it was not possible to see outside) directly inside the training facility somewhere in Memphis. The Memphis officers couldn't understand the reason for the cloak and dagger behavior. It occurred to me that these were typical of the training sessions mentioned earlier that the CIA conducted during this period for selected city and county police forces. Such sessions were coordinated by its Office of Security (OS), often in conjunction with the FBI and army intelligence which had similar programs.

Smith also told me of a shadowy federal contract agent who was assigned to run some of these sessions. Cooper, who went by the name of Coop, arrived in January 1968. Jim thought it strange that, unlike the other trainers, Coop didn't stay at an up-market hotel but rather at the Ambassador Hotel on South Main Street, in the area of Jim's Grill. He remembered meeting Coop at Jim's Grill, in the Arcade Restaurant, and at the Green Beetle. When Smith asked why he "hung out" in such places, Coop replied that this was where he had to go to get information he needed. Coop drew detailed maps of the area, and told Smith that he was with army intelligence before he became an FBI agent. He had been dismissed because of a drinking problem, and he seemed to drift into this contract work. It occurred to Smith that Coop was really on some sort of intelligence gathering mission and that the training activity was a cover.

Coop dropped out of sight just before the assassination. Smith never saw him again.

Since there was considerable confusion about where Dr. King stayed in his previous trips to Memphis, I asked Jim Smith what he knew. He knew that on at least one occasion—the evening of March 18, 1968—Dr. King stayed at the Rivermont. Smith knew this because he was assisting a surveillance monitoring team. The unit operated with the collaboration of the hotel and placed microphones throughout the suite. The conversations in Dr. King's penthouse suite were monitored from a van parked across the street from the hotel. Since Smith hadn't placed the devices he didn't know exactly where they were. Another source—who must remain nameless—described the layout to me. Every room in Dr. King's suite was bugged, even the bathroom. My source said they had microphones in the elevators, under the table where he ate his breakfast, in the conference room next to his suite, and in all the rooms of his entourage. Even the balcony was covered by a parabolic mike mounted on top of the van. That mike was designed to pick up conversations without including a lot of extraneous noise because it used microwaves that allowed it to zero in on conversations.

The surveillance team had about a dozen microphones—"bugs"—each transmitting on a different frequency, which prevented feedback. The multiple bugs enhanced the recording by providing a stereo effect, which was a trick allegedly learned from the movie industry. There was a repeater transmitter mounted on top of the hotel, which picked up each transmission and relayed it to one of the voice-activated recorders in the van. The recorders were all labeled according to where their respective bugs were located, and a light on the control panel came on when activity was being recorded from a particular bug. The person monitoring listened to it for a moment to decide whether something was being said that needed to be reported immediately. If it didn't seem urgent, it was simply recorded and at the end of the shift it was sent to the office to be transcribed and filed for future reference.

The surveillance detection equipment generally available wasn't sophisticated enough to pick up the bugs used, because they emitted a very weak signal. In fact, they transmitted the signal only about forty or fifty feet, to the rooftop repeater. My source said that there was nothing on the market at that time that would allow them to pick up such a weak signal.

The source said the repeater on the roof picked up the weak signal and amplified it many times before transmitting it to the van. Since the bugs could transmit about fifty feet and the ceilings in King's suite were about eight feet high with the repeater directly above them, there was forty feet or so to spare.

If Dr. King hadn't been on the top floor, the repeater would have been placed in the room directly above him or in one of the rooms on either side of his room.

I was advised that this surveillance effort wasn't undertaken to learn about Dr. King's strategies. The intelligence operation was mounted to catch him in sexually compromising situations which could be exploited at the right time.

At the time of the surveillance Jim Smith was detailed to special services and assigned to the MPD intelligence bureau. He said he actually acted as a gofer for the two federal agents who ran the surveillance and manned the headphones. They told him that they were instructed to obtain any incriminating information they could about Dr. King's personal activities, plans, and movements. They operated from a van parked near the hotel. This confirmed what I had suspected for years.

Dr. King also stayed at the Rivermont on the night of March 28, just after the march. As mentioned earlier, he was routed there by the MPD, led by motorcycle lieutenant Marion Nichols, who also arranged for his suite. Although Smith wasn't detailed to the surveillance team on that evening, it is reasonable to assume that the same surveillance program was in effect.

Smith, of course, was aware that the bureau had electronically surveilled Dr. King all over the country, and he quite rightly believed that these activities were no longer a secret. He may not have appreciated that the bureau had always denied there had been any electronic surveillance in Memphis. Illegal electronic surveillance conducted so close to the time of the assassination wasn't an operation with which the bureau would want to be associated. At the time Smith and I assumed that the surveillance was being conducted by the FBI, because the operation appeared to have their "M.O." stamped all over it.

I now understood why Dr. King was routed to the Rivermont on March 28 (where he had no reservation) instead of the Peabody (where he was supposed to stay that evening). The change had never made sense to me because the Peabody was sufficiently removed from the violence and was accessible. Lt. Marion Nichols wasn't available for an interview at any time before the trial. When interviewed subsequently he denied any personal or departmental responsibility for the decision to go to the Rivermont, stating that it was a decision made by someone in Dr. King's party.

After checking with his chief, Fred Wall, who had no idea what he would say but told him to go ahead and just tell the truth, Jim Smith agreed to testify.

Smith also recalled the outbreak of violence in the march of March 28 when he was part of a phalanx of police officers stretching across South Main Street at McCall as the marchers came up Beale Street. He said that he and his fellow officers were told not to break ranks even though some isolated individuals between them and the main line of the march began to break windows.

The violent disruption of that march was of interest because there were indications that *provocateurs* were present. This was the only violent march ever led by Dr. King, the violence coming apparently from within the group itself. It necessitated his return to Memphis on April 3, when he was moved to a highly visible accommodation in a most vulnerable motel where he wouldn't normally have stayed.

Rev. Jim Lawson's recollections dovetailed with Jim Smith's. He remembered leading the marchers up Beale Street and out to Main, where they were confronted by riot police. This was ominous in itself to those committed to a peaceful march, but then Lawson saw a group of youths on the sidewalk in the area between the marchers and the police. He knew the Invaders and most of the other young black activists but did not recognize any of these youths as being from Memphis. They had begun to break shop windows, yet the police remained impassively in place, just watching.

Lawson knew then that the police were going to use the gang activity as a justification to turn on the marchers. He stopped the march and tried to turn the line around, worried as much about Dr. King's safety as anything else. King didn't want to leave but eventually let himself be spirited away by Bernard Lee and Ralph Abernathy.

On another tack Jim Lawson agreed to travel to Washington to speak with Walter Fauntroy, intending to explore the entire

HSCA investigation with him, and assess his willingness to help. Lawson and I agreed to meet in Memphis in late December.

THE DEFENSE HAD TO BE CONCERNED about the statement of the prosecution's only eyewitness. Under our rules of procedure, in Stephens's absence his official statement could be read into the record. His drunkenness wouldn't be evident in a statement taken after the event. He would have to be impeached.

I saw Grace Walden, Stephens's common-law wife, on November 29 at the convalescent home where she now lived. She again confirmed that Charlie Stephens was drunk on the afternoon of April 4 and that he didn't see anything. This corroborated information already gathered through interviews with Wayne Chastain, MPD captain Jewell Ray and homicide detective Roy Davis and his partner, lieutenant Tommy Smith. Captain Ray had gone into the rooming house before 6:30 p.m. He was unable to interview Charlie Stephens because he was so drunk. Detective Davis tried to interview Stephens that evening too but also found he was simply too drunk, and lieutenant Smith confirmed that he had tried to interview Stephens on that evening but found him incoherent and barely able to stand up.

Tommy Smith offered another unsettling revelation relating to a photograph I found in the attorney general's file showing a lump just below Dr. King's shoulder blade. It appeared to be where the death slug had come to rest just under the skin (see photograph #16.) Smith confirmed that fact and said that he pinched the skin and rolled what appeared to him to be an intact slug beneath his fingers. He said that at the time he was certain they had a good evidentiary bullet.

The death slug in the clerk's office was in three fragments and the official story that had evolved was that it had **always** been in three fragments. However, in the HSCA volumes there was a photograph of the slug, apparently taken at the time of removal by Dr. Francisco, showing it to be in one piece at that point. Francisco's report referred to a single slug.

* * *

WHEN I INTERVIEWED CAPTAIN JEWELL RAY I told him that I had noticed in one report that he had met with an army intelligence officer named Bray on the evening of the murder. He confirmed the meeting. He said that Bray was the liaison with the Tennessee National Guard.

Jewell Ray was Lt. E. H. Arkin's superior in the MPD intelligence bureau. He said that Arkin was so close to the FBI that he (Jewell) locked his desk drawer to prevent documents from being routinely turned over to Bill Lawrence of the local FBI field office. Captain Ray resented the FBI's practice of taking everything and giving little or nothing in return. Arkin wouldn't agree to be interviewed before the trial.

CALVIN BROWN HAD LIVED AT THE LORRAINE after the assassination. I asked Ken Herman to locate him to see if he knew or heard anything during that time about the death of Mrs. Bailey or the killing itself. I eventually interviewed him sitting in Herman's car in front of Brown's house. Brown surprised me by declaring that he had heard that Jowers, the owner of Jim's Grill, did it. He couldn't recall the source of his information.

I LOCATED A TELEPHONE REPAIRMAN named Hasel Huckaby who according to a supplement to the MPD report was working near the scene of the crime on April 4. Huckaby said that on April 4 he and his partner, Paul Clay, were assigned to complete some work at Fred P. Gattas's premises on the corner of Huling and South Main Streets. At one point Huckaby noticed a well-dressed though apparently intoxicated person sitting on the steps by a side entrance of Gattas's place on Huling. Parked across the street was a plain dark-blue sedan that Huckaby associated with the man. Huckaby said that the man would occasionally stagger over to him and pass some inane remark. He felt there was something phoney about the person. He was too well-dressed for the neighborhood and his behavior didn't ring true.

The man was still there when Huckaby and Clay left late

that afternoon. Huckaby gave a routine statement following the assassination but was puzzled as to why MPD detective J. D. Hamby wanted him to detail each minute of his working assignments for a period of two weeks prior to the day of the assassination. About five years later, he was working on a line in the central headquarters of the police department when he saw Lt. Hamby. On impulse he asked Hamby if he had ever found out who the "drunk" was whom he saw on April 4, 1968. He was told that the man's name was Smith and that he was really an FBI agent under cover. If true, this was the first indication of an FBI presence at the scene prior to the shooting.

Apparently this was information that Huckaby shouldn't have learned—later he received a package in the mail containing half a burned match, half of a smoked cigarette, and rattles from a rattlesnake. After asking around, he came to believe that this parcel was a threat; a warning for him to keep his mouth shut about what he had learned if he wanted to finish the rest of his life. I found it interesting that none of this information appeared in his MPD statement. Huckaby agreed to testify.

Another person whose name appeared in the MPD report with no apparent significance was Robert Hagerty, who at the time was employed at the Lucky Electric Supply Company on Butler, just behind the Lorraine. During the afternoon of April 4 he noticed a sedan parked diagonally across from his shop just off Butler Street in such a way as to allow anyone inside a clear view of the balcony of the Lorraine Motel. There were two men dressed in civilian clothes sitting in the car, holding walkie-talkies. Hagerty didn't recognize the men as local detectives. The issue of walkie-talkies to MPD officers at that time was very limited. This was another indication that they could have been federal officers.

A second surveillance team, then, seemed to be operating on Butler, so that the Lorraine was literally sandwiched in between the two posts. We had apparently stumbled upon the first indications of a federal surveillance presence in the proximity of the Lorraine within hours of the assassination.

This surveillance presence must be viewed along with five

other factors: (1) the removal of security for Dr. King, (2) the removal of Detective Redditt from his surveillance detail, (3) the transfer of firemen Newsom and Wallace, (4) the pullback of the TACT units, particularly TACT 10 and (5) the presence of Chief MacDonald in the area of the Lorraine with a walkie-talkie in hand.

Chief William Crumby had told me in 1988 that a pullback of the TACT units had occurred and that the request came in "the day before." As to who made the request, he said, as noted earlier, "It could have been Kyles." He noted, however, that the emergency vehicles were under the direct command of Inspector Sam Evans. Crumby was willing to testify to what he knew about the pullback. Inspector Sam Evans had died in 1993.

I was astounded to hear for the first time in late 1992 that Dr. King had always been provided with a small personal security force of black homicide detectives when he came to Memphis. Its very existence and function had never been made public or mentioned. The only security unit referred to by the HSCA or otherwise publicly known was the squad of white detectives formed and removed by Inspector Don Smith on the first day of Dr. King's last visit.

It was obviously important to speak with the small cadre of black homicide detectives on the force in 1968. After two interviews with officers who were not on duty on the 4th, Tom Marshall and Wendell Robinson, I met with one who was: Captain Jerry Williams, now retired from the MPD. He described how as a young homicide detective in the 1960s he was given the task by Inspector Don Smith to put together a team of four black plainclothes homicide officers to provide security for Dr. King when he came to Memphis. Such visits were infrequent; King had been in the city only a handful of times before the visits connected with the sanitation workers' strike. The four-man team would apparently remain with Dr. King wherever he went, on a twenty-four-hour detail, staying in the same hotel. Williams recalled organizing a group on two previous occasions when Dr. King was in the city. Jim Lawson subsequently told me that he remembered this group of detectives as sincere and proud of being assigned to guard Dr. King.

I told Williams that for a number of years I had been very interested in where Dr. King stayed on his various visits to Memphis. In light of the FBI-generated criticism of him prior to his decision to stay at the Lorraine on his last visit, I wanted to know whether he had, in fact, ever stayed at that motel before.

Williams said that on the previous visits he remembered Dr. King staying at the Rivermont and the Admiral Benbow Inn but didn't recall him ever staying overnight at the Lorraine Motel. He said, however, that he might take a room there to receive local blacks who could visit more comfortably than in the white-owned hotels. (At that time, only a couple of motels didn't exclude blacks.) As Williams spoke, I remembered seeing a photograph taken by Ernest Withers of Dr. King during such a visit standing at the door of room 307.

"I was always troubled that I wasn't instructed to put together the security team for Dr. King's last visit," Williams said. He was certain that no one else had been given the assignment because he had discussed it with various black officers after the killing. When asked whether he ever asked Don Smith why the detail wasn't formed, he smiled and gently said no, that it wasn't something you would do in those days. Back then a black police officer couldn't even arrest a white person. The most he could do was to detain a suspect and call for a white officer to arrive.

Williams had formed the detail at Inspector Smith's request as recently as March 18, when Dr. King came to town to address a strike rally for the first time. On that visit Dr. King stayed in the top floor suite at the Holiday Inn Rivermont Hotel, and Detective Williams and his team posted a man in front of his door and stayed in nearby rooms. Williams believed that a unit was also in place on the evening of March 28, after the march broke up in violence, but he didn't recall who formed it, speculating that it was R. J. Turner, who had since died.

In his testimony before the HSCA, Inspector Smith stated that he had put together a security group that met Dr. King at the airport and followed him to the Lorraine on April 3. This detail consisted entirely of white detectives. They were Lt. George Kelly Davis, Lt. William Schultz, and Detective Ronald B. Howell, joined by Inspector J. S. Gagliano and lieutenants Hamby and Tucker at the Lorraine. Not one of them had any previous history of being assigned to Dr. King, nor would they have been regarded as suitable in terms of relating to the civil rights leader or his purposes. But since information about this previous black security detail had been concealed until now, Smith's white security force was never viewed in its proper context.

The detail was removed at Smith's own request later that same afternoon when he stated that he believed that the King party wasn't cooperating with them. (Jim Lawson and Hosea Williams maintain that there was no lack of cooperation from the King party.)

According to the HSCA report, when Inspector Smith asked for permission to withdraw the detail, chief of detectives William Huston allegedly conferred with Chief MacDonald who gave permission for the withdrawal, though MacDonald maintained that he did not recall the request, or removal. The HSCA also noted that Director Holloman maintained that he knew nothing about these decisions[8] and further stated that it ". . . tried to determine if Dr. King was provided protection by the MPD on earlier trips to Memphis but it could not resolve the question."[9]

This wasn't surprising, since no one from the FBI or the HSCA ever questioned Jerry Williams or any member of the previous security details he pulled together: Elmo Berkley, Melvyn Burgess, Wendell Robinson, Tom Marshall, R. J. Turner, Caro Harris, Ben Whitney, and Emmett J. Winters.

Williams was certain that if his usual team had been in place it could not and would not have been removed as easily as could some other white officers. The prosecution would say it was another coincidence. I regarded the omission of black security officers on Dr. King's last visit as one of the most sinister discoveries yet.

*　　*　　*

I SPENT SIX HOURS WITH MORRIS DAVIS in Birmingham on November 28. As previously mentioned years earlier, I had acquired an affidavit in which Davis contended that he had become aware of a plot to kill Dr. King involving Birmingham medical doctor Gus Prosch, a Frank Liberto, Ralph Abernathy and Fred Shuttlesworth. The HSCA had summarized Davis's allegations in its report, before dismissing them. Though giving little credence to most of his allegations, I was interested to learn what he knew about any involvement of Frank Liberto.

He said that in 1967 and 1968 he frequented the Gulas Lounge in Birmingham. There he became friendly with a Dr. Gus Prosch, who some years later would be convicted for illegal gun dealing and income tax evasion. Prosch introduced him to a man named Frank Liberto.

It soon became clear to me that Davis wasn't talking about any of the three Memphis Frank Libertos we had come across, but another Frank Liberto, whom he described as being dark haired and dark complected, between thirty-five and forty years old, about six feet tall and around 190 pounds. This Liberto allegedly had businesses in both Memphis and New Orleans.

Davis had earlier in the 1960s acted as a paid informant for the Secret Service, in counterfeiting matters, and the Drug Enforcement Agency (DEA). He said he assisted the Birmingham police in their investigation of the bombing of the 16th Avenue Church in which four children died, and they fed him information on various matters which interested him, some of which he would pass on to his federal agency contacts.

Davis maintained that the DEA files showed that one Frank Liberto was part of a major international drug trafficking operation associated with the Luigi Greco family in Montreal and that his operation spread from Corpus Christi, Texas, to Memphis, New Orleans, and Los Angeles, with family contacts in Detroit and Toronto. He said that Liberto was based primarily in New Orleans and had a home on Lake Ponchartrain outside of New Orleans.

Davis said that he had gone to Memphis in 1977–78 at his own expense to investigate the King assassination as part of some informal arrangement with the HSCA. In Memphis he met a Liberto flunky he knew only as Ed. He first saw Ed coming out of Frank's [Frank Liberto's] liquor store at 327 South Main Street. Ed outlined the gunrunning and drug operations of Frank Liberto. He said that guns were smuggled into Latin America over the border near Corpus Christi, Texas, in exchange for cocaine and marijuana. Ed also said that Liberto ran a number of gambling operations in various sections of Memphis.

Ed then took Morris Davis to the Liberto business where Ezell Smith worked. He told Davis that around 7:30 p.m. on March 30 James delivered to those premises the rifle he had purchased earlier that day. It was kept there until the morning of April 4, when it was fired once and the cartridge left in the gun. Its sole purpose was to be a throwdown gun for the cover-up of the killing.

I stiffened. Once again, the same building was being raised. The photograph of that building and its handwritten note flashed in my mind. Had Davis been the source of that photocopy? Subsequently, he was to say that he was not, although there was some similarity in the handwriting. (As mentioned earlier, the building was the one in the photograph which turned out to be the same one also allegedly referred to by Ezell Smith and of course owned by a relative of produce man Frank Liberto.)

Davis said that he confirmed at the Memphis land records office that most of the buildings in the 300 to 400 block of South Main Street—including the Merchant's Lounge, the liquor store and the Green Beetle—were owned by Frank Liberto, although a number were in his father's name. His father, according to Davis, was also Frank Liberto (Frank H.), who lived on the Memphis-Arlington Road in a large estate purchased in 1974. Davis knew nothing more about the father. I knew that the person at this address was auto dealer Frank Liberto, who in 1992 was in his eighties. There was no way this Liberto could have been the father of the Frank Liberto who owned the liquor store and the Green Beetle, who in 1992 was dead but would have also been around eighty years old.

Ed said that a person named Jim Bo Stewart handled business for Liberto when he was away. He also confirmed that

James was a patsy/decoy and that they meant to kill him after the job was completed. Ed claimed at one point to have been sent inside the prison by Frank Liberto on an arranged drug charge to kill James in 1969.

Davis then went on to say that some details that HSCA investigator Al Hack gave him began to corroborate what he himself had observed in March 1968 as well as what he had learned from Ed and his own DEA sources. Hack told him that he had obtained two phone numbers called by James before he left Puerto Vallarta for Los Angeles, which numbers appeared to be related to the Liberto family.

Davis said that after taking in all of his information, the HSCA buried his story and canceled his testimony on the day before it was scheduled.

There was no way that we could use any of Morris's information without obtaining specific corroboration. Even if the judge would have allowed his testimony, it would have been irresponsible to put this man on the stand. Davis understood and offered his full assistance in seeking corroboration. He suggested that I speak with Robert Long and Oscar Kent, each of whom knew about some aspect of the story. Davis also agreed to let me have his entire set of files on the case.

I couldn't locate Robert Long, and though Oscar Kent was still in the area I wasn't able to catch up with him at this time. I set about attempting to see what could be corroborated.

As for the gambling dens Davis described, S. O. Blackburn, a former MPD officer who had been assigned to investigate illegal gambling operations, later confirmed that there was a good deal of it going on during the time. At least two of the Frank Libertos (produce man and liquor man) and another member of the Liberto family were involved, and one of the gambling dens frequented was the Check Off (formerly the Tremont Cafe) which had been owned at the time by Loyd Jowers.

Ken Herman said that former Birmingham detective Rich Gianetti remembered Davis as a person who sold information and whose accounts were truthful. Gianetti also remembered a Frank Liberto who said he was from New Orleans and who visited the Gulas Lounge and spent money liberally. He said he was a good dresser and his description roughly matched the one Davis gave. When I later spoke with Gianetti, however, he said he only vaguely remembered the name of Frank Liberto.

Davis had maintained that HSCA counsel and staff had visited him at various times and he had provided the names and dates of these visits. Since these men were federal employees, there would be a public record of their expense requests and payments. An analysis of the General Services Administration (GSA) disbursement records for special and select committees obtained by D. C. investigator Kevin Walsh basically confirmed Davis's recollections and notes. It was obvious that the HSCA had devoted a considerable amount of time to Morris Davis. The principal HSCA investigator assigned to Davis was Al Hack. Subsequently I spoke to Hack, who admitted that Davis had appeared to have credibility as an informant for other federal agencies and that he did trade in information but try as they might, they could not confirm Davis's allegations. Hack's partner in the investigation was an Atlanta policeman named Rosie Walker who had since died. I suspected his files on the case might help us and asked our Atlanta private investigator to try to obtain them.

Aside from the Liberto allegations, some of which would be corroborated, Davis's statements about Abernathy, Shuttlesworth, and a range of other people and events, were, for one reason or another, not believable. Whether this was the result of honest mistakes, deliberate fabrication or official disinformation was not clear. Davis stood by his story and said that he recorded a number of his conversations with HSCA staff which would substantiate his claims. I could not listen to them because the equipment required had long ago ceased to be manufactured, though Davis's lawyer undertook to try to find a compatible machine.

THE EVIDENCE WE HAD UNEARTHED up until now tied together and strengthened evidence discovered earlier. Some startling contradictions to the official case had developed. There could no longer be any doubt that the chief prosecution witness had been drunk and unable to observe anything. Also it was clear that Chastain's earlier information about there being a change of Dr. King's room at the Lorraine was correct. Somehow he had been mysteriously moved from a secluded, ground-level courtyard room to a highly exposed balcony room. Lorraine employee Olivia Hayes recalled this and then Leon Cohen confirmed it, recounting his conversation at the time with Walter Bailey, the owner of the Lorraine.

As a result of the observations of Solomon Jones, James Orange, and Earl Caldwell, it now appeared conclusive that the fatal shot was fired from the brush area and not from the bathroom. We had seen evidence of the fresh footprints found in that brush area, which as Kay Black and James Orange alleged fourteen years earlier, was cut down and cleared early the morning after the killing, possibly along with an inconveniently placed tree branch.

A number of suspicious events were confirmed. The only two black firemen had been taken off their posts the night before the killing. These reassignments—considered along with the removal of black detective Ed Redditt from his surveillance post and the failure of the MPD to form the usual security squad of black detectives for Dr. King—were ominous. The emergency TACT units were also pulled back, with TACT 10 being moved from the Lorraine to the fire station. Finally, on Butler and Huling streets bordering the Lorraine, there were apparently surveillance details of some federal agency that afternoon.

In addition, for the first time evidence had been uncovered that the CB hoax broadcast, which drew police attention to the northeastern side of the city, had been transmitted from downtown near the scene of the killing.

Former FBI agent Arthur Murtagh personally confirmed a range of harassment and surveillance activity by the bureau against Dr. King, and MPD special services/intelligence bureau officer Jim Smith confirmed that Dr. King's usual suite at the Rivermont was under electronic surveillance by federal agents.

There were increasing indications that members of the Liberto family at least in Memphis and New Orleans, were implicated in the killing. For example, we learned that a rifle connected with the killing—perhaps the murder weapon—appeared to have been stored in the premises of a Liberto business only a few blocks from the Lorraine.

Jim's Grill owner Loyd Jowers, whose behavior had always seemed curious, seemed increasingly likely to have played a role. Not only was his involvement rumored locally, but a bailbondsman quoted one of Jowers's waitresses as pointing the finger at her boss. Taxi driver McCraw had earlier claimed that Jowers showed him a rifle he had under the counter in the grill that he contended was the murder weapon.

21

Making A Case: December 1992

ON DECEMBER 1, 1992, in St. Louis, Susan Wadsworth, a friend of FBI and HSCA informant Oliver Patterson, who had since died, confirmed her knowledge of his covert, dirty-tricks activities but refused to testify at the television trial for personal reasons. I also spoke with St. Louis television reporter John Auble who confirmed the incident, discussed earlier, where *New York Times* reporter Tony Marro was sent to a St. Louis hotel to interview Patterson and obtain derogatory information about Mark Lane. Auble, who had filmed the incident, was willing to testify and agreed to provide the footage.

The next day in New York I talked with Bill Schaap of the Institute for Media Analysis. Schaap and his colleague Ellen Ray (no relation to James) had agreed to be our experts on the role and use of the media in this case. I asked them to analyze the media's treatment of Dr. King during his last year, as well as that of James Earl Ray from the time of his identification to his conviction. I thought it was important to reveal that government manipulation of the media was part and parcel of the ongoing conspiracy. I intended to put Bill Schaap on the stand. He had an international reputation on the political use of the mass media and had testified as an expert in the *Spycatcher* case in Australia, where the British government had attempted to stop publication of former MI-5 agent Peter Wright's book.

FOR SOME TIME I'd been interested in finding out whether any foreign intelligence agencies had any information in their archives about the assassination of Dr. King. The previous summer I had traveled to Moscow to meet with ranking KGB officials who had come to treat long-held secrets as a commercial commodity and a source of income. Despite their willingness to search, it appeared that they knew little about the assassination.

On December 4 I flew to Paris to meet with French lawyer (avocat) Marcel Sorrequere and Pierre Marion, the former head of SDECE—the French equivalent of the CIA. Sorrequere had been personal lawyer to French president Charles DeGualle as well as to SDECE superintendent Ducret, who in 1968 was head of SDECE and had since died. Marion insisted on intense secrecy. He agreed to tap his sources in French and Israeli intelligence. At one point he said to me, "You are in great danger." I realized that he had already concluded that some part of the U.S. intelligence community had been involved in, if not responsible for, the assassination of King. Marion had no reason to overstate himself. Sometime afterward France went through a turbulent change of government. Marion's inside sources became very nervous about discussing anything sensitive. His Israeli sources claimed to have no information.

BACK IN MEMPHIS, after many tears and much soul searching, Betty Spates had finally agreed to tell all. In an interview with Ken Herman, she revealed that she had had an affair with Loyd Jowers which began when she first went to work at the grill in

1967 when she was about seventeen years old. She said she only "helped out" and couldn't be formally employed in a place where beer was served because of her age. She also worked part-time across the street at the Seabrook Wallpaper Company. She said that she believed that on the day of the assassination she went to the grill around 5:30 a.m. to help Jowers prepare for the day. As was their custom, she thought that they went to the small storage room at the back of the kitchen, where Jowers kept a cot, and "fooled around." Jowers would sometimes also use the room for a catnap in the afternoon. On other occasions he would go home during his break—usually around 2:30 p.m.—or go off to the Tremont Cafe on Calhoun, which he also owned.

That afternoon Spates came over from Seabrook to Jim's Grill several times. She knew that prostitutes had been working in the Huling/Mulberry area and was determined to keep an eye on Loyd. She said that he had been spending a lot of time in the backyard that week and she was worried that he might be two-timing her. Around 2:30 in the afternoon Jowers announced that he was closing up for a while and ordered everyone out, including her.

She went back to Seabrook and returned again around 5:00. Around 6:00 she noticed that Jowers had disappeared from the grill and she went to the kitchen to look for him. She was standing in the kitchen when she heard what sounded like a shot and then, within seconds, Jowers burst into the kitchen through the back door with a rifle. "What are you doing with the gun?" she asked. He said, "If I catch you with a nigger, I'll kill you." She was frightened. "Loyd, I ain't doing nothing," she said. He said softly, "I wouldn't hurt you."

Jowers was pale, "real white," and nervous. In front of her he broke the gun down into at least two pieces and then without a word held them close to his chest and walked briskly through the grill and out the front door. She watched through the front window as he turned right and walked the short distance to his brown and white station wagon parked north of the grill. She saw him open the hatch of the wagon and put the pieces of the gun inside. He then came back into the grill. The entire series of events—from the time he entered the kitchen until he put the pieces of the gun in the wagon and came back inside—took only seconds.

Spates recalled that Jowers's wife used to come to Memphis every Thursday to have her hair done; Spates assumed that she also did so on that day, and at the time she thought that was the reason for Jowers's more than usual efforts to keep her out of the grill. He was always more cautious on Thursdays. Jowers's wife owned the white Cadillac that was parked that day close to the fire hydrant, behind James's Mustang, but Spates wasn't certain whether his wife (who has since died) had parked it herself or whether Jowers had done so, as he claimed.

She also remembered finding around this time a large sum of cash, "more money than I ever saw," in an old suitcase in a disused stove in the kitchen.

Spates was afraid of Jowers. Jowers told her that he'd kill her if she ever talked about what she had seen. Over the years she'd been visited at each new job by Jowers's "heavy," Willie Akins. She believed that this was Jowers's way of telling her that he was keeping an eye on her. She also said that in 1969 he bought a house for her on Oakview to keep her quiet. It was put in her sisters' names because she was underage.

Betty Spates elaborated on her story when I interviewed her on December 16. She said she and her sisters Bobbi and Alda had begun to work at the grill in 1967. On the afternoon of April 4 she remembered waitresses Rosie Lee Dabney and Rosetta working in the morning but leaving around 3:30 p.m. She believed that Bobbi was there in the afternoon.

She said that during the time she was having an affair with Jowers he rented an apartment for her on Peabody. After the lease was up Jowers moved her upstairs to the rooming house for a while, and then in 1969 he bought the house on Oakview for her—or so he told her.

Then in the spring of 1969 she recalled that two men came by to visit at the new Oakview house, one of whom was black. They said that if she and her sisters would tell all they knew, they would get money, new identities, and be moved away. Betty didn't want to leave Memphis, so she refused. Since that time, she insisted no one had ever talked to her about this case other than in her discussions with Herman and me. Even on the night of the killing, when the police came in they told all the blacks in the grill, "You niggers don't know anything, get in the back." She said she and a number of the blacks went into the kitchen and were never interviewed.

She also remembered going through a marriage ceremony arranged by Jowers which was conducted in the Oakview house in November 1969 (Jowers, who she said had begun to drink heavily in 1968, divorced his first wife around this time).

One evening in January 1972 when Betty was working at the Arcade Restaurant she met a Mexican named Luis Ortiz, whom she took home with her. Jowers must have seen his car parked in front of the house; he came in, drew a gun, and took Ortiz away with him. Betty never saw Ortiz again and believed that Jowers killed him that night. His car remained there for some time.

Betty said that Jowers eventually put out a contract on her life. She said Willie Akins was supposed to do the job but mistook her sister Bobbi for her and tried to get Bobbi to go out with him so he could better arrange the killing. When Akins did finally meet Betty, he realized his mistake. During a subsequent interview she provided details of what she said were two attempts by Akins to kill her by shooting at her on one occasion and again at her and her two sons in 1983. I resolved to learn more about Akins.

Betty told me that Jowers had remarried within the last year and moved to the country. He had forgotten all of his black friends. She currently had no contact with him but seemed relieved when I told her that we didn't believe that Jowers had actually shot Dr. King. It was obvious that she still had some feelings for Jowers. She said that until he remarried earlier that year he had provided support for two of her children.

I had instructed Ken Herman to interview Rosie Lee Dabney, another waitress from Jim's Grill. A few days later he reported on his interview with her. Rosie Lee was off at the time of the shooting and knew nothing about the gun, but she was aware of the affair between Jowers and Betty. She confirmed serving eggs and sausage that afternoon to a stranger.

In interviews, Bobbi told us that she went to work early on the day of the shooting. She remembered that a priest came into the grill early in the morning asking where a certain church was located. She thought that was strange since there were no churches in that downtown area. She also remembered seeing James Earl Ray come in for a cup of coffee during the afternoon.

She was sure Jowers had gone out for a while in the morning because she remembered that Rosie Lee had to pay the beer man when he came in between 9:00 and 10:00. She said the beer man pulled into the spot where Jowers's old station wagon had been parked.

Bobbi also said that Jowers told her first thing that morning not to take breakfast up to Grace Walden, who lived in room 6-B on the second floor of the rooming house, as was her custom. He made it clear that he wanted no one to go upstairs into the rooming house on that day.

Jowers drove Bobbi to work the next day, April 5, in his old brown and white station wagon and told her that he had found the gun out back that was used to kill Dr. King and had turned it over to the police. He told her to be careful when she spoke about these events. Other than being interviewed by two men in 1968 who asked her if she saw Ray (not wanting to get involved she said no), no one had ever talked to her about the case.

James McCraw had stated that Jowers showed him a rifle in a box on a shelf under the cash register, contending that he had found it out back and later that he had turned it over to the police. Thus, if Betty ever raised a question, both Bobbi and McCraw would state that he'd told them about finding a gun and turning it in. It was a rudimentary cover-up at best, but Jowers probably thought it was better than nothing.

As for the Oakview house, Bobbi believed that she and her sister Alda had bought the house. She paid $200 for the $9,000 property purchase. The whole family lived in the house, and Jowers stayed there many times. Bobbi recalled that Jowers fired her soon after April 4, 1968, but did not remember any wedding of Betty and Jowers.

Bobbi confirmed that Jowers had also owned the Tremont Cafe on Calhoun, and MPD officer S. O. Blackburn disclosed that the cafe was a gambling den used by Jowers, both Frank Libertos and another member of the Liberto family. This information was the first indication that Jowers had any association with the Libertos.

Betty's other sister, Alda, refused to talk during this period.

The indications were that Jowers had no facility with a rifle. It also seemed clear that there were other people in the brush area and that the large footprints in the alley couldn't have belonged to the diminutive Jowers, who apparently usually had others do his dirty work. Jowers, then, seemed much more likely to be an accomplice than the shooter.

ON DECEMBER 5, Dale Dougherty called me from Waco, very excited. The hospital postmortem report on the death of his friend Bill Sartor had finally been pried loose after twenty-one years. It showed that Sartor had a lethal dose of methaqualone in his system when he died. Since Sartor had no history of any such drug use, Dougherty believed that it had been administered to him—either in the drinks he had at the Hickory Stick bar before he arrived home, or forcibly later that evening as he lay in bed.

Ken Abels, the Waco district attorney, officially declared the death a homicide. He assigned his chief investigator, J. C. Rappe, to work with Dougherty and coordinate the inquiry.

Since much of Sartor's work prior to and at the time of his death involved the killing of Dr. King and focused on Shelby County, Dougherty asked J. C. Rappe if he would formally request help from the Shelby County attorney general's investigative staff. This he did, requesting help from Shelby County attorney general's investigator Jim Smith who had been designated as that office's liaison to our work on the King case. Smith went to his chief who in turn secured the attorney general's permission for the cooperation.

I saw the investigation of Bill Sartor's death as being complementary to my inquiry into Dr. King's murder. The Waco investigation would be assisted by the knowledge I had about the King case, and I would have access to witnesses not previously available.

We went to see Robert Patrick Lyons, who Sartor had maintained was attacked by a Liberto hit man who held a knife to his throat and said he was ordered to kill him for helping Sartor learn things he had no business knowing. Lyons had earlier rebuffed Kenny and Dale Dougherty. Jim Smith and I, as a special counsel to the Sartor family, now would have several meetings with him. It was obvious that Lyons was still deathly afraid. He denied knowing any of the persons or the events concerning him described by Sartor.

In a session a few months later he told Jim Smith that he remembered Sartor calling him just before he died, saying he was coming to Memphis. Lyons thought Sartor mentioned the name of a person in the Waco area called Sam Termine with whom he was going to meet. When Dougherty mentioned this name to J. C. Rappe, it rang a bell. Termine was a club owner and one of Carlos Marcello's operatives in Waco. It was clear that Lyons knew far more than he was willing to admit.

DURING THIS TIME WE SEARCHED for Gene Pearson Crawford, who we learned from the attorney general's files was allegedly the "eggs and sausage" man who ate in Jim's Grill on the afternoon of the fourth and the morning of the fifth. (Now it appeared that although Jack Youngblood could possibly have been the person who successively visited attorney Russell X. Thompson and Reverends Latimer and Baltensprager on the morning of April 11, it was unlikely that he was, as we had earlier suspected, the "eggs and sausage" man.) Crawford was picked up by the police after Loyd Jowers called them on April 5, only to be promptly released. He had vanished, but when we found out that he was a drifter from Jackson, Tennessee, whose father had been known by the woman who managed the Ambassador Hotel, his potential significance greatly diminished. There was, however, no indication that Crawford was a gun collector, as FBI special agent in charge Jensen had maintained to Wayne Chastain was the case with the man whom they arrested.

KEN HERMAN CALLED former LL&L Produce Company vice president and Liberto partner James Latch, only to be told that he was under a doctor's care and that he couldn't discuss anything that happened in 1968. Besides, he said, he had suffered a heart attack and his memory was faulty.

Latch obviously knew a good deal. An FBI 302 report (302 reports are not signed statements but rather an FBI agent's summary of what a person allegedly said) on him in the attorney general's file confirmed that he was working at LL&L on the afternoon of April 4 and that he had a long scar on his neck. John McFerren's 302 report of the late-night interview the Sunday following the killing noted that McFerren had described the man who answered the phone and passed it over to "fat Frank" as "one of the bosses" and as having such a scar. He had to have been describing James Latch. I was determined to go to Mississippi to see Mr. Latch, but that would have to wait until after the trial.

I WAS AFRAID that Hickman might introduce statements of questionable validity from some of James's fellow prisoners. Under our rules, FBI 302 interview reports were admissable. When we asked James about particular individuals whose 302 interviews we had read, he genuinely seemed not to know them at all or only remotely. This included the informant Raymond Curtis, whose story, as previously noted, had been widely quoted by UPI in a wire service release. It would have taken UPI very little checking to learn that, though they were both in Jefferson City prison at the time, Curtis never knew James and that certainly James never spoke to him about anything. UPI's FBI contacts could have confirmed, however, that Curtis was well known to the bureau. Harold Weisberg obtained the FBI file on Curtis (C.A. 75-1996), and it revealed that he was determined to make a name for himself in this case. He apparently began his endeavors with an effort to defraud *Ebony* magazine by attempting to sell a false story of a "contract" offer to kill Dr. King. According to Weisberg, the FBI records even characterized Curtis as a "pathological liar,"[10] but this didn't deter the media from spreading his blatant lies about James, nor did it cause the bureau to reveal that it knew he was lying. Curtis's account reinforced the image they wanted of the lone assassin.

I obtained the testimony of one or more prisoners who actually knew James well. One was J. J. Maloney, a former multiple murderer and armed robber who had rehabilitated himself, becoming a published author and poet and a reporter for the *Kansas City Star.* He confirmed James's story about his escape in the bread box from Missouri State Penitentiary on April 23, and said positively that James was not a racist, that he kept to himself in prison, didn't use drugs, and had no problem with black inmates. When we asked him what he knew about particular prisoners who had made negative statements about James, he commented that those inmates didn't know James nor did they have contact with him. He questioned why prisoners who knew James well and moved in his circle weren't interviewed by the FBI.

Maloney was a find. He had been sent by the *Star* to cover the story of James's 1977 escape from Brushy Mountain. When he arrived, he saw upwards of fifty flack-jacketed, heavily armed FBI agents already on the scene. They had established a base camp, and some of them had gone into the hills where the escapees had fled. Maloney didn't know why they were there. James and the others were, after all, state prisoners, and there had been no call for federal assistance. He recalled that a highly vexed Tennessee governor Ray Blanton showed up and ordered the FBI out. When they didn't leave, he threatened to put them in the cell vacated by James.

Maloney agreed to testify.

Ken Herman and I met with another former inmate, Don Wolverton, at his automobile garage. Wolverton had shared a cell with James at Brushy Mountain off and on for three and a half years. He knew him well and liked him. He also confirmed that James wasn't a racist, didn't use drugs, and had no difficulty with blacks. After he and James were thrown in the hole for eighteen months following a botched escape attempt, they celled alongside each other.

In 1981 James had been the victim of a stabbing at Brushy Mountain Penitentiary, allegedly by some members of a militant black organization—the Akabulon group. Wolverton remembered that three or four days before the stabbing, Doc Walker, one of the assailants, was moved next to James. Two days before the incident, Wolverton (who had put in for a transfer nearer home one and a half years earlier) was suddenly transferred to Nashville. Wolverton said this was ominous because he always looked out for James.

Wolverton agreed to take the stand.

In conversations with one of my investigators Jim Johnson, Jules Ricco Kimbel, expanding on the story he had earlier told English producer John Edginton's researchers, said that he had piloted a Cessna owned by a company controlled by Carlos Marcello and flown two shooters in and out of Memphis on April 4. He provided specific details of his route—Three Rivers, Detroit, Atlanta, New Orleans, and west Memphis. I had doubts about Kimbel's truthfulness. When Canadian investigator Alec Lomonosof checked on the street where Kimbel originally said he took James to get identification documents, it was clear that he was mistaken or fabricating. Later, after viewing photographs of James, he decided that James was not the person he took to get identification. Further, in his story about flying in the shooters from Canada, he said he took off from an airport near Three Rivers, an area he said the CIA used for training operations. Eventually we learned that apparently no such training activity was conducted there.

However, some of Kimbel's information seemed to have the ring of truth, because certain aspects dovetailed with information we had obtained from other sources.

Kimbel continually referred to the Liberto family, and in particular, Sal Liberto of New Orleans, whom we knew to be one of Frank Camille Liberto's brothers. He stated that Sal was connected to Carlos Marcello. Kimbel took "assignments" from H. L. Hunt's Placid Oil Company over a period of twenty years, and he referred to Hunt as an implacable foe of Dr. King who, with Leander Perez, the powerful Louisiana racist, wanted King out of the way.

Kimbel described Marcello as having extensive business operations in Texas. He said that in all likelihood Marcello and Hunt were in business together in Louisiana and possibly elsewhere. Kimbel confirmed knowing Sal Liberto and said he was aware that Hunt's chief of staff, John Curington, posing as a Dallas private investigator, handled the contracts for a variety of unpleasant tasks the old man required.

Of great interest was Kimbel's description of a hunting camp where he said H. L. Hunt would occasionally meet and play cards with Carlos Marcello. Investigator Jim Johnson had once told me that he remembered being taken by his uncle to an east Texas ranch in the 1950s where he and his uncle and the owner of the ranch, Monroe Walridge, went dove hunting and where he saw Hunt and Hoover playing poker.

Writer Anthony Summers had earlier shown me his research on J. Edgar Hoover, which included evidence of Hoover's connections to the Texas oil barons, even to the point of them making gifts to him of shares in a number of their companies. He provided a copy of Hoover's last will and testament, which showed his oil company shareholdings. Summers also documented Hoover's closeness to senior mob leaders and their control over him. Among those figures exerting power over the nation's top law enforcement officer was Carlos Marcello.

In late October I had instructed Johnson to make initial contact with John Curington, who lived on a ranch in Big Sandy, Texas. Curington, along with Paul Rothermel, Hunt's chief of security, left the Hunts in 1969, falling into disfavor with the family (in particular, with sons Bunker and Herbert) over alleged managerial improprieties of the subsidiary HLH Foods. Rothermel had been seconded to H. L. Hunt by Hoover in 1954, leaving the bureau to take over security for the Hunt organization. In the course of the dispute, Bunker and Herbert had resorted to wiretapping Rothermel. When Rothermel discovered this he brought criminal proceedings against them. One of the lawyers the Hunt brothers hired in 1969 (to represent one of their investigators charged) was none other than James's second attorney, Percy Foreman, who had often represented the Hunts.

Curington, a native Texan, had attempted to trade in information at various times and on one occasion provided material for a *National Enquirer* article on the Kennedy assassination linking Hunt financing to that event. Jim Johnson was unable to make contact with him because he was serving a sentence for a white-collar crime and was unable or unwilling to meet until he was released. Any discussions with Curington would have to take place after the trial.

AT ERNESTINE AND HAZEL'S RESTAURANT, a longstanding black-owned cafe on South Main Street about three hundred yards from the rooming house, I spoke with patron William L. Ross, who told me that he was around the Lorraine at the time of the killing. He had gotten off work and taken the bus to Butler and South Main, arriving around 5:45. He began to walk down Butler to Mulberry, then turned left on Mulberry, crossed the street to the Lorraine side, and walked alongside the wall. There were a lot of people in the parking lot below the balcony. He heard the shot, ducked down, then straightened up and ran the fifty or so feet back to the driveway, where he saw Dr. King down on the balcony and people milling everywhere. Ross recalled seeing uniformed police coming up Mulberry.

Ross remembered talking with a woman who told him of a conversation that took place in the lobby of the Lorraine at the time of the shooting. A phone call allegedly had been put through to room 306 just before Dr. King went out on the balcony for the last time. This was the first I had heard about this message being relayed to Dr. King's room.

Since Ross was closer to the brush area than anyone else I had found, I wanted him to undergo hypnosis in order to learn if he saw anything or anyone right after the shooting. He agreed to try it. Ross also pointed me to Ernestine Campbell, whom I would interview soon afterward.

In 1968 Ernestine Campbell and her husband owned the Trumpet Hotel which abutted the Lorraine. No one had ever talked to her or asked her about what she saw on that fateful afternoon. Ernestine said she left the hotel and started for home just before 6:00 p.m., driving her gold-bronze Cadillac up Butler and turning right on Mulberry. As she passed the Lorraine driveway on Butler, she saw Dr. King standing on the balcony. She didn't hear anything because she had the car windows up and the radio on. As she turned the corner onto Mulberry she looked up and saw Dr. King lying on the balcony. She thought he'd had a heart attack. She stopped for a minute or two at the driveway, wondering why people weren't racing to the balcony. Possibly she had arrived at the driveway when everyone was still in a state of shock.

Her attention was in particular drawn to Jesse Jackson whom she said had one foot on the first step of the stairway looking up to the balcony while bent over ". . . putting something into a suit bag." Her pause was brief, and she drove on without seeing any policemen or really noticing anyone at all.

JIM LAWSON TOLD ME THAT WALTER FAUNTROY, the former HSCA head of the King investigation, wanted to cooperate, and we set up a meeting. I had not seen Fauntroy for fifteen years, and I was surprised and encouraged by his friendliness and receptivity. We were joined by his personal lawyer, Harley Daniels, who had been examining a wide range of HSCA "sealed" raw files that Walter had secured following the completion of the committee's work. It appeared to me that Daniels had been trying, for the better part of a year, to investigate the King case solely through files and documentation. (They were planning to write a book based on this research.)

One of them told me that Hoover used to receive daily army intelligence reports on Dr. King's activities in 1967–1968. I had discovered a document in the attorney general's file showing that MPD intelligence officer Captain Jewell Ray had met after the killing with a Colonel Bray, who was identified as being with army intelligence. At the time, I put it down to the plan, as Captain Ray had claimed, to move the Tennessee National Guard into Memphis to control any possible riots arising from the planned march. Now I began to believe that the army may have played a wider role.

It was curious, I thought at the time, that Hoover would have needed to receive reports from army intelligence surveillance when he appeared to have his own FBI operation in place (the surveillance activity at the Rivermont described by Jim Smith).

I TRIED TO CHECK OUT THE POSSIBLE INVOLVEMENT of an elusive character named J. C. Hardin. According to an FBI memo, in March 1968 while James was living at the St. Francis Hotel in Los Angeles a person named J. C. Hardin, who had spoken with the manager, Alan Thompson, had inquired about James. I learned that produce man Frank C. Liberto's mother's maiden name was Hardin. The fact that a Hardin had married into the Liberto family may have no bearing on the King case, of course, but I thought it should be checked out. Attorney Jim Lesar who was James's lawyer in the mid-1970s, was familiar with an interview of a former Tampa-based FBI agent, John Hartingh, who was alleged to have remarked, upon being asked about J. C. Hardin, that he was an asset of the bureau. I asked James about this matter, and he denied any knowledge of J. C. Hardin or anyone else inquiring after him at the hotel during this time. The Hardin name would come up later in our investigation in another context.

Another stranger allegedly visited James in Toronto (giving him an envelope) shortly before James flew to England. For a very long time there had been publicity and rumors about this visit by a so-called "fat man." I finally learned the identity and address of the visitor, Robert McDoulton, from files in the attorney general's office. When I called McDoulton and introduced myself, he was abrupt and, I thought, fearful, saying he didn't want to talk about the incident. Then he hung up.

*   *   *

As 1992 WAS DRAWING TO A CLOSE, former Seabrook employee
Frances Thompson was located and agreed to testify as to what
she observed on the afternoon of April 4. She seemed convinced that she had seen a man sitting in a Mustang parked
on South Main Street opposite the Seabrook offices where she
was employed. One of my investigators seemed convinced that
the man was James Earl Ray.

Former FBI agent Bill Turner agreed to testify from personal
experience about the extensive use of electronic surveillance
and "black bag jobs" (illegal break-ins) by specially trained
units of the bureau. Turner had been an agent for about ten
years but became appalled at the way Hoover ran the bureau and
sought a congressional investigation. Consequently he was forced
out of the FBI.

So, then, by the end of December, Betty Spates for the first time had
directly implicated her former boss and lover, Loyd Jowers, in the mur-
der, admitting that after hearing what sounded like a shot she saw
him run into the kitchen from the brush area carrying a rifle.

Her sister Bobbi had confirmed in part, telling of being driven to
work the next morning by Jowers, who admitted finding a rifle out
back. The new information seemed to fit with cab driver McCraw's
earlier revelation about being shown a gun under the counter of the
grill by Jowers on the morning after the killing. Bobbi had pointed to
some sinister activity going on upstairs on the day of the killing, recall-
ing that Jowers put the second floor off limits. Further, S. O. Black-
burn's information had revealed that Jowers's other cafe had been a
gambling den frequented by, among others, two Frank Libertos and
another member of the Liberto family. Also surfacing (from HSCA files
retained by Walter Fauntroy) was the surveillance by army intelligence
on Dr. King in collaboration with Hoover.

Finally, Bill Sartor's death had been confirmed to be a homicide. It
became apparent that early on, though without hard factual evidence,
he was on the trail of a Marcello/Liberto connection in the murder of
Dr. King.

22

The Trial Approaches: January 1993

As THE NEW YEAR began we were just twenty-four days from the trial. I came again to Memphis and wouldn't return to England until the jury reached a verdict. For James and me the trial was the culmination of years of waiting and work, and I believed it could result in rewriting the history of one of the republic's most tragic periods.

We opened an office on the lower floor of James E. "Jeb" Blount III's law offices, a few blocks from the court. I insisted on having a 6'×4' security safe moved in to house our most sensitive files. We would also have the offices swept for the presence of any electronic surveillance devices.

I finally interviewed former MPD detective Edward Redditt, now a schoolteacher in Somerville, Tennessee. He told me that in early 1968 he had been on regular assignment as a community relations officer on the Memphis police force. During the time of the sanitation workers' strike he had been seconded to the intelligence bureau, reporting directly to Lt. E. H. Arkin. Arkin was in day-to-day operational control and was also the designated liaison officer to the FBI and its local office intelligence specialist, William Lawrence.

Redditt was assigned the task of conducting surveillance on the striking sanitation workers. When Dr. King and his party returned to Memphis, he was ordered to take up a surveillance post along with black patrolman Willie B. Richmond, who was a regular member of the MPD intelligence bureau, in the locker room at the rear of fire station 2, on the corner of Butler and South Main streets. From this vantage point they could see the Lorraine Motel through a peephole in a paper put over the glass of a rear locked door. There were small windows as well near the ceiling on that back wall, but to see through them one had to lie on top of the lockers. As we have seen, this is what fireman Charles Stone was doing at the time of the shooting.

Thus the two-man team of Redditt and Richmond was on duty on April 3 and April 4, keeping an eye on the movements of Dr. King's party and the Invaders in and around the motel. On April 4 Richmond arrived late—probably between 2:00 and 3:00 p.m. Redditt was on duty, however, covering for his partner, whom he didn't really know or trust. He has since come to believe that Richmond was primarily assigned by Arkin to keep an eye on him.

Redditt told a familiar story: sometime after 4:00 p.m. on the afternoon of April 4, Arkin appeared at the fire station and told Redditt to follow him to headquarters. Redditt went along and was led into a large conference room where he said he saw assembled twenty or more people, many of whom he didn't recognize. Some of them were in military uniforms. MPD director Holloman told Redditt that a contract had been put out on his life and that security was going to be arranged for him and his family. Holloman said that a secret service agent had flown in from Washington to tell them of this threat. Redditt's first reaction was disbelief. He had been threatened from time to time by community activists who thought he had sold out, but hostility came with the turf. It never occurred to him that either he or his family would be in such danger as to require protection. When Redditt protested, Holloman ordered him home. He was officially off duty, and there would be no further discussion.

Arkin drove him home. They arrived in front of his house shortly before 6:00 p.m. and while still sitting in the car a report of the assassination came over the radio. Redditt was told to remain off work until further notice. Three days later he was called back and not a word was mentioned about the threat on his life. It seemed to disappear as quickly as it came. At various times he asked about it, only to be told that it had all been a mistake; the report had confused him with another black officer in another city. To this day he regards the incident as a mystery, and he considers the timing of his removal as sinister.

The HSCA report disclosed that the man identified as the Washington "secret service" agent wasn't a secret service agent at all. He was Phillip Manuel, the chief investigator for Arkansas senator John McClellan's Permanent Subcommittee on Investigations. Manuel's role has never been satisfactorily explained. He has admitted to being in Memphis on the day of the assassination, but has never been able to provide a reason. Director Holloman's recollections over the years have been similarly unrevealing.

The HSCA reviewed an internal MPD memorandum establishing that Arkin had in fact received conclusive information on April 4 that there was no threat on Detective Redditt's life. If there was any relevant threat at all it was against another black police officer in another city. The HSCA noted that ". . . this information was being received by Arkin as Holloman was holding his meeting with Redditt."[11]

The committee took the issue no further.

Redditt brought up an even stranger event. Sometime in the mid-1970s, prior to the HSCA investigation, he was asked to go over to the Federal Building in Memphis where he was shown a photograph by a person who he believes was a Justice Department official. (The Justice Department conducted an investigation of the FBI's investigation of the case during that period.)

The photograph was of a bundle **lying on the corner of Huling and Mulberry streets**. The bundle was being watched over or guarded by a uniformed Memphis police officer holding a shotgun whom Redditt identified with certainty as Louis MacKay, the same black patrolman who had been assigned to guard the evidence found in front of Canipe's until homicide chief Zachary took charge of it and carried it away. A well-circulated photograph shows officer MacKay, shotgun at the ready, in front of Canipe's.

I had never heard even a rumor about this extraordinary incident. At the end of our session Redditt agreed to testify about both experiences.

Louis MacKay was still an active MPD officer in 1993. Reviewing the events of that April 4 evening, he was positive that he guarded the bundle only on South Main Street by Canipe's and nowhere else. He has no explanation for the photograph described by Redditt. That photograph has never been seen again.

The obvious question is whether the photograph of Louis MacKay at Canipe's doorway and possibly the bundle itself could have been superimposed on a photograph of the corner at Huling and Mulberry. But for what purpose? Could this have been an alternate "official" escape route?

BETTY SPATES'S SISTER Alda finally spoke to me, adding new elements to Betty's story. She said that after the killing, Jowers fired Bobbi, Rosie Lee, and Rosetta. Contrary to what Betty and Bobbi had said, however, Alda contended (though I didn't believe her) that she had herself only begun work at the grill seven months after the event. Working with her at the time were Big Lena (the head cook) and Joy. She said that Betty used to come around and try to "supervise" things, taking advantage of her relationship with Jowers.

Alda recalled finding money in a suitcase in an old stove and telling Betty about it. Betty told Jowers and Jowers quickly fired both Lena and Alda. Alda recalled Jowers getting a phone call, going away and returning with the suitcase. She also recalled that Jowers told her not to go out the back door into the rear yard area. She added that Betty had a gun with a scope on it back in the 1970s and sometimes kept it under her bed. Alda couldn't recall any wedding at the Oakview house and had never heard about Jowers buying it. She believed that she and Bobbi had purchased the house by themselves.

Finally, Alda told us that Coy Love, a black street-artist, saw a man run across South Main Street just after the killing, continue up the alleyway by Seabrook, and then take off a hooded sweatshirt and throw it into a dumpster. To his later amazement, she said, Coy saw that the man was black.

Solomon Jones's story about seeing a man in the bushes with a hood or something around his head came to mind. In a statement to the MPD, Jones said he saw a man heading back toward the rooming house. This could explain the footprints in the alley as being left by someone heading into Jim's Grill and to South Main Street. In his statement given to the media on the evening of the shooting, he said he saw a man come down over the wall and onto or near the Lorraine property, only to drift away. We continued to look for Jones without success.

I was concerned that some of Alda's recollections seemed to contradict parts of Betty's statement, although it appeared that Alda was trying to distance herself from the events of April 4. Betty hadn't mentioned having a rifle, and we also wondered if either Betty or Alda was confused about the time when Jowers placed money in the stove—or whether there could have been two lots of stashed bills. Lastly, we didn't know what to make of Betty's uncorroborated insistence that a wedding took place.

At the risk of offending Betty, Kenny, local black investigator Cliff Dates, and I went to the Shelby County Jail to talk to her son, John Spates. He had been incarcerated there since October on what appeared to be a frivolous complaint by an acquaintance of his. Spates confirmed Akins's attempt to shoot him, his brother, and his mother back in 1983 but said he didn't understand why—one moment Akins seemed to be their friend and the next he seemed determined to kill all three of them. His mother had obviously been reluctant to tell any of them about what she saw, afraid that it would also put their lives in danger. I felt more confident about Betty's story after talking with her son. They seemed to be mutually protective, and I believed that, whatever the reason, Akins was likely to have made an attempt on John's life. We were still confused about when Jowers's cash appeared, as well as about the possible significance of the second-hand Coy Love story and were concerned about whether or not Betty was in possession of a rifle after the killing. We would eventually learn that Coy Love had died and we were unable to locate any surviving family he had.

Betty soon learned about our visit with John and was upset. It was clear that she had tried to shelter John from the underlying reason for the murder attempt in 1983. She believed that if he didn't know what she saw around 6:00 p.m. on April 4, 1968, he would be safe. She didn't recall ever having a rifle, and insisted that she had seen the cash in the stove prior to the killing.

Meanwhile, Ken Herman had located Bessie Brewer, the manager of the rooming house at 422 ½ South Main at the time of the shooting, and we set out to see her. Apparently her husband Frank had died and she now lived alone. Herman reported that according to her daughter, Bessie had been told by the FBI back in 1968 not to talk to anyone, and she had followed those instructions to this day.

When Herman introduced us she announced that she was not the Bessie Brewer that we wanted, but that she and her late husband had frequently been confused with the other Bessie and Frank, who were black. As we chipped away at that transparent story, I showed her a photograph of the area of the rooming house and detected a clear sense of recognition in her eyes; but she wouldn't relent. Bessie wasn't talking.

A NUMBER OF LOOSE ENDS began to come together. James Orange confirmed that he had seen smoke rising from the bushes right after the shot and then noticed the disappearance of those bushes the next morning. He would provide a statement, since

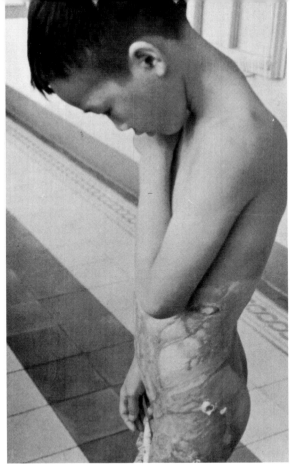

1. *left:* Napalm bombing and burning of innocent civilians in Vietnam moved Dr. King to become unconditionally opposed to the war.

(Photo by the author)

2. *below:* The author and Dr. King conversing before the keynote address at the 1967 NCNP national convention.

(Photo by Ben Fernandez)

3. *above:* The platform at the opening of the NCNP convention— Dick Gregory, Dr. Benjamin Spock, the Reverend Ralph Abernathy, the author, and Dr. Martin Luther King, Jr.

(Photo by Ben Fernandez)

4. *left:* The Reverend James Lawson in 1989—Dr. King's closest and most trusted colleague in Memphis in 1968.

(Photo by David Barker)

5. *above:* Dr. Benjamin Spock and the author in Memphis for the Memorial March after the assassination of Dr. King. *(Memphis State University Collection)*

6. *below:* South Main Street in front of Jim's Grill, the rooming house, and Canipe Amusement Company. *(UPI/Bettman)*

7. Attorney Wayne Chastain in 1995—now author's co-counsel in Memphis. Chastain was a reporter in 1968 and one of the first people on the scene.

(Photo by the author)

8. Solomon Jones, Dr. King's driver in Memphis, quoted as having seen someone in the bushes at the time of the shooting and also as having observed a man come down over the wall.

(Photo by the author)

9. John McFerren in 1995—a local businessman who just over an hour before the killing heard Memphis produce dealer Frank C. Liberto talking on the telephone and ordering someone to "…shoot the son of a bitch when he comes on the balcony."

(Photo by the author)

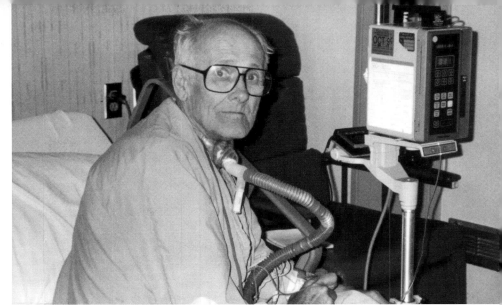

10. James McCraw in 1995, the Yellow Cab driver who minutes before the shooting saw the bathroom empty and State's chief witness Charlie Stephens drunk, and who was shown the murder weapon by Loyd Jowers. *(Photo by the author)*

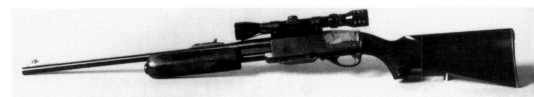

11. The "throwdown" gun bought by James Earl Ray and found in a bundle dropped in a doorway on South Main Street, alleged by the State to be the murder weapon.

(Memphis Police Department Evidence Files)

12. The area behind the rooming house and Jim's Grill, after the cutting of the brush and showing both wings of the rooming house with the alleyway in between.

(Memphis Police Department Evidence Files)

13. View from the balcony of the Lorraine where Dr. King was standing when he was shot, looking across Mulberry Street to the area behind the rooming house and Jim's Grill. Note the eight foot retaining wall with a large tree branch hanging over the edge. *(Memphis Police Department Evidence Files)*

15. The death slug in three fragments, taken in 1992.
(Author collection)

16. Autopsy photograph where the death slug is plainly visible just beneath the skin under Dr. King's left shoulder blade. *(Memphis Police Department Evidence Files)*

14. Frank Holloman circa 1968, Director of Memphis Police and Fire Departments in 1967-68.
(Memphis State University Collection)

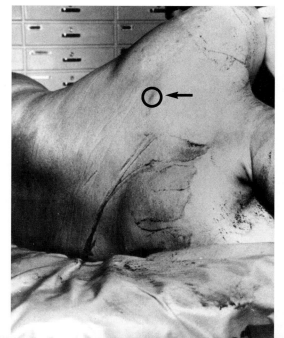

17. *above:* James Earl Ray and the author preparing for the television trial in a counsel's interview room at the Riverbend Maximum Security Prison.

(Photo by Jean Obray)

18. *left:* Frank C. Liberto, Memphis produce dealer initially implicated in the assassination by John McFerren. Photo taken in 1978 in Lavada Whitlock's restaurant which Liberto frequented on a daily basis.

(Courtesy of Sunday Express)

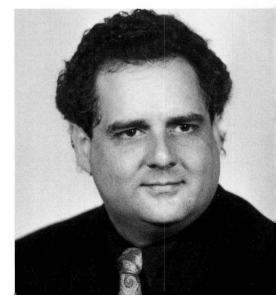

19. Nathan Whitlock, to whom Memphis produce dealer Frank C. Liberto admitted involvement in the assassination.

(Courtesy of Nathan Whitlock)

20. Memphis Police Department officer Louis McKay standing guard over the bundle dropped in Canipe's doorway—note the hedge in the upper right corner.
(*Photo by* Sam Melhorne, *Commercial Appeal*)

21. The hedge having been cut down shortly after the shooting.
(*Memphis Police Department Evidence Files*)

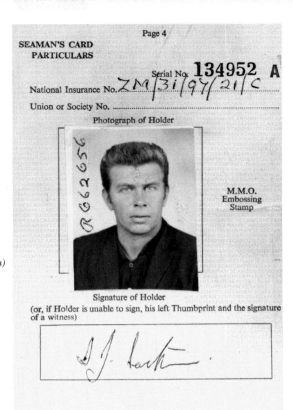

22. British Merchant Seaman's identity card of Sid Carthew in 1964. Raul approached Carthew in the Neptune Bar, Montreal in 1967, offering to sell him guns.

(Author collection)

SEAMAN'S CARD
PARTICULARS

Page 4

Serial No. **134952** **A**

National Insurance No. ZM/31/94/21/C

Union or Society No. ....

Photograph of Holder

M.M.O.
Embossing
Stamp

Signature of Holder
(or, if Holder is unable to sign, his left Thumbprint and the signature
of a witness)

23. Staged photograph of MPD cruiser pulled up to the sidewalk and clearly visible by anyone exiting the rooming house. Photo taken after hedge was cut thus supporting official conclusion that James Earl Ray saw MPD car and panicked, dropping the bundle. *(Memphis Police Department Evidence Files)*

24. Cheryl in 1995 executing her affidavit which alleged her acquaintance with Raul and his admission of being the assassin as well as Percy Foreman's admission to her that James Earl Ray was innocent and that Foreman also knew Raul. *(Photo by the author)*

25. Loyd Jowers (left)—the owner of Jim's Grill in 1968 who in 1993 finally admitted his involvement in the assassination—shown here attending a deposition in 1995 in the case of *Ray v. Jowers et al* with his attorney, Lewis Garrison.

(Photo by the author)

26. Felix Torrino's house where Raul and associates allegedly regularly met to assemble weapons, and where, according to Cheryl, Raul admitted the killing.

(Photo by the author)

27. Sketch of Percy Foreman
which he autographed
and gave to Glenda Grabow
in 1979.

(Artist: Robert McSorley)

28. Carlos Marcello, former New Orleans
crime boss whose empire included
Memphis and the Southwest, and who
agreed to carry out the contract. ultimately using associates in Memphis and Raul.

(Photo by Christopher R. Harris)

29. Arthur Wayne Baldwin in 1995,
former mob associated Memphis
topless club owner who was offered
two separate contracts (mob and FBI)
to have James Earl Ray killed in prison.

(Photo by the author)

US ARMY

John F. Kennedy Center for Special Warfare

FORT BRAGG, NORTH CAROLINA

30. Special Forces officers at Ft. Bragg including Colonel Henry Cobb (C. O. of the 20th SFG) fifth from left, and General Yarborough ninth from left.

(Yarborough Collection, Boston University)

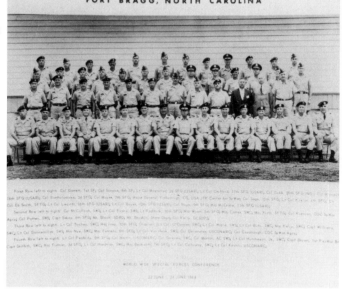

31. Major General William P. Yarborough (second left) and J. Edgar Hoover flanked by aides Colonel F. Van Tassell (left) and M. K. Hanson (right).

(Yarborough Collection, Boston University)

32. Lieutenant Eli H. Arkin circa 1968, senior Memphis Police Department Intelligence Officer.

33. The formal orders issued to Warren and other 20th SFG Alpha 184 team members.

```
     B816H          JCS004/30/R2
EWT
CO RUEPJS
DE RUEDPSA 65809
ZNY CCC
0 301442Z April 1968
TO RUEOEIA/CINCARSTRIKE
FM LANTCOMN/CINCSPECOPS
INFO/JCS
RUCIAUA/MAC
RUEPJS/NMCC
BT
TOP SECRET/CRYPTO 6880.      SUBJECT:      LANTCOM/CINCSTRIKE
OPLAN GARDEN PLOT 33-75,   WASHINGTON (U).
     REFERENCES:
     A.      LANTCOM 5673, DTD
     B.      CINCSTRIKE GARDEN
     1.      (C) MISSION: RECON RIOT SITE MEMPHIS PRIOR TO
KING, MARTIN L. ARRIVAL.
     2.      (C) CONCEPT OF OPERATOIN: CAS SUPPORT AT
NAS/RIVERSITE. NO, REPEAT, NO AUTHORIZATION BEYOND BRIEF AT
0430 UNLESS COMDED. CHOPPED AVAIL ON NOTICE CHANNEL 012.
     3.      (R) SITUATION: DEPLOYMENT MAIN FORCE MUST HAVE
LOCAL INTEL.
     4.      (P) OUT NOT SZNR 23. WILL ADVISE IF CHANGE.


     INFO: CJCS-1  DJS-3   SJCS-1  SACSA-3  NMCC-1  SECDEF-7
     ASD/ISA-9   WHOUSE-4      FILE-1(68)JJF/RAD/LANTCOM
```

34. *above:* The Illinois Central Railroad Building, as seen in 1968 from the balcony of the Lorraine Motel—20th SFG Alpha 184 team members Warren and Murphy's rooftop position at the time of the killing. *(Memphis State University collection)*

35. *below:* MPD Inspector Sam Evans in 1989. Evans ran the TACT units and briefed the 20th SFG Alpha 184 team members Warren and Murphy on the afternoon of the killing. *(Photo by David Barker)*

36. *above:* Marrell McCullough of the 111th Military Intelligence Group kneeling over the fallen Dr. King less than a minute after the shooting. *(Photo by Joseph Louw)*

37. *below:* View from flat roof of Fire Station 2 where Reynolds and Norton photographed the shooting and the assassin in the bushes. *(Photo by the author)*

38. The real Eric Galt
as shown in a 1967
photograph from his
Top Secret NSA file.

39. Two officers coming down
over the wall minutes after the
shooting, one identified by
Warren in 1994 as being a
CIA/NSA operative.

*(Memphis Police Department
Evidence Files)*

a previously scheduled trip to South Africa made it impossible for him to testify in person at the trial.

James's former attorney Jack Kershaw confirmed Jerry Ray's story about the offer made to him by William Bradford Huie in a meeting in Nashville. On offer was: $220,000 as well as pardons from Missouri and Tennessee in exchange for James's admissions that he was the killer. Jack told me that he took the offer to James who dismissed it out of hand. (Later, as we have seen, Huie came back again with the offer but would go through Jerry.) Kershaw believed that the two other men present at the meeting might well have been federal agents. He had no doubt that Huie was acting as an intermediary for the federal government since he reasoned that only the government could arrange the pardons and the protection. I recalled that Huie had previously developed a close working relationship with the FBI.

Former Louisville policeman Clifton Baird agreed to try to set out the details of the 1965 conspiracy to kill Dr. King in Louisville, although he was concerned that severely impaired speech caused by two strokes could detract from his credibility as a witness. Ultimately I was forced to abandon hope of even obtaining a statement from him. His wife said he was too unwell to consider the matter.

ON JANUARY 10 came the revelation from former MPD homicide detective Barry Neal Linville. Linville and his partner, J. D. Hamby, were present along with Lt. Tommy Smith at the city morgue on the evening of the murder. He and Hamby watched Shelby County coroner Dr. Jerry Francisco extract the death slug in one piece and hand it over to them for tagging as evidence and delivery to the FBI laboratory in Washington, D.C. Dr. Francisco also took photographs of the bullet, which he turned over to homicide inspector Zachary and to the FBI. Though of poor quality, there is a photograph taken by Francisco at the time of the removal of the slug from Dr. King's body in the HSCA volumes. There are no such photographs in the attorney general's file, having mysteriously disappeared.

When I showed the now retired Barry Linville a photograph

of the three bullet fragments presently under the control of the clerk of the criminal court, which are identified as Q-64, the FBI marking for the death slug (see photograph #15), Linville was incredulous. "That's not the bullet I saw taken from the body," he said. "The slug I saw was in one piece and in very good condition." The only visible defect, he maintained, was that the exposed lead in the nose of the bullet was flattened. On a scale of one to ten he rated the slug as a nine. I was impressed with Linville's forthrightness and certainty. Here was an experienced homicide officer who had seen thousands of evidence bullets, and he was amazed at the changes that had somehow occurred to the death slug he saw being removed from Dr. King's body. He could offer no explanation for this alteration of a vital piece of evidence. Neither could he explain why during the past twenty-five years no one had contacted him as one of the original MPD homicide investigators about what he saw and knew.

Barry Linville readily agreed to take the stand.

I FINALLY CAUGHT UP WITH MAYNARD STILES, who in 1968 was the deputy director of the Memphis City Public Works Department, and conclusively learned that early on Friday morning, April 5, a two-man team was sent out to cut and clean up the entire backyard at 422 ½ South Main Street. Stiles told me that the predawn request came from the police department, and that he immediately assigned the task to Dutch Goodman and Willie Crawford. Dutch Goodman had since died, but Willie Crawford was still working for the Public Works Department. According to Ken Herman he confirmed that he and Goodman did the cleanup under police supervision.

Having learned about the footprints near the edge of the alleyway between the two wings of the rooming house and that three patrolmen had been in the area, I had been trying to locate the only one who was still alive, former MPD officer Joe "J. B." Hodges. We finally found him. He said that a short time after the killing, he climbed on top of some drums at the base of the wall under the bushes and entered the backyard of the rooming house from the Mulberry Street side to join TACT 10 member patrolman Torrence N. Landers, who was already there. Hodges remembered having considerable difficulty in getting through the thick mulberry bushes.

Hodges told me that, contrary to earlier reports, he and not Landers had discovered the very large footprints in the mud just inside the alleyway. They appeared to him to be freshly made. He secured that area until a plaster cast was made of the prints, which turned out to be very large—one foot was 13½" and the other 14" long.

Hodges agreed to testify.

Keep in mind that it had rained heavily the night before the killing, and in his statement Torrence Landers had said that the ground was wet. It appeared that the heavy rain had washed mud inside the entrance of the alleyway. Here was yet another clear indication of the presence of a person in that area behind the rooming house. Along with the previous observations of Caldwell, Jones, Orange, and Ross (all of which had somehow eluded official investigators for twenty-five years), the significance of the brush area as the likely scene of the shooting was again enhanced.

MY INTERVIEWS WITH THE INVADERS turned up a few notable observations. Charles "Izzy" Harrington was one of the Invaders occupying rooms 315 and 316 farther along the balcony from Dr. King's room 306 on April 3 and 4. On April 3, he stayed around the motel and thought he heard sounds and activity in the bushes on the other side of Mulberry Street behind the rooming house. I was interested in the recollection but didn't think it particularly significant because the night of April 3 had been a stormy one and the rustling of the bushes could have been caused by the wind.

Izzy said that at about 5:45 or 5:50 p.m. on April 4, a maid knocked on his door and told him that the Invaders were going to have to leave the motel, because Dr. King's group was no longer going to pay their bill (previously, Invader Charles Ballard had also recalled this incident). When Izzy asked who had given her those instructions, she said Reverend (Jesse) Jackson. Izzy and the rest of the Invaders gathered up their things and left, some in Cabbage's blue Mustang, others on foot. This explained the sudden departure recorded in Patrolman Richmond's log, which was compiled from his surveillance post in the fire station across the street.

Izzy recalled that they had only been off the motel property for about fifteen minutes when they heard the sirens and learned about the shooting. They ran back toward the motel only to find that roadblocks (Public Works Department wooden horses) were in place on Mulberry Street. He said it couldn't have been more than ten minutes after the shooting that they were put up. His opinion was that someone knew what was going to happen and had them ready.

Calvin Taylor, another Invader, remembered the March 29 meeting with Dr. King with a feeling of awe.

FBI agent Bill Lawrence, who was the Memphis field office's intelligence liaison with the MPD, had testified before the HSCA that the MPD knew everything that was said at that meeting because "they had someone there." Before I was able to confirm the electronic surveillance of Dr. King's suite, I assumed that he meant that one of those present was reporting to him. Even with the electronic surveillance I believed it likely that they had an informant at the meeting. The bugging of course provided an opportunity for them to check the accuracy of their source's report. Such checking was routine. One of my MPD sources confided to me that on occasion he was assigned to an army intelligence officer he only knew as Hamilton. On this detail, one of his assignments was to follow an informant named "Copperhead" so that the intelligence section could evaluate his reports and work. Copperhead is now a popular Democratic legislator. His adherents would likely say that he acted like many others who manipulated the system to their own ends. I heard allegations of this type of collaboration regularly leveled at many of the "established" civil rights leaders in Memphis.

I indicated to Taylor that I knew the Invaders were infiltrated not only by the MPD through McCollough but also by the FBI, which had its own informant. Taylor became nervous and asked me if I knew who the person was. I said that I had a good idea but it wasn't my intent to follow it up. He seemed to relax, and the discussion continued. In 1968 he was a copy boy for the *Commercial Appeal*. His editor at the time told him that Bill Lawrence of the FBI had said he should watch his step because he was associating with the wrong people. He continued to associate with the Invaders and after the assassination he was made a full-fledged reporter.

"Big John" Smith, a native Memphian, had returned to Memphis from the West Coast where he had joined the Black Panthers. He came back to work with the Invaders and assist in their local organizing efforts. During early 1968 he was under nearly constant surveillance—physical (from the moment he left his home each day) and, he suspected, electronic as well.

He said that on the afternoon of April 4 he arrived at the Lorraine to meet other Invaders at about 4:45. A number of MPD officers were there when he arrived. He particularly remembered seeing Caro Harris sitting in the lobby. At about 5:30 he came downstairs to the restaurant to have something to eat with his wife and friends. He remembered noting that at that time all the police had disappeared. A kind of stillness had descended over the motel. "It was eerie," he said.

He agreed to testify.

RUFUS BRADSHAW, the police officer who had relayed the hoax message to central dispatcher Billy Tucker on April 4, confirmed that he had been flagged down by passing motorist William Austein, who then proceeded to relay the CB transmission to him, which he passed on as he was given it. To protect himself, Bradshaw said he pulled a private citizen into the car so that if he ever needed an independent statement of the event he could produce it. He had guaranteed anonymity to this person unless the necessity arose.

He had particularly hostile words for the FBI's treatment of

Austein, which he couldn't understand and he believed was unwarranted. He agreed to testify.

FORMER GOVERNOR RAY BLANTON confirmed J. J. Maloney's story about the massive FBI SWAT team which quickly appeared after James's escape in June 1977. He said that he was motivated to go to the prison immediately after the escape by a phone call from Louis Stokes, the HSCA chairman. Stokes told him that if he didn't get over to the prison, he was likely to lose his most famous prisoner and the HSCA was going to lose its star witness. Stokes's staff had learned that the FBI team was sent to Brushy Mountain with instructions to find James and not bring him back alive. Blanton said that because Stokes treated the FBI presence so seriously it was clear that there was no time to lose. He immediately took a helicopter from the capitol to the prison. He found it unprecedented that the FBI would come in uninvited and with such force on a state prison escape. Upon arriving he realized that Stokes had been right—he too concluded that the bureau wanted James dead.

The governor was reluctant to testify, though, wanting to keep a low profile, since he had one remaining criminal count pending before an appellate court, which if reversed would completely overturn his conviction on charges of corruption.

In my second meeting with Walter Fauntroy he said he was willing to testify for the defense at the trial. He said that in recent years he had reanalyzed some HSCA documentation and had become convinced that James was innocent. I was elated. He said he had concluded that much of the material had been withheld from the committee by its staff, who manipulated the HSCA's findings and report. He also confirmed governor Blanton's story, saying that it was he (Fauntroy) who first received the reports about the FBI's determination to kill James after his escape and that he caused Louis Stokes to alert the governor. I continued to press Fauntroy for information he said he had pertaining to the surveillance communications generated by army intelligence on Dr. King's activities.

*   *   *

THE TRIAL was now less than two weeks away. We had found Randy Rosenson, whose memory had clearly been affected by a long history of drug abuse. Rosenson stated that he was interviewed by the HSCA several times. He eventually recalled that on some of these occasions, he was represented by Knoxville attorney Gene Stanley. He agreed to allow Stanley to testify at the trial to provide evidence of the HSCA's apparent knowledge about the existence of Raul. Rosenson himself agreed to give an affidavit about these matters, since he couldn't travel to Memphis as he was in a daily outpatient methadone treatment program and running a business. Rosenson's and Stanley's recollection of the HSCA interviews in Knoxville, Atlanta, and elsewhere were confirmed by the General Services Administration (GSA) expenditure reports.

Rosenson also recalled an American Indian who lived in Miami in 1968 and who had substantial contacts in Latin and South America, and was involved in drug smuggling and gunrunning. Rosenson said that during this time he made frequent trips to Mexico with this person. Curiously enough, this individual owned a white Mustang. Rosenson also stated that prior to an HSCA interview in Richmond, he was visited by a big man who told him he should admit to having known James when asked. It would solve many problems. Rosenson said he refused. The man was introduced to him as a high-level Tennessee state official.

In subsequent telephone conversations with investigator Jim Johnson, inmate Jules "Ricco" Kimbel stated that he too knew the American Indian referred to by Randy Rosenson, whom I will call Harry. He said Harry was associated with Carlos Marcello and was a very dangerous man. A criminal record check showed that this person's files had been "cleaned," indicating that he also had, or had previously, some relationship with one or another federal agency. Such associations are for life, and their existence and any resulting activity are usually jealously protected. The "sanitizing" of files is just one way of ensuring secrecy. The discovery was exciting, but it was clear that it would be long after the trial before we would be able to investigate in detail this person's role, if any, in the case.

*   *   *

By January 16 I had prepared final affidavits for Jules "Ricco" Kimbel, Randy Rosenson, inmate Tim Kirk, and Marie Martin and Charlie Stein whom James had known in Los Angeles. Martin and Stein had previously been interviewed by investigator Jim Johnson. I thought statements from them might be necessary to rebut racist allegations contained in FBI 302 reports of their interviews which the prosecution might introduce. Martin, in particular, said that the FBI report of their interview with her, which she hadn't previously seen, was inaccurate and incomplete. She remembered James as being totally different from the media descriptions of him. She said that, far from being racist or violent, he danced with black women and played pool with black customers who "hung out" in the lounge of the St. Francis Hotel, where she tended bar. She never saw or heard of him displaying even a hint of violence. He was, on the contrary, quiet and somewhat shy.

We wanted several witnesses to be hypnotized to determine whether they could remember anything further. The state of Tennessee allows the introduction of evidence given following memory enhancement through hypnosis if a prescribed process is scrupulously followed and the sessions videotaped. As required, Dr. Joseph Cassius, who had experience in conducting this kind of exercise, knew nothing about the significance of the questions we had prepared.

Charles Hurley, who had picked up his wife at Seabrook Wallpaper on April 5, was among those hypnotized. Under hypnosis he remembered the first letter of the license plate on the Mustang parked in front of him, which he couldn't remember before being hypnotized but which was the same letter (A) he identified in his 1968 statement where he also identified the second letter as L. He now described for the first time that, as he pulled out from behind the white Mustang with a man sitting in it, he saw an old brown station wagon parked just north and on the same side of the street as Jim's Grill. My assistant Jean and I looked at each other in amazement. It appeared that Charles Hurley had just substantiated the presence of Jowers's old brown station wagon in the approximate location where Betty Spates had said it was when she saw Jowers deposit a broken-down rifle in the trunk. Later, Hurley agreed to accompany us on a brief visit to the South Main Street area. Fully conscious, he noticed the alteration of the billboard area from the way it was.

Ernestine and Hazel's cafe patron William Ross also underwent hypnosis. He recalled details with astonishing precision. Ross described hearing the shot as he reached the Mulberry Street door of the Lorraine on foot. He ducked down and then turned to the left, enabling him to look westward toward the brush. He insisted that from this vantage point, only a few feet from the wall, he had no doubt that the shot came from the brush in the area just behind and on top of the wall. He also remembered seeing a "pale goldish-brown" Cadillac on the same side of the street. This would likely have been the goldish-brown Cadillac driven by Ernestine Campbell as she was going home.

Ross learned from Walter Bailey sometime after the shooting about a phone call that had come through the switchboard for Dr. King's room just before 6:00 p.m. He recalled being told that the call or a message was relayed to the room by either Mrs. Bailey or someone relieving her. Under hypnosis, he was certain that the message for Dr. King was, "They're ready for him now" or words to that effect.

Ross said someone called Catherine who apparently worked at the Lorraine in 1976 had also heard about the phone call from Walter Bailey and also from Walter's brother Theotis. I looked for her but was unable to find her.

FOR THE FIRST TIME Ken Herman and I were able to inspect the cellar underneath Jim's Grill and the two businesses nextdoor, including Canipe's. We confirmed that the door from the alleyway between the buildings opened into a ground-level landing. Off the landing, on the right, a door led into Jim's Grill. Straight ahead from the landing there was a flight of stairs that led to the cellar underneath the grill. We also discovered long-unused coal chutes in front of the cellars. These chutes opened onto the sidewalk in front of the buildings. Considering the failure of the police on the scene to properly inspect the cellar and the presence of the footprints heading toward the alleyway door, I thought that this layout could be significant. Subsequently, we were to learn that in the rear of the grill—in the kitchen—there was a trapdoor, which also led to the cellar.

It was a labyrinth. In 1968 there were three doors leading to the outside at the rear of the northern wing of the building where James's room 5-B was located—one in the alleyway, one at the bottom of the rear rooming house stairs, and one leading directly from the grill itself through the storage room at the back of the kitchen. (See photograph #12)

Although there is a question of whether it was blocked up in 1968, at one time there was another inside door on the north rear side of the kitchen, which opened to the foot of the rear stairway of the rooming house as well as to the back door at the foot of the rooming-house stairs.

Only after this extensive examination could we appreciate the possible shooting locations and escape routes. The assassination had to have been well planned because it was undeniable that the MPD was there in force very quickly after the shot was fired.

On one occasion, when I was exploring the dingy cellar of the rooming-house building, a caretaker told me that prosecutor Hickman Ewing too was interested in the backyard as the possible scene of the shooting. A chill shot through me. Was it possible that he was going to abandon the shot-from-the-bathroom scenario, which had always been a cornerstone of the state's case? To flush him out, I proposed to him that we save the court's time and stipulate that the shot didn't come from the bathroom. Ewing's response was unequivocal: "Ludicrous." Our concern was finally put to rest when he said he was going to introduce a photograph that allegedly showed footprints in the bathtub.

We interviewed a former office manager for Jowers's cab company. (Jowers was one of the founders of the Veterans Cab company.) Aside from his stories about various criminal activities of Jowers and Willie Akins in the early 1970s, he also said that Jowers's and Akins's involvement in the killing of Dr. King was widely rumored among the drivers.

We obtained a photograph and rap sheet on Willie Akins. He was clearly a big man and a nasty piece of work, with a history of violence. Had we found the owner of the mysterious footprints found by J. B. Hodges in the alleyway?

JOHN LIGHT AGREED TO TESTIFY. He had been a senior officer in the Alton Police Department in 1978 when the *New York Times,* the HSCA, and the FBI all tried to establish that James and Jerry Ray were responsible for the Alton, Illinois, bank robbery. He confirmed Lt. Walter Conrad's statement to me that neither the *Times,* the HSCA, nor the FBI had made any contact with them in an effort to check out the allegations.

It was agreed that the prosecution was to receive Tim Kirk's statement in advance. On the day it was delivered, I drove with Ken Herman and an Invader intermediary, Abdul Yawee, to visit Doc Walker in another Tennessee prison. Walker had been one of the members of the black Akabulon group convicted of attempting to murder James in the Brushy Mountain prison library back in 1981. I needed to explore the possibility of another contract having been put out on James, either to intimidate or actually to eliminate him, as had occurred with Art Baldwin's offer to Tim Kirk in 1978.

At the time of the Baldwin contract James was about to testify in public before the HSCA for the first time. I am certain there was considerable fear in some quarters about what he might say. In 1981, however, there was no indication that James had any intention or opportunity to come forward with any revelations. It had been characterized as racially motivated by a small, well-known group of black militants, determined to gain public attention. The result was that two of them, Partee and Doc Walker, each received an additional sentence of sixty-six years while one of their number, Ransom, received a considerably smaller term. James had refused to testify against them, insisting that he couldn't identify any of his assailants.

Until I spoke with Doc Walker, the incident made no sense

at all. Walker admitted that he was moved next to James just before the assault. It was, he said, an administrative decision. (Recall that James's "protector," Don Wolverton, had been transferred to Nashville just before this event.) At the time of the attack James had been allowed to enter the library, even though it had somehow been stripped of security.

Walker maintained that the attack took place behind a partition. He wasn't in that area but two of his friends, Partee and Ransom, were there, as were a couple of white prisoners who testified against them. The result of the attack on James was that their group was effectively destroyed—they were split up and the leadership received long sentences.

The assault enabled the prison authorities to deal harshly with a small group of black militants who were a constant source of unrest inside the walls of Brushy Mountain. Although it's true that James had some twenty-two knife wounds, not one was life-threatening. If they had really wanted to kill James, they could have done so easily. The role of the white prisoners, except as informants to provide evidence against the three blacks, wasn't clear. Neither was it understandable why one member of the group received only a fraction of the sentence that was meted out to Walker, who wasn't even directly present at the attack.

BACK IN MEMPHIS, Ken Herman met me with a chilling story. The security officer hired by the HBO/Thames producers was Jim Nichols, an MPD officer Herman knew and trusted. Since the jury was arriving in Memphis on January 24 and being taken directly to their hotel—the Hilton—he did a routine check on the upcoming reservations. No one connected with the defense or the prosecution was to know where the jury was being housed. These arrangements were made by the producers with maximum secrecy. The Hilton was definitely not regarded as among Memphis's first-class hotels. The producers believed that its out-of-the-way location near the airport would best ensure the jury's sequestration.

When Nichols examined the reservation list he realized that

on the seventh floor, where the entire jury was to be housed, five rooms had been reserved for the same week in the name of William Sessions, the director of the FBI. Nichols was dumbfounded. When he commented on the illustrious guest, the hotel security officer was clearly proud. He said that an electronics team had come in from Washington earlier that week and had gone through every room on that floor in preparation for the visit by the director and his four agents.

Never had I expected this. The potential for tampering with the jury or some of its members was considerable, and it was likely that at least their private conversations and possibly their formal deliberations would be monitored.

Nichols had reported the FBI reservations to producer Saltman, who canceled the Hilton reservations and put the jury elsewhere. Nichols had checked the schedule of the Memphis director of police and fire, Melvin Burgess, to see if there was any note or indication of the Sessions visit, since it would be unprecedented for the director of the FBI to come to a city and not notify the local police chief. Nichols said he found nothing indicating the visit during the week of January 24, nor did Burgess know anything about it.

Saltman confirmed the story but asked me not to mention it until he had the opportunity to bring it up at our final pretrial meeting scheduled for Sunday, January 24. Nichols reported that the FBI reservations were canceled shortly after the jury was scheduled to stay at another hotel.

BALLISTICS EXPERT CHUCK MORTON arrived from California to examine and photograph the death-slug fragments and the other evidence bullets found in the bundle left in Canipe's doorway. The latter, he agreed, had been subjected to neutron activation tests, indicated by the uniform slicing open of cartridge jackets and the removal of lead samples. Morton's initial reaction, refuting the FBI's story, was that there were enough individual stria or markings on the remains of the death slug for a determination to be made as to whether it came from the Remington Gamemaster 760 30.06 evidence rifle. (The FBI had stated in their report that: "the bullet, Q64, from the victim . . . has been distorted due to mutilation and insufficient marks of value for identification remain on this bullet. Therefore, it was not possible to determine whether or not Q64 was fired from the Q2 rifle.")

I FLEW TO NASHVILLE TO finally prepare James for his testimony. He was basically in good spirits, anticipating what would effectively be, at long last, his trial on the charge of the murder of Dr. King.

I explained that one of our Memphis investigators, John Billings, would be at his side throughout the proceedings. James would have a direct communications link to the defense table via a one-way earpiece that my assistant Jean would wear throughout the trial, and would have direct two-way contact by portable telephone with me during the court breaks.

While at the prison I also visited Tim Kirk and got his answers to the prosecution's queries about his original affidavit. Since Kirk wouldn't be on the stand, this was the closest they would get to cross-examining him. The session was stressful. One of my aides, Ray Kohlman, accompanied me. Certain information prosecutor Ewing sought would have identified Kirk as its source and put him in serious danger inside the walls. We followed a tenuous line.

At one question, concerning the killing of a Memphis club owner who was a rival of Art Baldwin, he blurted out, "This son of a bitch is trying to get me killed." I explained to him that nothing would please Ewing more than his failure to provide this evidence. I continued to believe that his testimony about the contract offer on James's life, which was communicated to him by Baldwin in 1978 just before James's scheduled HSCA testimony, was a striking example of the ongoing cover-up of the existence of a conspiracy in this case.

BACK IN MEMPHIS I was debriefed on the discovery meeting, which had been conducted by Jean in my absence, during the course of which each side had an opportunity to examine the documentary evidence of the other.

I learned that in the prosecution's bundle of evidence was a photograph that showed a police car in the forecourt of the fire station, pulled right up to and facing the curb of South Main Street. The photograph had been taken after the assassination, and it was taken from the area of sidewalk near Canipe's. (See photograph #23) Its presence told us that the prosecution was considering introducing it as a true representation of Emmett Douglass's cruiser, which we had determined was parked way back by the north side door, out of the line of sight of anyone leaving the rooming house. The thought that the prosecution might infer that the photograph was taken shortly after the shooting was alarming. I had to wonder whether they really believed this evidence.

IT HAD BEEN NEARLY FOUR YEARS since I had seen Hosea Williams. Now he agreed to try to convince his former roommate, SCLC chief accountant and FBI informant Jim Harrison, to testify at the trial. Recalling Dr. King's last visit to Memphis, Hosea said he was surprised to learn that they weren't going to stay at the Rivermont but that their reservations had been changed to a motel called the Lorraine. Though in pain from a back injury, he would testify "come hell or high water," and later he would thank me for the "privilege."

DURING THE LAST WEEK BEFORE THE TRIAL, we broadcast an appeal on a popular local radio talk show for anyone with any information about the case to come forward. It resulted in one new witness. Emmanuel White remembered attending the sanitation workers' march on March 28. He said that he and his family pushed toward the front of the line to get closer to Dr. King, wanting to touch him. Near the front of the line, White saw some young men between the marchers and the police begin to break store windows. The person who started the vandalism was white, but blacks quickly followed suit. He subsequently observed mass looting, with the stolen goods being loaded into cars and vans, with Illinois, Michigan, Missouri, and other out-of-state license plates. He had heard that a number of these people came from Chicago, Detroit, and St. Louis. Emmanuel White was eager to testify.

White's observations fitted in with comments of former senior Invader leader Dr. Coby Smith, who in an interview on January 9 had said that the Invaders leadership left participation in the march up to their members' discretion but deliberately stayed away themselves. They were fearful that disruption was going to take place and that they would be blamed. Afterward, the Invaders conducted their own investigation, which established the presence in the area that day of a number of cars with Illinois license plates and a number of youths who weren't known to any of the Invaders. When Smith told me this in 1992, I recalled the 1967 Labor Day weekend in Chicago, the NCNP convention, the Black Caucus, and the Blackstone Rangers' participation in the government-sponsored provocation.

AS WE NEARED THE END OF OUR INVESTIGATION, we couldn't help being struck by the absence of any reference in the attorney general's files, including the MPD and FBI investigation reports, to certain issues, events, and persons of significance:

- The changing of Dr. King's motel room.
- Taxi driver James McCraw's observations.
- The observations of *New York Times* reporter Earl Caldwell.
- The complete story of Solomon Jones.
- The observations of Kay Black or Maynard Stiles, or indeed any reference to the brush having been cut.
- The observations of Rev. James Orange.
- Charlie Stephens's intoxication that evening.
- The strange visits to attorney Russell X. Thompson and Rev. James Latimer.

AS THE INVESTIGATION ALMOST completely gave way to the trial itself, it was apparent that much was yet to be done. The four-month intensive investigative period had seemingly disappeared in an instant. Had we another three months and the necessary resources to follow through on the plethora of loose ends and newly generated leads, I believed that it might have been possible to pull off a "Perry Mason" courtroom performance, as a result of which James's innocence would be established. But at this point, only Betty Spates's testimony could provide this result.

We tried every way to convince Betty and Bobbi to testify. Betty said she would come forward if Bobbi agreed. Bobbi was reluctant. We offered to have their faces blocked out or to provide a screen. They thought about it. Finally, Betty said she would testify if we blocked out her face. But I still sensed uncertainty.

Jowers could not know that Betty was testifying. The plan was to bring Jowers and his wife up from the country and put them up at a hotel the night before. Betty would take the stand just before lunch and then leave the court. Jowers would be the first witness after lunch, being brought to the waiting room for defense witnesses and then straight into court.

Jowers would be told that he would be testifying generally about the events of the day. He had been approached in a very nonthreatening way. Initially we had hoped that the prosecution could convince him to testify. They did indeed want him as a witness, knowing nothing about the real course of events, but when Hickman Ewing approached him, Ken Herman said that Jowers apparently told him to "go fuck himself."

The jury, having already heard Betty's and possibly Bobbi's, and McCraw's testimony about Jowers's actions and involvement in the killing, would be primed for Jowers's testimony. I planned to end up treating Jowers as a hostile witness and to break him down, step by step. But it all depended on the participation of Betty and Bobbi.

Even knowing that so much was left to be done, as we approached the trial I believed that we had advanced the defense case to a point it had never reached before. My concerns now were to hold on to witnesses, to expand that list by convincing others to testify, and to get the judge to allow various aspects of evidence before the jury.

It wouldn't be long before I was informed that Jowers was insisting on having his lawyer present in the courtroom for the entirety of his testimony.

23

The Eve of the Trial:
January 24, 1993

THOUGH THE INVESTIGATION CONTINUED, twenty-four hours before the trial was to begin we believed that our case contained a few surprises for the prosecution.

We intended to show, through his own testimony and that of others, that James Earl Ray, a fugitive on the run with few options, was a patsy. At some point he was targeted by persons involved in a conspiracy to kill Martin Luther King and kept on a string with the unfulfilled promise of travel documents and the ongoing payment of relatively small sums of money for the performance of routine tasks as requested. He was moved around the country by a handler he knew only as Raul. An affidavit sworn by Randy Rosenson and the testimony of his former lawyer, Gene Stanley, would not only confirm the existence of Raul but indicate that the HSCA had known of his existence.

Finally, when it was decided that the assassination would be carried out in Memphis, James was given specific instructions to buy a particular rifle within a few days of the killing, and to rent a room in the rooming house on the day itself.

We would attack head-on the conclusions of the prosecution's case and the HSCA report by introducing available evidence. We would show that there was no ballistics evidence to establish that the death slug was fired from the rifle purchased by James and found with the dropped bundle. In addition, although the death slug had frequently been described as being fragmented, or in three pieces, we had evidence that the bullet taken from Dr. King's body was in one piece when it was sent to the FBI laboratory in Washington.

We had developed substantial evidence to cast doubt on the prosecution's contention that the shot came from the bathroom. There was no fingerprint evidence in the room and, most important, an eyewitness—taxi driver James McCraw— would testify that the bathroom was empty and the door was open a few minutes before 6:00 p.m. McCraw would also testify that on the morning of April 5 Jowers showed him a rifle in a box under the cash register in Jim's Grill. We believed that the prosecution was going to rely on the affidavit statement of Charlie Stephens, which purported to identify a profile of James. Since Stephens had made contradictory statements and was drunk at the time, we would destroy his credibility. Our evidence would include testimony from reporter Wayne Chastain, McCraw, and police detective Tommy Smith, who saw Charlie Stephens drunk within minutes of the shooting.

We intended to assert that James Earl Ray was gone from the area by the time of the shooting. Eyewitnesses William Reed and Ray Hendrix would testify through their statements that his Mustang came up South Main Street and turned onto Vance sometime before 6:00.

Through the testimony of former *Press Scimitar* photographer/reporter Jim Reid we would seek to introduce evidence of gas station attendant Willie Green, who allegedly saw James and who we had come to believe had died. Reid told me that Green had excitedly identified James from a photo Reid showed him, saying that he was the man at his gas station around 6:00 p.m. on the day of the murder. (We had some reservations about this identification because we had finally been able to view the NBC/Earl Wells interview of Willie Green. Even though Green had clearly identified a photograph of James as the person he saw, he also said that the man had used the telephone, which didn't jive with James's recollections.)

We knew that the prosecution was going to maintain that the Mustang which was seen leaving from just south of Canipe's, after the bundle was dropped, was driven by James. We would produce evidence that it was another virtually identical vehicle to that of James, which arrived in the area shortly after 4:30 that afternoon and which had Arkansas plates.

WE WERE PREPARED to introduce evidence to show that the assassination was the result of a conspiracy that orchestrated a number of significant events leading up to the slaying.

Eyewitnesses would confirm that the demonstration of March 28 was sabotaged by *provocateurs*. Evidence would be advanced that in preparation for his return to Memphis Dr. King was manipulated into staying at the Lorraine Motel and that the room originally reserved for him in a protected, ground-level area was changed to a highly exposed, second-floor balcony room.

MPD surveillance logs indicated that Rev. Billy Kyles had not been truthful about his movements within the last hour of Dr. King's life, and this was confirmed by Ralph Abernathy and Hosea Williams. Kyles had, in fact, however innocent it may have been, called Dr. King out of his room minutes before the shooting and then concocted a story about talking to him in the room. There was some indication from MPD inspector Sam Evans that it was Kyles who requested the TACT units be pulled back (although I questioned whether there was any such request and Kyles has denied making it). We also knew that Reverend Kyles had taken a room (312) at the Lorraine on April 3 and 4, even though he lived in Memphis. We knew that Reverend Kyles was to be the prosecution's first witness, and I was eager to have an opportunity to raise these issues with him.

The defense would show that the shot actually came from the brush area behind the rooming house, with witnesses testifying that they had seen a person or persons there. Smoke was seen rising from the bushes right after the shooting. There were also the fresh footprints found at the beginning of the alleyway; we planned to introduce photographs of the plaster casts through the testimony of MPD dog officer J. B. Hodges, who discovered them.

Most explosive of all would be the testimony of Betty Spates, if she would actually come forward. She believed that her life had been in jeopardy ever since April 4, 1968, because of what she saw that day. She could positively identify a conspirator to the killing, if not the shooter himself, who appeared to take immediate possession of the murder rifle, break it down, and carry it away.

Betty Spates's sister Bobbi could substantiate elements of her story, and she'd also be able to testify that the manager of Jim's Grill had put the second floor of the rooming house off-limits on that day, preventing the delivery of food to a recuperating tenant—Grace Walden. But Bobbi, too, was afraid.

Evidence of the involvement of organized crime figures would be introduced through the testimony of John McFerren if we could get him to testify about what he heard and saw late on the afternoon of April 4 at the LL&L Produce Company in Memphis.

The role of the local police in the assassination would be raised by evidence about the unexplained transfer on April 4 of two black firemen from their usual duty assignment at fire station 2 and the forced removal of black detective Ed Redditt from his surveillance post in the fire station two hours before the shooting. In addition, there was the pull back of the TACT units from around the Lorraine, the absence of the usual security unit of black homicide detectives, and the disappearance of all police from the motel within an hour of the shooting.

Contrasted with the removal of the local police and their security personnel was the presence on April 4 of FBI or other federal agents in unmarked cars on Huling and Butler streets, with the Lorraine situated in between. We referred to this impinging presence as a "surveillance sandwich."

The Invaders abruptly left the hotel only to return to the area shortly after the shooting and be stopped by barricades that appeared within ten minutes. We learned that it ordinarily took about thirty minutes for them to be brought from their storage depot and put in place.

The defense would present evidence of the predisposition of the federal government to harm and discredit Dr. King. The use of electronic surveillance, wiretapping, and diversified harassment activities against Dr. King for a number of years before 1968 would be documented. (Former FBI special agents Arthur Murtagh and Bill Turner would substantiate these assertions.)

We would also call as a witness Jim Smith, the local MPD special services intelligence bureau officer, who along with federal agents participated in the electronic surveillance of Dr. King in Memphis. The FBI had always vehemently denied that King was ever electronically surveilled in Memphis. Our surprise evidence would establish this as yet other long-standing lie and establish the interest the FBI or other collaborating federal agency took in Dr. King while he was in Memphis.

The plethora of strange events involving government officials, at one level or another, would be capped by the bizarre disclosure of Ed Redditt concerning a photograph of MPD officer Louis MacKay standing guard over the well-known bundle of evidence lying not in front of Canipe's but on the corner of Huling and Mulberry streets.

The existence of a previous assassination effort against Dr. King would be put into evidence through the affidavit of Myron Billet.

We would also seek to introduce the affidavit of Jules "Ricco" Kimbel who claimed to have piloted the plane, owned by a company of New Orleans mob boss Carlos Marcello, that flew two shooters to Memphis from Canada. Kimbel's statement conflicted in part with our developing understanding of the events, but he was adamant about the involvement of government assets in coordinating and executing the assassination.

Finally, the defense would provide a range of evidence about the cover-up, official dirty tricks, and the suppression of the truth about what took place on that afternoon, starting with the hoax broadcast that diverted police attention to the northern part of the city away from the crime scene and the logical escape route to the south. This would be presented in conjunction with the failure of the MPD to follow some of its standard emergency procedures designed to facilitate the apprehension of a fleeing suspect. We would give evidence establishing the cutting down of the brush the morning after the shooting, and we would show that it was at the request of the police.

Then there were the efforts to kill James or to buy him off with an offer of money, a pardon, and a new identity for a detailed confession. Testimony from James's previous attorney Jack Kershaw about William Bradford Huie's offer of money was planned. Evidence about the contract offer on James's life that was offered to inmate Tim Kirk, and the events surrounding James's escape from Brushy Mountain Penitentiary at a time when the HSCA was being founded, was to be introduced.

James's lawyers and his brother weren't immune from dirty tricks. St. Louis television reporter John Auble was scheduled to testify about specific instances of HSCA dirty tricks set up against Mark Lane in 1978 and also against James's brother Jerry, through the use of an informant, Oliver Patterson, who admitted his role. Former Alton, Illinois, police officer John Light was scheduled to testify about the HSCA, FBI, and *New York Times* collaborating to falsely lay the blame for the Alton bank robbery on James and Jerry Ray. We believed that all this evidence was relevant because it showed external, even official, interest in establishing James Earl Ray as the lone assassin or in getting him out of the way.

The bureau's manipulation of the media's coverage of Dr. King and James was to be the subject of testimony researched and prepared by Bill Schaap of the Institute of Media Analysis in New York. Schaap's research had documented a campaign of hate and distortion against King and a gradual reconstruction of James's image from that of a petty criminal to a lone, racist assassin.

Our concluding evidence was to be provided by Walter Fauntroy himself, who said that he and the other HSCA members were misled by the staff and their own counsel. Fauntroy would say that his review of the evidence now indicated to him that James was not guilty.

PRINCIPAL PARTICIPANTS ON both sides of the case held one final pretrial meeting on Sunday morning, January 24.

Hickman Ewing had been provided in discovery with our documentation that dealt with the bureau's COINTELPRO activities against Dr. King, as well as Bill Schaap's research on the manipulation of the media and the Jerry Ray/William Bradford Huie telephone conversation transcripts. As a result, I believe he thought we were going to defend James by putting the government on trial; to a certain extent, of course, this was true.

Ewing told the judge he believed that much of our evidence wasn't relevant to any trial of James Earl Ray for murder. He admitted, for example, that FBI harassment of Dr. King was well known but maintained that it was irrelevant and that there was no evidence of any such activity against Dr. King in Memphis. I replied that there was indeed. The prosecutor looked skeptical.

I told the judge that I did intend to introduce such evidence, that I believed to be relevant since a significant aspect of the defense case pointed to the involvement of the bureau and perhaps other intelligence agencies in the murder of Dr. King and its cover-up. The judge proposed a private meeting with the defense after this session in order to ascertain specifically what evidence we were seeking to introduce.

The two sides had basically agreed on the trial procedures to be followed, but a few areas had not been clearly defined. Perhaps the main concern was the introduction of statements from witnesses who for one reason or another couldn't attend and therefore couldn't be cross-examined. We formally requested that FBI 302 interview reports be excluded because our investigation had located witnesses who repudiated 302 statements attributed to them that they had never seen.

It wasn't as though exclusion of 302 reports wouldn't have hurt our case. Our team had tried feverishly, without success, to locate alibi witnesses William Reed and Ray Hendrix. If the 302s were inadmissible, we knew we'd have lost their alibi statements, but we'd come to believe that some of the 302s were so unreliable that they might cast doubt on the trial itself. The judge ruled that such reports of interviews, since they were taken by law enforcement officers, had a basic presumption of credibility and should be admissable.

Throughout the meeting I waited for producer Jack Saltman to bring up the fact that the FBI had made reservations in the same hotel and on the same floor as the jury and had a technical surveillance team go through each of the rooms reserved for the jurors. It began to appear that he wasn't going to raise the issue at all. It may have been that he was afraid of the impact on the judge or even on Ewing. Ultimately, I forced the issue and he finally reluctantly mentioned it. The revelation was greeted with blank stares and no comment at all by the judge or the prosecutor.

IN OUR PRIVATE CONFERENCE with the judge, I outlined the conspiracy-related elements of the case, and in so doing summarized evidence on the following issues we intended to introduce:

- Government intelligence agency operations directed against Dr. King, as well as the FBI's specific COINTELPRO, COMIN-FIL, and other programs of harassment and electronic surveillance, including activities carried out in Memphis.

- Previous FBI and other governmental intelligence agency efforts to facilitate or arrange the murder of Dr. King.

- The changing of Dr. King's hotel as well as his room.

- The manipulation and use of the print and visual media by the FBI and intelligence agencies.

- Specific attempts to either buy off or kill the defendant.

- The expert opinion of the chairman of the subcommittee of the HSCA, Walter Fauntroy, that the committee was misled by its staff.

The judge was negative about allowing in any of this evidence, questioning its relevance to the specific charge of murder. The more he heard, the more rigid he seemed to become. He asked if we had evidence of any COINTELPRO activities against Dr. King in Memphis. I said we did. He asked what form it took. I said the evidence came from a participant in the activity. Reluctantly, he admitted that he might let such evidence in if we could concretely show it was done in Memphis.

It was difficult to remain restrained, particularly in light of the disclosures of FBI activity regarding the trial jury's security. If anything, I expected that this revelation would enhance the relevance and credibility of the point we sought to make. In retrospect, the incident might have made the judge even more cautious. He promised a ruling by 6:00 p.m.

I left the conference more depressed than at any time since we had begun to work on the trial. If the judge ruled against us, our case would be severely crippled; the entire trial could have become a farce. I believed that my obligations as a lawyer would require me to go immediately to the prison and confer with James. I'd have to put everything on the table and let him decide whether he wished to go ahead. Since the idea of the trial itself had originated with me, I certainly was not going to collaborate in its subversion.

At about 2:45 that afternoon, as we waited in the corridor for a pretrial press conference to begin, my frustration must have been obvious. There was no telling what I would do, or what I would say to the media.

Just before the press conference began, the judge called Ewing and me aside. He was going to let the defense put on its case, but he was ordering us to reveal the names of all of our witnesses, except the "security" witnesses, to the prosecution by the next morning.

The press conference went ahead in a spirited, upbeat manner, and when we left the courthouse late that afternoon I believed we had the court's approval for putting forward a wide-ranging defense.

24

The Trial: January 25–February 5, 1993

JUDGE MARVIN FRANKEL CALLED THE COURT TO ORDER at 9:30 a.m., Monday, January 25, 1993.

In his opening remarks the prosecutor forcefully contended that James was guilty. He said the defense would be "Anybody but me"; James would have them believe that the responsibility for Dr. King's murder was with the FBI, the CIA, or some guy named Raul.

I asked the jury to keep open minds and promised to take them on a journey that would boggle the imagination. I told them Dr. King had been a lamb led to slaughter by forces he knew only too well but that the defendant was also manipulated and controlled by forces that to this very day he didn't understand and couldn't identify.

The prosecution's first witness was Rev. Samuel "Billy" Kyles. Ewing led him through the sanitation workers' strike and Dr. King's agreement to come to Memphis. Kyles outlined the idea behind the Poor People's Campaign and said that, in his view, it was ". . . too much for the powers that be, to bring these poor people to Washington, to embarrass this nation by camping out on the mall in Washington." Ewing then moved on to the details of the march.

To our astonishment, Kyles blurted out that he had learned later that the FBI had hired *provocateurs* to disrupt the march. We'd fought to have such evidence admitted on behalf of the defense, and here it was being volunteered by the prosecution's very first witness. Judge Frankel seemed uncomfortable. Ewing, obviously unwilling to challenge his first witness, tried to ignore the statement.

In discussing events close to April 4, Kyles volunteered that they had boycotted one of the local newspapers, the *Commercial Appeal,* because it had engaged in character assassination of Dr. King. This was an example of just the sort of media manipulation we were planning to introduce.

The questioning quickly moved Kyles to April 4. The preacher described his supposed conversation in room 306 with King and Abernathy, and his position on the balcony some feet away from where King was shot just after 6:00 p.m. I began cross-examination by asking Kyles if he was familiar with Dr. King's speech at the Riverside Church on April 4, 1967. He said it was King's first major speech against the war and admitted that it had engendered a great deal of hostility. Kyles then volunteered that Hoover had made no secret of his dislike for King, whom he had called the most notorious liar in the country.

Kyles confirmed the fact that there was usually a black security squad formed to protect Dr. King in Memphis. He testified that he didn't remember there being any security on April 4 and that he was aware that the TACT units had been pulled back.

I countered Kyles's assertion that Dr. King had always stayed at the Lorraine, and he had to admit that in fact, at least on the two occasions before his final visit, he had stayed at the Rivermont.

I asked Kyles why, when he lived in Memphis, he had registered in room 312 at the Lorraine. He answered that he took a room in the event that someone else coming in without a reservation might need it. But in the next breath he went on to say, "As it turned out, A. D. King did come in, his brother came in," implying that A. D. was going to take the room. He further stated that he ended up taking A. D. to his home. In fact A. D. had registered in room 201.

Finally, I challenged his description of his activities on the fateful afternoon. I raised the MPD surveillance reports, which recorded him not as being in the room with Martin, but rather knocking on his door at 5:50 and calling him outside.

The dilemma for the defense, of course, was that by undermining Kyles's credibility, we could erode one of our basic themes of the FBI's anti-King activity. Kyles stuck to his story.

My exchange with the first witness would be one of the most heated of the trial. It was a dramatic start.

The court recessed after Kyles's testimony. On the steps of the courthouse Kyles said it was a real trial in every way, that the defense didn't pull any punches, and that his cross-examination was rigorous.

After the recess Ewing read into the record the statements of Ralph Abernathy and MPD intelligence officer Willie B. Richmond, which contained his surveillance report. Richmond's statement revealed that Billy Kyles had not been inside Dr. King's room at any time but that he had knocked on Dr. King's door around 5:50—about eleven minutes before the shooting. Dr. King answered the door, peered out, closed the door and emerged a few minutes later, shortly before 6:00, ready to leave for a soul food dinner at Kyles's home.

Abernathy's statement confirmed that he and King hurriedly prepared to go after the SCLC staff meeting broke up. He remembered Dr. King going outside and waiting for him on the balcony.

Lt. George Loenneke was brought on to describe his observations of Dr. King when he was struck. Loenneke stated that he had been watching Dr. King's party and the Lorraine from a peephole at fire station 2 when he saw King shot. As we have seen, two other firemen (Charles Stone and William King) said that the lieutenant was fiddling with his locker at the moment Dr. King was hit.

It wasn't significant, but something else that the lieutenant knew was important. He had told me about the Seabrook sales-girl who volunteered that she saw a man park a white Mustang in front of Canipe's amusement company and go upstairs in the rooming house. She was certain that the man was not James Earl Ray.

I wanted this story on the record. The problem was that it was hearsay. Ewing clearly knew about it because before the lieutenant could answer my eliciting question he was on his feet objecting to "anything that someone at Seabrook suppos-edly told him." The judge promptly sustained.

The prosecution established the presence of the bundle in front of Canipe's and introduced testimony relating to how soon after the shot was heard that it was found. Through the testimony of Deputy Sheriff Vernon Dollahite, Ewing did in-deed introduce a photograph—for illustrative purposes—of the general area around the time, showing a police car parked up on the sidewalk of the fire station parking lot. This was the photograph he had shown us in discovery and I thought it was misleading because he appeared to be using it to imply that the police car was in that spot at the time that James was alleg-edly fleeing. In fact, the photograph was taken at an entirely different time because the car in the picture was not that driven by Lt. Emmett Douglass, which at the time was parked much farther back and adjacent to the northwest door on the side of the fire station.

Former MPD lieutenant and FBI Academy graduate James Papia took the stand. He was one of the first officers on the scene and in the rooming house, and he testified that there was discoloration in the bathtub; he said it appeared someone had stood in it with shoes on.

During my cross-examination he admitted that he had no idea about where the rear stairway of the rooming house led and whether the back door at the foot of these stairs was locked or open. He also said he never entered Charlie Stephens's and Grace Walden's room 6-B, which overlooked the Lorraine and adjoined the room James rented as well as the bathroom. Papia was thus unable to offer any opinion on the sobriety of the state's main witness, Charlie Stephens.

The prosecution introduced statements of Willie Anschutz, a now deceased tenant of the rooming house, which said that after hearing the shot he saw a man run from room 5-B down the hall toward the front of the building, carrying some sort of package.

This was followed by former MPD homicide detective and FBI Academy graduate Glynn King, another one of the first police officers on the scene. He confirmed the presence of scuff marks in the bathtub and told of interviewing the landlady, Bessie Brewer, and Charlie Stephens, who he insisted did not appear to be even slightly intoxicated.

On cross-examination he said he remembered seeing the register for the rooming house. Since that book was not in the evidence in the clerk's office, I asked why he had not taken possession of it. His reply was simply, "You know, I don't know why."

Next, since Charlie Stephens was dead, the prosecution introduced his 1968 statement, for which I had ample refutation.

Homicide inspector N. E. Zachary detailed the items found in the bundle he took away from Canipe's door. Included were a number of personal effects belonging to James and, of course, the 30.06 Remington rifle he purchased in Birmingham. All of this physical evidence was, he said, turned over to the FBI for forensic analysis by their laboratory in Washington. Also sent to the bureau's lab, according to Zachary, was the death slug **in three fragments.**

Ewing read a statement of the now deceased Lt. J. D. Hamby in which he asserted that he turned over to Zachary **"one battered lead slug"** he received from the coroner, Dr. Jerry Francisco, after Francisco removed it from Dr. King's body.

James's purchase of the gun from Aeromarine Supply, his rental of a room at the new Rebel Motel on April 3, and his rental of the "sleeping room" in the South Main Street rooming house the next day were established, as was his purchase of the binoculars found in the bundle. We had offered to stipulate to these facts, which were not at issue, but the prosecutor refused, wanting to lay his proof before the jury.

Former Memphis field office special agent Joe Hester headed up the FBI's investigation of Dr. King's murder, and in the witness chair he said he would have hated to be known as the man who couldn't find the murderer of Martin Luther King. He discussed the extent of the search for the killer, and the resources expended. Under cross-examination he conceded that there were two white Mustangs in front of the rooming house on the afternoon of the assassination but called it a "coincidence." He contended that the bureau's COINTELPRO program was directed against communists, not Dr. King. He said there was no organized crime in Memphis, and he categorically asserted that there was no electronic surveillance of Dr. King in Memphis; without a doubt, he said, if there was he would have known about it.

The prosecution called Donald Champagne. He had been the head of the HSCA's ballistics panel and was well respected. He testified to the process followed by the panel.

On cross-examination he conceded that the results of the panel's analysis were inconclusive. They couldn't match the death slug to the evidence rifle. Champagne confirmed that the death slug provided to them was in three fragments.

The prosecution's next witness, New York forensic pathologist Dr. Michael Baden (who headed the HSCA's forensic panel), volunteered on direct examination that the bullet extracted from Dr. King was originally in one piece. Here again, the prosecutor was impeaching one of his own witnesses: Zachary.

Ewing closed his case with statements and testimony on a series of issues. One involved the date on which James put in his laundry when he was in Atlanta (James saying March 27 or thereabouts, and the state contending April 1). We had difficulty with this point because James had always insisted that he wasn't in Atlanta on April 1, and the tangible evidence of the laundry receipt seemed to indicate that he was. We felt that the date itself wasn't really important, but it had become an issue.

As to the circles drawn on the Atlanta map found in James's

room in the Atlanta rooming house, which the prosecution contended were near Dr. King's house, the SCLC offices, and around James's own current location on 14th Street at the time, the prosecution witness had to admit that the circles didn't enclose or pinpoint the areas at all.

The prosecution's last live witness was former FBI fingerprint expert George Bonebrake, who had worked on the evidence back in 1968. As expected, he identified one print of James on the evidence rifle and one on the scope, as well as others on some of the personal items in the bundle. He admitted on cross-examination that no prints of James were found in the rented room 5-B, the bathroom or anywhere else in the rooming house. He also had to admit that there were numerous other fingerprints found in the rooming house and lifted from the Mustang itself that he never identified and wasn't asked to identify.

The prosecution's case of circumstantial evidence was completed in three days, following the testimony of eighteen live witnesses and the introduction of twenty-two statements from unavailable witnesses.

WE OPENED THE DEFENSE CASE ON THURSDAY, January 28. Before we had even started, we lost one witness—our CB expert, Carroll Carroll, who refused to testify because of the publicity surrounding the trial. Much more worrisome was that we were also dangerously close to losing Betty Spates, whose nervousness was also compounded by the publicity.

After the testimony of J. J. Maloney and Don Wolverton, two former inmates who had known James quite well and attested that he was neither a racist nor a violent person, the trial was preoccupied for two days with the direct and cross-examination of James, conducted by satellite from the prison in Nashville. He was able to view the entire trial on a monitor in the prison and appeared on a monitor in the courtroom throughout the proceedings.

Immediately following James's testimony I explained how and why he had originally agreed to the guilty plea only to withdraw it and request a trial three days later. In his rebuttal, Hickman Ewing basically said that the plea was freely and intelligently given.

There were scheduled to be forty-nine live defense witnesses and nine statements from unavailable witnesses following James. (At the outset when Ewing's assistant Glenn Wright, a former prosecutor on the attorney general's staff, learned about the large number of proposed witnesses, he was incredulous. He asked Jean, "How can you get anyone to testify for James Earl Ray?" She replied, "It's called conducting an investigation.")

In an effort to give credibility to our contention that Raul existed, Knoxville attorney and former assistant U.S. attorney for eastern Tennessee Gene Stanley was put on the stand. The judge was furious about Stanley's attempt to narrate his representation of Randy Rosenson during his interrogation by the HSCA which included particular hearsay statements by committee staffers who confirmed the existence of Raul. We thought the statements should be admitted because they were against the interests of the speaker and therefore admissable, even though hearsay.

Our sworn statement from Rosenson dated January 20, 1993, confirmed his questioning by the HSCA staff, his involvement in smuggling activity in 1967–1968 across the Mexican border, and his travels with an American Indian who had both mob and FBI connections and who owned a white Mustang. Over our objections, the judge excluded the following part of the statement, which dealt with his HSCA interviews: "During these sessions the HSCA staff were primarily interested in having me identify an associate of James Earl Ray whose existence they acknowledged and whom they called Raul.

SHOCK WAVES WENT THROUGH THE COURTROOM when our witness Barry Neal Linville, the former MPD homicide detective, looked at the photograph I showed him of the three fragments of the bullet alleged to be the death slug and stated, "That's not the bullet I saw." He said that he had seen thousands of bullets in his career and that except for some flattening of the lead at the top, the bullet he and his partner saw the coroner take from Dr. King's body was a near-perfect evidence bullet.

Ewing tried to discredit Linville and failed. When asked if anyone else saw the bullet, Linville reeled off a list of MPD officers. The homicide office had been full of FBI officers, and there had been numerous photographs depicting the slug. "We felt that we found a piece of gold," he added.

Our ballistics expert, Chuck Morton, confirmed prosecution expert Champagne's statement that it was not possible to conclude that the death slug was fired from the rifle found in front of Canipe's.

Prosecutor Ewing asked about the degree of intactness of the bullet. Morton testified that according to the HSCA report the total weight of the three fragments was roughly half of a fully intact slug. Ewing used this to imply that the slug couldn't have been in such a pristine condition as Linville had stated. This really could only be explained by an inaccurate measurement taken by Hamby or as a result of the breaking off on impact and dispersal in the victim's body of most of the lead from the soft nose of the bullet that Linville admitted had been flattened.

In light of Linville's startling testimony, Ewing did the best he could with what he had, but he wasn't able to deal with the fact that the bullet when removed had been in one piece and was now in three fragments.

Linville's observations were supported by MPD captain Tommy Smith, who described how upon pinching the lump of skin below the shoulder blade covering the bullet and rolling the slug between his fingers, he had no doubt that it was in one piece. He went on to testify that Charlie Stephens was so drunk that he could hardly stand up when he tried to interview him shortly after the killing. He further confirmed the presence of thick bushes at the rear of the rooming house.

My co-counsel, April Ferguson, read into the record the affidavits of William Reed and Ray Hendrix, which confirmed their observation of the white Mustang leaving the scene minutes before the shooting.

We had next planned to show, through the testimony of

former taxi driver James McCraw, that the shot couldn't have come from the bathroom window because the bathroom was empty just before 6:00 p.m. However, McCraw had a heart attack in the witness room and had to be rushed to intensive care. We had taken an extensive statement from him, but we held off introducing it at this point, hoping that he might recover sufficiently to testify before the trial ended.

We put Capt. Emmett Douglass on the stand to counter the prosecution's contention that the person who dropped the bundle in front of Canipe's did so in panic upon seeing a police cruiser pulled up to the sidewalk. Douglass was adamant that his car wasn't pulled up to the sidewalk and wouldn't have been visible to anyone looking along the street in the position of the person fleeing the scene.

In his cross-examination, Ewing confronted Douglass with a previous statement in which he had said he thought he saw more than one gun when he looked at the bundle. Douglass himself readily admitted that his mind had been "playing tricks" on him.

The judge refused to allow the testimony of Jim Reid regarding his interview of gas station attendant Willie Green. It was hearsay, he ruled, refusing to accept our argument that the testimony was covered by the excited utterance exception to the hearsay rule. On balance, however, the ruling by the judge in this instance probably served to keep untrustworthy evidence from the jury.

He also refused to allow testimony of Wayne Chastain and Leon Cohen relating to their separate conversations with Walter Bailey, the owner of the Lorraine Motel, concerning the change in King's room. Again the judge considered it hearsay, and denied our argument that an exception applied.

We proceeded with testimony from Charles and Peggy Hurley and later Jimmy Walker showing that there were in fact two Mustangs parked in front of the rooming house on the afternoon of the shooting. By establishing the presence of two Mustangs and that the Mustang in front of Canipe's was not James's, it followed that James had in fact parked in front of the grill as he maintained. As further evidence that it was the

Mustang in front of Jim's Grill that belonged to James, we later called Frances Thompson to the stand. She had worked at Seabrook Wallpaper in 1968. The FBI 302 report of her interview at the time stated that she said she had seen a man sitting in the Mustang parked just south of Canipe's, at around 4:30-5:00 on the afternoon of April 4. When our investigators interviewed her she said that that was wrong and that in fact, she saw the man sitting in the Mustang parked in front of Jim's Grill. I was concerned about this apparent discrepancy.

When I raised the FBI report of her interview with her, she said it was incorrect and was quite definite that the car was in fact in front of Jim's Grill.

On cross-examination she confused Ewing with the prosecutor who had taken her statement originally. Ewing sought to discredit her with this and she became flustered, but she unwaveringly stood by her testimony that she saw a man in the car in front of Jim's Grill.

WE MOVED ON TO ESTABLISH OUR affirmative defense—that the assassination was the result of an elaborate conspiracy. The testimony of former policeman Jim Smith, the Rev. James Lawson, Emmanuel White, and Dr. Coby Smith all combined to show that *provocateurs* were at work in causing the sanitation workers' march to break up in violence. This was considerably bolstered by the previous testimony of Reverend Kyles.

Wayne Chastain testified about Stephens's intoxicated condition and his observation of the dense bushes, which he viewed from the Stephens's kitchen window just after the killing.

The defense found itself in an unusual situation. While virtually all the live witnesses for the prosecution were former policemen or FBI agents, the defense witnesses were from both sides and included a considerable number of policemen on duty during the time. This was particularly evident in the testimony concerning the disruption of the march. Dr. Coby Smith, while waiting to testify, told Jean how the Invaders were constantly under surveillance by the MPD and how young black men who had gone into the army were also used to spy on them. Meanwhile Jim Smith, who was also waiting to testify, was surreptitiously tugging at Jean's sleeve and trying to tell her that the practice Coby Smith described was true because Jim himself had been assigned to spy on the Invaders.

With one notable exception, all the policemen whom I had interviewed in preparation for the trial either believed that James was innocent or had serious doubts about his guilt. The exception, ironically, was Detective J. C. Davis, who at the time was an officer assigned to the intelligence bureau and who drafted the memo I found in the attorney general's office which referred to Betty Spates's statement contending James's innocence and her boss's culpability.

Jim Smith was later recalled to testify about his assignment to assist a team of federal agents conducting electronic surveillance on Dr. King in his suite at the Holiday Inn Rivermont Hotel on the evening of March 18. Smith stated that while he was assisting the agents he came to learn that they were hoping to pick up personal dirt on the civil rights leader. They were receiving in a van not far from the hotel. He referred to them only as "federal agents" until I inquired if they were FBI and he said they were. The basis of his knowledge was hearsay, and I felt sure that if Ewing had objected the judge would have sustained. Afterward, outside the courtroom, Ewing's assistant Glenn Wright attacked Smith, saying, "I thought you were supposed to be on our side."

The two men working in the area on the afternoon of April 4—Hasel Huckaby and Robert Hagerty—testified to their observations, which helped establish that surveillance activities were conducted on the streets immediately north and south of the Lorraine.

The jury could see a pattern of intelligence activity directed against Dr. King up to the moment of his death. I hoped that they would contrast this evidence of unofficial presence with the testimony we were to introduce of the stripping away of any official protective security presence around Dr. King and the Lorraine. Jerry Williams would testify about the absence of the special security unit of black homicide detectives usually provided to Dr. King in Memphis, and John Smith would recall that any remaining security/police around the motel disappeared within twenty minutes of the shooting.

Black firemen Floyd Newsom and Norvell Wallace, and black MPD officer Ed Redditt later testified that they were transferred and removed from duty assignments at fire station 2 during the last twenty-four hours of Dr. King's life.

Former chief William O. Crumby, who was going to testify about the pull back of the TACT units, was unable to do so at the last minute. He was not well.

BY THE THIRD DAY OF THE defense, we were experiencing major setbacks. McCraw was still in intensive care, so his statement was read into the record. The judge refused to allow the part describing the rifle Jowers kept in a box under the cash register. I have never understood this ruling. This hurt, but far worse was to come. John McFerren fled in fear and couldn't be persuaded to return to give evidence. Fear had also silenced Betty and Bobbi, who were due to testify that day. Betty had refused to answer the phone and wouldn't come to the door.

We had Loyd Jowers waiting to testify and had to put him on. He lived some distance away, and if we didn't call him now he would leave and we would miss the chance. We hoped against hope that somehow Betty and Bobbi could be persuaded to testify or at least give sworn statements so that Jowers would be impeached. If necessary, we could even recall him. As he had previously requested, he insisted on having his lawyer present in the courtroom for the duration of his testimony. His attorney, Lewis Garrison, had represented Jowers for years on his various civil matters. Jowers made the most of a hearing problem, which gave him ample time to reflect on the questions. It was interesting that Jowers lied about a number of matters—some seemingly insignificant but some clearly of importance. For example, at one point he denied that there was a rear exit at the foot of the back stairs. At another point he said he always kept the door leading from the kitchen to the rear stairs locked and barred. He said he had no staff at all working on the afternoon of April 4. Not wanting him to become aware of the degree of communication I had had with the waitresses who were in fact working that day, I didn't press him.

WE RETURNED TO THE TRIAL office that evening to learn that Hosea Williams, who should have arrived that day, was in too much pain even to get to the airport. He asked if he was really needed and was told yes. We rescheduled his appearance.

Meanwhile, Oscar Kent had arrived from Birmingham and was waiting to talk to us. (We had earlier made contact with him because Morris Davis had told us that he could corroborate Davis's allegations about Dr. Gus Prosch. After considering for some time, he offered to come to Memphis to talk to us.) He remembered seeing Davis and Prosch at the Gulas Lounge but said he didn't know anything about their business or any connection they might have with the King case. He went on to reveal an extraordinary story of his own. He said that he had been involved in illegal activity with some Birmingham police detectives. They had a falling-out and tried to set him up, charging him with a number of crimes over a period of years, all subsequent to 1968. The significance of this, he said, was that on March 30, 1968 he delivered a payoff to two detectives in a parking area near the Aeromarine Supply Company when they were on a stakeout waiting for James Earl Ray to appear. James did appear and entered the store. Kent said the detectives, whom he named, had James's photograph and real name. They told him it was not their intention to pick up James but merely to confirm his appearance. If true (the members of our team had different views as to this), it was a startling disclosure, one that indicated foreknowledge of the killing by the police department. There was no time to do any corroboration on Oscar Kent. I decided he would go on the stand.

FEBRUARY 1 WAS ANOTHER difficult day for the defense. It started well, with former FBI agent Arthur Murtagh movingly recalling the bureau's extensive unconstititional efforts to discredit Dr. King. At various points he broke down and sobbed.

Ewing again tried to prevent any evidence of the FBI's illegal activity against Dr. King, but the judge overruled him. However, he wouldn't let Murtagh mention the spontaneous remark of fellow agent James Rose, who upon hearing about the assassination exclaimed, "We [or they] finally got the son of a bitch!"

Former FBI agent Bill Turner's testimony was abbreviated after Ewing raised an objection as to relevance after only a few minutes, but not before Turner had described the FBI's "black bag" operations during this period.

St. Louis newscaster John Auble, who was prepared to testify about the incident of "dirty tricks" by the HSCA using the *New York Times,* was thrown off the stand by the judge virtually before he could open his mouth. The judge maintained that such post-assassination activities were not material to the charge of murder, despite our argument that as evidence of a cover-up they were relevant to the existence of a conspiracy.

The judge ordered a recess and asked the defense where it was going. We then told him we planned to call Bill Schaap as an expert on the political uses and manipulations of the media in influencing mass public opinion about Dr. King and James Earl Ray. The judge commented that author Gerold Frank had convicted James in his book. We told him that that was precisely the point. Jean produced the FBI memo from DeLoach to Hoover (dated the day after Ray's guilty plea hearing) proposing that an official record of the case be written by a friendly writer, and suggesting Gerold Frank. We knew the judge had read the book and so we had been waiting for an opportunity to introduce the memo. To his credit the judge allowed us to introduce it over Ewing's objection. He refused, however, to allow us to call Bill Schaap.

He treated the same way defense evidence pertaining to the efforts of the HSCA and the media to tie the Ray brothers to the Alton bank robbery. Former Alton policeman John Light's testimony was not to be heard.

We pressed on with testimony indicating that in all likelihood the shot came from the brush area opposite the Lorraine. We introduced the statements of Solomon Jones and Rev. James Orange. Kay Black also testified to having observed the area on the morning of April 5 after it had been cut and cleared up. Retired police officer J. B. Hodges testified to finding fresh footprints in the alleyway, and Maynard Stiles testified that the brush and the bushes were cut to the ground early the next morning.

William Ross came to testify about his enhanced recollection that the shot came from the bushes. Unfortunately, earlier Ewing had requested a conference in chambers to object to this testimony because Ross didn't remember where he thought the shot came from until after he was hypnotized. We thought that was the idea: that the subjects' recollections were sharper after hypnosis. We allowed the prosecution to view the video of our hypnosis sessions and though he talked generally about procedures his objections seemed to be more result-driven. The judge affirmed: Ross was out, even though Hurley and Walker, who had also been hypnotized, had been allowed in.

Oscar Kent took the stand and testified to his business relationship with particular Birmingham detectives in 1968 and to having observed two of them surveilling James Earl Ray as he entered and left the Aeromarine store on March 29. Kent testified that he had been charged with a number of fabricated crimes after this episode, but that the charges were ultimately dropped. He said that prior to his Aeromarine observations, with the exception of traffic violations, he had never been charged with a crime. On cross-examination Ewing asked Kent to provide details. In the course of doing so he described James as wearing khaki trousers and a lightweight light blue windbreaker. Though Ewing did not follow it up, this statement gave us concern because Donald Wood, the manager of Aeromarine, had clearly described James as being dressed in a dark suit, white shirt and tie, which, in fact, was James's usual dress during this time. (James later confirmed to us that he had never owned the type of clothes described by Kent.)

SINCE SO MANY WITNESSES HAD BEEN EXCLUDED, the defense was running short. We were anxiously awaiting the arrival of Hosea

Williams. Meanwhile, another crisis had emerged. Earl Caldwell had begged off, saying he was suffering from the flu. The defense staff pleaded and offered to provide local medical care. We held our breath.

Williams, having been met at the arrivals gate by a wheelchair, was driven straight to the courthouse. He testified that he arrived with Dr. King on April 3, that they were looking forward to staying at the Rivermont Holiday Inn, and that he was surprised that they were taken to the Lorraine Motel. He said that neither he nor anyone else in the entourage was familiar with the Lorraine and no one understood why the change was made.

In response to a question about room assignments, he said that Dr. King was "initially" given a room on the ground floor but ". . . for some strange reason, his room was changed."

He recounted the events in the hours before the assassination.

On cross-examination Ewing concentrated on Dr. King's itinerary in the months and weeks prior to the killing, apparently attempting to establish that his movements were public knowledge.

During my re-direct, Williams confirmed that there was an FBI informant employed as an accountant under Ralph Abernathy, SCLC's treasurer.

In addition to the losses already mentioned, the judge ruled that the defense couldn't introduce the affidavit of Tim Kirk relating to the contract offer on James's life; or Jack Kershaw's testimony about the offer of money and a pardon for James on the condition he admitted guilt; or Myron Billet's film interview and affidavit relating to a previous conspiracy to kill King; or Jules "Ricco" Kimbel's affidavit about flying in two shooters. We didn't even bother raising the issue of Oliver Patterson's affidavit, which outlined dirty tricks by the HSCA against Jerry Ray, including the taking of hair samples, theft of correspondence, and the introduction to him of a female agent for purposes of gathering information in exchange for sex.

It was the exclusion of evidence about the hoax broadcast that most upset James. The broadcast within minutes of the shooting was obviously of crucial importance. We had the dispatcher, William Tucker, ready to testify. The transcripts of the tapes had long been publicized and known. We also had the policeman in the field, Rufus Bradshaw, who received and radioed in the false CB account of a car chase involving a white Mustang. But the judge said, "Your client has benefited once from this hoax by being able to escape. I'll not let him benefit twice." The legal reasoning escaped me. James was so angry that he wanted to withdraw from the case.

John Billings called late at night to say that James was threatening not to appear the next day. I called James and told him that I shared his frustration but believed that the jury was with us. I agreed to recall him to the stand to give him an opportunity to ventilate.

Betty and Bobbi continued to avoid us. We prepared an affidavit for Betty to sign, but she refused. She spoke to to our investigator Cliff Dates on February 2, apologizing for any inconvenience caused and stating that she had finally decided not to cooperate, fearing that if she did so Jowers would "surely kill her." She also stated her belief that if the trial went well, James would be paroled in two years' time.

On James's recall the next morning, Ewing spent more time on his feet objecting than he did in his chair. James was determined to talk about the hoax, and Ewing and the judge were determined that he would not.

Ken Herman said he noticed a look of interest on the jurors' faces when the prosecutor tried to shut James up. He said the look asked, "What are they trying to keep from us?"

I later learned that when James showed up that morning he had with him a book with a sign inside it on which the following words were printed: THIS TRIAL IS A FARCE. He intended to flash it in front of the cameras if things continued the way they had. John Billings did his best to stabilize the situation.

Next on the stand was fireman William King. He testified that the day after the shooting he walked down Mulberry Street and noticed that "bushes" behind the rooming house had been freshly cut. When asked, he said that he was talking about trees rather than bushes, and he identified a long tree branch that appeared to have been recently cut and that hung over the wall.

I was thankful that Earl Caldwell finally appeared. He told how *New York Times* editor Claude Sitton had told him to "nail Dr. King." He vividly described how after the shot he saw a crouching man rising up from the bushes and staring at the balcony until he was distracted by Solomon Jones furiously driving the car back and forth. On cross-examination Caldwell testified that he had learned that the King party was to stay at the Lorraine Motel on or around April 1. He repeatedly stressed the height and thickness of the bushes in which he saw the crouching man.

The judge had repeatedly told me he wouldn't allow former congressman Walter Fauntroy to testify for the defense. However, I went ahead and called him. If the judge didn't want him to testify he would have to take him off the stand in front of the jury. Fauntroy had direct personal knowledge of the bureau's activities against Dr. King and of Hoover's attitude, because he had been the SCLC's man in Washington and had even attended the one meeting between Dr. King and Hoover. He had also had an opportunity to review a great deal of documentation from the HSCA's classified files and had become convinced that James was not guilty. As I attempted to elicit these facts, Ewing had hardly voiced his objection when the judge sustained.

In fairness, it seemed that the judge became increasingly committed to holding the evidence to that which was strictly relevant to a charge of murder. The judge's rulings severely limited our effort to demonstrate a very wide range of conspiratorial evidence related to the planning, execution, and ongoing cover-up of the truth about Dr. King's murder.

It's always tempting to second-guess the man in the robe, and in fact some of his rulings made good sense and were (even if intuitively so) well-founded in the rules of evidence. For example, Jules "Ricco" Kimbel's allegations of his involvement in a conspiracy as the pilot who flew the shooters in and out of Memphis had taken on material aspects of unreliability. As is often the case, particular aspects of his story had the ring and feel of truth but courtroom proof certainly requires and deserves a higher standard. The judge viewed these submissions more objectively than I did at the time. (Eventually I concluded that Kimbel may have provided me with some false information in the hope of inducing me to provide legal assistance to his brother, who was also in prison.)

I believe that the tightness of the judge's procedures, however, was overdone in some instances. The change of Dr. King's room was raised by Hosea Williams in his testimony, but the background for the change wasn't only material to the affirmative defense but highly significant. The events were set out by the now deceased manager of the Lorraine, Walter Bailey, in his conversations with investigator Leon Cohen and reporter Wayne Chastain, but these conversations were excluded by the court even though they were clearly against the interests of Mr. Bailey. Tim Kirk's affidavit setting out the details of the contract on James back in 1978 by U.S. government informant/operative Art Baldwin was always agreed to be allowed in if Hickman was permitted to ask questions to which Kirk would respond. This was done, and still the affidavit was kept out, despite it being extraordinarily contrary to Kirk's interests.

In rebuttal, Ewing attacked Oscar Kent's testimony by introducing a statement from Johnny C. Woods, one of the Birmingham detectives Kent had named. He denied being involved in any stakeout looking for James Earl Ray and noted that the Aeromarine Supply Store in 1968 was located near the Birmingham airport and not in a mall, where it is now. He further contended that he didn't meet Oscar Kent until the 1970s.

In their strident closing, the prosecutors kept the emotional level high, lamenting the loss to King's widow and his orphaned children. Their pretensions were sickening, particularly because throughout the trial I wasn't allowed even to hint at the personal relationship between myself and Martin and the impact that his death had had on me.

In the absence of any evidence, the prosecution referred to James's "racism" and made a great deal of the fact that James supposedly "stalked" Dr. King. The main thrust of their closing was in trying to discredit the defense witnesses or to dismiss the significance of their testimony. In the words of journalist Andrew Billen of the English newspaper the *Observer,* "They spend [sic] most of their allotted hour colourfully rubbishing the defense case rather than establishing their own."

IN MY CLOSING STATEMENT, I asked the jury to put aside the heat and consider the case carefully. I asked them first to consider the type of person James Earl Ray was, to think about his behavior in the context of his circumstances, and I urged them to ask themselves whether he was capable of pulling off such a crime.

The prosecution hadn't introduced a shred of evidence of any motive, I said, and pointed out the absurdity of their argument that James had stalked Dr. King. He had, for example, been in Los Angeles before Dr. King arrived, and when Dr. King arrived, he left. Also, there was no evidence to indicate that James even knew Dr. King was in Atlanta at the beginning of April, less than three weeks before the killing; when examined, the marks on James's map of Atlanta were clearly not around Dr. King's home or church. Further, the HSCA had considered the map to be such a flimsy piece of evidence that the members dismissed it. I went over the many holes in the prosecution's admittedly circumstantial case, including the failure to match the evidence slug to the rifle at the scene; the fact that none of James's fingerprints were found in the rooming house; the fact that the state's chief witness was falling-down drunk; that the bathroom was empty just before the shot was fired; that there were three eyewitnesses to activity in the bushes; and that two eyewitnesses saw James's white Mustang being driven away from the rooming house minutes before the shooting.

I moved on to catalog the wide variety of strange events surrounding the case, including the apparent tampering with the evidence slug, the cutting of the tree and bushes, the change of motel and room, and the removal of security, Detective Redditt, and the two black firemen, asking if any of these actions could really have been arranged by James acting alone.

I also reminded the jury about the revelation of the conducting of electronic surveillance against Dr. King in Memphis and the denial of that activity by FBI agent Joe Hester.

The judge addressed the jury for a half hour, after which they retired to consider their verdict. During deliberations the jury asked to see again photographic evidence submitted by the defense showing the death slug lodged just under the skin in Dr. King's back, the death slug itself, and the footprints found in the alleyway at the rear of the rooming house.

After seven and a half hours they sent word that they had reached a verdict.

The trial had run for over fifty hours during ten days, and when it ended we knew we would have to wait nearly two months to learn the result, as it would be revealed only when HBO and Channel 4 in England aired the trial on April 4, 1993. In spite of the fact that the greater part of our evidence concerning conspiracy had been excluded, and we couldn't put on our most explosive testimony because the witnesses were too afraid to testify, we believed we had put forward a good case.

25

The Verdict:
February–July 1993

I HAD BEEN BACK IN ENGLAND for less than a week when Jim Smith
called. After the trial he was harassed and closely watched in
the attorney general's office. Meanwhile, Ewing tried his utmost
to have Smith's testimony excluded from the program. The
rules required that the two sides sign off on the final version
as being representative and fair, and Ewing wrote a blistering
memo virtually accusing Smith of lying. He stated that after his
testimony Smith had said to Glenn Wright (Ewing's co-counsel)
that he really didn't know who the federal agents operating
the surveillance of King worked for, but had assumed it was
the FBI. He also said that it was rumored they were with the
army. Jack Saltman told me that he was angry and disappointed
with Ewing. He and Thames's legal advisor, Peter Smith, told
Ewing that just as the defense wouldn't be allowed to edit his
case, neither would he be allowed to edit defense testimony.
Eventually, one bit of Smith's testimony was edited out at Pe-

ter's suggestion and my reluctant agreement; at the time, I hoped that it might help to ease pressure on Smith. It consisted of a few lines where I had asked him how he would characterize the statement of an FBI official who said categorically that there was no electronic surveillance on Dr. King; Smith had replied that the agent either would have been lying or didn't know about it. On cross-examination (of which Smith was not aware) Joe Hester had said categorically that there was no such surveillance and if there had been he would have known about it.

Joe Hester had been made to look like either a liar or a fool, and he was still close to that office and to the former agents who had gone to work there. One way or another Jim Smith feared that they were going to get him—by setting him up in some way.

When I raised the issue of Smith's ongoing harassment with Jack Saltman, he was livid. He promised Smith that if it continued he would himself go and call a press conference in Memphis to blast the FBI. I mentioned Smith's concern that Hickman Ewing might have played a role. Jack took it up with Ewing, who said that the attorney general's office was indeed furious with Smith but that he had advised them that it would only look worse if they attempted to harass or penalize him in any way.

More than once after the program aired Jim Smith was called over to the FBI office and was actually grilled on his testimony as though the FBI was trying to learn what else he might know. He said they were acting as though he might have gone through their files and uncovered other information that could have been damaging to the bureau. He was told that if he didn't cooperate he'd never get his security clearance renewed.

ON SUNDAY, MARCH 21, 1993, two weeks before the trial was aired, the Memphis *Commercial Appeal* published the results of an eighteen-month investigation on the activities of army intelligence related to the civil rights movement. The article by Steve Tompkins concluded that army intelligence, which had a close working relationship with the FBI and J. Edgar Hoover (who

was himself made an officer), had kept Dr. King under electronic surveillance while he was in Memphis and elsewhere,
even up to the day of his assassination. Walter Fauntroy had
told me in preparation for his testimony that he had obtained
copies of army intelligence reports that went straight to Hoover's desk each morning. The *Commercial Appeal* article noted
that the close working relationship between the army and the
FBI often meant that the army, with its far greater manpower,
conducted these types of surveillance operations for Hoover, all
over the country. Agents were for all practical purposes made
available for Hoover's use.

In addition, the piece reported that army intelligence des-
patched Green Beret teams to thirty-nine racially explosive U.S.
cities, including Memphis, with instructions to make detailed
maps, identify landing zones for riot troops, and scout sniper
sites.

Jim Smith's testimony concerning his association with such
a surveillance team operating on March 18 against Dr. King at
the Rivermont Hotel, and the map-drawing agent Coop, was
confirmed. He was personally vindicated. Martin Luther King
was, without doubt, under electronic surveillance while in Memphis, and the collaborators were the MPD (which employed
Smith at the time), the FBI (which received the surveillance
tapes and transcripts), and U.S. army intelligence.

THE PROGRAM WAS SCHEDULED FOR SUNDAY EVENING, April 4, the
twenty-fifth anniversary of Dr. King's death. The plan was for
James, Hickman Ewing, and me to sit in the parole board's
conference room at the prison for a special viewing before
television cameras set up to record the first reactions to the
verdict. Afterward Sheena MacDonald of Channel 4 in England
would interview each of us, and this was to be transmitted by
satellite to the U.K. viewing audience.

I was running slightly late on Sunday morning, and when I
arrived at the prison, a little after nine, the screening had already begun. Except for minor breaks, the program was uninterrupted for nearly three hours. By the time the jury went out,

the viewing room had filled up. Even warden Mike Dutton had come in. The jury returned to the courtroom, announcing that they had reached a verdict. The court clerk collected the verdict and passed it to the judge who read aloud: "The Jury finds the Defendant Not Guilty."

There was a moment of silence and then James grinned. I smacked him on the back. Ewing's head just dropped. His chin lay buried in his chest for some time.

MacDonald moved quickly to ask the usual questions. I spoke about presenting an application for exoneration to the governor. James, somewhat at cross-purposes, said that perhaps he could now have a real trial. I stressed that the state had put forward its best case.

Ewing, now recovered, admitted that the program was well done and was good as far as it went. Then he began to backtrack with excuses. Any trial so long after the fact hurts the prosecution. He had no subpoena power. Eventually, in another forum, he stated that "at least" one defense witness "flat-out lied."

He stated that if the governor ever granted our proposed application, then he should be "impeached." Later in the interview, although throughout the trial he had vehemently opposed the idea that a conspiracy existed, he (apparently obliquely referring to the recent *Commercial Appeal* army intelligence article) now stated that it was quite possible that there was a conspiracy but that James was definitely involved. Incredibly, he went on to say that James may have been helped or hired by the Klan or the U.S. army to do the job.

Not unexpectedly, the verdict wasn't covered as a news event. It was virtually ignored by the media, with the exception of the NBC *Today Show*. In the days before the verdict was announced the phones were ringing off the hook with media inquiries, but when the verdict was made public the silence was deafening.

At the first opportunity I began to prepare the application to the governor for exoneration, and on Thursday, May 6, 1993, at 10:00 a.m., I entered the offices of Governor Ned McWerter's counsel, David Wells. I explained that we wished the governor quietly and seriously consider to the information that I was going to leave with Wells, and to do so with an open mind. I informed him that the investigation for the trial had produced a considerable body of new evidence but that there seemed no possibility, in our view, that the courts could reconsider the King case with the degree of objectivity required.

Counsel Wells assured me that he would place the issues before the governor. He said he would himself have to read the documents, and since I was filing an application and exhibits totaling nearly seven hundred pages, this would take him some time. He indicated that other work would make it impossible for him to begin for the next two weeks.

After the meeting, I returned to the hotel to meet Jim Lawson and the Rev. Will Avery, who were to participate in a press conference about the application at 3:00 that afternoon.

The governor had made a statement about two hours earlier that appeared to be deliberately timed to undercut our efforts. When asked by the press about the application, he responded that James Earl Ray was in prison when he entered the governor's office and James would still be inside when he left. I was forced to dismiss the statement as an impromptu remark not worthy of his office or the trust and responsibilities it conveyed. I had to disclose that counsel Wells had assured me that no matter what the governor said publicly the issues raised by the application would be brought to his attention.

The story was confined to the local area. Associated Press staff were present, but the details of the application weren't picked up. The networks ran none of the local footage. The news of the application to the governor was barely out there.

I decided to submit a petition to Amnesty International to take up the case. I had done so on two other occasions only to be refused. James was not, Amnesty had decided, a true "prisoner of conscience"—imprisoned or kept in prison because of his political beliefs. Now, after speaking with Dina Coloma, a researcher in the International Secretariat of Amnesty International, I thought that we might have a chance.

Coloma had seen the trial and admitted that as it had proceeded she had tried herself to conceive how the defendant might fit the Amnesty criteria. For Amnesty to consider intervening, it would be necessary for me to submit a formal petition establishing that James was a political pawn. I did so. The petition set out the basic political issues that have long been a part of the case. It raised a serious question about the occurrence and perpetuation of a miscarriage of justice as a result of governmental intervention. It detailed the tampering with some items of evidence and the suppression of other evidence.

Subsequently Coloma asked me if I would be willing to prepare a further submission on the issue of the guilty plea and set out in detail precisely how that came about. If it was clear that James had been railroaded into entering the plea, that was an issue which Amnesty could seize upon. I asked her if I might not also submit a note on the extradition issue, since James had been extradited largely, if not entirely, on the basis of the fraudulent and false affidavit of Charlie Q. Stephens. I briefed both issues, delivered the further submissions on June 25, and waited.

On July 14, Amnesty's head of research, Martin Smart, wrote saying that limited resources made it impossible for Amnesty in the short term to dedicate the staff necessary to examine and verify the allegations contained in the application.

DESPITE THE LACK OF NEWS COVERAGE, I considered the trial a success. Its preparation had provided a foundation for the opening up of the case as had never before been possible.

PART V

The Continuing Investigation

26

Loyd Jowers's Involvement: August– December, 1993

IN THE TRIAL'S AFTERMATH I had begun to focus on Loyd Jowers. I wanted to find a way to put the evidence that we had uncovered about his involvement on the record. In addition we needed to learn as much as possible about what he knew in order to get to the bottom of the conspiracy in Memphis. Though we already had enough evidence to establish James's innocence, the closer we could get to solving the crime, the better our chances of securing freedom for James.

Wayne Chastain knew Jowers's lawyer, Lewis Garrison, and frequently Garrison would discuss the case with him. Garrison told him that his client had dropped hints that he knew much more about the events of April 4 than anyone else. Garrison said that he seemed to be looking for a way to open up.

Ken Herman told me that on his own initiative he had gone to see Garrison and had a discussion with him about the alleged involvement of his client in the killing. He said Garrison somehow had learned about what we knew (I didn't understand how this could be so but I was later to find out). Garrison told him that he had advised Jowers and Willie Akins (who was also a client of his) not to say anything until a grant of immunity was obtained. He had undertaken to his clients to approach the Tennessee attorney general John Pierotti with such a request. John Billings asked his next door neighbor—black judge and founder of the National Civil Rights Museum, D'Army Bailey—to quietly ask the attorney general to review the request for immunity, which would shortly be submitted.

I was annoyed that Herman and Billings had taken all of these actions on their own, without instructions. They had both worked for me through the end of the trial. After April 4, 1993 not only did I not have funds to continue to use their services but as a result of the budgetary shortfall previous monies were owed to them and others. Herman and Billings had, however, a continuing legal and ethical responsibility to James which derived from their association with his defense and myself as his lawyer. Not only had they indirectly tipped-off Jowers and Akins to what we knew, but it was quite possible they had put essential witnesses, already fearful, at risk. If Betty and Bobbi knew that Jowers and Akins had become aware of their cooperation with us, we had little chance of convincing them to cooperate further.

Though I did not learn about this until October 4, sometime in May 1993 Garrison decided to include James McCraw, Bobbi Smith, and Betty Spates in the request for immunity. It was not clear to me how or even whether he had been authorized to act on behalf of Smith and Spates, but I knew that he had represented the three men on personal injury cases. I also didn't see how any of the people other than Jowers could be charged with any crime, since the statute of limitations had run out on any criminal charges stemming from acts committed after the crime.

I didn't expect attorney general Pierotti to approve the request for immunity, since he and his office had long been closely associated with the official "solution" of the case. Pierotti was a young prosecutor in the office in 1968 when Phil Canale was the attorney general. I was advised by Jim Smith that during the pretrial period Canale kept in touch with developments.

My early contacts with attorney general Pierotti were concerned with gaining access to the evidence for the TV trial, and he appeared to be most reasonable. Eventually, however, he opposed any testing of evidence whatsoever, and would only let us examine it in the Clerk of Court's office where it was stored. I also learned after the trial that his office had unofficially assigned a staffer to assist Hickman Ewing with his prosecution.

Jim Smith also told me that over the years a number of former FBI men had come to work for the office and this group was very protective of the status quo. In fact, it was the ex-FBI cabal and others who made life miserable for Smith after the trial, and caused the renewal of his security clearance to be denied. (By late May 1993 he was getting such hostility from his colleagues that he feared that he might be set up and his career finished. He had seen it happen to others. He therefore provided notice of his intention to leave after the new year and began to job hunt.)

I had no involvement in Garrison's request, but was anxious for the truth to come out, and hoped that all of the possibilities would be fully explored. It was obvious that Jowers would not reveal what he knew unless some sort of satisfactory immunity or plea arrangement could be obtained. There were any number of plea-bargaining possibilities open to the prosecutor and Garrison.

I discovered an alternative route for obtaining immunity. A little-known Tennessee statute provides that:

40-12-106. Prosecution of persons applying to testify not barred—Express immunity.—Notwithstanding any contrary provision of law, no person applying to testify before the grand jury shall be immune from prosecution based upon testimony subsequently given pursuant to such application, **except under express grant of immunity by the grand jury**. (emphasis added)

This allowed us to sidestep the attorney general's office and approach the grand jury directly and ask that body to hear evidence on the case. Ken Herman said he mentioned my suggestion to Garrison, but the lawyer insisted on going the conventional route. Herman said that he and Garrison both believed that the story was too big for Pierotti to suppress.

Garrison met with Pierotti at 3:00 p.m. on June 3 and laid out the request, stating that his unnamed clients wished to provide specific evidence pertaining to the killing of Martin Luther King in exchange for a grant of immunity from the state and federal governments. Pierotti asked Garrison for a brief statement outlining the evidence. Herman said Garrison quoted the attorney general as having said that once Garrison provided this there would be no problem issuing the grant. Garrison submitted the formal written request on June 22, 1993.

Meanwhile bits and pieces of Jowers's and Akins's story began to be passed on to me (usually now through Wayne Chastain, to whom Herman and gradually Lewis Garrison would talk). The allegation surfaced that Jowers had hired Frank Holt, a black produce-truck unloader, to do the shooting. (This report brought instantly to mind Coy Love's story about seeing a black man throw a hooded sweatshirt into a dumpster behind the Tayloe Paper Company.) Holt worked at the time for M. E. Carter Produce Company, which was located on Front Street (which ran parallel to South Main and was the next block east). We had come across Holt's name in an FBI 302 report, which stated that he had been in front of Jim's Grill immediately after the shooting and was told by the police to go inside the grill and stay out of the way. I had asked Ken Herman to look for Holt as a possible witness in our pretrial investigation but Herman couldn't locate him. According to Herman, Jowers told Garrison that Frank Liberto (the produce man) had given him the contract to murder King, thus apparently independently confirming John McFerren's story.

Jowers apparently acknowledged having seen James in the grill on April 4 seated at a table with a dark-haired Latino. This was almost exactly as James had described his meeting with Raul on the afternoon of the killing. Jowers also indicated that the money for the contract came from New Orleans and was delivered to Memphis in an M. E. Carter Produce Company truck carrying produce from that city. Herman also reported that Jowers had confirmed Betty's story about the events of April 4 leading up to the shooting.

There was no indication where and with whom the contract originated and it was quite possible that the information Jowers knew extended only to the local details of the actual killing. In any case, Jowers was insisting that he wouldn't reveal all he knew until he was granted immunity.

It transpired that Akins did not know Jowers at the time of the killing, but only became involved with him about a year later.

IN LATE JULY, I widened the focus of my investigation. I met with Steve Tompkins, the former *Commercial Appeal* investigative reporter, whose front-page piece on the active role of army intelligence since the end of World War I in surveilling and infiltrating black organizations and civil rights groups had been published on March 21, 1993.

Army intelligence had spied on Dr. King's family for three generations. The article noted that there was an extraordinary fear in official circles of what would happen if Dr. King was allowed to lead masses of American poor into Washington that spring. It stated that army intelligence was "... desperately searching for a way to stop him. ..."

I wanted to learn whether Tompkins, who had spent eighteen months researching his piece, knew anything about the King killing and if so whether he could open up some doors for me. Since Dr. King had been under army surveillance I wondered if the killing had been seen and even photographed. I had earlier read about this possibility in Douglas Valentine's book, *The Phoenix Program*, though at the time it appeared to be too speculative.[1]

Tompkins, a lanky, guardedly friendly man, had gone to work for the Tennessee Governor's Economic Development Department. I noted that he had confirmed the presence in Memphis that day of a number of army intelligence operatives. I needed to know their roles and, if possible, who they were. He would not give me their names but he did offer an observation that surprised and chilled me. He explained that he had stumbled on certain information which he was unable to print because of the lack of corroboration. He said that he had come to believe that in addition to surveilling Dr. King on April 4, 1968, the army presence in Memphis had a more sinister mission related to the assassination.

He had come to this conclusion after a conversation with a former Special Forces soldier now living in Latin America. The nervous ex-soldier had showed up with an AK-47 rifle which he kept near at hand throughout the interview. This man was the only member of the army unit whom Tompkins had been able to interview. Another member had been shot in the back of the head in New Orleans. The ex-soldier told Tompkins that he decided to leave the country after one of the members of the unit deployed to Memphis had been killed. He said it appeared that a "cleanup" operation was underway and that he had better get out.

I was at once excited and frustrated because this important information greatly complicated the picture. It was imperative that I investigate it as far as I could. Tompkins warned me that, if publicly questioned, he would deny telling me the information. As we parted, he said he was relieved to be away from the project, stating, "These people are incredibly dangerous. They'd kill you, your mother or your kids, as soon as look at you. You have to be very careful."

In a subsequent conversation I asked him if he would take me to his contacts or at least provide me with the names of people involved so that I might seek them out myself. I hoped he would become involved since he himself had been in naval intelligence and so had initial credibility and military access. He also understood far better than I could the mentality of that special community and how they operated. He reluctantly agreed to think about it.

*   *   *

TWO AND A HALF MONTHS after Garrison met with Pierotti there was no sign that the attorney general was going to act or even that he was seriously considering Garrison's request. I had therefore begun to think about ways of applying pressure in an attempt to force his hand.

On August 16 I wrote to him, informing him that I was aware of Garrison's petition, calling on him to grant the petition (or make a plea bargain arrangement with Jowers) and pointing out its potential impact, both in setting the record straight and in bringing about the release of a man who had been unjustly imprisoned for almost a quarter century. I also pointed out that the individuals concerned were effectively benefiting from *de facto* immunity.

Pierotti was on holiday at the time. He responded on September 8:

> Some months ago an attorney came to my office and stated that he knew of people who had knowledge of the murder of Dr. King which had heretofore not been revealed. He asked me if I would be interested in this information, to which I replied affirmatively. He stated that he could not reveal these people's identity unless I was in a position to seek, from the Courts or through Grand Jury proceeding, a grant of immunity from prosecution.
>
> I told this attorney that I would not consider immunity unless I had a full and complete statement detailing their knowledge of this matter. I would further only be interested in considering immunity if the information they provided could be corroborated by independent sources and documents. I asked this attorney if he was working with you or working independently. He replied he was working independently, so we therefore must be referring to different people. . . .
>
> As you state in your letter, your client has been incarcerated for over twenty-four (24) years and you believe him to be innocent. However, I have not been presented with any information or documentation to support your belief. I, therefore, have no reason to consider granting anyone immunity, and I

will not consider any such action unless and until I have evidence which can be proven beyond a reasonable doubt and to a moral certainty.

Correspondence continued. It became clear that he had no intention of considering the request. On September 15 he even denied having anything to consider, stating that: "... I have not been presented with any document requesting formal immunity for anyone in connection with this case, nor have I been presented with a summary of the evidence which any such applicant might possess which would cause me to consider immunity should such an application be made. If and when such evidence is presented to me I will consider it carefully but at this time I have nothing to consider."

I wrote back that, sadly, I had to conclude that he was being economical with the truth. He promptly replied that he had to hear from the federal government and that there was no use in continuing the exchange of letters until then.

I believed that Pierotti was seeking to make the federal government a scapegoat for his own inaction. In fact if immunity was granted for a state crime and a federal grant of immunity then requested in respect of other lesser federal offenses, it would be unusual for the federal government not to accede to the state's request.

On October 4, at the request of Lewis Garrison and Ken Herman, Wayne Chastain met both men in Garrison's office. To Chastain's surprise, Garrison provided him with a copy of the actual request for immunity submitted to the attorney general on June 22. Despite Pierotti's representations in his letter to me of September 15, the request was indeed a document asking for immunity and it contained a summary of the evidence on which the request was based.

It stated that Jowers (designated as Witness Green) was approached before the assassination and offered money to locate a person to assassinate Dr. King. The funds would come from another city through a local person or persons. Jowers, who had close contact with some persons in the MPD, was advised that he was in a strategic location to assist and that Dr. King would be a guest at the Lorraine Motel from a certain date. Jowers was to be provided with a weapon. Jowers located a person to do the job and funds were delivered to Jowers before the assassination in stacks of large bills. At the time of the shooting Jowers was stationed close to the assassin and once the shot was fired, the weapon was passed to Jowers who disassembled it and wrapped it in a covering. Jowers had been advised by other conspirators that there would be no reason to suspect him or any of the other participants in the actual assassination since there would be a decoy following the assassination.

The proposal next recounted information allegedly known by Betty Spates (designated as "Witness Brown . . . a close acquaintance of Jowers"). She would state that she was "within a few feet of the location where the shot was fired." Betty would also testify that she saw Witness Green with a rifle immediately after hearing the shot. She would state that she saw a large amount of money that had been delivered to Jowers. The money was in stacks of large-denomination bills. McCraw stated (he was Witness Black) that on the day after the killing Jowers showed him the gun and told him that it was the one used to assassinate Dr. King. Willie Akins (Witness White) would testify that he was asked, after the fact, by Jowers to take care of certain people "who knew too much." He was also told by Jowers that Jowers received the gun after the killing from the actual assassin. Bobbi Smith (Witness Gray) allegedly would testify that she was aware of the large amount of money paid to Jowers just before the assassination and that she had knowledge of other details about the actual killing.

The submission ended with a formal request for immunity for all five persons.

Jowers's story, as summed up for Chastain by Garrison, was that he had agreed at the request of produce-man Frank Liberto to hire a man to kill Dr. King on his last visit to Memphis. He had received $100,000 for his facilitation and he had paid a certain amount to the assassin, Frank Holt, who had worked as a loader for the M. E. Carter Company.

Jowers also contended that he tried to have Holt done away

with; a task he gave to his heavy Willie Akins. Akins apparently confirmed this assignment although he said at first that he didn't know why Jowers wanted the man killed. Akins said that before he could carry out the job the man disappeared.

Since I had no doubt that the attorney general would continue to stonewall any action based upon this evidence, I had to take steps on behalf of James. I retained Wayne Chastain as local counsel to approach the grand jury on James's behalf. I planned to ask the grand jury to subpoena attorney Garrison, at which time, if he so chose, he could request immunity for his client(s) in exchange for their testimony. I also formally asked the governor's counsel to ask the governor to hold off on issuing any ruling on our Motion for Exoneration since new evidence was forthcoming. I suggested that the governor could look foolish if he went ahead and ruled against us in light of information that would shortly be revealed.

By October 17 Wayne Chastain and I had agreed on the text of his submission to the grand jury. I would also provide Wayne with the names and addresses of the five people to be subpoenaed (which Garrison had not given to him) and a list of suggested questions. I suggested that Wayne ask the grand jury to formally request that federal immunity also be granted. In any event, once primary immunity was granted on behalf of the state, the witnesses would have no choice. Under pain of contempt they would have to tell all that they knew.

We delayed our actual submission because Wayne advised giving the attorney general every chance to act. In any event I believed that because most grand juries were closely controlled by the prosecutor it would be desirable to focus some publicity on the request in order to maximize the possibility of the members taking our submission seriously and acting independently. I therefore began to brief certain representatives of the American mass media.

By the beginning of December I was increasingly frustrated by the lack of any progress concerning the request for immunity and the unwillingness of the media to take up the issue.

On Tuesday evening December 7, I gave Wayne the go-ahead for the grand jury submission. He was to deliver the request (in the form of a letter and an affidavit) to testify the next day. He rushed it in and, on his own initiative, attached the names and addresses of the people to be subpoenaed. (I would have preferred that he had provided the names while testifying, but he thought that their inclusion would increase the sense of urgency.)

Later that day Wayne urged me to allow him to go to see the attorney general. I exploded. It was beyond me how he could believe there was a scintilla of hope that the attorney general would act. I was concerned that Pierotti knew the names of the witnesses and resolved to write to him to put him on notice that any contact with these witnesses outside of the grand jury room would be closely scrutinized. I explained to Wayne that on a previous occasion when one of these witnesses had tried in her way to come forward and get the truth out in order to clear James, she was visited unofficially in her home and, the record indicates, then called in officially and interrogated. Frightened off, it took twenty years for her to begin to come around again. I obviously had to do everything possible to prevent this happening again. My client was unlikely to survive another such period of recalcitrance.

I called Andrew Billen at the London *Observer,* one of England's oldest and most reputable broadsheets, to see if they would be interested. Billen had covered the trial and had a good working knowledge of the case. He was excited. So was his editor. It was clearly front-page material. Convinced that no American media entity would break the story, I gave the *Observer* the go-ahead.

Around this time I learned from some American contacts that Jack Saltman was talking to various media people, trying to sell the story and name the witnesses. I was also advised that Herman and Saltman had been working together for some time.

I was appalled. The privilege of confidentiality to James had been cast to the wind. Saltman had violated the rules established for the TV trial with regard to security witnesses. In confidence I had disclosed the existence of the security witnesses and the nature of their testimony. My trust was being flouted. Such a disclosure was likely to drive all of the witnesses away. In that event James would be the clear loser.

I confronted Herman. Our relationship, which had been strained since the trial, was now irreparably damaged.

I instructed Wayne to add the names of Ken Herman and Jack Saltman to the list of those persons to be subpoenaed. The next day, Thursday, December 9th, Wayne delivered the names directly to an attendant at the entrance to the grand jury room and waited. He was not called.

On Friday, Jim Smith told me that the attorney general and his number two, Strother, were closeted together continually and the local FBI special agent in charge had also been in for meetings. Jim said they seemed to have a "bunker mentality." I had no doubt that Wayne's request to appear before the grand jury was a source of their anxiety. The pressure was building.

Next, I became aware of and increasingly concerned about the rogue efforts of Herman and John Billings to locate Frank Holt. We all believed that Holt was in the Orlando area. Since, for their own reasons, they were determined to find Holt, I believed it essential that I exercise control over how he was approached. I was aware of a witness who saw a black man in the room James had rented. It could have been Holt. I needed to know exactly what he was going to say. I told them that I would go to Orlando to approach and personally interview Holt if he could be found.

I also sent them formal notices asserting attorney's privilege over everything they knew or had connected with the case.

I would bring black investigator Cliff Dates with me. If Holt could be found, Dates would approach him in as nonthreatening a manner as possible and begin to discuss his problem, which was not going to go away.

The Memphis *Commercial Appeal* quoted Pierotti as having denounced both Garrison and me, calling the entire story a "fraud" or "scam."

* * *

ON THE MORNING the *Observer* hit the newstands, I caught the flight to Orlando. C. D. "Buck" Buchanan, the Orlando P.I. I had hired for the job, had come up with an address for Holt. Memphis investigator Cliff Dates met me in Orlando and we went to 32 North Terry, a small transient boarding house, and walked up to the porch where we found a fairly intoxicated Jimmie Lee Branner, his sister, and Theresa, a young boarder. A paper bag filled with empty beer cans lay on one side. Jimmie Lee said Holt had not been there for months. Theresa pulled us aside and told us about some "crooks" who had been looking for Holt. They said they were from the church, but they weren't because they gave Jimmie whiskey and money and told him not to tell anyone else that they were looking for Holt.

We continued to comb the streets of the area. Later, as we drove around, we saw a grey Cadillac approaching. We both recognized Ken Herman in the back, sitting between a black man in a baseball cap and John Billings. I thought that they must have seen us. We pulled over opposite the boarding house and Cliff Dates went up to the porch to see Theresa. I remained in the car. Over my right shoulder I saw the grey Cadillac approaching up the side street just behind us. The back of my head was clearly visible. As the car reached Terry Street and turned left to go in the opposite direction, it burned rubber.

AFTER TAKING DATES to the airport so that he could catch his plane back to Memphis, I returned to the area that night and scoured the streets and checked two homeless centers in the area, with no success.

I was hindered in my search for Frank Holt by having to spend part of the next two days (December 14 and 15) negotiating with the ABC *Prime Time Live* producers. I had learned that Jack Saltman had sold the story and his consulting services to them. I saw the program as potentially being useful to the effort to free James, but I was afraid that they might name the witnesses. This would likely hurt our legal efforts, since if Betty and Bobbi were named without their consent and before their statements could be heard in a courtroom, they would probably repudiate earlier statements, or not discuss the matter at all. This, of course, is exactly what had happened before. The two sisters had been scheduled to testify at the trial only to back out in fear at the last minute.

I contacted the ABC producer. Eventually he promised that only the witnesses they actually interviewed would be named. I was told that they planned to interview only Jowers and Akins. In fact senior correspondent Sam Donaldson was already interviewing Jowers and Akins, preparing to move on to Pierotti late that afternoon.

On the program, which aired nationwide on Thursday, December 16, 1993, Loyd Jowers cleared James Earl Ray, saying that he did not shoot Dr. King but that he, Jowers, had hired a shooter, after he was approached by Memphis produce man Frank Liberto and paid $100,000 to facilitate the assassination. He also said that he had been visited by a man named Raul who delivered a rifle to him and asked him to hold it until final arrangements were made.

Loyd's cleanup man Akins confirmed he was ordered to kill the unnamed shooter but before Akins could get him in a place where he could "pop" him, the shooter disappeared, running off to Florida.

The producer's promise was worthless. Betty had been surreptitiously filmed leaving her place of work. Though partially obscured, she was recognizable and she was named. I was apprehensive about the effect.

The next morning I asked Cliff Dates to contact Betty and gauge her reaction to the show. He reported back that she was hurt and hostile and blamed me. She didn't realize that Herman and Saltman hadn't worked with me for eight months. Since she wouldn't talk to me I sent her a letter explaining the facts. From 6 a.m. to 9 a.m. that morning while doing other things I flipped back and forth from CNN to CBS to NBC and ABC. Incredible as it seemed, there was no news coverage of the previous night's program; not even on ABC. A review of the day's newspapers including the *New York Times, U.S.A. Today,* and the *Washington Post* showed only small mentions in the latter two, featuring Pierotti's new willingness not to reopen the case but to investigate further. Here was a confession, on prime-time television, to one of the most heinous crimes in the history of the republic—and there was virtually no American mass media coverage. The story was buried.

Andrew Billen, who thought the silence of the American media extraordinary, wrote a follow-up article on the television revelations in the *Observer*.

Having concluded that the governor would not seriously consider the basis for the motion for exoneration, I filed a petition on James's behalf seeking a trial on the basis of the new evidence discovered during the course of our investigation as well as the sensational public admissions of Loyd Jowers.

On the night the program aired (December 16) John Billings, who was trying to keep lines of communication open, called to tell me that they had still not found Holt. He said that the leads were strong and it was only a question of time before he surfaced. He insisted that when they found him I would be the first to know. I just listened. Earlier that morning Jim Smith had said that it was all over Memphis that Holt was the person implicated. He also said that he had heard that Holt had been found.

I was scheduled to fly back to London on Friday, December 17. About an hour before the flight I learned that Dwight Lewis of the *Nashville Tennessean* newspaper had left a message on the office answering machine: they had found Frank Holt and he wanted to get my reaction to Holt's statement. My heart stopped.

I called Lewis, who told me that two of the *Tennessean*'s reporters and a photographer had located Holt that day at the men's homeless center on Central Boulevard in Orlando, one of the shelters where I had "hung out" earlier in the week. He would move from one shelter to another since any semblance of continuing stay was not allowed. He apparently said that he had been inside Jim's Grill on the afternoon of April 4 but knew nothing about the assassination. The *Tennessean* had flown him to Nashville where he had taken and passed a lie detector test.

I was concerned about Holt's safety and pleaded with Lewis

not to mention his most recent address in the piece they were going to run the next day. Lewis said he would raise my concern with his editor. It was obvious that the decision was not his to make.

The *Tennessean* published a feature article on their interview with Frank Holt on Sunday, December 19. That morning I learned that Lewis had gone to the airport to put Holt on a plane bound for Orlando. Checking the schedules of flights to Orlando that day, I concluded that Holt had likely been put on a direct American flight. I asked Buck Buchanan to meet the flight and offer Holt a temporary safe house. Though the *Tennessean* had not printed Holt's address, since his name and general location were public and he had publicly refuted the allegations that he was the shooter, I thought his life might very well be in danger. After all, Akins had contended that Jowers had asked him in 1974 to get rid of Holt.

Buchanan met the plane and Frank Holt accepted the offer of protection and temporary accommodation until I could arrive to interview him on Wednesday. Buck settled him into a motel just outside of Orlando.

On Tuesday, Buchanan was contacted by the *Tennessean* as well as by investigators from Attorney General Pierotti's office. He had left his name at the homeless center the previous week when searching for Holt, and both the newspaper and the Shelby County officials had become aware of his interest.

The prosecutor had had five witnesses under his nose for over six months and had made no move to interview them, yet the *Tennessean*'s story was not even two days old and Pierotti had already sent a team to another state to search him out to, as he put it, "shoot full of holes" the story told by Loyd Jowers.

Buchanan told the reporter that he could give him no information unless authorized to do so by his client, and he told the Memphis investigators that he was instructed by an attorney and bound by the privilege. (I found this investigator's attitude refreshing.) He advised me that they did not ask him to request my permission to allow them to have access to Holt, nor did I ever receive any request from the attorney general or any member of his staff. They went away empty-handed.

Buchanan met me on my arrival in Orlando around 7:00 p.m. on Wednesday, December 23, and we took Holt out to dinner. He was a generally placid, almost expressionless man, and as we talked over the next three and one half hours, rapport was gradually established. He was concerned about his safety, saying that he wanted to leave the Orlando area and go to Tampa or elsewhere in the state.

The next morning Buck brought Holt around to my motel, where from about 8 a.m. until noon I interviewed him. He was uneasy about the tape recorder so I kept it off, taking notes instead. I had the benefit of informal comments he had volunteered to Buchanan before I arrived, including his impression that I had some responsibility to stop Jowers from telling lies about him.

Though I questioned him repeatedly, his story never varied. He said that he had left his home in Darling, Mississippi, in the mid-1950s and ended up in the Jacksonville area, which he had come to regard as a second home. In the early 1960s he went to Memphis and eventually took a job at the M. E. Carter Produce Company as a driver's helper, going on deliveries to towns in Arkansas and Mississippi.

Occasionally he would travel with the truck to Gulfport, Mississippi, and New Orleans where they would pick up some produce and bring it back to Memphis. This was the job he was doing in 1968 at the time of the assassination.

He had the impression that Frank Liberto, who had his own produce business (LL&L) out on Scott Street in the market, also had some interest in M. E. Carter because he frequently came around to the company's Front Street offices. Occasionally, he overheard conversations between Liberto and the "big wheels" of M. E. Carter, and on one occasion during the sanitation workers' strike he heard Liberto say, "King is a troublemaker and he should be killed. If he is killed then he will cause no more trouble." Holt also recalled that Charles Liberto, whom he thought was Frank Liberto's brother, seemed to have a negative feeling about Dr. King.

Holt said that he drank beer at Jim's Grill two or three times a week and had frequented the cafe before Jowers took it over after Jim's death. He insisted that he didn't really know Jowers and that Jowers certainly didn't know him except to serve him.

He remembered Betty Spates and her sister, who were waitresses in the grill. He knew that Jowers had something going with Betty, and he recalled that he had heard that this was why Jowers split up with his wife. He recalled that Betty and Bobbi were always friendly to him when Jowers was not around but that they were less so when he was present.

He recalled going upstairs in the rooming house to visit and drink beer with two friends—Applebooty and Commodore. Applebooty had worked at the warehouse at M. E. Carter. The last time Holt remembered being upstairs in the rooming house was before Commodore moved, which was sometime before the shooting. From his description of the layout, it appeared clear that Commodore had occupied room 5-B, the room rented by James on the afternoon of April 4, under the name John Willard. Bessie Brewer, the manager of the rooming house, had stated that the occupant of the room before James was named Commodore, except she said that he had become ill and was taken to the hospital where he died.

Holt said that on the day before the shooting he had gone on a delivery run deep into Mississippi and that they did not return until late morning or early afternoon of the following day, Thursday, April 4. When he reached Memphis he made the rounds of a few bars and eventually ended up in Jim's Grill late in the afternoon. To the best of his recollection he was inside the grill at the time of the shooting and could not explain the reference in the FBI report that he was passing the grill on his way to work. He did not recall ever being interviewed by the police or FBI. I found his recollections somewhat worrying, but the discrepancy could have been explained by Holt's own faulty memory, hampered by the passage of time and his alcohol abuse.

He remembered another Frank who had worked at M. E. Carter. He was also tall, and only had one eye. He didn't know him well but thought he was married and lived in the area. (For some time Ken Herman and John Billings had been looking for a one-eyed Frank Holt with a street name of Chicken Hawk. I wondered if they could have confused the two.) Holt even said that he had seen the other Frank on the afternoon of April 4 and believed that he was wearing a lumber jacket of some sort. He did not think that the other Frank was any more likely to have been involved in the shooting than he was. (I resolved to try to locate him, nevertheless, but we were unable to do so.)

Holt said that he had no gun of any kind at that time. He had hunted rabbits and squirrels in Mississippi with a single-shot .22 rifle years ago but had no experience with larger caliber guns such as that which was used to kill Dr. King.

He said he had known Coy Love, the street artist, but didn't recall seeing him on April 4.

When asked why Loyd Jowers or anyone would have named him, he was puzzled. "They probably thought I was dead," he said. Holt had been gone from Memphis for 24 years, leaving in late 1969, and returning only for a few hours in 1993 to visit a sick friend.

He had no interest in notoriety and abhorred being linked to the assassination. My impression after our interview was that he was credible and that I was not likely to see a more unpromising candidate for the assassin.

Buck and I spent that afternoon with Holt, as he took another lie detector test, essentially covering the same ground as the *Tennessean*'s had, and underwent hypnosis. Both sessions were videotaped, and both the hypnotist and the polygrapher involved concluded that Frank Holt was not involved in the crime.

Late in the afternoon of December 23, I shook hands with Frank Holt and said good-bye. I told him that I believed that he had further assisted in the clearing of his name.

I returned to England for Christmas believing that Jowers was either covering up his own role as the shooter or was protecting someone else. Akins's claim that he tried to find Holt and kill him in 1974 was incredible. By that time Holt had been gone from Memphis for five years.

In 1974, Jowers may have been constructing one of his self-protective stories, for around this time James was about to obtain a habeas corpus hearing. When threatened by events over the almost twenty-six–year history of this case, Jowers had always developed such stories. The morning after the shooting he told Bobbi that he had found a gun in the back and turned it over to the police. On that day he told cab driver McCraw a similar story. In 1968–1969 he identified Jack Youngblood to Wayne Chastain as the mysterious stranger who was in the grill and who had been picked up by the police, only to deny it to Wayne and reporter Jeff Cohen in 1972. He then confirmed the Youngblood story to me in 1978 when the HSCA investigation was preparing to call James. Regarding the presence of the waitresses in the grill on April 4, Jowers was strikingly inconsistent. In 1982, as I was pursuing some other leads in Memphis, he apparently instructed Akins to kill Betty. Six years later he finally tried to obstruct my locating Betty as well as her sisters Bobbi and Alda and the other waitress, Rosie Lee Dabney. It is thus possible to see an erratic pattern of cover-up or attempted cover-up activity by Loyd Jowers over the entire history of the case. This conduct has only begun to make sense in the perspective of the events of the last two years.

27

Breakthroughs: January–April 15, 1994

IN AN INTERVIEW with the *Tennessean* on January 7, 1994, attorney general Pierotti said that he was going to tell the grand jury to go ahead and listen to what Chastain had to say. The foreman, Herbert Robinson, said that even though Chastain was "a pain" they would hear him sometime after January 18, when the new grand jury was formed. (At the time of this book going to press Wayne would still be waiting to be called.) I found this appalling in light of attorney general Canale's strong undertaking to the jury at James's March 10, 1969, guilty plea hearing. At that time he pledged that "if any evidence was ever presented that showed there was a conspiracy" he would take "prompt and vigorous action in searching out and asking that an indictment be returned. . . ."

Fortunately we had already decided not to wait for this to happen but to proceed with the filing of a petition for a trial.

On January 7, I flew to Nashville and met with James for

about two hours before participating with him in a public television interview, which was to be aired on the following Sunday. He was in good spirits and was particularly interested in the possibility of using the imminent petition as a means of obtaining the declassification of relevant files, reports, and documents.

The interview went well. When the interviewer raised a question about James's ex-wife Anna's claim that he confessed to her over a prison telephone, James pointed out that these telephone calls were monitored and that there was a sign stating this by each phone, so that he was unlikely to discuss anything of a sensitive nature on the phone, much less confess guilt.

I also met again with former *Commercial Appeal* reporter Steve Tompkins. We had spoken several times by telephone during the intervening months, and he had decided to assist me in his spare time. He agreed to reach out to certain contacts of his in greatly varying positions in army intelligence, the Pentagon, and the Special Forces. He had no way of knowing what the response would be, and though he would try to put me in touch with the various people who might have answers to some of my questions, he doubted that they would meet with me face to face. First of all, he said, this was because I was a lawyer—and these guys distrusted all lawyers. Secondly, I was James Earl Ray's attorney and this made their assistance even more risky.

Tompkins said that from his experience these people had always kept their word. Though they would not volunteer any information, they had always answered his questions truthfully.

A couple of the Special Forces "grunts" (noncommissioned officers) would likely cooperate. In addition to covert operations relating to domestic turbulence in 1967, they had been involved in gunrunning activities into New Orleans. The operations were coordinated by a master sergeant who was a part of their group. The sales were made to Carlos Marcello's operation and delivered to barges in a cove bordering property owned by Marcello. A man named Zippy or Zip Chimento handled these transactions for Marcello. The soldiers were given the name of Joe Coppola, who was connected with the Louisiana Highway Patrol, in case they had any trouble transporting the guns by truck. When I checked I learned that Zip Chimento was in fact a confidant and associate of Marcello and Joe Coppola was the commissioner of the Highway Patrol.

ON MONDAY, January 10, Wayne filed the petition for the trial along with five volumes of exhibits and two video exhibits. Wayne and I then drove out to Jim Lawson's old church, Centenary Methodist, where a press conference had been scheduled to call for an independent grand jury investigation. When we got there a number of participants, including Jim Lawson, who had flown in from Los Angeles, had already arrived. The Reverend William Sloane Coffin, the former chaplain of Yale University and pastor of Riverside Church in New York, whom I had not seen in sixteen years, came in shortly after with John Frohnmeyer, a lawyer who had resigned from his post as the Bush administration's appointee to the National Endowment for the Humanities and was in the Freedom Forum First Amendment Center at Vanderbilt. Rev. Coffin had just arrived to take up a post there on sabbatical. The group also included Rev. C. T. Vivian, Dr. King's former aide; Rev. Joseph Agne, director of racial justice for the National Council of Churches in New York; Rev. Ken Sehested of the Baptist Peace Fellowship in Memphis; Rev. Mark Matheny, chairman of the Asbury United Methodist District Council on Ministries in Memphis; Rev. Herbert Lester, pastor of Centenary United Methodist; and Rev. William Vaughan III, pastor of Good Samaritan United Methodist Church.

I briefed the group and answered questions for about two hours. The following two-hour press conference focused on the group's commitment that a grand jury should independently investigate the murder of Dr. King under the leadership of its own foreman and an independent prosecutor not associated in any way with the Shelby County district attorney general. All agreed that the Shelby County D.A. couldn't be regarded as an objective, impartial investigator.

Wayne and I left the meeting feeling uplifted. Later that day we learned that the petition had gone to the court of Judge

Joe Brown, whom Wayne held in high regard, and a hearing had been scheduled for the following morning.

The next morning Wayne and I arrived at the Criminal Justice Center to find television cameras already ensconced in the courtroom. During the brief hearing, the judge raised the question of whether or not our petition could prevail because of prior decisions that had been reached on some of the issues, primarily related to overturning a plea of guilty. We argued that those prior decisions were made without the benefit of the new evidence we now sought to produce which proved James's actual innocence of the crime. The judge asked both sides to prepare memoranda of law on the issues, scheduling a hearing for April 4, the twenty-sixth anniversary of the assassination.

Early that afternoon John McFerren and a friend, Freddie Granberry, came down from Somerville for a meeting in the restaurant at the Ramada hotel. McFerren promised that this time he would not "chicken out" and that he was ready to sing like a bird. He said that he recalled hearing from a local man, Tommy Wright, that on Saturday mornings Liberto would meet with a high-level Tennessee state official at his law office in Fayette County. Tommy said that they would meet regularly on Saturday mornings. Alarm bells went off. I recalled that Randy Rosenson had insisted that in 1978, around the time of his interviews by HSCA staff, he had been visited by the same high-level Tennessee state official, who tried to get him to say that he had been acquainted with James Earl Ray. If Rosenson had known James then he could have dropped the cigarette pack containing the card himself. If he didn't know James then someone else had to have left the pack and card behind. James had always stated that he believed the card was linked to Raul. Since the state and the HSCA had taken the position that Raul did not exist, any evidence to the contrary had to be a problem for them.

In retrospect this could explain why official pressure might have been put on Rosenson to say that he knew James. At the time I couldn't understand why this official would be at all interested in this matter. In light of the connection now being alleged between Liberto and the official, it made more sense.

McFerren said that another source of information was his lawyer from Jackson, Tennessee, Mr H. Ragan. Ragan had handled
McFerren's divorce and had become quite friendly with him.
He had told McFerren quietly, years ago, that the same state
official "handled" matters and looked out for the interests of
organized crime in Tennessee. McFerren thought that Ragan
would confirm the relationship. Ragan repeatedly refused to
speak with me. He appeared frightened and certainly did not
want to continue the discussion he had previously had with
John McFerren.

I had better luck with Tommy Wright. He remembered
seeing "fat" Frank, the produce man, in 1968 at the law offices
of the high-level Tennessee state official who had allegedly visited Randy Rosenson prior to one of his HSCA interviews.

At 2:30, I parted with McFerren and Granberry and met with
retired MPD Captain Tommy Smith. In response to my question, Smith confided that various senior officers of the MPD
were regularly on the take back in 1968, but he didn't know
any details. He said that he was out of the loop because they
knew that he wasn't interested.

He also said that the police officers who went to the FBI
Academy—N. E. Zachary, Robert Cochran, Glynn King and others—formed a special clique.

Tommy Smith then surprised me by saying that Zachary had
called him before he testified at the TV trial, apparently in an
attempt to influence what he would say. Tommy said that was
probably one of the reasons for his decision to testify. He said
he told Zachary that he wasn't going to say what Zachary
wanted him to confirm. My mind flashed back to Glynn King's
testimony and his explicit statement that Charles Stephens was
sober just after the assassination. In light of what so many other
witnesses said, King's observations were inexplicable.

That evening, Wayne and I went to visit John McFerren's
sister Sallie Boyd, who had arranged for us to interview Margaret Toler. As the assistant director of food services for St. Jude's
hospital, Toler used to order food from M. E. Carter but, she
said, the food was always delivered in Frank Liberto's trucks.
The invoices were also sent by Liberto's company, and fre-

quently some of them were for food and produce that was never delivered. She estimated that the hospital lost between $90,000 and $100,000 per year as a result of this scam. Jowers had maintained that the money for his operation was brought to Memphis in an M. E. Carter truck. Frank Holt had earlier described to me Frank Liberto's regular presence at M. E. Carter. Toler's recollections seemed to confirm the relationship between M. E. Carter and Liberto.

IN LATE JANUARY I WAS finally able to speak with Betty Spates. After reading the letter I sent to her, she had told Cliff Dates that she and Bobbi would only talk to me. She said that Jowers, Akins, and others said they were interested in doing a book or movie about the case, and wanted her to change her story to say that she saw a black man hand the rifle to Loyd in the doorway of the kitchen, seconds after the shooting. She refused.

Jowers himself had called her and asked her to tell this story, and Willie Akins came around with a tape recorder and a tape that she was supposed to listen to help her get the story straight. When she refused to go along with this farce, Akins told her that she had "blown it" for all of them. He said that they could have split $300,000 if she had cooperated.

Just before Jowers went on *Prime Time Live,* when Sam Donaldson was in Memphis filming interviews for the program, Akins brought Donaldson or someone from the program around to Spates's house. She wouldn't let them in though Akins began to bang on the windows. She even heard the ABC person say, "I don't want to bother this lady, if she doesn't want to talk to me." Eventually they left.

Betty totally refuted Jowers's claims about Frank Holt and strongly insisted, as before, that when she saw Jowers running toward the back door there was no one with him. We agreed to meet the next time I was in Memphis.

In a telephone conversation in mid-January Betty told me that the Tennessee Bureau of Investigation (TBI) had called her and wanted to interview her. She wanted to know what I thought she should do. I advised her to see them and answer their questions truthfully.

Then, over the last weekend of January, John Billings told me that he learned that Pierotti had asked the TBI to conduct an investigation into the new Jowers evidence. He said that they had already spoken to McCraw on two occasions and McCraw said he had stuck to his story. Billings called the Memphis TBI office and spoke with the investigator, who appeared to have very little knowledge about the case. When he offered to be interviewed and volunteered Ken Herman as well, Billings was told that the attorney general would have to approve such an interview. He would check. The impression Billings received was that they wouldn't be interviewed, and that by using the TBI Pierotti was distancing himself from direct responsibility for the investigation while still controlling the enquiry. As it turned out, they were never interviewed.

I wrote to Pierotti offering any reasonable assistance to the TBI investigation of the new evidence. I told him that James was interested in being released and not in solving the murder. I also advised Pierotti (hoping that the word would reach others) that if released, James intended to leave the country, but while he stayed inside the investigation aimed at establishing his innocence would, of course, continue.

When questioned by the *Tennessean* about the results of his investigation, Pierotti had claimed that the witnesses had retracted their stories. Following this comment I called Betty and asked her what had happened in her interview. She told me that they only asked her about statements Ken Herman had made about what she had said. Since she was angry with him, believing that he had betrayed her trust, I was concerned about what her responses might have been.

DURING THIS TIME STEVE TOMPKINS called and left an urgent message. When I returned his call he said that to his surprise he had received a telegram from a Special Forces contact he had previously interviewed, whom I will call Warren, who now lived in Latin America. The message was simply that "... he now knew who Dr. William Pepper was'' and that he was prepared to answer any questions I would put to him through Tompkins. Under no circumstances would he meet directly with me. The date he set for the meeting, outside of the U.S., was the last weekend in March. Steve Tompkins was willing to go as a consultant and put my questions to Warren, who he said had never lied to him, although, on occasion, he would refuse to discuss a matter or say that he did not know. Based on what Tompkins had told me about him, I knew that he and his partner, whom I will call Murphy, who lived in the same country but who had never met Tompkins, had vital information. He said that though I would have the names of and personal details about Warren, Murphy, and perhaps others, one of the conditions would be that I agree not to name them. Without that understanding there could be no cooperation. If I broke my word on this issue he thought it likely that both of us would be killed. I agreed to the condition but was unclear on whether I could name any participants who had since died. He said simply, ''That's your call.'' Since he would be working for me, he had no problem with my using his name. He would provide detailed written reports.

Through James, I got another lead on the army's role. He had asked me to contact a private investigator named Alexander Taylor following a meeting he had had with him some while ago. The former intelligence officer told me he would do what he could to help our investigation and mentioned a telephone discussion he recently had had with the retired former Army Assistant Chief of Staff for Intelligence Major General William P. Yarborough. Taylor reported that Yarborough believed that it was time for the American people to be told how close America was to civil war during the late 1960s and how extensive was the military preparation. Taylor said he had heard independently in the autumn of last year that ''someone new'' (he assumed it was me) had come on the scene and was particularly thorough. As a result, he thought the whole picture of the role of the military might evolve. With respect to the King case, Taylor volunteered that the time could well be right for a deal to be made, as a result of which James might walk.

Taylor offered to reach out for a meeting with Vice President Gore through his congressman. I was unclear about Taylor's motivation and pessimistic about the chance of success but not opposed to such an effort being made. In any event, nothing came of it.

THEN, on February 22, 1994, after nearly six years of my urging, Amnesty International entered the case and wrote to the attorney general. They specifically asked him what he was doing about the new evidence and expressed their wish that it be thoroughly aired in open court.

Pierotti wrote back on February 28 advising Amnesty that James was in prison not because he was a political prisoner but because he murdered Dr. King. He termed the new evidence "baseless fabrications." After a further exchange of letters, it became clear that he was not going to answer their specific questions. Amnesty decided not to pursue the matter further. There seemed to be no end to Pierotti's arrogance. I believed he knew that aspects of Jowers's story had been confirmed, and yet he continued to maintain that it was all a sham.

ON MARCH 7, 8, and 9 I spent a total of thirteen hours with Betty Spates. She agreed to tell me her story from the beginning, adding that she had been racking her brains, trying to remember each detail about what she observed on April 4, 1968. I met her in her darkened home and for the entirety of my visits we sat at her dining room table, interrupted from time to time by one or another of her adult children. She told the story of her involvement with Jowers and the grill as she had always told it, adding details. She said, for example, that after Loyd's wife divorced him, he bought a white Cadillac identical to the one that she had owned and driven when they were married. There were a few surprises, however, when she related the events of April 4, 1968.

Now Betty remembered going over to the grill just before noon on that day and noticing that Loyd was nowhere around.

She went back to the kitchen at the rear to look for him. The door was slightly ajar. She was only in the kitchen for a short time when Loyd came through the back door carrying a rifle. The gun had a fairly light brown stock and handle and a barrel that appeared to be of normal length; she did not remember seeing a scope. She said that Loyd did not appear to be in a hurry, nor did he seem to be under stress. He was almost nonchalant.

She was startled and asked, "Loyd, what are you doing with that gun?" He replied, half jokingly, "I'm going to use it on you, if I catch you with a nigger." She said, "Loyd, you know I wouldn't do that," and he said he was only kidding, that she knew he'd never hurt her.

He put the gun down alongside a keg of beer and then, as though he had second thoughts, picked it up again and proceeded to break it down in front of her. He then carried the pieces through the grill, went out the front door, and turned left, walking several feet to where his old brown station wagon was parked. As she watched through the window he put the broken-down rifle into the back of the wagon, looking around afterward to see if anyone was watching. Then he came back inside.

She confirmed that during the course of that afternoon she was in and out of the grill, going back and forth to Seabrook. Although Jowers always discouraged her from being around on Thursdays when his wife would drop by, that Thursday he seemed especially ill at ease and kept chasing her out. That only made Betty more suspicious that he was cheating on her, and she was in the grill when Jowers's wife came in around 4:00 p.m. Mrs. Jowers walked straight up to her and called her a whore and told her to get out. Loyd intervened, telling his wife to get out herself and directing Betty to get behind the counter. Sullen and speechless, Loyd's wife stalked out.

After a while Betty went back across the street to Seabrook, returning to the grill to check on Loyd sometime before 6:00. She recalled Bobbi was still there. She often "hung on" to maximize her tips after her shift finished at 3:30. Rosetta and Rosie Lee had gone home. Loyd, however, was again nowhere in sight.

Eventually, she went back toward the kitchen, noticing that this time the door between the restaurant section and the kitchen was tightly closed. Thinking that this was unusual, she made her way into the kitchen where she noticed that the door leading to the backyard was ajar. Soon after, she recalled hearing what sounded like a loud firecracker, and then within seconds she looked out and saw Jowers rushing from the brush area through the door, carrying another rifle. When she first saw him he was about ten to fifteen feet from the door. He was out of breath, she said, and white as a ghost. His hair was in disarray, and the knees of his trousers were wet and muddy as though he had been kneeling in the soggy grass or brush area.

When he caught his breath he didn't appear angry, but plaintively said to her, "You wouldn't ever do anything to hurt me, would you?" She said, "Of course I wouldn't, Loyd." Without another word he moved quickly to the door leading into the grill, which opened right next to the counter on the left. In one quick step, with the rifle at his side, he was behind the counter and she saw him place the gun on a shelf under the counter and push it farther back.

She remembered that the rifle was distinctive. It had a dark mahogany-brown stock, a scope, and a short barrel that made the gun look like a toy gun. There was something screwed or fixed onto the barrel somehow, fitting over it and increasing its diameter.

In this statement, for the first time, Betty had spoken of two separate instances of seeing Loyd Jowers bringing a gun in from the brush area behind the kitchen. It was somewhat worrying that this was the first time she had mentioned a second gun. On the other hand, this account corroborated what McCraw had said all along about Jowers showing him the gun under the counter.

Betty went on to say that a few months after the killing in 1968, she was visited by three persons who she believed were government officials. One was black, another white, and the third appeared to be Spanish or Latino. They offered her and her sisters new identities, relocation, and money for, it was said, their own protection. They refused, supported by their mother, and the men left.

Two of the same men returned about five years later. (This would have been around the time that James was being given an evidentiary hearing in federal court.) The offer was repeated and again refused.

In the early 1980s, in addition to the incident when Akins fired at her and her two sons, one evening he came in through the back door of her house when she had just returned, exhausted, from work. As she was seated on her sofa, he pulled out his pistol and fired three shots into the sofa, missing her by inches. As she thought about it, Betty believed that Akins was only trying to frighten and not to kill her.

Betty signed detailed affidavits in support of all of these events.

When we filed Betty's primary affidavit with the court the *Tennessean* published its contents. Shortly afterward attorney general Pierotti leaked a statement taken by the TBI on January 25 that we found distressing. It was purportedly under oath, handwritten by TBI special agent John Simmons and witnessed by one of Pierotti's investigators, Mark Glanker. In it Betty denied seeing Jowers with the rifle at 6:00 p.m. and further denied having any information supporting James's innocence.

When I asked Betty about it she did not recall giving the specific answers recorded. Once again she said they only asked her to respond to specific points in Ken Herman's statement.

It did appear, however, that she had signed the TBI statement. I realized that I would not get to the bottom of the discrepancies until I could obtain the statement and copies of the complete tape recordings of the TBI interview. This latter would not be possible unless we had an evidentiary hearing and we could obtain them in discovery. At the end of March, however, I was able to obtain a copy of the TBI interview statement of Betty Spates. On its face the handwritten statement dated January 25, 1994 appeared to contradict the affidavit she had given me on March 8, 1994. When I showed it to her and asked her how she could have signed it, she said she didn't read it because her glasses were broken. It was read to her, and the investigator wrote as he asked her questions, telling her not to volunteer information but to simply answer questions about Herman's statement. She said the men from the attorney general's office and the TBI made her afraid. Betty went out of her way to assure me that she now wanted to testify and to clear her name of any hint of her being a liar.

For some time I had known that Betty had a brain tumor that affected her memory from time to time, but until then I had not taken it seriously. The tumor also resulted in her having blinding headaches. She was afraid to undergo surgery because of what she believed was the risk of permanent brain damage.

SID CARTHEW LIVES IN ENGLAND. In 1967-1968 he was a merchant seaman sailing on both cargo and passenger ships destined for ports around the world. He frequently traveled to North America and spent time in the U.S. Gulf ports as well as in Montreal. In Montreal he would frequent the Neptune Tavern on West Commissioner's Street, because it was right down near the docks, and was a hangout for merchant seamen. It was in that bar on two occasions that he met a man named Raul.

Carthew came upon the TV trial by accident. Knowing nothing about the case before seeing the trial, Carthew became interested when he heard James Earl Ray testify about being in the Neptune in late July and August of 1967. His interest was heightened when James went on to describe his meetings in that bar with Raul. Then Carthew heard prosecutor Hickman Ewing ridicule James's contention not only that Raul could have manipulated James into being a patsy for the killing of Dr. King, but that he even existed.

Carthew tried desperately to contact me, getting nowhere until he contacted the General Council of the Bar in London which gave him my address. He assured me that Raul did indeed exist. Carthew said Raul approached him at the Neptune sometime in 1967. Raul had struck up a conversation about the sale of guns. Carthew had a passing interest, and Raul said he would sell him some Browning 9mm handguns. Carthew said he would take four, and Raul, apparently thinking he meant four boxes, entered into negotiations. He quickly turned off, however, when it became clear that Carthew was only talking about four weapons rather than boxes. Carthew said Raul muttered something about it being typical of the English, who never had enough money to pay for anything.

Sid Carthew described Raul as being about 5'8" tall and weighing approximately 145 pounds. He had a dark, Mediterraneanlike complexion and dark brown hair. (This was consistant with James's description of Raul.) Carthew remembered him saying that the guns were stolen from a military base and that the price included the fee for the master sergeant who organized the supply and who, according to Raul, would deliver them himself to his ship in exchange for cash. This dovetailed with Tompkins's account of the New Orleans gunrunning activity of the Special Forces soldiers.

In addition Carthew remembered Raul asking him about the possibility of someone going to England on board a ship such as his. He told him that it would not be a problem, insisting that seamen tried to help out any person in trouble. He said that Raul seemed skeptical about the arrangements. It was as though he was looking for an assurance that it wouldn't work. In any event he did not pursue the matter.

I couldn't believe my good fortune. Carthew said that he believed that a shipmate and friend of his named Joe Sheehan, with whom Carthew had lost touch, was also present at the table in the bar when the discussion about the guns was going on. We eventually tracked down Sheehan, who said he wasn't at the Neptune that particular night but confirmed that Carthew had mentioned the incident to him sometime afterward at the annual general meeting of the National Union of Seamen in May 1968.

THE HEARING ORIGINALLY SCHEDULED FOR April 4 had been put off until April 15. Judge Joe Brown's courtroom was practically empty at 11 a.m. that morning except the jury box which was jammed with the media. The state's side of the table had the attorney general and two assistant attorneys general crammed together, with Wayne and me sitting on the defense side. The handful of spectators included Ken Herman, John Billings, Lewis Garrison, and, to my surprise, Willie Akins.

After the preliminaries, the state (through assistant attorney general William Campbell) argued on behalf of its motion to dismiss the petition. Their argument was that on a strict interpretation of Tennessee law the petition had to be denied. While admitting that James might claim relief under federal law, Campbell argued that after all the time that had elapsed he was technically precluded under state law, essentially because he had entered a plea of guilty.

This would mean that anyone who had pleaded guilty, whether that plea was coerced or not, would never be entitled to a trial, even in a case like this where new evidence of actual innocence came to light.

When my turn came, I reviewed the factual history of the case and argued for relief based upon the guarantees of rights contained in both the Tennessee and U.S. constitutions. I contended that the court should examine the new evidence pertaining to the actual innocence of James. I argued that it was now substantially clear that the guilty plea was coerced and that in any event the state should not be allowed to deny a trial in a case where the defendant is actually innocent. The state's blatant attempt to separate Tennessee law and procedure from the minimal obligations required under federal law was unconstitutional.

Though the hearing was to focus on the law, I argued the law by substantially elaborating upon and applying the facts. This enabled me to put a long list of suppressed factual evidence and factual discrepancies on the record and of course to be heard by the judge and the media.

Pierotti spoke for about 15 minutes as part of the state's rebuttal argument and clearly appeared to be agitated. He made the mistake of actually addressing me, asking whether or not I had represented one of the Ray brothers before the HSCA. This allowed me to rise and interrupt him to explain to the court (and put on the record) the circumstances that led to my representing Jerry Ray.

At the end of the argument the judge complimented both sides and then, referring to lengthy notes, stated that although the state might be technically correct, requiring him to deny the petition, nevertheless he was going to allow us to put forward evidence. This evidentiary record would be available to an appellate court, he said, as well as to history. In an impassioned reference to the importance of Dr. King, he said history compelled him to allow as much information as possible to be placed before the public under the auspices of his court.

The state was stunned. Campbell inquired what this meant. The judge said that he would not finalize or file any order until after the proffer (submission of evidence) was over. We were elated.

When asked by reporters outside of the courtroom what he was going to do, the attorney general responded that he was ". . . going to pull out the rest of my hair," and labeled our case "garbage."

It was an extraordinary result. If he had explicitly ruled in our favor and granted a trial or a full evidentiary hearing, the state would have appealed, and considering the inclination of the court of appeals and the Supreme Court, he would likely have been overturned. In any event we would have been off on the appellate trail. By not finalizing any ruling (effectively pocketing it), he kept the matter before him and could thus allow us to call witnesses and submit evidence. We intended, for example, to file a motion asking to test the rifle and the bullets in evidence. Whether or not the judge would go so far as to order a trial at the conclusion of our evidence remained to be seen, but following the hearing on April 15 I believed that there was a chance.

28

Setbacks and Surprises: April 16– October 30, 1994

YEARS EARLIER JOHN MCFERREN HAD TOLD ME (as he had also told writer Bill Sartor in 1968) about an incident that occurred shortly after James's capture in 1968. He was produce shopping in Palazolla's market store when suddenly the manager saw him and began to cry. Startled, McFerren asked one of the black employees (Robert Tyus), whom he knew as Old Pal, what the problem was. Old Pal took him aside and explained that seeing him must have reminded Mr. Palazolla about the death of his teenage son. The boy had had a stall in Frank Liberto's LL& L wholesale produce store in the market at 815 Scott Street and might have learned too much about Liberto's involvement in the killing of Dr. King. Shortly after McFerren had given his statement setting out the conversation he overheard on April 4, in which Liberto told someone ''to shoot the son of a bitch when he comes on the balcony,'' the Palazolla boy died, supposedly in an automobile accident. By making his statement

McFerren had put Frank Liberto clearly in the frame with regard to the King killing. The tightly knit section of the Italian community involved in the produce business knew about McFerren's allegations. Old Pal implied that the death was arranged by Liberto to ensure his silence.

I had long been unable to corroborate this death. When I asked Ken Herman to check it out in 1992 he told me that there was no record of it. Over the years McFerren had become unable to remember the details of the incident. Then, when I asked him about the management of the Palazolla operation, McFerren spontaneously said that Mr. Bob Palazolla, who was running the business for his father, was the one who cried. McFerren said he remembered now that he was told that Mr. Palazolla broke down because the death of his son was somehow associated with him learning information about Liberto's role in the killing of Dr. King. Robert Chapman, a restaurateur who was a friend of Wayne's and a longtime large-volume customer of the Palazolla Produce Company, offered to ask Michael Palazolla, who currently runs the business, about the death of a youngster around that time. He was told that family patriarch Walter had a grandson who had died as a teenager. Walter's son, the boy's father, was Bob Palazolla. John agreed to try to locate 'Old Pal' and see what further information he could obtain.

ON APRIL 22, 1994 I left for Dallas to meet with oil man H. L. Hunt's former chief aide John Curington. We would meet again the following November 6, at which time he brought along Clyde Lovingood a former aide and close friend of Mr Hunt. Months earlier I had instructed one of my investigators Jim Johnson, to raise certain preliminary questions with him when he was available to be interviewed. In meetings that lasted more than thirteen hours, he expanded considerably on the information he'd given my investigator and offered many new revelations on the billionaire oil man's close ties to several of the institutions and individuals that were emerging as having involvement in the conspiracy—in particular the FBI and the Mafia.

Curington had worked for Hunt Oil for fifteen years and for nearly thirteen of these had worked for H. L. Hunt personally, occupying the office right next to him, only by a door, which usually stood open. As was not unusual with such an employer, he frequently worked eighteen-hour days and seven-day weeks and often traveled with him. In such a position few things should have escaped his notice.

As he explained it, he was basically Mr. Hunt's "follow-through" guy. He did whatever was necessary to get a job done. While not engaging in the dirty work himself, he made the arrangements at the old man's request. My investigator had said at one point that he had even referred to himself as Hunt's "bag man," saying that he carried and delivered cash, sometimes in very large amounts, to any number of places, organizations, and individuals in support of right-wing activities as well as to pay for specific operations. Curington insisted that no one knew all of the old man's business since he would frequently assign confidential tasks to particular individuals whom he trusted.

Though Curington was clearly concerned about his own legal position, since he had participated in many of the illegal activities he detailed, he was remarkably frank overall. While continually referring to documents in an old brown leather suitcase, the sixty-seven-year-old Texan confirmed that a closer relationship than had ever been publicly known existed between his ex-boss and FBI director J. Edgar Hoover. Their association went back to the early 1950s. My investigator Jim Johnson had witnessed this relationship during his boyhood visit to Monroe Waldridge's east Texas ranch. Apparently they had been poker-playing friends for many years, and their compatible right-wing political views made them allies. Hoover had even seconded a trusted FBI agent, Paul Rothermel, to Hunt as his head of security. Rothermel left the bureau in late 1954 and joined Hunt in 1955.

Curington was present at various meetings between the two men when Martin Luther King was discussed. Usually Hoover came to the old man's hotel room. While the two men shared a dislike for Dr. King, Hoover's animosity was more passionate and obsessive, more personal. Hoover regularly provided Hunt with a considerable amount of documentation and material to be used as ammunition against Dr. King in the oil baron's extreme right-wing, daily nationally syndicated *Life Line* radio broadcasts. King was a favorite and a regular target of *Life Line* venom, and Hoover provided the poison. Curington recalled one meeting in Chicago between Hunt and Hoover, which to the best of his recollection was held around the time of the American Medical Association national convention in the year that Milford Rouse was elected president (upon checking I learned that that convention was held in June 1967). At that meeting in Hunt's hotel room, he recalled Hunt telling Hoover that he could finish King by constantly attacking him on his daily radio broadcasts. Hoover replied that it would not work. He said the only way to stop King would be to "completely silence" him. After King's murder, Hunt acknowledged to Curington that Hoover had won that argument.

He also said that the old man had a private telephone that he kept in his desk drawer. The phone was in the name of a dead man, John McKinley. It was on this phone that he would receive and occasionally place phone calls about sensitive matters. Very few people had the McKinley phone number. Hoover was one and he would call only on this phone.

In April 1968, *Life Line* produced a fifteen-minute daily program, six days a week, on 429 stations in 398 cities across America. Between 1967 and 1968 Hunt spent nearly $2,000,000 on this program alone. Curington revealed that the entire effort, as well as other shadowy, often deeply covert political activity, was funded by monies diverted by Hunt from H.L.H. Products Inc. Curington ran this company, which the "old man" had established as a front for funding such political activity. This is why Curington found charges of embezzlement made by Hunt's sons Bunker and Herbert and nephew Tom Hunt in 1969 against himself and Paul Rothermel hard to take: funds were routinely siphoned off, and kickbacks from purchasers were collected and diverted, on the old man's instructions. James's former lawyer, Percy Foreman, who also represented the Hunts, was ultimately indicted for charges connected with the wiretapping of Hunt aides Curington and Rothermel as a part of the effort to prove the embezzlement charges.

Curington also acknowledged that his boss and Hoover shared many of the same friends, including several kingpins of organized crime. Not only was Hunt close to gamblers Frank Erickson (to whom he once owed $400,000) and Ray Ryan (who at the same time owed him a large amount), but he associated with Frank Costello (the mob's liaison to Hoover) and Meyer Lansky. Clyde Lovingood, who handled other sensitive assignments for Hunt, confirmed that he was the direct liaison with Lansky. Hunt's top-level mob ties also included Carlos Marcello and Dallas boss Joe Civello.

Subsequently, in Curington's file I found a *Dallas Morning News* obituary for Civello, dated January 19, 1970, which indicated that one of H.L.H. Products' senior officers, John H. Brown, was a pallbearer at Civello's funeral. Other pallbearers included Civello's Baton Rouge relatives, the Polito family, long associated with Carlos Marcello. Brown lived across the street from Civello, and when the FBI wanted an informant on Civello, Curington arranged for Brown—with Civello's permission—to provide innocuous bits and pieces of information, so that the Hunt relationship with both the bureau and Civello was enhanced. According to Curington, it was not as though Hoover would ever do anything contrary to Civello's interests, but he realized that information was power and he liked to know as much as possible. Hunt also knew and closely relied upon certain Houston individuals who were very close to Marcello.

In politics, he noted that Sam Rayburn, the former speaker of the House of Representatives, and his protégé Lyndon Johnson were both lifelong close political assets of Mr. Hunt.

Other political allies of Hunt, and the beneficiaries of his largesse, across the nation, included John Connally in Texas and Senator James Eastland of Mississippi, who headed the right-wing Senate Internal Security Subcommittee. Curington said that all these people received payoffs or unrecorded contributions from Hunt, delivered in a variety of ways. Connally or Eastland, for example, might sell cattle to Hunt, who would vastly overpay them. He said that a Louisiana state official was the conduit for cash payments to Jimmy Hoffa and the Teamsters Union, whose assistance was bought for the purpose of dealing with labor problems at any of the Hunt operations. In one instance, Hoffa actually pulled the union out of a Hunt operation in Muncie, Indiana. The Teamsters connections were often used to beat up or kill people who created problems at any of the Hunt operations.

Curington also said that H. L. Hunt's daily liaison with President Lyndon Johnson on political matters was former FBI agent Booth Mooney, who was personally close to the president. Mooney not only delivered communications back and forth between Johnson and Hunt but also wrote over half of the *Life Line* broadcast tracts, including many of those attacking Dr. King.

Turning to the killing of Dr. King, Curington said that on the evening of the assassination, shortly after the shooting, Hoover called Hunt and advised him to cancel his anti-King "Life Line" programs that were to be aired that evening and the morning of April 5. After that call Curington said he was called to Hunt's home and given the task of putting together a team of secretaries to call the radio stations. Then on April 5, the day after the assassination, Hunt told him to make arrangements for him (Hunt) and his wife to travel to a Holiday Inn resort hotel in El Paso, Texas. The tickets were in the names of Curington and his wife, and he took Curington's American Express card with him. They checked in at the Holiday Inn on April 5 in the names of John and Mary Ann Curington. Curington said the hotel was on 6655 Gateway East, El Paso. Providing a copy of the hotel bill, Curington pointed out that before Hunt checked out of the Holiday Inn in El Paso, Texas on April 6 he engaged in a lengthy long-distance telephone call. Curington speculated that whoever was on the other end of that call must have given Hunt a grave message, which caused him to leave the hotel suddenly. He then disappeared for about ten days. In my review of sections of the Hunt organization file provided to me by Curington, I found a memo that Curington stated had been prepared by Paul Rothermel dated April 9, 1968. It revealed that Martin Luther King was very much on his mind on the morning of April 6. It began,

"At 6:50 a.m. April 6, Mr. Hunt called from El Paso, Texas and said that a book on Martin Luther King absolutely had to be written." He wanted the book to prove King ". . . to be practically a communist . . ." The memo recorded a further call at 8:00 a.m. and even "several times" more leaving messages ". . . always to the effecct that the book must be written . . ." Hunt was noted as suggesting that the book be called "The Career of King or Martin Luther King."

Curington said he also spoke with Hunt that morning, and all he wanted to talk about was the book on King. Then after a full weekend of work on the project he called it off as abruptly as he began. Curington speculated that someone, perhaps Hoover, pointed out to him that he should distance himself from King at that time and not call attention to his animosity toward him. It is clear that H. L. Hunt was enormously preoccupied with Dr. King during that first weekend after his death.

By the end of our session, I concluded that John Curington, twenty-five years later, still appeared to be in awe of the man who he said moved on an entirely different level from "the rest of us."

THAT LAST WEEK IN APRIL I flew from Dallas to Miami and met Jim Johnson at the Hilton in Fort Lauderdale. He had spent the day talking with Harry, the American Indian with whom Rosenson had said he travelled to Mexico for various types of smuggling and gunrunning operations. In 1968 Harry lived in Miami and owned a white Mustang. Johnson told me that he was convinced that he was Raul. I thought it unlikely. The next morning I interviewed him for four hours. Though he had been involved in a wide range of covert activities for government agencies, Carlos Marcello, and even the Dixie Mafia (a loosely knit group of professional criminals-for-hire), he was clearly not Raul. Like many others, however, he may have come into contact with individuals who had some connection to the King killing.

Next I traveled to New Orleans to interview Randy Rosenson to see if he could identify the high-level Tennessee state official as the man who, just prior to him being interviewed by the

HSCA in Richmond, Virginia, had urged him to admit knowing Ray. He was unable to do so.

A PAROLE HEARING FOR James was set for May 25. This would be the first time he had appeared before the board. Such hearings are confined to a review of conduct during time served and other factors related to an assessment of whether or not a person should be released. They are not concerned with any determination of guilt or innocence. I had no doubt that the decision would be made on purely political grounds and that the board would have made its decision before the hearing began. Consequently, we decided to use this hearing as a forum to focus on James's innocence.

I was struck by the extent of media coverage, which included Court TV broadcasting throughout and extensive newspaper coverage, particularly in light of the fact that Jowers's admissions on network television had been virtually ignored. Jim Lawson and Hosea Williams testified in favor of James being released. James's former wife Anna was her usual vitriolic self in opposition. Attorney general John Pierotti—attending, so I was told, his first parole hearing—read from a prepared text and waxed on about the terrible loss of Dr. King. He maintained that James could never even in a hundred years repay his debt to society. Being well aware of the politics represented by the attorney general, I was sickened.

I challenged the board to act independently of the governor who appointed them and who had publicly expressed his wish that they deny parole, and also to disavow the previous statements of the board's former executive director, who said James would not be paroled unless he admitted guilt. After three hours of the board focusing on James's past record, it became clear that the decision had indeed been made before the hearing began. In fact, this was confirmed by a slip of the tongue of one of the members near the end of the hearing. Parole was denied. James was told he could apply again in five years after he had served a full thirty years. James, understandably, reacted angrily.

At a posthearing press conference, in response to a question about the testing of the rifle, Pierotti made the extraordinary statement that he didn't know if James was guilty and he didn't have to prove it. So much for the requirement that prosecutors shall be primarily concerned with justice.

I was more convinced than ever that our best hope lay in Judge Brown's courtroom. Judge Brown had been pressing us for some time to submit our draft order for the testing of the rifle and the bullets in evidence. I believed it likely that once the judge granted our request the state would appeal his order and seek a delay pending review. It had therefore seemed advisable to submit our motion after the parole hearing so that the parole board would rule prior to any setback in the appellate courts, which I thought was distinctly possible.

I RETURNED HOME TO ENGLAND only to turn around eight days later and fly back to Memphis to prepare for the test-firing of the rifle which we planned to attempt on Monday morning, June 6. The judge had ordered the rifle to be tested in Shelby County (preferably at the sheriff's department firing range), but there was no adequate facility there to accomplish this. After consulting with our ballistics expert, Chuck Morton, I decided to build one myself in a designated area at the sheriff's range. We acquired a 600-pound bale of cotton and seventeen 2' × 3' × 1.5' cardboard boxes, which I planned to pack with cotton and join together to form a cotton tunnel receptacle into which the experimental bullets would be fired by investigator Cliff Dates, who had agreed to be the shooter. I bought a box of 150-grain Remington soft points bullets and at Morton's suggestion another box of bronze tips, or military bullets. He advised firing the different bullets in alternate fashion, with each test-fire being retrieved and sealed in an evidence packet before the next one was fired.

Local teacher Wallace Milam, who was knowledgeable about trace element analysis in general and the process of neutron activation analysis in particular, agreed to coordinate the taking of lead samples from the evidence bullets, to weigh and seal them, and then deliver them to a designated laboratory. It would have been preferable, of course, to have the chemist performing the analysis collect the sample himself, and I would have preferred to have Chuck Morton present at all stages of the ballistics test activity, but there were simply no funds available for this.

AROUND 10:30 THAT SATURDAY evening (June 4) I received a call from Nathan Whitlock, who had known Frank Liberto in the 1970s, and who I heard had been told by Liberto himself that he had arranged to have King killed. Whitlock usually drove a cab at night; on that evening he was driving a limousine and I rode with him so we could talk. He told me about his conversation with "Mr. Frank" (Frank C. Liberto) some sixteen years earlier. He said that his mother, Lavada, had owned a restaurant that lay on the route between Liberto's home and his LL&L produce company business in the Scott Street market. Nearly every day the produce man would stop in there for breakfast in the morning on his way to LL&L and for drinks in the afternoon on his way home. Nathan said that when he had had a few drinks, Liberto took to baring his soul to Lavada. She would often leave her post at the bar, sit down at a table, and talk with him. His conversation ranged from complaints about his wife (who he said was a compulsive gambler) and his girlfriend (who he said was only interested in his money) to his admission that he arranged for the killing of Martin Luther King. Nathan said that when his mother told him about this he became upset that Mr. Frank would involve his mother in this "gangster" talk. Nathan played guitar and used to travel, but in between trips he would help out in the restaurant, where he would often serve beer to Mr. Frank. Occasionally he would play the guitar for him—Liberto, he said, liked to hear "Malaguena." Nathan would sometimes also drive Liberto's truck back to the market to pick up something Liberto had forgotten. For these favors Liberto would tip him ten or twenty dollars.

Nathan said Liberto wanted to appear to be a big shot around him. He showed off a thick roll of bills and a jade, diamond, and gold ring purportedly given to him by Elvis Presley. They became reasonably friendly. Liberto told Nathan that his relationship with his mother reminded him of Liberto's relationship with his own mother.

Another customer of the restaurant once quietly advised Nathan to be careful since Liberto was in the Mafia. Nathan, who was about eighteen at the time, once asked Liberto if indeed he was in the Mafia and what the Mafia was, anyhow. Liberto told him that the Mafia was a group of businessmen who "took care of business." He added that as a youngster he used to push a vegetable cart with Carlos Marcello in New Orleans. At the time this meant nothing to Nathan because he didn't know who Marcello was.

Because he was upset about Mr. Frank's conversation with his mother, he decided to confront him. One afternoon in 1978, just before Nathan was scheduled to go away on a trip, Liberto came in and ordered a beer and sat down at a table in front of his photograph, which hung on the wall along with those of other regular patrons. Nathan engaged the 300-pound produce dealer in conversation and then asked him directly if he had killed Dr. King. He said Mr. Frank looked as though he was going to be sick to his stomach. He immediately asked Nathan if he was wired. The boy thought Liberto wanted to know if he was on drugs, which he denied.

Then Liberto said, "You've been talking to your mother, haven't you?" Nathan admitted that he had, and Liberto then told him, "I didn't kill the nigger, but I had it done."

Nathan said, "Well, that S.O.B. is taking credit for it," (referring to James), to which Liberto responded, "Oh, he wasn't nothing but a troublemaker from Missouri." He added that James was a "front man," a "set-up man." Then Nathan said Mr. Frank turned on him, saying, "You don't need to know about this," and after jumping to his feet and drawing his right hand back as though to hit him, he said, "Don't you say nothin,' boy," and glared at him. He stomped around, thinking for a minute or so, and then said, "You're going to Canada, aren't you?" Nathan said he was. Liberto became quiet and Nathan went to the back of the restaurant to take care of something. When he returned, Liberto's beer was still on the table but Mr. Frank was gone.

He never saw Liberto again, but in early 1979 during his trip his mother sent him a letter stating that Frank Liberto had died. Nathan said he was somewhat sad because they had parted with some hostility between them.

On Monday Nathan gave me a written account of his encounter with Frank Liberto and also showed me photographs of Liberto sitting at a table in his mother's restaurant. (See photograph #18.)

Sometime later Nathan would tell this story directly to the attorney general, after which he was interrogated by members of Pierotti's staff. He said they tried to break down his account, but he stuck to his guns. (Later both Nathan and his mother told their stories under oath.)

On June 5, Wayne Chastain and I met for the first time with Willie Akins. In a three-hour session he discussed how he had come to know Loyd Jowers and how he gradually learned about Jowers's involvement in the killing. He basically confirmed the acts of violence against Betty but cast them in a different context. He said that he never took a contract on her life but admitted that he had fired shots into Betty's sofa late one afternoon—but not because he was trying to kill her. He wouldn't have missed if he was really trying to kill her. He had been going with her at the time and found her with someone else on the sofa when he came in. He said that the cause of the later incident, in the early 1980s, was his anger with her for intruding when he was with another woman in a bus belonging to Jowers.

It appeared that Jowers had only fairly recently begun to open up to him regarding the King case. He said that on the evening John Edginton's documentary aired in the States (in which Earl Caldwell spoke about seeing a figure in the bushes), Jowers called him and said, "Big N [Jowers always called him that, he said it stood for Big Nigger], you know that figure in the bushes he talked about—that was me."

Akins left me in no doubt that he had come to learn that Betty's story was true. Jowers was out in the bushes at the time of the shooting. He said that on one occasion Jowers told him that the person who could do him the most damage was the chauffeur. He was, of course, referring to the long-missing Solomon Jones. Akins also commented on the whereabouts of the actual murder weapon, contending that so far as he understood it, Jowers had kept control of it for a period of time. He said he believed that even today Jowers knew where the gun was. I thought that was unlikely, considering the fact that Jowers was probably a low-level participant.

Akins continued to pay lip service to the story about being asked to get rid of Frank Holt. My sense was that Akins had pieced part of the story together but that Jowers certainly had not told him everything.

Although he was clearly lying about some things, Akins's information only added more corroboration to Jowers's involvement. The question still remaining about the actual killing, however, was whether or not he had been out there alone and whether he himself had pulled the trigger. I increasingly believed that the answer to both questions was no. Someone, or some others, were there as well.

THAT MONDAY MORNING, June 6, after having breakfast with Nathan Whitlock, I went out to the sheriff's range with investigator Cliff Dates and began to build the bullet trap. Wayne went along to court with Wallace Milam and his associate.

Dates and I were in the process of hand-packing the boxes when a sheriff's deputy came out to tell us that there would be no firing of the rifle that day. The attorney general had requested that an FBI ballistics expert be present, and this would require time to arrange. Though this issue had never been raised before, the judge thought it was a reasonable request and granted it, not only with respect to the ballistics firing but also the taking of the lead sample for trace element analysis. Once again we were on hold. I returned to London.

While Dates and I had been at the rifle range, a man named

Robert McCoy arrived at the courthouse looking for me. He had driven all the way from Milwaukee to tell me his story. Being unable to find me he returned home, leaving a message on Chastain's answering machine. I spoke to him five days later on June 11. He said he believed that in 1967, as an eighteen-year-old black civil rights activist in Carthage, Mississippi, he had stumbled on the conspiracy to kill Dr. King. The local sheriff regarded him as a troublemaker and had picked him up on the evening of December 1 on a phoney charge. This allowed them to hold him until an FBI agent was brought in to interview him. McCoy said they threatened to put him away unless he agreed to go undercover and work for them. In order to get out of the tight spot he was in, he agreed. The agent pulled out a black book and asked him about a number of black leaders and their influence on local movements. Specifically, they wanted him to become involved with the SCLC and to keep them informed about Dr. King's movements and when he would be returning to Mississippi.

He said they were very interested in whether he had heard anything about Dr. King running for president or vice president with Robert Kennedy. After leaving the sheriff's office, McCoy fled the area. Eventually he went to Wisconsin. McCoy's experience only made it more evident how concerned the bureau and its allies were over the possible national political plans of Dr. King.

Early the following week the attorney general notified us that an FBI ballistics expert would be in Memphis on Thursday, June 16, in order to observe the test-firing of the rifle as well as the taking of lead scrapings from the evidence bullet and the death slug. At the same time, however, Pierotti indicated that he was going to appeal Judge Brown's interlocutory order allowing ballistics testing and the proffer of evidence by the defense.

I left London on Wednesday to carry out the testing, but by the time I arrived, a stay had been granted by the Court of Criminal Appeals. There was little else to do but hold a press conference in order to object to the bad faith of the attorney general. He had obtained a delay on what appeared to be the pretext of getting an FBI expert to attend the testing, allowing him time to obtain a stay. We prepared a motion requesting that we be allowed to proceed.

Wayne and I met the local press corps. Two TBI agents sat off to one side taking notes during the entire press conference. I stated that the desperate action of the attorney general was a continuation of the historical cover-up of the truth and angrily challenged them to ask Pierotti why he was so afraid of allowing the weapon to be tested. In their session with the attorney general, the local reporters went no further than to ask him how he thought I could get this evidence out in the open. He replied tersely that I could always publish. It seemed to me that this might indeed be our best way forward now.

I also advised the media that I was going to ask the United States attorney general to enter the case, not by means of a Justice Department investigation but rather by empowering a federal grand jury to hear testimony. The following week this request was formalized.

Once again I had that old feeling—the fix was in. My apprehension increased when Wayne gave me a set of the state's motion papers. In sworn affidavits Pierotti had stated that our testing would "irretrievably damage evidence" (categorically untrue), rendering it unavailable for "future proceedings." Would the court of appeals be naive enough to accept this rationale?

I WENT TO SEE Art Hanes, Sr., and Art Hanes, Jr. (now a judge). I hadn't seen them in sixteen years but they graciously received me on short notice. I thought it would be useful to obtain any remaining defense file materials that could assist James. I was out of luck. In 1977 their entire file containing all of their initial investigation interview statements was sent off to the HSCA and never returned. Subsequently, it was sealed with the rest of the HSCA investigative files. This meant that James's subsequent attorneys who were entitled to receive that file would be barred from having and using it. This was one more example of a violation of James's sixth amendment right to a full and fair defense.

*   *   *

WAYNE CHASTAIN AND I finalized the response to the attorney general's appeal against Judge Joe Brown's decision to allow a proffer of evidence in support of James's actual innocence.

The Tennessee court of appeals had set August 16 for oral argument of the state's appeal. Since I had a conflict on that date we submitted a motion for a one-week continuance. It was denied because the court ruled that my admission on motion to appear before the lower court in this case was not binding on the appellate courts in the state. Thus, I would have to apply separately to each state appellate court, and there wasn't time. Wayne had never heard of this technicality being asserted before. Consequently, Wayne appeared alone and argued. As expected, the court was hostile. A ruling was promised in September.

I decided to open up another legal front and bring a civil action against Loyd Jowers on behalf of James. Jowers had, after all, actually admitted on national prime-time television that he played a key role in the case for which James had spent twenty-five years in prison. Jowers had also publicly admitted that James was a patsy and did not know what was going on. Thus Jowers's acts and his continued silence had resulted in the unjust imprisonment of James.

We filed the complaint for the civil suit against Loyd Jowers, Raul _____ and other unknown parties on Thursday, August 25. We alleged that Jowers had participated in the tort of conspiracy as a result of which James had been deprived of his liberty and been wrongly imprisoned for twenty-five years. On top of that we added the newly developed ancillary tort of outrage, which was justified by the very nature and continuation of the wrongful acts. Damages sought were $6,500,000 actual and compensatory and $39,500,000 punitive.

BACK IN LONDON IN SEPTEMBER, we came across a photograph in the *Commercial Appeal*'s pictorial history, *I Am A Man*.[2] It was a shot of MPD officer Louis McKay guarding the bundle in Canipe's doorway. At first glance I thought I had seen this photo dozens of times before. Then I noticed that unlike other photographs I had seen, this shot was taken looking south toward the fire station, and in the background in the upper right was a hedge running down to the sidewalk between the parking lot and the fire station. I was curious. Although there had been rumors of a hedge in that spot we had never seen any photographs of it. Upon checking the evidence photographs from the attorney general's office, this hedge did not appear standing in any of the evidence photos. Then I came across a photograph of the hedge having been cut down to its very roots. I was amazed, and wondered how I could have overlooked it before. From all of the other photographs one would never know that a hedge had ever been there. The significance, of course, is that the official investigators had contended that on leaving the rooming house James had seen a police car parked up near the sidewalk which caused him to panic and drop the bundle. As we have seen, there was no police car in this position (it being parked about sixty-feet back from the sidewalk) but even if there had been, the hedge would have obstructed the view and made the official story untenable.

It was clear as could be. At the time of the killing a hedge was there. Sometime shortly thereafter (probably the next morning when the bushes at the rear of the rooming house were cut) it was cut to the ground and all trace of its existence obliterated. The photograph which Ewing used for illustrative purposes at the television trial showed a police car in clear view pulled up to the sidewalk. That photograph and others like it must have been staged, taken after the scene had been physically altered. In fact, in the staged photographs where the billboards are visible the billboard advertisements are different from the ones in place on the day of the killing and the day after. The photographs of the cut hedge reveal the same billboard ads as those in place at the time of the killing. Further confirmation of the existence of the hedge is provided by the HSCA drawing of the crime scene (MLK Exhibit F-19)[3] which actually depicts it in place. Later, former fireman William King also confirmed the existence of the hedge. So it was not only the rear brush area of the rooming house that had been changed to suit the state's case but the South Main Street side as well. (See photographs #20, 21, and 23.) It was scandalous, but par for the course.

BY A 2 TO 1 VOTE the court of appeals made permanent the temporary restraining stay that prevented us from testing the weapon, and also prevented Judge Brown from holding the evidentiary hearing that would have allowed us to present a wide range of evidence. Strangely enough, a vitriolic dissent was written by Judge Summers, who had signed the initial stay. In his dissent he said that it was outrageous that the appellate court should go so far as to actually overrule a trial court judge's historic right to control evidence in his court. The judge thought it was a dangerous and unconstitutional action and indicated that we (defense counsel) would be derelict in our duty if we did not appeal the matter to the Supreme Court. We filed an appeal requesting an emergency hearing..

CHASTAIN, I, AND LOCAL INTERMEDIARY Thurston Hill finally met with Willie Crawford in his living room, where we visited for over an hour. I wanted to ask him about the cutting down of the hedge as well as about who from the MPD actually oversaw the cutting of the brush.

During the course of this session, the retired former Memphis sanitation department supervisor alternately praised Dr. King and denied being anywhere near the brush area behind the rooming house at any time. There was, he said, no way that he was part of a two-man cleanup team dispatched to raze the area which backed on to Mulberry Street and overlooked the Lorraine. He admitted knowing Dutch Goodman, who Director Stiles had said was the other member of the team, but denied that he would be sent on such a duty. He kept insisting that their total focus was on picking up garbage and not cutting down weeds.

When I confronted him with Stiles's comments, he became aggravated and defensive in his denial. Anyway, he said, the right man was in jail and none of this mattered anyway. He also denied making any admission of being there to Ken Herman, who had reported such a statement to me prior to the trial. Crawford was obviously frightened and determined not to admit having been on the scene.

JIM LAWSON'S OLD FRIEND JOHN T. FISHER represents the old-time Memphis establishment and wealth. They had become friends at the time of the sanitation workers' strike. Lawson suggested that I speak with him to get a first-hand account of his conversation with Percy Foreman in January 1969 as they sat next to each other on a flight from Houston to Memphis.

Fisher pulled no punches. He said that Foreman was very direct. He said that he had made a mistake agreeing to represent Ray. He did not, as a rule, represent white trash because they couldn't pay. He said that he was going to get rid of Ray for good by arranging for him to plead guilty. Then, because of the virtual impossibility of opening up the case again under Tennessee law, Ray would be inside and out of his hair for good. Foreman told him that it made no difference whether Ray was guilty or not—he was going to finish him.

Fisher had been astounded and not a little uncomfortable about a lawyer talking that way about his client. He said it was deplorable and that he was willing to provide a sworn statement.

ON THE DAY OF OCTOBER 15, I drove out to the Shelby County Correctional Center—the "Penal Farm"—in order to meet with Arthur Wayne Baldwin. I had wanted to talk to Art Baldwin for a very long time, having first heard about him as a result of Tim Kirk's first affidavit in 1978 concerning a contract on James's life. The timing had never been right. For a number of years Baldwin had been on top of the world, running a very lucrative topless club in Memphis. During those years he certainly was not approachable. Then, when he came under the control of the federal government in their effort to convict Governor Ray Blanton and members of his staff, he was, if anything, more unavailable. Not seeing a way through to him during all of this time, I just waited.

Now, sixteen years later, Art Baldwin appeared to be at his lowest point ever, having been locked up for a relatively minor theft. I thought that this would be as good a time as any to meet him face-to-face but I was prepared to be disappointed. I wasn't.

Sitting in the small attorney's-interview room, with several days' growth of beard, Baldwin was soft-spoken and alert. He said that he now sympathized with James. He volunteered having heard that James was assisted in escaping from Brushy Mountain Penitentiary in June 1977 and that he was not supposed to be brought back alive. I told him that I had also come to believe that this was the case. (I had been told by Steve Jacks, James's counsellor at the time, that the tower nearest the escape route had been unmanned, and I was aware of the large FBI SWAT team which took up their positions immediately after the escape.) I told him that it seemed that some people feared what James might have testified to before the HSCA. At the time of the escape the committee's investigation was just getting underway. Baldwin nodded. Referring to the escape, he said, "They tried to get me that way too." He then went on to describe how during his sentence in Nashville, after he had finally turned down the "Ray contract" (believing that he was being set up), he was offered an opportunity to escape but refused because he learned that a team of shooters was waiting for him just outside the walls.

He then told me about two contracts on James's life with which he was involved. The first, he now clarified for me, came from the "Memphis Godfather" who in 1977 told him that the people in New Orleans wanted this matter cleared up once and for all. He quoted him as saying that the killing had been botched up. Ray was supposed to have been killed in Memphis. The Godfather reportedly said, "One, two, three, *bam*," slamming his fist on the table. "It was simple." Since it didn't get done as planned it had been an embarrassment ever since and he wanted it ended. It was like "a stone in his shoe which he wanted out," and he said that if Baldwin could accomplish it for him he would forever be in a good position.

Baldwin was not keen to get involved but did not want to offend the man. He had been present on other occasions when the Godfather talked to produce man Frank Liberto on other matters. He said that the Godfather treated Liberto like a "puppy dog," ordering him about in brutal fashion. Baldwin said he offered the contract to Tim Kirk in a face-to-face meeting in the autumn of 1977. Some months later he raised it again with him on the telephone. This was the approach reported by Kirk. Ultimately it went nowhere.

The approach from the bureau came some months later. Though it clearly came from Washington and had to come through both the Nashville and Memphis SAC's, it was broached by one of the agents who were controlling him in 1978 at the time he was their key witness during the prosecution of Governor Ray Blanton. He said that the agent raised it with him as they drove from Memphis to Nashville during this time. The scheme proposed was that he and a state official would go to Brushy Mountain prison with transfer papers for James who ostensibly was to be moved to Nashville. They would arrive around 3 a.m. and take him. Baldwin was expected to kill James en route. They would bury him. He would go out of the Brushy Mountain population count, and since Nashville was not expecting him he would not be missed for some time. The transfer papers at Brushy Mountain would then be pulled. Baldwin said he became uneasy when he could not get answers to questions concerning how long they expected the story to be kept quiet and what the ultimate explanation was to be. He began to believe that perhaps he and even the official were to be killed as well as James. He pulled back.

He said they offered him lifetime immunity from all prosecution. The second FBI control agent also knew about the scheme, he said, and he said he heard the two agents discussing the other efforts to get rid of James (the June 10, 1977 prison escape and the Godfather's plans). James's continued presence was a sore spot for all concerned. Both the mob and the government wanted him dead because they believed that it was only his continued presence that kept questions about Dr. King's assassination alive. In their view the doubts would largely die with James.

Eventually, after James testified and nothing startling came out, the idea of killing him seemed to go away. It was not raised again and it appeared to me that perhaps all concerned had come to realize that James was not going to reveal even the peripheral information he might have learned or pieced together after the fact.

Baldwin was willing to take a lie detector test. His candor surprised me. It was obvious that he was fed up with being used by the government. His disclosure was the first time that I had heard about the Memphis Godfather's involvement in the case.

I NEXT WENT TO ORLANDO for one of the most sensitive meetings to date. I met for three hours on October 16 with a man whom I will call Carson, who I believed had vital information that could confirm—and provide independent verification of—the military presence in Memphis around the time of the sanitation workers' strike.

Carson and I fenced for some time. He was one of those bright, initially idealistic and patriotic warriors who almost inevitably reach a point where they can no longer swallow the corruption, deceit, and sheer criminal activity that often characterizes official but deniable covert operations. Carson began slowly but then opened up. His story was more than I hoped for. Because of the compatibility of the details with those emerging from other sources, it swept away any lingering doubts I had about the picture of events that was developing. I asked him to check out some details and he reluctantly agreed, being very uneasy about becoming involved. Carson agreed to fax the information to me.

Just before we ended, Carson said, "This meeting never took place." I agreed. "You have to be very careful," he said. "They'll drop you where you stand."

NEW ORLEANS HADN'T CHANGED. It was a living testament to the consequences of the type of all-pervasive corruption that not only permeated every aspect of life but was accepted as inevitable by its citizens. There were potholes the size of which I had not seen outside of the Bronx or a third world city. Bridges were decaying, brownouts occurred regularly, and in 1994 Louisianans had the worst health in the nation. Carlos Marcello, who had treated New Orleans as his private fiefdom, had died, but the culture of crime, violence, greed, and official corruption that he institutionalized lived on.

The New Orleans Metropolitan Crime Commission had been forged into an active watchdog by its executive director in the 1960s, Aaron Kohn, who was now dead. Kohn was constantly critical of D.A. Jim Garrison's failure to go after organized crime or even to acknowledge its existence. In my meeting with commission investigator Tony Radosti (who, having become disgusted by the corruption, left the New Orleans police department to go to work for the commission), I learned that Kohn had also produced a highly sensitive investigatory report on the Kennedy assassination which, he said, "made a number of people in Texas very unhappy." Radosti had not seen the report, however, and did not know where it was. The commission had recently begun to restrict access to its anecdotal files as a result of lawsuits. With respect to my particular interest it was agreed that Tony would pull specific files I requested, examine them, and unless there was some reason for them to be withheld, allow me to read them. We found a very thin, basically uninformative file on the Libertos, but there was a good deal of information on the criminal activities of Marcello associate Joe "Zip" Chimento (who according to 20th SFG soldier Warren was the contact man in New Orleans for their gunrunning) and Randy Rosenson, who was often represented by Marcello's lawyer—C. Wray Gill—mostly concerning drug possession and dealing. I found it interesting that Carlos Marcello had yet another connection to a person who had surfaced in this case.

I found Charlie Stein in a rehabilitation hospital and interviewed him at length. A stroke had affected his memory but he was clear about certain things. James, whom he had known as Eric Galt, was no racist. He got along well with blacks, particularly with black women. On the trip from Los Angeles to New Orleans, James did make a telephone call to the people—"contractors" or "engineers"—he was to meet in New Orleans, but Stein did not observe the number he dialed. One evening in New Orleans James told him that while he (James) was in a meeting in a bar in lower Canal Street (Le Bunny Lounge), he saw Stein pass by and wanted to call to him but the person with him (presumably Raul) did not want to be seen and so he did not call out. Stein said he believed that James went to a meeting in a huge building at the end of Canal Street and that he also met with some people from Gentilly Road. (He believed that James told him about this activity but he really wasn't certain how he learned about it.)

I next spent some hours going through the New Orleans street directory in the public library and despite a brownout which interrupted the work, I learned that the big building Charlie Stein was talking about could only have been the International Trade Mart, which in 1967 was still run by none other than Clay Shaw, the long-time CIA asset prosecuted by Jim Garrison for conspiracy to assassinate President Kennedy. I noted the names and telephone numbers of a number of the tenant companies. Right around the corner from the Trade Mart were the offices of Buck Kreihs Machine Company, whose vice president and general manager was Salvatore J. Liberto.

As noted earlier, James had long thought that the back up Baton Rouge telephone number which Raul had given him belonged to a man named Herman Thompson who, at the time, was Baton Rogue Deputy Sheriff. Thompson was a close friend of Edward Grady Partin, the Baton Rouge Teamsters leader whose testimony for the government resulted in Jimmy Hoffa being put away on jury tampering charges. During the 1960s Ed Partin was clearly controlled by the government which had enough on him to put him away for a very long time. There had long been rumors about Partin's possible involvement in the killing.

In a telephone conversation and subsequent meeting, Doug Partin (who in 1994 was the business manager of the Baton Rouge Teamsters local number five, which had been run for years by his brother) was very candid. His brother Ed had engaged in a great deal of activity of which he disapproved and much that he knew nothing about. He surprised me by saying that it was not impossible that his brother might have had some role to play in the killing, though he had no indication of this.

I asked him about Herman Thompson and he confirmed that Thompson had been a local deputy sheriff and at the time was close to his brother. He also confirmed that Ed had had a relationship with Carlos Marcello that he said was probably driven by the fact that nothing happened in Baton Rouge in those days without Ed's approval. After a local investigation, that included a discussion with a local investigative reporter who observed Partin clearly, I found no indication of any involvement of Thompson or Partin in the conspiracy.

29

Raul: October 31, 1994–July 5, 1995

On October 31, 1994, as a part of our discovery in the civil suit against Loyd Jowers, Raul___ and others, I prepared to take the deposition (examination under oath) of a woman who allegedly had known a person named Raul in Houston, Texas, in the 1960s and who had come to learn that he was involved in the killing of Dr. King. In the autumn of 1993 she had contacted Lewis Garrison, whose name she had seen in the newspaper in conjunction with Loyd Jowers's request for immunity. For some reason, Garrison had brought Ken Herman into his first meeting with her in 1993 and she believed (as apparently did Lewis Garrison) that he was still working as my investigator. I only gradually learned about her existence and had been denied access to her. Lewis Garrison finally had agreed to facilitate the taking of her deposition.

The next morning, November 1, the woman had apparently become ill and had returned home with her husband. Garrison, embarrassed and upset, gave Chastain and me their names and telephone number. He said that Herman had told him categorically that the witnesses would not talk to us. In case they were trying to avoid us, Chastain and I immediately prepared a summons for the woman and her husband, whom I will call Cheryl and Bob, and set out for the town where they lived, which was a few hours from Memphis.

We arrived at their home as a school bus pulled up to drop off a youngster who we would learn was their grandson, and whom they looked after until his mother finished work.

As Bob greeted the boy on the sidewalk I approached and called his name. He didn't seem to be surprised in the slightest, indicating that he recognized me from television. I introduced Wayne and said that I believed that someone might have been feeding them misinformation. He said casually, "Come on in." We sat down in the living room and he introduced his wife to us.

They both insisted that she had not been well and on Monday had not felt up to the formal deposition. They appeared pleased to meet us and said that after that first meeting in Garrison's office they only met with Herman and former Thames Television producer Jack Saltman, with meetings being held at Herman's home with no lawyers present. They said that they had wondered where the lawyers were, since they had come forward for the express purpose of trying to help free an innocent man.

In this and subsequent sessions I learned about Cheryl's experiences as a young woman. She almost always appeared to be nervous and frequently glanced at her husband for support as she recalled events.

She said that in 1962 when she was fourteen years old she met a man who went by the nickname of Dago. Years later she learned his real name which she told me. His first name was Raul but I will use the pseudonym Pereira for his family name. Each day she would walk from her home on Hanson Road to South Houston Junior High School, passing a small gas station on the corner of East Haven and College Boulevard. Dago didn't seem to work at that station but just sat around in front. Since he was friendly to her and she was having a difficult time living with her aunt and uncle, where a pattern of abuse had been established over a number of years, she was happy to know him. She recalled that he was about 5'9" tall, a bit wiry, and weighed 155–160 pounds. His hair was dark with a reddish tint and she thought that he would have been around thirty years old. (I recalled that this matched James's description of Raul, particularly with respect to hair color). In a year's time when she was fifteen she met and married Bob, who by his own admission drank continually and stayed out a good deal.

Soon after they were married Cheryl and Bob moved to a small house on East Haven, near the gas station. During this period she only saw Dago occasionally, and between 1966 and 1970 he disappeared from the area. She did not see him at all, but in 1969 or 1970 she did come to know a man whom she and Bob called Armando.

Armando began to hang around a good deal; and with Bob gone much of the time Cheryl was very lonely and began to spend more and more time with Armando and his friends and appears to have been exploited by them and some of their associates. Since Armando did not drive at all she frequently drove him places. One of the places they visited was the rented house of Felix Torrino [sic] on the corner of 74th Street and Avenue L. It was at Torrino's house sometime in 1970 that she recalled seeing Dago again for the first time following his absence. At that time Armando told her that Dago, who was much younger, was his cousin with the same family name and that Dago's real name was Raul Pereira. He said that they emigrated to the United States from Brazil or Portugal, though Raul came over many years after Armando. Cheryl said that Armando was quite proud of the fact that he once lived in Chicago and worked for Al Capone's organization.

After she had spent some time with them, Armando and Torrino independently told her that Raul had actually killed Martin Luther King. They even told her some details, mentioning some bushes and trees at the rear of the rooming house and saying that Raul had leaned on and broken a tree branch while carrying out the shooting. When she heard this she was shocked. Raul did not know that they had told her and they did not want him to know.

Cheryl became increasingly close to this group between 1970 and 1978 and knew that they were involved in different illegal activities which included gunrunning, forging passports, and even the making of pornographic films. She assisted in some of this activity, including the passport forging and gunrunning. When a shipment of guns was arriving from New Orleans she would drive down to the Houston ship's channel, go on to the docks, and allow the boxes to be loaded into the trunk of her car. Often making several trips as instructed, she would deliver the guns, which were either in cardboard boxes or crates, to Torrino's house where, she said, Raul Pereira, Torrino, and their associates would assemble them. She would only go to pick up the guns when particular customs agents were on duty so that she would just be waved through. Though she never asked questions, she heard the men comment that it was safer to ship the weapons around the coast by boat than to truck them in by road. (I recalled the information provided by Warren about the gun-running operation which was run for Marcello by Zip Chimento, as a result of which stolen military weapons were delivered by Warren and other 20th SFG officers to barges in a cove which bordered property owned by Marcello. Too, there was British merchant seaman Sid Carthew's account of being approached in the Neptune Bar in Montreal by a man who introduced himself as Raul, who offered to sell him new military-issue handguns. Carthew said Raul told him that the guns were stolen from a military base and that a master sergeant had to be paid off. The degree of independent corroboration of this activity appeared to be staggering.)

Cheryl said that during this period Raul Pereira lived or at least spent a good deal of time in a second-floor apartment in a house on Navigation near 75th Street, close to the docks.

Though Raul did drive, she frequently drove him and Armando wherever they wanted to go. She recalled dropping Raul off at the Alabama movie theater where he would often go in the morning to meet with Houston associates of Carlos Marcello. Included in this group were the theater manager, Ross

Vallone, who seemed to be Marcello's main man in Houston, and another man, Joe Bacile, who at one point asked Cheryl to marry him. She refused, electing to stay with Bob. Bob said that Marcello owned a number of these movie theaters in Houston, and Cheryl thought there was some pornographic movie production activity going on at the Alabama. Cheryl actually saw Marcello in Houston on a couple of occasions with Armando, Raul, and their friends, at a fruit stand on Navigation and in a bar next door. She said that on another occasion it was arranged for her to spend time with Marcello at a house in the area.

One day in the early 1970s, around 1:00 p.m., she drove Armando over to Torrino's house where the usual group had gathered. Her car keys were on a ring which had a plastic viewfinder containing miniature photos of John and Robert Kennedy and Martin Luther King. One of those seated around the table (she believed his name was Manuel) picked up the keys which she had put down on the table, looked into the viewfinder and then tossed it to Raul. Cheryl said when Raul saw it he became angrier than she had ever seen him.

She didn't recall everything he said but did remember him shouting, "I killed that black son of a bitch once and it looks like I'll have to do it again." He dropped the keys on the floor and stamped on the plastic viewfinder. Then he grabbed her, put a gun to her head, and forced her into a bedroom where he proceeded to rape her. She said she left Torrino's house that afternoon shattered by the experience. Bob pressed her to tell him what was wrong but she didn't because she feared he might do something which they would regret.

From that point on, although she still associated with the group, she tried to keep her distance from Raul who behaved as though nothing had happened.

She recalled that in 1978 and 1979 two of Bob's brothers got into trouble and were prosecuted. Bob and Cheryl asked Houston attorney Percy Foreman to defend them. Foreman became attracted to Cheryl and even offered her a job. She wanted to decorate houses which Foreman owned and rented out but he wanted her to work in his office. He was trying to impress her and even gave her an original sketch of himself which he personally signed on June 22, 1979 (see photograph #27).

After a while she learned that Foreman had been James Earl Ray's lawyer. He told her that one day white Americans would learn that Ray was a "sacrifice" or had to be "sacrificed" for their welfare. He even told her that he knew Ray was innocent, but that it didn't matter. Cheryl, who had been harboring the terrible secret about who she really believed killed Dr. King, decided finally to unburden herself. She told Foreman. Shortly afterward Foreman informed her that he had spoken with Raul Pereira. To her horror, he appeared to have known him for some time. Thereafter Foreman called her at home several times a week to talk to her about Raul and tell her to be careful. She had the impression that he spoke regularly with Raul, and was trying to take advantage of her plight to get her into bed. She was afraid of alienating him but wasn't interested and tried to keep her distance. Finally, at one point in 1979, Foreman told her in no uncertain terms that if she and Bob did not leave Houston, they would be dead within the year.

They prepared to leave and put their house up for sale. In a matter of weeks Cheryl was driving on the expressway and a wheel simply fell off her car, nearly causing her to be annihilated by an eighteen wheel tractor-trailer. She believed this was no accident because every one of the nuts came off. Since Bob regularly serviced the car and checked the wheels, the lug nuts must have been deliberately loosened.

They left, only returning to sell their house, and in 1981 resettled in their present home. They had no further contact with either Armando or Raul Pereira.

Cheryl and Bob also told me that they had seen the Edginton/BBC documentary and in it recognized a photograph of Jules "Ricco" Kimbel taken over twenty years ago, as being someone they had seen in Houston associating with Raul, Armando, and their crowd.

They said that they had told their story to Herman and Saltman when they first met them a year earlier. Recently they had been shown an old photograph by them which Cheryl recognized as being of Raul Pereira. It was obvious that Herman and Saltman wanted to develop a commercial production based upon Cheryl's story.

CHERYL APPEARED to have no reason to lie and she did not ask for money. Percy Foreman did dedicate the sketch of himself to her so there was obviously some relationship there, but the other details of her extraordinary story required checking to the extent possible.

I contacted Houston investigator Jim Carter and asked him to check out some leads. I authorized him to call Ross Vallone who still lived in Houston. Pretending to be an old friend of Raul Pereira's, Carter first established Vallone's connection with the Alabama theater and then told him that he was trying to locate their mutual friend. Vallone went silent for a moment and then said that he really didn't know where he was. Carter said there was no doubt that he knew him.

I located a telephone listing in Houston in the name of Amaro Pereira and when I raised it with Bob, he said, "Oh yeah, Armando's name was Amaro but we always called him 'Armando.'" When Carter checked it out he learned that an Amaro Pereira had lived at the address but had been gone for a number of years. The present residents had kept the phone in his name rather than changing it and having to put up a deposit.

Next I gave Carter the task of checking out a number of people in Houston with the name Pereira.

DURING THIS TIME WAYNE AND I drove to Corinth, Mississippi, for an unannounced visit to the home of James Latch, the former vice president of LL&L (Liberto, Liberto and Latch) Produce Company. Wayne was uneasy about doing so but I pressed for the visit, since Frank Liberto's old partner had avoiding me for some time. We found the house and knocked on the door. Eventually Mr. Latch appeared and, somewhat guardedly, invited us in. Wayne's uneasiness could only have increased when the phone rang as we entered and before we even sat down. We had given Mr. Latch our business cards and in response to the caller's questions he read out our details over the phone. After this conversation, while we were in the beginning stages of our interview, the phone rang again and he repeated the process. Finally we began an uninterrupted session.

Latch was clearly trying to distance himself from Frank Liberto by claiming ignorance of Liberto's activities and saying that Liberto had not dealt fairly with him on financial matters. He insisted that two heart attacks and a stroke had severely affected his memory. Consequently, he said he did not recall who was on the phone to his partner on the afternoon of April 4 when his partner received two telephone calls, or even if he had answered the phone as John McFerren insisted he had done. He did recall occasional visits by Liberto's brother, Tony, from New Orleans as well as from his mother. He also recalled that Liberto occasionally visited his father who, divorced from his mother, lived in Beaumont, Texas.

Gladys, Liberto's wife, also worked in the business, he said, and was an inveterate gambler. Liberto once told him that she gambled heavily in Las Vegas at the local dog track, sometimes losing substantial sums of money. One time she even pawned the valuable jade ring given to him by Elvis Presley. (This confirmed Nathan Whitlock's recollections.)

IN THEIR DEPOSITIONS IN THE CIVIL CASE *(Ray v. Jowers et al.)* Nathan Whitlock and his mother told their stories. Nathan confirmed his earlier account of Frank Liberto's admissions. Lavada Whitlock Addison said she ran a restaurant which Frank Liberto frequented in 1977–78. He would regularly stop in early in the morning on his way to work and have oatmeal prepared specially. He would also come in for a late afternoon beer or two on his way home from the market. Gradually, he developed a friendship of sorts with Mrs. Whitlock and he would occasionally be candid with her and her son Nathan. He complained, for example, about his wife—who he said was a compulsive gambler—and his mistress (whom he kept in a condo at the

Lynton Square development on the corner of Macon and Graham) who he said was only interested in his money.

When serving him and other customers, Mrs. Whitlock would often sit down at the table with them to chat. On one occasion she recalled that something about the King assassination came on the television and Liberto calmly commented, partly to Mrs. Whitlock and partly to no one in particular, "I had Martin Luther King killed." Startled, she responded instantly, rising at the same time, saying, "Don't tell me such things," and "I don't believe it anyway."

CHASTAIN HAD PREVIOUSLY TOLD ME that at the October 1994 meeting in Garrison's office when he was given a copy of the request for immunity, Herman had made a point of telling Garrison that he had informed him about his client's—Jowers's—involvement in the killing as soon as he had learned about it. Herman told the attorney that he felt that he had an obligation to do so because he had done investigatory work for Garrison's law office. I wondered what had happened to his obligation to James Earl Ray. It was this foreknowledge that put Jowers on his guard and caused him to require Garrison to be present during his testimony at the television trial and also explained Herman's earlier statement in the aftermath of the television trial that somehow Garrison had found out about Jowers's involvement.

Just prior to Jowers's deposition, attorney Garrison confirmed to me that Herman had told him about the existence of the waitresses who could implicate his client, as a result of which Jowers insisted that he be present as a condition of testifying.

Loyd Jowers was deposed over a nine and one-half-hour period. He had with him a typed clause asserting his Fifth Amendment rights ready for use. Nine hours would pass before he would use it. We began at a gentle pace as I took him from his childhood and early life in a large rural family to his days on the police force, which roughly lasted from 1946–1948. After that he formed his own "Veterans Cab Company" whose initial members were all World War II veterans. It was during his brief career as a police officer that he met Memphis produce dealer Frank C. Liberto in 1946 or 1947. He denied knowing any other Frank Liberto. When I asked him about the liquor man up the street he said he knew him and made purchases from him, sometimes daily, but that until my question he had not known that "Frank" (as he knew him) was a Liberto. He simply didn't know his last name.

He said that back in 1946 he knew both patrolman N. E. Zachary and Sam Evans. He also knew inspector Don Smith when he was a patrolman. He became particularly close to G. P. Tines, who years later became an inspector in charge of the intelligence bureau. The friendship developed because Tines's wife and Jowers's first wife went to school together. Jowers supplied details of his six marriages (three to the same woman).

He recalled Frank C. Liberto in the late 1940s as a prominent produce man whose business was located downtown in the market near central police headquarters. Later the market moved to Scott Street and Liberto moved his business there. Jowers believed that the Scott Street produce business LL&L was owned by Frank Liberto and his brother, but he didn't remember the brother's name. He denied knowing Frank Liberto well, although he believed that "Frank," as he called him, did help him get some taxi business from the market.

He said that he didn't see Frank Liberto again until 1965. He refused to acknowledge any business dealings with him. In 1966 he left Veterans Cab and went to work for the Yellow Cab Company, owned by Hamilton Smythe, as a dispatcher. The next year (1967) he opened a restaurant called the Check Off Inn on 153 East Calhoun Street, the site of the old Tremont Cafe. He maintained that when he eventually opened Jim's Grill in the summer of 1967 his wife ran the Check Off Inn, but it was not clear how she could have done this while working full-time for the Memphis Stone and Gravel Company. He also denied that there had been any gambling going on at the Check Off.

When he opened Jim's Grill he moved Lena, a cook from the Check Off, over to the grill. He also hired Betty Spates and her sisters Alda Mae Washington and Bobbi Smith. At the time a white woman also worked for him as a waitress, but he couldn't remember her name.

He described an Esso gas station on the corner of Vance and Second, and he remembered another station on Vance and Third which he thought was a Shell station. (I thought that either of these could have been where James went to try to have his spare tire repaired around the time of the shooting.)

He acknowledged driving both a white Cadillac and a brown Rambler station wagon and said that it was possible that the Cadillac was in his wife's name. He confirmed that his wife, Dorothy, had her hair done every Thursday. (April 4, 1968, was a Thursday.)

Though he bought most of his supplies from Montesi's supermarket, he said that fresh vegetables came from M. E. Carter and that deliveries were made every day.

He said that the back door from the rooming house was boarded up, but he couldn't explain why it appeared to be open in police evidence photographs I showed to him taken shortly after the killing.

Jowers said that on April 4 he drove the white Cadillac to work and that Bobbi Smith worked on the morning of April 4 but left around 4:00 p.m. He said Betty Spates did not work at all that day because one of her children was sick. Also, he said that Big Lena and Rosie Lee had gone from his employ months earlier and that he himself had fixed breakfast for the "eggs and sausage" man. (Sometime prior to Jowers's deposition I had located Rosie Lee Dabney and she confirmed that she was waiting on tables in Jim's Grill on the afternoon of April 4. She said she served eggs and sausage to a stranger on the afternoon of the shooting and again the next morning. An MPD report dated April 6 stated that Dabney was on duty all day on April 4 and that she had served eggs and sausage to a stranger.) Jowers could not identify a photograph of Jack Youngblood as the "eggs and sausage man." At the time of the gunshot he said that he was drawing a pitcher of beer.

Jowers confirmed with certainty that the bushes in the backyard had been cut down. He actually drew a line surprisingly close to the building up to where he said the thick bushes came. He acknowledged that the waitresses probably did take food up to Grace Walden but denied telling Bobbi not to take food up to her on the morning of April 4.

He denied driving Bobbi to work on the morning of April 5 or going out to the back or even looking out there on the morning after the shooting. He said he drove the white Cadillac that day.

Incredibly, he categorically denied having any relationship with Betty Spates. He also denied knowing anything about the Oakview house and ever staying overnight there. He did, however, admit to speaking with Spates on December 13, 1993, the night the *Prime Time Live* program was filmed, to warn her, he said, that reporters were on the way to her house.

I showed Jowers a copy of the transcript of the ABC *Prime Time Live* program and he agreed it was an accurate statement. I then entered it into the record. When I began to question him on the statements he made on the program, he invoked the Fifth Amendment. I noted for the record that the transcript had already been agreed to and entered into evidence and that in my opinion the protection of the Fifth Amendment was not available to him. Garrison then agreed to stipulate "... that the questions were asked and Mr. Jowers gave these answers" (the answers being those responses given during the television program).

Jowers's testimony was extraordinary for the number of untruths he told, many of which were clearly contradicted by other evidence and testimony and some of which contradicted his earlier statements.

Jowers, for reasons best known to himself and his counsel, insisted on deposing Betty Spates. Lewis Garrison served a subpoena on her, and she came along in a hostile frame of mind. Before beginning, I took her aside and explained that Jowers, who had denied having any relationship with her, had insisted that she be called. Initially, she was inclined not to remember anything, but gradually she decided to cooperate. She confirmed the factual truthfulness of the affidavit she had given to me which I have discussed in detail earlier.

Willie Akins was also deposed and stated that years after the event Jowers admitted to him that he was involved in the killing. Jowers described his meeting with Raul, Raul having brought the gun to him at the grill, and Frank Liberto arranging for a delivery of a large sum of money in a produce box which was included in a regular delivery. The scene was striking. Jowers greeted Akins cordially and then Akins, under oath, proceeded to directly incriminate his old friend. Akins continued to maintain that years later he had been asked by Jowers to kill Frank Holt. At the end of the deposition Jowers and Akins went off together talking about old times.

Betty's sister Bobbi Smith was also subpoenaed and appeared as scheduled on December 22. Under oath she confirmed what she had told me in an informal interview on December 18, 1992, two years earlier. Jowers had told her not to take breakfast upstairs to Grace Walden on the morning of April 4. She usually did this about twice a week around 10–10:30 a.m., after the morning rush was over. I had always thought that this was significant because it meant that something was going on up there well before noon that day, some four or more hours before James arrived to rent the room. Bobbi also said that Jowers picked her up on the mornings of April 4 and 5, as usual, in his brown station wagon which on April 4 he parked just north of the grill in front of the U.S. fixtures store. (I remembered that during and after hypnosis Charles Hurley, who was picking up his wife Peggy on South Main Street that afternoon, recalled seeing a brown station wagon on that side of the street.) On the way in on the morning of April 5, Jowers told Bobbi about the rifle being found in the backyard after the killing. She also confirmed that Jowers often spent the night at the Oakview house where she lived with her mother and Betty in 1969, and that he had a longstanding affair with Betty during all of this time. She also said that at the time of the killing Betty did have a job at the Seabrook Wallpaper company across the street from Jim's Grill.

Finally, she said that she had told the same story to the TBI investigators sent by Pierotti and she did not understand why they would say that she knew nothing or had retracted her story. They told her not to discuss the matter with anyone.

SOMETIME AFTER TELLING ME his story about Frank Liberto, Nathan Whitlock told me about a rumor of an earlier King murder contract put out to a member of a family named Nix who lived in Tipton County, Tennessee. Nathan said he understood that Red Nix had been given a new car and a rifle and was paid $500 a week to track and kill King. If he succeeded he was to get $50,000. Whitlock thought the offer came from Frank C. Liberto. Red had been killed not too long after Dr. King was shot. At Whitlock's suggestion I met with Red's brother, Norris, and Bobby Kizer, who jointly owned and ran the Neon Moon nightclub on Sycamore View in East Memphis. They confirmed that Red was given a new car and was put on a payroll for a job. "He was after someone all right," said Norris Nix, "but I don't know who." They believed that Tim Kirk, who was a friend of Red Nix, would know who hired him, and offered to ask him to tell me what he knew. He could, they said, free my client. Bobby Kizer even offered to go up to the prison with me to talk to Kirk.

I was surprised. I thought I knew everything Kirk had to say. Eventually I visited him again to ask him about the Red Nix murder contract. He said with certainty that the contract was put out by Carlos Marcello, not Frank C. Liberto. It was sometime in mid-1967. He said Nix knew Marcello and undertook various jobs for him. A car had indeed been provided. This was the first indication directly linking Marcello to a contract on Dr. King. Nathan Whitlock had been under the impression that Frank C. Liberto had also been behind the Nix contract. Kirk said there was no way. It came directly from New Orleans and Carlos Marcello.

Kirk said that Red Nix was set up and killed sometime after the assassination and that it could well have been related to his knowledge about the contract. He promised to try to check out what was behind Red's murder. Try as he did, he was unable to learn anything.

Information about the Marcello/Red Nix contract reminded my assistant Jean about something that Memphis investigator Jim Kellum had included in one of his reports in 1992 before he asked to be released. It concerned an informant who had allegedly mentioned a similar contract which was put out at a meeting in Jackson, Tennessee. Kellum agreed to arrange a meeting. On the morning of December 20, 1994, Kellum brought to breakfast "Jerry," a longtime trusted informant of his. Jerry told of attending a meeting in Jackson, Mississippi, in mid-1967 at the Blue Note Lounge. There, a wheelchair paraplegic named Joe "Buck" Buchanan, who was into a variety of illegal activities and well connected in New Orleans, put out a $50,000 contract on Dr. King, which Jerry believed had come from that city. Jerry also said that Tim Kirk was at that meeting, as was one of the Tiller brothers from Memphis (who we knew had some association with Kirk). When I raised the meeting with Kirk he said he had a vague recollection of the event. It seemed that this contract was later picked up by Red Nix, possibly directly from Marcello.

Jerry said that Joe Buchanan was killed some years later, shot sitting in his wheelchair in his front yard, after being set up by a woman he knew well. Jerry said that she was probably still alive and would likely know why Buchanan was killed and who ordered him to be shot. Jerry agreed to try to locate her and find out. He ultimately became unable or unwilling to do so.

More than ever the trail of the Memphis contract that actually resulted in Dr. King's death led to New Orleans and pointed toward the involvement of the Mafia organization of Carlos Marcello. Marcello had not just given his approval but had taken on the job and had attempted to subcontract it on more than one occasion—the last time being through his Memphis associates which included Frank C. Liberto and the Memphis Godfather.

FOR A NUMBER OF YEARS THERE had been rumors about a Yellow Cab taxi driver having seen someone going down over the wall just after the shooting. As part of the investigation for the television trial, I had asked two of my investigators, Herman and

Billings, to get the names of Yellow Cab drivers working on April 4. They were not forthcoming.

Finally, in autumn of 1994 a driver came forward of his own volition. At first, he tried to tell his story to the attorney general but he encountered total disinterest. Then, after spotting Lewis Garrison's name in the local paper in an article about the case, he telephoned him and left his name. Garrison duly passed it on to me and I spoke to him on November 5, 1994.

Louie Ward told me a story he had held back, out of fear, for twenty-six years. He had been driving on the night of April 4 and around 6:00 p.m. he was parked near the corner of Perkins and Quince. Suddenly he heard the dispatcher come on the radio, obviously responding to a driver's call about an emergency (the drivers could only hear the dispatcher's side of conversations with the other drivers). He heard the dispatcher say that he would send an ambulance and then, in response to something else the driver said, the dispatcher said he would send one anyway and call the police. From what he had heard Ward learned that the emergency was the shooting of Martin Luther King. He also realized that the driver was taking a fare to the airport. Ward went straight to the airport and met up with the driver who told him his story. Ward said that the driver, whose name he could not recall and who probably was in his early sixties, was driving car 58. The driver said that he had gone to the Lorraine shortly before 6:00 p.m. to pick up a passenger with an enormous amount of luggage. As they finished loading up his taxi in the Lorraine parking lot, the driver turned to look at the area of dense brush and trees opposite the motel. His passenger quickly punched him on the arm in order to get his attention and (so the driver later thought) distract him from looking at the brush, saying, "Look up there—Dr. King's standing alone on the balcony. Everybody's always saying how difficult it would be to shoot him since he is always in a crowd. Now look at him." At that precise moment the shot rang out and the driver saw Dr. King get struck in the jaw and fall. The driver said he grabbed his microphone and told his dispatcher that Dr. King had been shot. The dispatcher said he would call an ambulance, and the driver said that considering the wound he didn't think it would do much good. Then Ward said the driver told him that he saw a man come down over the wall empty-handed, run north on Mulberry Street, and get into a black and white MPD traffic police car which was parked across the middle of the intersection of Mulberry and Huling. At that point the driver told the dispatcher to tell the police that one of their units had the man. Meanwhile, the passenger was becoming irritable, saying that they had to leave immediately because otherwise the ambulance and other cars would box them in and he had to make his plane. They left.

Ward heard the driver repeat the story to three MPD officers at the airport, and observed a second interview being conducted later that evening in the Yellow Cab office by other policemen. After that evening Ward said he never even saw the driver of car 58 again. Ward was working full-time at the Memphis army depot and was on the job round the clock the next two or three days. It was only after this period that he was able to return to his part-time taxi driving. When he went back to the South Second Street Yellow Cab office for the first time after the killing he asked after the car 58 driver. Three or four of the drivers in the office told him that he had fallen or had been pushed from a speeding car onto the Memphis-Arkansas bridge late on the evening of April 4. Ward also said that at that time there was speculation by some of the drivers that since the man seen fleeing the area wasn't carrying a gun that perhaps it was hidden in the back of Loyd Jowers's café because all of this activity took place behind that building.

Ward agreed to undergo hypnosis in order to see if he could recollect the names of the driver of car 58 and the dispatcher. Subsequently, under hypnosis, he recalled that the driver's name was Paul, and that after the fleeing man got into the passenger side of the MPD traffic car, the car headed north at top speed. Louie Ward agreed to try to help us locate the dispatcher on duty.

I did manage to locate and depose a former Yellow Cab dispatcher named Prentice Purdy. Under oath in May 1995 Purdy stated that he nearly always worked the 7 a.m. to 3 p.m.

shift and that was his schedule on the day of the assassination. He did recall a full-time driver named Paul and said that he believed that he almost exclusively did airport runs. He said that he could not specifically recall ever seeing Paul after April 4, but he did not know if or when he had died. He said he was unable to remember Paul's last name, though he did agree to continue to think about it. I telephoned him a few days later and he still was unable to recall the name but within the week he had left a message on Chastain's answerphone and I called him back. He said Paul's last name was Butler.

Telephone records indicated that a Paul Butler who was a driver for the Yellow Cab company was listed in the 1967 Memphis residential telephone directory. His wife, Betty, continued to be listed in 1968 as his widow. According to social security death listings Paul Butler died in August 1967. He obviously could not have been the driver of car 58 on April 4, 1968. We were back to square one.

The story was consistent with Solomon Jones's observations, but I wondered why Ernestine Campbell or William Ross would not have seen this person. When asked, Ernestine said that at that time she had focused her entire attention on the balcony and then on Jesse Jackson's actions at the foot of the stairs. I also recalled that immediately after the shot William Ross had turned and run back to the driveway, so within seconds of the shooting as he stared at the balcony his back would have been to the wall on the opposite side of the street. The fleeing man could well have been missed by Ross though seen by Jones, who had stared at the area of the origin of the shot for a brief while after it was fired.

I recalled the curious photograph shown to Ed Redditt during the course of the investigation by the Justice Department, which showed the evidence bundle on the corner of Mulberry and Huling. The chain of events recounted by Ward might explain why at some time there could have been a plan to drop the incriminating evidence bundle on this street corner which now appeared to be on the actual escape route of the assassin.

*　　*　　*

ON THE MORNING OF NOVEMBER 9, I met with Steve Tompkins in his G-10 office in the Tennessee State Capitol Building. He had prepared a chronology of events for me, which I was eager to analyze and discuss. He had printed it out before he left the office the previous night. He looked everywhere but couldn't find it. When he thought about it he remembered placing it on a desk in the office with his secretary's resume on top of a manila legal size folder. Both were gone. He was convinced that his office had been entered and the file taken.

I had recently had a similar experience. On one visit to Birmingham my address/appointment book had disappeared. I had come to make it a habit to carry with me at all times the most sensitive working files. After completing a number of telephone calls I left the room, taking the file bag with me, but leaving the address book behind, lying on the unmade bed.

When I returned I needed a phone number and looked for the book. It was nowhere to be found.

I located the housekeeper who had, in my absence, cleaned the room and made the bed. She remembered seeing the book and moving it before changing the sheets. She returned to the room with me and showed me the end table against the wall where she had placed the book on top of a sweater which I had also left lying on the bed. The sweater was there exactly where she had placed it, but the book was missing. She and I looked behind and under the table and the bed and all over the room. It remained missing and has never turned up.

Reluctantly, I had to conclude that it had been surreptitiously removed. For some time I had followed the practice of registering in an assumed name. On this occasion, since I was only in Birmingham for one night and only a couple of people knew I was in the city and no one knew where I was staying, I had not taken this precaution. Even though the book contained little relevant or indispensable information, and my writing was often illegible anyway, it was an ominous indication that a closer look was being taken at my activity.

In addition, one day later a Memphis friend who was holding material from a source for me, told me that the "eyes only" file was missing. These incidents were worrying. Steve Tompkins was concerned but could do nothing except print out another copy. Security would now have to be a more important concern than ever before.

JUST BEFORE THE COURTS CLOSED for Christmas, attorney Garrison filed a motion in the civil suit on behalf of defendant Jowers asking for the right to test the rifle in evidence. His rationale was that if in fact this was the murder weapon, then he could have no liability since it was the rifle purchased by James. Since we had been trying to have the weapon tested for some time, we did not object. The court said it would consider the motion but at the time of this book going to press no ruling had been made.

SOME MONTHS BEFORE, Richard Bakst, a Maryland taxi cab driver, had told me about one of his passengers who claimed he knew a Memphis policeman who was on duty in the area of the Lorraine Motel on the day of the killing. The passenger had said that the officer, who was a family friend, had seen, just after the shooting, a man running in the brush area toward South Main Street. He was carrying a rifle. When, shortly afterward, the officer told his superior on the scene about the incident, he was told to forget about it, because they already knew who did it. Bakst had consistently refused to name his passenger, who he said did not want to discuss the matter further.

On December 17, Bakst finally disclosed the identity of his passenger, Michael. Eventually I spoke with Michael and he agreed to talk to the former MPD officer. In 1968, the policeman was a motorcycle officer and was, Michael believed, assigned to Dr. King's escort unit. Michael basically confirmed Bakst's account, including the order from a superior officer to say nothing about seeing a man with a rifle in the bushes. According to Michael, the policeman was willing to talk to me. I left Chastain's phone number and my own but again as this book goes to press we have not heard from him.

*　　*　　*

JIM KELLUM, WHO HAD WORKED with the MPD intelligence bureau, confirmed to me for the first time on December 20, 1994, that he had learned that Reverend Billy Kyles had been an informant during 1967–1968. His source, who had been an administrative aide and secretary in the intelligence bureau, confirmed to me that Kyles had indeed supplied them with information on a regular basis but was unclear as to the precise dates of this service and appeared too nervous about going into detail.

I NEXT RETURNED TO THE STORY about a rifle having been stored, for a time, in the premises of another Liberto family member's business where Ezell Smith had worked. We finally learned that Ezell had died. One of his friends (who was also a friend of John McFerren) was O. D. Hester, whose street name was "Slim." Slim now lived in Illinois, outside of Chicago. John McFerren called him. Slim said he knew all about the rifle kept in this building. "Tango," who ran a store in the produce-market area, disclosed to John McFerren that he also knew all about the gun being kept in the Liberto business premises. When I met with Tango late one evening in February 1995, he told me that a man named Columbus Jones had told him about a rifle being carried to those premises around the time of the killing, although he did not know any details about the weapon. Jones said his source was Ezell. He said that it was rumored that this was the gun that had killed Martin Luther King. Columbus Jones died in early 1995 before I could speak to him. I did speak with Slim. Ezell had told him that the murder weapon was kept and assembled at the Liberto premises where he worked. He promised to speak with another man who had worked for that business to try to obtain details about the rifle, but he was unable to locate him.

ON SATURDAY, MARCH 11, 1995, attorney Lewis Garrison, with Loyd Jowers present, began to depose James in a small conference room at the Riverbend Penitentiary. The deposition continued until noon the following day. Throughout the session Jowers listened intently as James gave the usual answers to the questions he had heard a thousand times before. As he left the prison that Sunday afternoon for what was described as a 500 mile drive to his current home, Loyd Jowers seemed to be more amenable than ever before to revealing details which I believed would ultimately establish James's innocence.

Jowers agreed to answer some questions about the killing through his lawyer. There would be no recordings of his statement and the attorney Lewis Garrison would take the follow-up questions to him for his response. On March 14, 1995, the process began in Garrison's 400 North Main Street office. While he provided some new details of the conspiracy, much of what he said confirmed information obtained previously from Betty Spates, Betty's sister Bobbi Smith, and taxi driver James McCraw.

At the outset Garrison stressed that the Holt story did not originate with Jowers. He was uncertain whose brainstorm it was, but believed it originated with Willie Akins and Ken Herman. Though he emphasized that it was not concocted by Jowers he had to acknowledge that his client did go along with it for a while.

Jowers contended that in March 1968 he was first approached by a local businessman who dealt in securities and bonds and whom he had come to know from his gambling activity with Frank Liberto.

This man told him that because of the location of Jim's Grill he was going to be asked to provide certain assistance in the carrying out of a contract to assassinate Martin Luther King. In exchange for this assistance he would be paid handsomely.

On March 15, soon after this conversation, Jowers was approached by produce man Frank C. Liberto to whom he owed a very large gambling debt. This debt would be forgiven, Liberto told him, and he would receive a large amount of money if he would provide the assistance initially mentioned by the messenger. Specifically Liberto said:

1. $100,000 would be delivered to him in cash in the bottom of an M. E. Carter vegetable produce box. The money came from New Orleans, as did the contract on King's life.

2. He would be visited by a man who would bring the murder

weapon—a rifle—and leave it with him for pickup at the right time.

3. There would be a patsy or decoy to distract attention.

4. The police—some of whom were involved—would be nowhere in sight.

Jowers agreed. As Liberto said, a man did come to see him. In fact he met with this man on two occasions before April 4. Jowers thought that he introduced himself as "Raul" or "Royal." Jowers said he appeared to have a Latin/Indian appearance. He was about 5'9" in height and weighed approximately 145-155 pounds. He had dark hair and appeared to be between thirty-five and forty years old. (This description matched that provided by Cheryl and James.)

They discussed the plans for the killing. Raul told Jowers that his role would be to receive and hold the murder weapon on the day of the killing until Raul picked it up. After the shooting Jowers would have to take charge of it again and keep it concealed until Raul came to take it away. Jowers was also expected to keep his staff out of the way at all times. He confirmed Bobbi's story that he instructed her not to follow her usual practice of taking food to Grace Walden.

On the morning of April 4, sometime around 11:00 a.m. after the rush was over, Raul, according to plan, came into Jim's Grill, bringing with him a rifle concealed in a box which he turned over to Jowers to hold. Jowers said that Raul told him that he would be back later that afternoon to pick it up. Jowers put the gun under the counter and carried on with his work. He next admitted that he took his nap in the back room sometime around or after 1:00 p.m. when the lunch crowd had gone. He woke and began to work again around 4:00 p.m. Sometime later, Raul returned briefly and took the gun from him and went back into the kitchen area with it. Jowers claimed to be uncertain as to whether he remained in the rear of the grill, or went upstairs by the back stairway. (According to James's recollections, Raul was upstairs off and on during the afternoon. It therefore seems more likely that Raul took the gun upstairs to room 5-B and concealed it there).

Jowers said that sometime before 6:00 p.m. he went out into the brush where he joined another person.

He did not provide any more details except to admit that immediately after the shot he picked up the rifle which had been placed on the ground and carried it on the run in through the back door of Jim's Grill. As he ran into the back of the grill, he was confronted by Betty who, as she had said, stood near him as he broke the gun down, wrapped it in a cloth and quickly put it under the counter in the grill itself. Jowers finally confirmed that her recollection of the events was basically correct.

He also admitted that the next morning between 10 and 11 a.m. he showed the rifle, which was in a box under the counter, to taxi driver James McCraw, thus confirming McCraw's recollection. Sometime later that morning but before noon, Raul reappeared in the grill, picked up the gun and took it away. He said he never saw the rifle again and had no idea where it was taken or where it is today. (When McCraw was deposed in mid June 1995 Jowers in front of Chastain and Garrison explicitly threatened McCraw just prior to the deposition beginning. He said to McCraw, who was rising to greet him, something like, "You'd better stand up while you can, 'cause if you continue to run your mouth, you won't be able to stand up again.")

The version of events just laid out was completely at odds with the answers Jowers gave in his deposition. Though his most recent statements were consistent with information and accounts of other less self-interested persons it had to be borne in mind that Jowers was aware of many of the other statements.

ON APRIL 15, 1995, THE United States Attorney General's office finally replied to my earlier letter requesting a federal grand jury. Basically, the letter said that the federal government could do nothing and that it was well known that a state investigation was in process and a post conviction relief petition pending. I was urged to provide my evidence to the state authorities. I really expected nothing else from the administration which had just taken former Tennessee Governor Ned McWerter to Washington as a special consultant to the president.

On May 8, 1995, the Tennessee Supreme Court denied our application for Extraordinary Appeal. The Court of Criminal Appeals's injunction remained in effect, prohibiting trial court judge Joe Brown from issuing any order concerning evidence before his court. The judge was also ordered to issue a final order on our petition. The action of the appellate courts appeared to me to be an unprecedented draconian stripping away of a trial court's authority. Because the judge's decision to allow the petitioner an opportunity to put on (proffer) evidence had been reversed by the appellate courts, it was generally assumed that the judge would now have no alternative but to dismiss the petition. I believed that the judge could still order an evidentiary hearing or even a trial. I planned to request a hearing so that full oral argument could take place.

ON THURSDAY JUNE 1, 1995, a former client of Lewis Garrison whom I will call "Chuck" walked into Garrison's law offices in Memphis. Some years ago Chuck had injured his leg while working and Garrison had obtained disability benefits for him. He was looking for some additional legal assistance on this matter. In the course of their meeting the subject of the King assassination came up, apparently prompted by a telephone call to Garrison from Loyd Jowers. Chuck told Garrison about something he observed related to the killing. Garrison urged Chuck to talk to me. He was very afraid. Garrison and Chuck's common-law wife told me that a number of people had told him that he would be killed if he told what he saw. Eventually, under threat of subpoena, he called me and we spoke for nearly an hour.

He said that in 1968 he was six years old. On April 4 of that year he rode from Tunica, Mississippi, to Memphis with his father who made the journey in order to meet with Dr. King. He did not know why his father was meeting with Dr. King on that day but remembers being excited about the trip. Chuck, now about thirty-five years old, said at that time his hair was in plaits, which were cut off soon after that day. His father drove up to Memphis, eventually reaching Mulberry Street and going south toward the Lorraine. He parked opposite but just south of room 306 in the shade of the trees and bushes just above and behind the wall. (I realized that at that time in the afternoon the sun would have been in the west behind the brush and trees on the wall which would have provided shade in the spot he described). Chuck said his father told him to wait in the car. He said his father went onto the motel property through a southern entrance near the corner of Butler and Mulberry and ascended the southernmost staircase leading to the balcony. He walked north along the balcony to Dr. King's room 306. Chuck said that after he saw his father enter the room he lay down on the front seat and took a nap. He believed that it was around 4 p.m. He didn't know how long he slept. When he woke up he sat up on the open window frame of the front passenger door and with a child's curiosity began to look all around. In a short while his attention was drawn to a man in the brush and trees area above the wall about five or six feet in front (south) of him. He said the man stood looking directly across at the motel. He was a few feet back from the edge of the wall and partially obscured by the trees and bushes. He was of medium build, had dark hair and a black moustache and appeared to be Arab or Mexican. He was dressed in khaki trousers and a short-sleeved shirt and wore an army officer's style (Garrison) peaked hat. Holding a rifle close in up against his stomach, he stood there for a while looking across at the Lorraine and then disappeared, going back into the bushes and trees. Chuck thought that he was hunting birds. He came from a rural area and was used to seeing people with rifles hunting birds or rabbits, so this did not seem unusual to him. Chuck thought that a long time passed before the man reappeared. He thought it must have been about an hour, but it is obviously difficult for him twenty-seven years later to assess his sense of time when he was six years old.

He recalled seeing a photographer/reporter walk down Mulberry Street from Butler. The reporter looked at him as he walked right past him. He urged me to find this reporter who he thought would at least be able to establish his presence. I was unable to do so.

At one point he saw his daddy leave Dr. King's room and begin to walk toward the same southernmost stairway at the far end of the balcony he had climbed earlier. He also saw Dr. King come out onto the balcony and stand at the railing. Just at this time the man reappeared, clearly visible just a few feet back from the wall, though partially obscured by the bushes. Chuck's attention was drawn at this time because at that moment birds flew up from the trees, apparently disturbed by the man. The man raised the rifle and took aim and as he did so Chuck said even today he can vividly recall his fear that the man (who he thought was going to shoot at a bird) might hit his daddy because he was pointing his gun in the direction of the Lorraine balcony. The man seemed to take his time. He was facing Chuck who was staring at him from a sloping distance of about twelve to fifteen feet. The man's right hand held the stock of the gun and his left-hand trigger finger was on the rifle trigger. He fired and Chuck saw two puffs of smoke come from the barrel of the gun and linger even after the man was gone. Strangely, Chuck did not recall hearing the shot. The man moved instantly back into the bushes and disappeared.

Chuck said that he lost sight of the man but then no more than two to three minutes later, he saw the man run up to a white car parked on the far (south) side of Butler Street, opposite the fire station. (To get there, if the alleged shooter was in front of the fence he would have had to either run along the wall under cover of the bushes, jump down at the back of the fire station and continue running north to Butler, or scale the fence at its lowest point in the corner at the rear of Canipe's, cut through the parking lot and round the front of the fire station to Butler. If he was behind the fence he would already be in the parking lot and follow the latter route. Either route would have put him and the rifle he carried in clear view of any passers-by for a period of time. Chuck specifically stated he did not see him running along Mulberry Street.) Chuck said that having reached the car the man opened the driver's side front door and threw the rifle across into the passenger's side of the front seat, then jumped in and drove away heading east on Butler. Glancing behind him he said he saw a white man with a white tee shirt and a big belly standing in the brush area some distance in front of Jim's Grill. About this time his father, who was running, bent over up Mulberry Street, reached the car and got in, yelling at Chuck to get down on the floor of the car, which he did. His father drove away at high speed.

Chuck raised the fact that in the famous Joseph Louw photograph showing people on the balcony pointing in the direction of the shot, one person, the young woman Mary Hunt, though pointing straight ahead was looking off to the left—in the direction of Butler Street and the white car. I had tried many years earlier to find Mary Hunt but was unable to do so and eventually learned that she had died of cancer. In any event, since the photograph was not shot immediately after Dr. King was hit, it was likely that the man would have already departed the scene.

Chuck said that he had told Reverend Kyles about what he saw and Kyles advised him to keep his silence. Kyles told him that the government had Dr. King killed and the elimination of one more black man wouldn't be a problem for them. Chuck said that a number of people had told him to say nothing if he wanted to remain alive. His daddy had him tell what he saw to several people. Because his father believed that the boy's life was in danger as a result of his observations, those told were sworn to secrecy. One of those he said he told very many years ago was Ralph Abernathy. If this was true, I wondered why Abernathy had never mentioned or even hinted at the story to me.

Chuck was very apprehensive about being seen with me but he consented to go with me to the scene. We parked in what he thought was the exact spot on Mulberry Street where his father had parked. Dr. King's room would have been slightly behind him or north of where he would have been sitting in the front seat (see chart 6). From this position he would have been able to see a car parked in the spot where he said he saw the white car.

It was obvious to me that in 1995, twenty-seven years later,

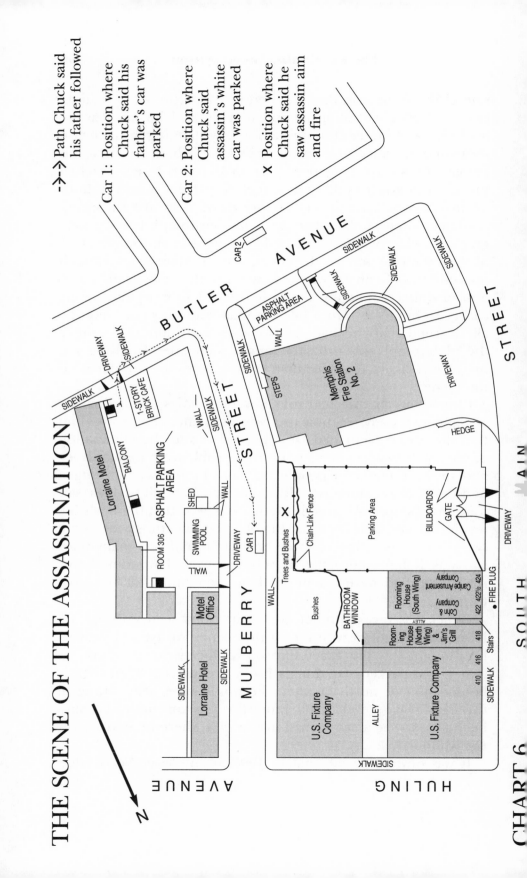

THE SCENE OF THE ASSASSINATION

->-> Path Chuck said his father followed

Car 1: Position where Chuck said his father's car was parked

Car 2: Position where Chuck said assassin's white car was parked

x Position where Chuck said he saw assassin aim and fire

CHART 6

Chuck was somewhat disoriented with respect to the physical scene. He thought that there was a second driveway into the Lorraine off Mulberry Street. There wasn't, although there was an entrance from Butler near the southern stairway. More importantly, he didn't initially appreciate the fact that the fire station backed right down onto Mulberry Street, neither did he realize how large it was. On the Mulberry Street side the parking lot was closed in by a tall chain-link fence which was set back a short distance (around four feet) from the wall. Though the fence was mostly covered by brush and weeds it was bare and clearly visible near the north corner bordering the rooming house rear yard. Chuck said that he never noticed the fence and that the man he saw simply went back into the brush away from the wall.

I recalled that the area where Reverend James Orange had always insisted that he saw the smoke appeared to be very close to the spot where Chuck said he had seen the shooter. I had always assumed that Orange had been mistaken and that he must have meant the bushes behind Jim's Grill and the north wing of the rooming house, because the trajectory of the bullet and observations of other witnesses pointed to the shot having been fired from further north. I couldn't conceive how a shot fired from a point that far south, which would have been to his left, could have struck Dr. King in the right cheek, exited below the right jawbone and reentered the right side of his neck. For this to happen he would have had to turn considerably to his left just before being hit and there is no eyewitness indication of this.

I was also unable to find anyone who remembered seeing Chuck's father's car parked on the west side of Mulberry.

When I interviewed Carthel Weeden, who was in charge of fire station 2 in 1968, he said that immediately after the shooting he ran across to the Lorraine and helped Benny Thornton put Dr. King on the stretcher for transportation to the hospital. At one point he was confronted by a hysterical, somewhat heavy-set black woman dressed in black. He learned that her name was Catherine. She was screaming that, "he was shot in a white car." Weeden thought she meant that the shot came from below from a passing white car. I thought this must have been the young woman referred to in a note in 1968 defense co-counsel Hugh Stanton's file, who was identified as a LeMoyne college student and described as screaming at the police to go after a man she saw getting away. As discussed earlier, I had tried unsuccessfully to locate her. It was possible that she meant that the shooter was leaving in a white car.

I had never heard any report about Chuck's father participating in any meeting with Dr. King on that day. For at least some of the time that Chuck said his father was meeting with Dr. King there was an SCLC executive staff meeting in progress. Reverend Hosea Williams did not recall any outsiders being present during the meeting but believed that some people from Mississippi had been called to Memphis. Reverend Lawson was not at the meeting but said that people often drove long distances to see Dr. King about any number of things. Such a visit would not have been unusual at that time since the southern leg of the Poor People's march was starting in Mississippi. I spoke with some black leaders in Tunica who knew Chuck's family. No one said that they had heard about his father ever meeting with Dr. King. One community leader even said that the family left the area in the early 1960s, moving to Memphis. One of Chuck's brothers, who was three years older than Chuck, said that they were tenant farmers in Tunica in 1968 but that it was very unlikely that his father would leave the farm to go to Memphis in April. He said that he certainly did not remember it happening.

Chuck's elderly mother, on the other hand, did recall her husband saying that he had met with Dr. King. She said he mentioned it more than once but she was not certain when the meeting or meetings took place. She also vaguely remembered hearing about something that Chuck saw that was kept secret, but she could not, or would not, recall any details. She did say that during this time she was ill and away from the family and she believed that her husband and the younger children did live in Memphis for a while. She also remembered that six-year-old Chuck did have plaited hair for a while.

I discussed these conversations with Chuck on Sunday, July

2. He told me that he had gone to a funeral the day before at which his brother and one or more of the community leaders with whom I had spoken told him that if he continued to talk he would get himself killed. Chuck had the impression that their concern was centered round secrets other than the King assassination that he might have heard when he was around his father. They also invited him to join the local Masonic lodge where previously he had been excluded from membership. His brother pressed him to join. As a "brother" in the lodge he would be bound to secrecy.

When I spoke with Chuck's common-law wife she confirmed that Chuck had told her this story many years ago. She had known him since about 1979 and she believed that he first unburdened himself about what he saw in 1987 or 1988. She also said that at the time of the television trial she went with Chuck to visit his family and during that visit he brought up the experience. The family members did not want it raised and advised Chuck for his own good to keep quiet. She had always found Chuck to be truthful. Whatever his faults, lying was not one of them. His attorney, Lewis Garrison, basically confirmed his reliability but noted that he had had a minor drug problem and had recently served a short jail term.

Chuck seemed sincere but corroboration was virtually nonexistent and his story implausible. On the face of it, the degree of specificity seemed impressive but even if he was telling the truth he could easily have been mistaken as to the details, particularly since he was only six years old at the time. He had no apparent reason to lie but it was possible that the entire story was a fabrication. In light of all the available conflicting information, and absent additional corroboration, I had to discount Chuck's story.

BY MAY 1995 THE INVESTIGATION in Houston had not borne fruit. In the interim Garrison said he had been told by Herman that the man they believed to be Raul who they were looking at lived in Detroit, was using the name Diablo, and was in the import/export business specializing in a particular product. A search of those businesses led nowhere and I assumed that Herman was putting out disinformation. Too, James had told me that Herman and Saltman had shown him an old photograph which he said was the same picture he had seen in 1979 and which he had recognized as being of Raul. He could not however recognize a 1994 photograph they showed him of a man they claimed was the same person.

At the time of Loyd Jowers's deposition on November 2, 1994, Garrison showed Jowers the 1994 photograph which was provided to him by Herman and returned to him. Jowers said that he could not make a positive identification. Garrison also showed me the photograph which was of a relatively slim man dressed in a blue jacket, white shirt and tie, with graying brown hair.

Sometime later attorney Garrison informed me that Jowers was later shown the earlier photograph of the man alleged to be the younger Raul Pereira and he tentatively said that he was the man named "Raul" or "Royal" who he knew was involved with the crime.

Cheryl told me that she too had been shown the more recent photograph. At first she said she couldn't be certain because the greying hair confused her. She likened it to someone wearing a wig. Subsequently, she told me that the similarity of the facial structure convinced her that it was the Raul Pereira she knew.

I decided to go to Houston myself with Cheryl and Bob. We retraced Cheryl's movements from the time she first moved to Houston at age fourteen. A Waffle House restaurant now stood on the spot where the gas station had been located. We spent time in the area of the docks and Navigation Avenue observing an old house which was one of the places where she said Raul stayed during the time she saw him in Houston. We also drove past the house rented by Torrino where Cheryl said Raul allegedly admitted the killing and she was raped. It was now painted a grayish blue color (see photograph #26). The places Raul Pereira used in Houston appeared to be temporary accommodations. I had the impression that he might have had a permanent base elsewhere. Cheryl and Bob were nervous being in the obviously rough and hostile area, where strangers, particularly those with cameras, were regarded as the enemy and often subjected to drive-by shootings. The scene, they said, was very much as it was back then, incredibly poor and dilapidated. The Alabama Theatre was now a bookstore but Cheryl was able to point out Ross Vallone's old office where he held court, always seated in a recliner chair.

Bob tried to talk to some of the people who had been around during the 1960s and 1970s. The few he located were reluctant to talk, with the exception of one person who did talk and even gave him a photograph of Amaro which he gave to me.

Before parting company Cheryl executed an affidavit which set out her story in detail and said that she knew James Earl Ray was innocent and that she was prepared to testify in court on his behalf and tell what she knew.

Upon my return to England, a Houston area lawyer confirmed in a lengthy telephone conversation that Percy Foreman had become in the 1960s and 1970s the foremost lawyer for organized crime figures. Former mob lawyer Frank Ragano, who had represented Carlos Marcello and Santo Trafficante, had previously told me about Foreman's role as a lawyer for prominent mob figures. (He also revealed their extensive dissatisfaction with his services.)

I heard a rumor that the man I was looking for lived in the Northeast. I began a computerized state-by-state, name and residence check and cross-referenced search, using the name of Raul Pereira provided by Cheryl. It was a long shot that the man might be using his real name but there was always a chance. A small number of people named Raul Pereira surfaced. I instituted credit and other checks on these persons. By a process of elimination based primarily on age, ethnic origin (I had decided to focus only on white male immigrants between fifty-five and sixty-eight years of age with Portuguese or Brazilian origins), the list gradually reduced. The search was completed in early June and one person remained who satisfied the basic criteria. He appeared to be a relatively successful businessman, nearly sixty-one years old. He jointly owned his home, which was in a middle to upper middle class neighborhood in a city in the Northeast, with his wife. He had two grown children, one a twenty-five-year-old daughter and a son who appeared to be thirty-three. I then did a yellow pages search of import/export companies specializing in a particular product in that man's county. One possibility came up. When I called the business number an answer machine referred me to the home telephone number of the man I was focusing on.

I turned my attention to gathering more information about his personal life as well as his business. He owned another property on the same street where his import/export business was located in one of the city's poorest areas. He was reportedly a member of the local Portuguese American society and had no criminal record. From immigration records I learned that he had entered the United States from Portugal through New York City. His social security number had been issued in New York between 1961 and 1963 and he first appeared in his city telephone directory in 1965. (I recalled that Cheryl had said she first met this man she knew as Raul Pereira in Houston in 1962.) If this was James's Raul then for at least twenty years he had clearly led a double life.

A letter arrived from James in which he said that he had received a letter from Saltman stating that he and Herman had confronted Raul. He had apparently been hostile, taken photographs of them, and had his Spanish-speaking wife ask them to leave.

I wanted to obtain a current photograph of the Raul Pereira I was looking at in order to show it to Cheryl and also to determine whether this was the same man whom Herman and Saltman were considering, whose photograph I had seen at Jowers's deposition. So, in June 1995 I instructed a surveillance team to take photographs of him. When the photographs arrived at my office in London, I anxiously opened the courier pack. I was virtually certain it was the same man whose photograph I saw at the time of Jowers's deposition. The man I had begun to focus on earlier that spring clearly appeared to be the same person Herman and Saltman were looking at.

I decided to call Herman. He put Saltman on and they confirmed the visit and the hostile reception. Raul would not come to the door. His daughter spoke to them, lying in response to even the most simple and apparently nonthreatening questions. Giving no indication of where the man was or the man's identity, they both assured me that the man that they had found was Cheryl's Raul. When I expressed skepticism designed to draw out information, they jointly confirmed to me that the birth date and social security number of the man in the older photograph were identical to the birth date and the social security number of the man they had recently visited and who was the man in the more recent photographs. Herman later said that a C.I.A. contact of his told him that there was an active C.I.A. file on this person. The file reportedly indicated that Raul had worked for the Portuguese Government's national munitions company with some coordinating responsibility for weapons sales and distribution between October 1957 and December 1961.

Immediately thereafter I spoke with Cheryl. She told me that prior to Herman and Saltman's visit to Raul, they arranged for her to participate in a telephone conversation which was put through to Raul Pereira's home. She believed various members of his family, including himself, his wife, his daughter and son-in-law, were on various extensions and participated at different times. Cheryl said when Raul came on the phone she knew it was the Raul Pereira she had known in Houston, because of the way he pronounced her name. He never could pronounce it correctly. Despite what became hysterical denials of knowing her and ever being in Houston, she said she had no doubt this was the man.

It was obvious that Raul Pereira had been well and truly alerted and I was concerned that he might flee. This, of course, would allow the state to continue to contend that he was not the right man and that James's Raul never existed. In addition, since Herman and Saltman said they did not have enough to satisfy their television producers I was apprehensive about what further action they might take which could induce him to flee.

There therefore appeared to be little choice but to promptly join Raul Pereira as a party in the civil action against Jowers. We prepared a summons to go along with the original complaint in which he had been named, and a notice of deposition. The complaint against Raul alleged that:

1. He entered into a conspiracy with others to kill Dr. Martin Luther King, Jr.

2. In furtherance of his participation in this conspiracy he instructed, controlled, and orchestrated the movements of James Earl Ray in such manner as to arrange for a rifle with Ray's fingerprints on it to be found near the scene of the crime and for Ray to be charged with said crime.

3. In collusion with other codefendants he participated in providing and taking away a second rifle which may have been the actual murder weapon.

There was, however, always the possibility that he was not the right man and we had to acknowledge it. A mistake could greatly destroy our credibility, yet inaction could lose for us one of the most, if not the most, significant on-the-scene player whose very existence had been denied by the MPD, the FBI, and the HSCA.

I decided upon a middle ground. At the time he was being served he would be handed a letter informing him that if he was not the man we sought and was willing to talk to us and confirm the fact that we were in error, then we would withdraw the action against him. In the meantime we would request an order from the court sealing the file so that the fact that a summons and complaint and a notice of deposition had been issued and served upon him would not be made public.

Accordingly, Chastain and Garrison went into the judge's chambers on Friday, June 23, and secured an order sealing the file until further order of the court.

Around this time private investigator Bob Cruz told me that a source of his inside the Immigration and Naturalization Service (INS) had informed him that Raul Pereira had come into the United States on December 11, 1961. His source also said that Raul's INS file had been transferred in October 1994 to Memphis, Tennessee. He commented that there was no apparent reason for sending the file to Memphis and that the file would only be transferred at the request of another federal agency.

With time of the essence, I arranged a meeting with Cheryl and Bob in Memphis on the weekend of June 24. I showed Cheryl the photographs I had obtained of Raul Pereira. I was virtually certain that they were of the same man Herman and Saltman had photographed but she would not confirm that this was the Raul she knew. She did say once again that the man she talked to on the telephone call was the Raul she knew, and stated that the phone call was actually made from her home. This meant that the number would have been on a recent month's bill. She and Bob promised to give us the number so that we could compare it with the number we had for the Raul Pereira we had located.

Cheryl executed an affidavit in which she stated she recognized Raul from a 1960s photograph and also recognized the facial features of the man in a 1994 photograph she had been shown by Ken Herman. She further stated that she participated in a telephone conversation with Raul Pereira and that she was positive that this was the Raul she knew in Houston because of his inability to correctly pronounce her name, and that based upon her identification she understood we were preparing to bring him into the law suit against Loyd Jowers and others.

The following Sunday evening I called for the phone number but Bob said he could not find the bill.

On Monday at 7:45 a.m. we met Bob Cruz, who had organized the surveillance detail. He reported that the mother and daughter had already gone out, apparently leaving Raul at home alone. Before approving the final arrangements for service I needed to be absolutely certain that this was the same man being looked at by Saltman and Herman. I decided to call Raul myself and talk to him on the telephone. I did so and adopted a sympathetic tone, saying that I believed that he may have been harassed unjustly and I wanted him to know that though these people had once been associated with me as a lawyer in the case they were no longer working with me and were off on their own. He ponderously took down Chastain's and my details. He spoke with a fairly heavy accent and did not appear to be flustered. It was difficult to tell how much, if any, of Raul Pereira's language problem was feigned. (The surveillance team had told me that he demonstrated a high degree of street smarts when they tried to tail him. They said he knew exactly which moves to make to shake them off.) He seemed puzzled that I knew about his "problem" and confirmed that he had been bothered by some people and that this was upsetting him and his family. He expressed surprise that things thirty years old were being raised now and denied ever being in Houston. I asked him to meet with Chastain and me privately in order to try to clear up any question of his involvement and he asked me to call him back that evening after 7 p.m. when he would have had a chance to talk to his "kids" and his wife. I agreed and we held off any attempt at service that day. At 7:15 p.m. his daughter answered and said, in effect, that her father did not have to prove anything and his word denying any knowledge of the events would be good enough. She confirmed that a man named Saltman had appeared at their front door wanting to question her father and she said that she told him that if he published or released any information about her father they would sue him.

My impression was that she was well trained and intelligent. Mr. Pereira knew what he was doing by putting her forward. Toward the end of the conversation she said that they might ask their lawyer about talking to me, though she would not give me his name. At that point I concluded that we would have to serve Raul Pereira.

I left the papers with P.I. Cruz to formally serve.

The man I have called Raul Pereira was served on July 5 and made a party defendant in the *Ray v. Jowers et al.* lawsuit.

30

Orders to Kill

OVER A PERIOD OF TWENTY-FOUR months from June, 1993, while all of the other investigative activity was proceeding, information was obtained from a number of sources inside the army. These sources included the two former Special Forces members living in Latin America, whom I have called Warren and Murphy, who answered questions I put to them through Steve Tompkins. Their responses and some corresponding documentation (supplied by Warren) revealed not only the extent of their covert activity in various parts of the U.S. in 1967–68 but also detailed their involvement in the events surrounding Dr. King's assassination.

First hinted at by the Memphis *Commercial Appeal* in 1993, the role of the army and the other cooperating government agencies in the assassination of Dr. King has been one of our nation's deepest, darkest secrets. I have only been able to uncover it by piecing together the accounts of Warren and Murphy with those of other participants and persons who were in strategic positions with access to information, and analyzing relevant army intelligence documents, files and other official records which have never been made public. Wherever possible I have used independent corroboration. I have adopted the policy of not disclosing the names of the most sensitive team members who are still living, but I have named those who are dead in the belief that historical truth requires no less.

BEFORE SETTING OUT THE DETAILS, however, I believe that it will be useful to lay out the organizational structure which drove the events.

During the 1960s a highly secret federal organizational structure, with army intelligence in the forefront, carried out officially approved tasks which ranged from conventional intelligence activity—"eye-to-eye" surveillance and information gathering and analysis—to blatantly illegal covert operations. I have been surprised to discover the degree of official cooperation that existed during the time between what have often been publicly portrayed as exclusively competing agencies and officials.

Military Organization

In October 1961 Secretary of Defense Robert McNamara, with a view to eventually consolidating all intelligence functions of the individual armed services under one joint service organization, established the Defense Intelligence Agency (DIA). By 1965, however, the DIA had only taken over the U.S. Army's Strategic Intelligence School and the administration of the military attache system. The individual armed services, particularly the army, strove to retain their own intelligence apparatus. The army established its own intelligence and security branch on July 1, 1962. Following the Oxford, Mississippi, racial riots of 1963 when the 101st Airborne was deployed, Major General Creighton V. Abrams, the on-scene commander, wrote a highly critical assessment of the state and performance of army intelligence at Oxford. In part he stated:

"We in the Army should launch a major intelligence project, without delay, to identify personalities, both black and white, and develop analyses of the various civil rights situations in which they become involved."

His report received serious attention that resulted in the army intelligence machine that was in place in 1967–68. The intelligence and security branch was a group of professional intelligence officers who were fulfilling the role of the Military Intelligence Division created by its World War I chief lieutenant Colonel Ralph Van Deman. Van Deman, the father of army intelligence, began sixty years earlier to work closely with city police departments. In 1967 it was renamed the Military Intelligence Branch, and it formed part of the U.S. Army Intelligence Command (USAINTC) based at Fort Holabird, Maryland. Fort Holabird is a ninety-six-acre military compound where by 1968 in a huge steel two-story room, one city block in length, was housed the Investigative Records Repository (IRR). The IRR then contained more than seven million brown-jacketed dossiers on American citizens and organizations, including subversive files on individuals who—according to army intelligence—were "persons considered to constitute a threat to the security and defense of the United States." There were files on the entire King family in the IRR.

At that time USAINTC took over control of seven of the eight existing counterintelligence or U.S. army military intelligence groups (MIGs) in the Continental United States (CONUS) and Germany (the 66th MIG). The eighth MIG—the 902nd—was under the command of the army's Assistant Chief of Staff for Intelligence (ACSI) who from December 1966 until July 1968 was Major General William P. Yarborough. He had run the John F. Kennedy Special Warfare School at Fort Bragg, North Carolina, between 1961 and 1965 and was the founder of those units known as the Green Berets. By 1967 the MIGs employed 798 army officers, 1,573 enlisted men, and 1,532 civilians, including sixty-seven black undercover agents. Of this total force, 1,576 were directly involved in domestic intelligence gathering activities, and of these "spies" some 260 were civilians. I was provided with a copy of the ACSI command structure and table of organization as it existed in 1967.

The MIG officers were responsible for "eye-to-eye" surveillance operations, which included audio and visual recording of people and events designated as targets. Dr. King was a target, and throughout the last year of his life he was under the surveillance of one or another MIG team. Thus, in New York he was surveilled by the 108th MIG; in Los Angeles the 115th; Tennessee, Georgia, Alabama and the South, the 111th; in Chicago the 113th; in Washington, D.C., the 116th; in Newark, New Jersey, the 109th; and in Germany the 66th which was based in Stuttgart, Germany. I set out in Chart 7 (see Appendix) a map showing the territorial areas and headquarter bases of the MIGs inside the CONUS and in Charts 8, 9, and 10 in the Appendix the USAINTC Table of Organization in 1967, the USAINTC Field Offices and the USAINTC communications network.

Closely related to the USAINTC structure at the time was the separate intelligence office of the army chief of staff commanded by ACSI Yarborough. In addition to his control of the 902nd MIG, he supervised the Counterintelligence Analysis Board (CIAB), both of which were based in Falls Church, Virginia, though the CIAB was also secretly housed in a red brick warehouse at 1430 S. Eads Street in Arlington, Virginia. The CIAB analyzed a wide range of MIG-produced intelligence and forwarded reports usually directly to the ACSI. The 902nd MIG was a highly secretive operation, which I have learned carried out some of the most sensitive assignments.

Intelligence gathering was also done in 1967 (at least from June 12, when formally assigned the task) by the 20th Special Forces Group (20th SFG) headquartered in Birmingham, Alabama. As we will see, this function was in addition to the provision by the 20th SFG of small specialized teams for other "behind the fence" (covert) operations. This group was made up of reservists from Alabama, Mississippi, Florida, and Louisiana. The Alabama reservists were part of the third largest state National Guard unit in the country (20,016 members—surpassed only by New York and California). (From the early 1960s in Southeast Asia the Special Forces (Green Berets) began to be used for specialized intelligence-gathering functions in addition to their covert mission activity.)

The Klan had a special arrangement with the 20th SFG. The 20th SFG actually trained klansmen in the use of firearms and other military skills at a secret camp near Cullman, Alabama, in return for intelligence on local black leaders. The earliest of such training exercises began on November 12, 1966. Some members of the 20th SFG also used these sessions for illegal weapons sales.

The U.S. Strike Command (CINCSTRIKE) was the overall coordinating command (which could call upon all military forces on U.S. soil) for the purpose of responding to urban riots in 1967–1968. At that time it included liaison officers from the CIA, FBI, and other nonmilitary state and federal agencies. It was headquartered at MacDill air force base in Tampa, Florida, and the ACSI and USAINTC commanders were primary leaders in developing CINCSTRIKE strategy for the mobilization of forces as required for defensive action inside CONUS.

The United States Army Security Agency (ASA) headquartered at Fort Meade, Maryland, which in 1964 became a major command field operating agency under the control of the army chief of Staff, carried out all "non eye-to-eye" or ELINT (electronic intelligence surveillance). The ASA employed expert wiretappers, eavesdroppers, and safecrackers. The surveillance included wiretapping and electronic eavesdropping such as that carried out against Dr. King on March 18 and March 28, 1967, when he stayed at the Rivermont Hotel in Memphis (and, as we shall see, on April 3 and 4 at the Lorraine Motel). Thus, the "federal" agents with whom MPD special services/intelligence officer Jim Smith was working on March 18, whom we had initially believed to be FBI agents, were almost certainly ASA agents though probably assigned to work with the 111th MIG. In the field, the members of the ASA were also housed, though always in a distinctly separate working area, with the MIG operations. At Fort McPherson in Atlanta, for example, they were in the same building as the headquarters of the 111th MIG but worked clandestinely and were entirely separated by a floor-to-ceiling chain-link fence.

Finally, in terms of this story, there was the Psychological

Operations (Psy Ops) section. This group was primarily used for highly sensitive and technical photographic surveillance and reports. Psy Ops teams were used by MIGs or for other special missions, including those run out of the ACSI's office.

Interagency Structure

Alongside this multifaceted army structure were the National Security Agency (NSA), the CIA, the FBI, and the Office of Naval Intelligence (ONI). The NSA monitored and analyzed all targeted international cable, telephone, telex, teletype, and telefax communications as well as, on occasion, specified, sensitive domestic telecommunications traffic. As discussed earlier (see chapter 11) the CIA, through its clandestine Office of Security and the Domestic Operations Division, carried on extensive domestic operations interfacing on domestic activity (as did each of the army operating commands) with the FBI and ONI. These operations were carried out on a project-by-project basis, usually through specially created SOGs (Special Operations Groups). The interagency umbrella or coordinating intelligence body was the United States Intelligence Board (USIB). Represented on the USIB were the CIA (whose Director Richard Helms was its chairman), the NSA Director, the National Security Adviser to the president, the ACSI, the FBI, the ASA, USAINTC, the DIA and ONI.

This overall military/law enforcement and intelligence agency structure determined and controlled the planning and implementation of the range of military operations in Memphis, including the use of the Tennessee National Guard. Riot control in Memphis was accomplished through the use of the Tennessee National Guard.

The Principal Senior Officials

Mayor General Yarborough took over in December 1966, as ACSI, coming from command of the 66th MIG in Stuttgart, where his primary duty was to catch communist spies and run agents in East Germany. A limited number of key officers served under him. The commanding officer of USAINTC, the overall army intelligence organization, was Brigadier General William Blakefield, who was not a trained or experienced intelligence officer and who seemed to have been chosen for that position by army chief of staff Harold Johnson precisely because he was an outsider. The impression I have formed is that General Blakefield was uncomfortable with this command area and that he followed the ACSI General Yarborough on most issues.

The director of the CIA at the time was Richard Helms, and J. Edgar Hoover, of course, led the FBI. Though a closely guarded secret, FBI director Hoover seconded a trusted agent, Patrick D. Putnam, to Yarborough's ACSI staff in the Pentagon in order to ensure the closest working relationship. Putnam began this assignment in December 1966 with Yarborough's arrival and continued until his departure in July 1968.

The commanding officer of the 111th MIG (the group which covered all of the Deep South and so was most often engaged in surveilling Martin King) was Colonel Robert McBride.

From 1959 to 1971, the commander of the 20th SFG was Colonel Henry H. Cobb, Jr. (service number 0000514383) of Montgomery, Alabama, who retired as a Major General. His second in command was Major Bert E. Wride (service number 0002267592). The Alabama Army National Guard, which contained the 20th SFG, was per capita the nation's largest in 1968. Alabama also had the largest number of armories (140) of any state in America. In 1968 the Alabama Guard operated on a $150 million budget.

In 1979, after his retirement, Cobb became Alabama Adjutant General—the highest ranking member of the Alabama Army National Guard, appointed by Governor Fob James.

The 20th SFG Professionals

Warren and Murphy, the two members of the Special Forces team deployed to Memphis on April 4 who had agreed to discuss the mission, had been active in covert Special Operation Group (SOG) missions in Vietnam. They were hardened, highly skilled veterans; Warren was a sniper. Both were from the 5th Special Forces Group in Vietnam, and part of a Mobile Strike Force Team involved in cross-border covert operations in 1965–66. They were reassigned in 1967 as reservists to the 20th SFG, with Camp Shelby, Mississippi, as their training base, although they also secretly trained, according to Warren, at Mississippi Senator James Eastland's plantation near Rosedale in Sunflower County. I obtained a copy of the 20th SFG roster of Alabama soldiers around the time and their names appeared.

Other Domestic Missions

Warren and Murphy stated that throughout 1967 they were deployed in 902nd covert operations as members of small specialized "alpha team" units in a number of cities where violence was breaking out. They were issued photographs of black militants in each city they entered, and in some instances particular individuals were designated as targets to be taken out (killed) if an opportunity arose in the course of a disruption or riot. During this time, army intelligence published green and white books ("mug bugs") on black radicals, which contained photographs, family history, political philosophy, personal finances, and updated surveillance information in order to facilitate their identification by army commanders and intelligence personnel.

An example given by Warren was his mission in Los Angeles in February 1968, when there was a major black conference at the L.A. Sports Arena. SNCC leaders Stokely Carmichael and H. Rap Brown were there. The 20th SFG had the arena staked out in case of trouble. Surveillance pictures of a militant black group called the Brown Berets were passed out to the members of the team. The group's borrowing of the Green Beret symbol "pissed all of us off," Warren said. One target was a man named Karenga (Ron Karenga) whose organization's headquarters were down on South Broadway near some strip joints. The

20th SFG had a team across the street waiting for him, but he never showed up. Warren said that on that occasion they also had a secondary mission, which was to do recon. (reconnaissance) of a home up in the western hills near the UCLA campus. The recon was to determine the feasibility for a future "wet insert ops determined" operation ("wet insert ops determined" means that the unit carries out a surreptitious entry at night into the targeted residence, kills everyone there, and leaves without a trace). He said their recon confirmed the feasibility of such an operation. Warren subsequently learned that the house was used by Senator Robert Kennedy when he was in Los Angeles in 1967–68. (Shortly after the recon Kennedy would declare for the Presidency.)

Warren said that in 1967 he was also similarly deployed on other sensitive operations in:

Tampa, Florida (June 12–15, 1967—riots)
Detroit, Michigan (July 23, 1967—riot)
Washington, D.C. (October, 1967—riot)
Chicago, Illinois (December, 1967—recon)

The Memphis Mission

In successive sessions, Warren, eventually joined by Murphy, set out the details they personally knew about the Memphis deployment. They were part of an eight-man "Operation Detachment Alpha 184 team." This was a Special Forces field training team in specialized civilian disguise. The unit consisted of: a captain (as CO); a second lieutenant; two staff sergeants; two buck sergeants, and two corporals. (From a source inside the ACSI's office whom I will call "Herbert," I learned that a key aide of the 902nd MIG [whom I will call "Gardner"] had personally selected the team from the roster of the 20th SFG, which was provided at the request of the ACSI's office and sent to him at 6:15 p.m., October 23, 1967, by an AUTOVON dispatch from 20th SFG headquarters in Birmingham [an AUTOVON is a first-generation fax machine, which was state of the art at the time]).

A two-man recon unit of the Alpha 184 recon team consisting, they believed, of the second in command (who I was to learn from Herbert was the now deceased Second Lt. Robert Worley) and one other entered Memphis on February 25 through the Trailways Bus Terminal, completed recon on the downtown hotel area, and mapped egress routes to the north of the city. (It will be remembered that the "hoax" automobile chase took place in the northern section of Memphis and concentrated attention on this area of the city.) The team leader (who I learned from Herbert was Captain Billy R. Eidson—service number 0002282683), who is also now dead, was apparently given the final orders for the deployment at 7:30 a.m. on March 29, and Warren and Murphy stated that the team was specifically briefed before departing from Camp Shelby for Memphis at 4:30 a.m. on the morning of April 4, 1968.

During the approximately thirty-minute session the team was left in no doubt as to its mission. On the order they were to shoot to kill—"body mass" (center, chest cavity)—Dr. Martin Luther King, Jr., and, to my surprise, the Reverend Andrew Young, who was to be Warren's target. They were shown "target acquisition photos" of the two men and the Lorraine Motel. Eidson's pep talk stressed how they were enemies of the United States who were determined to bring down the government. Warren said that no one on the team had any hesitancy about killing the two "sacks of shit." Warren and Murphy stated that immediately after the briefing the team left by car from Camp Shelby for Memphis, carrying the following weapons in suitcases: standard .45 caliber firearms, M-16 sniper rifles with 8-power scopes (the closest civilian equivalent would be the Remington 30.06 700 series—remember that James was instructed to buy a Remington 760); K-bars (military knives); "frags" (fragmentation grenades); and one or two LAWS (light anti-tank weapon rockets). It appeared they were prepared for all contingencies. They were dressed as working "stiffs," similar to those day laborers who worked on the barges or in the warehouses down by the river near President's Island.

Warren remembered having a late breakfast at a Howard Johnson's restaurant when they arrived in the city. Captain Eidson arranged for Warren and Murphy to meet with a senior MPD officer who they believed was attached to the MPD's intelligence bureau and who told them that their presence was essential to save the city from burning down in the riot which Dr. King's forces were preparing. Warren later identified Lieutenant E. H. Arkin from a photograph as being the officer they met. (Arkin was also the MPD's chief liaison with special agent William Lawrence, the local FBI field office's intelligence specialist. When I interviewed Arkin he did not acknowledge any such meeting.)

Sometime after noon Warren and Murphy met their contact down near the railroad tracks. Warren named the man, whom he called a "spook" (army slang for CIA). He said he remembered this person because he closely resembled one of his best friends. The contact took them to the roof of a tall building that dominated that downtown area and loomed over the Lorraine. Their guide provided them with a detailed area-of-operations map, pictures of cars used by the King group, and the Memphis police TAC radio frequencies.

He didn't know the building's name, but I realized that it could only have been the Illinois Central Railroad Building, a structure with eight stories on top of a mezzanine, which lay diagonally southwest of the Lorraine (see photograph #34). Murphy agreed that they were in position by 1:00 p.m. and remained on their rooftop perch for over five hours. In their two-man sniper unit Warren was the shooter and Murphy the "spotter" and radio man. Murphy's job was to relay orders to Warren from the coordinating central radio man as well as to pick out or "spot" the target through binoculars. The central radio man, a corporal, is living in Canada in an intelligence officers protection program. I know his name and service number but have been unable to locate him.

Also during the course of that afternoon Warren had spoken over the radio with an MPD officer whose first name he believed was "Sam" who was the head of the city TAC. (This had to be Sam Evans, head of the MPD tactical units). Warren said

that Sam provided details about the physical structure and layout of the Lorraine. He also told Warren that "friendlies were
not wearing ties." Warren took this to mean that there was an
informant or informants inside the King group.

For the balance of the afternoon, he and Murphy waited. (I
learned from other sources inside the 111th MIG that ASA
agents monitored the discussions going on in Dr. King's room
[306], which was one of three rooms in the Lorraine they had
bugged. I learned that the telephones in each of the three
rooms were also tapped and that the agents kept a separate
folder for the transcripts of the conversations for each room.
Presumably these discussions and telephone conversations were
being passed on to Captain Eidson through his central radio
man. Though I cannot be certain of this, the two civilians
parked in the Butler/Mulberry Street area that afternoon who
were noticed by Robert Hagerty may well have been ASA
agents, since Hagerty also saw them with walkie-talkies. Similarly, the man seen loitering near his parked car on Huling
Street at the same time by telephone repairman Hasel Huckaby
may well have been a member of the 111th MIG team in the
area.)

Subsequently, my private investigator Jim Kellum reported
that former members of the MPD intelligence bureau, including senior officer Lieutenant Eli Arkin, confirmed to him that
all during this time agents of the 111th were in their offices
working with them. Arkin later confirmed their presence to me
and said that he had requested that they be moved to another
office in the central headquarters because they were interfering
with the work of his staff. I learned that "Intelligence Emergency Operation Centers" (IEOCs) were set up within a MIG
when a crisis was anticipated in that MIG area city. All intelligence information—in and out—was routed through the IEOC
and troop deployment communications passed through this operations center as well. From what Lieutenant Arkin told me,
it appears that in Memphis, true to the Van Deman tradition,
the IEOC was located in the MPD central headquarters, initially
in the intelligence bureau office.

Finally, near what Warren termed the "TTH" (top of the

hour—6.p.m.) the King group emerged from a lengthy meeting.

Warren recognized his target, Andrew Young, and took aim, holding him in his sights. Radio man Murphy waited for the order to fire, which he was expecting Captain Billy Eidson to give and which he was prepared to relay. It didn't come, and as usual in such circumstances the seconds seemed like hours. Warren kept Andy Young in the crosshairs of his scope, and then he said, just after TTH, a shot rang out. It sounded like a military weapon, and Warren assumed that the other sniper unit had jumped the gun and fired too soon because the plan was always for a simultaneous shooting. He said he never knew where the other sniper unit had been placed, but they would also have been above the target and at least 300 yards from it. A less well-trained soldier hearing that shot might have fired, but Warren said he had to have the direct order before he would pull the trigger. Murphy asked for instructions, and there was a long silence. Then Eidson came on and ordered the team to disengage in an orderly fashion and follow the egress routes assigned to them out of South Memphis where they were located. Warren and Murphy packed up and went down the same stairs they had climbed more than five hours earlier. They went across Riverside Drive and down to the river, where a boat was waiting. Eidson joined them and they quickly went some distance downstream to a prearranged point where cars were waiting. Eidson ordered complete silence for the return trip. No one was allowed to speak. Only some of the team went out this way. Warren said the rest obviously went out another way, but he had no idea how they returned. He said that his immediate impression that the other team had "screwed up" continued until later that evening when he heard that some "wacko civilian" had apparently done the shooting.

When asked, he said he believed that it was entirely possible that the Alpha 184 team mission could have been a backup operation to an officially deniable, though jointly coordinated, civilian scenario. Warren said that he had seen Captain Eidson on only two other occasions after April 4, and he refused to talk to him about what had happened.

As noncommissioned officers, staff sergeants Warren and Murphy were "grunts." They would only have been told what they needed to know in order to carry out their particular task on the day. Warren stressed that April 4 was the first time he had been in Memphis, and that he had not participated in any recon activity. He said that though their operation was a military one, so far as he knew there was some interservice cooperation since they were coordinating with Tennessee National Guard units and NAS—the Millington Naval Air Station.

Warren provided a copy of the orders for the April 4 mission in Memphis, which I include as photograph #33. They confirm the following statements he made:

1. A team was in Memphis.
2. Reference was made to a 4:30 a.m. briefing.
3. The brief at 4:30 was controlling unless so ordered otherwise.
4. NAS support (Millington Naval Air Station support was on line).
5. Support services were provided at the "Riversite."
6. Local intelligence was needed.
7. Recon on the site was required ". . . prior to King, Martin L. Arrival."
8. Termination of mission was available on radio notice channel 012.

I was advised that "chopped" referred to the availability upon request of removal by NAS helicopter.

The orders appeared to come from the office of the Joint Chiefs of Staff and were issued under the umbrella of the anti-black terrorist operation "Garden Plot" which was a part of the overall U.S. Command antiriot operation CINCSTRIKE which was activated with the outbreak of any major riot. The document has been checked by a Pentagon source in intelligence who confirmed its authenticity.

The orders were clearly well circulated, reaching the highest levels of government. They were even sent to the White House. The Pentagon source provided a decoding of the initials used to indicate where the orders were sent and confirmed the following: CJCS stood for the Chairman of the Joint Chiefs of Staff; DJS meant the Director of the Joint Chiefs of Staff; SJCS meant the Secretary of the Joint Chiefs of Staff; SACSA was the FBI's Special Agent in Charge of Security Affairs; NMCC referred to the National Military Command Center; SECDEF indicated the Secretary of Defense; ASD/ISA was the designation for the Assistant Secretary of Defense for International Security Affairs, and WHouse referred to the White House.

The origin of the orders LANTCOMN/CINCSPECOPS revealed knowledge and involvement of the Atlantic Command as well as a special operations section of CINCSTRIKE. The critical reference is to the 4:30 a.m. briefing at which time sources said the deadly nature of the operation was explicitly laid out and "target acquisition photos" of the two targets and their location were shown.

WARREN HAD HEARD ABOUT one other time when a 20th SFG unit had almost "taken out" Dr. King. This was during the Selma march in 1965. Warren said the sniper, who was also a member of the Memphis Alpha 184 team, claimed that on that occasion he actually had the SCLC leader "center mass" (the center of his chest in the crosshairs of his scope) in his sights awaiting the order to fire, which never came because Dr. King turned sharply away at the opportune moment and was closely surrounded thereafter on the march. Warren would not name this soldier or any other member of the team except his expatriate buddy Murphy, who consented and also provided information. Though he was unaware of it, the names of all eight, including his own, had been independently provided by Herbert (the officer in the ACSI office), who corroborated their active duty presence in Memphis on April 4 as members of the Alpha 184 team which had been selected and coordinated by Gardner of the 902nd MIG. Herbert's further check of the files revealed that the 20th SFG did indeed have a sniper team deployed to the Selma area for the beginning of the march from Selma to Montgomery. Two of the members of that Selma team confirmed that King was being targeted until he turned left, at one point, and crossed a bridge.

There was one soldier on both that Selma 20th SFG team and the April 4, Alpha 184 team in Memphis. His name was John D. Hill (J. D.), a buck sergeant who was murdered in 1979. As mentioned earlier, on October 16, 1994, I made contact with a man whom I will call Carson who knew J. D. well. More importantly, J. D. had shared with him what he personally knew about the King assassination plan.

When I raised the subject of J. D.'s involvement in the killing of Dr. King and asked him whether J. D. had ever discussed the operation with him, he sighed, and was silent for a while. He said the subject had come up, but he was reluctant to open up this can of worms since it could lead to the two of us being killed. He uttered the familiar phrase, "You don't know who you're dealing with." I told him that by now I was getting the idea. The problem was that my client was innocent of this crime and had served nearly twenty-six years in prison and that even though his innocence was becoming ever more obvious the state had spurned every face-saving opportunity to free him which I had put forward. Consequently, I had little choice and certain risks were necessary. I believed that the only way to free him would be to solve the case conclusively and that we had progressed very far toward this goal.

Carson gradually came around. He said that in the mid-70s J. D. appeared to want to shed some baggage about his past. He told Carson about an assassination mission he had trained for over a period of many months, to be carried out on a moment's notice. He was in training with a small unit selected for the mission because they were all members of the 20th SFG.

He said that J. D. was a member of the 20th SFG which, Carson came to learn, though officially a Special Forces Reserve unit, actually was used for a wide range of covert special or "behind the fence" operations inside and outside of the U.S. J. D. told him that on April 4 the main body of the Alpha 184 team arrived in cars from Camp Shelby, which was their staging base and the training home for the 20th SFG reservists. Each year the 20th SFG traveled to Camp Shelby for two weeks of field training with other units. Shelby was used because of the size of the facility which allowed for the live firing of long-range weapons within the compound.

With respect to the Memphis mission, he said that all weapons, material, and immediate orders were generated from the base, although the actual preparation for a triangulation shooting had been previously practiced at a site near Pocatello, Idaho. At an early stage the scenario called for a triangular shot at a moving vehicle in an urban setting. At the time no official details were provided about the mission and the men believed it was to be directed at an Arab target. J. D. said that, though he soon learned that the mission was to be executed in Memphis, Tennessee, the target still remained a mystery. He believed that some of the team had gone to the city earlier. Carson had the impression that the team consisted of seven, not eight, persons and that there were three shooters, a communications specialist, logistical and transportation officers, and a unit commander. Since each of the soldiers was trained in at least three MOS's (military skills), some members would have doubled up as spotters, as this function was always required.

He said that J. D. identified the sites as a rooftop, a water tower, and a third-story window, with the team expecting to have to fire upon and hit their targets (there was more than one) when they were in a moving car entering or leaving the motel parking lot. The team knew that the King party was going to dinner that evening, and they didn't believe for a minute that Dr. King would appear on the balcony in such an exposed position. They were convinced that it was a kill for which they were going to have to work.

The weapons that Carson said J. D. told him were carried by the team were in line with the list provided by Warren, down to and including the LAWS (light antitank weapon rockets). Carson said it was obvious from the way J. D. spoke that something went wrong and that they had to leave unexpectedly and quickly. They (or some members of the team) were flown out from West Memphis.

Carson agreed to fax the information to me and to include the name and address of J. D.'s unit partner, who he said was very different from J. D. Conditioned by his experiences in Vietnam, he was apparently a stone killer; a "psycho," said Carson.

Carson said he had always had reservations about J. D.'s death. He said the official account made no sense to him. J. D. was allegedly shot to death at point-blank range by his wife, sometime after midnight on January 12, 1979. She apparently fired five bullets from his .357 Magnum into a closely confined area of his chest. He was dead before he hit the floor. Carson said it had all the signs of a professional killing. He had known J. D.'s wife and did not believe that she had the strength or the capability to handle the large firearm with the precision described. He recalled that she left or was taken out of town shortly afterward and that she was never indicted for the crime. Carson believed that J. D., a heavy drinker, might have begun to talk to others about the Memphis operation and that this could have been the reason he was killed. I remembered that Warren had said that he had left the country because he believed a cleanup process had begun within a year of the assassination and that if he returned to the United States he would be "immediately killed." Though he wouldn't name the team member who he said was shot in the back of the head in New Orleans, I noted that Eidson and Worley were also both dead. My investigator Buck Buchanan spoke with the first officer on the scene after the shooting of J. D., Donald Freshaur, who arrived only minutes after. He said that Janice Hill told him that she "couldn't take it any more." Her husband J. D. had a history of heavy drinking and abusive behavior. I obtained a copy of the court records relating to the death and confirmed that there was no indictment. She was released and lives today in another town in Mississippi.

As mentioned earlier, just before we ended Carson said, "This meeting never took place. You have to be very careful," he said. "They'll drop you where you stand."

When Carson's faxed note came through on plain paper a couple of weeks later it confirmed what he told me and provided further information. J. D.'s team was positioned on a Tayloe Paper Company water tower.

J. D. thought that the other two teams were on a rooftop and a third-story window. (I knew that there was a cluster of water towers on top of the various Tayloe Paper Company buildings which stretched westward, back toward Front Street and the river.) Carson wrote that J. D. confirmed that something had gone wrong and the mission was aborted. They disengaged, were picked up and driven out of South Memphis to West Memphis Arkansas airport where they were placed on a small aircraft and flown to Amory, Mississippi, after releasing their weapons and other gear to the logistics officer who remained behind. They apparently dispersed at that point, J. D. returning to his home in Columbus. J. D. told Carson that everything that had transpired during the training phase up to and including the mission was classified as Top Secret. J. D. learned upon his arrival in Columbus that Dr. King had been assassinated.

I had no information about the inclusion on the Alpha 184 team of a third shooter, and Warren had always firmly believed that there were only two shooters. Two of the locations described to Carson by J. D. were credible, since we know that Warren and Murphy were on the roof of the Central Illinois Railroad building, and the main Tayloe Paper Company Water Tower also met the criteria for a perch.

It was remarkable that J. D.'s account, coming to me twenty years after Carson had heard it, independently confirmed the presence of a Camp Shelby-based 20th SFG Alpha 184 shooting team in Memphis on April 4, 1968, which had been drawn from crack reserves of the 20th with Martin King as a target. Further, J. D. had said that a team had been training for that mission for a period of several months. (This time frame is in line with the date [October 23, 1967] when Gardner of the 902nd MIG got the 20th SFG roster and began to handpick the team.) When subsequently asked, Warren confirmed that Pocatello, Idaho, was a training area.

Warren and Murphy never knew that I had access to J. D.'s story, neither did they or Carson know that the names of each member of the Alpha 184 team had been provided to me by Herbert. One of the names on that list also matched the name of the person independently named by Carson as J. D.'s unit partner.

IN RESPONSE TO A QUESTION about whether or not he knew or had known Jack Youngblood, the onetime government operative and mercenary who had long been on the periphery of the King case, Warren said he remembered him well from the time they served together in Vietnam when Youngblood was assigned to a highly classified covert Special Operations Group based in Can Tho (1st SOG), which was financed and controlled by the CIA and involved in dirty work—sabotage, assassinations, and special operations—throughout Southeast Asia. Warren also flew several missions with Youngblood when the latter was with the "Air Studies Group" based at Nha Trang. He said that he had last seen Youngblood in the summer or early fall of 1967 on one of his gunrunning deliveries to New Orleans. He saw Youngblood with Zippy Chimento, the coordinator of Carlos Marcello's gunrunning operations in which Warren and (from what Sid Carthew and Cheryl independently said), apparently, Raul Pereira, were also involved. He recalled that Youngblood had flown in with "Ken Burns or something." [I came to believe that he was referring to Ken Burnstein, who was involved both in gunrunning and drug smuggling. Burnstein hired Youngblood as a pilot for his Ft. Lauderdale airplane taxi company—Florida Atlanta Airlines—but Youngblood also worked for an Alabama arms dealer by the name of Stuart F. Graydon. Burnstein, who was convicted of drug smuggling in 1974, died in a plane crash in 1976. He was also the main illegal weapons procurer for Mitchel Livingston WerBell III, who was a key freelance asset of the CIA and who built and supplied weapons through Central America and eventually Southeast Asia for the agency in the 1960s.]

Now, sixteen years after I first met and interviewed him in

1978, it appeared clear that though apparently not himself involved, Jack Youngblood did know at least one of the people on the scene at the time of the killing. It occurred to me that the people he talked about my obtaining information from in 1978 could very well have been these former Vietnam war buddies Warren and Murphy since Youngblood had said that the people he wanted me to meet believed they had been sold down the river by their government after many years of faithful service and now lived outside of the country. Warren and Murphy certainly had a grievance against the government, having left the country because they believed that they were to be killed. It was ironic that sixteen years later, I would independently obtain their story.

Warren also said that he had heard "scuttlebutt" (rumors) that the 111th Military Intelligence Group (MIG) had a black agent inside Dr. King's group. Using an intelligence source with access to different personnel data banks, I asked for a check to be completed on Marrell McCollough who I had previously confirmed from two independent sources had gone to work for the CIA in the 1970s. The report bore fruit. McCollough was not who he appeared to be. He had been in the regular army between February 1964 and December 1966 and was a military policeman (an MP). Then on June 16, 1967, he was reactivated and hired as an army intelligence informant and attached to the 111th MIG headquartered at Camp McPherson, Georgia.

Thus McCollough had ultimate reporting responsibility to the 111th MIG, though he was deployed to the MPD as an undercover agent, and officially reported to MPD lieutenant E. H. Arkin. He was apparently shocked and surprised when the shooting occurred. It is unlikely that he was aware as he knelt over Dr. King (see photograph #36) that the 20th SFG sniper teams were in the wings with the prone body of Martin King and the erect form of Andrew Young center mass in their scopes.

I forwarded a photograph to Warren to see if he could identify either of two persons coming down over the wall, quite obviously shortly after the killing since uniformed police were shown in the photograph running up Mulberry Street. The two figures were hatless and wearing some kind of uniform. One of them appeared to be wearing a small miltary issue side-arm. (See photograph #39) Warren was quick to respond. He didn't recognize the figure farthest away, but the man closest to the camera, bending over as he prepared to jump down from the wall, he knew from his days in Vietnam as someone who had been assigned to the 1st SOG in Can Tho. He named him and said he believed that in Vietnam he was associated with either the CIA or the NSA, and that in 1968 he was work-ing for the NSA. I thought it possible that he might have been seconded to another agency for this operation. Interagency sharing or secondment of such personnel was a regular practice.

Warren, who I had come to believe was credible and reliable, also said that a photograph of the actual shooting from the brush area existed and that sometime after the event he had seen it. He said the shooter was not James Earl Ray. I recalled that Doug Valentine had reported in his book *The Phoenix Pro-gram* that there was a rumor that such a photograph had been taken.[68] Warren provided the name and address of the now retired officer who supposedly had a copy, and agreed to ap-proach him.

The former Psy Ops officer whom I will call ''Reynolds'' agreed to have contact, but initially he insisted on the same procedure that had been used with his Latin American buddies. My questions would be carried to him by a former intelligence officer whom we both trusted. The meeting was set for early December 1994 in the coffee shop of the Hyatt Regency Hotel near Michigan Avenue in Chicago.

REYNOLDS WAS ABOUT 5'10" TALL, 160–170 pounds, with grey, short-cropped hair. He said that in Vietnam he had been as-signed to the 1st SOG (Special Operations Group) based in Can Tho and that he worked for the 525th Psychological Oper-ations Battalion.

Reynolds said that he and his partner (whom I will call ''Norton'') were deployed to Memphis on April 3 as a part of a wider mission they believed was under the overall command of Gardner of the 902nd MIG whom Reynolds knew and for whom he had worked on a number of assignments. They carried the necessary camera equipment and were armed with standard issue .45 caliber automatics. Norton also carried a small revolver in a holster in the small of his back. They arrived before noon on that day and went directly to fire station 2 where the captain, Carthel Weeden, whose name had never surfaced in any official report or file that I have seen, facilitated their access to the flat roof. They took up their positions on the east side of the roof. From that vantage point they overlooked the Lorraine and were well placed to carry out their mission, which was to visually and photographically surveil the King group at the Lorraine Motel and pick out any individuals in photos who might be identified as a communist or national security threat. (In the spring of 1995 I went up onto the roof. I was impressed with the completely unobstructed view of the balcony in front of Dr. King's room 306 [see photograph #37]) From 1:00 p.m. they began forwarding reports to the local IEOC office from which they were sent on to the headquarters of the 111th MIG in Fort McPherson and then to Gardner of the 902nd MIG. Sources inside the 111th MIG confirmed that regular reports were received on April 3 and 4.

This surveillance continued throughout the afternoon and resumed again the next morning, April 4. It was in place throughout the day and the same process of transmitting information was followed. Because of Jim Kellum's information and Eli Arkin's admission to me that agents of the 111th had been inside the offices of the MPD intelligence bureau, I have come to believe it likely that in the first instance the reports were called in to them at MPD headquarters from the fire station and then transmitted onward. This process would conform to the chain of communications for such activity described in the 1973 Senate Judiciary Subcommittee Report on Constitutional Rights. There would have been no reason for Captain Weeden to have been told or know about the assassination plot, and I have no reason to believe that he did know. When I visited

Weeden in June 1995 he indicated his awareness of the photographers on the roof except that when the discussion turned to how they got up there he talked in terms of how it "could" or "would" have happened. He said they would not have gone up on the roof using the inside vertical ladder in the garage but would have been given a "short" ladder in order to climb up from the side of the building.

From what Reynolds said, at the very moment that we now know the 20th SFG Alpha 184 snipers had Dr. King and Andrew Young center mass in the crosshairs of their M-16 scopes, his camera was trained on Dr. King as he stood on the balcony, while Norton was watching and shooting any arriving cars. At 6:01 p.m., the fatal moment when the shot rang out, Reynolds said he was surprised and in rapid succession quickly snapped four or five photos following Dr. King as he fell to the balcony floor. Reynolds said Norton almost instinctively swung his camera from its parking lot focus to the left and, focusing on the brush area, caught the assassin (a white man) on film as he was lowering his rifle. He then took several shots of him as he was leaving the scene. Reynolds said that though Norton had caught the assassin clearly in his camera he personally only saw the back of the shooter as he left the scene. He said that they hand delivered the pictures to Gardner but Norton kept the negatives and made another set of prints which Reynolds said he had seen (I recalled that Warren had also said that he had viewed them). Reynolds categorically stated, as had Warren earlier, that the sniper in the photograph was not James Earl Ray.

Eric S. Galt

At one point during my investigation of the involvement of the army, a source placed a photograph in front of me, and asked, "Do you know who this is?" It was a full frontal head shot of Eric St. Vincent Galt—the man whose name James had assumed and used for most of the time between July 18, 1967, and April 4, 1968 (see photograph #38). I was told not to ask any questions because it had come from and was part of an

NSA file. I learned that Galt, who as we know was the executive warehouse operator at Union Carbide's factory in Toronto, had top secret security clearance. The warehouse he ran housed an extremely top secret munitions project funded by the CIA, the U.S. Naval Surface Weapons Center, and the Army Electronics Research and Development Command. The work involved the production and storage of "proximity fuses" used in surface-to-air missiles, artillery shells, and LAWS. Galt had worked for Union Carbide of Canada Ltd, which was 75% owned by Union Carbide Inc. of the U.S. since the early 1980s. The company was engaged in high-security research projects controlled by the U.S. parent. Galt's top secret security clearance was actually conducted by the Royal Canadian Mounted Police, and his last security check had been in 1961. Union Carbide's nuclear division ran the Oak Ridge National Laboratory in Oak Ridge, Tennessee.

I learned that in August 1967 (shortly after the time when James assumed the Galt identity) the real Eric Galt met with Gardner's aide and that they met again in September. At that time Galt was cooperating with another 902nd MIG operation that involved the theft of some of these proximity fuses and their covert delivery to Israel. (I have obtained a confidential memorandum issued by the 902nd MIG on 17 October 1967 which confirms and discusses this operation, Project MEXPO, which was defined as a "military material exploitation project of the Scientific and Technical Division (S&T) . . . in Israel." The file and project number was 10518S-MAIN. The memo indicated that pursuant to a conference held on July 12, 1967, it was agreed that the 902nd would provide administrative support services to the project.)

The real Eric Galt was listed in the Toronto telephone directory in 1967—68 as "Eric Galt" with no middle name or initial, and in 1967 he had begun to use the initial S., dropping his middle name, St. Vincent, entirely. When James in July 1967 assumed the alias Eric S. Galt, he was signing the name in the same way as the real Galt had recently adopted.

The coincidence was impressive. James had somehow acquired the name of a highly placed Canadian operative of U.S.

army intelligence. Further, he began using the name on July 18, 1967, around the time the real Eric Galt was meeting with Gardner's aide.

I had to finally conclude that though James likely obtained the other aliases by himself, there was little likelihood that he, on his own, had accidentally chosen the Galt identity. He was, however, as was his right, apparently determined to protect someone or some persons who he believed had tried to help him (though he almost certainly did not know who ultimately provided the alias to him). By protecting his supplier he would also avoid the potential hell of protective custody. This was the status given prisoners who appeared to be informants. Once in this situation the correctional authorities can exert total control over the prisoner for his own "protection," even requiring him to be housed in the most austere conditions with his movements totally restricted. It can be a living hell. Those of us not familiar with this reality cannot appreciate it. Aside from the fact that James has strong views about never being a "snitch," he has also been determined never to provide any reason for protective custody to be imposed upon him. It has only been fairly recently that I have come to appreciate this position.

Previously I had no doubt that James was used and manipulated, but now it was apparent that his manipulation involved not only elements of organized crime but also a specific, senior level, highly covert military intelligence group, the involvement of which could be traced back at least to July 18, 1967, when he began to use the Galt identity.

Suddenly Galt appeared to be a critical link, facilitating the use of James Earl Ray as a patsy by a covert part of army intelligence and involving the 20th SFG, the FBI, and the other associated and collaborating members of the government and intelligence community involved with the assassination of Martin Luther King.

I raised the connection with deep cover source Herbert. He nodded and said, "James Earl Ray was a dead man." The identity was not to have mattered. He was to have been blown away either in Memphis or in Africa, if he made it that far.

But why was Eric St. Vincent Galt's identity chosen for the

patsy? It finally made sense when I realized that the use of an identity with top secret clearance was a means of securing and protecting the patsy from any mistakes or problems he would encounter before he was needed. Any routine police check would come up against a protected file, and the result would be that the government agency (in this instance the NSA and the army through the ACSI's office) could control the situation and instruct any law enforcement authorities to let the patsy go. Galt, a Canadian citizen with some physical resemblance to James, would have no need to know about the use of his name, and it was therefore unlikely that he would be told. James would also most likely not have known anything about Eric S. Galt.

The fact that the NSA had a file on Eric Galt reminded me that James Bamford, in his research for his book, *The Puzzle Palace,*[69] had stumbled upon a very well-kept, highly classified secret—the surreptitious involvement of the NSA in the effort to locate James after the assassination.

As early as 1962 the NSA had systematically begun to include in a "watch list" the names of persons and organizations who were engaged in dissent against America's Vietnam policy. In 1967 this list and its focus increased sharply. On October 20 of that year General Yarborough sent a "TOP SECRET COMINT CHANNELS ONLY" message to NSA director Marshal Carter requesting that the NSA provide any available information about possible foreign communications to and influence on individuals associated with civil disturbances in the United States.[70]

This request was apparently unprecedented. The army began to send over page after page of the names of protestors gathered by army intelligence units from all over the country whom they wanted surveilled. The CIA, the Secret Service, the FBI, and the DIA followed suit. The result was that this "watch list" grew enormously and went far beyond its original purpose. The NSA had a vacuum cleaner approach to intelligence gathering, sucking up all telecommunications of targeted individuals into the system. The use of a targeted person's or organization's name triggered the interception and recording of the conversation which was then subsequently analyzed. Thus, if an organization or a person was targeted, the communications of everyone in contact with them would be subject to this process. Thousands upon thousands of private communications were scooped up and scrutinized by the big ear of the government.

The NSA became involved in the search for James Earl Ray in May 1968. Attorney General Ramsey Clark and a number of Supreme Court decisions had frustrated the FBI's efforts to institute microphone and electronic surveillance of James's brothers and sisters. Eventually an FBI internal memorandum conceded that such a measure would likely be unconstitutional, and it was dropped.

Then, however, Frank Raven, the NSA's officer who received the watch lists from the rest of the law enforcement and intelligence community and acted upon them, received a direct order to place Ray's name, along with several aliases, on the watch list. What was unusual about this occurrence was that it was not a request from the FBI or the Justice Department but an order directly from the office of the Secretary of Defense, Clark M. Clifford, who has no recollection of issuing it.[71] Raven said that he tried to object to the order on constitutional grounds but was told that ". . . you couldn't argue with it—it came from the highest level."[72]

The NSA's involvement in the investigation of James Earl Ray has never been revealed in any official investigation. What was emerging, then, was the involvement of army intelligence (more precisely the 902nd MIG)—which was under the direct control of the Assistant Chief of Staff for Intelligence (Mayor General William P. Yarborough)—with James from at least July 1967, through his use of the identity of one of the 902nd's assets who had top secret security clearance. This led to the subsequent unconstitutional involvement of the NSA to use the watch list to locate him. It appears likely that the order which was routed through the Defense Secretary's office found its way there from the office of the ACSI.

The scope and complexity of this operation was literally mind-boggling. I needed to understand how it had all developed during that last year.

Chronology of Relevant Events

From the time that the eyewitness accounts of the Alpha 184 team members and related personnel began to become available to me, I set about the task of acquiring from other sources information and documentation (some of which is still classified 28 years later) which revealed what was happening in 1967–68 at senior levels of the government and the intelligence community.

As noted earlier, at the same time that General Yarborough took over as ACSI in December 1966, director Hoover seconded to Yarborough's staff a trusted and, until now, virtually unknown agent named Patrick D. Putnam. (It should be remembered that Hoover had had a close working relationship with the army since the late 1920s, when his number one, Clyde Tolson, came over from army intelligence to join the bureau and established the tie for his boss, who was gratuitously given and maintained the rank of Lieutenant colonel in army Intelligence until after the Second World War.) Putnam was to remain as the daily liaison between Hoover and Yarborough until the latter left the office of ACSI in July 1968, at which time he wrote to Hoover lavishly praising agent Putnam. A copy of this letter dated 2 July, 1968, was among the documents provided to me.

The senior staff of the 111th MIG met on January 17, 1967, at their Fort McPherson headquarters to look at photographs that were part of a surveillance summary report of Martin Luther King's arrival in Jamaica. The 111th had been on his trail as he left, and then continued surveillance in the Caribbean.

The next day at FBI Headquarters, starting at 11:00 a.m., General Yarborough met in his new capacity for the first time with director Hoover. Also present was CIAB head Colonel F. E. Van Tassell. The discussion focused on the army and the bureau working together to counter the growing antiwar movement, which Yarborough and Hoover agreed was the result of a communist conspiracy. They were kindred spirits. The importance of this strong anticommunist, anti-civil rights, pro-war attitude, which dominated Hoover's FBI and the army's intelligence staff in 1967, should not be underestimated.

They agreed that information produced by the massive army intelligence surveillance operation of Dr. King was to be routinely and regularly shared with the bureau. (Walter Fauntroy had told me during my preparation for the television trial that in the documents obtained as a part of the HSCA investigation—though mentioned nowhere in the committee's report—he had seen examples of such army intelligence reports which were sent to Hoover).

In February, wiretapping and ELINT (covert electronic surveillance) were carried out by the ASA. The tapes and transcripts were reviewed at Fort Meade, though often passed through the MIG in which area the activity took place. For example, a telephone conversation between Dr. King and his friend New York lawyer Stanley Levison on February 18 was recorded by the ASA and passed through the 108th MIG. In this particular conversation army intelligence, the FBI, and other intelligence agencies in the loop learned about Dr. King's emerging awareness that many blacks considered the war to be a form of genocide and of his determination to participate in the April 15 antiwar demonstration at the United Nations where I would float his and Ben Spock's names on a third party ticket.

The various components of the intelligence community seemed to be in nonstop meetings concerning the antiwar movement at this time.

On February 23 at 10:30 a.m. the umbrella organization, the USIB, held its weekly meeting with both the CIA's Richard Helms and ACSI Yarborough attending.

The 115th MIG photographed and recorded a speech of Dr. King's in Los Angeles on February 25 when he shared the platform with antiwar senators Eugene McCarthy and George McGovern. The photos and transcript sent to the Pentagon for analysis revealed King's contention that the war was a manifestation of "white colonialism," and reported his statement that "We must demonstrate, teach, and preach until the very foundations of our nation are shaken."

The analysis of these remarks, completed two days later at CIAB headquarters at Bailey's Crossroads, Virginia, concluded that Dr. King's speech was "a call to armed aggression by negroes against the American people." At 10:30 a.m. this report and analysis was sent over to ACSI Yarborough. At 2:30 p.m. that day, the 111th MIG out of Fort McPherson sent a report identifying two black agents who were available to infiltrate the SCLC.

IN EARLY 1967, though the American people were regularly given optimistic forecasts regarding the war, army intelligence was very much aware of how badly it was actually going. On March 18 Vietnam Commander General William Westmoreland sent a request to the Joint Chiefs of Staff for 201,250 more troops (4.5 additional divisions). At the same time antiwar pressures were also steadily building at home.

In Chicago six days later on March 24, members of the 113th MIG (headquartered at Fort Sheridan, Illinois) photographed and recorded Drs. King and Spock addressing the rally of 5,000, during which Dr. King called for the fervor of the civil rights movement to now be applied to the antiwar movement. Surveillance continued on the 25th of March and then, as we have seen, on April 4 at Riverside Church in New York Dr. King delivered his formal and most powerful denunciation of the war up to that time, personally committing himself to the effort to end it. The speech was photographed and recorded by agents of the 108th MIG.

Since the devastating effects of the war on Vietnamese civilians were being highlighted by Dr. King's speeches everywhere he went, at 10:30 a.m. on April 7 Colonel Van Tassell and his staff at the CIAB reviewed the massive photographic evidence of the effects of the bombing on women and children in Vietnam, which were now, more and more, becoming available for the masses to see. Napalm-burned children (such as that set out in photograph 1) figured prominently. (I had helped to form a nationwide Committee of Responsibility, backed by prominent Americans, which began to bring badly burned and injured children to hospitals all over the United States. Consequently, horrifically injured children became increasingly visible in America's towns and cities.) A strategy was obviously needed to counter the growing sympathy of American public opinion for the plight of Vietnamese civilians. One week later, on April 14 at 4:00 p.m., Colonel Van Tassell's CIAB staff met with General Yarborough and staff from the DIA and the Joint Chiefs of Staff Intelligence Unit. The focus of this meeting was to discuss ways and means of infiltrating the antiwar movement for purposes of intelligence gathering and subversion.

ALL OF THE ACTIVITY surrounding the massive April 15 antiwar march and rally in front of the United Nations was recorded and photographed by the 108th MIG. The 108th MIG photos and transcripts routinely went off for CIAB analysis, which when they landed on Yarborough's desk, contained the analysis that Martin Luther King was continuing to work with subversive groups which were planning "war in the streets of our towns and cities." The analysis also tied together Dr. King and SNCC leader Stokely Carmichael, calling them "allies in a role of subversion and revolution."

Five days before the launching at Harvard of "Vietnam Summer" (the student-driven series of antiwar educational activities) Hoover sent a memo on King to the White House, with a shortened version being delivered by Putnam to Yarborough. In it Hoover contended that King "is an instrument in the hands of subversive forces seeking to undermine our nation."

On April 30 Dr. King's sermon at Ebenezer Baptist Church was recorded by ASA microphones and sent from the 111th MIG at Fort McPherson to the CIAB. In that session, with Stokely Carmichael in the congregation, Dr. King called America "the greatest purveyor of violence in the world today."

On May 16 Hoover declared before the House Appropriations Committee that Stokely Carmichael, whom he labeled as Dr. King's ally, was secretly recruiting a black army to wage a revolution against white America.

The 66th MIG in Stuttgart, West Germany, recorded Dr. King's antiwar speech in Germany on May 29.

On June 6 in a 2:00 p.m. meeting General Yarborough formally approved an ambitious plan to plant HUMINTS (informers) inside major black nationalist groups. Half an hour later he met with his close ally and confidant USAINTC Commander Blakefield.

As THINGS BEGAN TO HEAT UP in the cities, all sectors of the administration feared that riots would break out that summer. The president, looking for preemptive answers, convened a high level meeting on June 12. In attendance were Chairman of the Joint Chiefs of Staff Earle Wheeler, the director of the CIA Richard Helms, Secretary of Defense Robert McNamara, and National Security Advisor McGeorge Bundy. Out of this session, which focused on ever-growing combined antiwar and civil rights movements, decisions were made to mobilize the 20th SFG for special duty assignments in urban areas and for the 111th MIG to provide a new analysis of the intentions of Dr. King and his organization. This order was given on that day to his staff by the commanding officer of the 111th, Colonel Robert McBride.

The first report by a 20th SFG unit from the area of a racial disturbance in Prattville, Alabama, arrived at the 111th MIG Headquarters on June 13 and stated that blacks involved in rioting were quoting Dr. King's comments against the war. Between June 12 and June 15 the 20th SFG also deployed two alpha sniper teams to Tampa during riots in that city. Warren was on one of those teams, which I learned from an independent intelligence source in that city were under the control of the 902nd MIG.

Three days later, on June 16, former Military Policeman Marrell McCollough, who had been discharged in December 1966, was brought back to active duty and assigned to the 111th MIG and onward to the Memphis Police Department.

Newark exploded on July 12, and no end of meetings took place at the headquarters of the 109th MIG in that city, at the

Pentagon, and elsewhere in Washington. The primary issues were how to keep the lid on the situation, how to preempt the outbreaks, and how to efficiently suppress them.

On July 18, 1967, after arriving in Canada, James Earl Ray began to use the name Eric S. Galt. In August 1967 and again in September, the real Eric S. Galt (who had top secret security clearance and a classified NSA personnel file) met with Gardner's aide.

Detroit exploded on July 23, and the 82nd Airborne under Lieutenant General John L. Throckmorton was sent in. The 20th SFG was sent there as well, and in that team was staff sergeant Warren. The 113th MIG began to interrogate apprehended rioters, preparing extensive transcripts and reports for transmission to Washington. At midnight on July 23 Yarborough entered the army's Operations Center in the Pentagon and declared that a revolution was underway by blacks. That night Yarborough ordered all MIGs to be put on full alert and all potential guerilla targets—armories, power stations, gun shops, radio and television stations, and other vital installations—to be put under surveillance.

During this week Dr. King, along with civil rights leaders Whitney Young, A. Philip Randolph, and Roy Wilkins, issued a joint appeal for the riots to stop, terming them dangerous to the civil rights movement and to the nation. At the same time SNCC leaders Carmichael (in Havana on July 25) and H. Rap Brown (in Washington, D.C., on July 27) spoke of a guerilla force and black revolution. On July 25 rioting also broke out in Cleveland, Phoenix, and in both Flint and Saginaw, Michigan. On July 26 violence erupted in South Bend, Indiana.

ON JULY 28 MEMPHIS was added to the 111th MIG's "watch city" list, and at 8:00 a.m. General Yarborough convened a meeting of his senior staff to consider the Detroit crisis. Feedback from the 113th MIG clearly indicated that no foreign or domestic enemy of the United States was behind the riots, which the agents saw as being entirely homegrown and a result of deteriorating living conditions and hostility over the war. CIAB analyses of the June 21, 1943, Detroit riot and the Watts riots in 1965 produced the same conclusions. Yarborough was advised that there was no credible evidence that these uprisings were planned or premeditated by subversive elements, but rather that they spontaneously flowed from isolated incidents.

Yarborough rejected this analysis and insisted to the group that either Havana or Peking would ultimately be found to have been behind an urban conspiracy. He went on to state that "there are indications weapons have been stolen from a number of military ports including Dugway Proving Grounds where there are some pretty sophisticated weapons." (Ironically, much of the theft was the result of operations carried out from inside the army itself by a number of people including the army's own Provost marshall, who was eventually charged and convicted for armaments thefts and sales.)

During all of this period, the uniformity of the positions taken by ACSI Yarborough, Hoover, and even the CIA is striking. (Remember the Jay Richard Kennedy information to the agency's Office of Security which alleged that Dr. King was controlled by Peking line communists.) Throughout the turmoil, and in spite of the availability of intelligence reports to the contrary, it seemed necessary for these leaders to blame all the troubles on a foreign enemy.

Because of the official mindset that was conveniently determined to treat King, Carmichael, and H. Rap Brown as one and the same, Stokely Carmichael's meetings with North Vietnamese Premier Phan Van Dong and Dong's July 31 broadcasts, which were relayed by the NSA and which associated his government with the "anti-imperialist" struggle of black people in America, were taken as also representing Dr. King's position. Animosity was further heightened by alleged threats by Carmichael in Havana against President Johnson and Secretary of Defense Robert McNamara.

On August 8 the CIAB reported on the survey of 496 men arrested in Detroit at the time of the riots. The revelation that King, not Carmichael or Brown, was the black leader most admired by the rioters, was greeted with shock.

Two days later, in the course of the weekly USIB meeting

chaired by CIA director Helms, the discussion focused on the CIA setting up a special group to work with army intelligence in order to infiltrate antiwar groups and also identify subversive radicals and groups. Five days later, on August 15, Helms ordered one of his agents, Thomas Karamessines, to set up a Special Operations Group (SOG) to penetrate the domestic movement. I was advised that the operation was housed at 1770 I Street in N. W. Washington. Under its umbrella, among others, came: Operation CHAOS, devoted to mail opening and developing files on U.S. citizens, and Project MERRIMAC, whose goal was to infiltrate and spy on ten major peace and civil rights groups. It appears that at some time between the beginning of the riots in Newark on July 12, and the middle of August [after Detroit had exploded and been analyzed] the decision was made to establish the domestic SOG. The purpose of this joint effort was to counter what was regarded as revolutionary activity in CONUS. The SOG combined intelligence operations and resources of the CIA, the army and the FBI, as well as those of other agencies which though in the informational loop were on the periphery of actual operations.

On August 31, unknown to us, the 113th were present at the NCNP convention opening meeting and they photographed and recorded Dr. King's keynote address. Earlier that day, ACSI General Yarborough met with NSA representatives and urged them to monitor international cable traffic to support the army's counterintelligence operations and pinpoint the foreign governments that were helping black radicals and the antiwar movement (this became known as Operation MINARET).

ON SEPTEMBER 5 ACSI Yarborough first began to seriously consider the major upcoming antiwar demonstration developed by the umbrella antiwar organization, the National Mobilization Committee, and planned to take place at the Pentagon on October 21. He immediately called a staff meeting. On September 13 Yarborough, Lt. General L. J. Lincoln—commanding general of the fourth army—and their staffs journeyed to Mexico, where they stayed for five days.

Upon his return, General Yarborough arranged (through army vice chief of staff General Ralph E. Haines, Jr.) for the stockpiling of tear gas and riot-control equipment at twelve strategic locations around the U.S.

On October 3 at 6:10 the president met with Secretary of Defense McNamara, Secretary of State Dean Rusk, and National Security Advisor Walt Rostow. He reported that the congressional leadership had told him that they will "not tolerate the large demonstration which is planned for late October." He wanted contingency plans developed to protect the White House, the Pentagon, and the Capitol.

That day there was a rebellion inside the 198th Light Infantry Brigade at Fort Hood, Texas, with many men saying that they would rather go to the stockade than leave for Vietnam the next day. A riot broke out, with shooting and firebombs being used.

Between the Fort Hood riots and October 14, numerous meetings took place between members of the president's cabinet and staff and at many levels of ACSI staff and USAINTC personnel. In every instance the focus was on the upcoming Washington demonstration and the growing antiwar movement in the cities and—at the beginning of a new academic year—on the campuses. On October 14, to some extent in collaboration with USAINTC, Yarborough dispatched forty-five undercover agents to principal U.S. cities where demonstrators were getting ready to depart for Washington. The agents were ordered to infiltrate the antiwar group, and travel with them. They were given counterfeit draft cards and IDs. Another group of agents of the 116th MIG began preparation for march infiltration.

The very next day, October 15, 1967, saw Frank C. Holloman take over as city Fire and Police Commissioner in Memphis. Though an FBI agent for twenty-five years, for seven of those he had been attached to J. Edgar Hoover's office in Washington and had by all accounts continued to be loyal to Hoover and trusted by the director.

On October 19 at 2:30 a.m. DEFCON 2 status was declared with respect to the preparations for the demonstration. (DEFCON designations indicate the degree of seriousness attached to a perceived threat to national security. Ascending DEFCON designations [which then went from 1 to 5] indicate a heightened threat.) On that day two C-130 aircraft carrying 89 persons took off from Pope Air Force Base, landing at Andrews Air Force Base outside of Washington.

DEFCON 3 orders were received by the 82nd Airborne at Fort Bragg, North Carolina on October 20. The unit's commander, Lt. General Throckmorton (the on-scene commander during the Detroit riots), left the headquarters of the 111th MIG at Fort McPherson and flew directly to Fort Myers, where the army Command Center had been established. He was met by Army Chief of Staff Harold Johnson, and they began a tour of the capitol area. At 5:02 p.m. that day General Throckmorton arrived at the White House for a visit with the president.

On October 21 at 10:00 a.m. the demonstrations got under way. Army leaders began watching on closed-circuit television (cameras were mounted on helicopter gunbags and the roof of the Pentagon). Eventually, Secretary of Defense McNamara, army Chief of Staff Johnson, ACSI Yarborough, and aides went onto the roof of the Pentagon to observe. The massive demonstration clearly shook those leaders. The mere presence of such an outpouring of citizens publicly condemning the government, its policies and leaders emphasized official impotence. Yarborough was subsequently quoted in the *Commercial Appeal*, describing the scene as follows:

> It looked like a castle where the Huns had gathered around; as far as the eye could reach, there they were, shaking their bony fists. There were American Nazis. There were communists. There were hippies . . . I can assure you it was a sight to make you stop to think. As we looked at this great horde below us, waving their battering rams, so to speak . . . the Secretary of Defense [McNamara] turned to the Chief of Staff of the Army [General Johnson] and said, "Johnny, what are we going to do about this?" Johnny said, "I'm damned if I know."

According to an inside source, the chief of staff promptly

turned to his ACSI and said, "Bill, what are you going to do about this?"

Dr. King's press conference on October 23, which followed his testimony before the National Advisory Committee on Civil Disorders, only added to the anxiety of both the military and civilian leadership. In the press conference Martin unequivocally said that he would lead prolonged massive demonstrations in Washington with the purpose of shutting down the government. He was determined that if the government would not shut down the war, then the government itself would be shut down.

At 1:04 p.m. on that October 23, in the wake of the press conference, President Johnson met in emergency session with the CIA's Richard Helms, Joint Chiefs of Staff Chairman Earle Wheeler, and National Security Advisor Walt Rostow and various aides. At that meeting Johnson said, "We've almost lost the war in the last two months in the court of public opinion. These demonstrators and others are trying to show that we need somebody else to take over the country ... We've got to do something about public opinion."

At 3:30 on that same day a call went from the ACSI's office to the office of the 20th SFG in Birmingham, requesting that the roster of 20th SFG be sent to Gardner at the 902nd MIG's offices at the Pentagon. At 6:15 p.m. an AUTOVON dispatch went off with the roster. (I learned that the process of selection of the supersecret 20th SFG Alpha 184 team began with the arrival of that roster and that the team was handpicked by Gardner.)

The next morning, at about 10:30 a.m., Yarborough arrived at CIA headquarters in Langley for a special meeting with director Helms to discuss the backing of the marchers by communists. Upon his return to his office Yarborough openly declared, "We have the means to stop these bastards, all I need is the word go."

Two mornings later (Thursday, October 26) the ACSI was back at Langley for the weekly USIB meeting with Helms in the chair. At 4:00 p.m. on that day he met with Gardner of the 902nd MIG.

Yarborough went to Vietnam on November 8 for a firsthand observation of the conflict. He was confronted with low morale everywhere. Then on November 11, the Vietnamese, rubbing salt in his wounds, released three prisoners of war, including two blacks, following negotiations in which Dr. King had participated. The National Liberation Front (NLF) said the blacks were released because of the "courageous struggle" of blacks in the U.S.

On November 17 at 5:10 p.m., in response to a report that armed blacks were preparing to target key public facilities, Special Forces teams were deployed to conduct reconnaissance in cities that it was believed could explode that spring and summer. They were ordered to make precise maps, take aerial photos, set up communication nets, command points, sniper sites, and formulate operational plans. This was exactly the activity that MPD special services/intelligence officer Jim Smith described "Coop" as doing around this time and later. They also stockpiled weapons and antiriot gear. The Special Forces teams used were the 20th from Birmingham, the 10th at Fort Devins, Massachusetts, and the 5th at Fort Bragg, North Carolina. By early 1968 this information had been compiled on 124 cities throughout the country.

Later that day, the ACSI's office received a report that the regular army units left in CONUS (parts of the 82nd Airborne, the 1st and 2nd Armored Divisions and the 5th mechanized Infantry Division at Fort Carson, Colorado) were understrength and underequipped.

ON THE HOME FRONT, so far as the army was concerned, the prognosis worsened. On November 30, Senator Eugene McCarthy announced that he was going to run against Lyndon Johnson in the Democratic primaries as an antiwar candidate, and on December 4 in Atlanta, Martin Luther King announced the plan to hold massive demonstrations in the capitol during the spring of 1968.

On December 5 the CIA issued a report stating that $300 million worth of damage had been imposed on Hanoi as a result of 800 tons of bombs and missiles dropped each day on North Vietnam since March 1965. The cost to the U.S., however, had been the loss of 700 aircraft worth $900 million. The exercise had thus resulted in a net loss of $600 million. The aircraft industry was hardly lamenting the nation's losses.

On December 10 Martin King kept up the pressure in speeches at his old Dexter Avenue Baptist church in Montgomery, Alabama (recorded and photographed by the 111th MIG) and at the Sheraton Hotel in Chicago (surveilled by the 113th MIG).

On December 12, the army, in a major reassessment of its domestic intelligence operation, went on a CONUS war footing. Updating of all recon information was ordered, as was the classification of cities and groups for subversive potential. Then on December 28, as 1967 was drawing to a close, Yarborough and Gardner met at 2:00 p.m.

On January 2 Patrick Putnam delivered a bureau memorandum to Yarborough, which stated that King "will create massive civil disobedience in the nation's capitol and in ten to fifteen major cities through the U.S. in the spring of 1968 if certain commitments are not forthcoming from Congress in the civil rights field."

That day, after General Westmoreland's year-end report stating that the U.S. was winning, the National Liberation Front (NLF) attacked in regimental strength within fifty miles of Saigon. The ensuing battle in a rubber plantation resulted in twenty-six American soldiers being killed and 111 wounded.

ON JANUARY 10 PRESIDENT JOHNSON ORDERED army Chief of Staff Harold Johnson to "use every resource" to diffuse the civil disturbances planned and projected by Dr. King for the spring. Some of those in the loop have confirmed that there was no longer any doubt that at the highest levels it was understood that the gloves were off—no holds were barred in the effort to stop Dr. King's "invasion" of the capitol.

On the next day the ACSI Yarborough attended the regular weekly USIB meeting at Langley and later that same day under the surveilling eyes, microphones, and cameras of the 115th MIG and oblivious to the storm gathering around him, Dr. King spoke at the Belmont Plaza Hotel in New York City, calling for the war to end or the government to be shut down.

On January 12 at 2:00 p.m. Yarborough met with and briefed army Chief of Staff Johnson. Then, a new crisis arose. The number of "fragging" incidents (black enlisted men shooting/killing their white officers) was climbing dramatically, and ACSI senior staff met to discuss this problem. Yarborough was particularly incensed that the army's own newspaper, *Stars and Stripes*, was printing stories about black unrest at home.

On January 15 the International Association of Police Chiefs held a four-day conference on the prevention and control of civil disorders at Warrenton, Virginia. In attendance were Memphis Police Chief J. C. MacDonald and Frank C. Holloman. With the conference in its first morning Mrs. Martin Luther King led a march on the Capitol of five thousand women all clad in black to protest against the war in Vietnam.

On January 26 at 4:45 Yarborough briefed his staff on his CIAB's new intelligence assessment of Dr. King. The assessment noted Martin King's increasing emphasis on the theme of "genocide," since 22% of the total American soldiers killed were black, more than double the proportion of black soldiers. A copy was sent to Westmoreland's J-2 (intelligence chief).

Patrick Putnam and Yarborough met at 3:00 p.m. on January 29 to discuss FBI/army-coordinated action to counter the expected urban civil disturbances.

On January 31, word of the NLF's Tet (new year) Offensive shook the army and Washington. Five of South Vietnam's largest cities were attacked along with thirty-six of forty-four provincial capitals and 25% of its 242 district capitals. The offensive involved 70,000 NLF troops which overran U.S. and South Vietnam forces. Westmoreland's continued positive reports and claims of imminent victory were dramatically shown to be blatantly false.

*   *   *

IN FEBRUARY, ACSI Yarborough and his staff began to spend an increasing amount of time on CINCSTRIKE preparation for the anticipated riots. As noted earlier, CINCSTRIKE operations were the overall CONUS armed forces coordinated response to the domestic rebellions. Based at MacDill Air Force Base in Tampa, Florida, all domestic forces were deployed according to the plans developed there. During this period Yarborough spent on average about three hours a day on the planning and specifically on February 2, 5, 6, 7, and 8 he was locked into these sessions. Most meetings were in the Pentagon but on February 7, at 4:15 p.m., Yarborough flew to Tampa for on-site meetings on February 8.

On the evening of February 7, the 116th MIG surveilled Martin King as he spoke at the Vermont Baptist Church in Washington, D.C., strongly challenging the government. An hour before his speech he met with SNCC leader H. Rap Brown and Stokely Carmichael in Brown's room at the Pitts Motor Hotel in northeast Washington. In the conversation the difference in philosophy and strategy between Martin King, Brown and Carmichael was clearly revealed. From a transcript of that session:

> BROWN: "We stop the fuckers here. Right here . . ."
> CARMICHAEL (came in, saying): "No more Uncle Tom dammit. This let them shit on you shit . . . ain't working. You know it and so does everybody . . ."
> King (cut in): "Is killing and burning (unintelligible) in your own people's streets, your answer?"
> Carmichael: "It's time. We can't wait any more."
> KING: "Nobody is as tired of waiting as me."
> CARMICHAEL: "Then let's shut the honkies down. They bring the army, we fight the fuckers with ours. We got guns. Marching for peace—shit, you seen it. What's it got us?"

MARTIN'S APPROACH NEVER WAVERED. He wanted to include the more violent of the dissident leaders and work with them to maximize the impact of the Washington demonstration planned for the spring, but not on their terms. This was clear from the ASA and MIG surveillance of him, yet ACSI Yarborough and his colleagues on the USIB continued to lump him together with Brown, Carmichael, and others who advocated a violent strategy. It suited all of their interests and preconceptions: Hoover's, Yarborough's, Helms's, and Lyndon Johnson's as well.

Also on that day the ACSI's office received an internal report that in 1967 the army suffered a record 40,227 desertions and 155,536 soldiers absent without leave.

On February 9, the quagmire deepened. At 11:02 a.m. Joint Chiefs of Staff Chairman Wheeler delivered to President Johnson Westmoreland's request for the 82nd Airborne and the 69th Marine division (fifteen battalions, 40,000 more troops) to save the situation. Wheeler advised against the deployment and told Johnson if he sent these troops "you will have no readily deployable strategic reserves" for use in CONUS. The new Secretary of Defense Clark Clifford was also critical of the request.

Three days later, on February 12, 1968, 1,300 sanitation workers in Memphis, Tennessee, went out on strike. At its Fort McPherson, Atlanta, headquarters the 111th MIG established a "special security detachment" under the direct control of ACSI Yarborough for immediate deployment and use in emergencies.

On February 15, 111th MIG agents followed and surveilled Martin King as he spoke at St. Thomas AME Church in Birmingham and Maggie Street Baptist Church in Montgomery, Alabama. Then on February 19 the 111th picked up the surveillance of him as he addressed a gathering of 150 black ministers in Miami. The next day ACSI Yarborough received the latest FBI study of King, which basically called him a communist and a sex fiend.

INTELLIGENCE FILES noted information as of February 22, without naming the source, that Dr. King would be coming to Memphis to lend support to the sanitation workers' strike.

Then, as recounted by Warren, quietly, on February 25, a

20th SFG recon. team entered the city of Memphis through the Trailways bus terminal. They conducted reconnaissance of the downtown hotel area and mapped egress routes north.

Three days later, on February 28, President Johnson was confronted with Westmoreland's request for 200,000 more men, which he was advised by Wheeler meant a call-up of 250,000 and an additional $2.5 billion to the budget and possibly even the call-up of the Korean War veterans.

Also on that day at 10:30 a.m. Gardner met with CIAB chief Colonel Van Tassell and FBI liaison Patrick Putnam to discuss the latest progress on the plans to abort the planned Washington demonstration later that spring.

On March 1, Secretary of Defense Clark Clifford called the army's Vietnam policy bankrupt. (It appears that during this time he was studiously kept outside of the loop of information and bypassed within the department.) Meanwhile in Cullman, Alabama, six members of the 20th SFG met with the Tuscumbia-based Knights of the Ku Klux Klan in highly secret and covert "Klan Special Forces" exercises in which the SFG soldiers provided two days of firearms and explosives training for the klan members present.

On March 4 at 2:30 p.m. Yarborough met with Gardner, and four days later he hosted a luncheon party beginning at 12:30 p.m. with the FBI's William Sullivan (domestic intelligence chief), Patrick Putnam, and Merrill Kelly of his staff. On March 11, Chairman William Fulbright of the Senate Foreign Relations Committee opened hearings on the war. In his opening statement Fulbright stated, "The signs of rebellion are all around us, not just in the hippie movement and in the emergence of an angry New Left, but in the sharp decline of applications to the Peace Corps, in the turning away of promising students from careers in government, in letters of protest against the war and troubled consciences about the draft."

The next day Senator McCarthy got a shocking 42% of the vote in the New Hampshire presidential primary.

On March 14 at 8:00 a.m. a CIAB report was delivered to ACSI Yarborough stating that thirty people were arrested after a breakout of violence in the Memphis sanitation workers' strike. No early settlement was in sight and the report suggested the deployment of additional personnel from the 111th MIG to work with the MPD and the FBI to keep the city under control.

The next day, March 15, FBI Director Hoover met one-on-one with Gardner of the 902nd MIG.

On the morning of March 16 the massacre of the village of My Lai began. (Though known virtually immediately by army intelligence, it was initially covered up and would only be brought to public attention when journalist Seymour Hersh broke the story on November 13, 1969.) That day in Washington Senator Robert Kennedy announced that he was running for president and in Anaheim, California, Dr. King spoke to the powerful California Democratic State Council while agents of the 115th MIG watched and recorded.

On March 17, Reverend James Lawson in Memphis telephoned Martin King in Los Angeles to give him an update on the strike. King had agreed to address the strikers and their supporters in Memphis at a rally on March 18. The conversation was recorded by ASA agents on Dr. King's end. Then the 115th MIG photographed and recorded King's speech at Los Angeles' Second Baptist Church.

On March 18 King arrived in Memphis at 7 p.m. under the surveillance of the 111th MIG and spoke at a rally of 15,000 people at the Mason Temple Church. In the audience was the 111th MIG's undercover agent Marrell McCollough. Martin pledged to return and lead a march four days later. After the speech he went to the Lorraine Motel to meet with community leaders. Then he went to the Rivermont Holiday Inn where he stayed that night under electronic and wiretap surveillance conducted by ASA agents assisted by MPD special services/intelligence bureau officer Jim Smith.

The next morning at 10:00 a.m. ACSI Yarborough hosted a two-hour meeting on the growing domestic turbulence held in Pentagon Conference Room 2E687 (office of Major W. M. Vickers, Chief, Consolidated Intelligence Support Facility). At 2:30 p.m. on that day, there was a fifteen-minute telephone conversation between the office of the 20th SFG and the Pentagon's National Defense Center regarding deployment plans.

On March 20 former Marine Corps commandant and Medal of Honor winner David M. Shoup virtually pronounced the Vietnam War incapable of being won. His comments deepened public depression and army frustration over the seemingly endless quagmire of Vietnam.

On March 21 the president replaced Westmoreland as commander, kicking him upstairs, making him chief of staff. Also on that day at 3:30 p.m. senior 20th SFG staff met for two hours to discuss the Memphis situation. Simultaneously, at Camp Ravenswood, Illinois, according to a report by a black undercover agent of the 113th MIG, 175 white and fifty black community leaders met secretly to plan protest activity for the Democratic National Convention. Dr. King had two representatives in attendance.

Four days later on March 25, President Johnson appeared to be a beaten man as he met in the White House dining room at 10:30 a.m. with Joint Chiefs Chairman Wheeler and new Vietnam Commander General Creighton Abrams. He said, "Our strategic reserves . . . are down to nothing. Our fiscal situation is abominable . . . the country is demoralized. You must know about it. . . . The [New York] *Times* and the [Washington] *Post* are all against us. Most of the press is against us."

That evening, in an upbeat mood, Dr. King spoke at the Convent Avenue Baptist Church in New York City. Recorded by the 108th MIG, he announced that his nonviolent, civil disobedience campaign had targeted Washington, D.C., as well as both major party political conventions.

ON MARCH 28 KING ARRIVED in Memphis at 10:30 a.m. to lead the march, which had been rearranged because of snow, beginning at Clayborn Temple at 11:06 a.m. Violence instigated by *provocateurs* broke out, and he was taken to the Rivermont Holiday Inn, where his suite and phones were bugged by ASA agents. On that day, 68 C-130 and C-5 troop transports were placed on alert to move army troops to Memphis, and FBI Division 5 Section Chief George C. Moore sent Yarborough a report on the riot. Yarborough also obtained a report that day

that the army's strategic U.S. reserves were down to 60,000 men
and these troops were not front-line quality. They were in need
of training and up-to-date weapons. The report questioned
whether the army had enough regular forces left in CONUS
to be able to put down major simultaneous riots in American
cities.

Finally, on March 28 at 6:45 p.m. Gardner of the 902nd MIG
met with the FBI's Division Five Chief George C. Moore and
Special Agent Steve Lancaster to discuss the final arrangements
for the 902nd's Memphis deployment.

At 7:30 a.m. March 29 at the Camp Shelby, Mississippi, training base for the 20th SFG, Captain Billy R. Eidson was given
his orders on the Memphis deployment and mission of the
Alpha 184 unit he was to lead. Later that morning at 9:45 a.m.
at the Falls Church, Virginia, headquarters of the 902nd MIG,
Gardner received a current briefing report on the plans for
the 20th SFG Alpha 184 team deployment in Memphis.

At 10:00 a.m. in his suite at the Rivermont Hotel, while being
electronically surveilled by ASA agents, King met with Charles
Cabbage, Calvin Taylor, and Charles "Izzy" Harrington, and
committed himself to return to Memphis to lead another
march on April 5. Transcripts of this meeting were cabled to
the Pentagon.

Also that day at the MacDill Air Force Base in Tampa CINCS-
TRIKE went on a DEFCON 1 alert and at SCLC headquarters
in Atlanta a letter arrived from Vice President Hubert Humphrey to Dr. King, urging him to postpone his Poor People's
Campaign.

On Sunday morning, March 31, Dr. King preached at the
National Episcopal Cathedral in Washington, D.C. That evening Lyndon Johnson announced that he would not seek reelection. The Reverends Andrew Young, James Orange, and
Jim Bevel flew to Memphis and on arrival were placed under
surveillance by the 111th MIG agents who followed and
watched them check into the Lorraine Motel. (In anticipation
of their arrival, ASA agents, with local MPD assistance, had
installed hidden microphones in three rooms of the Lorraine

Motel, one of which was Room 306, where Dr. King was to be placed upon his arrival on April 3.)

The next morning ASA agents electronically surveilled the SCLC staff members meeting with the Invaders as they began preparations for the march. At the same time tensions in Washington and around the country were heightened by black Congressman Adam Clayton Powell's speech, at Florida A&M University in Tallahassee, in which he called for the "total revolution of young people black and white against the sick society of America." Agents of the 111th MIG in attendance recorded his remarks.

On APRIL 3 AT 9:30 A.M. CINCSTRIKE met in Tampa on the mobilization plans for an anticipated riot in Memphis. Two hours later Dr. King and his SCLC party arrived in Memphis from Atlanta. Under the watchful eye of agents of the 111th MIG, he held a brief press conference and then went to the Lorraine Motel where he was checked into balcony room 306 (though, as we know, initially he had been scheduled to occupy the more cloistered and protected ground level room 202). Throughout the day he attended various planning meetings. Those at the Lorraine as well as telephone conversations were recorded and monitored by ASA agents from a vehicle parked in the area.

Around noon, Carthel Weeden, the captain at fire station 2 (which backed onto Mulberry Street and overlooked the Lorraine Motel) discreetly showed Reynolds and Norton, the two Psy Ops officers under Gardner's command, to the roof on the east side of the station from which vantage point they would begin to conduct visual and photographic surveillance of activity at the Lorraine Motel. (To appreciate their vantage point, see photograph #37.) Beginning at 1:00 p.m. there began the transmission of the Psy Ops surveillance reports to the 111th MIG headquarters at Fort McPherson via 111th MIG officers in the IEOC office located in the MPD's headquarters.

Also during the day SCLC controller and FBI paid informant

Jim Harrison, after arriving with Dr. King, checked in with Memphis FBI Special Agent in Charge Robert Jensen.

ON THE MORNING OF APRIL 4, at 4:30 a.m. at Camp Shelby, Captain Billy Eidson briefed his seven other Alpha 184 team members on their mission. The team left by cars for Memphis around 5:00 a.m. They would be met by on-site handlers and taken to their perches. Also that morning all of the surveillance teams and activities were back in place.

At 3 p.m. Phillip R. Manuel, a former army intelligence officer and in 1968 chief investigator for the McClellan (Senate Permanent Investigations) Committee who had been in Memphis for two days, met with MPD intelligence bureau Lieutenant E. H. Arkin.

Martin King and most of the SCLC executive staff remained in meetings, in room 306 during that afternoon, electronically surveilled by the ASA agents and visually observed by the MPD officers in the fire station, the Psy Ops agents on the roof of the fire station and the Alpha 184 sniper teams on their perches on the roof of the Illinois Central Railroad building, and the Tayloe Paper Company water tower.

At 5:50 p.m. the Rev. Billy Kyles, an MPD intelligence bureau informant, was observed by the various surveillance personnel knocking on the door of room 306 with Dr. King answering and then going back inside. Shortly afterward the SCLC staff meeting broke up and the various participants left to go to their rooms.

AT 6:01 P.M. A SNIPER FIRED a single shot which struck Dr. King at the same time the Alpha 184 snipers had King and Young in the crosshairs of their scopes. Reynolds's camera instantly photographed the falling King, taking four or five photographs, as Norton panned the brush area, catching the sniper as he lowered his rifle and left the scene.

Also immediately after the shot 111th MIG/undercover MPD

agent Marrell McCollough raced up the stairs and knelt over the prone body of Dr. King.

Around 6:04 p.m., after a pause following the shot, Captain Eidson ordered his men to disengage, pack up, and withdraw according to their egress plans. Part of the team met at the river and went on the water by boat to waiting cars. The other group went by road to West Memphis airport, where they were flown to Amory, Mississippi.

Around 6:30 p.m. a police broadcast described a false chase of a suspect in the northern section of the city, diverting attention from the downtown area (these egress routes had previously been surveyed by the 20th SFG recon. team).

At 7:05 p.m. the Rev. Dr. Martin Luther King was pronounced dead at St. Joseph's Hospital.

The "invasion" of the nation's capitol greatly feared by its military and intelligence leaders became a nonevent without the leadership of Dr. King. The fires, the anger, and the rebellions of the 1960s faded away after his death. Calm slowly returned to the nation, and the rights of people at home and in Vietnam, once in the forefront of public attention, disappeared once again from view.

31

Chronology

1995 WOULD HAVE BEEN DR. KING'S sixty-sixth year. Now, nearly eighteen years after I began this journey, I set out in chronological order the details of how and why I believe he was assassinated.

AS EARLY AS 1957 the FBI identified the SCLC as a potential target for communist infiltration. In 1962 the bureau established a COMINFIL file on the organization and Dr. King, and in 1963 it increased its attention. A wide range of COINTELPRO activities was used in an effort to harass, discredit, and demoralize Dr. King.

Through 1964 the focus of the government's activity was aimed at discrediting and removing him from any position of prominence or leadership in the civil rights movement. By early 1965, however, they were no longer dealing with just a black Baptist preacher, for on December 10, 1964, Dr. King was a Nobel Peace Prize winner with international stature. The strategy became redirected toward his elimination.

It is now clear that two attempts to kill Martin Luther King took place in 1965. There may have been others. The 20th SFG was present during the early stage of the Selma-to-Montgomery march which began on March 21, 1965. One of the members of a sniper team in that unit, J. D., briefly had Dr. King center mass before he turned away.

The second attempt was in September 1965, when an effort was made to involve Louisville police officer Clifton Baird. It was only because Baird tape-recorded and disclosed the actual approach, which emanated from named Louisville police officers who were collaborating with FBI agents from the Louisville field office, that it became known.

ELECTRONIC SURVEILLANCE CONTINUED on Dr. King. In the fall of 1966 Acting U.S. Attorney General Ramsey Clark refused to grant the bureau permission to bug and wiretap Dr. King. However, J. Edgar Hoover had access to army intelligence and ASA surveillance which had vastly more resources. In addition, the CIA's Office of Security was developing its own file.

From the beginning of 1967 until his assassination on April 4, 1968, King was subjected to a massive blanket of surveillance through the army MIG network and the ASA. The often daily reports were shared with FBI director Hoover (who had also seconded a trusted agent, Patrick Putnam, to Yarborough's staff) and with CIA director and USIB chairman Richard Helms. ACSI Yarborough appeared to be the bridge not only between Hoover and Helms but also between army intelligence and each of the other national intelligence entities.

From early 1967, King tied civil rights, peace, and economic justice together. While H. Rap Brown, Stokely Carmichael and others advocated a more violent response, they were seen as fringe figures with relatively small followings. Dr. King spoke to and bridged the poor and the middle classes, blacks, whites and Hispanics, the young generally and students in particular. His base was broad and his credibility as a moral leader (despite the FBI's dirty tricks and smear campaigns) was unequalled.

During this time every record of every meeting involving government intelligence officials reflects the conclusion that he was the enemy—a dangerous revolutionary controlled by communists. At the top, against all reason, there were no doubts, no second thoughts, and only minimal dissent in the ranks. His antiwar speech in Los Angeles on February 25—which focused on the Vietnamese casualties—advocated teaching, preaching, and demonstrating, yet the ACSI's counterintelligence analysis incredibly called it "a call to armed aggression by negroes against the American people." Four hours later, the 111th MIG at Fort McPherson, in Atlanta, had two black agents ready to infiltrate the SCLC. Jim Harrison, the SCLC controller, had already become a deep cover FBI informant under the control of special agent Al Sentinella. Other informants were run by special agent Art Murtagh of the Atlanta field office.

ACSI Yarborough, CIA director Helms, and the FBI's Hoover became increasingly alarmed as Dr. King increased the pressure on the administration during 1967, even considering running as a potential presidential candidate.

When in June, during the AMA national convention in Chicago, Director Hoover met with fellow gambler, friend, and political ally Texas oil billionaire H. L. Hunt (whose daily syndicated *Life Line* radio programs frequently attacked King), Hoover said he thought a final solution was necessary. Only that action would stop King.

Other attempts to assassinate Dr. King originated during this period, apparently involving elements of organized crime for the first time. A meeting was held at the Blue Note Lounge in Jackson, Mississippi. Joe "Buck" Buchanan, a paraplegic involved in various Dixie Mafia criminal activities throughout the South, including New Orleans, offered a $50,000 murder contract. Present at the meeting were Tim Kirk and one of the Tiller brothers. The contract came out of New Orleans directly from Carlos Marcello and was eventually picked up by Red Nix of Tipton County, Tennessee, who was given a car and a gun to enable him to stalk and shoot Dr. King.

*   *   *

IN RESPONSE TO HEIGHTENED tensions throughout the country, the 20th SFG was mobilized on June 12 with a unit being sent to Tampa. Warren, a sniper, was a member of one of the 20th SFG alpha teams run by the 902nd MIG and sent to that city (the 902nd MIG was attached directly to the ACSI's office). Riots continued in Tampa from June 12–June 16.

On June 15, Raul Pereira became a naturalized American citizen.

On June 16, in the midst of the escalating turbulence, Marrell McCollough, a discharged black soldier, was brought back on active duty. Assigned to the 111th MIG, he was deployed to the Memphis Police Department to engage in undercover work.

In July and August 1967, Gardner's aide of the 902nd MIG met with Eric S. Galt, an employee of U.S. defense contractor Union Carbide with top secret security clearance. Also sometime in mid July, James Earl Ray, who following his escape in April had worked his way to Montreal, somehow obtained and began to use the name Eric S. Galt as an alias.

In 1967, Warren participated in the delivery of weapons to New Orleans. The equipment was stolen from his 20th SFG Camp Shelby training base and the theft was organized by a master sergeant. The deliveries were made to Marcello's associate Zippy Chimento on property owned by the New Orleans Mafia leader. Army intelligence/CIA operative Jack Youngblood was also present on occasion.

During this time Raul Pereira and his cousin Amaro were receiving some of these weapons at the Port of Houston which were shipped by water from New Orleans. Raul and Amaro also met during this time with Carlos Marcello in Houston.

RIOTS BROKE OUT ACROSS the country that summer, with the most serious explosions taking place in Newark and Detroit (where Warren was also deployed). Despite contrary intelligence reports, Martin Luther King was branded as the source of the disruptions and as being under the control of foreign communist elements.

In response, Generals Yarborough (ACSI) and Blakefield (USAINTC), and CIA director Helms pushed a new domestic

Special Operations Group (SOG) into high gear. Projects CHAOS and MERRIMAC focused on spying upon dissenting citizens and infiltrating the ten major peace and civil rights organizations, including NCNP whose preparations for a national convention scheduled for the Labor Day weekend were well under way.

In August, James Earl Ray, who was now using the alias Eric S. Galt, had meetings with Raul in the Neptune Bar on West Commissioners Street in Montreal. He entered into discussions with Raul, who said he could provide him with money and travel documents in exchange for James's assistance in certain smuggling activity. Desperate for money and a way to Europe, James agreed, and finally left Montreal around the end of August to travel to Birmingham where he was to meet up with Raul. Raul gave James a New Orleans telephone contact number.

On August 31, Dr. King delivered a forceful keynote address opening the NCNP convention at the Palmer House in Chicago. A "Black Caucus" which appeared to come out of nowhere was formed, and arriving black delegates were forcibly brought under its control. The group, which appeared to be dominated by urban blacks (the provocateurs were later identified as Chicago Blackstone Ranger gang members and other inner-city thugs) was led by an unknown political cadre and immediately took on a disruptive policy. I received word of their intention to kidnap Dr. King and hold him until a range of their demands was met. King's exit was quickly organized immediately after he spoke. In retrospect, this was exactly what the *provocateurs* wanted. King was a bridge, he had the ability to bring people together. His presence was therefore contrary to the interests of the government *provocateurs* who only wanted to break up the convention and defeat its purpose. They succeeded.

On that last day of August the National Security Agency (NSA) was formally brought into the recently formed SOG loop of the combined intelligence agency effort to counter the ever-growing antiwar/economic justice forces. Following a meeting with Yarborough, the NSA launched Operation MINARET to monitor international cable traffic and assist the efforts of the ACSI counterintelligence section to identify foreign governments helping "black radicals" and antiwar groups.

IN EARLY SEPTEMBER Yarborough learned about the plans for a massive antiwar demonstration to be addressed by Dr. King on October 21 at the Pentagon. He began to prepare for the confrontation by increasing surveillance and developing a program of infiltration of antiwar groups.

The government's worst fears were realized in the October 21 demonstration. The sight of masses of people attacking the citadel of American power not only appalled but, because of their impotence, humiliated the senior government and military officials who observed them. They believed that there was every possibility that what they viewed as a revolutionary force might not be consistently contained, particularly in light of the depletion of available trained forces in CONUS due to the war. Secretary McNamara asked Chief of Staff Harold Johnson what he was going to do about the rising emergency. Johnson turned and asked the same question to his ACSI—Yarborough.

The shock of the demonstration reverberated throughout official Washington, and at a senior level the decision to form and use a specialized 20th SFG alpha team was clearly made. On October 23, Gardner, following a request from the ACSI's office, received the roster of the 20th SFG and selected the eight-man Memphis team which was to become Alpha 184.

MEANWHILE, in Birmingham Raul gave James money to buy the Mustang and asked James (who was puzzled by the request) to buy some photographic equipment which he ordered by mail from a Chicago company. Since Raul may have been involved in pornography in Houston, this could explain why he wanted the equipment, or it may have been simply to make it appear that James was involved in stalking activity.

James was keeping in touch occasionally with Raul. Following his instructions he went to Mexico, arriving on October 7. He remained there until he went to Los Angeles on November 19. As he cleaned out his car before crossing the border, he discovered the L.E.A.A. business card with the name and address of Randy Rosen(son) written on it.

As James made his way to California, units of the 20th SFG containing specialized sniper teams were deployed to recon cities that the army contended might "explode" next spring and summer. The teams were ordered to make street maps, take aerial photos, establish communications nets, command posts, sniper sites, and operational plans.

In autumn and early winter of 1967 some of the members of the 902nd MIG's Alpha 184 team were practicing daily for their mission at a site near Pocatello, Idaho. The "shoot" was from a triangular formation, and during these sessions at least, though this seems to have ultimately changed, three shooters were practicing.

In autumn 1967, James's relationship and activities with Raul were on hold. Raul, however, knew how to contact him (through L.A. general delivery) and James had the New Orleans telephone contact number.

In early December James was instructed by Raul to travel to New Orleans. This he did, sharing the driving with Charlie Stein, a briefly known acquaintance. During that visit to New Orleans, James met with Raul. Raul told him that he would be needed for another gunrunning job into Mexico and that he would contact him in a few months' time.

ON DECEMBER 4, in Atlanta, as President Johnson was meeting with the Joint Chiefs of Staff, Martin Luther King announced the formation of SCLC's Poor People's Campaign with demonstrations planned for Washington, D.C., in the spring.

On January 10, an increasingly nervous president ordered Chief of Staff Harold Johnson to "use every resource" under his command to defuse the anticipated spring civil disturbances.

Around this time another approach to the mob was made. A contract was offered to kill Dr. King, previous efforts having been unsuccessful. Minor gangster Myron Billet attended a meeting in the small town of Apalachin, New York, a favorite mob meeting place. Though most of the time was spent on other matters, three government agents (from the CIA and FBI) offered one million dollars to Carlo Gambino and Sam Giancana to arrange for the killing of Dr. King. The offer was not accepted. The agents indicated that it would be placed elsewhere.

Presumably Marcello, whose operative Red Nix had failed to carry out the earlier contract, was approached, since he eventually came back into the frame and turned to members of his organization in Memphis to finally complete this contract.

ON FEBRUARY 12, the day the Memphis sanitation workers went out on strike, the 111th established a "special security detachment" to be under the direct control of the ACSI, General Yarborough, for "immediate deployment" in emergencies.

Ten days later on February 22, an informant of the 111th MIG reportedly indicated that Martin Luther King would become involved in supporting the strikers. This was almost a month before he actually came to Memphis.

Three days later, a 20th SFG recon team entered Memphis, coming in through the Trailways bus terminal. One of their tasks was to map egress routes in the northern section of the city.

On February 28 Hoover's seconded FBI agent Patrick Putnam met with the 902nd MIG's Gardner and CIAB director Colonel Van Tassell.

ON THE WEEKEND of March 15 James was instructed by Raul to leave Los Angeles and drive to New Orleans where he would receive further instructions. At this time Memphis produce man Frank Liberto asked Loyd Jowers to repay a "big" favor. Jowers, who had been alerted earlier by another mutual acquaintance, was told by Liberto that the brush area behind his Jim's Grill was to be used as a sniper's lair for the assassination of Dr. King, who would at some time in the next three to four weeks be staying at the Lorraine Motel which was directly opposite the brush area. A gun would be provided.

Jowers was told that the police would not be there. A patsy was also going to be provided and Jowers would be handsomely paid. Liberto explained that the money came out of New Orleans.

Also on that March 15, J. Edgar Hoover met one-on-one with the 902nd MIG's Gardner, who was the coordinator of the military mission.

It is clear that by March 15, not only had the die been cast but various wheels had been put in motion so that the assassination would be carried out in Memphis during the course of Dr. King's visits to that city in support of the strikers.

On the next day, Saturday, March 16, the massacre of civilians began in the village of My Lai, Vietnam, and Senator Robert Kennedy announced his candidacy for the presidency on an antiwar platform. Dr. King addressed the powerful California democratic state council on that day and on the following Sunday, March 17, as ASA agents listened, he discussed on the telephone the arrangements for his travel from L.A. to Memphis, where he was scheduled to address a strikers' rally on Monday evening (March 18) at Mason Temple.

Dr. King flew to Memphis and addressed nearly 15,000 people. 111th MIG agent Marrell McCollough was in the audience. King promised to return to lead the march which was planned for March 22. He then went to the Lorraine Motel where he met with local leaders, after which he went to the Rivermont Hotel where the four-man black detective team led by Jerry Williams provided security all night. During this stay he was electronically surveilled and the phones in his suite were tapped and monitored by ASA agents, with the assistance of Jim Smith of the MPD special services/intelligence bureau.

On March 22 the planned march to Memphis was cancelled due to a heavy snowstorm and rescheduled for March 28. Also on March 22 James arrived in New Orleans, a day late. Raul had already gone to Birmingham with instructions for James to meet him there at the Starlight Lounge, the next day. They met and at Raul's insistence set out immediately for Atlanta.

In Atlanta Raul told James to stay close to the rooming house because he might be needed quickly to go on a trip to Miami. He also asked James to leave the side door open so that he (Raul) could come and go without being seen.

IN BIRMINGHAM, on March 22, 20th SFG second in command Major Bert E. Wride conducted a two-hour briefing on the Memphis situation and plans. At the same time, President Johnson announced that General Westmoreland had been replaced by General Creighton Abrams, as commander of the Vietnam forces.

At 7:30 a.m. on March 28 in Camp Shelby, 20th SFG Alpha 184 team captain Billy R. Eidson was given his orders on the Memphis deployment. Later that day, the rescheduled march was broken up by *provocateurs* and Dr. King was led to the Rivermont Hotel by an MPD motorcycle officer, even though he had reservations at the Peabody Hotel. He was given his usual suite, making it possible once again for his activities and conversations to be monitored by the waiting ASA agents. The disruption of the march placed the army on "full alert focus" in Memphis. George C. Moore of the FBI's Division Five (counterintelligence) sent a Memphis field office report to Yarborough and then late that afternoon Moore went over to Falls Church, Virginia, to meet with Gardner of the 902nd MIG.

The day after the aborted march, Dr. King tried to bring things together in a meeting with the Invaders who he tended to believe (incorrectly) were responsible for the previous day's violence. The session at the Rivermont was overheard and taped by ASA agents who cabled the transcripts to the Pentagon. They learned that King was personally determined to return to Memphis and complete his march on Friday, April 5.

That same day, March 29, Raul, whom James hadn't seen for over five days, returned and announced that the gunrunning operation was set. He said they had to leave immediately for Birmingham. Once there, he instructed James to buy a rifle at the Aeromarine Supply Store. When James came back with a .243 caliber Raul told him to arrange to exchange it for a 30.06, which James did the following day. Before departing, Raul instructed James to meet him on April 3 at the New Rebel Motel in Memphis and bring the gun with him.

ON MARCH 29, even as Dr. King was addressing the problem of provoked violence in Memphis, various congressmen and senators delivered scathing attacks on him. The media picked up the theme.

On that day the FBI prepared a draft article for placement through "cooperative" sources, taking Dr. King to task for leading a violent march and also for staying at white-owned hotels. It urged him to stay at the "fine Hotel Lorraine." The combination of the bureau and the press (articles appeared across the country) was formidable. Subsequently, a decision to stay at the Lorraine was made.

Around this time Jowers received a regular produce delivery from the Liberto-controlled M. E. Carter produce company which contained in the bottom of the box the sum of $100,000 in cash, which had been delivered from New Orleans. Considering Jowers's role this appears to be a lot of money and raises the possibility that Jowers may also have been disbursing funds under instructions to designated MPD and possibly other officials. During this period Jowers was visited on two occasions by Raul, who discussed details of the proposed hit with him.

On March 31, while Martin King preached at the Episcopal Cathedral in Washington, D.C., his aides Andrew Young, James Orange, and James Bevel flew to Memphis to begin preparations for the march. Their meeting that evening in the Lorraine with the Invaders was overheard by ASA agents. At some point the reservation for Dr. King's room was changed from a cloistered secure room (202) to a highly exposed one (306).

ON THE MORNING OF APRIL 3, Dr. King arrived in Memphis where he was met not by the usual security team of black detectives, but by a specially formed group of white detectives who had never before been used as a security detail for Dr. King. They would be removed late that afternoon and were not formed the next day. This was significant. The black detectives had been assigned to protect Dr. King on previous visits. Now, during a visit when the tension in the city and hostility toward him was at an all-time high, the special black security team was not formed.

Shortly after King arrived at the motel, checking into room 306, Psy Ops officers Reynolds and his partner Norton were met around noon (when the firemen on duty had begun their afternoon—noon to 5 p.m.—nap) by fire station 2 Fire Captain Carthel Weeden, who provided them with an observation post on the flat roof on the east side of the fire station, overlooking the Lorraine. Hourly surveillance reports on activities at the motel began to be transmitted to 111th MIG agents stationed in the IEOC inside the MPD's central headquarters.

Soon after the SCLC group arrived in Memphis that morning, one of their number, controller Jim Harrison, the deep cover FBI informant inside SCLC, called the Memphis SAC Robert Jensen, in order to check in and tell him that he was in town with the group in case he was needed for anything.

Also on this day, in the back of the fire station, MPD intelligence bureau officer Detective Ed Redditt and patrolman Willie Richmond surveilled all activity going on at the motel. The TACT units were pulled back on the orders of Inspector Sam Evans who controlled those units. TACT 10, which had used the Lorraine as its base, was ordered out of the immediate area of the Lorraine Motel. Its new base, beginning on April 4, was to be the fire station. This pullback constituted a further removal of a security force from the immediate area of the Lorraine.

On April 3, James, transporting the Aeromarine rifle, checked into the New Rebel Motel where he was joined by Raul late that evening. At that meeting Raul told James to meet him at Jim's Grill at 3:00 p.m. the next afternoon and wrote the address down for him. Raul left, taking the rifle with him.

Sometime around this time a rifle connected with the assassination scenario may have been stored on the premises of a Liberto business located within blocks of the Lorraine.

Martin Luther King, whose room was under constant eye-to-eye MPD and 111th MIG surveillance as well as electronic surveillance by ASA agents, went that evening (April 3) to address an overflow crowd at Mason Temple in the presence of an 111th MIG team and 111th MIG/MPD undercover agent Marrell McCollough.

At the request of the MPD, between 10 and 11 p.m. that evening the only two black firemen at fire station 2—Floyd Newsom and Norvell Wallace—were ordered not to report to their regular station the next day, April 4. Their new assignments were to fire stations in distant parts of the city. It appears likely that Newsom and Wallace were removed because they were potential witnesses who could not be controlled.

ON APRIL 4, Captain Eidson began briefing his Alpha 184 team at 4:30 a.m. at Camp Shelby. They were shown target acquisition photos of the Lorraine Motel and their targets Dr. King and Andrew Young, who were described as enemies of the government. Young was a target as he was viewed as potentially the most effective successor of those likely to pick up the torch. No firing was to occur until the order was given by Eidson. Each member of the team was told where to go when they arrived in Memphis. They would be met and taken to their prearranged positions.

Within thirty-five to forty minutes they were on their way. Shortly after in Memphis, Loyd Jowers got ready to open up Jim's Grill for the day and began to prepare, as usual, for the breakfast crowd. He told Bobbi Smith not to follow her usual routine of taking breakfast upstairs to recuperating rooming house tenant Grace Walden. Presumably this was because the area was to be used for some staging activity for the operation.

At 10 a.m., even as the Alpha 184 team drew nearer to Memphis, ACSI Yarborough and USAINTC commander Blakefield left the Pentagon for what was to be a nearly four-hour meeting at Bailey's Crossroads with senior CIAB officers and others. At 2:10 p.m. the meeting broke up and they returned to the Pentagon.

At the fire station Reynolds and Norton climbed back up to their surveillance perch on the roof and continued the routine established the day before, passing reports along to the MPD-based agents of the 111th MIG. The 111th MIG and ASA agents were also in place from early morning in the immediate area of the Lorraine. Also in position was the MPD surveillance team (Redditt and Richmond) in the rear of the fire station.

SOMETIME in late morning Jowers was visited by Raul who gave him a rifle to hold, saying he would pick it up later. Jowers dutifully put it on the shelf under his counter.

Dr. King got up late that morning. There was an SCLC executive staff meeting set for the afternoon and a court hearing on the city's application to enjoin the march was scheduled for that morning. Andy Young had been assigned the task of attending the hearing and reporting back. Sometime after he left, MPD chief MacDonald took up a position near the Butler Street entrance to the Lorraine, walkie-talkie in hand.

In Memphis, Captain Billy Eidson introduced Warren and Murphy to Lieutenant Eli Arkin of the MPD intelligence bureau. Arkin reportedly told them that their assistance was essential to save the city that Dr. King's forces were preparing to burn down. They then met up with their contact around 1:00 p.m. Warren named him and said he believed he was a CIA agent. They were taken to their perch on top of the Illinois Central Railroad building where they assumed a state of readiness. In the course of the afternoon Captain Eidson put Warren on the radio with MPD inspector Sam Evans who described the layout of the Lorraine. He also advised them that "friendlies would not be wearing ties." (The only government agent we have identified who was physically close to Dr. King at the time of the killing was Marrell McCollough who was not wearing a tie. It is also interesting to note that James was wearing a tie although Raul, reportedly, was not.)

[Inspector Evans (whose son Sam Jr. is currently an investigator for attorney general Pierotti's office) was a significant MPD senior officer and a link between the army and civilian operations. Jowers had been told by Liberto that no police would be around at the time of the killing. Evans was in charge of MPD special services including the emergency TACT units, and on April 3 he ordered the TACT units in and around the area of the Lorraine Motel to pull back. The closest unit—TACT 10—moved its base from the Lorraine to the fire station, thus providing the civilian shooter with more of an opportunity to escape. Also Evans's introduction to Warren by the alpha team's CO Captain Billy Eidson, clearly placed him in the loop regarding the army operation.]

Around this time J. D. and his partner were met by their contact officer and taken to their perch on the Tayloe Paper Company water tower.

James, having run some errands earlier that morning, made his way downtown to look for Jim's Grill where he was to meet Raul in mid afternoon. On the way, he stopped to change a slowly leaking tire, which made him late. James arrived on South Main Street and after going to the wrong bar eventually entered Jim's Grill. Not seeing Raul inside, he retrieved his car and finally parked it in front of Jim's Grill around 3:30 p.m. By that time Raul had shown up in the grill. He instructed James to rent a room in the rooming house upstairs which he did under the name of John Willard, although Raul had initially wanted James to rent the room using the Galt alias. James was dressed in a dark suit with a white shirt and tie and looked out of place. Raul was also wearing a dark suit and light shirt but was not wearing a tie.

Loyd Jowers pretty much followed his routine most of the day, except for meeting with Raul and spending time out in the back brush area behind Jim's Grill.

Raul sent James to purchase binoculars and then instructed him to bring his bag upstairs to the room. James also carried a bedspread up to the room in case he had to sleep there since he didn't want to sleep on the one provided.

By this time all of the preparations for James to be set up were completed. He had rented the room which was to be the staging area, brought some of his physical possessions into it so that they were available to be planted, and purchased a set of binoculars which could be used to support the allegation that he was surveilling the motel.

AROUND 4:00 P.M. Andrew Young returned from court and joined the SCLC meeting in room 306.

Between 3:00 and 4:00 p.m. MPD intelligence bureau lieutenant E. H. Arkin met with Phillip R. Manuel (former army counterintelligence officer and investigator for the U.S. Senate Committee on Permanent Investigations). Manuel had been in Memphis for a couple of days. Sometime after 4:30 p.m. Arkin appeared at fire station 2 and ordered Redditt to go with him to central police headquarters. Between 5:00 and 5:30 p.m. at a headquarters conference room filled with military brass, the Director of Police and Fire Frank Holloman ordered Redditt to go home for his own protection, indicating that there had been a threat on his life. Redditt resisted but was finally driven home by Arkin, who had already learned that the threat was bogus.

Around 4:40–4:45 p.m., a man in a dark blue windbreaker drove up South Main Street in a white Mustang with Arkansas plates and parked it just south of Canipe's in front of the billboards and just north of the parking lot driveway. He sat in the car for some time and then eventually got out and entered the rooming house, going up to room 5-B where he would join Raul. This white Mustang driver was clearly not James, who was dressed in a suit and tie on that day.

Sometime late that afternoon Raul visited Jowers again in the grill. This time he picked up the rifle he had left earlier. He carried it into the back of the grill and apparently upstairs to James's room.

Around 5:00 p.m. James Latch answered the phone in the LL& L office and handed it to Frank Liberto. An agitated Liberto yelled at the party on the other end of the phone, "I told you not to call me here, shoot the son of a bitch when he comes on the balcony." He then told the caller that he should collect his money from his (Liberto's) brother in New Orleans after he had finished the job. The sum mentioned was $5,000. It appears that Liberto was speaking to the shooter, who may have been Raul.

Meanwhile, also around 5:00 p.m. or shortly afterward, Invader Big John Smith arrived at the Lorraine Motel. Passing through the lobby on his way to a meeting room, he noticed a number of MPD officers around the motel, particularly officer Caro Harris. When he came down from the meeting about thirty minutes later (5:30–5:45 p.m.) the officers, including Harris, had all disappeared.

By this time, then, all security had been stripped away from Dr. King's immediate area. In contrast, massive surveillance units were in place. Three rooms at the Lorraine, including Dr. King's room, 306, were bugged and the telephones tapped. Eye-to-eye physical surveillance was in place from units on Butler and Huling Streets and photographic surveillance was in process from the roof of the fire station. Also still in place were the Alpha 184 sniper teams.

SOMETIME AROUND 5:15 P.M. Raul gave James $200 and told him to go to the movies as he wanted to meet alone with a gunrunner. Raul also told James to leave the car, as he would be using it later. Instructed to return in two to three hours, James left the rooming house around 5:20, got a quick bite to eat, and then remembered the flat spare tire. Deciding to try to have it repaired, he went looking for a gas station. He drove north on South Main for two blocks and then at Vance Avenue turned right at about 5:50–5:55 directly in front of two Jim's Grill customers (Ray Hendrix and William Reed) who were walking to their hotel—Clarks Hotel.

Between 5:30–5:50 p.m., with James out of the way, the shooter was in the brush area with the murder weapon, where he was joined by Loyd Jowers. The two began to watch the motel, waiting for Dr. King to come outside.

Meanwhile, another person waited in room 5-B, prepared to take the bundle containing the rifle James bought and other items of his downstairs to plant them.

Also at 5:50 p.m., as J. Edgar Hoover was settling in at his favorite Washington eating and drinking place (Harvey's Restaurant), ACSI Yarborough was en route to attend a reception for the Chinese Ambassador at 3225 Woodley Road N.W.

Back in Memphis, around 5:45–5:50 p.m., Redditt's surveillance partner Richmond observed the hurried departure of the Invaders from their motel rooms 315 and 316. Some left in Charles Cabbage's car and others departed on foot. Soon after they left, Richmond observed Reverend Billy Kyles knock on the door of room 306. He saw Dr. King answer the door, speak briefly with Kyles and then go back inside, closing the door behind him. Right around then, the 111th MIG undercover agent Marrell McCollough drove into the parking lot of the Lorraine with SCLC's Jim Orange and Jim Bevel.

Shortly afterwards the SCLC staff meeting broke up. Reverend Kyles was on the balcony some fifteen to twenty feet north of Dr. King's room. The exiting staff members left Dr. King's room quickly and headed for their rooms to freshen up in preparation for the soul food dinner planned at Reverend Kyles's home.

A minute or two before 6:00 p.m. Dr. King came out on the balcony, leaned on the railing, and began to talk to people in the group right below him in the parking lot, one of whom was Andy Young.

Betty Spates had entered the grill just before 6:00 p.m., coming across the street from the Seabrook Wallpaper Company looking for Jowers. She made her way back into the kitchen, noting that the kitchen door, which was always open or at least ajar, was closed. Jowers was nowhere to be seen.

As Dr. King stood at the railing at 6:00 p.m. he was center mass in J. D.'s sights. J. D. waited for the order to fire. At the same time Andrew Young, who was standing in the motel parking area, was also held center mass in Warren's sights.

Unknown to either army sniper, the civilian shooter was also "drawing a bead" on Dr. King from the brush area, with Loyd Jowers kneeling nearby.

At exactly 6:01 the shooter fired and his bullet struck Martin King in the side of the face. The impact rocked him back and then he fell where he had been standing.

As the impact rocked Dr. King backward and he began to fall, Reynolds snapped four or five shots catching Dr. King as he fell. Norton then swung his camera from the direction of the parking lot of the Lorraine to the left, focusing on the brush area to catch the shooter lowering his rifle and leaving the scene. After dropping the gun on the ground, the shooter scrambled through the brush and down the wall. Jumping down onto Mulberry Street he ran north to Huling and went around the front of a waiting MPD car to get into it on the passenger side. The car then drove quickly away, heading north on Mulberry Street.

Paul, the Yellow Cab driver of car number 58, who was picking up a fare at the Lorraine, saw the shooter coming over the wall and into the police car and immediately reported it to his dispatcher over his radio.

Meanwhile Loyd Jowers had picked up the murder weapon which had been left on the ground by the shooter and began to run back to the rear door of his kitchen. Inside, Betty, hearing a shot and seeing the back door open, went to it and looked out. Jowers was then about ten to fifteen feet away, coming toward her. She stepped back and he ran into the building. He was white as a ghost, out of breath, and his hair was in disarray. The knees of his trousers were muddy. In the kitchen he turned to her and said plaintively, "You wouldn't ever do anything to hurt me, would you? She replied, "You know I wouldn't Loyd." In front of her, he quickly broke down the gun into two or three pieces and covered it with a cloth. He left the kitchen, stepping quickly behind the counter under which he placed the gun on a shelf, pushing it back out of sight.

Immediately after the shot, 111th MIG agent Marrell McCollough raced up the stairs to reach the fallen Dr. King and knelt over him, apparently checking him for life signs.

Very close to the time of the shot, a person dressed in a dark suit exited James's room 5-B, went down the stairs, out of the building, and dropped the bundle in the recessed doorway of Canipe's store. He then got into the Mustang just south of Canipe's and drove away, going north on South Main Street.

*   *   *

IN THE FIVE MINUTES immediately following the shooting (TTH+6), Warren and Murphy on the Illinois Central Railroad building and J. D. and his partner on the water tower were ordered by Captain Billy Eidson to disengage and proceed to their respective preassigned egress routes. Sometime thereafter Reynolds and Norton made their descent from the roof of the fire station.

MPD officers Joe Hodges, Torrence Landers, and Carroll Dunn, having penetrated the thick brush at the rear of the rooming house, found what appeared to be a fresh set of large footprints. One was 13 1/2 inches long and the other nearly 14 inches. They were at the top of the alley which ran between the buildings and pointed in the direction of the door at the end (which led to the basement and also into the grill). No proper search was conducted of the basement of the rooming house.

Dr. King was rushed to St. Joseph's Hospital.

James, returning to the rooming house area, saw a policeman blocking traffic on South Main Street. Constantly aware of his fugitive status, he headed south out of the area, intending to call his New Orleans contact number in order to learn what had happened. When he heard on the radio that Dr. King had been shot and that the police were looking for a white man in a white Mustang, he decided to head straight for Atlanta.

Inexplicably no all points bulletin (APB) and no signal Y (blocking exit routes from the city) were issued by the MPD. Within half an hour after the killing, a hoax CB broadcast took place depicting a car chase on an outward egress route in the northern end of the city. (Remember that the Alpha 184 recon team had on February 25 mapped egress routes in that section of the city.)

Yellow Cab driver Paul dropped his Lorraine fare off at the airport and reported what he had seen, first to another Yellow Cab driver, Louie Ward, and then to three MPD officers. He was subsequently also interviewed that evening by the police at the Yellow Cab offices on South Second Street. Paul reportedly died late on the night of April 4, either falling or being pushed out of a car on the Memphis Arkansas bridge.

On the evening of April 4, H. L. Hunt was called by J. Edgar Hoover and advised to pull off the air all anti-King *Life Line* radio programs being aired in the next twenty-four hours. Hunt immediately summoned John Curington to his home and gave him the assignment of organizing a group of secretaries to make the radio station calls. Hunt began feverishly working on an anti-King book on the day after the assassination, only to abruptly abandon the project.

In the course of the rest of the evening, Dr. King was pronounced dead at St. Joseph's and his friends paid their last respects. In performing the autopsy the coroner would strangely fail to trace the path of the bullet in Dr. King's body. The death slug was removed in one piece from Dr. King's back where it came to rest just under his left shoulder blade. MPD officers, often accompanied by FBI agents, began to take statements from witnesses in the area, and the rifle, death slug, and items found in the bundle in front of Canipe's were sent off to the FBI laboratory for forensic examination.

VERY EARLY THE NEXT MORNING, in response to a request from the MPD, Memphis Public Works deputy director Maynard Stiles assigned two supervisory workers Dutch Goodman and Willie Crawford (remember non supervisory workers were on strike) to go to the rear of the rooming house where under MPD supervision they cut the brush to the ground. The tall hedge which ran between the fire station and the parking area immediately adjoining the rooming house was also cut to the ground. A large tree branch between the bathroom window and the Lorraine may also have been cut down sometime after the killing, thus eliminating an apparent obstacle to a clear shot from the bathroom window.

The MPD investigation was aborted almost from the outset, taken over and controlled by the FBI, even though the murder was a state and not a federal crime. Though detectives conducted numerous interviews, glaringly obvious leads and significant witnesses were ignored, and the drunkenness of the state's main witness, Charlie Stephens, was concealed. The investigation files were also clearly sanitized. Where, for example, are: the interviews conducted of Yellow Cab driver Paul; the photographs of the bullet removed from Dr. King's body; the photographs of the scene of the crime as it was at the time, before the bushes at the back of the rooming house and the hedge between the parking lot and the fire station had been cut down?

Loyd Jowers opened the grill the morning after the shooting after driving Bobbi to work. On the way he told her about finding a gun out back which he said he had turned over to the police. Sometime in late morning he lifted the lid of a box and showed Yellow Cab driver James McCraw the rifle he had hidden under his counter within a minute or two immediately after the shooting. A scope was also in the box but it was not attached to the rifle. Jowers told McCraw that this was the rifle which had been used to kill Dr. King and that he had found it out back and was going to turn it over to the police. It seems that Jowers was already beginning to construct a cover story.

OBVIOUSLY IT IS TOO MUCH of a coincidence for the Alpha 184 army snipers and the "civilian" assassin to have been there independently taking aim at Dr. King at the same moment. The whole arrangement: the manipulation of Martin Luther King into the exposed balcony room; the stripping away of security and potential witnesses who could not be controlled; the provision of a patsy; the positioning of massive surveillance and a sniper team; the provision of local intelligence and logistical assistance; the restriction of the investigation by FBI control; the ignoring of leads and evidence begging for attention; the alteration of the scene of the crime could only have been possible with the knowledge and cooperation of the FBI, army intelligence, the ASA, the 20th SFG, elements of the ACSI's office, the CIA, the mob, and senior officers of the MPD. Further, we know from Warren's orders that the White House, the Secretary of Defense, the FBI, and officials of the Joint Chiefs of Staff, among others, were aware of the Memphis army deployment. The relationship between the army and the civilian assassination operations is further revealed by James's use of the alias of Eric S. Galt. Galt, holding top secret clearance, was at the time involved in another covert operation (Project MEXPO) with the same unit (the 902nd MIG) which carried out the Memphis deployment and coordinated the 111th MIG, ASA, and 20th SFG forces on-site. In fact, Gardner of the 902nd MIG himself selected the eight-man Alpha 184 sniper team.

It clearly appears that the hit was to be carried out by the civilian contract killer with the army snipers there as backup shooters if the contract shooter could not make the shot or if he failed to kill King. How two snipers shooting from different locations could take out both King and Young and still pin the shooting on James Earl Ray is difficult to reconcile until one remembers that the initial plan appeared to be to shoot at a moving target in a car. Because of the movement of the car and the fact that bullets would be deflected back and forth inside, it would be virtually impossible to determine the origin of the shots. The army snipers were surprised that their targets Dr. King and Andy Young were outside of their rooms in exposed positions just before six p.m. Not believing their luck, they quickly got them in their sights and waited for the order to fire. They were amazed when this did not come.

While particular senior level officials must have been aware of the whole picture, the lower level participants only knew what their particular roles were. Thus, the army snipers knew nothing of the local subcontract and Warren assumed when King was shot that it was one of their snipers who had fired too early. Similarly, the civilian operatives were unlikely to have known about the military presence. Even if the fiction of the lone assassin James Earl Ray could not be sustained there was at the next level, already in place, an officially deniable local contract and assassination operation ostensibly carried out exclusively by organized crime.

As to organized crime, the mob would not be involved without being paid. Though it appears that the payment was organized from official sources, unvouchered and thus untraceable funds would have been used.

In one sense the killing itself was the easy part. The difficulty in such operations is how to cover up the truth and keep it covered up so that the official involvement does not surface. In order to accomplish this, strict control must be exercised over any investigation. Such control characterized the original FBI-directed MPD investigation and the subsequent Justice Department and HSCA investigations.

It is important to realize that much of the subsequent cover-up activity took place after a number of key officials in 1967–68 had gone from the scene. Director Hoover died in 1972. Lyndon Johnson did not run for reelection and died in 1973. H. L. Hunt passed away in 1974 and by then Richard Helms, army chief of staff General Harold Johnson and ACSI General William Yarborough were long gone from the official positions they held at the time. Gardner faded away and eventually disappeared. Finally, in the years following the events of April 4, 1968, two members of the Alpha 184 team (Captain Billy Eidson and 2nd Lieutenant Robert Worley) died or were killed, leaving Warren and Murphy in no doubt that a cleanup operation was under way. They left the country. A third member— the central communications operator—also went into hiding in Canada, and a fourth, J. D., was also killed some years later.

The exception, however, was outside of government where Carlos Marcello, though in prison for part of the time, remained active in running his New Orleans criminal enterprise and the same Memphis Godfather continued to be his main man in Memphis. Produce man Frank C. Liberto also continued to "take care of business" in that city with the Godfather's blessing, until he died in 1978, the year he admitted his role in the killing to the Whitlocks.

The point is that insofar as the government is concerned, the personalities—heinous though many of them were— changed, but a consistent policy of covering up the truth by the use of every possible means (including further murders) was continued. In every sense the cover-up has been institutionalized, and is not dependent upon the actions of particular individuals who were involved and determined to protect themselves.

JAMES EARL RAY ABANDONED the Eric S. Galt alias, and after going from Atlanta to Canada, fled to England using the name Ramon George Sneyd. Media coverage, often using FBI-planted stories, generally depicted him as a racist, violent, cold-blooded killer, who had dealt in and used drugs. This coverage would continue beyond his conviction. The public image of James was not the only one being molded by the mass media. It would also consistently record and remember Dr. King's pre-1966 Southern civil rights work, ignoring his formidable commitment to end the war and economic injustice at home. James was ultimately arrested on June 8, extradited to the United States on July 19, arriving in Memphis around 3:00 a.m. Only hours before, when tipped off about Ray's return, Memphis produce man Frank Liberto flew to Detroit. After James's capture all FBI work on the case ceased.

At no time in the pretrial period or since was the defense allowed to test the rifle or the bullets in evidence. James found himself housed in oppressive conditions, with his lawyers (first the Haneses and then Percy Foreman) being paid pursuant to a contract with an author who he gradually came to believe was providing information to the FBI. James would eventually be coerced into pleading guilty by his second lawyer, Percy Foreman. It finally emerged that at least by 1977–78, Foreman apparently knew Raul and had no doubt that his former client was innocent.

The day after the guilty plea hearing, the FBI put in motion the production of an official version of the case. The author proposed was Gerold Frank, whose book did indeed become the official version. The case was closed.

Three days after the guilty plea James petitioned the court to set aside his plea and grant him a trial. He was denied relief and has been seeking a trial ever since.

*   *   *

SOMETIME IN 1969 OR 1970 on separate occasions Amaro Pereira and Felix Torrino independently told Cheryl that Raul had assassinated Martin Luther King.

IN 1971 writer William Sartor, who had begun to focus on the involvement of Carlos Marcello and the Libertos in the assassination, died mysteriously in Waco, Texas, the night before he was to interview a significant witness. Twenty-one years later an autopsy report was finally obtained and it appeared that he had been murdered. A homicide investigation was opened.

In the early 1970s Marrell McCollough, then working for the CIA, returned to Memphis as part of a covert operation directed against certain antiwar activity in that city.

In 1974, Raul, in a rage, admitted to Cheryl in the presence of Amaro, Torrino and others that he was Dr. King's assassin, confirming what Amaro and Torrino had told her years earlier.

In 1976, in response to public outcry over the FBI's COIN-TELPRO excesses against Dr. King, the Justice Department began an investigation of the FBI's investigation of the assassination. In a report issued on January 11, 1977, the Justice Department found nothing wrong with the "technical competence of the investigation," and also found no new evidence which called for an investigation by state or federal authorities.

In 1977 author William Bradford Huie scheduled a small private meeting with James's lawyer Jack Kershaw. It was held in Nashville with two strangers present who may well have been federal agents. Huie asked Kershaw to take an offer to James of a sum of money, a pardon, and a new identity, if James would admit guilt. Only the federal government could arrange the deal Huie proposed. James rejected the offer out of hand, and it was later repeated by Huie in a tape-recorded and transcribed conversation with James's brother Jerry.

The HSCA investigation itself constituted the next cover-up. Early on, Richard Sprague, who had indicated his determination to acquire all relevant CIA and FBI and other intelligence files, was summarily removed. He was even escorted under armed guard from his office in the Capitol, presumably because they were afraid that he might remove sensitive documents which the committee would not want revealed. Under the new chief counsel Robert Blakey, no threat was posed to the interests of the intelligence community or the FBI. The committee undertook a tightly controlled investigation which focused on closing doors rather than following up leads, and sealing files, which incredibly included James's lawyer Art Hanes's trial file. Then, the "dirty tricks" activity of Oliver Patterson was deplorable, as was the refusal to seriously investigate and follow obvious leads pointing to the involvement of organized crime in the killing. Equally reprehensible was the HSCA's irrational adherence to the Alton bank robbery as a source of money for James when he was never a suspect and was not charged and in fact was not involved. By HSCA's King subcommittee chairman Walter Fauntroy's own admission, the HSCA knew at least about some of the 111th MIG surveillance activity and yet this significant and dramatic information was buried. The HSCA also clearly knew about the FBI's plan in 1977 to kill James when he was on escape but never mentioned it. In addition, staff investigators had admitted that they knew that Raul existed and that they knew who he was, yet in the final report they denied his existence and said that if he did exist he was one of James's brothers.

With all of this information, counsel Blakey was still prepared to unequivocally state that the HSCA had found no evidence of any involvement on the part of any agency of the U.S. government and the HSCA postulated an incredible conspiracy theory which purported to involve James with some St. Louis individuals without a shred of evidence that he had ever met with them or even knew of their existence. Conveniently the alleged conspirators were dead at the time of the investigation.

DURING THE TIME that the HSCA investigation was in operation, there was a series of efforts to silence James Earl Ray prior to his testifying in public in August 1978. It is important to note that there have been efforts to silence James at critical times during the history of the case. James Earl Ray was supposed to have been killed before he could be captured. One official source (Herbert) said that the reason the Galt alias and its tie to the 902nd MIG was never considered a problem, was because James was to have been killed, either in Memphis or in Africa.

There would obviously have been concern in official circles about what James might testify to at his trial. This was taken care of by the orchestration of his guilty plea.

Then, in June 1977, James escaped with others from Brushy Mountain Penitentiary and all the indications are that he was not supposed to return alive. He was no sooner over the wall (the nearest guard tower was curiously unmanned at the time) and into the hills behind the prison when a large SWAT team (upwards of thirty FBI snipers) took up position in the area. The function of snipers is not to apprehend. It is to kill. On the day of the escape Governor Ray Blanton received a call from HSCA chairman Louis Stokes who told him that HSCA staff believed that the FBI went to the area with instructions to kill James. The governor immediately went to the prison and ordered the agents to leave. Some years later when the federal agents controlling Arthur Baldwin discussed Ray with him, Baldwin said they made it clear that on that occasion James was not meant to be brought back alive. The escape, Baldwin understood, was staged for the purpose of killing James and putting an end to the problem. James's luck held up once again. He was actually captured by a prison guard. The plan failed.

The next attempt to close the case once and for all by eliminating James arose in the autumn of 1977. The Mafia Godfather in Memphis told Art Baldwin that if he (Baldwin) could clean up the problem he would be very amply rewarded. He told him that the people in New Orleans found Ray's continued visibility worrying—they wanted the problem to be over. The Godfather felt an obligation because the "screw up" happened in his town and area of responsibility. Baldwin approached Tim Kirk with whom he said he had worked on some other matters. They met and discussed the problem but it went no further. Some months later (in June 1978), Baldwin spoke by telephone with Kirk who by then was in the Shelby County Jail. Though Baldwin was offered $50,000 to get the job done, he told Kirk that the contract price was $5,000. Kirk became suspicious because of Baldwin's known ties to federal agents and let James's lawyers in on the plot. If Kirk knew that the Godfather had put out the contract, he never let on.

The third and final attempt, of course, involved an offer made to Baldwin by his FBI control agent some six or seven months after the Godfather's approach. It was first set out during a car journey to Nashville, and Baldwin subsequently overheard it being discussed by agents involved in the prosecution of Governor Ray Blanton. Baldwin backed off because he could not get satisfactory answers to material questions. Though promised lifelong immunity from all prosecution, Baldwin increasingly began to suspect that he, and possibly the other person who would be working with him, would not survive the operation.

In 1980, Cheryl and Bob, following the advice of Houston attorney Percy Foreman (who seemed to know Raul) and in fear for their lives, left Houston and resettled in another state where Bob had family.

In 1989 JAMES's latest appeal for a trial based on a clear violation of his Sixth Amendment rights was denied by the Supreme Court of the United States.

Frustrated in the courts, the 1993 Thames/HBO teletrial provided an opportunity for at least some of James's case to be put to the public.

Even then, however, cover-up attempts continued. The rooms of the television trial jury were visited and "inspected" by "technical staff" of the FBI from Washington, during the week prior to the jury's arrival. In addition, rooms on the same floor were reserved in the name of William Sessions (then director of the FBI) for himself and four agents. Cover-up by interference with the jury or some members of it, appeared to be the order of the day in mid January 1993. This failed.

BETWEEN 1993 AND 1995 the most recent cover-up has been successfully orchestrated at the local level by Shelby County District Attorney General John Pierotti. The appearance of Wayne Chastain before a grand jury was blocked in contravention of the right of a citizen under Tennessee law. Then, of course, the American media would not break the story of Loyd Jowers's involvement and his application for immunity, necessitating the breaking of the story in the London *Observer*. Following the *Observer* story, when ABC's *Prime Time Live* program aired the television admissions of Loyd Jowers, they were totally ignored by CBS, NBC, and even ABC news itself as well as the overwhelming mass print media throughout the nation. Despite Pierotti admitting that he would be derelict in his duty if he did not investigate the new evidence, he never talked to Jowers and the public reports from his office distorted the actual statements of James McCraw and Bobbi Smith. Subsequently, the attorney general's office ignored Nathan and Lavada Whitlock's statements about the local Mafia contract and Louie Ward's attempt to tell about the man his fellow cab driver Paul saw coming down over the wall and getting into a police car right after the shooting. Finally, the attorney general's office has blocked every attempt to allow material evidence of James's innocence to be put on in court, as well as continuing to prevent the testing of the rifle (which twenty-seven years after the crime has yet to be independently tested by the defense).

Further, the federal government continued to be unhelpful. My appeal to Attorney General Janet Reno guaranteeing federal civil rights indictments if she formed a grand jury, was met with brush-offs.

So, the cover-up is alive and well in the State of Tennessee and the United States, and consequently, throughout the world. Its effectiveness continues to be a testament to the comprehensive efficiency of senior law enforcement officials and the general collaboration of the mass newspaper, magazine, and television and radio broadcast media.

HOWEVER, an innocent man remains in prison and the case will not go away. In the spring and summer of 1995 Raul appears to have been located. On July 5, 1995, he was served with a summons and complaint and made a co-defendant in James Earl Ray's civil action against Loyd Jowers, Raul, and others. Though James has to date been denied a trial in the criminal courts, new arguments will soon take place in Judge Brown's court and the civil action is moving forward and will shortly come to trial. The investigation also continues.

Some questions will likely always remain unanswered, but as new evidence inevitably comes to light the history of the assassination will continue to be rewritten.

32

Conclusion

As THIS STORY COMES TO A CLOSE the next millenium is less than five years away.

Nearly forty years ago Americans and the world began an extraordinary decade. It was a time when no problem seemed insolvable, and no obstacle insurmountable. It is difficult now to recall, much less understand, those times when there was so much hope for the future and an unbridled passion for life dominated our daily lives. Masses of people, long suppressed, came out in full view. Their presence was frightening to an alliance of the corporate elite and their agents in government which long ago had come to dominate American public and private life. Legions of the poor, blacks, women, Native Americans, disaffected soldiers, students, and even prisoners represented a new, vital force which would inevitably clash head-on with the nation's leaders who, in the face of increasing economic hardship at home, were advocating a growing war effort in Vietnam.

When Martin Luther King only preached about morality and led his people, Southern blacks, down the road of realizing their basic civil rights, he could be tolerated. He was a nuisance but the cooptive power of the society could well allow for long overdue concessions to be given to blacks in order to head off any potentially serious disruptive activity. This coopting facility of the American system has, historically, been extraordinarily successful. It is the most subtle and effective apparatus of control that the world has ever seen. The system's flexibility allows for basic reforms to take place as they become necessary, with the distribution of just enough wealth to enough people so that only a troublesome but manageable minority remains to act on their discontent.

When, however, Dr. King began to assert his moral leadership on the issues of peace and economic justice, he became intolerable. Then the massive weight of the American government came down on him. As we have seen he and his followers were subjected to harassment, infiltration, surveillance, and wiretapping. Finally he was killed—and for what? For seeking peace and justice in his native land which had rejected one and denied the other.

The amount of money spent on the government's multiplicity of anti-King operations, not to mention the expenditure of the HSCA's and other cover-up activities, is incalculable. The average citizen would be staggered, as was I, by the number of different intelligence units and operations. Shock turns to horror when one becomes aware that the pervasive spying on Dr. King was only the tip of the iceberg and that massive surveillance operations were mounted against huge numbers of American citizens with most of the spying done on Americans who were themselves paying for it. Thus, American taxpayers were paying for their own government to spy on themselves.

When the Senate Judiciary Subcommittee on Constitutional Rights issued its 1973 report detailing the massive spying on civilians by army intelligence, the nation was shocked. The practices were soon put down to the excesses of General Yarborough, his successor General Joseph McChristian, General Blakefield, and other individuals, and were soon forgotten. The fact is that from what we now know, the report hardly scratched the surface.

It is too easy and all too prevalent to blame such past abuses and excesses on the likes of Hoover, Yarborough, or other individuals wielding power at the time. The clear, however unwelcome, indications are that the problem is a systemic one.

In 1968 the last serious effort to change American society led by Dr. King came to an end with his death. American cities burned for a while, but the Washington "invasion" fizzled out. The force that died early that evening of April 4, 1968, has never been revived.

Now it may be too late. The corporate elite, their lawyers and bankers, as well as their assets in government who have led us into the abyss may quite simply be too strong to dislodge, too powerful to unseat, at least in our lifetimes. We now appreciate as never before the power of the "establishment."

James Madison's worst fears appear to have been realized. He, the Republic's fourth President, the father of the Bill of Rights and the Constitution itself, warned about the very danger which has consumed our representative democracy. He noted that when any faction becomes so powerful, beyond its legitimate numerical presence, that it can dominate the branches of government and the political parties, so that dissent is suppressed, then tyranny will thrive. The system of government which results is a democracy in name only.

Under the Constitution of the United States, Madison and his founding colleagues attempted to provide for the problem by establishing a structure of government with a separation of powers, so that theoretically the executive, legislative, and judicial branches may each act as a check on the others.

What was not envisioned, however, was that an increasingly powerful corporate elite would develop which would not only formulate and act upon common policies, values, and goals, but also lend its senior representatives to government service. The power and influence of this corporate faction extends across all branches of government into virtually every agency and department. Governmental policies and activities in the service of these powerful private economic interests have, where those interests required, continually lied, and deceived the people as to the true state of events at home and abroad.

Thus, the enormous power and wealth of the government has been used for purposes and ends which all too often have been directly contrary to the interests of the masses of Americans.

With all of this history laid bare and the details of the abuse of power clearly revealed, the inevitable conclusion will still be very difficult for many Americans to accept. Representative democracy, as practiced in the United States, has failed.

I believe that the revival of democracy in America can only be accomplished by the people taking actual control over their public affairs. Time and again, I have been impressed with the ability of juries comprised of ordinary people provided with a full presentation of the facts to thoughtfully administer justice. I remain confident that if provided with all of the facts the people are still democracy's best hope.

By 1995, however, a significant obstacle exists in the fact that the public information put out on sensitive issues is rarely complete, balanced, and comprehensive. It is usually skewed in order to obtain the desired public response. This must be addressed. It goes without saying that control of the major media companies by multinational conglomerates will never ensure the objectivity required to enable the citizens to make informed decisions.

This was a problem which faced Dr. King daily between 1965–68 as he argued for the commitment of the nation's wealth to the alleviation of misery at home rather than the infliction of barbarism abroad.

Dr. King is gone forever. He can never be brought back to us, however much the memory of his quest for justice lives on. James Earl Ray will remain in prison unless the outrage of ordinary people reaches such a crescendo that he is at last either given the trial denied to him for twenty-six years or, based upon all that we now know, he is offered a pardon or clemency. Until that day, justice will continue to be denied in this case.

As for the cancer afflicting the body politic and democracy in America, only the people in their millions can affect a cure. Rather than mourning the passing of liberty I hope they begin to organize its rebirth.

APPENDIX

MAP 1 - USAINTC DEPLOYMENT

Area of Jurisdiction - CONUS Military Intelligence Groups

HQ, 108th MI Gp, Ft Devans, Mass.

HQ, 109th MI Gp, Ft Meade, Maryland

HQ, 116th MI Gp, Washington, D.C

HQ, 111th MI Gp, Fort McPherson, Georgia

HQ, 113th MI Gp, Fort Sheridan, Illinois

HQ, 112th MI Gp, Ft Sam Houston, Texas

HQ, 115th MI Gp, Presidio of San Francisco, California

CHART 7

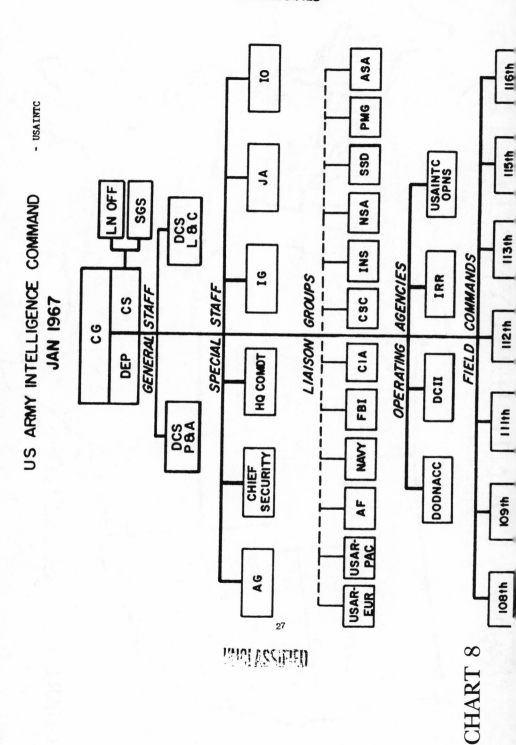

US ARMY INTELLIGENCE COMMAND
JAN 1967   - USAINTC

GENERAL STAFF

SPECIAL STAFF

LIAISON GROUPS

OPERATING AGENCIES

FIELD COMMANDS

CG
DEP
CS

LN OFF
SGS

DCS P&A
DCS L&C

AG
CHIEF SECURITY
HQ COMDT
IG
JA
IO

USAR-EUR
USAR-PAC
AF
NAVY
FBI
CIA
CSC
INS
NSA
SSD
PMG
ASA

DODNACC
DCII
IRR
USAINTC OPNS

108th
109th
111th
112th
113th
115th
116th

27

CHART 8

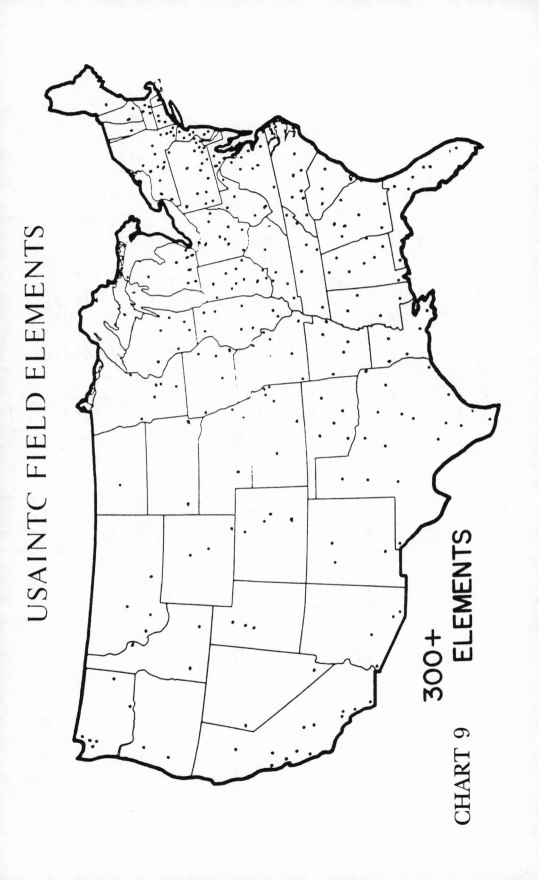

USAINTC FIELD ELEMENTS

300+
ELEMENTS

CHART 9

USAINTC COMMUNICATIONS

EXPANDED AUTOVON NETWORK

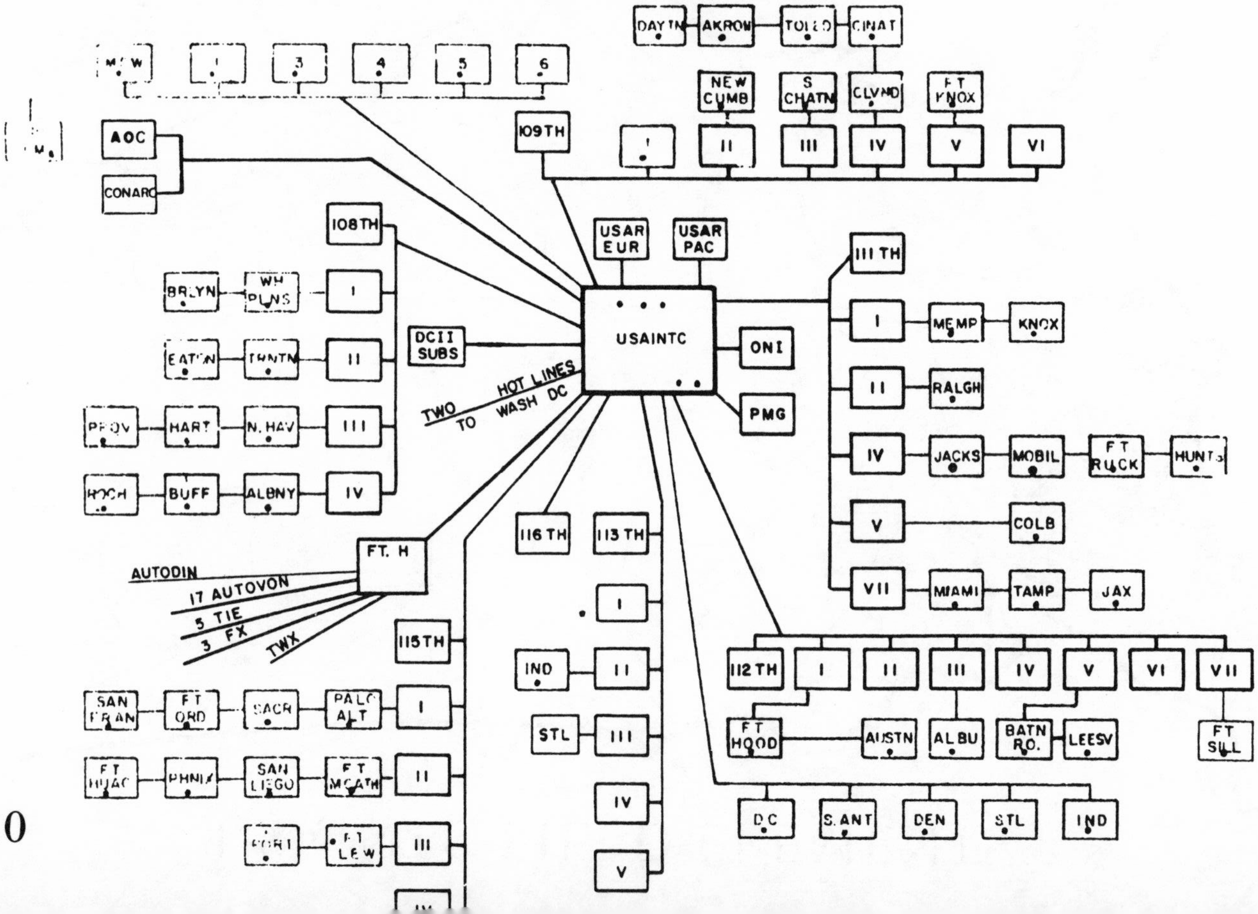

CHART 10

NOTES

1 David J. Garrow, *Bearing the Cross* (New York: Vintage Books, 1988). p. 543.
2 Ibid. p. 545.
3 FBI Memorandum Report from Cartha DeLoach to Mr Mohr dated November 27, 1964.
4 Joan Turner Beifuss, *At the River I Stand* (Memphis, TN.: St. Lukes Press, 1990) pp. 382–383.
5 Gerold Frank, *An American Death* (New York: Doubleday & Company, Inc., 1972) p. 172. 6 UPI April 24, 1968.
6 UPI April 24, 1968.
7 Drew Pearson/Jack Anderson, *The Washington Post*, July 22, 1968.
8 Gerold Frank, op. cit.
9 FBI letter from Cartha DeLoach to Clyde Tolson dated March 11, 1969.
10 Addendum to letter from DeLoach to Tolson dated March 12, 1969.
11 George McMillan, *The Making of an Assassin* (Boston: Little, Brown, 1976).

12 William Bradford Huie, *He Slew the Dreamer* (Nashville: Thomas Nelson Inc. Publishers, 1968).

13 Harold Weisberg, *Frame-Up* (New York: Outerbridge & Dienstfrey 1971).

14 Mark Lane/Dick Gregory, *Code Name "Zorro"* (Englewood-Cliffs, N.J.: Prentice-Hall Inc. 1977.

15 George McMillan, op. cit.

16 *St. Louis Post-Dispatch,* January 20, 1976.

17 Affidavit of G. Robert Blakey, Rancho La Costa, Inc. et al. v. Penthouse International Ltd. et al.

18 *Penthouse* magazine March 1975.

19 Blakey affidavit, op. cit.

20 Jim Hougan, *Spooks* (New York: William Morrow & Co. Inc. 1978) pp. 533–534.

21 Thomas Plate, Andrea Darvi, *Secret Police* (London: Robert Hale 1982) p. 294.

22 Memorandum 15 March 1968 from Acting Director of Security to Deputy Director for Support.

23 David Wise, Thomas B. Ross, *The Espionage Establishment* (New York: Random House, 1967) p. 143.

24 David Wise, Thomas B. Ross, op. cit.

25 David Wise, Thomas B. Ross, op. cit. pp. 143–160.

26 Morton Mintz, Jerry S. Cohen, *Power, Inc.* (New York: Viking Press, 1976) p. 283.

27 U.S. Department of Justice, Report of the Justice Department Task Force to Review FBI Martin Luther King Jr., Security and Assassination Investigations, Washington, D.C., January 11, 1977.

28 U.S. Senate Committee on the Judiciary, FBI Statutory Charter—Appendix to Hearings Before the Subcommittee on Administrative Practice and Procedure Part 3, 95th Cong. 2d Sess. U.S. Court Print pp. 33–75.

29 HSCA Report Vol VI p. 138, MLK Exhibit F-436D.

30 Memo to A. E. Belmont from W.C. Sullivan December 24, 1963.

31 Ibid.

32 Memo to W. C. Sullivan from C. D. Brennan 4/18/68.

33 Memo to W. C. Sullivan from C. D. Brennan 12/15/68.

34 File Memo June 23, 1966 to Atlanta S.A.C. Joseph K. Ponder.

35 Memos to W. C. Sullivan from G. C. Moore 12/13/67 and 12/29/67; Memo to Attorney General Clark 1/2/68 and his response 1/3/68.

36 HSCA Report Vol. VI, p. 67.

37 The details of these contacts are set out in a series of Memoranda from F. J. Baumgardner to W. C. Sullivan dated: 11/10/64, 12/6/64, 2/1/64, 3/2/65, 4/23/65, 5/24/65, and 8/14/65.

38 *New York Times,* November 19, 1964.
39 Memorandum from Baumgardner to William Sullivan November 3, 1966.
40 Memorandum from Robert Wick to Cartha DeLoach November 9, 1966.
41 Memorandum from Charles Brennan to William Sullivan March 8, 1967.
42 Philip Melanson, *The Martin Luther King Assassination* (New York: Shapolsky Publishers 1991) p. 132.
43 Memorandum from SAC Chicago to Director FBI June 1, 1967.
44 Melanson, op. cit. p. 132.
45 Memorandum from George Moore to William Sullivan October 25, 1967.
46 Memorandum from George Moore to William Sullivan March 26, 1968.
47 HSCA Report Vol. IV p. 200.
48 Memoranda from Milton Jones to Thomas Bishop 3/18/69.
49 Jack Anderson and Les Whitten, *The Washington Post* 12/17/75.
50 Memos F. J. Baumgardner to W. C. Sullivan dated 9/8/64 and 9/17/64.
51 HSCA Final Report p. 573.
52 Curt Gentry, J. Edgar Hoover, *The Man and the Secrets* (New York: W. W. Norton & Company 1991) p. 572.
53 HSCA Report Vol. VI p. 125.
54 HSCA Final Report p. 377.
55 HSCA Final Report p. 376.
56 Melanson, op. cit. p. 73.
57 Garrow, op. cit. p. 468
58 Deposition of Percy Foreman April 3, 1974, in case of *James Earl Ray v. Jimmy H. Rose* No. C-74-166, United States District Court, Western District of Tennessee, Western Division p. 154.
59 *Ibid.* p. 167.
60 *Ibid* p. 182.
61 HSCA Final Report pp. 548–549.
62 HSCA Final Report p. 547 (footnote).
63 HSCA Report Vol. VIII p. 608.
64 HSCA Final Report p. 555.
65 Douglas Valentine, *The Phoenix Program,* (New York: William Morrow and Company, 1990) p. 338.
66 *I Am A Man* (Memphis, TN: Memphis Publishing Company, 1993) p. 104.
67 HSCA Vol. I p. 77.

68 Douglas Valentine, *The Phoenix Program*, op. cit.
69 James Bamford, *The Puzzle Palace*, (New York: Penguin Books USA, 1983) p. 321
70 Ibid. p. 317
71 Ibid. p. 321
72 Ibid. p. 321

ACKNOWLEDGMENTS

DURING THE PERIOD OF eighteen years my work on this case has bene-fited from the assistance of a large number of people to whom I am grateful. Though it is not possible to mention everyone individually, the contributions and sacrifices of some particular individuals have been so significant that they must be recorded.

I wish to acknowledge the courage of John McFerren, "Cheryl" and "Bob," Betty Spates, Louie Ward, Nathan Whitlock, Clifton Baird, Art Murtagh, Bill Turner, Daniel Ellsberg, and William Sartor, as well as my Tennessee associate counsel Wayne Chastain. Each has demonstrated, often under great pressure, the fortitude necessary to try to right the twenty-six year old wrong which both deprived the nation of the unique leadership skills and vision of Martin Luther King and sent an innocent man to prison.

Credit and appreciation is also extended to a number of local law enforcement and intelligence officials who have disclosed pieces of the story or otherwise assisted. This list includes present and former Memphis Police Department officers such as Tommy Smith, Barry Neal Linville, Jim Nichols, Ed Atkinson, Ed Redditt, Jerry Williams, Joe Hodges, Emmett Douglass, and Alex McCollum. A special note of thanks is owed to former MPD officer Jim Smith who told the truth and suffered professional harassment as a result. Too, there was former Memphis Deputy Director of Public Works Maynard Stiles and former Fire Department officers whose contributions were significant including William King, Charles Stone, Floyd Newsom, Chief Norvell Wallace and Lieutenant George Loenneke.

Many people from all walks of life were willing to share what they knew about the case and/or provided an essential base of grass roots support and encouragement. I am particularly grateful to Sid Carthew whose conscience compelled him to take great pains to search me out and Ray Kohlman who gave unstintingly of his time. Among others I am grateful to: James McCraw, Peggy and Charles Hurley, William Ross, Ernestine Campbell, John "Bill" McAfee, John Fisher, "Tango," Tommy Wright, Jerry Little, Hazel Sweeney, Kay Black and the Invaders, particularly Charles Cabbage, Big John Smith, Izzy Harrington, Dr. Coby Smith and Abdul Yawee.

A number of former friends and associates of Dr. King have provided invaluable assistance. It was with Ralph Abernathy that I initially met and interrogated James Earl Ray, and through the years the Reverend Jim Lawson has been a constant pillar of strength and support. Jim's integrity and capacity for love is unmatched in my experience. In his unswerving commitment to the legacy of Dr. King, the Reverend Hosea Williams has been a constant reminder to me of what this is all about. Whenever needed he has been there, occasionally in great physical pain. The Reverend James Orange is another who has gone out of his way to try to tell what he saw at the time of the killing.

The considerable previous research and investigative efforts particularly of Harold Weisberg as well as Mark Lane have provided an essential foundation for my own work.

More recently, the work of English television producer John Edginton and author Philip Melanson have kept some significant issues alive. English reporters Andrew Billen of the London *Observer* who broke a key aspect of the story and Oonagh Blackman of the London *Sunday Express* have demonstrated a degree of interest and independence rarely seen in the American press. Other researchers and authors whose work has occasionally overlapped with my own have been a welcome source of information and general encouragement. Among others are Anthony Summers, Jim Hougan, Colonel Fletcher Prouty USAF ret., James Bamford, Peter Dale Scott, Dan Moldea, Douglas Valentine and Dick Russell.

Home Box Office and Thames Television provided James with his only trial up to the present time. This effort (and my work generally) was greatly facilitated by the Tennessee Department of Corrections Deputy Director Mike Dutton who was previously warden of Riverbend Penitentiary where James is incarcerated, and Mary Dennis the Warden's assistant. Memphis attorney April Ferguson, who has had a long standing interest in the case, assisted as co–counsel.

Previous lawyers of James Earl Ray, Arthur Hanes Sr., his son Judge Art Hanes Jr., Jack Kershaw and Jim Lesar were gracious with their time and information.

I reserve a special note of thanks for former Memphis journalist Steve Tompkins, whose earlier work opened the door to the most sensitive, deeply hidden area of my investigation. For me Steve epitomizes the very best of a dying breed in America—the investigative journalist who is only restricted in the pursuit of the truth by his conscience.

I am also indebted to and wish to acknowledge the contributions of a number of other serving and former military officers, intelligence and other government officials who must remain anonymous but without whose courage the full story could not have been told.

This book would not have been written in its present form without the herculean efforts of my assistant for the last nine years, Jean Hazel Obray. Her singleminded, unselfish dedication to the defense of James Earl Ray, the investigation of the case and the completion of the book has been matched by her creative contributions and insights into people and events. Where my performance has been lacking in any respect she has enhanced it and where it has been good she has pushed for excellence.

To her goes my heartfelt gratitude.

Index

A

Abels, Ken, 206, 240
Abernathy, Ralph, 17, 18, 19, 21,
    22–23, 27, 29, 30, 31, 32, 35,
    51, 119, 160, 220, 227, 230,
    274, 282, 399
  assassination and, 134
  conspiracy theory and, 47, 53
  Ellsberg affidavit and, 91, 92
  FBI and, 297
  Harrison and, 158–159
  HSCA and, 52
  King's last hours and, 160, 283
  as King's successor, 33
  meeting with Ray, 51–53, 66–82
Abrams, Creighton V., 412–413 457,
    471
Academic community, CIA and, 87
Addison, Lavada Whitlock, *see*
    Whitlock, Lavada
Admiral Benbow Inn, 225
Aeromarine Supply Store, 34–35,
    36, 76, 125, 127–128, 211, 285,
    294, 296, 300, 471, 473
Agent(s) provocateur
  Black Caucus and, 466
  Invaders and, 9, 61, 130
  McCullough as, 130
  March 28 march (Memphis) and,
    117, 220, 282, 291, 458, 470–471

Agne, Joseph, 334
Akabulon group, 243, 265–266
Akins, Willie, 236, 237, 253–254,
    264–265, 313, 315, 316,
    320–321, 325, 331, 337, 343,
    345, 359–360, 384, 393
Alabama Army National Guard, 417
Albert, Carl, 90
Alibi witnesses for Ray, 139–140,
    193, 195–196, 204, 279
Alton, Illinois bank robbery, 44,
    107–109, 125, 265, 277, 295,
    487
Ambassador Hotel, 217, 240
American Death, An (Frank), 53
American Independence Party, 124
Amnesty International, 307–308,
    340
Anderson, Jack, 39, 43, 119
Anschutz, Willie, 59, 288
Antipoverty program, 4
  King and, 4, 10, 14
Antiwar demonstrations, 5, 441, 442,
    443, 447–450, 452, 466–467
Appeal, 148, 150, 158, 174–175,
    182, 183, 491
Applebooty, 329
Arcade Restaurant, 217, 237
Arkin, Eli H., 14, 126, 129, 222,
    250, 251, 421, 422, 431, 460,
    475, 477

Armando, *see* Pereira, Armaro
Army, 412–461
  assassination and, 413–414,
    421–436, 456, 460–461, 469,
    467–468, 469, 470, 472, 473,
    471, 474, 477, 481–483,
    485–488
  chronology of relevant events
    and, 439–461
  domestic missions of, 419–420
  Galt and, 435–439, 444, 465, 484,
    486
  intelligence organization,
    411–418
  King and, 415, 469, 487, *see also*
    surveillance of King and, *berlow*
  Ku Klux Klan and, 415, 455
  Memphis Police Department and,
    465
  senior officials of, 417–419
  Southern Christian Leadership
    Conference and, 458, 460, 462,
    464, 468, 473, 475
  Special Forces Group and, 317,
    333, 338–339, 345, 347, 412,
    415, 418–419, 420, 444,
    450–451, 455
  surveillance of King and,
    246–247, 248, 304–305,
    316–317, 414, 415, 416, 423,
    432, 433–434, 441, 442, 443,
    452, 454–455, 456–457, 458,
    459, 460, 463, 469, 470, 471,
    473, 477, 478, 487
  urban riots and, 444–445, 446,
    450–451, 458, 464, 465, 467
  Vietnam War opposition and,
    440–444, 445–450, 452–453,
    465, 466–467, 493
Assassination, 27–33, 460, 478–479,
    480, 481, 482–484, 494
  aftermath of, 34–38
  Army and, 412–413, 420–435,
    456, 459–461, 467–468, 469,
    471, 474–475, 477, 478, 479,
    480, 481 483–485

BBC documentary on, 160–165,
    175, 184, 377
books on, 53–61, 104–105, 148,
    166–167, 170, 295, 337, 362,
    482, 486
chronology of, 462–481
cover-up of, 485–491, 494
evidence of, 190–191, 199–201
foreign intelligence agencies and,
    234
Invaders and, 98, 250, 257–259,
    276
Jowers and, 157, 195, 264–265,
    315–316, 319–320, 324, 325,
    326–331, 341, 342, 343, 380,
    384, 469, 475–477, 478, 479,
    480, 482, 491–492
King's last hours before, 28–29,
    95, 159–160, 245, 274, 282–283,
    460, 478–479
location of shot and, 56, 93–94,
    129, 153–154, 163, 165, 186,
    190, 191, 211, 231, 263–264,
    273, 274–275, 296
Mafia and, 102–103, 131–136,
    137–139, 145–148, 380–381,
    386–387, 393, 394–395, 464,
    465, 468, 476, 477, 484, 486,
    487
media and, 53–54
Memphis Police Department and,
    30–31, 126, 185–186, 190–191,
    275, 294, 392–393, 460–461,
    472, 473, 474, 475, 478, 480,
    482
phone call preceding, 263
photographs relating to, 139,
    190–191, 364, 483
posture of King when shot and,
    93
prior attempts at, 140–144, 243,
    386–387, 395, 426, 462–463,
    464, 468
Raul and, 375–376, 377, 378
Ray's story on, 66–82, 139–140,
    148, 188

scene of, 93, 97–98
Selma, Alabama and, 426
state's case on, 55–59, 94–97
throwdown rifle and, 228, 231
witnesses of, 94–97, 149, 174,
    184–185, 188, 201–202, 208,
    210, 221, 230–231, 245–246,
    253, 283–284, 396–402, 474,
    481, *see also* Jones, Solomon;
    Stephens, Charles Quitman
Yellow Cab Company and,
    388–390
see also Ballistics; Bushes, between
    rooming house and Lorraine
    Motel; Conspiracy theory;
    Footprints, between Lorraine
    Motel and rooming house;
    Rifle, for assassination
Assistant Chief of Staff for
    Intelligence (ACSI), 415, 416,
    417, 437, 439, 440, 441, 447,
    448, 450, 452, 453, 454
Association of Federal, State,
    County and Municipal
    Employees (AFSCME), 13
Atkinson, Ed, 210–211
Atlanta
    map of, 55–56, 187–188, 200,
        286–287, 301, 304
    Ray in, 55–56, 75, 129, 212,
        286-287, 301, 470, 471, 486
At the River I Stand (Beifuss), 28–29
Auble, John, 233, 277, 295
Austein, William, 152, 199, 259–260
Avery, Will, 307

B

Bacile, Joe, 376
Baden, Michael, 286
Bailey, D'Army, 313
Bailey, F. Lee, 42, 166
Bailey, Lorraine ("Lurlee"), 22, 31,
    203–204, 222, 263
Bailey, Theotis, 263

Bailey, Walter, 22, 97–98, 151,
    203–204, 231, 263, 290, 300
Baird, Clifton, 140–144, 255, 463
Baker, William, 142–143
Bakst, Richard, 391–392
Baldwin, Arthur Wayne, 134–135,
    190, 212, 265, 300, 366–369,
    489–490
Ballard, Charles, 257
Ballistics
    assassination rifle identification
        and, 128, 136–137, 163,
        199–200, 255–256, 267–268,
        273, 284, 285, 288
    rifle tested for evidentiary record
        and, 347, 356–357, 360,
        361–362, 392, 486, 491
    state's case disproved with,
        136–137
    television trial and, 289–290
Baltensprager, John, 101, 102, 240
Bamford, James, 437
Bank robberies, 59
    Alton, Illinois, 44, 107–109, 125,
        265, 277, 295, 488
Baptist World Alliance, 121
Barksdale, Gene, 212, 213
Barr v. Matteo, 85
Bathroom window, shot fired from,
    94, 129, 153–154, 163, 165,
    186, 190, 191, 211, 263, 273
Battle, Preston, 44–45, 167, 169,
    172, 173–174
BBC documentary, on assassination,
    160–165, 175, 184, 377
Bearing the Cross (Garrow), 4
Beasley, James, 45, 46, 96, 180
Beifuss, Joan, 28–29
Belafonte, Harry, 117
Benavites, Tony, 102
Bennett, John, 10
Berens, Howard, 66, 68, 80, 81
Bergard, Coleman, 31–32
Berkley, Elmo, 226
Bevel, James, 21, 28, 98, 130, 472
Bevel, Jim, 458, 479

Big Lena, 252, 254, 255, 382
Billen, Andrew, 304, 322, 326
Billet, Myron "Paul Bucilli," 146,
    147–148, 161, 276, 297, 468
Billings, John, 268, 298, 313, 321,
    322, 326, 329, 338, 345, 387
Binoculars, 35, 56, 78, 128, 186,
    188, 285, 476–477
Birch, Philip, 42
Bishop, Martin, 147
Black, Kay, 61, 98, 119, 129, 156,
    209, 231, 296
Blackburn, S. O., 229, 239, 249
Black Caucus, 8, 9, 84, 270, 466
Black Organizing Project (BOP), 14
Black Power movement, 9
"Black probe" operation, 123
Blackstone Rangers, 9, 270
Blair, Arlie, 140–144
Blakefield, William, 417, 443, 465,
    474, 494
Blakey, G. Robert, 61, 63–64, 65,
    91–92, 108, 111, 123, 125, 488
Blanton, Ray, 134, 212, 242, 260,
    366, 368, 489, 490
Blount, James E. "Jeb", III, 249
Blue Note Lounge (Jackson,
    Mississippi), 386, 464
Bob (husband of Cheryl), 374, 376,
    377, 378, 404–405, 409, 490
Bonebrake, George, 287
Bonnevecche, J. Christ, 102–103
Books
    on assassination, 53–61, 104–105,
        148, 166–167, 170, 295, 337,
        362, 486
    on King, 353–354, 481
Boycotts, 20
Boyd, Sallie, 336
Bradshaw, Rufus, 152, 199, 259,
    298
Branner, Jimmie Lee, 322
Brantman, Alfred L., 109
Bray, Colonel, 222, 247
Brennan, C. D., 120

Brewer, Bessie, 56, 95, 96, 97, 193,
    254, 285, 329
Brewer, Frank, 254
Bridgeman, Paul Edward, 40, 80
Brown, Bailey, 21, 22, 27, 35
Brown Berets, 419
Brown, Bernard, 141, 142, 143
Brown, Calvin, 222
Brown, H. Rap, 419, 445, 446,
    453–454, 463
Brown, Joe, 335, 345, 356, 361, 363,
    365, 396
Brown, John H., 352
Brush, see Bushes, between rooming
    house and Lorraine Motel
Brushy Mountain State Penitentiary,
    Ray in, 68–82, 136, 148, 243,
    367, 489
    Ray's attempted murder at,
        134–136, 212, 243, 265–266,
        268, 275, 297, 300, 365–368,
        488–489
    Ray's escape from (1977), 68,
        242–243, 277, 360, 366–368,
        489
Bryan, George, 155
Bryant, Baxton, 133
Buchanan, Joe "Buck," 321,
    327–328, 330, 386, 428, 464
Buck Kreihs Machine Company,
    371
Buford, Walter, 101, 148
Bundy, McGeorge, 444
Burgess, Melvin, 226, 267
Burnstein, Ken, 431
Bushes, between rooming house
    and Lorraine Motel, 93, 95,
        184, 208–211, 256–257, 289,
        291, 387, 397
    cut down, 61, 98, 129, 156, 184,
        190, 201–202, 214, 254, 277,
        296, 298–299, 364–365,
        481–482
    shot fired from, 102, 129, 136,
        165, 231, 254, 274–275
Butler, Betty, 389

Butler, Paul, 389, 481, 482, 491
Butler, Thomas, 42, 43

C

Cabbage, Charles, 20, 196, 258,
458, 479
Caldwell, Earl, 163, 184–185, 210,
231, 257, 297, 299, 359
Campbell, Ernestine, 246, 263, 389
Campbell, William, 346, 347
Camp, George M., 62
Canada
Kimbel in, 163, 164
Ray in, 39–40, 59, 71, 79–80, 107,
162–163, 193, 243, 247,
465–466, 486
Canale, Phil M., Jr., 45, 47,
173–174, 181, 314, 332
Canipe, Guy, 30, 35, 136–137, 155
Canipe's Amusement Company
bundle (rifle) dropped at, 30, 59,
94, 136–137, 154, 155, 214,
252, 267, 274, 284, 285, 286,
290, 363–364, 478, 480
layout, 265–266
Mustang parked in front of, 30,
56, 59, 60, 153, 154, 155, 156,
186, 197, 199, 202, 214, 236,
262, 274, 284, 477
Capone, Al, 374
Carlisle, John, 195
Carmichael, Stokely, 418, 444, 445,
453–454, 463
Carroll, Carroll, 199, 208, 287
Carson, 369, 427–430
Carter, Jim, 378
Carter, M. E., Produce Company,
315, 316, 320, 328, 329,
336–337, 382, 393, 472
Carter, Marshal, 437
Carthew, Sid, 344–345, 375, 430
Cassius, Joseph, 262
Castro, Fidel, 83
Catherine, 265, 402
Caywood, David, 133

CB radio broadcast, *see* Hoax CB
radio broadcast
CBS, Stephens interviewed on, 97
Center for National Security
Studies, 83
Central Intelligence Act, 88
Central Intelligence Agency (CIA),
416, 417
Blakey and, 63–64
domestic activity of, 85–88
establishment of, 85–86
Kimbel and, 162–163
King and, 83–85, 463, 464
Mafia and, 146–147, 161–162
Operation CHAOS and, 9, 84,
85, 446, 466
police force training sessions and,
217
Special Operations Groups, 85,
88, 416, 417–418, 419, 446–448,
465, 466
Vietnam War opposition and,
441–444, 446–447, 449, 450,
451, 465, 466–467
Youngblood and, 100–104
see also Office of Security
Cessna, 243
Champagne, Donald, 286, 289
Champion, Carolyn, 204
Chapman, Leonard E., 114
Chapman, Robert, 349
Chastain, Wayne, 94, 95–96, 97,
100, 101, 127, 149, 156, 157,
164, 203–204, 209, 221, 231,
241, 273, 290, 291, 300, 312,
315, 319, 320, 321–322, 323,
331, 332, 334–335, 336, 345,
349, 359, 361, 363, 365, 373,
378, 380, 389, 391, 395, 408,
410, 491
Check Off Inn (Memphis), 229,
381, 382
Cheryl, 373–378, 404–405, 406, 409,
430, 487, 490
Chicago, antiwar march in (1967),
5

"Children of Vietnam, The"
  (*Ramparts*), 4–5
Chimento, Joe "Zip," 333–334, 370,
  375, 430, 465
Chuck, 396–404
Church Committee Report, 52
Civello, Joe, 352
Civil rights
  CIA and, 84
  Johnson and, 6
Claridge Hotel, 61
Clark, Earl, 211
Clark, Ramsey, 46, 93, 113, 438,
  463
Clarks Hotel, 478
Clay, Paul, 222
Clifford, Clark M., 438, 454, 455
Cobb, Henry H., Jr., 417
Cochran, Robert, 336
Code Name Zorro (Lane), 60–61
Cody, Archbishop, 121
Coffin, William Sloane, 4, 334
Cohen, Jeff, 60, 101, 149, 331
Cohen, Leon, 203, 231, 290, 300
COINTELPRO, 52, 112–114, 161,
  216, 275, 277, 281, 286, 462,
  487
Colacurcio, Frank, 212
Cole, Echole, 13
Collins, LeRoy, 114
Coloma, Dina, 307–308
Colton, John P., Jr., 181–183
COMINFIL, 112, 462
Commercial Appeal, 117, 119, 128,
  155
Commodore, 329
Communist Party
  King and, 112
  Southern Christian Leadership
    Conference and, 112–114
Community on the Move for
  Equality (COME), 15
Connally, John, 352
Conrad, Walter, 107–108, 265
Conspiracy theory, 45, 46–47, 48,
  53, 60, 141

Abernathy on, 81–82
alibi for Ray and, 139–140
Baird/Blair story and, 140–144
ballistics evidence and, 136–137
Brushy Mountain attack on Ray
  and, 265–266
cover-up of, 268
Ellsberg affidavit and, 88–93,
  98–100
evidence for, 93–104, 131–144,
  196
Hays and, 148–150
hoax CB radio broadcast and, 31,
  54, 60, 152, 199, 207–208, 231,
  259–260, 277, 287, 297–298
HSCA and, 107–110, 124–130,
  487
Kirk and, 134–136
Mafia and, 102–103, 131–136,
  137–139, 145–148, 161–162
Memphis Police Department and,
  51, 152, 293, *see also* TACT
  forces withdrawal and, *below*
opposition to, *see* House Select
  Committee on Assassinations;
  State's case
Ray involved in, 272
Betty Spates and, 275
TACT forces withdrawal and, 30,
  130, 151–152, 163, 213–216,
  224, 231, 274, 275, 282, 293,
  296
television trial and, 194, 274, 276,
  291, 295, 299, 301–302, 306
Cooks, Stoney, 89, 90, 92, 98, 99
"Coop," 217, 305, 450
"Copperhead," 258
Coppola, Joe, 333–334
Costello, Frank, 352
Counterintelligence Analysis Board
  (CIAB), 414, 441, 442, 444,
  445, 446, 455
Cover-up, of assassination, 485–492,
  494
Crawford, Gene Pearson, 240–241
Crawford, Willie, 256, 365, 481

Crumby, William O., 130, 151, 152, 224, 293
Cruz, Bob, 409, 410
Cupples, Steve, 197
Curington, John, 244–245, 349–354, 482
Curtis, Raymond, 42, 241–242

D

Dabney, Rosie Lee, 100, 236, 237–238, 252, 341, 382
Dago, 373–374
Daily News, FBI and, 115
Daley, Richard, 9
Dalitz, Morris, 63–64
Daniels, Harley, 246
Dates, Cliff, 204, 253, 298, 321, 322, 325, 337, 356, 360
Davis, George Kelly, 226
Davis, J. C., 194–195, 292
Davis, Morris, 134, 193, 211, 227–230, 294
Davis, Roy, 221
Death slug, assassination rifle identification and, 221, 255–256, 267, 273, 285, 286, 289, 482
DeLoach, Cartha, 6, 37, 53–54, 115, 121, 295
Democracy, failure of, 493–496
Denaro, Tina, 65
DeSoto Motel (Mississippi), 77
Diablo, 405
Disinformation, 111
  Herman and, 406
  photocopy of building in crime scene and, 139
  Youngblood and, 104
Dixie Mafia, 354
Dollahite, Vernon, 30, 154, 186, 284
Domestic Operations Division, of CIA, 86
Donaldson, Sam, 325, 337
Dougherty, Dale, 205–206, 239

Douglass, Emmett, 30, 213–216, 269, 284, 290
Draft, Spock on resistance to, 11
Ducret, 234
Duncan, William, 141, 142
Dunn, Carroll, 191, 481
Dutton, Mike, 306
Dwyer, Robert "Buzzy," 45, 180

E

Eastland, James, 355, 418
"Ed," 228–229
Edginton, John, 160–165, 243, 359
"Eggs and sausage man," at Jim's Grill, 100–101, 164, 238, 240, 383–384
Eidson, Billy R., 420–421, 428, 458, 460, 461, 471, 474, 475, 481, 485
Eisenhower, Dwight D., 87
Eldridge, Eddie Lee, 194
Electronic surveillance, 161
  "ELINT," 415, 440
  of Invaders, 258–259
  of King, 36, 113, 115, 122, 126, 161, 217–220, 231, 246, 258, 261, 276, 292, 303–305, 463
  of television trial jury, 266–267, 276, 277
  see also Surveillance
"ELINT" (electronic intelligence surveillance), 415, 440
Ellington, Buford, 19
Ellsberg, Daniel, 88–93, 98–100, 144
England, 247
  extradition from, 40, 43, 59, 68, 80, 94, 167, 205, 308, 485
Erickson, Frank, 352
Ernestine and Hazel's Restaurant, 245, 263
Eskridge, Chauncey, 30–31, 46
Esquivel, Raul, Jr., 161
Esquivel, Raul, Sr., 60, 149, 161–162
Eugene, Michael, 43
Evans, Edward, 138

Evans, Sam, 14, 18, 20, 151, 152,
    163, 224, 274, 381, 421, 473,
    475
Evans, Sam, Jr., 475
Evidence
    of assassination, 190–191,
        199–201
    for television trial, 181–183
Evidentiary record, establishment
        of, 346–347, 355–356
    delay in, 361–363, 365
    denial of, 396
    rifle and bullets tested for,
        346–347, 356–357, 360,
        361–362, 486
Ewing, Hickman, 180, 181, 189,
    190, 192–193, 264, 265, 271,
    276, 277, 281, 282, 283, 284,
    285, 286, 288, 289, 290, 292,
    295, 296, 298, 300, 303, 305,
    344
Exoneration, from government,
    306–307, 321, 326
Extramarital sexual activity, King
    and, 113–114, 119–120, 122,
    219, 292

F

"Fat" Frank, 336
Fauntroy, Walter, 52, 89, 90, 91, 92,
    98, 99, 100, 220, 246, 248, 260,
    277–278, 299, 305, 440, 488
    see also House Select Committee
        on Assassinations
Federal Bureau of Investigation
        (FBI), 47, 60, 68, 417, 416
    Alton, Illinois bank robbery and,
        108, 265
    assassination and, 223, 231, 486
    Austein and, 259–260
    Baird and, 141, 143
    ballistics and, 128, 136–137, 200,
        255–256, 267–268, 273, 288,
        289–290, 361–362
    "black bag" operations, 295

Blakey and, 63–64
books on assassination and,
    53–54, 295
Bessie Brewer and, 254
COINTELPRO and, 52, 112–114,
    161, 216, 275, 277, 281, 286,
    462, 487
COMINFIL and, 112, 462
Cupples and, 197
Curtis and, 241–242
electronic surveillance of King
    and, 217–219, 231, 249, 258,
    279, 463
Hardin and, 247
Holloman and, 14
HSCA investigation and, 99, 487
Huie and, 169, 255
Hunt and, 349, 350, 353
Invaders and, 258–259
Kimbel and, 161–162
King and, 4, 36, 60, 85, 88–93,
    96, 98–100, 112–124, 128,
    216–220, 231, 247, 248, 250,
    258–259, 275, 276, 282, 286,
    292, 295, 299, 303–305,
    350–351, 353, 361, 454, 462,
    463, 471
William King and, 201
King-Spock presidential ticket
    and, 116
Latch and, 241
Latimer and, 203
location of shot and, 93
McCoy and, 361
McFerren and, 133, 134
Mafia and, 146–147
media and, 53–54, 277
Memphis and, 455, 456, 457–458
Memphis march (March 28) and,
    282
Memphis Police Force and,
    221–222
Office of Security and, 83–84
police force training sessions and,
    217
Ray and, 36–37, 38–39, 40, 41,

43–44, 47, 60, 68, 242, 260, 436, 437–438, 470–471, 486, 488, 488
Ray's prison escape (June 1977) and, 68, 260, 487, 489
Southern Christian Leadership Conference and, 112–113, 115–117, 123, 158–159, 297, 459–460, 462
Stephens and, 184
television trial jury tampering and, 266–267, 489
302 interview reports and, 275–276
Vietnam War opposition and, 449–440, 445–447, 450–451
Wilkins and, 6
See also Hoover, J. Edgar
Fensterwald, Bud, 77
Ferguson, April, 131, 135, 148, 181, 289
Fingerprints, 128–129
Mustang and, 129, 287
rifle for assassination and, 128, 173, 287
Finley, Bernell, 155
Fireman
black boy telling shooting account to, 54, 149
transfer of Newsom and Wallace and, 23, 126, 150, 196, 224, 231, 275, 293, 474
Fisher, John T., 366
Florida Atlanta Airlines, 430
Footprints, between Lorraine Motel and rooming house, 196, 239, 253, 256–257, 296, 330, 481
Ford, Harold, 99
Foreign intelligence agencies, assassination and, 234
Foreman, Percy, 44, 45, 46–47, 137, 168–171, 172–174, 245, 351–352, 366, 376–377, 405, 486, 490
Foster, Kenneth, 196–197
Frame Up (Weisberg), 60

France, assassination and, 234
Francisco, Jerry, 33, 46, 129, 221, 255, 285
Frankel, Marvin E., 181, 281, 282
Frank, Gerold, 37, 53, 54, 295, 486
Freedom of Information Act, 83, 85, 109, 116, 125
Freshaur, Donald, 428
Frohnmeyer, John, 334
Fulbright, William, 455
Funeral, for King, 31, 35–36

G

Gagliano, J. S., 226
Galt, Eric S., 71, 73, 76, 434–438, 444, 465, 475, 483, 485, 488–489
Galt, Eric St. Vincent, 40, 434
Galt, Eric Starvo, 36–37
Gambino, Carlo, 146, 147, 469
"Garden Plot," 424
Gardner, 419, 425, 429, 433, 435, 436, 444, 450, 451, 455, 456, 458, 459, 467, 470, 471, 484
Garner, James, 37, 75
Garner rooming house, 200
Garrison, Jim, 52, 162, 370, 373
Garrison, Lewis, 293, 312, 313, 314, 315, 318, 319, 320, 321, 345, 372–373, 380, 383, 387, 391, 393–395, 396, 403, 404, 408
Garrow, David, 4, 158
Gattas, Fred P., 222
Gaynor, Paul, 84
Getz, George, 44
Ghormley, Judson "Bud," 30, 94, 154, 155, 186
Giancana, Sam, 83, 146, 147, 469
Gianetti, Rich, 229–230
Gianotti, Frank, 21–22
Gill, C. Wray, 370
Gioia, Frederick, 31
Glanker, Mark, 343
Globe-Democrat, 118
Goodman, Dutch, 256, 365, 482

Gore, Albert, 340
Grady, Edward, 371
Graham, Julius, 155
Granberry, Freddie, 335, 336
Grand Jury investigation, 332, 333,
    334, 362, 395–396, 490–491
    see also Evidentiary record,
    establishment of
Grapevine Tavern, 124
Graydon, Stuart F., 431
Greco, Luigi, 227
Green Beetle Tavern, 213, 217, 228
Green Berets, 413, 414
    Memphis and, 305
Green, Willie, 156–157, 193, 204,
    208, 273–274, 290
Gregory, Dick, 91
Guaranteed income, King on, 4, 10,
    14
Guilty plea, Ray entering, 44–48,
    53, 59, 80, 96, 104–105, 137,
    166–174, 189, 225, 287–288,
    297, 308, 332, 335, 346, 367,
    486, 487
Gulas Lounge, 134, 227, 230, 294

H

Hack, Al, 229, 230
Hagerty, Robert, 223, 292, 422
Haines, Ralph E., Jr., 447
Halperin, Morton, 83
Hamby, J. D., 223, 226, 255, 285,
    289
"Hamilton," 258
Hamilton High School (Memphis),
    18
Hanes, Arthur, Jr., 43, 44, 166–167,
    168, 169, 173, 362, 486
Hanes, Arthur J., Sr., 43, 44,
    136–137, 148, 155, 166–167,
    168, 169, 170, 172, 173, 362,
    486, 488
Hardin, J. C., 247
Harrington, Charles "Izzy," 20,
    257–258, 458

Harris, Caro, 226, 259, 478
Harrison, James, 158–159, 269, 460,
    464, 473
Harry, 261, 354
Hartingh, John, 247
Hayes, Olivia, 196, 203, 231
Hays, Renfro, 44, 100, 148–150, 150
Helms, Richard McGarrah, 85, 87,
    88, 416, 417, 440, 443, 446,
    449, 454, 463, 464, 465, 485
Hendrix, Ray Alvis, 139, 193, 276,
    289, 478
Herbert, 419, 420, 425, 430, 436,
    489
Herman, Ken, 150–151, 152, 157,
    180, 182, 183, 184, 193, 202,
    211–212, 213, 222, 227, 229,
    234, 237, 240, 241, 242, 253,
    254, 256, 263, 265, 266, 298,
    313, 315, 316, 319, 322–323,
    329, 338, 343, 345, 349,
    365–366, 373, 374, 378–380,
    387, 393, 403, 406, 409
Herron, Matt, 59–60
Hersh, Seymour, 456
He Slew the Dreamer (Huie), 54–55
Hester, Joe, 286, 304
Hester, O. D., 393
Heymann, Philip, 108, 109
Hickory Stick bar, 205, 239
Hill, Janice, 429
Hill, John D., 426, 427, 428,
    429–430, 479
Hill, Thurston, 365
Hilton Hotel, television trial jury
    and, 266–267, 276, 277
H.L.H. Products Inc., 244, 351
Hoax CB radio broadcast, 31, 54,
    60, 152, 199, 207–208, 231,
    259–260, 277, 287, 297–298,
    481
Hodges, Joe "J. B.," 191, 210,
    256–257, 265, 275, 296, 481
Hoffa, Jimmy, 115–116, 355, 371
Holiday Inn Rivermont Hotel, 225,
    457

electronic surveillance of,
    217–220, 246, 292, 305, 415,
    457, 458, 470–471
King's speech at, 19
reservation at, 118–119, 470
reservation change to Lorraine
    Motel, 60, 269, 274, 282, 297
Holloman, Frank C., 14, 19, 31,
    101, 126, 133, 210, 217, 226,
    250–252, 447, 452, 477
Holt, Frank, 315, 320–321, 320–322,
    323–324, 326–330, 339, 360,
    384, 393
Home Box Office (HBO), television
    trial and, 181, 183, 188, 191,
    490
Honorary degrees, to King, 121
Hood, Clement, Sr., 162
Hoover, J. Edgar, 14, 21, 248, 417,
    447, 456, 478, 485, 495
Army and, 440
books on assassination and, 295
conspiracy theory and, 46
electronic surveillance of King
    and, 248, 304–305, 463
fingerprints of Ray and, 37
Harvey's Restaurant and, 28
Hunt and, 350–351, 352,
    353–354, 464, 481
King and, 4, 36, 60, 88–93,
    98–100, 113, 115, 119, 121,
    122, 143, 246–247, 248, 282,
    299, 304–305, 350–351, 353,
    354, 442, 453–454, 463, 464,
    469
Mafia and, 146, 244, 352
Marquette honorary degree and,
    121
media and, 115–117, 119–120
Office of Security and, 83–84
Southern Christian Leadership
    Conference and, 112, 123
Vietnam War opposition and,
    440–441, 493
House Intelligence Committee
    report, 52

House Judiciary Committee, 52
House Select Committee on
    Assassinations (HSCA), 52,
    62–65, 68, 163, 487–488
Alton, Illinois bank robbery and,
    265, 295, 48–4887
ancillary volumes, 112, 126–130
Baird and, 140, 141, 142
ballistics and, 286, 289
Blakey and, 61, 63–64, 65, 91–92,
    108, 111, 123, 125, 487
COINTELPRO and, 161
conspiracy theory and, 107–110,
    124–130, 487
Davis and, 227, 229, 230
death slug and, 221
Ellsberg affidavit and, 90, 91–92,
    99, 100
Fauntroy and, 89, 90, 91, 92, 98,
    99, 100, 277–278, 299, 487
FBI involvement and, 99, 487
Kimbel and, 162
Lane and, 277
Liberto and, 131–134
Mafia and, 146, 147
Mustang and, 155
Patterson and, 64–65, 487
Raul and, 261, 272
Jerry Ray and, 62, 64, 106–110,
    125, 277, 295, 298
John Ray and, 62, 108–109, 125,
    277, 295
Ray's files sealed by, 362
Ray's innocence and, 260
Ray's prison escape (June 1977)
    and, 260, 368
Redditt and, 251
report, 111–127, 487
Rosenson and, 137–139, 261, 288
Sartor and, 205
security for King and, 226
Sprague and, 63, 487–488
Howell, Ronald B., 226
Huckaby, Hasel, 222–224, 292, 423
Huie, William Bradford, 54–55, 60,

Huie, William Bradford (*Cont.*)
104–105, 166–167, 168, 169,
255, 277, 487
Human, Kenneth, 42
HUMINTS, 443
Humphrey, Hubert, 35, 458
Hunt, Bunker, 244–245, 351
Hunt, E. Howard, 147
Hunt, H. L., 162, 244–245,
349–354, 464, 482, 485
Hunt, Mary, 399
Hunt Oil, 350
Hunt, Tom, 351
Hurley, Charles, 156, 199, 202,
262–263, 290, 296, 384
Hurley, Peggy, 156, 199, 202, 290,
384
Huston, William, 226
Hypnosis, for television trial,
262–263, 296, 384, 387

I

I Am A Man, 363
Illinois Central Railroad building,
421, 429, 458, 460, 475, 481
Immunity, for Jowers, 312–315, 316,
372, 381, 491
Indian Trail restaurant (Winnetka),
70, 186
Ingram, William, 12, 98, 209
*Inside Story: Who Killed Martin Luther
King*, 160–165, 175, 184
Institute for Media Analysis, 233
Intelligence Emergency Operation
Center (IEOC), 424
International Association of Police
Chiefs, 452
International Trade Mart, 374
Invaders, 9–10, 15, 193, 220, 265,
459, 471, 479
agent(s) provocateurs and, 9, 61,
130
assassination and, 98, 250,
257–259, 276
FBI and, 258–259

March 28 march and, 270, 471
Memphis sanitation workers'
strike and, 14–15, 20, 27, 28
surveillance of, 9–10, 129–130,
152, 258–259, 291–292, 458
television trial and, 196
Investigative Records Repository
(IRR), 413

J

Jackson, Jesse, 20–21, 246, 258, 389
Jacks, Steve, 367
James, Fob, 417
J.D., 463, 476, 479, 481, 484, 485
Jefferson, Thomas, 10
Jensen, Robert G., 46, 101, 159,
460, 473
Jerry, 387
Jim's Club, 78
Jim's Grill, 30, 56, 60, 77, 78, 79,
96, 100–101, 102, 139, 140,
153, 154, 155, 157, 163–165,
186, 191, 193, 196–197, 209,
213, 217, 222, 232, 248, 262,
275, 381, 382, 473, 476, 477
Big Lena, 252, 254, 255, 382
Rosie Lee Dabney and, 100, 236,
237–238, 252, 341, 382
"eggs and sausage" man in,
100–101, 164, 238, 240, 382
Holt and, 315, 326, 328
layout, 265–266
Mustang in front of, 157,
290–291, 477
rifle for assassination at, 232,
235–236, 238, 273, 342, 389,
394, 395, 397, 477, 478, 479,
480, 482
Rosetta and, 252, 341
see also Jowers, Loyd; Spates, Alda;
Spates, Betty; Smith, Bobbi
Jim's Place, 102
John, Jim, 349
Johnican, Minerva, 181, 199, 200,
201

Johnson, Harold, 417, 448, 451, 467, 468, 485
Johnson, Jim, 243, 244, 245, 261, 262, 350
Johnson, Lyndon B., 87, 451, 454, 459, 484, 485
 antiwar groups and, 84
 civil rights and, 6
 decision against reelection and, 21
 Hunt and, 353
 King and, 4, 5, 34, 452, 454
 New Politics versus, 5
 urban riots and, 468
 Vietnam War and, 4, 445, 446, 447, 449–450, 451, 454–455, 457, 467, 470
Johnson, O. B., 133
Jones, Columbus, 393
Jones, Solomon, 29, 31, 60, 94, 95, 97, 126, 129, 151, 159, 160, 185, 193, 208, 210, 231, 253, 257, 296, 299, 360, 390
Jones, T. O., 13
Jowers, Loyd, 30, 96, 100, 101, 229, 232, 234, 235–236, 312–328, 337–338, 474
 Akins and, 316, 320–321, 325, 327, 360, 384, 393
 assassination and, 157, 195, 222, 235, 264–265, 315–316, 319–320, 324, 325, 326–331, 341, 342, 343, 384, 385, 469, 478, 479, 483
 book or movie on case by, 337
 deposition, 380–384, 385, 405
 Garrison and, 393–3965
 Holt and, 315, 320–321, 323, 326–330, 339, 360, 385, 394
 immunity for, 312–315, 316, 318–322, 372, 380, 491
 Frank Liberto and, 239, 320, 381, 384, 393–394, 469, 472, 476
 Pierotti and, 340
 Raul and, 394–395, 404, 472, 475–476

Ray v. Jowers et als. and, 363, 379, 407–408, 410, 490–491
rifle for assassination and, 164–165, 232, 235–236, 238, 239, 248, 262–263, 273, 275, 293, 341, 342, 343, 360, 391, 394–395, 475, 480, 482, 483
television trial and, 271, 296–297, 298
see also Jim's Grill; Spates, Betty
Justice Department, 389, 485

K

Karamessines, Thomas, 446
Karenga (Ron Karenga), 419
Kauffmann, John, 124
Kellum, Jim, 212, 386, 392, 422, 433
Kelly, J. K., 112
Kelly, Merrill, 455
Kennedy, Edward M., 4
Kennedy, Florence, 106–107, 109–110
Kennedy, Jay Richard, 84, 446
Kennedy, John F., 52
 assassination of, 103, 112, 162, 370, 371
Kennedy, Robert, 33, 420
 assassination of, 103
 King and, 21, 36
 Mafia and, 63
 presidency and, 21, 456, 470
Kennedy Travel Bureau, 40
Kent, Oscar, 229, 294, 296, 300
Kershaw, Jack, 104, 255, 277, 297, 486
KGB, assassination and, 234
Kimbel, Jules "Ricco," 161–162, 193, 243–244, 261–262, 276, 297, 299–300, 378
King, Alfred Daniel ("A.D."), 27, 31, 142, 283
King, Coretta, 32, 33, 47, 53
King, George, 44
King, Glynn, 288, 336

King, Martin Luther, Jr., 458–461,
462–463, 493–494, 494, 496
attempts to kill, 140–144,
462–463
birthday of as national holiday,
119
"black probe" operation and,
123
books on, 353–354
CIA and, 83–85, 463, 464
contract to kill, 243, 386–387,
393–394, 395, 464, 468
extramarital sexual activity,
113–114, 119–120, 122, 219,
292
FBI and, 36, 60, 85, 88–93, 96,
98–100, 112–124, 128, 216–220,
223, 232, 247, 248, 250,
258–259, 275, 276, 282, 286,
292, 295, 299, 303–305,
350–351, 352–353, 361, 454,
462, 464, 469, 471
funeral, 31, 35–36
Grand Jury investigation and,
332, 334, 362, *see also*
Evidentiary record,
establishment of
honorary degrees to, 121
Hunt and, 244–245
media and, 114–119, 233, 277,
282, 299, 470, 475, 486
Memphis sanitation workers'
strike and, 11–18, 27, 117–118,
454, 455, 456, 469–470
National Conference for New
Politics and, 466
Nobel Peace Prize to, 122, 143,
462
nonviolence and, 28, 220, 451–
452, 457, 469, *see also* Marches,
in Memphis
Office of Security and, 83–85
Poor People's Campaign and, 10,
14, 15, 18, 20, 21, 22, 55, 113,
117, 282, 458, 468

as presidential candidate, 4, 5, 7,
84, 116, 464
security for, 54, 61, 126, 130,
224–226, 231, 249–252, 274,
275, 282, 296, 472, 473, 477
surveillance of, 36, 113, 115, 122,
126, 161, 217–219, 231, 258,
261, 276, 292, 303–305, 414,
415, 416, 424, 432, 432–434,
440, 441, 442, 443, 451,
454–455, 456–457, 458, 460,
463, 469, 470, 471, 473, 487
urban riots and, 444, 445,
451–452, 465
Vietnam War opposition and,
4–5, 6–7, 10–11, 113, 116, 441,
442, 443, 444, 446, 449, 451,
452–453, 464
see also Army; Assassination;
Conspiracy theory
King, William B., 201–202, 283,
298–299, 364
Kirk, William "Tim," 135–136, 189,
190, 212, 262, 265, 268, 277,
297, 300, 366, 368, 385–386,
464, 489–490
Kizer, Bobby, 385
Kohlman, Ray, 268
Kohn, Aaron, 370
Ku Klux Klan, Army and, 415, 454
Kyles, Samuel "Billy," 19, 29,
151–152, 224, 281–283, 392,
399, 460, 479
King's last hours and, 28–29, 95,
159–161, 274, 478–479

L

Lancaster, Steve, 458
Landers, Torrence N., 191,
256–257, 480
Lane, Mark, 53, 60–61, 64, 66, 68,
88, 91, 92, 105, 106, 129, 135,
138, 148, 233, 277
Lansky, Meyer, 352
LANTCOMN/CINCSPECOPS, 426

Latch, James, 205, 241, 378–379, 477

Latimer, James M., 101, 102–103, 202–203, 240

Laue, James, 22

Lau, Thomas Reyes, 37

Lawrence, William, 102, 222, 250, 258, 259, 422

Lawson, James, 12, 13–14, 15, 16, 19, 20, 22, 68, 90–91, 92, 131, 132, 220–221, 224–225, 226, 246, 291, 307, 334, 355, 366, 456

Le Bunny Lounge (New Orleans), 371

Lee, Bernard, 4, 21, 30, 31, 220

Lehner, Robert, 62, 138

Leland, Lee, 147

LeMoyne College, 208

Lesar, James, 77, 247

Lester, Herbert, 334

Levinson, Stanley, 5, 6, 441

Lewis, Dwight, 326–327

Liberto, Frank Camille, 131–134, 162, 163, 193, 205, 206, 212–213, 227–230, 231, 239, 244, 247, 249, 315, 320, 325, 328, 335, 336–337, 348, 349, 357–359, 367–368, 379, 380–381, 382, 385, 386, 387, 393–394, 469, 477, 485

Liberto, Frank (in automobile business), 212

Liberto, Frank (owner of Frank's liquor store and Green Beetle Tavern), 212

Liberto, Gladys, 379

Liberto, Liberto and Latch (LL&L) Produce Company, 24, 132, 248, 257, 275, 379, 382, 477

Liberto, Salvatore J., 134, 161–162, 163, 243–244, 371

Liberto, Tony, 379

"Life Line" programs, 351, 353, 464, 481

Light, Job, 277

Light, John, 265, 295

Lincoln, L. J., 446

Linville, Barry Neal, 255–256, 288–289

Liuzzo, Viola, 166

LL&L Produce Company, *see* Liberto, Liberto and Latch Produce Company

Locke, Harvey "Ace," 149–150

Loeb, Henry, 12, 13, 21, 31

Loenneke, Ed, 202, 283–284

Lomonosof, Alec, 243

Long, Huey, 149

Long, Robert, 229

Lorraine Motel, 22, 61, 98, 119, 151, 159, 193, 222, 245, 246, 387, 388, 398, 401, 456, 470, 472, 473, 475

  Caldwell at, 163, 184, 185

  FBI on, 118, 471

  Kyles staying at, 28–29, 160, 282–283

  MacDonald at, 224

  Ray's rooming house having view of, 56, 94–95, 149, 190

  reason for King staying at, 225

  reservation change from Holiday Inn Rivermont Hotel to, 60, 269, 274, 282, 297

  room change at, 60, 97–98, 119, 196, 203–204, 231, 274, 297, 300, 459, 472

  security at, 54, 56, 130, 207, 226, 249–252, 282, 472, 473, 475, 478

  surveillance of, 416, 421, 422, 433–435, 459

Los Angeles, Army presence in 1968 in, 418–419

Los Angeles Times, 39

Louisville, Kentucky, assassination attempt on King in, 140–144, 463

Louw, Joseph, 22, 29, 400

Love, Coy, 254, 255, 315, 330

Lovingood, Clyde, 349, 352

Lowery, Joseph, 91
Lowmeyer, Harvey, 35, 36–37, 76
Lucky Electric Supply Company,
223
Lyons, Robert Patrick, 206, 240

M

McAfee, John "Bill," 207–208
McBride, Robert, 443
McCarthy, Eugene, 440, 450, 455
McChristian, Joseph, 493
McClellan, John, 126, 251
McCollough, Marrell, 28, 98,
128–129, 152, 258, 431, 443,
456, 461, 465, 470, 474, 475,
479–480, 487
McCormack, John, 114
McCoy, Robert, 361–362
McCracken, Maurice, 161
McCraw, James, 55, 153–154, 156,
164–165, 186, 191, 199, 209,
232, 238, 249, 273, 290, 293,
313, 320, 331, 338, 342, 393,
395, 483, 491
MacDonald, J. C., 14, 207, 224, 226,
452, 475
MacDonald, Sheena, 305, 306
McDoulton, Robert, 247–248
McFerren, John, 131–133, 134, 161,
162, 189, 193, 205, 212, 213,
241, 275, 293, 315, 335, 336,
348–349, 380, 393
McGovern, George, 441
MacKay, Louis, 252, 276, 363
McKinley, John, 351
McMillan, George E., 54, 62, 170
McNamara, Robert, 412, 443, 445,
447, 448, 467
McWerter, Ned, 306–307, 321, 326,
397
McWilliams, Carey, 4
Madison, Commander, 4
Madison, James, 494
Mafia, 103, 130, 161–162, 243–244,
336

assassination and, 102–103,
131–136, 137–139, 145–148,
380–381, 385–386, 393 395,
464, 465, 468–469, 477–478,
484–485, 487
Blakey and, 63
contract on King's life and,
386–387
contract on Ray's life and,
367–369, 368, 369, 488–489
Hardin and, 247
Hoover and, 146, 244, 352
Hunt and, 244–245, 349, 352
Kimbel and, 243–244
Latch and, 241
McFerren and, 132
New Orleans and, 369–371, 385,
386, 464, 465, 485
Office of Security and, 83
Pepper and, 145
Rosenson and, 138
Sartor and, 100–101, 134,
239–240, 248
Special Forces and, 333
television trial and, 193–194,
204–206, 212–213, 275
see also under Liberto
Mail, *see* Operation CHAOS
Major, 95–96
Making of an Assassin, The
(McMillan), 54
Malone, John, 120
Maloney, J. J., 242, 260, 287
Manuel, Phillip R., 126, 251, 377,
460, 476
Maori, Raul, 163
Marcello, Carlos, 134, 194, 205,
212, 240, 243, 244, 248, 261,
276, 333, 352, 354, 358, 370,
375–376, 385, 386, 405, 430,
464, 465, 467, 483, 487
"March against fear", in Memphis,
15
Marches, in Memphis
April 8, 21, 22, 27–28, 35,
458–459

March 28, 18–20, 117–118, 220, 274, 282, 291, 458, 470, 471
"March against fear," 115
Marion, Pierre, 234
Marquette University, 121
Marro, Anthony J., 64, 223
Marshall, Tom, 224, 226
Martin, Marie, 74–75, 262
Mason Temple (Memphis), King speaking in, 17–18, 22–23
Matheny, Mark, 334
Maxey, Hugh, 124
Media
    Ellsberg affidavit and, 91, 92
    FBI and, 53–54, 277
    Grand Jury investigation and, 362
    King and, 114–119, 233, 277, 282, 299, 471, 484
    Ray and, 38–39, 40–42, 43–44, 47, 62–63, 74, 82, 171, 233–234, 322–327, 333, 355, 484, 485, 490–491
    television trial and, 233–234, 306, 307, 308
Melanson, Philip, 151–152, 163
Memphis
    Green Berets and, 305
    Invaders, 129–130, 152, 220, 250
    Ray in, 34–35, 37, 43–48, 56, 59, 77–79
    sanitation workers' strike in, 11–18, 27, 36, 117–118, 133, 250, 454, 455, 469–470
    Tennessee National Guard in, 19, 20, 247, 416, 424
    see also Assassination; Invaders; Marches, in Memphis
Memphis City Public Works Department, bush clearing and, 210, 256
"Memphis Godfather," 306, 484
    contract on Ray's life and, 367, 368, 369, 488–489
Memphis Police Department
    Army and, 420, 422, 423, 424, 425, 433, 434, 460, 465, 475

assassination and, 30, 31, 93, 126, 185–186, 190–191, 275, 294, 392, 460–461, 474, 478, 480, 481, 482
    bribery and, 336
    burning of intelligence bureau files and, 61, 482
    bush clearing and, 211, 256, 277, 481
    death slug and, 255–256, 290
    Douglass and, 213–216
    FBI and, 221–222
    Hagerty and, 223
    hoax CB radio broadcast and, 31, 54, 60, 152, 199, 207–208, 231, 259–260, 277, 287, 297–298, 480
    Huckaby and, 222–223
    Invaders and, 259–260, 291–292
    at Jim's Grill, 196
    Kyles and, 393
    March 28 march and, 18–20, 220
    Mustang and, 31, 152, 155
    Redditt and, 61, 126, 129, 201, 223, 231, 249–252, 275, 296, 473, 477
    riot control training for, 217
    security for King and, 54, 56, 126, 130, 207, 224–226, 231, 292–293, 474, 478
    Smith and, 216–217, 219, 220
    Stephens and, 97
    surveillance of King and, 305
    TACT forces withdrawal and, 30, 130, 151–152, 163, 213–216, 224, 231, 274, 275, 282, 293, 296, 473, 476
    walkie-talkies and, 223, 224
    Youngblood and, 100, 101, 102, 103
Memphis Stone and Gravel Company, 381
Merchant's Lounge, 228
Meredith, James, 15
Michael, 392–393
Milam, Wallace, 356, 360

Military intelligence groups
("MIGs"), 413, 414, 415, 416, 417,
418, 422, 424, 429, 431, 434,
435, 438, 439, 440, 441, 442,
443, 444, 453, 454, 456
Missouri State Penitentiary, Ray's
escape from, 7, 39, 67–68, 70,
242, 488
Montesi's supermarket, 383
Moooney, Booth, 353
Moore, George C., 458, 471
Morris, Bill, 31, 169
Morton, Chuck, 267, 289, 356
Murphy, 411, 417–419, 420,
421–424, 425, 429, 431, 475,
481, 485
Murphy, Charles, 149, 339
Murtagh, Arthur, 123, 216, 232,
276, 294–295, 464
Mustang(s), 248, 289, 467, 476,
477, 480
  in Atlanta, 36–37, 200, 481
  at Canipe's Amusement
    Company, 30, 56, 59, 60, 153,
    154, 155, 156, 186, 197, 199,
    202, 214, 236, 262, 274, 284,
    477
  cigarette butts and ashes in, 36,
    200
  existence of two, 36, 153,
    155–156, 186, 197–199, 202,
    274, 286, 290–291
  fingerprints and, 129, 287
  at Jim's Grill, 257, 290–291, 475
  police chasing, 31, 152
  Ray's story on, 72, 78–79, 140
  Rosenson on, 261, 288
  spare tire repair at gas station
    and, 140, 156–157, 204, 230,
    273–274, 383, 476, 477, 478
  television trial and, 196–199

N

Nashville Tennessean, 326
Nation, 5

National Association for the
  Advancement of Colored
  People (NAACP), 6, 15
National Civil Rights Museum, 22
National Conference for New
  Politics (NCNP), 5, 8–9, 10, 84,
  270, 447, 465, 466
National Council of Churches, 121
National holiday, King's birthday as,
  119
National Mobilization Committee,
  447
National Security Act, 85
National Security Agency (NSA),
  416, 437–438, 445, 446, 466
National Student Association, CIA
  and, 87
Neptune Bar (Montreal), 71, 181,
  344–345, 375, 466
New Moonnight club (Memphis),
  386
New Orleans
  Mafia in, 213, 369–373, 385, 386,
    393–395, 466, 465, 485
  Ray in, 75, 466, 471, 470
New Politics, 5, 7, 8–11, 84
  see also National Conference for
    New Politics (NCNP)
New Rebel Motel (Memphis), 77,
  78, 285, 471, 472
Newsom, Floyd, 150, 196, 293, 474
Newsweek, 41
New York, Spring Mobilization
  demonstration in, 5, 6–7
New York Times, 38, 115
Nichols, Jim, 266–267
Nichols, Marion, 19, 219
Nick, 103
Nix, Norris, 386
Nixon, Richard M., 116
Nix, Red, 385–386, 464, 469
Nobel Peace Prize, to King, 122,
  143, 462
Nonviolence, of King, 28, 220, 454,
  457, 472
  see also Marches, in Memphis

Norton, 433, 434, 459, 460, 473, 475, 481

O

Oakview house, 236, 237, 384, 385
Obray, Jean, 146, 191, 262, 268, 288, 291–292, 295, 387
Observer, Ray and, 322–323, 325, 491
Office of Naval Intelligence (ONI), 416
Office of Security (OS)
King and, 83–85
Operation CHAOS, 9, 84, 85
police force training sessions and, 217
Project RESISTANCE, 84
O'Leary, Jeremiah, 41
O'Neill, Tip, 62
Operation CHAOS, 9, 84, 85, 446, 465
Operation MINARET, 447, 466
Orange, James, 21, 28, 98, 130, 209, 231, 254, 257, 296, 401, 458, 472, 479
Organized crime, *see* Mafia
Ortiz, Luis, 237
Osborn, Howard, 84
Otmoor Production, 161

P

Palazolla, Bob, 349
Palazolla, Michael, 349
Palazolla Produce Company, 348, 349
Palazolla, Walter, 349
Papia, James, 285
Partee, 265–266
Partin, Doug, 371–373
Patriarca, Raymond, 145
Patterson, Oliver, 64–65, 233, 277, 297, 487
Payne, Larry, 20, 21
Peabody Motel, 19, 133, 219, 470
Pearson, Drew, 39, 43

Pennington, Lee, 84
Pentagon, assassination and, 425–426
Penthouse, Dalitz and, 63
Pepper, William, 32
as appeals lawyer, 148, 150, 151–152, 158, 174–175, 182, 183
as attorney of record for television trial, 188–189
closing statement in television trial and, 304–305
Robert Kennedy and, 36
King and, 6–7, 10
Mafia and, 145
meeting with Ray, 51–53, 66–82
Memphis memorial march and, 35
National Conference for New Politics and, 5
Jerry Ray and HSCA and, 106–110
security for, 391–392
Vietnam War and, 3–5
Pereira, Amaro (Armando), 375, 376, 377, 378, 405, 465, 486, 490
Pereira, Raul, 373–379, 404–410, 465, 466
Peretz, Martin, 9
Perez, Leander, 162, 244
Pete, 102
Peters, Estelle, 129
Peters, Robert, 141, 142
Phoenix Program, The (Valentine), 316
Photographs, staged, 139, 190–191, 364
Piedmont Laundry (Atlanta), 55, 129, 286
Pierotti, John, 181, 255, 313–314, 315, 318, 319, 322, 325–326, 327, 332, 338, 340, 346, 361, 362, 385, 475, 491
Placid Oil Company, 244
Political leaders

Political leaders (*Cont.*)
  Hunt and, 352–353
  King discredited to, 114
Polito family, 352
Poor People's Campaign, 10, 14,
  15, 18, 20, 21, 22, 55, 113, 117,
  282, 402, 450, 451, 454, 457,
  468
Pope, King meeting with, 120–121
Portugal, Ray in, 40, 80
Powell, Adam Clayton, 459
Presidential candidacy
  of Robert Kennedy, 21, 456, 470
  of King, 4, 5, 7, 84, 116, 464
Presley, Elvis, 380
Press Scimitar, 98, 156
Prime Time Live, 322–325, 337, 383,
  491
Prisoners, statements of, 241–242
Project MERRIMAC, 446, 466
Project RESISTANCE, 84
Prosch, Gus, 134, 211–212, 227,
  294
Provincial Motel (New Orleans),
  75
Pseudonyms, Ray using
  Paul Edward Bridgeman, 40, 80
  Eric S. Galt, 71, 73, 76, 434–438,
    444, 466, 476, 484, 486,
    488–489
  Harvey Lowmeyer, 35, 36–37, 76
  John L. Rayns, 70, 73
  Ramon George Sneyd, 39–40, 80,
    486
  John Willard, 56, 77, 78, 475
Psychological Operations (Psy Ops)
  section, 416, 459–460
Public television, Ray interviewed
  on, 333
Public Workers Federal Credit
  Union, 36
Purdy, Prentice, 390
Putnam, Patrick D., 417, 439, 442,
  451, 452, 455, 463, 469
Puzzle Palace, The (Bamford), 437

R

Rabbito, Barbara, 68, 131, 135, 136
Raborn, William P. "Red," 87
Racism, Ray and, 59, 68, 82, 124,
  243, 287, 300, 370
Radio broadcast, *see* Hoax CB radio
  broadcast
Radosti, Tony, 370
Ragan, H., 336
Ragano, Frank, 406
Ramparts, 87
  "The Children of Vietnam," 4–5
Rancho La Costa California, 63
Randolph, A. Philip, 6, 445
Ransom, 266
Rappe, J. C., 206, 239
Raul, 55, 64, 71–79, 120, 125, 128,
  138–139, 149, 155, 187, 188,
  261, 272, 288, 316, 325, 335,
  344–345, 354, 363, 371, 372,
  373, 384, 394–395, 405, 430,
  465–466, 467, 468, 469, 470,
  471, 472, 473, 475–476, 477,
  486, 487, 488, 490
  Pereira, 373–378, 405–411, 465
Raven, Frank, 438
Rawls, Wendel, Jr., 107, 108
Ray, Anna, 68, 137–138, 139, 255,
  333
Ray, Ellen, 233
Ray, Franklin, 197
Ray, James Earl, 377
  alibi witnesses for, 139–140, 193,
    195–196, 204, 279
  appeal, 139–140, 148, 150, 158,
    174–175, 182, 183
  deposition (March 1995), 393
  extradition from England, 40, 43,
    59, 68, 80, 94, 167, 205, 308,
    486
  FBI and, 36–37, 38–39, 40, 41,
    43–44, 47, 60, 68, 242, 260,
    368, 438, 486, 487, 488
  guilty plea of, 44–48, 53, 59, 80,
    96, 104–105, 137, 166–174, 189,

255, 287–288, 297, 308, 332, 335, 346, 367, 486, 489

innocence of, 53, 68, 69, 79, 81–82, 179, 377, 404, 483, 488, *see also* Appeal; Conspiracy theory; Evidentiary record, establishment of; Television trial

life, 37, 66–67, 186–188, *see also* own story on assassination, *below*

media coverage of, 38–39, 40–42, 43–44, 47, 62–63, 74, 82, 171, 233–234, 277, 333, 486, 490, 491

Missouri State Penitentiary escape and, 7, 39, 67–68, 70, 242, 488, 489

murder contract on, 134–136, 212, 265–266, 268, 275, 297, 300, 365–368, 487–489

own story on assassination, 66–82, 139–140, 148, 188

parole hearing for, 355

racism and, 59, 68, 82, 124, 243, 287, 300, 370

release of, 338, 339–340

search for, 38–40, 42–43

setup of, 475–477

state's case against, 55–59, 94–97, *see also* Stephens, Charles

see also Bank robberies; Brushy Mountain State Penitentiary; Conspiracy theory; House Select Committee on Assassinations; Pseudonyms, Ray using; Raul

Ray, Jerry, 62, 64–65, 71, 74, 81, 487

Alton, Illinois bank robbery and, 107–109, 265, 277, 295

Foreman and, 168–169, 170, 171

HSCA and, 106–110, 125, 277, 297

Huie and, 104, 105, 168, 255

letter on Ray's trial and, 170, 172

Pepper and, 346

Raul and, 138

St. Louis conspiracy and, 124

Ray, Jewell, 221–222, 247

Ray, John, 62, 70, 81

Alton, Illinois bank robbery and, 107, 108–109, 125, 265, 295

Foreman and, 169

HSCA and, 125

St. Louis conspiracy and, 124

Rayns, John L., 70, 73

Ray v. Jowers et als., 363, 379, 408–409, 410, 490–492

Redditt, Edward, 54, 61, 126, 129, 201, 224, 231, 249–252, 275, 276, 293, 389, 473, 475, 477

Reed, William Zenie, 139–140, 193, 276, 289, 478

Reid, Jim, 156–157, 210, 273, 290

Religious leaders, King discredited to, 120–121

Reno, Janet, 491

Reward, for capture and conviction of assassin, 35

Reynolds, 432–434, 459, 460, 473, 475, 480

Rhodesia, Ray going to, 42, 59, 71

Richmond, Willie B., 30, 160, 250, 258, 283, 473, 475, 479

Rife, Walter, 67

Rifle, for assassination, 55–56, 78, 102, 103, 129, 134, 139, 173, 191, 196, 213, 385, 472, 473

at Canipe's, 30, 59, 94, 136–137, 154, 155, 186, 214, 236–237, 252, 267, 274, 284, 285, 290, 363–364, 477, 480

at corner of Huling and Mulberry Streets, 252, 390–391

identifying, 128, 163, 199–200, 221, 255–256, 267–268, 273, 284, 285, 288, 289, 482

Jowers and, 164–165, 232, 235–236, 238, 239, 248, 262–263, 264–265, 273, 275,

Rifle (*Cont.*)
  341, 342, 343, 360, 389,
    394–395, 474, 477, 479, 482
  at Liberto family business, 393
  purchase of, 34–35, 36–37, 55,
    76–77, 125, 127–128, 211, 273,
    285, 294, 296, 300, 471
  Ray's fingerprints on, 128, 173,
    287
  testing for evidentiary record,
    347, 356–357, 360, 361–362,
    392, 486, 491
  throwdown rife, 228, 231
Riley, John, Mrs., 36
Riverbend Penitentiary, Ray at, 394
Rivermont Hotel, *see* Holiday Inn
  Rivermont Hotel
Riverside Church, King's antiwar
  speech at, 6, 282, 443
Robberies, 67, 71, 107, 187
  Montreal brothel, 107
  see also Bank robberies
Robinson, Cleveland, 5
Robinson, Herbert, 332
Robinson, Wendell, 224, 226
Rockefeller Commission Report, 52
Rockefeller, Nelson, 114
Rose, James, 123, 295
Roselli, John, 83, 146, 147
Rosen, Randy, 74, 467
  see also Rosenson, Randy
Rosenson, Randy, 74, 127, 137–139,
    193, 261, 262, 272, 288, 335,
    336, 354–355, 370
Rosetta, 252, 341
Ross, William L., 204, 245–246, 257,
    263, 296, 389
Rostow, Walt, 447, 449
Rothermel, Paul, 244–245, 350, 351,
    353–354
Rouse, Milford, 351
Royal Canadian Mounted Police
  (RCMP), search for Ray by,
    39–40
Rumbaut, Carlos Hernandez, 81
Rusk, Dean, 114, 447

Rustin, Bayard, 6, 15
Ryan, Ray, 352
Ryan, Richard J., 168, 171, 172

S

St. Francis Hotel (Los Angeles), 75,
    104, 247, 262
St. Joseph's Hospital, 30, 31, 95
St. Louis conspiracy theory,
    124–125, 487
St. Louis hotel, 64
St. Louis Post-Dispatch, 62
Saltman, Jack, 180, 181, 188, 267,
    276, 303, 304, 322–325, 373,
    377–378, 404, 406, 407, 409,
    410
San Francisco Chronicle, 39
Sanitation workers' strike
  (Memphis), 11–18, 27, 36,
    117–118, 133, 250, 369, 454,
    456
Sartor, William, 100–101, 134,
    204–206, 239–240, 248, 348,
    487
Satchfield, Caroll, 199
  see also Carroll, Carroll
Schaap, Bill, 233–234, 275, 277, 295
Schultz, William, 226
Scotland Yard, 40, 42
SDECE, assassination and, 234
Seabrook Wallpaper Company, 157,
    193, 202, 235, 248, 262, 284,
    291, 341, 384, 479
Security, for King, 54, 61, 126, 130,
    224–226, 231, 249–252, 274,
    275, 282, 296, 472, 473, 478
Sehested, Ken, 334
Selma, Alabama, attempted
  assassination and, 426
Senate Judiciary Sub-Committee
  Report, 52
Senate Select Committee on
  Intelligence Activities, CIA and,
    88
Sentinella, Al, 123, 158, 464

Sessions, William, 267, 276, 490
Sheehan, Joe, 345
Shelby County Jail, Ray in, 43–48,
    166–167
Shoup, David M., 457
Shuttlesworth, Fred, 134, 227, 230
Siegel, Ben "Bugsy," 146
Silberg, Earl, 109
Simmons, John, 343
Sitton, Claude, 184, 299
Slim, 393
    see also Hester, O. D.
Smith, "Big John," 259
Smith, Bobbi, 236, 238–239, 249,
    252, 313, 320, 325, 331, 337,
    341, 382, 384, 385, 393, 474,
    483, 491
    Holt and, 328
    immunity for, 313
    television trial and, 271, 275,
        293–294, 298
Smith, Coby, 270, 291
Smith, Don, 126, 224, 225–226, 382
Smith, Ezell, 213, 228, 393
Smith, Jim, 216–218, 219, 220, 231,
    239, 247, 276, 291, 292,
    303–304, 314, 321, 326, 415,
    450, 456, 470
Smith, John, 292–293, 478
Smith, Peter, 303
Smith, Tommy, 127, 209–210, 221,
    255, 273, 289, 336
Smythe, Hamilton, 382
SNCC, 445, 453
Sneyd, Ramon George, 39–40, 59,
    80, 486
Sorrequere, Marcel, 234
Southern Christian Leadership
    Conference (SCLC), 11, 13–14,
    29, 402, 460, 473, 477
    Abernathy and, 51
    assassination and, 33
    conspiracy theory and, 53
    FBI and, 112–113, 115–117, 123,
        158–159, 297, 440, 462, 464
    Invaders and, 28, 459

Lowery and, 91
Memphis marches and, 20–21, 22
Memphis sanitation workers'
    strike and, 15, 16
security for King and, 126
surveillance of, 459, 464
Southern Motel (Corinth), 77
Spates, Alda, 236, 238, 239,
    252–253, 331, 383
Spates, Betty, 157, 163, 189, 193,
    287, 292, 313, 316, 320, 331,
    338, 383, 384–385, 393, 479,
    480
    Akins and, 343, 359–360
    Holt and, 328–329
    immunity for, 313, 320
    Jowers and, 164, 165, 234–237,
        238, 252–253, 384, 395
    Jowers' book and, 339
    media and, 325
    John Spates and, 253–254
    story of to Pepper, 340–344
    television trial and, 194–196, 271,
        275, 293–294, 298
    Tennessee Bureau of
        Investigation and, 337–338,
        343–344
Spates, Bobbi, see Smith, Bobbi
Spates, John, 253–254
Special Forces Group (SFG), of
    Army, 317, 333, 338–339, 345,
    347, 411, 415, 417–418, 419,
    443, 449–450, 455
Special Operations Group (SOG),
    85, 88, 416, 418, 446,465, 466
Speiser, Mark, 109
Spellman, Francis Cardinal,
    120–121
Spica, John Paul, 124
Spock, Benjamin
    Memphis memorial march and,
        32, 35
    as presidential running mate, 5,
        7, 84, 116–117, 441
    Vietnam War opposition and, 11,
        442

Sprague, Richard, 62, 487–488
Spring Mobilization demonstration, 5, 6–7
Stanley, Gene, 137, 138, 139, 261, 272, 288
Stanton, Hugh, Jr., 44
Stanton, Hugh, Sr., 44, 173, 208, 402
Starlight Lounge (Birmingham), 72, 75, 76, 470
State's case, 55–60, 136
  appeal of, 148, 150, 158, 174–175, 182, 183
  ballistics evidence against, 136–137
  dissent, 59–63
  evidence against, 94–105, 136–137, 139–140, 153–157
  Stephens as witness for, 94–97, 153–154, 174, 221, 231
  television trial and, 189
Stein, Charles, 60, 74–75, 127, 162, 262, 370–371, 468
Stein, Rita, 75
Stephens, Charles Quitman, 43, 55, 56, 59, 94–97, 127, 153–154, 157, 167, 174, 183–184, 191, 209, 221, 230–231, 273, 284–285, 289, 291, 308, 336, 483
Stewart, Jim Bo, 228
Stiles, Maynard, 13, 210, 256, 296, 365, 421
Stokes, Louis, 138, 147, 260, 488
Stone, Charles, 201, 202, 250, 283
Stout, Bill, 97–98
Strother, 321
Subcommittee to Investigate Problems Connected with Refugees and Escapees, 4
Sullivan, William C., 113, 455
Summers, Anthony, 244, 365
Supreme Court, appeal and, 175, 365, 490
Surveillance, 275

assassination and, 223–224, 231, 246–247, 248
interagency structure for, 416, see also Central Intelligence Agency; Federal Bureau of Investigation; Office of Naval Intelligence
of Invaders, 292–293
of King, 249, see also Army; Electronic surveillance; Federal Bureau of Investigation
on striking sanitation workers, 250
Sutherland, John, 124

T

T. J., 103, 161
TACT forces, withdrawal of, 30, 130, 151–152, 163, 213–216, 224, 231, 274, 275, 282, 293, 296, 473, 476
"Tango," 392
Tayloe Paper Company water tower, 193, 196–197, 315, 429, 460, 476
Taylor, Alexander, 339–340
Taylor, Calvin, 20, 258–259, 458
Teale, Sarah, 208
Teale Productions, 208
Teamsters, Hunt and, 355
Television trial, 179–308, 490
  corroboration and new evidence and, 207–232
  defense case and, 233–248, 272–276
  exoneration application to governor and, 306–307, 321, 326
  jury tampering and, 266–267, 276, 277, 489
  media coverage of, 306, 307, 308
  Pepper's closing statement, 301–302
  preparations for, 179–191
  pretrial investigations, 192–206

Ray's reaction to, 298
  trial, 249–302
  verdict, 303–308
Tennessean, 332
Tennessee Bureau of Investigation
    (TBI), 385
  Jowers and, 337–338
  Latimer and, 203
  Betty Spates and, 337–338,
    343–344
Tennessee National Guard, in
    Memphis, 19, 20, 248, 416, 424
Tennessee Rules of Criminal
    Procedure ("TRCP"), for
    television trial, 188–189
Tennessee Waltz (Ray), 148
Termine, Sam, 240
Thames Television, 180, 181, 188,
    191, 490
  see also Television trial
Thomas, Norman, 4
Thompson, Alan, 247
Thompson, Frances, 248, 291
Thompson, Herman, 127, 373
Thompson, Kenneth, 42, 43
Thompson, Russell X., 101–102,
    103, 148, 150, 202, 240
Thornton, Benny, 401
Throckmorton, John L., 444, 448
Tiller brothers, 386, 464
Time, 40–41, 62, 134
Tines, Gradon, 381
Toler, Margaret, 336, 337
Tolson, Clyde, 53, 54, 439
Tompkins, Steve, 304, 316–317,
    333, 338–339, 345, 390, 411
Torrino, Felix, 374, 375, 376, 377,
    487
Trafficante, Santo, 406
Travelodge motel (Birmingham),
    76
Tremont Cafe, 229, 235, 239
Trial
  appeals denial and, 148, 150,
    158, 174–175, 182, 183, 490

guilty plea and, 44–48, 53, 60, 80,
    96–97, 104–105, 137, 167–175
  request for, 326, 331, 333,
    344–346, 486, *see also*
    Evidentiary record,
    establishment of
  see also Television trial
Truman, Harry, 85, 86–87
Trumpet Hotel (Memphis), 246
Tucker, William, 31, 152–153, 199,
    226, 259, 298
Turner, Bill, 249, 276, 295
Turner, Carl C., 114
Turner, R. J., 225, 226
Tyson, Brady, 89–90, 92, 98, 99, 144
Tyus, Robert ("Old Pal"), 348, 349

U

Union Theological Seminary, 10
U.S. Army Intelligence Command
    (USAINTC), 413, 414, 415,
    416, 417, 443, 447
U.S. Army Security Agency
    ("ASA"), 416, 440, 442
U.S. Intelligence Board (USIB), 416
U.S. News & World Report, 115
U.S. Strike Command
    (CINCSTRIKE), 415, 424, 425,
    453, 458, 459
University of Mississippi, 15, 31
UPI, Curtis and, 241
Urban riots, 444–445, 449–450, 451,
    452, 454–455, 457, 464, 465,
    467, 468

V

Valachi, Joe, 67
Valentine, Douglas, 316, 433
Vallone, Ross, 377, 379, 406
Van Deman, Ralph, 413
Van Tassell, F. E., 440, 442, 469
Vaughan, William, III, 334
Veterans Cab Company, 264, 381
Vickers, W. M., 456

Vietnam Summer, 7
Vietnam War, 441, 442, 446, 450,
    451,452, 454, 455, 457, 470,
    471
  CIA and, 88
  King's opposition to, 4–5, 6–7,
    10–11, 113, 116, 440, 441, 442,
    443, 444, 445, 446, 449, 450,
    451, 452–453, 464
  opposition to, 5, 437, 440,
    441–457, 465, 466–467, 493
  SOG operations in, 88
  Spock's opposition to, 11
  surveillance of antiwar groups
    and, 84
  U.S.-caused devastation and, 3–4,
    451
Violence
  after assassination, 32, 34
  antiwar demonstrations and, 441,
    443, 447–450, 452
  Memphis march (March 28) and,
    19–20, 117–118, 270, 274, 458
  urban riots and, 443, 444–445,
    450–452, 457, 406, 467, 468
  See also Nonviolence
Vivian, C. T., 334
Volpe, John A., 114

W

Wadsworth, Susan, 64, 233
Walden, Grace, 56, 94, 95, 97,
    126–127, 149, 221, 238, 275,
    284, 384, 394, 474
Waldridge, Monroe, 350
Waldron, Martin, 38
Walker, Doc, 243, 265–266
Walker, Jimmy, 197, 290, 296
Walker, Robert, 13
Walker, Rosie, 230
Wall, Fred, 220
Wallace, George, 124
Wallace, Norvell, 150, 196, 293, 473
Walridge, Monroe, 244
Walsh, Kevin, 230

Ward, Louie, 387–388, 481, 491
Warren, 338, 339, 375, 411,
    418–419, 420, 421–424, 425,
    428, 429, 430, 431–432, 434,
    443, 444, 455, 465, 475–476,
    479, 481, 483
Warren Commission Report, 52
Washington, Alda Mae, *see* Spates,
    Alda
Washington, D.C., *see* Poor People's
    Campaign
Washington Post, 47
Washington Star, 41
Watch list, Ray and, 437–438
Watergate, 52
Waters, Charlie, 352
Weeden, Carthel, 401–402, 433,
    433, 459, 473
Weisberg, Harold, 59–60, 77, 93,
    149, 241–242
Wells, David, 306–307
Wells, Earl, 208, 274
WerBell, Mitchel Livingston, III, 431
West Hunter Street Baptist Church,
    160
Westmoreland, William, 441, 452,
    454, 455, 457, 471
Wheeler, Earle, 443, 449, 454, 455,
    457
White, Emmanuel, 269–270, 291
White House, assassination and,
    425, 426
Whitlock, Lavada, 357, 358, 359,
    379–380, 485, 491
Whitlock, Nathan, 357–359,
    379–380, 385, 485
Whitney, Ben, 226
Wilkins, Roy, 6, 15, 445
Willard, John, 28, 30, 37, 56, 77,
    78, 329, 476
Williams, Hosea, 21, 28, 32, 158,
    226, 294, 296–297, 300, 402
  Harrison and, 158–159, 269
  King's last hours and, 159–160,
    274
  Ray's parole and, 355

Williams, Jerry, 224–226, 292, 470
Wilson, Harold, 114
Winters, Emmett J., 226
Withers, Ernest, 208, 225
Witnesses
  alibi, 139–140, 193, 195–196, 204, 279
  of assassination, 94–97, 149, 174, 184–185, 188, 201–202, 208, 210, 221, 230–231, 245–246, 253, 283–284, 396–403, 473, 481
  for television trial, 188–189
Wolverton, Don, 242–243, 266, 287
Wood, David, 196–197
Wood, Donald, 34–35, 125, 127–128, 211
Wood, Mike, 87
Woods, Johnny C., 300
Worley, Robert, 420, 428, 485
Wride, Bert E., 417, 471
Wright, Alexander, 194
Wright, Glenn, 180, 181, 288, 292, 303
Wright, James Alexander, 195
Wright, Tommy, 335, 336

Y

Yarborough, William P., 339, 413, 414, 416–417, 437, 438, 439, 440, 441, 442, 443, 444–445, 446, 447, 448, 449, 450, 451, 452, 453, 454, 455, 456, 458, 463, 464, 465, 466, 467, 471, 474, 479, 485, 494
Yawee, Abdul, 265
Yellow Cab Company, 381, 386–389, 480, 481, 483, 491
York Arms Store, 35, 56, 78, 186, 188
Young, Andrew, 10, 18, 28, 29, 31, 32, 89, 90, 92, 98, 99, 159, 160, 459, 472, 474, 475, 477, 479, 484
  Army and, 420, 423, 431, 434, 460, 472
Young, Whitney, 6, 445
Youngblood, Walter Alfred "Jack," 100–104, 148–149, 164, 203, 240, 247, 331, 382, 431, 465

Z

Zachary, N. E., 46, 102, 103, 133, 203, 252, 255, 285, 336, 381